SLEAFORD CHURCH.

SLEAFORD,

AND THE

WAPENTAKES OF

FLAXWELL AND ASWARDHURN,

IN THE

COUNTY OF LINCOLN;

BY THE

VENERABLE EDWARD TROLLOPE, M.A., F.S.A.,

ARCHDEACON OF STOW.

LONDON:
W. KENT AND CO., 23, PATERNOSTER ROW;
SLEAFORD:
PRINTED AND PUBLISHED BY WILLIAM FAWCETT.
1872.

Original published by William Fawcett, in 1872.

This reprinted edition published in 1999 by:
Heritage Lincolnshire,
The Old School, Cameron Street, Heckington, Sleaford,
Lincolnshire, NG34 9RW.

British Library Cataloguing-in-Publication Data.
A CIP catalogue record for this book
is available from the British Library.

ISBN 0-948639-24-5

Design of jacket and additional pages by
The S S Crome, Alford, Lincolnshire.
Production by Nicholas Russell, Cambridge.
Printed in the UK by Woolnough Bookbinding Ltd,
Irthlingborough.

FOREWORD TO THE REPRINTED EDITION

IT is almost 130 years since Edward Trollope's "*Sleaford and the Wapentakes of Flaxwell and Aswardhurn*" was first published and it has now begun to acquire the status of a rare book. When antiquarian booksellers do obtain copies, they sell for increasingly high prices. For most people, it has become a volume to be consulted only in the reference section of a library. Yet Trollope's history, covering as it does a considerable part of central Kesteven, deserves to be much more widely read. A work of local history, it has itself become a part of local history.

In many ways, Trollope was a typical Victorian antiquarian. Born into a Lincolnshire baronet family, he pursued a long and distinguished career in the church, rising from his early days as the curate of Rauceby and rector of Leasingham to become Archdeacon of Stow and (in 1877) Suffragan Bishop of Nottingham. Yet he still found time to indulge his historical and antiquarian interests, publishing numerous books and articles on subjects as diverse as the life of Pope Adrian IV and the Battle of Bosworth Field. His history of Sleaford and its surrounding villages was partly the product of a lifelong attachment to the locality where he had begun his ecclesiastical career and partly the result of his desire to improve on a previous work of local history, which was published anonymously in 1825 by James Creasey but was largely the work of Dr Richard Yerburgh, then Vicar of Sleaford.

It is easy to dwell on the historical inaccuracies of Trollope's work with the benefit of modern scholarship: no doubt future generations will do no less for ours. In some respects, his predecessor Yerburgh was a better interpreter of evidence than Trollope, and readers are advised to treat passages such as his opening section on the Ancient Britons as examples of a very Victorian kind of antiquarian speculation rather than as accurate history.

However, that this book stood alone as the only attempt to write a full-scale history of the area for over a century tells us something of the importance and authority it quickly assumed, and what Trollope sometimes lacked as an interpreter he more than compensated for in his meticulous gathering of well-referenced evidence. For anybody interested in the history of Sleaford or the villages in the wapentakes of Flaxwell and Aswardhurn, Trollope remains an essential starting point and a vital reference tool. His occasional anecdotal digressions - like his memorable story of the drunken coach ride around Dunston pillar in the opening pages - reward readers in a way few modern historians can emulate.

As Newton commented, we see further now only by standing on the shoulders of giants. As the only person since Trollope's time with the audacity or impertinence to attempt to do this to him, it is a particular honour for me to have been asked to write a foreword to this reprint. Somehow, I think people will still be reading Trollope long after my own work is forgotten and I hope that this reprinted edition will help to prolong that process for another 130 years.

Simon Pawley
Sleaford
16th February 1999

CHRISTOPHER WORDSWORTH, D.D.,

LORD BISHOP OF LINCOLN.

BELIEVING your Lordship to be one of those who regret that there is no History of Lincolnshire worthy of such a designation, although I cannot supply that want, I beg leave most respectfully to dedicate this little volume to you, as one which may supply some materials towards a future History, and I trust prove useful in affording information respecting Sleaford, formerly a possession of the Bishops of Lincoln, and the parishes around it.

Looking back upon the past, as you are accustomed to do with a keen perception and deep interest, I fear your Lordship has found but little information gathered up ready for your use with respect to the important County of Lincoln, except the acts of some of the more distinguished of your predecessors, although from its size and wealth, and connection with the Royal House of Lancaster, it is one of the most important in England.

I have often been urged to undertake the task of compiling such a History; but have ever felt that the labour required would be too great for me, engaged as I constantly am in more urgent and ceaseless professional duties, as well as from the fact that the cost of its production would be very great, if illustrated and printed in a form worthy of the County of Lincoln, and of comparison with the already published Histories of other counties.

No doubt much has been lost through the delay that has occurred in the supply of such a work; but something also has been gained, because until of late years the knowledge of ecclesiastical architecture, and of archæology generally was so limited.

I fear that my task of attempting to describe the town of Sleaford and the parishes within the Wapentakes of Flaxwell and Aswardhurn, together with a few others, will not by any means be found faultless, and has certainly not been accomplished in so complete a manner as I could have wished; but yet considering the very great difficulties of compiling even a little work like this, arising from the scantiness of materials and other causes, I trust that you will accept it as a small mark of the deep respect I feel for your Lordship personally, as well as in your public capacity, as one of the most learned and excellent of that long series of Prelates who have successively presided over the great Diocese of Lincoln.

I am,

With the utmost respect,

Your obedient servant,

EDWARD TROLLOPE.

PREFACE.

I T is now forty-six years since the only work descriptive of
Sleaford and its vicinity was published by the late Mr.
James Creasey, so that had this been a perfect production originally, it would now require considerable revision and additions;
but as the knowledge of Ecclesiastical Architecture, of Antiquities,
and other kindred subjects, has in this interim very greatly advanced, and thus enabled us to describe the fabrics of churches
and relics of past ages with far greater accuracy than could have
been done half a century ago, a demand for a new History of
Sleaford and its vicinity has naturally arisen.

At first it was proposed to make the old work serve as a
foundation of a new one, in the hope that with alterations and
additions it might be reproduced in a more correct form; but by
degrees the old materials have almost entirely disappeared during
this process, except the extracts from Domesday book, Testa de
Nevill, and Gervase Holles, &c., which only required revision,
while even the limits of the area around Sleaford now described,
differ from those adopted in Creasey's work, so as distinctly to
confine these to two of the ancient Wapentakes or Hundreds of
Lincolnshire, although at the earnest desire of some, a few
parishes beyond those boundaries are described in a supplement
of this volume, because they were included in the old History,
but contrary to my own judgment, because this interferes with
the limits of other Wapentakes or Hundreds, the history of which
I hope may hereafter be written. As, however, by the arrangement adopted, the supplement can easily be detatched from this
volume whenever this work is undertaken, I am reconciled to its
temporary appearance in this volume.

Excepting the engravings of the Churches, taken from photographs, and a few others kindly drawn by the Rev. Charles
Terrot, all the illustrations have been engraved from the Author's
own drawings.

As the history of each parish usually begins with extracts from Domesday Book, a few words respecting the origin and character of that important work will perhaps be acceptable. It is not quite certain when its compilation was commenced, some asserting that this took place so early as the year 1080, but from the evidence of the following entry at the end of the second volume it certainly appears to have been finished in the year 1086. "Anno milessimo octogessimo sexto, ab incarnatione Domini facta est ipsa descriptio, non solum per hos tres Comitatus, sed etiam per alios." If so, it did not altogether owe its origin to the tyranny of the Conqueror as is usually supposed, but from the necessity of providing means for the defence of the of the kingdom against enemies, most probably when a Danish invasion was apprehended in 1085, and there was no national army to protect England, so that King William was forced to procure a large force from Normandy and Brittany ; but as these troops were quartered upon the English to their dislike and inconvenience they readily submitted to a measure providing for their future defence through themselves, according to the evidence of the Council of Sarum. To apportion this burden equitably a survey of England was ordered to be made, and the feudal tenure of its lands was then commenced, on the ground of the necessity for supplying the necessary means for the national defence.

This survey was made by Commissioners, of whom Remigius Bishop of Lincoln, Walter Gifford Earl of Buckingham, Henry de Ferrers and Adam the brother of Eudo Dapifer were appointed to survey the midland counties, including Lincolnshire, whence we may fairly assume that the first of these took a leading part in the compilation of the report referring to Lincolnshire. The name Domesday Book was not a novel one, for Alfred's Codex, or Liber Judicialis, consisting of his laws, was termed his "Dom-Boc ;" but king William's book is of a different character, consisting as it does, not of laws, but of a record of the quantity of the lands of England and of their value in the time of Edward the Confessor and when the record was taken, together with a description of the same and other particulars, as well as of their possessors, tenants and servants. Occasional reference is also made to the churches and priests of the places described, and other matters, but only in an incidental and imperfect manner. It was also called formerly by other names, viz., Liber Regis, Rotulus Wintoniæ, and Scriptura Thesauri Regis, &c.

It contains the united returns of the Commissioners employed in its production, who were empowered to summon all persons they pleased to give evidence as to the value, quantity and particulars of the lands and possessions of every lordship. These returns were transcribed into two volumes, one rather larger than the other, the first of which begins with Kent and ends with Lincolnshire, and was long kept in the royal Treasury at Winchester under the guardianship of the auditor, chamberlain, and deputy chamberlain of the Exchequer, but is now preserved in the new Record House attached to the Rolls Chapel.

The other earlier authorities often quoted are Testa de Nevill, compiled in 1270; Valor Ecclesiasticus, 1535; Leland's Itinerary, 1546; Willis's MS.

Some explanation of the character and quantity of the lands referred to in this volume under different terms may perhaps be useful. Of these the following are most frequently mentioned, viz:—

A soc, sock, or soke. This was a territory over which a lord exercised the right of administering justice, and in connection with which he possessed various privileges.

A manor is a lordship, the name of which is still in common use. It was first adopted in England in the reign of Edward the Confessor, and derives its name from tha French *manoir*.

Demesne, or demesne lands, a term retained in that of domain, consisted of a portion of a manor usually lying around or near to the aula of the lord, and cultivated for him by his servants.

A knight's fee consisted of 8 carucates or hides.

A carucate was a piece of plough land varying in quantity according to the character of its soil, but usually consisted of 120 acres.

An oxgang, or bovate, also varied in quantity according to the quality of the land, because it was computed to be as much land as an ox could plough annually, but most commonly consisted of 16 acres.

A selion was a ridge of land, or headland, lying between two furroughs of no definite extent.

A croft was a small home close.

A toft, a small plot of ground with a house upon it, or on which a house had once stood.

A curtilage, a garden, or yard, attached to a house.

Under the feudal system all subjects held their lands of the king, and these were usually granted by the holders to subtenants—wholly or in part. Below these were two classes of inferior tenants termed sokemen—*i.e.*, free sokemen, who simply paid rent for the land they held of a lord or sub-tenant; and base sokemen, who paid for their land in labour. Next in rank came bordars, who were small tenants or cottagers paying for their holdings in kind to their territorial lord. Lastly came villans, who were bondmen attached to their lord's land, and sold or given to others with the land on which they lived and died.

The right of "free warren" was a license from the king to preserve and kill game; and a license to "crenellate," was one sanctioning the fortification of a castle or house, also obtainable only through the king's consent.

One particular respecting a now well known house in Sleaford, that has come under the Author's notice since the description of the town has been printed, he desires now to record. About the year 1700, Mr. William Alvey, the founder of the school in Sleaford still bearing his name, built the handsome old house in Northgate next to the Sessions House, now used as Messrs. Peacock & Handley's banking house. He erected it on the site of an old inn called the Talbot, and lived in it until his death in 1729. Originally the door was in the middle of the house, and over it are the initials E. A. in a cipher, which were those of his wife, in compliment to whom they appear there. This noted Sleaford benefactor was succeeded by Mr. Alvey Darwin, probably a nephew of his; and then by a surgeon. In 1803, Messrs. Peacock & Handley's Bank, first established in the Market-place, April 2nd, 1792, was removed to this house, but its original character has been but little altered and is an excellent specimen of a small but handsome house of the 17th century, besides which the fact of its having been Alvey's house gives it additional value.

In 1723, a disastrous fire occurred at Sleaford, the recollection of which has now entirely passed away locally, but a record of which remains through the medium of the following advertisement in the *Stamford Mercury*, dated Thursday, March 26th, 1723-4: "These are to give notice to the several Towns and the Ministers and Churchwardens of the same, unto whom divers Letters Recommendatory have been sent, to collect their

charity for the relief of the sufferers by the late sad and violent
fire, which happened at New Sleeford in the County of Lincoln,
that such of the said Towns as have not collected or returned
their collections for the said fire, are desired to collect and pay
in their respective sums so to be gathered at the next Visitation,
viz., unto Mr. Joseph Williamson at Boston, the Reverend Mr.
Thomas Sellers at Sleeford, and Mr. John Algate at Grantham,
who will be there, and ready to receive the same."

Last year—1871, two large stones were found in Ruskington
opposite the churchyard gate, and about a foot below the surface
of the town street. These were a little more than 3 feet square.
In the centre of one was a socket about a foot square, which
seems to indicate that they once served as the base of a village
cross.

The William Benningworth, or Benniworth, mentioned in
the account of Howell as its first recorded rector, was the
founder of the Franciscan Friary at Lincoln, 1230.

ILLUSTRATIONS.

LIST OF SUBSCRIBERS.

Ashington, Rev. H., Anwick
Anders, Rev. H., Kirkby Laythorpe
Andrews, Mr., Osbournby
Amcotts, Colonel, M.P., Hackthorne Hall, Lincoln
Abraham, Mr., Sleaford
Adlard, Mr., Ruskington
Atkin, Miss A., Heckington
Almond, Mr., London
Allen, Mr. E., Sleaford
Allen, Mr. W., Sleaford
Appleby, Mr. E., Grantham
Bristol, the Most Noble the Marquis of
Brownlow, the Right Hon. the Earl of
Boot, J. H., Esq., M.D., Sleaford
Bedford, J., Esq., Sleaford
Barnes, Rev. C., Digby
Brewitt, Mr. Jno., Sleaford
Bampton, Mr. T., Sleaford
Barnes, Mr. Jas., Heckington
Bellamy, Mr., Spanby
Bennison, Mr. M., Sleaford
Blasson, G., Esq., Heckington
Blasson, Thos., Esq., Billingborough
Bettis, Rev. G. R., Doncaster
Bacon, Alfred, Esq., Cheadle, near Manchester
Brand, Mr. J., Billinghay
Brown, Mr. J. C., Sleaford
Buttifant, Mr. J. G., Romsey
Blaze, Mr., Louth
Baxter, Mr. John, Sleaford
Bell, Rev. James, Sleaford
Bacon, Mr. John, Sleaford
Bacon, Mr. John T., Sleaford
Chevin, Mr. H., Leasingham
Chamberlain, Mr. G., Sleaford
Cragg, E., Esq., Threckingham

Child, Rev. C., Sleaford
Cook, Mr., Heckington
Cameron, Rev. G. T., Heckington
Clarke, Miss, Scredington
Coney, Mr., Sleaford
Collinson, Mr. H., Burton-on-Trent
Collinson, Mr. F.
Clements, E., Esq., Sleaford
Chambers, Mr. John, South Kyme
Cumberworth, Mr. H., Heckington
Christopher, Mr. Z., Heckington
Cammack, T., Esq., M.D., Spalding
Clay, Mr., Holdingham
Count, Mr. J. C., Sleaford
Chapman, Mr.
Cartwright, Mr. E., Sleaford
Dolby, Rev. J. S., Howell
Dudding, W., Esq., Howell
Dibben, Mr. E. R., Sleaford
England, C., Esq., Sleaford
Elcombe, Mr. E., Sleaford
Evison, Mr., Ewerby
Ellwoood, Mr. D., Sleaford
Frudd, Mr. J., Bloxholm
Fawcett, Mr. T., Sleaford
Foster, W. H., Esq., Cranwell
Fane, W. D., Esq., Norwood, Southwell
Ffytche, J. L., Esq., Thorpe Hall, Louth
Fryer, Mr. W., Sleaford
Graves, Mr., Ashby
Gardner, Rev. H., B.A., Liverpool
Green, John, Esq., Knipton
Godson, G., Esq., Heckington
Gibson, Mr. Joseph, Sleaford
Goodacre, Mr. W., Sleaford
Green, Mr., Sleaford

Goodwin, Mr. Geo. P., Nottingham
Hamilton, Right Honble. R. C. N., Bloxholm Hall
Hervey, G. H. W., Esq., Sleaford
Holdich, W. H., Esq., Sleaford
Holdich, C. W., Esq., Sleaford
Holdich, Miss, Sleaford
Heald, Mr. B., Sleaford
Hervey, Mrs., Osbournby
Hine, Mrs., Sleaford
Hervey, Mrs., Cranwell
Hunt, Mr. W., Sleaford
Hubbard, Mr., Ewerby Thorpe
Harris, Mr. W. H., Sleaford
Harris, Mr. Thomas, Hale
Hudson, Mr., Ruskington
Hipkin, Mr. F., Sleaford
Harris, Mr., Heckington
Houson, Rev. H., Brant Broughton
Harris, Mr., Anwick
Hand, Mr., Billinghay
Hyde, Mr. John, Sleaford
Hoole, Miss, Heckington
Ingoldby, H., Esq., Sleaford
Jacobson, T. E., Esq., Sleaford (2)
Jackson, Mr. W., Sleaford
Jackson, Mr., Ipswich
Jenkins, Rev. E. C. F., Billinghay
Johnson, Mr., Sleaford
Jackson, Mr. John, Swineshead
Jackson, Mr., Vachery
Jackson, Mr. W., West-st., Sleaford
Kirk, C., Esq., Sleaford
Knight, H., Esq., Sleaford
Knapp, Rev. H., Swaton
Lambert, Mr. J. C., Sleaford
Lynes, Rev. W., Miningsby
Loder, R., Esq., London
Laurent, Rev. Felix, B.A., Saleby
Latham, Rev. F., Helpringham
Marston, J. T., Esq., Sleaford
Matson, Rev. W. T., Sleaford
Martin, Mr. R., Sleaford
Morris, Mr. Joseph, Sleaford
Mason, Rev. J. M., Silk Willoughby
Mutter, G., Esq , Aswarby
Morton, Mr. J., Boston (2)

Mitchell, Mr., Holbeach (2)
Mackinder, Mr.
Nickolls, Jno., Esq., Sleaford
Nightingarl, Mr., Sleaford
Ostick, Mr. M., Sleaford
Ogden, Mr., Ruskington
Onslow, Mrs., Leigh, Tunbridge Wells
Parry, Thos., Esq., Sleaford
Peake, H., Esq., Sleaford
Pickworth, Mr. James, Kirkby Laythorpe
Peacock, Edward, Esq., Bottesford Manor, near Brigg
Pogson, S., Esq., Anwick
Phillips, J., Esq., Stamford
Pattinson, Mr. S., Ruskington
Pattinson, Mr. W., Ruskington
Pearson, Mrs., Colsterworth, Grantham
Parkinson, Mr. J. H., East Sheen, Surrey
Paradise, T., Esq., Stamford
Parker, Mr., Fulbeck
Poucher, Mrs., Rauceby
Pogson, F. M., Esq., Anwick
Partridge, Mr. M., Heckington
Pedrette, Mr. Sleaford
Robinson, Mr. J. G., Sleaford
Reading, Mr., Heckington
Roberts, Mr. R., Sleaford
Rusby, Mr., London
Roberts, Mr. John, Sleaford
Robinson, Mrs., Kensington, London
Rippon, Mr. W., Burton Pedwardine
Roberts, Mr. A., Sleaford
Roberts, W. B., Esq., Park Hill, Streatham, Surrey
Rodgers, C., Esq., Sleaford
Repton, Mr. J. M., Sleaford
Roberts, Mr. W., Sleaford
Rest, Mr. M., London
Simpson, T., Esq., Sleaford
Snow, H., Esq., Sleaford
Sewards, Mr. J., Junr., Sleaford
Scarr, Rev. G., Ruskington
Salmon, Mr. J., Sleaford
Swiss, Mr., South Kyme
Smith, J., Esq., Birstal

Stacye, Rev. J. M., Shrewsbury Hospital, Sheffield
Smith, Miss C., Kensington Park Gardens, Notting Hill
Sandy, Mr., Haverholme
Smith, Mr., Junr., Ewerby
Sumner, Mr. Geo., Rauceby
Smith, H., Esq., Horbling
Snow, Rev. B., Burton Pedwardine
Simpson, Mr. Justin, Stamford
Struggles, Rev. T., Bakersville, U.S.
Stennett, Mr., Ewerby
Smedley, Miss, Sleaford
Stainer, Mr. W., Sleaford
Stout, Mr. W., Sleaford
Sneath, Mr., Senr., Sleaford
Sharpe, Mr. T., Sleaford
Sumner, Mrs. H.
Tindale, T. P., Esq., Sleaford (2)
Thoroton, Rev. C., Rauceby
Tomlinson, E., Esq., Helpringham

Thurlby, J., Esq., Rauceby
Thorpe, Mr. T., Ewerby
Tinley, J., Esq., Silk Willoughby
Torey, Mr., Billinghay
Tomlinson, B., Esq., Asgarby
Thorpe, Mr. R., Evedon
Tomlinson, J. H., Esq., Barton-on-Humber
Thompson, E., M., Esq,, Billinghay
Taylor, Mr. J., Quarrington
Whichcote, Sir Thos., Aswarby Park
Whichcote, Rev. C., Aswarby
Whichcote, G., Esq., Osbournby
Willson, M. W., Esq., Rauceby Hall
Welby, W. E., Esq., M.P., Newton House
Weaver, Mr. Jos., Sleaford
Williams, Mr. S., Sleaford
Wainer, Mr. T., Sleaford
Wells, Mr. S., Leasingham
Young, Rev. J. P. B., Wilsford

ERRATA.

Page 98, line 20—"Saxon" for "Roman."
Page 115, line 25—"1431" for "1820."
Page 333, line 15—"Angus" for "Anjou."
Page 421, liue 20—"Donington" for "Dorrington."

LIST OF SUBSCRIBERS TO THE REPRINTED EDITION

Rachael Affleck, Dunsby
St Andrew
Paul & Anthea Ashmore, Sleaford
Dr & Mrs R.K. Allday, Boston
Mrs P.A. Allpress, Sleaford
Simon Andrews, North Kyme
John Anthony, Pinchbeck
Betty Arnold, The Old Vicarage,
Howell Road, Heckington
Wendy J. Atkin, Sleaford
The Rev F.H. Bailey, Scopwick
Raymond Bailey, Sleaford
Nigel H. Ball, Ruskington
Keith Stanley Bampton,
Leasingham
P. Banister, Heckington
T.E. Barton, Sleaford & District
Civic Trust
George Charles Bason,
Bembridge, Isle of Wight
Malcolm Derek Baxter, Digby
Mark Bennet, Lincoln
Tim & Sindy Benton, Sleaford
R.J. Betteridge,
Welton By Lincoln
Anne P. Blanchard, N. Ferriby
Rebecka Blenntoft,
Heritage Lincolnshire
Revd D. F. Boutle
David G. Bramford, Dembleby
Mr & Mrs Brewster, Leasingham
Mr and Mrs J. Brock, Sleaford
& District Civic Trust
P.W.S. Brown, Frieston
Michael W. L. Brown
Dr J. Clevedon Brown, Sleaford
Miss S.B. Butler, Sleaford

P.G.D. Byllam-Barnes, Ashtead
Rodney & Janet Callow, Lincoln
Miss E.M. Chester, Spalding
Gerald Clarke, Sleaford
Graham H. Clay, Billingborough,
Gwen Clay, Boston
Patricia J. Clement, Sleaford &
District Civic Trust
A. Colahan, HADFAS,
Holland & Kesteven Branch
Mr & Mrs W.H. Collin,
Peterborough
Alan & Jill Cook, Sleaford
Peter & Julia Dabbs, Ruskington
R.W & Miss M.M. Dales,
Mablethorpe
Charles Arthur Daubney, Sleaford
June & Edward Dawes,
New Malden, Surrey
Miss E.M. Dickinson, Digby
George H. Dobbs, Leasingham
Mr & Mrs K. J. Dolby, Sleaford
Yvonne & Eddy Double, Sleaford
& District Civic Trust
Mrs Ruby Doughty, Sleaford
Christopher Edwards, S. Rauceby
Mrs D.R. Etienne, Scredington
Paul Everson, Nantwich
Mr & Mrs Fawcett, Baumber
Fred Felstead, Bourne
Mrs Lesley Fluck (Younger),
Newnham on Severn
Peter Freeman, Sleaford
Hugh Frost, Sleaford
John Gale O.B.E., Boston
Mrs Jean Garfoot, Navenby

James Walter Gash, Sleaford
Dr Richard Gill, Newbury
Glenn Anderson Associates
Roger Goodburn, Oxford
Mr & Mrs J.M. Goodin, Sleaford
Matt Green, Heckington
Margaret Green
M. & J. Greenfield, Dorrington
Pat Gregory, Nettleham
Mrs D.E. Gregson, Sleaford &
    District Civic Trust
Sheila & Harry Grossmith,
    Heckington
Jack Anthony Gunson, Spilsby
H.G. & M.W. Haines, Sleaford
Eleanor Hall, Newlandrig
Dr Alan A. Hall, Sleaford
Dr N.J. & Mrs E. Hards, Didcot
Hilary Healey
Bernice & Jim Hepple, Sleaford
Colin Hill, Sleaford
Mr C.J. Hillcoat, Ashby de la
    Launde
Val Hinkins, Cherry Willingham
Roy Hix, Sleaford
Douglas C. Hoare, Sleaford
Christopher J. Hodgson, Lincoln
Elizabeth Hodgson, Sleaford &
    District Civic Trust
Robert J.B. Hodgson, Sleaford &
    District Civic Trust
T.W. Hollingworth, Barrowby
Geoff Holmes, Heckington
Jim Holton, South Rauceby
Jim Hopkins, M.B.E. History of
    Boston Project
David W. Hopkins, Heckington
Mr & Mrs B Horgan, Sleaford
A.E. Horstead, Sleaford
Robert Hoyes, Stixwould
L. & M. Hulse, Heckington
Institute of Historical Research,
    University of London
Ian Jebbett, Sleaford
Mrs Ann Keighley, Hemingby

Margaret E. Kent (nee Beecroft),
    Colwall
Mr & Mrs J.O. Kirk, Sleaford &
    District Civic Trust
Mrs J. Kirkham, Sleaford
Josef & Helen Kirschner,
    Kirkby-La-Thorpe
Gavin Lawrence, Maidstone
John R. Lee, Sleaford
George Henry Lefley
Mark R. Leggott, Holland Fen
Library Services, Lincolnshire
    County Council
S.F. Long, Billingborough
M.J. Love
Mrs Elaine Y. Lovell,
    Eagle Moor, Lincoln
Eva Maplethorpe, Sleaford
Mr D. A. Marsh, Ruskington
Diana M. Marvin
Gordon & Kathleen Matthew,
    Sleaford
Keith & Sue May, Caythorpe
Mrs Sheila McAlpine Stevens,
    Leasingham
J.P. & W.L. McConnell,
    Kirkby-La-Thorpe
Mr P.G. Mead, Sleaford &
    District Civic Trust
L.F. & E.A. Mills, Sleaford
John Mitchell, Silk Willoughby
Godfrey Money, Bognor Regis
Peter & Phyl Montgomery,
    Scothern
J.C. Morgan, London
Mr & Mrs J. E. Morris,
    South Kyme
Revd Richard Morrison, Digby
Miss F.A.R. Murray, Lincoln
Mrs E.M. Nickols
Dr Margaret R. Nieke, York
Richard Oliver, University of
    Exeter
Mr & Mrs P. Onyon, Sleaford

Arthur & Dorothy Owen,
S.L.H.A & L.R.S.
Peter Paddison,
Southend on Sea
Nigel Panting, Roxholm
Stuart Parker, Lincoln
E.J. Patterson, Ruskington
Gordon Paul, Grantham
Simon Pawley, Sleaford
Alison Peach, Lincoln
Stephen Peatfield, Metheringham
G.I. Phillips, Lincoln
Angus Pilton, Heckington
Charles Pinchbeck, Heckington
Sue Pittendreigh, Billinghay Fen
Revd Gordon Plumb,
Saxby-All-Saints
Mrs Pat Pomeroy, Fishtoft
John N. Porter, Thornford
G.R. Prentice, Sleaford &
District Civic Trust
David Price, Harrington
His Hon. Judge A.J. Proctor,
Lancaster
P. Ratcliffe, Silk Willoughby
Alan Redmond Books,
Billingborough
Mrs Sheila Redshaw, Nocton
Mr James & Mrs Maureen
Renfrew, Sleaford
D.N. Robinson OBE, Louth
Mr & Mrs R. Ruck, Little Steeping
Mr A. & Mrs M. Ruck, Boston
Mr & Mrs A.W. Russell,
Helpringham
Mr E.W. & Mrs P.V. Rylatt,
Broughton
Alan Sagar, Wainfleet
Dr John Samuels, Normanton-
on-Trent
S.M.A. Sardeson, Howell
Trevor Sentence, Leasingham
Trevor & June Sharp, Pinchbeck
R.W. Shaw, Sleaford
Matt & Betty Skipp, Ewell, Surrey
David & Jane Smith, Sleaford

Mr & Mrs M.G. Smith, Sleaford
G.R. Smith
Gordon Smith, Leasingham
Mr C.M. Smith, Sleaford
Jane Smith, Kings Langley
Mr & Mrs H.S. Stanley,
Helpringham
D. Start, Heritage Lincolnshire
Jenny Stevens, Gosport
P.E. Stevenson
St George's College of
Technology, Sleaford
David Stocker, Oxford
Carole & Maurice Tennant,
Holbeach
J.R. Thompson, Sleaford
Simon G. Titley, Sleaford
Martin W. Titley, Sleaford
Mr & Mrs R. Tong, Dorrington
Michelle Towers, Sleaford
Jemma Louise Trollope, Sleaford
David & Ada Tretheway, Sleaford
& District Civic Trust
D.A. Turland, Sleaford
Michael Turland, Sleaford
Ralph Wadsworth, Potterhanworth
Mr J.M. Walker, Cardiff
Mrs E.M. Walker, Nettleham
Mrs Elizabeth Walters, Horbling
R.S.R. Warnes
R.J. Watts, Thorpe Latimer
Pearl Wheatley, Lincoln
George Henry Wilkinson, Boston
Mrs Mary Wilkinson,
R.J. Willars, King's Lynn
Alun Williams, Quarrington
Martin Williams & Gillian Darby,
Swinstead
Canon Tom Williamson,
Canon of Lincoln (retired)
F.A. & E.M. Winter, Sleaford
Margaret Withers, Sleaford
D.R. Woodthorpe, Digby
Edward Wreglesworth, Wellingore
Mrs Maureen Anne Young, Sleaford

HISTORY

SLEAFORD AND THE NEIGHBOURHOOD,

INCLUDED IN THE

WAPENTAKES OF FLAXWELL AND ASWARDHURN.

———————————

THE boundaries of the area around Sleaford proposed to be described, and lying within the Wapentakes of Flaxwell and Aswardhurn, are these, viz. :—the High Dyke on the west, Langoe Wapentake on the north, or a line just south of Wellingore, Kirkby Green, Thorpe Tilney, Walcot, and Billinghay, Kyme Eau and Holland Dyke on the east, separating the Division of Kesteven from that of Holland; and the Wapentakes of Winnibriggs with Threo and Aveland on the south, or a line a little to the north of the Bridgend road. This area constitutes nearly a perfect square, from 12 to 13 miles across, diagonally subdivided by the boundary between the two Wapentakes it comprises, with Sleaford almost exactly in the middle. In the Wapentake of Flaxwell there are 22 parishes or hamlets, containing in all 50,937 acres, and a population of 9,705; and in Aswardhurn 24 parishes or hamlets, an acreage of 48,134, and a population of 8,070. The soil of the first is heath over an

A

Oolite rock on the west, clay of various qualities and occasionally gravel in the middle, and peaty soil on the east over silt, gravel, or clay. That of the latter is for the most part clay, and fen towards the east over Oxford clay. Except the fen portion of these Wapentakes their surface slightly undulates and is scored by several small rivulets flowing from west to east towards the sea, of which the Slea is the chief.

As the heath and fen portions of the two Wapentakes are peculiar features some description of these will perhaps be acceptable. Formerly one continuous tract of light land called generally Lincoln Heath extended from the high table ground on the south of Lincoln and the Witham to Cranwell, or about 13 miles. It rises gradually from under the Oxford clay stratum on the east and terminates in a steep ridge as it sinks suddenly towards the Lias district on the west ; but besides this, its whole surface consists of a series of gentle undulations resembling those of the Atlantic after a storm, and the straight white road carried over these in succession on its way northwards, does not very inaptly represent the foamy track of some vast steam-ship, such as the Great Eastern leaves behind her in calm weather, while the shadows of the little clouds passing over the surface of the Heath, just as they do on the real ocean, add to the correctness of the comparison. Beneath a thin layer of light soil, from 9 to 18 inches in depth, is a thick stratum of limestone, belonging to what geologists call the series of the " Great Oolite." At some very remote period, and during countless centuries, water was gradually depositing the limy particles with which it was charged on the clay beneath it, until it formed a coating many feet in thickness, sometimes sympathising with the undulations of the subsoil, and sometimes drifting into its deeper hollows, so as to cause a considerable degree of variation in its thickness. It has also been subjected to other subsequent disturbing causes, from the pent-up powers of the earth's deeper recesses. A remarkable example of this may be seen in a railway-cutting between Ancaster and Wilsford, where an upward thrust from below is exhibited, forming a rounded eminence beset with fissures, now filled in with earth that has been washed in from the surface.

Many deeds of violence have been perpetrated on this heath. One was long recorded in the nave of Lincoln Minster to this effect : " Here lies John Ranceby, formerly Canon of this church, who was with malice prepense nefariously slain on the ' Haythe ' (spelt thus) in the year of our Lord 1388 by William ————. God have mercy upon his soul." The surname of the murderer had been effaced either by accident or design. In latter times it was men's purses rather than their lives that were in great danger on the heath—through highwaymen, by which it was infested. Even in the last century the Windmill House in the parish of Leasingham, was a favourite place of assemblage for these gentlemen of the road—as they were termed, and a little hollow on the Lincoln road in Dunsby parish, now marked by a row of cottages, was the most common scene of attack upon travellers. But there were also natural dangers arising from the character of the heath in olden days. When no well-kept roads traversed it, and it could boast of still fewer houses upon it than at present, poor folks were often lost upon its dreary expanse, and some died from prolonged exposure to cold and wind and snow on the heath. In the register of Leasingham parish are several evidences of such misfortunes, within a space of 53 years nine poor travellers having apparently just reached that place, on the southern confines of the heath, to die. They run as follows in the list of burials : —" Elizabeth Ping, a stranger ;" " Susanna Ellis, a traveller ;" " Dolton Pickworth, a poor stranger ;" and sometimes even still shorter, such as " A travelling woman," or " A travelling man," without a name at all ; yet these speak of unknown sufferings as well as of unknown persons. Two remarkable instances of thank-offerings for preservation from starvation on the heath still throw light upon this point : the first is connected with the parish of Blankney, where a small field was left by a female whose life had been saved through the tolling of its church bell, on condition that that bell should be rung every evening at 8 o'clock. The other case is connected with Potterhanworth, where 23 acres of land, called Culfrey-lands, were left by a traveller who had been rescued from the heath by hearing the sound of Potterhanworth church bell, on condition that that bell should be tolled every evening at 10 minutes to 7, by the oldest parishioner who had not received parochial relief, and who was to have the proceeds of the land as his fee. But at length a greater benefactor was found in the person of Sir Francis Dashwood, who erected Dunston Pillar, and placed upon its summit a

large glass lantern that was lighted every night for the purpose of
guiding benighted travellers on their way across the heath. And
no doubt it served that purpose well, but yet did not always
enable people to get to their own homes in safety, especially when
they had been carousing at the Green Man club—formerly much
frequented by the gentry of the neighbourhood, and when far
more liquor was unhappily consumed than now ; for it is recorded
that two of these on their way towards Lincoln, after they had been
assisted into their carriage, and their coachman had been previously assisted into his box, thought it prudent to give him the
following directions :—"John, be sure you keep the pillar light
upon your right, and then we shall get home safe," before sinking
into sleep. But when these sleepers awoke they found the sun
was rising, and that they were still near the Pillar, and still in
their carriage instead of being in their beds, one of them called
out, "Why, John, where are we ?" Upon which John answered,
"Oh, it's all right, sir, the light is upon my right ;" and so it was,
for he had been circling round it all night, and was not much
nearer home than when he began to drive. Violence and dangers
have now happily passed away, and there are no murderers or
robbers on the Heath, nor need even for a light on Dunston
Pillar.   Hence instead of a lantern, a statue of good King
George III. surmounts the Pillar at Dunston ; but could he see
the wonderful change that has taken place on the surrounding
district between the time of his accession to the throne and the
year 1870, he would be indeed greatly astonished ; and although
when it was told him that Lord Buckinghamshire intended to set
up a statue in his honour upon Lincoln Heath, he is reported to
have said, "Ah! Lincolnshire, all flats, fogs, and fens!" and did
not relish the idea at all ; could he now see the locality where
that statue still stands he might be justly proud of that portion
of his kingdom.

      Some notice of the character of the fen land of Lincolnshire,
a portion of which lies within the Wapentakes of Flaxwell and
Aswardhurn, is next required.

      A great contest between the sea and the land, leading to fre-
quent changes in their respective boundaries, had certainly been
raging upon the Lincolnshire coast for centuries before the arrival
of the Romans in Britain, and that period when written records
began to be kept.   Doubtless the ocean has there, from time to

time, swept far beyond its natural limits with an irresistible tide, reaching points in Lincolnshire now removed nearly twenty miles from it;* and yet, little by little, it has, through its very fury, aided to form a future barrier against itself. This it has done by the accumulation of the silt left upon its retreat, in concert with the earthy deposits caused by the continual flow of the inland waters, not only on either side of those points where they have respectively found an exit into the sea, but generally in that great bay of the Wash and its adjoining shores, reaching from Wainfleet to Hunstanton on the Norfolk coast, and so appropriately termed by Ptolemy "*Mentaris æstuarium,*" or bay of river mouths. In this manner a considerable portion of the division of Holland has gradually been gained, or perhaps we may say, *re*-gained from the bed of the sea, whilst the continued growth of its coast, as well as of that of the southern part of Lindsey, is evinced by the relative position of the sea-banks that have been successively raised for its defence.

The subsoil of this district is Oxford clay, lying in waves, and once forming the surface. Over this has swept at some very remote period a vast and violent tide of waters from the N.W. to the S.E. portion of the county, which has left thick beds of drift behind it, consisting of white silty clay, boulders, large yellow water-worn flints, numerous beds of gravel, intermingled with which are teeth and bones of elephants and various animals,† besides other deposits. Lincolnshire has, apparently, to thank Yorkshire, or some more northern locality for this furious inroad, for through some convulsion of nature a compound and chaotic marine flood once swept along the vale of York and the

---

* At Roxholme, near Sleaford, there exists a silty substratum abounding with cockle and other ordinary sea shells ; and at Holbeach Hurn, a distance of three miles from the sea, a seam of cockle shells, three inches thick, was traced by Dr. Latham two or three feet below the present surface. This was on land in the occupation of Mr. Baily, near Fleet Haven.

† At Partney, a fossil tooth was found, weighing two pounds three ounces, in the gravel bed near Partney Mill, in 1822, twelve feet below the surface. It was supposed to have been one of the grinders of a hippopotamus or elephant. —Oldfield Addenda, p. 20. Another similar tooth was found at Quarrington, a few years ago, also in the gravel ; and the skull of a cetacean, from the Lincolnshire fens, now in the Cambridge Museum, was supplied by the late Mr. Hopkinson, of Morton.

north-eastern portion of Lincolnshire, until, reaching that point
of the Cliff hills through which the Witham flows, at Lincoln,
it burst over the whole tract of the lowlands of this county,
and found an exit eventually in the sea. This will fully
account for the layer of white silty clay often found above the
Oxford clay, and filled with marine shells, as well as for the
boulders and beds of gravel, &c , such as those near Lincoln, at
Kyme, Tattershall, Edenham, Baston, Deeping, &c. So far the
sea had lorded it over a considerable portion of the Lincolnshire
soil, but a rival then became predominant, for fresh-water gained
the ascendancy, and has plainly left the mark of its reign behind
it in the form of a soapy blue clay, varying in tint and abounding
with fresh-water shells. This is doubtless the deposit of sluggish
streams and prevalent floods occasioned by the continual run of
waters from the higher lands of the county before they were
assisted on their way towards the sea by the hand of man ; but
the ocean was not tamed as yet, and we can see that it occasionally gave battle to the fresh waters and their prey, at this period,
by the existence of channels filled with marine silt running up
into the blue clay in the form of bays and creeks. This stratum
contained amply sufficient fertilizing matter for the sustenance of
the finest trees of various kinds, and from it sprang up oaks of
vast dimensions, lofty firs, alders, hazels, and birch trees, whose
roots are still firmly fixed in the soil that originally so amply
nourished them, whilst their innumerable trunks lie prostrate
beneath a funeral pall of black peaty earth created by the debris
of their own leaves mixed with decayed vegetable matter, such as
stagnant waters always produce.

Occasionally, but more rarely, the sea still disturbed these
vegetable cemeteries, for we find silty deposits of considerable
thickness in some portions of the fens above the peaty stratum,
and in a few instances alternating with it more than once.* How
long the lands we are speaking of remained at a sufficiently high
level above both fresh and sea waters to enable them to nourish
trees of great size, including oaks varying from one foot to ten in

* In Sutton St. Edmund's Parish, two strata of peat are found, alternating with others of silty clay, two or three feet thick ; also in Ramsey Fen,
where, below the peaty surface and a clay substratum, a second deep deposit
of peat exists.

diameter, is, of course, uncertain, but from their dimensions we may safely presume that this period of their growth lasted for at least five centuries. Again, how long these fen districts continued to be covered with stagnant fresh-water, after it had wrought such terrible ruin upon thousands of acres of the finest forest lands, is undeducible from any internal evidence, but they certainly were for the most part still prevalent, when a new and intelligent power drew near, already well practised in the art of combating with nature as well as with man, and that was the power of Rome. Probably the Romans were attracted to take possession of the rich Lincolnshire lowlands before the close of the first century, when they, no doubt, soon experienced considerable inconvenience from occasional irruptions of the sea, and from almost unceasing floods of fresh-water; but as they never submitted to such difficulties without a struggle, in which they were usually successful, they in this instance proceeded to encircle the whole coast of their new possession with a vast sea bank, capable of resisting all further encroachments of the sea,* and to deepen and defend the outfalls of its rivers. Next they began to gather up the valuable land they had by so much labour secured, and by the formation of a main drain, fifty-seven miles long, called the "Car Dyke," reaching from the Nen to the Witham, which caught all the waters flowing from the higher lands before they spread themselves over the lowlands, and by other drains, they completely secured for themselves the territorial fruits of their patient and enormous labours.

But, besides the coastal line of fen lands, there are vast tracts in the interior of Lincolnshire of a similar character, form-

---

* It is interesting to observe how cleverly the Romans took advantage of all such assistance from the hand of nature as could be rendered available in aiding them to form this marine barrier, incorporating in their work, as they did, every sand bank or range of Dunes tossed up upon the shore by the united agency of tides and violent winds, so as to save labour. In Tetney parish, one of these banks, about three acres in extent, and fourteen feet high, has thus been made use of, and still bears distinct evidences of having been occupied by the Britons. These consist of five circles of earth, from one to two feet high, and from nine to thirty-eight feet in diameter; and on a similar adjoining bank, upwards of four acres in extent, and divided from the first by a little streamlet, is another circle, thirty-six feet in diameter, and a large oval one, sixty-five feet long, by forty-seven in width.

ing together an aggregate of 522,000 acres, lying from four to
sixteen feet below high water level. The largest of these extends
from the Trent through the Isle of Axholme into Notts, and far
into Yorkshire, in the direction of Doncaster; De la Pryme, in his
Paper on Hatfield Chase (Philosophical Transactions, No. 275,
p. 980), observing,—"That round about by the skirts of the
Lincolnshire wolds unto Gainsburgh, Bawtry, Doncaster, Baln,
Snaith, and Holden, are found infinite millions of the roots and
bodies of trees, great and little, of most part of the sorts that this
island either formerly did, or at present does produce, as firs,
oaks, birch, beech, yew, winthorn, willow, ash, &c., the roots of
all, or most of which stand in the soil in their natural postures,
as thick as ever they could grow, as the bodies of most of them
lie by their proper roots. Most of the great trees lie all their
length about a yard from their great roots (unto which they did
most evidently belong, both by their situation and the sameness
of the wood,) with their tops most commonly north-east, though
the smaller trees lie almost every way cross those, some above,
some under, a third part of all of which are firs, some of which
have been found of 30 yards length and above, and have been
sold to make masts and keels for ships. Oaks have been found
twenty, thirty, and thirty-five yards long, yet wanting many yards
at the small end." But perhaps the monarch of all these submerged trees was an oak, also alluded to by De la Pryme, which
was fourteen yards in diameter, and forty yards long. This was
calculated to have been not less than seventy yards high, and to
have contained 1,080 feet of timber.*

From observations made in sinking a well in the Trent valley
it was found that a stone causeway existed on a shingly gravel
foundation, twenty-seven feet below the present level, above
which were fragments of Roman pottery, &c., then a thick

---

* During the year 1858 an oak was extracted from Conington Fen, Hunts,
sixty feet long to the collar, whence sprang two large limbs, each of which
alone would have formed tolerably large sized trees, the diameter of the trunk
was four feet. The level of Conington Fen has sunk five feet in consequence
of its drainage, from which cause the above-mentioned tree was revealed.
There the oaks alone are broken off from their roots, which remain embedded
in the clayey subsoil; the elms, firs, and yews, having been uprooted when
they fell, and lie prostrate in all directions.

stratum of bog earth divided into two layers by a thin intervening stratum of sand, next foundations of buildings and bones of domestic animals, then bog earth again, and finally evidences of modern cultivation. Hence it may fairly be assumed that during the Roman occupation of Britain, this vast tract of fen land bore quite a different character to what it has since done ; that it had a gravelly subsoil* and an ordinary earthy surface covered with trees, not usually if at all subject to floods, but that subsequently it became, more or less, constantly submerged so as to destroy its previous forest growth, and to cover the bodies of the former vegetable giants of the district beneath one uniform dark surface —the offspring of a very inferior annual vegetable growth and decay, mingled with earthy deposits.

This great change has usually been attributed to the burning of the forests by the Romans, on account of the covert it afforded to swarms of suffering Britons, who lost no opportunity of harassing the forces of their subjugators on their march along the great military road, or Ermine Street, between Lindum and Danum ; and there certainly are apparent signs of burning† about the stumps of some of these trees, but others have clearly been cut down, the marks of the axe still remaining perfect on their surfaces, and many more have been torn up by the roots, and occasionally splintered, perhaps by their fall. It is quite clear that the Britons and the Romans‡ used this great forest, traces of both having been discovered intermingled with its remains ; and to them may be attributed the marks of cutting and burning still apparent. But great though the power of Rome was, and abundant her supply of British slave labour, it is not possible to

---

* In the valley of the Witham, at Lincoln, all the burials in the southern Roman cemetery are in the sandy subsoil of that locale, and the sepulchral monuments, &c., of that people are always found *below* the present superincumbent moorish soil.

† It is very observable (says De la Pryme) and manifestly evident, that many of those trees, of all sorts, have been burnt, but especially the fir trees, some quite through, and some all on a side, some have been found chopped and squared, some bored through, others half riven with great wooden wedges and stones in them, and broken axe heads, somewhat like sacrificing axes in shape, and all this in such places and at such depths as could never be opened from the destruction of this forest until the time of the drainage.

‡ Close to one of the roots of the submerged trees in Hatfield, eight or nine Roman coins were found, also much Roman pottery at other spots.

conceive that such an enormous tract of woodland, as Hatfield
Chase, was destroyed by the hand of man, particularly as a
clearance of a few miles on either side of their military way and
around their various Stations by the Romans, would have answered every purpose of security ; nor would the felled trees ever
have so impeded the flow of the inland waters as to convert an
immense district of previously dry land into a permanent swamp,
as has been suggested. Another solution of this phenomenon,
therefore, must be suggested, in connection with a still more remarkable fact which remains to be described, namely, the
existence of a submarine forest off the present Lincolnshire coast.

At intervals along the shore of this county, from Sutton to
Clee-Thorpes, many banks or islands are from time to time exposed to view. These are usually covered with silt, but when
occasionally stripped of that marine deposit, they are found to
possess a substratum of moory vegetable soil, filled with the roots
of prostrate trees of very large size, accompanied by their
berries, nuts, and leaves. Some may be particularly instanced at
Huttoft, in Calceworth Hundred, and marked in Mitchell's chart
of this coast under the term of "Clay-huts," whence Huttoft
perhaps derives its name. These were visited in 1796 by Sir
Joseph Banks, and Corria de Serra, a scientific member of the
Society of Antiquaries, who published an account of his observations on that occasion in the Philosophical Transactions of the
Royal Society, whence we gather that these islands abounded
with the roots of oaks, firs, and birches, still firmly imbedded in
the soil where they grew, whilst their fallen trunks, covered with
bark in a very fresh condition, were lying near them in the midst
of a bed of partially decomposed leaves, mixed with decayed
rushes, sedges, and other vegetable matter, forming a black peaty
stratum ; the water was observed to deepen on the seaward side
of the line of islands, so as to form a steep bank, and the channels between them were from four to twelve feet deep. From
experiments made below the surface of the islands, as well as at
Sutton, Mablethorpe, and other spots on the mainland, it was
clearly ascertained that the subsoil of both was identical.

It will now be desirable to answer the very natural questions that may be put in connection with these facts, namely,
"When these districts were severally submerged by fresh and
salt water ?" and "By what agency ?"

Various theories have been advanced for the purpose of solving these problems, the principal of which are—

1. The interference of the Romans with the natural drainage.
2. A change in the coastal line through the action of the sea.
3. The agency of earthquakes causing subsidence of the earth.

Let us shortly consider each of these. There is no doubt that the Romans did raise a continuous sea bank along the greater portion of the Lincolnshire coastal line, of which considerable remains still exist; also that they deepened the outfalls of rivers and such drains as they chose to make or retain, so that in after times, during the Saxon period, should these have been neglected, as was most probably the case, the original evil would be greatly increased, because as the drainage of the whole lowland space within the sea bank was then dependent solely upon the artificial and not numerous outlets provided for them by the Romans, if these should be silted up, a permanent flood would be the consequence, bringing death and burial with its waters for the forests that once doubtless covered the fens of Lincolnshire, no tree being able to survive a continued immersion of its roots in water. This theory, however, respecting the subterranean forests of Holland and Kesteven, although very plausible, is not tenable, because it has been clearly ascertained that portions, at least, of the Roman bank are raised upon this very peaty stratum of which it has been supposed to be the originator,* so that the submersion of the forest land below, clearly belongs to a date anterior to the works above it; although from observations on the subsoil of Hatfield Chase, and portions of the Trent and Witham valleys, we have reason to suppose that a change of levels in those districts took place at a later period, Roman remains having been found there below the peat stratum very commonly, particularly when the enclosure of Austerfield was in progress.

Secondly, finding that the submersion of these forest lands was not affected by the agency of the Romans, also that large tracts of similar lands exist beyond the sea bank, and far below

---

* Farming of Lincolnshire, by John Algernon Clarke, Agricultural Journal, vol. 12.

the usual level of the sea, it has been suggested that a change in the coastal line has been effected by the action of the sea.

Great changes have no doubt taken place in the outline of the Lincolnshire coast, owing to the action of the sea on its exterior, and the ceaseless flow of the inland waters from its interior. Many large estuaries are now completely filled up, which are known to have formerly existed ;* whilst, from the remains of forests below the ordinary level of the sea, it is clear that the coastal boundary once extended far beyond its existing limits. To account for this last-named fact it has been supposed that a higher ridge of land may have once existed beyond the present tidal line, serving to protect a plain lying below the sea level, of which the islets still occasionally visible are a portion, and that this ridge was either gradually worn away by the continual action of the oceanic currents, which are remarkably strong off the Lincolnshire coast, or suddenly broken down by some extraordinary combination of wind and tide, upon which the low tract behind it would also of necessity become the prey of the ocean. It has also been suggested that as sandbanks off this shallow coast have been repeatedly known to disappear, and to form again on other spots with great rapidity in long lines parallel with the shore, a continuous barrier may have been thrown up under some extraordinary combination of wind and tide, behind whose sheltering limits vegetation might soon demonstrate its power, so as to gradually produce a forest that existed for some centuries, until at length that element from which it had been rescued, putting forth unwonted strength, broke through the boundary of its own creation, and again claimed its supremacy over the tract beyond it. This theory is supposed to have been strengthened by the fact of the destruction in the 11th century, of a great part of Earl Godwin's lands on the Kentish coast, the site of which is still so often and so fatally indicated by the Goodwin sands, off Deal, and exposed to view during low tides ; but I believe both this Kentish submersion of land and that of Lincolnshire arose from another cause, which now remains to be considered, namely,

---

* Such as Bicker Haven, seven miles long, which still remained a salt marsh in 1611, being marked as such, at that date, by Hondius, on a map of the lowlands of Lincolnshire, &c., published at Amsterdam, and which, when existing, must have entirely altered the outline of the Wash.

"Subsidence." This phenomenon of the existence of submarine forests is by no means a rare one, and may be witnessed at various points of the shores of Scotland, England, and Wales. On the northern shore of Fife, bordering the estuary of the Tay, such a forest may be seen occasionally, although usually concealed by a bed of stratified silty clay, from fifteen to twenty-five feet thick, interspersed with marine shells. In Hartlepool Bay, such another forest may be seen during the lowest neap tides, whose stumps of oaks, firs, alders, thorns, and hazels, intermixed with their berries, nuts, seeds, and also with the horns of the ox, red-deer, and even with the wing-cases of land beetles, not unfrequently excite considerable attention. In Yorkshire are several similar instances. Off Owthorne is a bed of fresh-water deposit, usually below the sea, containing roots of oaks, hazels, &c., and amongst their fallen nuts and leaves, a British "dug-out," or canoe, was discovered, together with the horns and bones of the red-deer; and I am informed that at other points, on the Holderness coast, submarine forests have also occasionally become visible, as well as at Holme, in Norfolk, on the southern side of the Wash. The south coast possesses many examples of the same character, of which Bournemouth offers one, and the tract between Newlyn and St. Michael's Mount another. This was once no doubt forest land, and confirms in a remarkable manner, the ancient title of that extraordinary eminence, which, according to Carew, was termed "the rock in the wood." Sir H. de la Beche says the shores of West Somerset, Devonshire, and Cornwall abound with instances of these submerged lands; and one has been recently observed in Padstow Harbour, on the northern coast of the last named county, which was suddenly exposed to view by the shifting of a sand bank. In South Wales, Giraldus de Barri, or Cambrensis, as he is usually termed, observed such a phenomenon so long ago as 1188. He says in his "Itinerary," chapter 13, page 217, "The sandy shores of South Wales being laid bare by the extraordinary violence of a storm, the surface of the earth which had been covered for many ages re-appeared, and discovered the trunks of trees cut off, standing in the very sea itself, the strokes of the hatchet appearing as if made only yesterday; the soil was very black, and the wood like ebony. By a wonderful revolution, the road for ships became impassable, and looked not like a shore, but like a grove, cut down perhaps at the time of the deluge, or not long after, but certainly in very remote times." In my opinion, however, these, and many other instances that might have been mentioned, of the present position of what have clearly once formed large forest districts, but are now far below the usual level of the sea, can only be satisfactorily accounted for by partial subsidences of the crust of the earth. This theory may indeed appear to be more marvellous than the preceding ones, and therefore less likely to be true in the opinion of those who are acquainted with geology; but when from the study of that science we find that certain strata, the undoubted deposit of water, are now upheaved far above the reach of that element, and that large tracts of land have sunk beneath it, we can only regard such changes as one of the usual, but always wonderful, operations of nature. Strabo was well acquainted with this motive power in the earth's crust, who says, "It is not because the lands covered by seas were originally at different altitudes that the waters have risen or subsided, or receded from some parts and inundated others; but the reason is that the land is sometimes raised up, and sometimes depressed, and the sea also is simultaneously raised and depressed, so that it either overflows or returns into its own place again." It may be said, however, these were old—perhaps antediluvian changes, and we are quite sure the earth has long stood firm. It will be well, therefore, to mention an instance of the subsidence and elevation of land during the historic period. Perhaps the most noted one is that which occurred at Pozzuoli, in the bay of Baiæ, as indicated by the pillars of the temple of Jupiter Serapis at that place, and certified by documentary evidence. Originally, that temple of course was built above the level of the sea; the site then sank twelve feet, so as to submerge its columns in a fresh-water deposit which protected them from future injury. The subsidence, however, continued, and then the sea swept over this newly-formed marshy surface, covering the columns of Jupiter's temple to a depth of nine feet more, and exposing them to the depredations of that destructive marine bivalve, the "Lithodomus" of Cuvier, from which they have greatly suffered. At one period then they were sunk twenty-one feet below the sea level,* leaving a little less

---

* Evidence of a most conclusive character was obtained by Mr. Babbage,

than half their original height above it; but then another change began, and the flat shore where this temple stands gradually rose again; a document of the reign of Ferdinand and Isabella of Spain, referring to a grant of land at Pozzuoli made to the University of that town "where the sea is drying up," and another of Ferdinand's alone, a little later, speaking of the same locale as one "where the ground was dried up." In the year 1538, the year of a great eruption of Vesuvius, the land about Pozzuoli rose rapidly, but it has since slightly sunk again, and now is apparently stationary. Again, an earthquake that occurred in 1819, on the Delta of the Indus, was followed by very extraordinary and permanent changes in the levels of the adjacent district; the eastern channel of that river bounding the province of Cutch, suddenly deepening at Luckput from one foot to eighteen feet, so as to render it navigable, and at the same time creating a large inland lake, whilst Sindree, above Luckput, together with its fort, gradually sank below the newly-created waters, until its angle towers alone appeared above their surface; but in exchange for this depression, an elevation fifty miles long appeared rising from a previously flat plain, at a distance of about five miles from Sindree, which the inhabitants very appropriately termed "Ullah Bund," or mound of God. Perhaps, however, the most striking modern illustration of what has once taken place in many portions of England, may at this time be witnessed in the United States. In 1811, the valley reaching from the mouth of the Ohio to that of the St. Francis (300 miles long), was convulsed, after which several new lakes were formed, such as Obion in Tennessee, twenty miles in length, and another near New Madrid, about ten miles west of the Mississippi in Missouri, termed "the sunk country." This is seventy or eighty miles long, and thirty wide, and from its placid surface rise the trunks of innumerable semi-submerged trees, all dead, and whitening in the wind previous to the final plunge they must all shortly make into that deadly element below, wherein so many of their brothers have already sunk before them.

---

as to the elevation of a considerable tract of land in the vicinity of this temple, for at thirty-two feet above the present sea level, he discovered a waveworn line covered with barnacles, and pierced by boring testacea on the face of the banks above the tract of land lying below them.

It may be remarked, however, that in these instances, volcanic agency was the cause of the subsidences spoken of, whereas no signs of such a power exist in the lowlands of Lincolnshire or on its coast. But neither are they to be found in that of the American sunk country, nor do earthquakes usually leave any direct evidences of their mighty agency behind them, although they often have been connected with permanent changes of the earth's surface of a great and extraordinary character. Again, even some natives of Lincolnshire may say "But when had we earthquakes?" I will therefore instance a few. In 1048 there was a serious convulsion in that county,* also another in 1117, that particularly affected the division of Holland, greatly endangering and injuring Croyland Abbey, portions of which, then just built, were with difficulty stayed up by vast timber props.† In 1185 Lincoln was much damaged by an earthquake.‡ In 1448 a violent shock was again felt in the southern parts of the county.§ In 1750 a shock occurred throughout its whole extent, and in parts of Lincolnshire and Northamptonshire, attended by a rumbling noise. It happened on a Sunday and the people ran out of churches from their devotions in great alarm ; chimneys fell ; houses tottered, and plates, &c., fell from shelves.‖ And so late as 1792, Bourne and the neighbouring towns experienced another shock of an earthquake. It is not necessary to point

---

* 1048. Quo anno terræmotus factus est magnus Cal. Martii die, Dominica.—Historia Ingulphi (Oxford edition, 1684), p. 64.

† Hoc terræmotu cum etiam Anglia in multis provinciis gravissime vexaretur, verum Ecclesiæ Croylandensis opus recens, et adhuc sine constabiliente nave tenerum, proh dolor! in australi muro corporis sui horribilibus orificiis dehiscens, proximam ruinam minabatur acturum, nisi Carpentariorum industria longissimis trabibus et tignis transversis stabili concordia, usque ad navis impositæ confœderatiorem deinceps solida constantia fulciretur.—Ibid, p. 129. Petri Blesensis continuatio.

‡ A.D. 1185. Terræ motus magnus auditus est fere per totam Angliam, qualis ab initio mundi in terra illa non erat auditus. Petræ enim scissæ sunt, domus apideæ ceciderunt, Ecclesia Lincolniensis metropolitana scissa est a summo deorsum. Contigit autem terræ motus iste in crastino diei dominicæ in ramis palmarum, viz. xvii Kal. Maii.—Roger Hoveden, 359.

§ Historia Croylandensis continuatio, p. 526.

‖ Collections for a Topographical History of the Hundred of Aveland, by John Moore.

to any instances of elevation of land in Lincolnshire as a counterpoise to the subsidence of others for the purpose of corroborating this theory which I have ventured to advance, because none was observable in the case of the Mississippi valley and other examples, but I am inclined to think that a slow upward movement has begun to take place in large districts of Lincolnshire long ago, and that by means of carefully conducted scientific observations this will be hereafter certainly proved, and accurately measured. The filling up of channels and estuaries of large size that formerly existed, and the rapid growth of its coasts at various points, apparently indicate this, whilst the known gradual but continually increasing elevation of the Danish coast, and parts of Norway, greatly strengthen such a supposition.* Nor need such an hypothesis be considered extravagant. There stands the fact of the existence of submarine forests. They must have acquired their present depression through some convulsion of nature, that I believe to be subsidence, and surely the upheaval of lands is not more extraordinary than their depression ; at all events both phenomena have repeatedly occurred on a very large scale ; and, in conclusion, I thankfully shelter my opinion behind the strong shield of Sir Charles Lyell, who says (Principles of Geology, page 289,) "If we could compare with equal accuracy the ancient and actual state of all the islands and continents, we should probably discover that millions

---

* Professor Worsaae, in his Primæval Antiquities of Denmark, page 9, says, —" Denmark seems to have been raised, by a powerful revolution of nature, from the bottom of the sea. By degrees its naked banks of gravel became covered with aspen forests. When the land rose still higher, and the dampness diminished, the aspen disappeared after having, by numerous growths, formed a way for the fir, which now spread all over the country. This species of tree continued for a very long period, but at length was compelled to give place to a very different and a higher class. At first the beech was unable to grow here. The earth was covered with oaks, of that species termed the winter oak, which differs from the now prevailing species the summer oak ; these were succeeded by groves of alders, until all was so prepared and developed that the light and beautiful beech spread its crowns over the whole country. That Denmark in its primæval times, before it possessed its present vegetation, had passed through these four periods, is clearly proved from the ancient peat bogs, in which are found stems of trees of each distinct period lying like beds one over the other."

B

of our race are now supported by lands situated where deep seas prevailed in earlier ages. In many districts not yet occupied by man, land animals and forests now abound, where ships once sailed ; and on the other hand we shall find on inquiry, that inroads of the ocean have been no less considerable. When, to these revolutions produced by aqueous causes, we add analogous changes wrought by igneous agency, we shall perhaps acknowledge the justice of the conclusion of Aristotle, who declared (Meteorics, chapter 12,) " That the whole land and sea on our globe periodically changed places."

THE BRITONS.

Chroniclers of all ages have usually been tempted to cast a glittering veil over the origin of the nations whose history they have undertaken to record, whence the truth is often with difficulty discovered after the mind of the reader has recovered from the influence of this medium, and gathered strength to view historic incidents in their just proportions. Such fictitious brightness was shed by the Roman Poets and Historians over their descriptions of the original colonization of their afterwards mighty capital, and nothing less than a semi-Divine semi-Heroic origin could be ascribed by them to so great a people as the Romans, or entertained by their countrymen, so that whilst their chroniclers gilded the stern, or perhaps really unknown truth, those for whom they wrote gladly fostered it.* Anchises and Venus were said to have been the progenitors of the Roman race ; and in like manner Brutus, the Great Grandson of these same illustrious personages, has been fixed upon by some of our earlier historians as the first British Colonist, and the founder of our nation.

---

* But few if any Nations know for certain the exact particulars of their first origin. Richard of Cirencester saying Cap. III. "Solis quippe Judæis, et per ipsos finitimis quibusdam gentibus, hoc contigit felicitatis, ut a primo inde mundi exordio gentis suæ originem continuâ serie ex infallibilibus deducere possint monumentis.

The time has however arrived when no such baseless fictions can be indulged in, and writers as a rule desire only to elicit and record the truth when speaking of the past, without prejudice or exaggeration.

The existence of Britain was known to several southern nations for five centuries before the Christian Æra, Herodotus alluding to it under the term of the Cassiterides, or tin-islands ; * but Aristotle, who lived B.C. 350, is the first author who mentions it by name, describing it as consisting of two very large islands Albion† and Ierne,‡ called the Britannic,§ and lying beyond the Celtæ.

Little however was known of this country for some centuries after this period, except by the Phœnicians, who had held communication with parts of Albion‖ from the time of Homer for the purpose of exporting tin, but they were probably only acquainted with some of its ports on the Cornish coast, the Scilly Isles, the Isle of Wight, and perhaps some portions of the Irish and Welsh coasts ; and what they did know they kept a profound secret from interested motives connected with their traffic ;¶ so that with the exception of a visit from Himilco sent from Carthage on an exploratory expedition between the years B.C. 362 and 350, and occasional visits from the traders of Massilia** and Narbona,

---

* Strictly speaking the Scilly Isles only were implied by this term.

† A term doubtless derived from the whiteness of its cliffs.

‡ Derived perhaps from "Hiera" or sacred, as being the supposed original seat of some of the Celtic Deities.

§ The Britons and their country are said by some to have received their name from the word "brit" or spotted, because of the devices they painted upon their bodies, Martial terming them "Cœrulei" and "Picti," Propertius "Infecti," and Ovid "Virides," from the same custom. But perhaps they were originally so termed from the name of one of their tribes, as was Brittany on the other side of the channel.

‖ From their celebrated settlement at Gades or Cadiz.

¶ It is narrated by Strabo, III. 175, that a Roman vessel continuing to follow a Phœnician one when on a cruise to Britain, the captain of this last purposely ran his Galley on shore so as not to disclose the position of that Island, and that he was most liberally rewarded for his patriotism on his return to Cadiz.

** Pythias, a Greek of Massilia, first uses the term Britannia, who coasted along its shores for six days, and reached "Thule" or the Shetland Isles.

Britain remained almost detached from the rest of the world*
until Julius Cæsar made his celebrated descent upon the Kentish
Coast, B.C. 55. He had previously discovered how the Phœnicians
reached Britain, and had learnt some particulars of their trade
through Publius Crassus whom he had left on the coast of Gaul
after his first campaign in that country; but when he was
advancing himself towards the British channel he could gather
no further particulars concerning the land beyond it he was
proposing to invade, although he summoned the chief merchants
and sea-faring people of the coast for this purpose; and as the
Belgæ who then occupied the nearest points of the opposite
shore, still kept up communication with their parent tribe on the
continent, it was probably through their influence that they
would not, rather than that they could not comply with his desire.
Whilst therefore Cæsar was assembling his troops on the plains
near Calais he sent Caius Volusenus in a Galley to explore the
opposite coast, who ran along it for five days, but never ventured
to disembark, as the coming invasion was well known, and the
Britons were generally prepared to offer a fierce resistance,
although some tribes had offered to submit and to give hostages
to the Roman Chief. Then followed the descent, Cæsar embark-
ing from the "Portus Iccius," or Boulogne in 80 vessels,
containing his 7th and 10th Legions, the issue of which adventure
we need not describe, but will pass on to the condition of
Britain and its inhabitants at this very important period of its
history.

There is little doubt but what this Island was originally
peopled by the Celtic Gauls,† perhaps by some, who worsted
in the contest with a stronger or more fortunate one pressing
upon it from the interior, boldly betook themselves to their boats,

---

* Scipio Africanus Minor, and Polybius the historian, during the interval,
viz : B.C. 150, had vainly endeavoured to find out the course to these islands
although they instituted inquiries concerning this point in the chief cities of
Gaul. Polybius however speaks of the manner in which tin was smelted in
Britain, and wrote a treatise upon the subject, which is now lost.

† The Celts were driven forward by the German tribes, who were themselves in some measure pressed upon by the Sarmatian race. Tacitus doubts
whether the Britons were immigrants or an indigenous people, he suggests
however that the Caledonians might be of German, the Welsh of Spanish,
and the remainder of Gaulish origin.

and ventured across the sea to that line of white cliffs occasionally appearing on the horizon, which seemed to offer them a peaceful asylum. Then other expeditionary parties followed no doubt, who also settled themselves in various parts of Albion, the fresh arrivers either driving forward the older settlers, or retreating inland themselves according to the issue of the encounters between them. Multitudes of Celtic Gauls were driven out from the district between the Rhine and the Seine, and took refuge in Britain B.C. 150, under pressure from the Belgæ,* ("Musgrave's Belgium Britannicum," page 94), whilst this strong and more than usually intelligent people, in its turn, had been compelled to cross the channel, and to settle themselves in the South Eastern portion of our Island, again expelling those feebler tribes from their new settlements whom they had previously driven from the Continent, not long before the period of Cæsar's landing on the Kentish Coast. That great man informs us that Britain was then very thickly peopled, that it abounded with habitations resembling those in Gaul, and with cattle, that the Belgæ, or inhabitants of the East Coast were the most civilized, and that those beyond them sowed no corn, and wore no woollen clothing, their food being flesh, milk, and fruit, their covering skins of deer and sheep, whilst they stained their persons with a blue dye to render their appearance more fearful on the battle field,† allowing their hair to flow freely over their shoulders and their moustaches to grow, but otherwise being completely shaved. In height they exceeded both the Romans and the Gauls. All were warriors, their frequent intestine wars having served as a school in which the art of war had been rudely but generally studied according to Gaulish rules, their women even being ready to join in the fray, who frequently contended side by side with the men They fought on horseback,

---

* Cæsar says, Lib. I, cap. I, "Gallia est omnis divisa in partes tres; quarum unam incolunt Belgæ, aliam Aquitani, tertiam, qui ipsorum lingua Celtæ, nostra Galli, adpellantur. Hi omnes linguâ, institutis, legibus inter se differunt. Wright, together with other authors, supposes that these first were of German origin.

† They deck out and paint their bodies with curious devices, and the shapes of all sorts of creatures, and are only partially clad, lest these ornaments should be concealed. Herodian Liber III.

in chariots, and on foot, the last being by far the most numerous, and from their extraordinary agility they were most formidable. Their arms were spears, huge pointless swords, and small shields. They commenced the combat by charging their opponents with their chariots, whence they first discharged their spears, and then rushed on foot into the midst of the enemy's ranks in the hope of throwing them into confusion ; but if they failed in this, they rapidly retreated to their chariots, in the management of which they were extraordinarily skilful, and fell back upon their infantry. Despising the aid of breast plate and helmet, they were the better able to execute all manœuvres requiring speed and agility. Herodian in his " Life of Severus, Liber II" gives the following interesting description of the Britons as soldiers when they were supporting the rebel Albians in Gaul against Severus. The British army, (says he) consisted of great and brave troops of most excellent soldiers, and though Severus in his speech to his army when about to commence his campaign against it affected to despise it, calling it a poor army of Islanders utterly unable to resist his Roman forces, when a great battle was fought between the two armies near Lyons, the encounter was so fierce and protracted, that it was for a long time doubtful which way the victory would incline; for, says this author, the Britons were not at all inferior to the Illyrians in manhood or martial ardour. Some historians indeed narrate that Severus was at one time put to flight, beaten off his horse, forced to throw off his imperial mantle, and hide himself; but that Lætus one of his commanders charging the conquering Britons with fresh troops, altered the fate of the day, put the Britons to flight, and pursuing them into Lyons sacked and burnt that town, whence he sent the head of Albinus to Rome. Herodian in his 3rd book also gives us the following particulars of the character of British Warriors and their country, which are particularly applicable to Lincolnshire. " The most part of Britain (says he), being surrounded by the ocean's continual irruption, is fenny and moorish. In those bogs the Barbarians are accustomed to swim and run up and down, plunging into them up to the middle, because being half naked they care not for mire and mud." Severus therefore to cope with such amphibious foes gave orders for the formation of Causeways and Bridges in the marsh districts before the opening of his campaign in Britain, so that his forces might have a better chance of standing upon solid ground.

The Government of the Britons was first in the hands of the Druids,* and secondly of the Chiefs of tribes, who often came into collision through their mutual struggles for supreme command. The Druids were exempt from serving in war, from tribute, and various liabilities to which all others were subject; their President or Chief being elected by the Druidical body. They held grand councils at certain times and places, a sacred oak grove in " Mona," or Anglesea, being held in the highest veneration for this purpose, when their most solemn decrees and judgments were delivered, which none dared to despise under fear of being in consequence excluded from the public sacrifices; when they were, they were regarded as outcasts, utterly unworthy of associating with their brethren living within the pale of Druidism. Their sacred rites were performed in the depths of ancient oak groves, a circle of huge stones indicating the limits of their sanctuaries; and if they found the misletoe growing upon an oak, esteeming it sent from heaven as a token of the Deity's selection of that particular spot to be worshipped in, they held it in the highest veneration, and after sacrificing two young white bulls, coming in white robes, they cut the sacred plant with a golden sickle, and placed it with much reverence upon a white cloth. But they had a far worse habit than this, namely the offering human sacrifices, which they believed to be necessary to appease the Gods when they were about to engage in war or any other dangerous enterprise, or when sickness prevailed, for which purpose they discreetly reserved thieves and other malefactors; but if this supply failed they scrupled not to offer up innocent persons as expiatory sacrifices. In their hands also were the interpretation of all portents, the administration of law, and the practice of medicine; so that enjoying as they did so many privileges and possessing so much power, it is not wonderful to find that their body was very numerous, and that multitudes of young men, amongst whom many came from Gaul, were committed to their care for instruction. These they taught orally, disallowing all written records, but teaching the mysteries of their Order, and preserving the annals of their country by the

---

* Lucan refers to the Druids, as does Pliny, Liber XXX.

aid of memory alone, they poured forth their learning in profuse *viva voce* versification. They also inculcated a belief in the transmigration of souls, as one lessening the fear of death, and were skilled in astronomy and natural philosophy. Besides the Druids, there were Bards, who sang of the heroic deeds of their countrymen in poetic strains, accompanied by the harp.* Polygamy appears to have widely prevailed among the Britons. Bright or golden coloured hair was common among both sexes, and it is a curious fact that the ladies of Rome, admiring this, dyed their hair in imitation of the British prevalent tint, just as some English ladies have of late given the same tint to their hair, through a foolish temporary fashion. To this Propertius alludes, saying :

"Nunc etiam infectos demens imitare Britannos
Ludis et externo tincta nitore caput."

The word infectos or, as some read "insectos;" referring to the blue dye procured from woad, still grown in Lincolnshire, with which the Britons tattooed their skins. Cattle and sheep were their chief wealth ; but some of the Eastern tribes wore a gold ring on the middle finger of their left hand, and their chiefs a torc of the same precious metal round their necks. The more northern natives wore rings of iron round their waists and necks (says Herodian) which they esteemed as valuable as other barbarians do gold. For money they used brass pieces, and iron rings of a fixed weight ; but they had also a coinage, whose character was rudely copied from classical types. Besides the tin, for which Britain has been ever justly celebrated, it is said to have produced thus early white lead, iron, and some gold and silver, as well as muscle pearls† of various hues, and a kind of cockle producing an unfading red dye. The Britons had also bracelets of glass, amber, ivory and jet, in great plenty, and of good quality ; but most of these were imported. Their habitations were log huts thatched with reeds, and defended by an inclosure of felled

---

* These, as well as the Druids, are alluded to by Lucan.

† These are said to have attracted Cæsar to make his invasion, and Pliny reports, Lib. IX. 35, that upon his return to Rome he dedicated a breastplate covered with British Pearls to the Goddess Venus Genetrix. Tacitus says the British Pearls were cloudy.

trees ; * these were not intended for permanent use, as the Britons were for the most part Nomades ; but some tribes of Kent and Cornwall had better houses, and were more cultivated and hospitable than those of the interior. They had boats, the keels and foot-stocks of which were of light wood, and the rest of wattles covered with hides, besides dug-outs or canoes hollowed out of whole trunks of trees. Several such canoes have been found at various times in the fens of Lincolnshire, and in 1828 a very perfect specimen was discovered at Horsey, near Peterborough, at the junction of the old river with the Nene. This is figured in Artis's Durobrivæ, from which Fig. 1 is taken. It was 30 feet long, 2 feet 8 inches across at the widest point, and formed out of the trunk of a tree. Fig. 2 gives the plan of the same. Near it were found part of another canoe, formed of two logs pinned together, the heads of two barbed fish spears, two spear heads, and two forks.

According to Solinus, the Britons, whenever they were making a voyage, abstained from food. They were of an inquisitive disposition, besetting such travellers or merchants as ventured amongst them with questions, and compelling them to disclose all they knew concerning

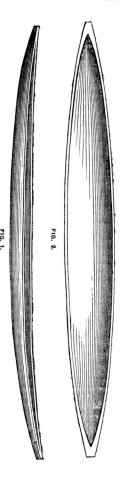

* Others were probably formed of withies or wattles covered with mud, their interiors being partly sunk in the ground, groups of shallow pits of a circular form still existing in various parts of this country, once forming the substructures of such dwellings, particularly in Wiltshire, and have been described by Sir Richard Colt Hoare, but as Roman vestigia have been found on the sites of many of these, there is often much difficulty in determining positively to what people such sites should be assigned.

foreign lands. Diodorus describes the corn growing tribes as storing up the produce of their fields in thatched houses, from which they took sufficient for their daily wants in the straw.

Some tribes burnt the bodies of the dead, and heaping up around them a pile of such articles as were pleasing or necessary to the deceased when living, viz : animals, arms, vessels, the whole were burnt together ; after which the ashes of each body were deposited in an earthen jar ; but other tribes deposited their dead in the ground accompanied by their arms, over which large tumuli were raised, subsequently termed, "beorh," or "bearw," by the Saxons, and now barrow, or else hlæw, now low or hoe. These often enclosed a "cromlech"* or rude sepulchral chamber formed of three or more huge stones, over which the earth was piled to a great height, and sometimes surrounded by a circle of stones, whilst in other cases a single flat stone covered the remains of the deceased. Such were the habits of the Britons, once termed by Virgil, "Penitus toto divisos orbe Britannos." The few particulars respecting the character of this country which may be gathered from ancient authors must next be recorded. Cæsar compares its form to a triangle, having its southern shore, or base, opposite to Gaul ; Livy and Fabius Rusticus to an oblong shield or a two edged axe, (bipennis) ; whilst Tacitus assents to this comparison should Calidonia be excepted, which he describes as stretching out far to the North, and terminating in a wedge-shaped form. As regards its climate, we find that the present common opinion respecting it, dates from a very early period. Herodian saying, Lib. III., "The pools and fens out of which the foggy vapours continually arise make the sky always cloudy." Strabo and Diodorus describe this Island as being for the most part flat and woody, but as having some strong places on the hills. Its salt and hot springs are also spoken of, as being used for baths, and also its profusion of birds and fish. Juvenal alludes to its whales and porpoises, Sat. X. 14, and other authors mention its "vituli marini," or seals, its salmon, herrings, eels, and oysters.† British dogs were famous, and highly prized by the Romans. Some of these, Strabo informs us, were trained for war, and used by the Gauls against their

---

* This is a Celtic term meaning a stone table.
† From "Rutupiæ," or Richborough.

enemies in battle, a custom still practised by the Spaniards in the 16th century against the American Indians under Vasquez, Nunez de Balboa and others; these were probably mastiffs; and Claudian, "II Consul Stilichonis, 301," refers to others as being employed against bulls, *i. e.* bull-dogs; these were required for the amphitheatre at Rome, and an officer or agent, termed "Curator Cynegii," was appointed to reside in Britain, for the express purpose of collecting them, and transmitting them to Rome to take part in the combats exhibited there. "Pennant's British Zoology, Vol. I. p. 80." Lastly, we gather that British funerals were magnificent, and especially those of great chiefs.

Lincolnshire, on the arrival of the Romans in Britain, was part of the territory of the Coritani, a Celtic race. The boundaries of this people no doubt varied at different times,* but their country certainly lay between that of the Brigantes on the north, and the Iceni on the south. Its seaboard reached from the Humber to the Wash; it was probably bounded by the Humber and Trent on the north and north west, the Severn on the west and south west, and the Avon and Welland on the south; thus including the counties of Lincoln and Leicester, and parts of Nottinghamshire, Derbyshire, Staffordshire, Worcestershire, and Warwickshire; although others think that it was bounded by the Dove and Goit on the west, and the Nene on the south, including within it Lincolnshire, Leicestershire, Rutlandshire, Nottinghamshire, Derbyshire, and part of Northamptonshire. Their chief towns were Lind-Coit or Lincoln, and Rage or Leicester. They were

---

* Bishop Gibson, in Camden Col., p. 433, observes, "The bounds of the ancient nations inhabiting Britain can not be nicely determined, for how can we hope exactly to distinguish them when our ancient authors only deliver at large in what quarter of the nation they were seated, without descending into their particular limits. Besides most of the barbarous nations seem according to their strength at different times to have had dominions larger and narrower. Especially in Britain (where were so many kings), we cannot imagine but that they were frequently making encroachments upon one another. The boundary west of the Humber seems to have been that mountainous country which stretches between the Doune and the 'Seteia' or Mersey, and afterwards the Mersey itself." This chain of rivers and mountains, which it is presumed continued afterwards to be the march or limits between the kingdoms of Mercia and Northumberland, seems to have been a sufficient security against mutual encroachments of the Brigantes and Coritani, and that this was really the limits of the kingdom of Mercia in the after times might be easily shown.

either a peaceful or a timid people, who through retiring before
their foreign invaders into the fastnesses of their forests, or the
ready asylum of those fens with which the eastern part of their
territory abounded, thus escaped defeat, and the bitter consequences of revolt against their better disciplined invaders, which
befel the more pugnacious Brigantes, and impatient Iceni.
When Ostorius Scapula, the Roman commander in Britain A.D. 50,
was securing the dominion of that great people here, and subdued
the Brigantes beyond them, the Coritani did not resist him, as
he passed through their country; and when Petilius Cerealis
subsequently made a successful campaign against the same people
the Coritani again refrained from resistance, as they did when
the famous Julius Agricola, in the year A.D. 78, and subsequently
not only pushed the victorious Roman arms far beyond all previous
limits, but consolidated the Roman dominion in Britain generally
by the formation of admirable military roads, and the construction
of permanent camps and stations along their lines, the remains of
which are still distinctly visible on the soil of Lincolnshire,
and especially in that portion of it about to be described. The
celebrated geographer, Ptolemy is, however, the first author that
actually speaks of the Coritani, A.D. 120, who in giving the names
of the British tribes, mentions the Ordovices, the Cornubii,
the Coritani, the Catyeuclani, and the Dobuni; of these the
Coritani appear to have possessed themselves of Lincolnshire and
Leicestershire. The greater part of their territory was covered
with a vast forest, which appears to have been termed Sylva
Calidonia, in common with another forest district so called in
Kent. L. Florus, Lib. III, describing Cæsar as following the
Britons " in Calidonias Sylvas,"* called after the actual Sylva
Calidonia of Scotland, while much later records refer to the great
forest formerly covering the present Division of Kesteven. This
woodland tract during the British period was tenanted by the
elk, red deer, wolf, and wild boar ;† and perhaps by the bear and
beaver, remains of all of which have been found beneath the

---

* Florus appears to speak of Calidonia Sylva in common with Saltus
Hercynius proverbially when he mentions a forest of any size. Camden
derives Calidonia from kaled—rough.

† To these we might perhaps add the great Irish Elk, " Cervus Megace-
ros," as its horns have been found in the adjoining County of York, viz., in

surface of its soil. Then also the eagle, bustard, stork, crane, bittern, kite, rough and reve, and heron abounded, besides water fowl, and fish in extraordinary profusion.

Cæsar was utterly unacquainted with the more remote Celtic tribes such as the Coritani,* and we have reason to think exaggerated their barbarous condition. The Druids were certainly acquainted with the use of letters, although they preferred oral instruction and learning gathered through that medium, they had considerable skill in constructing large sea-going vessels and war chariots, casting bronze weapons, stamping gold coins after Greek types, and making pottery; but above all in transporting and erecting huge stones for religious or sepulchral purposes, which still excite admiration, and in throwing up defensive earthworks of prodigious size and extent.

The Wapentakes of Flaxwell and Aswardhurn are not rich in British remains. A large mound or tumulus in Aswarby Park close to the Sleaford and Falkingham road, and now surmounted by a very large oak several hundred years old, may be of British origin, as tumuli of this size usually were. A large leaf-shaped sword was found with another less perfect specimen in 1852 in a field at Billinghay Dales, between the Tattershall turnpike road and Billinghay Skirth, about a mile and a half from Tattershall Bridge, and two miles from the Car Dyke. It was produced by casting, and still has a very sharp edge on both sides. It has lost its point, but when complete was 22 inches long without its handle, and 1¾ inches wide across the broadest part of the blade.

The handle is now gone, but some of the rivets that once fastened this on to the blade still remained when it was found. Two

---

Hornsea Mere, Holderness. Claudius Paulinus, the Proprætor, sent from Britain as a present to Solemnis, in Gaul, amongst other articles, the skin of a seal, six months old. This is recorded in an inscription on a marble slab found at Vieux, near Caen, in Normandy. Gold and silver are reported also to have been found in Britain, by Tacitus, in his "Life of Agricola."

* But little was known of the character of Britain at Rome for some time after its invasion by Julius Cæsar. Horace seems to speak of it as the very

brass daggers of British origin were found in removing a bank
in South Kyme, during the year 1820.   One is $10\frac{1}{2}$ inches long,
the other $7\frac{1}{2}$ inches. See Figs. 1 and 2, Plate II.   These are of
peculiar shape, from the great width of their bases originally
enclosed in handles, and the very bright colour of their platina,
which gives them a golden appearance.   They are now in the
Duke of Northumberland's Museum, at Alnwick.   An excellent
example of a grooved and looped brass palstave, or implement
used as an axe or chisel, when supplied with a wooden handle
attached to it by a thong passed through the metal loop, was
found in 1818, at the old ford of the river Slea.   A very fine flint
hammer was discovered in digging gravel on some rising ground
east of Sleaford by the Tattershall road ; Fig. 3, Plate I, and
a very beautiful vessel was found at Billinghay a few years ago ;
it is of pale dull red earthenware of the usual British form, and
carefully ornamented ; $7\frac{1}{4}$ inches high, and $5\frac{1}{4}$ inches diameter at
the widest part. Fig. 4, Plate I.

ROMAN   REMAINS.

The district we are describing has been indelibly scored by
the Romans, and is still interspersed with traces of their former
supreme dominion over it.   One of the greatest of their works
in Britain—the Ermine-Street, or High-Dyke, forms the western
boundary of the Wapentakes under notice ; a branch of it—now
represented by Mareham lane, intersects that of Aswardhurn, as
does another great Roman work unrivalled in England, viz : the
Car-Dyke—a long and broad navigable drain.   These must first
be described through their just claim to such preference.

---

end of the earth,

> " Serves iturum Cæsarem in ultimos
> Orbis Britannos."—Carm. Lib. I., Ode 15.

It was however in some measure described by Livy, Strabo, Fabius Rusticus,
Pomponius Mela, and Pliny, besides Cæsar, and Tacitus. This last author
agrees with Herodian in saying the sky was there cloudy and rainy, although
the cold was not so great as in Gaul.   He reports that its vegetable growth
was quick, but its maturation slow, also that the sea surrounding it was sluggish and laborious to the rower.

PLATE I.

FIG. 1.

FIG. 2.

FIG. 3.

FIG. 4.

THE ERMINE-STREET, OR OLD ROMAN ROAD.

This great work, constituting one of the four principal Roman Roads of Britain, may fairly vie with any of the other three, both as to length and grandeur of design.

Its Roman name is lost, but by the Saxons it was termed Earminga-Street, or Eormen-Street,* the terminal of which derived from the Roman *stratum*, is still represented by the modern word—street, or road. Perhaps the term Earminga or Eormen was derived from the name of some British tribe, as Wætlinga-Street was from Wætla, or from Eormen, a Saxon deity, or the same word applied to anything vast or noble. That portion of it running from Castor, near Peterborough, to the Humber, which will now be described, is called by various names in different localities, such as the Forty-foot or Norman-gate, the High-Dyke, the Old-Street, and the Ramper, but the whole constituted one continuous road, still usually designated the Ermine-Street. The Romans were certainly not the first road-makers in Britain, whence it is quite possible that part of the great military roads they constructed followed the lines of more ancient ones; but these Roman works so far surpassed all that had before existed, as to constitute a new era in British road-making,† which must have been regarded with wonder by the natives of this island, although they

---

* This term has often been given to one or more other ancient roads : but there is now a general agreement with Morton's opinion, who says, in his *History of Northamptonshire*, p. 502 : "Whether there be another Erming-street, or not, this I take to be the very Erming-street which is usually reckoned one of the four great Ways ; this being in many places as signal and considerable for its breadth and height as the Watling Street, and also paved as that is in some places."

† Hollinshed, in his *Chronicle*, V. I, p. 189, says that a British king, Dunwallon, commanded four principal roads to be formed in his dominions, B.C. 483, "which should lead such as trauelled into all parts thereof from sea

perhaps looked angrily upon them, as serving to confirm their
subjugation.*

Had not the Roman Itineraries served to prove the origin of
such roads, the remaining entrenched camps through which the
Ermine-Street passes, the inscribed stones, the articles of bronze,
iron, and pottery, together with the innumerable coins found,
and still being found along its line, would have proclaimed this
beyond doubt.   The great utility of such roads to the Romans is
palpable, for they at first needed these as subjugators, and subsequently as colonists, after the Britons had ceased to oppose them
openly, but were ready to make covert attacks upon them when
they could do so with any hope of success, and especially when
the nature of the country facilitated such movements.

In Lincolnshire this was peculiarly the case, where the great
forest of Kesteven offered shelter to the natives, who were intimately acquainted with its fastnesses, as well as with the fens and
estuaries with which it then abounded to a far greater extent
than at present, and were always safe from the avenging hand of
their subjugators, against whose iron sway they long chafed and
rebelled whenever they dared to do so.   To counteract such
natural advantages on the part of the Britons, the Romans

---

to sea, his subjects having been previously sorely oppressed by theives and
robbers as they trauelled to and fro. To these he gave sundrie large privileges,
whereby they became safe and verie much frequented, and caused the same to
be paued with hard stone of eighteene foot in breadth, ten foot in depth, and
in the bottom thereof hugh flint stones, also to be pitched, least the earth in
time should swallow up his workemanship, and the higher ground ouer-grow
their rising crests, and the names of these four waies are the Fosse, the
Gwethelin, or Watling, the Erming, and the Ikenild." The importance of
the Ermine-street, during the later Saxon period, is declared, by the more
severe penalties imposed upon persons guilty of assault or other misdemeanors
upon it, the Watling-Street, and the Foss Way, than elsewhere, as ordained
by Edward the Confessor, and confirmed by the Conqueror.

* Most bitterly must the British tribes have lamented over their own
want of union when they were subject to such hard masters as the Romans
were ; for as only a few tribes could be induced at one time to act in concert
against their foreign invaders, they were defeated in detail.   Their stubborn-
ness was subsequently manifested on many occasions, and they only submitted
to their conquerors through the severest pressure, being always eager to regain
their freedom, which, for want of wise counsel rather than of valour, they
had lost.

most wisely constructed roads, in connection with which they formed stations and entrenched camps at convenient intervals, whence forces could be sent from point to point as required; and thus the whole country was eventually supplied with a complete system of military roads. So well was this design planned and carried out, that considerable remains of these roads still exist, and especially of the Ermine-street, which serve to attest the energy and perseverance of those Roman Legions formerly stationed in Britain to secure its possession. The structure of the Ermine-Street was not so elaborate as that enjoined by Roman authorities on this art, for from a section of it discovered in the parish of Winterton, as carefully recorded by Mr. Padley, the earth had simply been excavated to the depth of seventeen inches, and then two layers of rough stones on edge, slanting in opposite directions, were laid to constitute the foundation of the road, which had no central rise, nor was there any trace found of the *summum dorsum*, or surface paving. The width of this paved portion of the road was between twelve and thirteen feet, and the ordinary height of its embankment three feet; but some portions of it are considerably higher. Of the date of this ancient work

we have no record. It is possible that its formation may have been commenced by the Proprætor Ostorius Scapula,* A.D. 50, in connection with his campaign against the Brigantes, and who on

---

* He was famed for his defeat of the Iceni, who had submitted to the Romans without giving battle, but who at length took courage to make irruptions into what had become Roman territory, and finally to revolt openly in concert with other tribes, after they had formed an entrenched stronghold, and thought that no Roman general would advance against them during the winter. Ostorius, however, did take action, and notwithstanding the great valour they exhibited, stormed their stronghold, and entirely routed their forces, so that all the wavering tribes were forced to declare for the Romans, among whom were, no doubt, the Coritanians of Lincolnshire. Then followed the campaign against the Cangi, or people of Cheshire and Lancashire, and that against Caractacus and the Silures. Ostorius died A.D. 55.—See *Tacit. Ann.*, L. XII., c. 31, 32, and L. XVI., c. 23.

his return, we are told, had time to give all due attention to the province committed to his charge : or it may have been begun or carried on during the subsequent campaigns of his successor, Didius, the ally of Cartismandua, queen of the Brigantes, against her husband Venusius, when Vettius Bolanus took the same course in the reign of Vitellius, or when Petilius Cerealis,* during his second stay in Britain, made his northern campaign : but if not made before, it certainly must have been constructed when Julius Cnæus Agricola, the celebrated Proprætor and nominee of Vitellius, had firmly established the Roman rule in Britain, who advanced three times towards the north of Britain before his removal from it, A.D. 85.† No doubt this road, in common with the other great Roman military roads, was subsequently extensively repaired, and perhaps added to or altered, according to Galen, Book IX, c. 13. Trajan, as we might have expected, desired such works to be carried out, when all roads that were wet or miry, were ordered to be either raised or paved, such as were overgrown with bushes were cleared, circuitous roads were made straight and their lines altered so as to avoid the ascent of steep hills, or desert districts troubled by wild beasts, and their surfaces were levelled. His great predecessor, Augustus, had ordered *mansiones* and *mutations*, or stations, to be erected along such roads ; and probably in Trajan's time, at least, such necessary adjuncts had been supplied for the use of the Roman army in Britain.

---

* Petilius Cerealis was by no means always a successful commander, for when in command of the 9th Legion, first sent to Britain by Claudius, A.D. 43, he advanced against the Iceni, under Boadicea and her allies, A.D. 61, the Romans suffered a signal defeat, of whose force 70,000, including their allies, are said to have fallen, and Petilius only saved his cavalry by flight ; but in a subsequent battle 80,000 Britons fell, which insured the supremacy of the Roman rule in Britain. As, however, the 9th Legion had been almost exterminated, it was subsequently largely recruited by Nero, who sent over 2,000 Legionary soldiers, eight cohorts of auxiliaries, and 1,000 horses from Germany, to strengthen it.—*Tacit. Ann.*, L. 14, c. 31—58. When Petilius came a second time to Britain, A.D. 71, he was victorious in a series of battles with the Brigantes.

† In the spurious *Chronicle* of Richard of Cirencester it is stated that Agricola *did* make roads to the north, for the purpose of conveying corn to the prætenturas of Scotland.—Stukeley's *Richard of Cirencester*, p. 120.

The Ermine-Street, in its entirety, may be reckoned to commence at Pevensey—*Anderida*, whence it ran to Chichester—*Regnum*, and London : passing along Bishopsgate-Street, it proceeded by Enfield, Cheshunt, Ware, Broughing—*Ad Fines*, Royston, where the Ikenild-Street crosses it, Caxton, Godmanchester—*Durolipons*, Huntingdon, Stukley, Sawtry, Stilton, to a point between Chesterton and Alwalton, or the site of the great station of *Durobrivæ*, close to the village of Castor,† in the county of Northampton. This, at least in part, existed before the Ermine-Street was constructed, as demonstrated by the remains of a Roman potter's kiln found by Artis beneath the bank of the Ermine-Street, and when made, was either carried through the centre of an entrenched camp, of an irregular oblong form, now called "the castles," or else the camp was subsequently formed to take advantage of the road.

The extensive remains of a town and numerous detached residences on this spot clearly prove the former existence of an important Roman station here, round which many wealthy colonists had subsequently settled; but these remains cannot now be noticed, because their description would unduly prolong this description of a portion of the Ermine-Street.

A little north of Castor this ancient road crosses the river Nene, and its bank is very perceptible, but soon after, that which may be regarded as the principal line, continues its course towards the north-west, while the other takes a due north direction. At first the bank of this last is entirely gone, although originally it appears to have been as important as the other road ;† but at a point called Lang-dyke, a mile north of Upton, it again becomes visible, and hereabouts it was itself called Lang-dyke according to Camden, and also High-Street. Passing by Hilly Wood, two miles eastward of Woodcroft, where a Roman flanged roof tile

* An abbreviation of Dorm-ceaster, by which name this place was originally known, and whence, in Camden's time, the term of Dormons was given to the Roman coins often found there.

† Stukeley thought that this was made first, from its being "Nearer the first intention of a meridian line than the other," which he supposed was subsequently struck out when the Romans had become better acquainted with the geography of the country, and upon their finding that they must incline the original line westward to reach Lincoln, as well as to avoid the fen district, where it would require constant reparation.

was found in 1867, bearing the stamp—LEG · IX · HIS.—of the 9th Legion, surnamed Hispanicus,—it then runs through the parish of Ashton,* where the foundations of a square structure, supposed to be Roman, formerly existed, and perhaps are still visible in a little wood called Ashton Lawn, and is intersected by the Syston and Peterborough railway, before it crosses the low meadows and bridge of Lollam, wrongly thought by Stukeley to retain a reminiscence of Lollius Urbicus. After reaching the Welland, where two Roman swords, two daggers, and what was thought to be the iron frame of the tablet of a vexillum, were found in 1740, also a large brass of Pertinax, and other Roman coins five years later, *(Gentlemen's Society of Spalding)* its first appearance on the soil of Lincolnshire is in the parish of West Deeping; whence, under the term of King-Street, it runs in a straight line, leaving Langtoft on the east, and Gretford, Braceborough, and Wilsthorpe on the west, at which last place Stukeley thought there had been a Roman station, and where many Roman coins have been found at intervals.   It crossed the Glen at Katesbridge, after which its bank is not distinguishable ; but it appears to have run parallel with the Car-Dyke† and the present road to Thurlby and Bourn. In and about Bourn many Roman coins have been occasionally found, including a gold one of Nero, and others of the Maximian and the Constantine period.

Marratt, in his *History of Lincolnshire*, Vol. III, p. 79, thus speaks of certain Roman remains at Bourn : "In what is called the Home Close, at the south end of the town, adjoining the turnpike road, there is a square entrenchment, single ditched. The rampart at each of the corners was formerly twice as high as the sides, but of late years it has been levelled, and the ditch

---

* This parish, with the adjoining ones of Ufford and Bainton, constituted the once royal manor of Torpell, now the property of Lord Kesteven.   When possessed by Margaret, Countess of Derby, a quadrangular mansion, surrounded by a moat, in Torpell park, stood on the west of the Ermine-street ; but her principal residence in this locality was at Colly-Weston, afterwards inherited by Henry VIII., and where he stayed from the 1st to the 5th of August, 1541, when on his way to meet the King of Scotland in the north.

† The celebrated Roman navigable drain, reaching from the Nene to the parish of Washingborough, on the Witham, a description of which will be subsequently given.

on the west side filled with earth;" and in the same vol., p. 81, says : "About 60 years ago a tesselated pavement was found in the Park grounds, but destroyed a few days after;—also, a large urn near it, containing coins in such a perishable condition that they soon fell to pieces. The stone that covered it was preserved; there appears to have been an inscription on it, but it was quite illegible." "Extensive potteries continued to exist at Bourn, until May 25, 1637, when a great fire broke out in Potter-street, Eastgate, which destroyed them, and they were never rebuilt."— *Ibid.*, III, p. 73.

From Bourn the Ermine-Street ran west of Morton and east of Stainfield, where there appears to have been a station from the evidence of Roman foundations, pottery, and innumerable coins found there, chiefly in a close called Blackfield.

Here there was also a branch road, or *via vicinalis,* running westward, described by Mr. Thomas Leman, in a letter to the Rev. Samuel E. Hopkinson, in the year 1819.

Perhaps this road first branched off a little to the north of Morton, or at a right angle from it on the line of the present road from Hacconby to Stainfield; but subsequently it certainly ran in a line towards Ponton. The first actual remains of this road Mr. Leman found just to the north of Norwood; he then traced it in the adjoining pasture field abutting upon the Grimsthorpe and Irnham road, next in two other small pasture closes on the east of that road, in the southern portion of Irnham Park, where it still retained its high ridge, and then, after a break, he found an equally well preserved portion of it in Corby low pasture, extending as far as the Corby and Irnham road, which it crossed about 100 yards south of a large pond. Beyond this it was lost in the arable ground, but it appears to have run thence a little to the north of Burton Coggles, and by Stony-lane towards the main line of the Ermine-Street in the direction of Ponton. After leaving this road to the west, what may be termed the eastern Ermine-Street, ran nearly on the line of the modern road between Morton, Hacconby, Dunsby, and Rippingale, on the east, and Hanthorpe and Kirkby Underwood on the west, as far as Graby toll-bar, at which place it now diverges into a grass field, where its bank is traceable. Passing the road leading to the hamlet of Graby, in the form of a grass lane, or riding, it runs northwards a little to the east of Aslackby, where it has been infringed upon by some cottage gardens. Hence it continues its course over a series of undulations, the highest of which is called Beacon Hill, near Sempringham,* whence the blue plains of the Division of Holland may be seen below, stretching out widely towards the east ; then intersecting a small brook, by what is still called the Street bridge, and crossing the road from Folkingham to Billingborough, it reaches Stow Green, celebrated for the decisive battle fought there between the Saxons and Danes, A.D. 870, and also for its fair. Next it surmounts the ridge on which stands Threckingham, and crosses another very ancient road, now called the Holland Road, but formerly the Salters' Way. This also was thought to be Roman by Stukeley; and was certainly, as the name implies, used by those engaged in the great salt trade formerly carried on between the Lincolnshire coast and the interior of the country. The position of Threckingham at the junction

---

* Famous as the birthplace of Gilbert de Sempringham, son of Joceline de Sempringham, rector of that place. Gilbert, having determined to retire from the world and lead a strictly religious life, built a retreat for himself on the north side of St. Andrew's Church, in his native village, where he could devote his whole time to prayer and holy meditation. Subsequently he admitted a certain number of persons of both sexes into his retreat, and thus founded a monastery whose inmates lived under one roof, but where the monks and nuns were most rigidly separated from each other, the latter receiving their food and other necessaries through a window. The Gilbertine rule may be considered as a distinct one, which received the sanction of Pope Eugenius III., by means of a bull to that effect ; but the monks nearly followed the rule of St. Austin, and the nuns that of St. Benedict. For the maintenance of Sempringham Priory, Gilbert de Gant gave its inmates three carucates of land, which gift was amplified by similar grants of land made by Reginald de Ba, Hugh de Baiocis, and the proceeds of the church of Fordham, given by Henry III. Gilbert de Sempringham was admitted as a saint into the Roman calendar by Pope Innocent III, A.D. 1202, and lived to see thirteen monasteries of his order founded, of which he was the master or grand prior. One very laudable object of the order was to foster learning ; to promote which Robert Lutteril, rector of Irnham, gave a house in St. Peter's parish, Stamford, together with lands and tenements in Ketton, Cottesmore, and Casterton, for the benefit of the Gilbertine scholars, studying divinity and philosophy in a school of this order at Stamford. To this was attached a chaplain, by a license of John Dalderby, Bishop of Lincoln, dated 1303. St. Gilbert was buried between the high altars of St. Mary and St. Andrew, of the monastic church of Sempringham, and beneath the wall separating the monks' from the nuns' choir, so that both could venerate his grave.

of these two ancient roads was an important one, and here many
Roman coins have been found.   From this point to Sleaford
the Roman road we are describing pursues a nearly straight course
in an embanked form, leaving Spanby and Scredington on the
right, and Osbournby and Aswarby on the left.   Between the
last named parish and Burton the base and part of the shaft of a

mediæval boundary cross stands by the side of the road, which is
here twenty-eight feet wide, with a grassy margin on either side
of nearly the same width.   Next the site of an old moated mansion, called Mareham Hall,* in the parish of Burton Pedwardine,
is passed, whence the whole of this ancient road from Graby bar
to Sleaford, thirteen miles in length, derives its present name.

---

* Mareham constituted a grange, granted to Sir Thomas Horseman in
1564.   Previously it belonged to Simon Hall.   Burton Pedwardine, of which
Mareham now forms a part, is so called from the Pedwardine family, who once
possessed it.   The manor of Burton was originally granted by the Conqueror
to Wido de Credon or Croun, whose descendants possessed it until the eventual
heiress of the family, Petronilla, married William de Longchamp, son of the

Here it is in a very perfect condition, because it has neither been disturbed by the plough, nor otherwise injured. Still continuing its straight course, and leaving the beautiful spire of Silk Willoughby Church on the left, at a point about half a mile from Sleaford, the modern road to that town has been diverted from the ancient one. The course of this last, however, may still be clearly traced on its way towards the site of an ancient moated mansion, now termed the Old Place, about half a mile eastward of Sleaford, which first belonged to Lord Hussey, subsequently to the family of Carre, and now to the Marquis of Bristol. Before crossing the Sleaford and Boston road, the old road under notice has degenerated into a worn hollow track, instead of standing upon a bank, and in the same condition, under the term of Old Eau Lane, it descends on the eastern side of the Old Place to the site of an ancient ford over the Slea, a little to the east of Cogglesford Mill, and used as such until 1792. On the grounds of the Old Place many Roman coins and occasionally fragments of Samian ware and other pottery have been found ; and in the river by the ford, a fine brass British celt was discovered in 1818, of which a cut is subjoined.

Before the inclosure of Sleaford and Leasingham Moors, a portion of the embankment of this ancient road leading towards Ruskington, was plainly visible. This ran nearly parallel with the present Tattershall road, and westward of it; but now the only remnant of this consists of a section of its bank in a hedgerow between two small fields south of the Moor-lane, in the

---

Abbot of Croyland. Their son, Henry Longchamp, had an only daughter and heiress, Alice, who, through her marriage with Roger Pedwardine, transferred the manor of Burton to her husband's family, and died 1330. The Pedwardines held Burton until the reign of Edward IV. For further particulars see subsequent account of Burton Pedwardine.

parish of Leasingham. Passing westward of Ruskington Church, it most probably was continued in some form towards the great Lindum Colonia, through the parishes of Dorrington, Bloxholm, Ashby, Scopwick, Blankney, Metheringham, Dunston, Nocton, Potterhanworth, and Branston, again joining the other and more important line of the Ermine-Street at a point about a mile south of Lincoln. No trace, however, of such a road now remains, and Roman vestiges have been found only in two of the above-named parishes, viz., Ashby and Potterhanworth. In the former, a portion of a tesselated pavement was discovered in 1831. It was 18 feet long by 6 feet wide, and consisted of black and white tesselæ, of different sizes forming bands of various widths. At Potterhanworth great quantities of Roman pottery of different kinds were found on the site of the parish school-house, when its foundations were laid.

Returning to the main line of the Ermine-Street a little north of Castor, we find that it passes Sutton Wood on the east, and runs through the hamlet of Southorpe, where coins of Antoni-nus Pius, Marcus Aurelius, Claudius Gothicus, Magnentius, and Constantine the Great have been found, together with Roman pottery, &c., chiefly in the pits on the eastern side of the road. Next it may be traced in the parish of Barnack as a wide bank, thus described in Gough's edition of *Camden*, II, p. 270,—" Here it rears a high ridge, particularly in the little wood of Barnack, where it has a watch-tower upon it." This so-called watch-tower, however, no longer exists, but a Roman fibula and some urns were found close to the Ermine-Street at Barnack, in 1731 ; since then many Roman coins have also been picked up here, and more recently the torso of a small nude male figure cut in Barnack stone was dug up, now in the possession of the Incumbent, the Rev. Canon Argles. Hence the Ermine-Street runs by Walcot Hall and through Burghley Park, since its enlargement by John, Earl of Exeter, in 1655, but before that time it formed part of the public road between Stamford and Peterborough. Here it is now not traceable, because its bank having been formed of gravelly materials, was carted away to make walls about Burghley House.—Bridge's *Northamptonshire*, II, p. 501* Next it may

---

* Portions of its materials were also subsequently used for the repair of a neighbouring road ; Stukeley in a MS. memorandum, when speaking of it,

be detected crossing a branch of the Welland, near Worthope
Park wall, where its bank is three feet high and twenty feet
wide, whence it descends the valley of the Welland, and crossing
that river at a spot on which Bredcroft Hall* formerly stood,
enters Lincolnshire, according to Stukeley's words, "with a broad
elated crest." Passing by the sites of the Benedictine Nunnery
of St. Michael and the Augustine Priory, it leaves the town of
Stamford† on the east, in the form of a broad raised bank, called
Green-bank, and then, as a turnpike road, reaches Casterton.
None of the Roman Itineraries mention the existence of any town
or station between Durobrivæ and Causennæ, yet there certainly
was a large camp at Casterton, ten miles north of Durobrivæ, or
Castor, a considerable portion of which still remains, close to
Ermine-Street. Probably this camp, like the one below Castor,
was made before the road that subsequently passed by it. It
is situated in a bend of the river Wash, which thus defended

---

says, "The overseers of the highways of St. Martin's parish, Stamford, had in
a sacrilegious manner digged it up to mend their wicked ways withal."

* This spot was so called in King John's reign, when it belonged to Lucy,
wife of William de Humet, lord of Stamford, who, out of her lands here, gave
half a mark of silver yearly to the nuns of St. Michael, on condition that they
should observe her anniversary with an obsequy ; half of which was to be expended on a pittance on that day, and the other half to be bestowed upon the
infirmary.—Peck's *Antiquarian Annals of Stamford*, Lib. VII., p. 11. Subsequently the sessions for the county of Rutland are said to have been held in
Bredcroft or Bradecroft Hall, the foundations of which were still visible on
the north bank of the adjacent water course in the last century.

† During the year 1868, a Roman stone coffin, lying east and west, was
discovered in a field of Mr. Gilchrist's farm, near Stamford, about half a mile
from the Ermine-street, through the grating of a plough against its lid.
Unfortunately it was immediately disinterred, and dragged out of its long
resting-place by horse-power, and then its contents were emptied out hurriedly
by persons wholly incompetent either to observe or report the result. It is of
a massive character, without ornament, and simply coarsely tooled, a flat slab
forming its lid. Within were remains of two bodies, a male and female,
whose skulls lay at each end of the coffin ; also about a dozen earthen vessels
—probably of Durobrivan ware, a glass lachrymatory, and some bone pins.
On the north side of this coffin other human remains were found, forming
portions of another skeleton ; and, from the fact of some large iron nails being
discovered with these, we may conclude they were originally deposited there
in a wooden coffin. Shortly after a tesselated pavement also was found near
this spot, indicating the former existence there of a Roman house.

nearly two-thirds of its circumference. Its area was about twenty-seven acres in extent, and it was probably wholly surrounded by a fosse and vallum. These still remain—so far as they existed on the north-eastern side of the turnpike-road passing through the village of Castor, beginning at a point a little to the south of the church, and joining it again after having enclosed an irregular shaped parallelogram just before the road to Ryhall branches off from it; but there are now no traces of the remainder. Its situation in a low valley, although objectionable in some respects, secured for it a plentiful supply of water, and also an additional source of strength from its proximity to the little river Wash. Stukeley thought that the Ermine-Street diverged from its direct course so that it might pass through this station, but in reality it is only the modern road that does so, which leaves the old *via* a little to the south of Casterton Church. This, pursuing a straighter course, must have crossed the Wash twice, although its bank here for some little way is lost; but near Tickencote it again becomes visible on the western side of the turnpike road from Stamford to Grantham, with which it is once more incorporated. Stukeley reports that many foundations of Roman buildings had been found at Casterton before he wrote his *Itinerarium*, and also many coins, of which he mentions a denarius of Pompey, a large brass of Nero, and specimens of the reigns of Trajan, Antoninus Pius, Severus, Claudius Gothicus, Maximianus, and Constantine.

North of Tickencote Hall the Ermine-Street, under the name of Horn Lane,* runs straight to Greetham Mill, leaving Bloody Oaks† on the west. At Greetham Mill it turns directly towards the north, and Gale thought that a branch road led hence to

---

* Horn was formerly a distinct parish, containing 830 acres of land, but is now included in the parish of Empingham, and the site of its church is in Exton Park, to which the successive rectors were long inducted under a certain old thorn bush in that park.

† So called from the slaughter of the Lancastrians here, after a desperate battle between Sir Robert Welles, placed at the head of 30,000 Lincolnshire men by the Earl of Warwick, and Edward IV. at the head of a still larger force, which was fought in Horn-field, March 12, 1470. In this battle King Henry's adherents were utterly defeated. Sir Robert Welles and his brother-in-law, Sir Thomas De la Launde, were taken prisoners, and beheaded at Doncaster three days later. The name of Bloody Oaks still commemorates the

Nottingham; but there are no traces of such a road now. Passing Stretton, or Street-town, on the east, and South Witham on the west, where it constitutes a portion of the old North-Road, and thence on between the site of Lobthorpe Hall* and North Witham, it reaches a point half-a-mile north of the once well-known Black Bull of Witham Common, where the modern road turns northward and passes through Colsterworth, and the old Roman *via* is difficult to trace for a space of about two miles, so that it will be well to describe this more particularly. On its first divergence from the North-Road, soon after passing Honypot-Lane on the right, it runs along the eastern side of a triangular field belonging to Earl Dysart, whence it proceeds as a grass lane until it reaches the Colsterworth and Bourn turnpike-road. On the north of this it has again ceased to exist as a road, but its line may still be traced, running through a field in which are some stone pits, belonging to Mr. J. Dove, two fields belonging to the Rev. J. Mirehouse, two others belonging to Christopher Turnor, Esq., and then between two old pasture fields (also Mr. Turnor's), where an oak tree stands on the right of the line. It continued to run in the same direction through the parish of Easton, having an old hedge there marking its eastern boundary, until it reached that point where it is still used as a modern road under the ancient term of the High Dyke, with which it now communicates by a short grass lane running abruptly westward, instead of running on straight as it did originally. In a field north of the road leading to the village of Easton, and about 150 yards from that road, was a Roman camp of considerable size, on the site of which Roman relics have been occasionally found, including a horse's bronze bit, broken in two, but otherwise in perfect condition. Here, also, among others, the following Roman coins have been discovered, viz. : a small silver one, having on the obverse the head of Nero, and the legend, "NERO· CÆSAR · AUGUSTUS" ; reverse, Jupiter seated, holding a bolt in

---

fall of the 10,000 men who fell in the conflict, and a field between Little Casterton and Stamford, is also called Losecote-field, from a local tradition that the Lancastrians here divested themselves of all that encumbered their flight from the battle field and their victorious foes.

* This was the ancient seat of the Sherard family. It is surrounded by a fosse originally nine yards wide, and is 130 yards long and 100 yards wide.

his right hand and a hasta pura in his left; legend, "JUPITER · CUSTOS." A small brass, having on the obverse the head of Licinus, and the legend, "LICINUS. JUN. NOB. C."; reverse, two trophies between two soldiers, each holding a spear in one hand and a shield in the other. In the exergue, "T. R. P.", and a star. Licinus became Cæsar A.D. 317, and was executed A.D. 326. After passing through Easton parish the Roman road shews itself clearly enough, sometimes a little on the right and sometimes on the left of its present representative, first leaving Stoke Rochford on the west, and next Great Ponton, where, according to Stukeley, many Roman vaults, tesselated pavements, urns, coins, bricks, &c., were found during the last century.* Then it passes by a group of cottages at Woodnook, a mile westward of Little Ponton,† and on to Cold Harbour,‡ two miles westward of Grantham, where it is intersected by the old Salter's Way—now called the Brigend-road § or Haydor-lane. Scarcely any Roman remains have been found at Grantham, but Burton,

---

* In the township of Little Humby, three and a half miles east of the Ermine-Street, and nearly parallel with Great Ponton, many Roman vestiges were found in 1828, such as pottery, pins, and coins, most of which were secured by the late Mr. William Cragg, of Threckingham. These last chiefly consisted of small brasses of Claudius Gothicus, Magnentius Posthumus, Constantinus Magnus, and Constantinus II.

† Four miles westward of Little Ponton, a Roman villa was discovered in the parish of Denton, during the year 1727. Two of its tesselated pavements were engraved by William Fowler, one from a drawing made by Dr. Stukeley, the other by himself, in 1800. These were both composed of grey tesselæ, with a centre-piece of richer work, the one being an oblong, nine feet by three, having long octagons and small squares designated by grey and white borders upon a red ground; the other a square of nine feet, having a star-like figure in the centre, surrounded by diamonds, each having an interlaced knot in its centre, within a square surrounded by a guilloche border, composed of grey, red, and yellow tesselæ.—See *Philosophical Transactions* for 1804.

‡ It is remarkable that spots so named are very frequently found near to ancient roads; one exists in Cammeringham parish, near Tillbridge Lane, a branch of the Ermine-Street, north of Lincoln; another near Stewton, by Louth; another near Hessle, Yorkshire; another near Wye, in Kent; and another at Titsey, by the Pilgrim's Way, in the same county.

§ Leading to Bridge end—or as it is commonly spelt Brigend Priory, from its nearness to Holland bridge. This was a Gilbertine House, founded in the reign of John, by Godwin, a rich citizen of Lincoln, in honour of Our Lord. At the dissolution, as parcel of Sempringham Abbey, it was granted

in his *Commentary on the Antonine Itinerary*, p. 216, states that a great stone trough, covered with a stone, and filled with Roman coins, was dug up there. He also remarks that one of its streets is called Castle-street; that between this and the river foundations of a castle were discovered, and that he had a piece of glass found in the Grange garden, which he believed to be Roman. The Ermine-Street, from the Brigend-road, takes a perfectly straight course northwards, over a series of undulations, leaving Welby on the east, and Londonthorpe, Belton, Syston, Barkston, and Honington on the west. On an eminence in this last-named parish, and a mile and a half westward of the Ermine-Street, is a strongly entrenched earthwork, pronounced to be a *castrum exploratorum* of the Romans, by Stukeley, but it must certainly be of British origin, and in no respect resembles a Roman camp. It consists of an area of irregular form, containing an acre and a quarter of ground, surrounded by a triple vallum and a double fosse, occupying two more acres. The average height of the outer vallum is three feet, that of the other two, seven feet, and the level of the enclosure is three and a half feet above that of the bottom of each fosse. The width of the inner vallum is nineteen feet four inches, of the middle one twenty-seven feet four inches, of the outer one fifteen feet four inches. As the slope of each vallum can be easily surmounted, perhaps there were no regular entrances to the central area, but there are slight depressions at four different points through these, which may or may not be of subsequent formation. The whole remains in a very perfect state, only a portion of the outer vallum having been partially cut away at two points. This earthwork was undoubtedly occupied by the Romans, as in 1691 an urn containing a peck of Roman coins was discovered within it, and subsequently others were found, a score of which Stukeley obtained in 1728. Amongst these he names a large brass of Agrippa, another of Julia, the daughter of Augustus, and one of Magnentius. Fragments also of weapons are said to have been ploughed up here.

---

to Edward Lord Clinton, up to which time prayers had been daily said by its inmates for travellers who had to encounter the dangers of the fens. The remains of its buildings were taken down in 1770, and were employed in building an adjacent farm house.

In a direct line between this earthwork and Ancaster, in a field called the Twelve Acre Close, a rudely formed Roman stone coffin was more lately discovered, still bearing upon its outer surface the tooling of its makers very distinctly. It is six feet ten inches long, two feet two inches wide at the head, diminishing to one foot ten inches at the foot, and one foot eight inches deep. The head is rounded like other examples of Roman stone coffins found at Bath. Upon it was a rude slab, four inches thick. It lay in a north and south direction, at so slight a depth as to have been discovered through the action of the plough, and contained the skeleton of a male, in a tolerable state of preservation. It now stands in Ancaster churchyard.

The Ermine-Street descends sharply before it passes through Ancaster, a once important Roman station, most probably that of *Causennis* or *Isinnis*, placed by the pseudo Richard of Cirencester and the *Antonine Itinerary* between *Lindum* and *Durobrivæ*, and estimated at thirty miles from the latter, which is nearly correct; but at twenty-six miles from the former, or twelve miles too much, probably through the interpolation of a superfluous Roman X.

Such a site was an excellent one for a Roman station, from its proximity to a never-failing streamlet, and its sheltered situation. Here, accordingly, an irregular parallelogram, containing nine acres of land, was surrounded by a fosse ten feet deep and fifty feet wide, affording a secure camp, through which the Ermine-Street ran.

Postponing a description of Ancaster, we must here advert to a *via vicinalis*, which branches off from the great Roman road at this place, and is now called the Potter-gate Road. This runs nearly on the edge of a high ridge on the west of the Ermine-Street, and overlooking the villages of Caythorpe, Fulbeck, Leadenham, and Welbourn, it passes close to the east of Wellingore, and rejoins the parent road at Navenby. Roman coins have frequently been found near this road, and in 1857 an interesting discovery was made within forty yards of it, in a field at Caythorpe, belonging to the Rev. C. D. Crofts, through the grating of a plough against a large stone. This, on examination, led to the uncovering of the base of a pillar two feet in diameter, upon which was another circular stone, containing within a cavity a small black earthenware olla, enclosing sixteen Roman coins, among which were a large brass of Faustina Junior

—reverse, Juno; a small brass of Constantius; one of Magnentius; one bearing on the obverse "URBS ROMA"; reverse, the wolf and twins; one of Gratianus, and another of Honorius or Arcadius. Here also were found a very small square incense altar, the base and feet of a statuette and portions of the legs and arms, cut in stone. This not improbably formed the sepulchral effigy of a Roman colonist, placed, as usual, within a niche.

After the Ermine-Street has emerged from the little valley in which Ancaster lies, its bank is both wide and high, and especially so on the summits of the natural undulations of the line it traverses. A quarter of a mile north of Ancaster, and

close to the edge of the old road we are describing, nearly the whole of a small rough stone, forming a milliary,* was discovered, bearing this inscription :— " IMP · C · FL · VAL · CONSTANTINO P · F · INV · AVG · DIVI · CONSTANTINI · PII · AVG · FILIO"; or, *Imperatori, Cæsari, Flavio, Valerio, Constantino, Pio, Felici, Invicto, Augusto, Divi, Constantii, Pii. Augusti, Filio.* This was not in its original position, and its base had been broken off. In size it is two feet three inches long, one foot wide, and seven inches thick. It was apparently used to mark the spot where a funeral deposit had been made, as some fragments of human bones and pottery, and also part of a red deer's horn sawn cleanly from the remainder, were found with it.

---

* Had this milliary stone been perfect, we might possibly have ascertained with certainty the Roman name of Ancaster, as in the case of the one found at Leicester, which bears the Roman name of that town, and formerly constituted the second milestone from it. These stones were renewed from time to time by the *curatores viarum*, or road surveyors.

Stukeley mentions the existence of stones by the side of the Ermine-Street in his time, but he never saw one with an inscription cut upon it, and perhaps in reality no milliary at all. In *Iter.* V., p. 87, he says, " Upon our road there are many stones placed, but most seem modern, and like stumps of crosses, yet probably are milestones ;" and speaks still more positively in *Iter.* I., p. 80, when describing this *via*, " I have seen bases of milliaries, and one or two fragments of milliaries on its sides." These are no tests of the date of a Roman road, as they were often replaced, and probably sometimes at least in anticipation or commemoration of the transit of some great personage, in whose honour they were inscribed ; but we are more fortunate than Stukeley was, for we may still see a milliary existing at Ancaster, bearing a complimentary legend cut in honour of Constantine the Great * and not improbably so cut by persons who actually saw him in company with his father Constantius, on their way from Boulogne to York, at the head of a large Roman force marching against the Calidonians, along the Ermine-Street, and through Ancaster ; or when, after the loss of his father, he hastened back to secure the empire for himself.

Between Ancaster and a spot called Bayard's Leap,† where the Ermine-Street is intersected by the Sleaford and Newark road, it presents a grand appearance, its well developed bank, from three to six feet high, and wide in proportion, remaining in nearly as perfect a condition as when it was first made by the Romans ; but before reaching the above-named spot, its bank has been partly destroyed. From this point the Ermine-Street is no longer stoned, and the whole space devoted to the public use

---

* Constantine had made a wonderfully fast journey from Nicomedia across Europe, by the aid of the imperial military roads, and the *mutationes agminales*, or posting houses, established along their lines, and was just in time to join the Emperor at Boulogne, or Gessoriacum, before he embarked for Britain. He accompanied him in his campaign against the Calidonians, and back to York, or Eboracum, where Constantius died, which occasioned Constantine's speedy return to Italy.

† Or the bay horse's leap, so called from a local tradition that a nameless horseman, pursued by a witch, who sprang upon his steed, fled towards the refuge of a cross road, over which both horse and man bounded with a prodigious leap—still marked upon the turf margins of that road—and at which point the supernatural assailant fell dead.

on either side of it is deeply scored with ruts.   Through this the
bank of the old road wends its way, but just before it reaches a
small planting called, from its shape, the Cocked-hat plantation,
near Temple Bruer* it inclines to the western side of its modern
area, and its bank has been partly carted away.   Beyond this
point it has been much injured, and sometimes almost obliterated,
until it reaches the turn to Wellingore, where it has been repaired
and stoned for a short distance.   Soon, however, it resumes its
former dilapidated condition, occasioned by turf-cutting and partial removal of its bank; and as a grassy way, but little used,
passes by Navenby and Boothby Graffoe on the west, where the
towers of Lincoln Minster begin to constitute a grand terminus
towards which this ancient road directly points, and Dunston
Pillar † is seen about two miles to the east.   Parallel with the
village of Harmston, on a slight eminence, the bank of the old
road is distinctly visible, where it extends into an adjoining field
on the right, and at another spot a little further on.   Hence it
continues its course northwards as a grassy way in a perfectly
straight line until it reaches a small house called Waterloo Cottage, from which point not even a footpath indicates the former
course of this great road ; yet some very slight traces of its bank
may be detected even here, pointing towards the west end of a
farm house, called Friezland, soon after which it begins to serve
its original purpose as a foundation to the road between Wad-
dington and Lincoln, which it will be observed has a higher bank
as long as it runs on the line of the old Roman road.   Before
approaching Red Hall these two roads again diverge, the Ermine-
Street pursuing its course northwards, which is marked by a
footpath in front of the above-named house, and terminates in an

---

* Temple Bruer, or the Temple Preceptory on the heath.   This was
founded by Elizabeth de Cauz, in the reign of Henry II., and afterwards richly
endowed with lands for the maintenance of the Templar fraternity.   In 1324
this establishment was granted to the Hospitallers, when it became a Commandery of that order, and so continued until its suppression in 1538.   A
small Early English tower is all that now remains of its once extensive buildings, the lower story of which is richly arcaded, and served as a chapel.

† Erected as a lighthouse for the benefit of persons travelling across the
formerly desolate Lincoln Heath, by Sir Francis Dashwood, in 1772.   Its
lantern was eventually blown down by a storm, and in 1810 the pillar was
surmounted by a statue, in terra cotta, of George III.

irregular strip of grass land by the side of the modern Sleaford and Lincoln turnpike-road, exactly on the summit of the high ground bordering the valley of the Witham, before it descends that valley.   There more care was required in making its bank, and more pains were taken in constructing the road itself, as it passed over the fenny soil through which the Witham flows, to the southern entrance of the important Roman colonial town of *Lindum.*   Here it was joined by the *via fossata,* or Foss-road, as it is still called, and crossing the two branches of the *Lindis, Victius,* or Witham river, whether by bridges or fords we know not, ran through the lower Roman town, then beneath the southern gateway of the upper town, which it nearly bisected, and its northern gateway, or Newport Arch, after which it continued its course northwards, through the centre of Lincolnshire, towards the *Abus,* or Humber, whence it has been called the Humber-Street, as well as the High-Street, and the Old-Street.

"The Hermen-Street," says Stukeley, "going northward from Lincoln, is scarce diminished because its materials are hard stones, and the heath on both side favours it."   *Itin.* V., p. 93. While Abraham de la Pryme, an antiquary of the last century, speaking of this ancient road, says, "It is cast up upon both sides with incredible labour to a great height, yet discontinued in many places, and then begun again. Where it runs over nothing but bare mould and plain heath, it then consists of nothing but earth thrown up ; but when it runs through the woods, there it is not only raised with earth, but faced with great stones set edgeways, very close together, the better to preserve it—its width being seven yards."   We have seen, however, that at one point the paved portion of this *via* did not exceed thirteen feet in width.   From a recent excavation it has been discovered that the Ermine-Street immediately after it left the Newport Arch, ran slightly to the east of the present road, but with this exception it followed the line of that road very exactly, and its swelling bank may still be seen in much perfection as it passes Riseholme, in a series of undulations on its way to the north.   At a point four miles distant from Lincoln is a Roman branch road, or *via vicinalis,* now called Till Bridge Lane, which leads to the Trent, and eventually to Doncaster.

It was naturally conjectured by Horsley, *Brit. Rom.*, III., c. 2, p. 434, that this road, sometimes called the Old-Street, ran *directly* from the great colonial city of *Lindum* to *Danum*, or Doncaster; but such was not the case, as it branched off from the Ermine-Street as above mentioned. The first mile-and-a-quarter of this old road is now disused, but may be detected in the fields through which it ran; and on its site various small brass Roman coins have been found of the Constantine period, as recorded by Archdeacon Illingworth, in his *Topographical Account of the Parish of Scampton*, p. 4. Half-a-mile northward of this point Till Bridge Lane branches off at a right angle from the Ermine-Street, and into this the old Roman road to Doncaster falls near to the village of Scampton, where, as one and the same road, it runs in a straight line to the Trent (*Trevona*), and Littleborough, on its western bank—the Roman *Agelocum* or *Segelocum*, its whole length being ten miles.—Stukeley thus describes it: "This ridge is likely to be of eternal duration, as wholly out of all roads, it proceeds directly on the heath, then descends the cliff through the rich country at bottom, between two hedge-rows, by the name of Till Bridge Lane. When you view it on the brink of the hill, 'tis as a vista or avenue running through a wood or garden, very straight, and pleasanter than when you come to travel, wanting a Roman Legion to repair it." *Iter*. V., p. 87.

At Scampton, the remains of a very large Roman villa were found in 1795, chiefly through the instrumentality of Archdeacon Illingworth, the then incumbent of Scampton, who published an account of that discovery. Having heard that some bricks had been turned up in getting stone from a pit, in a field lying southeast of the village, and north of Till Bridge Lane, he was led to examine them, and finding they were Roman, he ordered excavations to be made, which disclosed the foundations of a Roman house, that had occupied an elevated site about 200 feet square in area, and contained forty rooms. It was built of the stone of the district, and its walls were usually two to three feet thick, but one wall was from five to five-and-a-half feet thick. These foundations were from two to three feet below the surface, and from one to two feet only in height, chiefly forming the substructure of the house, so that it could not be ascertained how one room communicated with another, nor what was the character of the superstructure; but the sill of the principal doorway still remained in situ. Probably most of the hypocausts of this villa escaped notice, as the furnace of only one of these, on the eastern side, seems to have been discovered and noted. In all, the remains of thirteen tesselated pavements were laid bare, some of quite coarse work, but others of much beauty ; the white tesselæ being cut from the native limestone, and the red and grey being formed of terra cotta, or baked clay, varying from half an inch to an inch and-a-half in size. These pavements were laid upon a thick substratum of cement composed of lime, gravel, and pounded brick. The most beautiful of the pavements was engraved by Fowler. This was found in a room, fifty feet long, but only ten feet wide, on the eastern side of the house It was not quite perfect, but its general design, composed of grey, red, yellow, and white tesselæ—still retaining their original tints—was as perfect as ever. Portions of the fallen stucco, or plaster, with which some of the rooms were lined remained on the floors, and especially in the above named room. These were painted with various colours, such as green, or red and white, and blue and white in stripes. On the floors of the rooms also lay quantities of flanged and scored roof tiles, charred wood, and melted lead, clearly indicating the way in which this house, like almost all others of Roman origin eventually perished. Here also were found the shaft of a small pillar, a spear head, innumerable fragments of earthenware, and some glass vessels, fibulæ, bone pins, and many coins of the lower Empire. Since this many others have been found, and also the skeleton of a female, round the bone of one of the fingers of which still remained a small Roman bronze ring, now in the possession of the Diocesan Architectural Society. Many skeletons were disclosed during the excavations carried on in and about the site of this villa, but these were the remains of bodies buried in the cemetery of St. Pancras's Chapel, built in the twelfth century on this spot, which has also passed away. A well of Roman origin close by, called St. Pancras's Well, besides the adjacent chapel now unfortunately destroyed, thus commemorated that young Roman saint martyred in Diocletian's reign, to whom Augustine dedicated the first Christian church at Canterbury, and whose name was perhaps given to this well and chapel, as being appropriate in connection with the site of a Roman house, some remains of which may then have been apparent above ground.

Till Bridge Lane, after passing Scampton and crossing two branches of the little river Till, whence it derives its name, passes

through Sturton or Street-town, which evidently is so called
from its propinquity to the Roman road. North of this is Stow,
whose venerable church justly claims to be the mother church of
the Diocese of Lincoln, and probably stands on the site of the
Roman Sidnacester, although, so far, unfortunately, very few
Roman remains, such as coins, &c., have been found in or about
it, to confirm this belief.

Crossing the railway from Lincoln to Retford, this old road
passes near to Marton, situated on a ridge overlooking the valley
of the Trent. Here portions of the pavement of a Roman house
were remaining until the beginning of the last century, *Magna
Britannia*, II., p. 1454, and many Roman coins have since been
found in this parish, including a large brass of Hadrian, and
another of Carausius.

From Marton the road descends into the valley below, pointing directly to Littleborough, on the Nottinghamshire bank of the
Trent. Here was a ford made by the Romans in the manner
they usually adopted as an aid to the transit of rivers. On either
side the bank was sloped away, so as to make an easy descent
leading to a raised causeway in the bed of the river. This was
eighteen feet wide, and held up by strong stakes driven into the
soil on either side, and paved with stones. It existed until 1820,
when through the obstruction it created to the navigation of the
river during dry seasons, it was removed; but a portion of the
paved descent on the Nottinghamshire side still remains. Such
works were ordered to be constructed by the Emperor Hadrian,
during his visit to Britain, A.D. 120, when he directed the banks
of roads to be repaired, and their surfaces to be paved afresh,
built bridges over some rivers, and made paved causeways across
the beds of others, such as this at Littleborough. He therefore
may have been the author of this work, and it is a curious fact
that in a cleft of one of its piles, a large brass coin of his reign
was found, bearing a figure of Justice on the reverse. It afforded
the means of communication with a Roman station surrounded,
as usual, by a wall and deep fosse, of which some remains may
still be detected. It is generally agreed that this was the
Agelocum, of the *Antonine Itinerary*, or the *Argolico* of the pseudo
Richard of Cirencester, an opinion which is confirmed by its
relative distance from *Lindum Colonia*, or Lincoln, and *Danum*, or
Doncaster, viz., fourteen miles from the former and twenty one

from the latter. Many Roman relics have been found at various times on this spot, and especially on the eastern side of the village, where the river has disturbed part of its site. Here Stukeley observed foundations of buildings and portions of pavements projecting from the river bank, and here Gale likewise, when crossing the river, saw *a coraline urn, i.e.*, a piece of Samian ware, in its bank, "This (says he,) I pulled out, but it was broken in pieces, as it stood it had bones in it, and a coin of Domitian."— Gale's *It. Anton.*, p. 13. In 1718, part of a coarse gritstone altar was found in a sandpit here, whose *foculus,* or hollow for fire on the top, was perfect, and whose mouldings were quite entire, and clean as if newly cut, but nearly the whole of the inscription on it had been cut away, as if preparatory to cutting another upon it, but the end of the original one remained legible, viz., " LIS · ARAM · D · D." By this was found another wrought stone, which a contemporary antiquary, conceived to be of a monumental character. These formerly stood on each side of the steps leading from the ferry to the inn above, but have now disappeared. Perhaps one of these is what Stark, in his *History of the Bishopric of Lincoln*, p. 112, calls a milliary stone, and was used as a horse block. Ella, in a letter to Stukeley, contained in *Reliquiæ Galeanæ*, p. 118, thus speaks of his researches at Littleborough :—" Fragments of the finest coral coloured urns are frequently discovered, and some with curious *bassi relievi* upon them, and the workman's name generally impressed with extant letters at the inside of the bottom. I have in my hands the fragments of some urns and vessels, one of which is the largest part of a Roman *discus*, or sacrificing platter, another which seems to be a cover, but I never had the good fortune to meet with any urn or vessel complete, nor heard of any, except one of a singular make, with an Emperor's head embossed upon it, the same which Dr. Gale has given us the figure of, found at York."— Gale's *It. Anton.*, p. 23. " The urns, or vessels, are most of them of this coral colour, and but few of the coarse grey sort which are met with in other places ; though we might have expected great numbers of this coarse sort, this station being within a few miles of one of the most noted potteries in this island, Santon, near Brigg, in Lincolnshire, where these were made."—*Phil. Coll.*, N. IV. p. 88. " There are also found here, but very rarely, Roman signets of agate and cornelian ; one of the finest and largest I ever saw was found at this place; I thought it so valuable as to bestow the setting upon it, but the workmen did it so slightly, that, to my great regret, it dropped out, I know not when, and was lost. The engraving was well performed, and the polish, though it must have lain 1300 years at least in the soil, much exceeded anything I have seen of English workmanship. Here also a Roman medical seal or tally was found."—Gough's *Camden.*, II. p. 404. This station has produced a vast number of coins, especially about the year 1736, when the fields between the town and bridge were ploughed up, including many very minute pieces (minnims). They have also been picked up at the edge of the river, very commonly when the tide has been out, in dry seasons, besides being found in ploughing and digging, and used to be termed "Swine Pennies," because they were sometimes rooted up by those animals. Mr. Ella regrets that so many specimens were so covered with rust as to be of little use for the cabinet, and that no *Thecæ Nummariæ* had been discovered, the contents of which might be better preserved. Coins, however, have been found here of Nero, Vespasian, Domitian, Trajan, Hadrian, Marcus Aurelius, Faustina, Gallienus, Victorinus, Tetricus, Carausius, Allectus, Constantinus Magnus, Constantius, Constantinus Secundus, and Crispus, besides many of the Constantine period, having on the obverse a galeated head and " URBS ROMA "; reverse, the wolf and twins; and others with " CONSTANTINOPOLIS " as a legend. Two, struck in Trajan's reign, and described in a letter of Ella to Stukeley, are particularly interesting; the one—a large brass of that Emperor, bore on the reverse a representation of one of his great works, the mole at Ancona, and the other a figure of Britannia, holding a spear in her left hand, with a shield at her left foot, and the name " BRITANNIA " on the exergue. From Littleborough this Roman road may be distinctly traced on its way through a second Sturton, or Street-town—distinguished from the other by the addition to its name of " le steeple,"—South and North Wheatley, Doncaster, Castleford—*Legiolium*, Tadcaster—*Colearia,* to York—*Eburacum* or *Eboracum.*

Returning to the main line of the Ermine-Street, where Till Bridge-lane branches from it, this ancient road proceeds to Spital * after passing which it becomes very conspicuous from

* The usual abbreviation of hospital, a retreat or home for poor widows

the size of its bank, where, in some instances, it is very prominent. Blyborough is then left on the west, where part of a coarse
tesselated pavement was found some years ago, and then Kirton,
which lies a-mile-and-a-half westward of the Ermine-Street, and
was thought by Pegge to be the *In medium* of the spurious
Richard of Cirencester, as it is about half way between Lincoln
and the Humber. Opposite Kirton the Ermine-Street becomes
simply a grass lane, and part of its bank lies on the left of the
modern track; but when it reaches Redbourn the bank is on the
right of the present road, and planted with trees. About a mile
further northward, and on the west of the road, is Gainstrop, the
site of a destroyed village, where Roman coins, pottery, and
bricks, have at different times been discovered. Just beyond the
point where the Ermine-Street is intersected by the Manchester,
Sheffield, and Lincolnshire Railway, and in the parish of Hibaldstow, is an entrenched camp of Roman construction. This lies
low between two small streams, which probably led to its formation there. The northern and southern limits are traceable through
a slight rise and fall in the ground, still serving to indicate the
fosse and agger of those sides of the camp. The eastern boundary
is entirely gone; but its western one, four hundred yards long, is
quite discernible. Roman coins have occasionally been found
here, and the pavement and hypocaust of a Roman house were
laid bare near the camp, when the adjacent railway was made.
Two miles northward of this, two pavements, with hypocausts
beneath them, were discovered some years ago in the farm yard
of Mr. Grantham, of Scawby, and were engraved by Mr. W.

---

having been established here in the reign of Edward II. This charitable
institution was subsequently enriched by Thomas de Aston, Prebendary of
Centum Solidorum, Lincoln, Sept. 17th, 1390, but subsequently Prebendary
of Liddington, and Archdeacon of Stow. Born at Aston, Staffordshire, he
obtained a licence from Richard II., to build and endow a chapel there, as
well as to reconstruct and endow "a certain habitation at Spittall-o'-the-Strete
for poor men," in 1394. At both places daily prayers were to be offered up
for the king while living, and for his soul's salvation when dead, as well as
for the souls of the Prince of Wales his father, his grandfather Edward III.,
and others. This grant to the hospital consisted of four messuages in
Hemswell, one toft and thirty acres of land at Spital, and the profits of the
churches of Skellingthorpe and Carlton. Thomas de Aston died June 7th,
1401, and was buried in the nave of Lincoln Cathedral.

Fowler, in 1818. One was composed of a light grey or white ground, having an oblong compartment in the centre, filled with a scale pattern of black, red, and white tesselæ. The other had four central squares, filled with alternated devices, surrounded by the guilloche pattern, a wider border of the same device, a strip of chequered work on the sides, and then a narrow white and a broad red border, beyond which were coarser light grey tesselæ. A small camp is also said to have existed in Scawby parish, as well as some of the original stone pavement of the Ermine-Street, until the middle of the last century. After passing the turn to the village of Scawby, the bank of the old road becomes very conspicuous, being about five feet high here. Running past Twigmoor,* a long tract of woodland on the west, and then across a light sandy district, whose surface is liable to shift, through the action of the wind, the ancient road is partly buried by these sands. At Broughton is a conspicuous mound, looking like a barrow, but when it was opened some years ago no evidence appeared that it was of artificial origin. Here, however, some Roman vestiges have occasionally been discovered, such as fragments of pottery, and bricks or tiles.† Emerging from the sand, and as a gravelled road passing through a still sandy tract covered with wood, past the site of Gokewell Nunnery,‡ the

---

* A remarkable moor, in the centre of which is a piece of water, round which countless numbers of the *larus ridibundus*, or black-headed gull, have bred for many years. These birds arrive in February, and leave about the middle of July. The black patch on their heads disappears during the winter season. Some breed also in the adjoining parish of Manton. Two other instances of such inland gulleries exist in England, one at Scoulton Mere, near Hingham, Norfolk, twenty-five miles from the sea, and the other at Pallinsburn, the seat of A. Askew, Esq.

† Eight British barrows were opened in this parish during 1850, by Messrs. Arthur Trollope and Joseph Moore. Several vases of rude earthenware, flint implements, &c., were then discovered.—*Archæological Journal*, VIII., pp. 341, 351. In this parish also certain lands are held by an extraordinary manorial service of cracking a gad-whip in Caistor Church once a year, which service, however, has of late years been discontinued.—*Archæological Journal*, VI. pp. 239, 248.

‡ A Cistercian nunnery, founded by William de Alta Ripa, previous to 1185. At the Dissolution its prioress and six nuns were dispossessed of their home, and their house and lands were granted to Sir William Tyrwhit. A few years ago several stone coffins buried in the cemetery were brought to light.

Ermine-Street reaches a spot called Britons' Graves, on the edge of Thornholme Moor, whence the site of the once stately priory of Thornholme* may be seen. Here is another sandy district, often suffering much injury from its tendency to blow, appropriately called Santon,† where a Roman pottery, and several furnaces were discovered some years ago, also a brass grating of a cruciform shape, and many fragments of pottery, together with a few coins. Towards the summit of one of the numerous sand hills near the Ermine-Street a large flat stone was found some time since, probably indicating a sepulchral deposit below, but whether Roman or not is uncertain. A mile and a half north of Santon lies Appleby, where an earthern vase, surrounded by dark soil, and containing a considerable number of Roman silver coins, was discovered in a rabbit warren. Two miles north of Appleby, and a mile and a half to the west of the Ermine-Street, lies Roxby, where, in the last century, a labourer, in repairing the fence of a small field of Robert Cary Elwes, Esq., lying to the south-west of the church, discovered part of a Roman tesselated pavement, many large stones and roof-tiles of the house to which it belonged, and portions of its wall-plaster, painted red and yellow, near to which Roman coins have since been found. Subsequently this pavement was so far uncovered as to allow of its being copied and engraved in 1799, by Mr. William Fowler, of Winterton. After passing through Roxby pasture the Ermine-Street enters the next parish, Winterton, where very beautiful tesselated pavements have been discovered, indicative of the former existence there of a superior class of Roman Colonial houses, the whole of which were drawn and engraved by Mr. Fowler. In 1747 three more were uncovered just below the Cliff House, to the west of the village, and a mile and a half from the Roman road now being described. One is twenty-eight and a half feet long and nineteen feet wide; the

---

* This was an Augustine house founded by King Stephen, and dedicated to the Virgin Mary. At the Dissolution its site and lands were given to Charles Brandon, Duke of Suffolk.

† In dry times these sands drift so much as to injure the adjacent land greatly, and sometimes are so heaped up in ridges as to resemble snow drifts. In this parish there were three barrows previous to its inclosure, where proclamation was made of any straying cattle by a bellman, which cattle, if not redeemed within twelve months and a day, were sold by public auction.

second forty feet long and thirteen feet wide. In the centre is a bust of Ceres within a circle surrounded by a double guilloche border, placed within a square, flanked first by two narrow compartments, filled with a scale pattern formed by red and grey tesselæ, and then by two oblongs, ornamented with interlaced circles in a very pleasing manner; a plain border composed of red, white, and grey tesselæ, disposed in bands of various widths, surround the whole. The third was damaged, but it had a border composed of red, white, and grey squares, containing oblong compartments within, in one of which was a stag. Another pavement was found here in 1797. This had a figure of Apollo, within a circle, surrounded by a guilloche border of red, grey, and white tesselæ in the centre, a compartment on either side filled with an interlacing pattern, and a series of red, white, and grey bands round these, constituting the outer border. Other Roman remains have also been found here, such as a brass eagle, as recorded in the *Minutes of the Society of Antiquaries*, a spear head, much pottery, and many tiles, bricks, and coins, including a large brass of Vespasian, a silver one of Antoninus Pius, and many of the Constantine period. About half way between the Ermine-Street and these pavements, a Roman potter's kiln was accidentally discovered in 1868. It had been formed by excavating a hollow penetrating the surface soil, a thin stratum of clay, and the sand below, and resembled one or more found by the late Mr. Artis, at Castor *(Durobrivæ)*, in Northamptonshire. Its shape was that of an inverted cone, six feet deep, and the same in diameter at its widest part. Its wall was constructed of clay, mixed with gravel, four inches thick below, increasing to ten inches above. The floor of the furnace was covered with black ashes and broken pottery. With this a lateral flue communicated, formed of flat oolitic stones, whose blackened and reddened surface indicated the great heat to which they had been exposed. From the middle of the furnace rose a concave clay shaft, one foot nine inches high, whose widely spreading base and head enable it the better to support the floor of the piles above. This floor was broken, but appears to have been made, as usual, of tiles covered with clay. The domed top of the kiln had also disappeared, but its debris, consisting of broken tiles and pieces of plaster, lay within the kiln. The surface of the clay lining and the flue-shaft, was of a pale blue, fading off into red and ochreous yellow, occasioned by exposure to heat. Many fragments of pottery were found in and about this kiln, chiefly of grey ware, plain and scored, among which were some of vessels having compressed sides. Three miles and a half eastward of Winterton the tesselated pavement of a Roman villa was discovered in the parish of Horkstow. It was not wholly uncovered, but evidently belonged to a long narrow room, and was divided into three compartments, surrounded, first by a narrow grey and white border, and then by another of red and white. One of these compartments contains a most curious representation of a Roman chariot race. On a white ground the *cavea, carceres, spina,* and *metæ,* of the circus are depicted, and four drivers of *bigæ* are contending for a prize* The first of these is triumphantly pulling up his steeds opposite the winning point ; the second, when closely following, loses his advantage by the fall of one of his steeds, for the third, through this misadventure, will give him the go-by, and the fourth, through collision with one of the other chariots, or with the wall of the *spina,* is in the act of being thrown out of his chariot from the loss of one of its wheels, while two horsemen hasten to his assistance, one of whom is dismounted and is attending to this unfortunate competitor. A portion only of the corresponding compartment of this pavement remains, but its subject is that of the *Parcæ,* or Fates. The circular centrepiece pourtrays Genii preparing the thread of the Fates gathered from the contents of a high basket or *calathus.* Round this is a large circle divided into four compartments, each having a circular medallion within it. In one of these Clotho and Lathesis are represented with the thread of Fate between them, and in another Atropos, whose task it was to cut this vital thread. On either side of these medallions are Neriedes mounted on Seahorses, attended by Genii; in the angles of the squares without the wide interlaced border of this circle, are Tritons, in reference to the idea that the Fates were the daughters of the sea. Divided from the last-named subject by a narrow compartment composed of interlated circles, &c., is part of a circular subject within a square. In the middle is

---

* The charioteers of the circus were often distinguished by colours representing the four seasons of the year ; one set wearing green, for spring, termed the *factio prasina ;* a second red, for summer, termed *russata ;* a third blue, for autumn, termed *veneta ;* and a fourth white, for winter, termed *alba.*

a figure of Orpheus in a Phrygian cap, playing on a lyre, and attended by a peacock; in a circle around, divided into eight compartments, edged by a guilloche border, are various beasts and birds, supposed to have been attracted by Orpheus's strains. Among the former appear a dog, deer, boar, bear, and a young elephant. In the angles between this circle and the square compartment in which it is placed, are large busts composed of red tesselæ on a white ground, accompanied by small red circles, one bearing a white and the other a red cross, like a Christian dedication symbol.

The Ermine-Street can no longer be traced in Winteringham, its bank having been destroyed through the enclosure of that parish, and subsequent cultivation; but there is no doubt as to its line, and the spot where it reached the Humber; for, continuing its former straight course northwards, it would at length reach the summit of a small promontory on that great river, half a mile north-east of the village of Winteringham,* which formerly protected a little haven called Flashmire, now silted up. This terminal was marked by a Station, probably that of *Ad Abum*, which Stukeley states was ploughed up a few years before he wrote his *Itinerarium Curiosum*. In his account of this spot, he speaks of the existence of a fine spring here—always a desirable adjunct to a Station—of vast stones, pavements, and foundations, which often broke ploughers' shares, and of remains of streets or roads made of gravel or sea sand. He also gives an engraving of the appearance of this spot, dated 1776, and states that several intakes had been made here in the memory of man. Roman coins have not unfrequently been found at Winteringham; one of Claudius was brought to Stukeley, and a collection from Flashmire was brought to the author when he visited the site of *Ad Abum*, in 1855. Stukeley, speaking of Winteringham, says, " This place is over against Brough, the Roman town on the Yorkshire shore, but it is rather more eastward, so that, with the tide coming in, they ferried over very commodiously thither; " and, in confirmation of this opinion, a discovery was made here, and at Brough, during the remarkably dry summer of 1826, when the Humber

---

* In this parish is a tumulus near the Church, surrounded by a stone wall, and here, in north beach gravel-pit, a cinerary urn and twenty celts were discovered—probably British.

was very low, viz., the remains of a raised causeway, or jetty, stretching out from both places, similar to the *vadum* descent in the Trent at Littleborough, and apparently of Roman construction. Brough was undoubtedly a Roman Station— perhaps Prætorium. Hence the Ermine-Street ran to Market Weighton, where it divided; one branch leading thence, by Thorpe-on-the-Street and Wilberfoss, to York, the other by Londesborough, New Malton, and Cawthorn, to Whitby.

From Winteringham, in Stukeley's opinion, a Roman road ran over Whitton brook, not far from West Halton, where many Roman coins have occasionally been found, to Alkborough, where, on a commanding height overlooking the confluence of the Trent, Humber, and Ouse, as well as the whole Isle of Axholme, is a Roman camp, surrounded by a fosse and vallum, three hundred feet square, having an entrance on the north, and its western side protected by a steep declivity of the cliff on which it stands. The field in which this camp lies used to be called Countess Close, from a Countess of Warwick, who gave the manor of Alkborough to Magdalene College, Cambridge. Close to this camp is a turf labyrinth, thirty feet in diameter, of mediæval design, supposed to be of Roman origin, but in reality of later date.* These works were sometimes called Julian's bowers, or Troy towns, which helped to deceive Stukeley as to their extreme antiquity, and although there certainly were Roman labyrinthine devices, one of which has lately been discovered worked in a tesselated pavement at Caerleon, the turf labyrinth at Alkborough is distinctly a mediæval work, or at least a copy of one.

---

* For the history of such works, see *Archæological Journal*, vol. 15, p. 16, or *Architectural Societies' Papers*, vol. 4, p. 351.

THE CAR-DIKE.

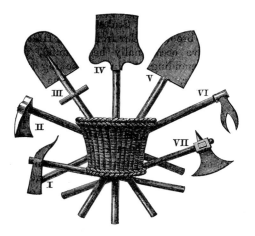

. Pickaxe from Trajan's Column. II. A Hoe from do. III. A Spade from a sepulchral bas-relief. IV. A Shovel from Pompeii. V. A Spade from a sepulchral painting. VI. A two-pronged Hoe from a gem. VII. A Hatchet from Trajan's Column. In the centre is a Labourer's Basket, also represented on Trajan's Column.

The fens of this portion of England afforded the means of exhibiting the versatile genius of the Romans during the period of their dominion in Britain. It was nature that here offered far greater difficulties to that people than the owners of the soil, for after the Romans had enforced the submission of the Girvii, or fen men, settled on the border of the Wash, they found that they had to control an element whose power had hitherto remained undisputed within their newly acquired territory and to rescue the fen lands of parts of Lincolnshire and Northamptonshire from the dominion of the upland waters, before much profit could be derived from the extraordinary fertility of their newly acquired lowlands.

An immense amount of labour was required to effect this design; but the Romans were not a people to shrink from its execution; and that they succeeded in accomplishing it is evident from the still existing testimony of one of their great earthworks, termed "the Car-Dike." This was once a wide and deep catchwater canal, commencing at a point on the Nene about half a mile from Peterborough, and terminating in the parish of Washingborough, near Lincoln, where it formerly communicated with the Witham after a course of 56 miles in length. Such being its character, we may perceive two additional inducements that would lead the Romans to carry out such a work. As the depth of the Car-Dike was amply sufficient to float boats of considerable size, such a canal, before the Coritani were completely subjugated, would afford a ready means of transporting military stores through a dangerous district, because here the light armed natives would, from the nature of the ground, possess unusual advantages over their heavily armed invaders; while afterwards, in peaceful times, such an inland navigation would be very valuable to the Romans for trading purposes, connecting as it did, the river Nene with the Witham, and thus affording a means of inland communication by water between the important cities of *Lindum Colonia* and *Durobrivæ*, whereby the dangers of the ocean were avoided, as well as the difficulties of land transportation.

Of the Roman origin of the Car-Dike there has never been any doubt, although the date of its formation is unrecorded, and the name of its originator unknown, because the Britons never dedicated so great an amount of labour as this required in behalf of a peaceful object, while the Roman remains and traces that have been left on or near it point most satisfactorily to the nation under whose auspices it was created.

It has been thought by some that the name Car-Dike may have been derived from some entrenched strongholds in its vicinity, as well as from its having afforded a means of transit between the British "Caer Dorm," or "Durobrivæ," and "Caer Lin," or "Lindum Colonia"; but it is far more likely that this name is of a much later date, and one that simply means fen-dike, or a cutting carried through the "cars," a term still commonly used in connection with fen lands.

This ancient work is also occasionally called "the Bell-Dike," from a tradition, partially prevalent, that the original large bell, or "Great Tom" of Lincoln Cathedral,* was floated on a raft or boat to its destination all the way from Peterborough by means of the Car-Dike canal; some adding that the bell was a present from an Abbot of Peterborough to the Cathedral of Lincoln, and others that it was forcibly abstracted from his Minster. Such a popular belief is probably founded on the fact of *some* bell having been floated along the Car-Dike, and certainly points to a time when this cutting was used as a navigation for the transmission of heavy goods.

Evidence on this head was also afforded some years ago by the discovery of a quantity of sculptured stones in that portion of the Car-Dike passing through the parish of Morton. These stones were clearly intended for the construction or reparation of some ecclesiastical building, but seem to have been accidentally sunk in the Car-Dike, in whose bed they remained for several centuries.

This great work was most probably formed under the supervision of a Roman military engineer, and in part by the actual labour of Roman troops, as they were habitually employed upon such works of utility, as well as of defence, when their services were not immediately required in the field; for instance, in the midst of a war with Gaul, the Senate, while it commissioned one of the Consuls, Lucius Anicius Gallus to prosecute the campaign ordered the other, Marcus Cornelius Cethegus, to superintend the drainage of the Pontine Marshes, " they thinking," as Livy informs us, "that they could in no way better prove themselves to be faithful supervisors of the Commonwealth than by redeeming a large tract of land for its use;" the same author also elsewhere states, " that the Roman Consuls, to prevent idleness on the part of the soldiery, habitually employed them in making highways, so that they were almost as well versed in the use of the spade as of the sword." The Romans were accustomed to take a part in works of drainage on a large scale, so that we need not be surprised at the magnitude of those they have left behind them in this part of

---

* The present bell, weighing 9894 lbs., was cast in a furnace erected in the Minster Yard, by Henry Holdfield, of Nottingham, and William Newcombe, of Leicester, who were co-contractors for this particular work alone, in the year 1610. It replaced one weighing 7807 lbs., which *possibly* may have been transported from Peterborough.

England. A large fenny district near Placentia in the valley of the Po was drained by Scaurus, and supplied with navigable canals. The Emperor Claudius undertook the drainage of the Fucine Lake, employing 30,000 men for eleven years upon the work, but yet was forced to leave its completion to Hadrian. "Sueton in vitâ Claudii." Tacitus alludes to the cutting of a canal between the Rhine and the Meuse, 23 miles long, by means of which, he adds, the dangers of the ocean were avoided, and we may remember that the navigable canal of the Pontine Marshes along which track boats plied, and made so familiar to us by Horace, was but the drain of that fen district to which we have before alluded.

But, although the Romans were fully accustomed to execute great works of drainage, no doubt they compelled the unfortunate natives of such countries as they had subdued to take a large share in the more laborious portions of these operations, and we actually find from the "Life of Agricola," that the Britons complained deeply of the Roman tyranny in this respect, declaring that their conquerors "wore out and consumed their bodies and hands in clearing the woods and embanking the fens."

Stukeley has suggested that both the Ermine-Street and the Car-Dike were works of the reign of Nero, and from the mere fact of finding a series of synonymous names of places, &c., in the vicinity of the latter, such as Catesbridge, Catwater, Catscove, Catley, &c., he has, with his usual fervid imagination, proposed to hail Catus Decianus a Procurator in the above named Emperor's reign as its author; all however that we know of that personage militates against such a decision, because during the short time of his administration he only exhibited his utter incapacity, having first allowed the Roman arms to be signally defeated, and then fled disgracefully into Gaul: In addition to which, as we find Stukeley afterwards proposing to make Carausius the constructor of the Car-Dike on equally insecure ground, and that thus his opinion was capable of oscillating between two dates about 200 years apart, we can not look upon him as a safe authority, or indeed any authority at all, on this point.

With far greater reason it may be surmised that the intelligent and indefatigable Cnæus Julius Agricola was the constructor of the Car-Dike, about the year A.D. 79, when he had succeeded in establishing the Roman rule almost universally in Britain, and was beginning to instruct its inhabitants in agriculture and commerce, at the same time that he was securing and consolidating his conquests by forming lines of communication through Britain, and when such a canal as the Car-Dike would be most useful for the transmission of stores to the north during his Scottish campaigns. Agricola was re-called by Domitian A.D. 84; hence, if he *was* the Car-Dike constructor, its date can thus be pretty accurately arrived at; and this hypothesis is strengthened by the testimony of the Roman coins that have been found in many instances, and occasionally in large quantities, near the banks of this originally vast fen-dike; but if after all it is of a later date, we can not possibly suppose it could have been carried out during the next 35 years when there was a temporary stagnation of Roman enterprise, and must therefore attribute it to Hadrian, when he visited Britain A.D. 120.

Stukeley has surmised that the Car-Dike was defended by a series of "forts"—that is military entrenchments, guarding its extremities, and commanding its navigation at intervals; these he fixes at Eye, Narborough, Billinghay and Walcot, simply from an idea he entertained that those names appeared to point to such works, and not from a personal inspection of the Car-Dike; but there are not the slightest traces of entrenchments at any of those places. His assumed Roman origin also of the " Low," the site of a mediæval building near Peterborough, is very doubtful: here, he says very positively, was a camp ditched about, just where the Car-Dike begins on one side of the river, and another such fortification at Horsey-bridge on the other side of the river."—*Iter.* I. p. 8. Whereas, although the Low moat certainly did once communicate with the Car-Dike, it is far more probable that it was cut in that situation simply for the purpose of drawing the amount of water necessary for its supply from the adjacent and more ancient work.

During the Saxon period the Car-Dike was no doubt entirely neglected in common with all the other great and useful Roman works; hence its channel gradually diminished in depth through the washing in of soil and the yearly growth of weeds, although, from the magnitude of its banks, neither the neglect of man, nor the re-action of nature during many centuries has been able to efface its original grandeur entirely; those evidences of its former importance still for the most part rising up boldly along the edge of the lowlands between Peterborough and Lincoln, in rivalry with the modern railway and drainage works in their vicinity, although their formation was the result of simple manual labour unaided by the various appliances of modern science, or the gigantic power of steam. The first written allusion to the Car-Dike is to be found in the pseudo Chronicle of Ingulphus, who was elected Abbot of Croyland Abbey, A.D. 1076. In that work it is said that "Richard de Rulos, Chamberlain to the Conqueror, enclosed all his lands eastward to Car-Dike, and beyond Car-Dike to Cleylake beyond Crammor, excluding the river Welland with a mighty bank." Afterwards it is occasionally alluded to in the reports of the various commissioners successively appointed to examine the condition of the drains and embankments of the Lincolnshire fens; whence we gather that it was considered to be an important feature in the then drainage of those lowlands for a considerable period, although its original use has now been superseded by more modern drains such as the Forty-foot and others.

As might be expected, the original depth and width of the channel of the Car-Dike have now been for the most part greatly reduced, while its banks have at some points been expanded and lowered by the action of the plough, and at others, either mutilated or entirely removed ; there are, however, but few spots where its course may not still be traced, and from a careful inspection of its now very varying outline, and from measurements at many different points, I am of opinion that, at first, its channel was fifty feet wide, and eight feet deep, and that its banks were thirty feet wide below, lessening to ten feet above, whence the height of the banks above the natural ground level would also be ten feet. (See Section I.)

As a rule, the Car-Dike forms the western boundary of the fens between Peterborough and Lincoln, the most trifling portions of rising land being carefully left on the west, except at Eye, Kyme, and a few other spots. The banks are entirely formed of the black fen soil, whenever this was of a sufficient depth for the purpose, but more usually of the silty clay forming the subsoil, strewn with the large flints and pebbles found between those strata ; hence they may be often readily discerned from the light colour and poor character of their soil, when their elevation can no longer be detected, as in Walcot and Timberland parishes.

CAR-DIKE SECTIONS.

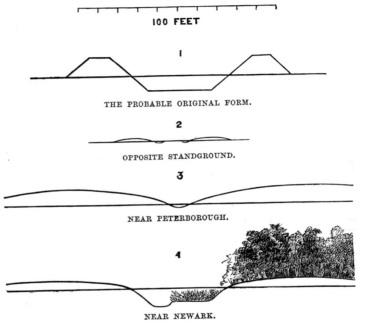

100 FEET

1

THE PROBABLE ORIGINAL FORM.

2

OPPOSITE STANDGROUND.

3

NEAR PETERBOROUGH.

4

NEAR NEWARK.

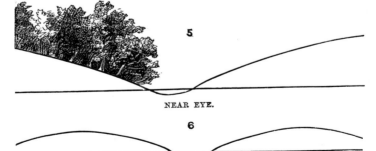

5

NEAR EYE.

6

NEAR NORWOOD.

7

NEAR THURLBY.

8

THE MIDDLE OF THE MIDFODDER BAR-DIKE.

9

NEAR HECKINGTON TUNNEL.

10

SOUTH KYME.

11

NORTH KYME.

12

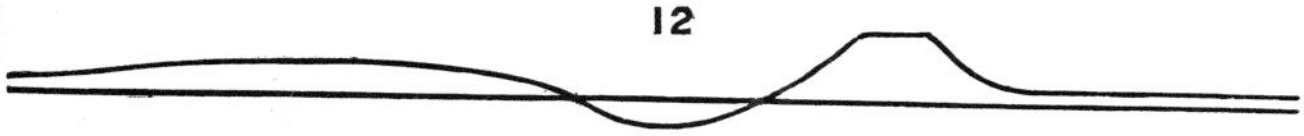

BILLINGHAY.

13

WALCOT.

14

MARTIN.

15

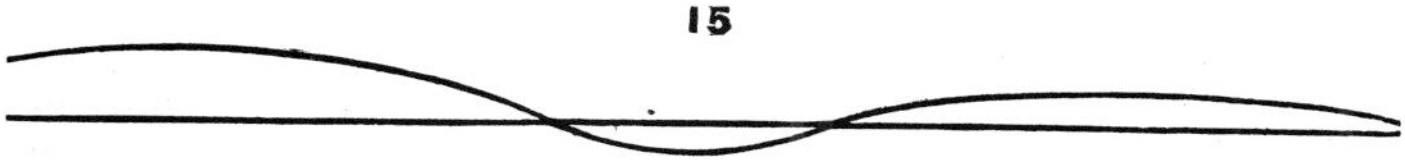

METHERINGHAM.

Rennie, the engineer, gave high praise to the originators of this ancient work; after he had inspected it professionally, pronouncing it "to have been well conceived," while even an ordinary observer can readily see how boldly it was executed.

The level throughout is nearly uniform; hence it has been a matter of surprise to some how it could have retained a supply of water sufficient to enable it to act as a navigation in summer, and yet to afford a means of exit to the upland waters during the winter months. It must, however, be remembered that as the Car-Dike was intersected by various natural streams, it would thus be kept full of water even in the driest seasons, and yet that through the same medium, as well as through its own natural terminals on the banks of the Nene and Witham, it would be able to pass off its redundant waters; in addition to which, it must be borne in mind, that if flood gates were formerly required for the occasional protection of the Car-Dike from the overflowing of the said rivers, the Romans were fully acquainted with the use of such artificial hydraulic aids, so that no doubt they adopted them, if needful, although no traces of these can now be discerned.

The southern end of the Car-Dike is close to Peterborough, but it was by no means out of any consideration for it that such a point was selected for the commencement of the canal under notice, because no such town as Peterborough was then in existence. *The* great town of this district during its Roman occupation was " Durobrivæ," whose site is now partly marked by the village of Caistor, six miles distant from Peterborough. This was one of the ten cities in Britain put under the Latin law by the Romans— " civitates Latio Jure donatæ," according to the pseudo Richard of Cirencester, whence its inhabitants enjoyed all the rights of Roman citizenship ; and perhaps it derived such a privilege from its situation on that great Roman via, the Ermine-Street, as well as on the Nene, then navigable up to its site, whence it enjoyed a means of water communication with "Lindum Colonia," through the Car-Dike.

The grandeur of "Durobrivæ" was partly revealed by the discoveries of the late Mr. E. T. Artis, while on the line between its site and Peterborough many Roman coins, vases, portions of pavements, &c., have occasionally been found, and especially in Longthorpe field. These coins belonged to the reigns of Augustus,

Claudius, Ælius the adopted son of Hadrian, &c. Descending the Nene to a point half a mile to the south east of Peterborough,* and opposite Standground sluice toll house, the southern entrance of the Car-Dike was reached, and there faint traces of its channel and banks may still be seen. (Sec. 2.)

These, after crossing a modern drain, become more conspicuous, the former being indicated by a shallow bed 30 feet wide, which afterwards resembles an ordinary ditch, and is flanked by some remains of its banks, until it approaches the Low, before alluded to, where a variety of Celtic implements and a boat, or dug-out, of the same period, were discovered, in the bed of the Nene, as recorded by Artis.

Running by a high modern bank in the direction of Wisbech, the Car-Dike may be clearly seen on its way towards Fen-gate, where its banks are now surmounted by a windmill and a few cottages, shortly beyond which they begin to assume a far more imposing character. (Sec. 3.) Passing through the Boon field, the channel then gradually increases in width, until upon approaching the village of Newark it is 50 feet wide, and is used as an osier bed. (Sec. 4.) Then contracting again, upon entering Newark, a turnpike road is carried along its eastern bank, which, with its companion bank, fringed with willows, thus runs nearly to Eye† There turning abruptly to the west, the Roman engineer boldly cut through a promontory of rising ground, instead of skirting it, according to the general rule observed, whence this is one of the most remarkable points of the Car-Dike, a lofty bank on one side, and a plantation on the other, here rising on either side of the canal. (Sec. 5.)

Afterwards the eastern bank is crowned for a short space by the modern Wirrington road, before it reaches Norwood. There both banks are very striking, particularly at a turn they make westward, (Sec. 6.,) whence they may be seen stretching over the plain to a considerable distance. Afterwards they decline in

---

* A silver coin of Antoninus was found near the Car-Dike at the back of Peterborough Minster, and many Roman coins about its precincts. *Iter Cur.*, I., p. 7., Note.

† Absurdly thought to derive its name from "agger," by Stukeley. Here sundry Celtic remains were found in the last century, consisting of brass spear heads and celts.

height, but not in width, making several turns for the purpose of leaving all the elevated ground on the west, and nothing but fen land on the east.

Opposite Wirrington this ancient work was remodelled about 30 years ago, so as to form a modern drain, termed, from its supposed unnecessary size, "the folly." This runs into the Welland a little above Peakirk, but the Car-Dike has been allowed to continue its course from a point about a mile south of that village, as an ordinary ditch accompanied by some traces of its banks, until it is entirely lost on the western side of the Railway Station. Thence it passed by Peakirk, towards the foot of the slight eminence crowned by Glinton; after which it again resumed its northern course, as it may next be traced, as a simple ditch flanked by slight remains of its banks, a little to the south east of Northborough, and as far as the junction of the Deeping and Maxey road with that leading from Northborough to Peakirk, where it is again lost.

It appears however to have pursued its course northwards, until it reached the Welland, and entered Lincolnshire at Market Deeping; after which it ran a little to the east of Towngate, on a line now designated by a perfectly straight road, as it may again be seen at the end of this, where it joins the Towngate Outgang road, at first as a ditch only, but afterwards flanked by portions of its old wide banks as far as Langtoft,* with one exception, about a mile south of that village, where a deep hollow now alone indicates its former existence. After crossing the Langtoft Outgang road, the Car-Dike has been forced to do service in connexion with a moat surrounding an old Mansion there, and also as a small fishpond. Hence it runs as a ditch, accompanied by slight signs of the ancient banks to Baston;† crossing the Baston road, it may be subsequently traced in the form

---

* At a spot about half a mile from the Car-Dike and Langtoft, an urn was found, some fifty years ago, containing about a thousand small brass Roman coins; since which time others of silver and brass have been occasionally found, as well as in Uffington parish near here, including one of Vespasian.

† Many Roman coins have been found in this parish, one person there now possessing about eighty of these, including a large brass Trajan, and several good specimens of Claudius Gothicus, Constantine the Great, Constantine the 2nd, Magnentius, and Valens.

of a wide hollow as far as Thetford Hall, where it becomes a long fishpond again, reaching nearly to the river Glen by Kates-bridge. After crossing that stream, the Car-Dike shrinks into the limits of an ordinary ditch, but, presently, its eastern bank again becomes apparent, at some spots being 90 feet wide and 5 feet high, while both banks are evident on approaching Thurlby, whose Church is built upon one, and the parsonage upon the other. Passing Thurlby Hall as a wide, bankless, and not very odoriferous ditch, it arrives opposite Elsea wood, where the eastern bank is 90 feet wide and 4 feet high (Sec. 7.), and is again occasionally visible until it reaches some garden ground in the immediate vicinity of Bourn,* whence it runs through the eastern suburb of that town to a point about a mile and a half further to the north, accompanied only by occasional traces of its original banks; but then they again become conspicuous and are 90 feet wide in the hamlet of Dyke. After passing Morton,† the banks sink, but still flanking a ditch between them, the Car-Dike passes through the parishes of Hacconby, Dunsby, and Dowsby;‡ in this last a modern road occasionally surmounts the eastern bank; then the channel continues in a dwindled form until it approaches Billingborough, where, for a short space, its ancient width is well defined, as well as the magnitude of its banks. After having been crossed by the Bridge-end road, or Salter's way, near Threekingham, its wide banks are still conspicuous in the parish of Swaton, and its

---

* The ancient course of the Car-Dike has been altered for a short space here, but is still well known from the difficulty it presents to persons wishing to build or rebuild on its site.

† In this parish many Roman coins have formerly been found, as well as in Grimsthorpe Park, including a fine large brass of Hadrian.—*Iter. Cur.*, I., ps. 7, 12." And this is not surprising, for at Stainfield, near Morton and Grimsthorpe, there was once clearly a considerable Roman Station as indicated by the blackness of the soil there, mingled with Roman pottery; this spot, indeed, used to be a perfect treasury of Roman coins, whence the market women brought many specimens for sale to Bourn on market days. There was an entrenched camp also at Edenham, a little to the south west of Stainfield.

‡ Between this village and Pointon, at a spot about half a mile from the Car-Dike, is a group of six tumuli, probably British, now termed "the Hoe Hills."

bed is used as a modern drain for about a mile, but this again
dwindles to a ditch between low banks in Helpringham parish
until it approaches the Great Hale road, where both the banks
and the channel are better defined; then again the latter lessens
and the former sink, although still wide, before they are crossed
by the Boston and Sleaford road and railway. This ancient
work then reaches a group of cottages in Star Fen, beyond the
Littleworth road, where its banks have been sadly mutilated, and
occasionally entirely removed. Hence passing by the Heckington*
Eau Dyke, and through the parish of Ewerby, it runs in a straight
line to Heckington tunnel a little to the west of South Kyme. At
first the banks of this portion of the Car-Dike, here termed the
Midfodder, are wide, but after awhile the western one has been
more or less removed, and then again both now present much the
same appearance as they originally did, having been remodelled
of late years and planted with a triple row of willows; but the
channel has here been divided by a central bank thrown up in
the midst of it. (Sec. 8.)

Before reaching Heckington tunnel the Car-Dike assumes a
less perfect form, (Sec. 9,) and next it constitutes a portion of the
Boston and Sleaford Navigation† for about a quarter of a mile

---

* In Heckington parish Roman coins are sometimes found, among which
one of Julia Mammæa, and also in the adjoining one of Kirkby-Laythorpe,
including some of Septimius, Severus, Fanstina the younger, and Constantine
the 2nd.

† From this point to its junction with the Witham, it is called the Kyme
Eau, which was used as a navigable canal in the early part of the 14th century,
as we gather from documentary evidence; in the 16th Ed. 3d., Gilbert de
Humfraville, Earl of Angus, then exhibiting a petition to the king, wherein he
set forth, that a certain water called the Ee of Kyme, between Doc-Dyke on
the east, and Brentfen on the south, which ran through his lands for the space
of six miles in length, was so obstructed and stopped by reason of mud and
other filth, that ships laden with wine, wool, and other merchandize, could
neither pass through the same in summer nor in winter, as they had been used
to do, except it were scoured and cleaned, and the banks so raised, that the
tops of them might appear to mariners passing that way, whensoever the
marshes there should be overflowed. And that as the said Earl had for the
common benefit of those parts bestowed no small cost towards the repair of
the said place, called the Ee, and heightening of those banks, so he intended
to be at much more, in case the said king would please to grant unto him and
his heirs for ever, certain customs of the merchandize passing in ships through

before reaching a house termed Halfpenny Hatch. In cleaning out its bed here a few years ago a small Roman vase of grey ware, was discovered, figured subsequently on page 79.

A hollow, 50 feet wide, there indicates its line, flanked by detached portions of the banks resembling a range of tumuli; but soon again, as a broad ditch between low wide banks, it reaches the Sleaford and Tattershall road. (Sec. 10.) Near this point, in the parish of North Kyme,* is a small entrenched camp, forming a parallelogram 554 feet long, and 354 feet wide (figured on the next page). This is formed by an outer agger, or bank, 20 feet wide, and an inner one, 13 feet wide, and 138 feet long. The angles of this last are rather higher than the other portions, to give additional security at those points, but the average height of both aggers is about 4 feet. It will be seen from the plan that the lines of the outer and inner aggers do not run at equal distances from each other, there being only a space 12 feet wide between these at the east end to correspond with one 47 feet wide at the west end. There are now gaps through both aggers, on the north, south, and west sides of the camp, of which the chief are on the south side and may be original. In the area so enclosed are traces of three mounds or tumuli, placed at nearly equal distances from one another.

A little to the north of this was formerly a tumulus 100 feet wide at its base. In 1820 some spear heads were found within

---

the same, to have and receive in form above said, viz : for every sack of wool carried through the channel, fourpence ; for every pocket of wool, twopence ; for every ton of wine, fourpence ; for every pipe of wine, twopence ; for every four quarters of corn, a penny ; for every thousand of turfs, a penny ; for every ship laden with cotton, fourpence ; and for every ship laden with other commodities than aforesaid, twopence.

Wherefore the said king directed his precept to William Fraunk, then his Escheator in this county, that he should forthwith make inquisition, and certify whether it would be to the damage of him the said king or his subjects, if the said customs were granted unto the before mentioned Gilbert for the purposes above expressed. And accordingly the said Escheator did certify that it would not be prejudicial to the said king or any others to make such a grant.—Gough's *History of Imbanking*, p. 196."

* In digging into a bank near the Car-Dike here, two bronze leaf-shaped swords were discovered, in 1820 ; the one was 1ft. 10½in. long, and the other 1ft. 7½in.

E.

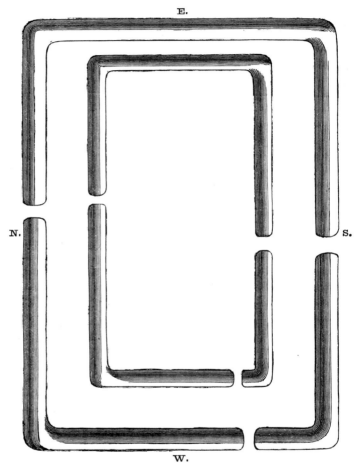

N. S.

W.

PLAN OF KYME CAMP.

it, probably of the British period; but when it was entirely removed, a few years ago, nothing further was discovered.

After crossing the Sleaford and Tattershall road the banks of the canal are more fully developed, especially when running parallel with the village of North Kyme, (Sec. 11,) but again sink, until they arrive at a point where they have been repaired for the purpose of forming a drain connected with the Billinghay Navigation. (Sec. 12.)

There the Tattershall road is carried along the eastern bank, but diverges from it again before it reaches Billinghay. In a gravel pit a little to the north of this village, and about a quarter of a mile from the Car-Dike, ten skeletons were recently found, lying north and south, within two feet of the surface, and with them a portion of a conglomerate quern, and three small vases of dark grey Durobrivan pottery; two of these are represented in the subjoined cuts, the tallest of which is 5 inches high, the other $3\frac{1}{2}$ inches high.

VASE FOUND AT HALFPENNY HATCH.   VASES FOUND AT BILLINGHAY.

After passing by the parsonage garden and some cottages built on its western bank, the channel, here resembling an ordinary ditch, turns abruptly to the north west, under a small tunnel near the church; but soon traces of its original wide banks again appear, and at a point about a mile and a half from Billinghay, are conspicuous from the poverty of the yellow silty clay of which they are made, as contrasted with the natural surface soil by the side of them.

After passing Walcot, the whole work still remains very perfect, (Sec. 13,) and forms a striking line of demarkation between the undulating ground on the left and the perfectly level fen lands on the right, extending almost as far as the eye can reach towards the Wolds; but before reaching Thorpe Tilney, it has been much mutilated. Here Walcot Delph, the first of several large modern drains, crosses the Car-Dike at right angles. Opposite Thorpe Tilney there are some sharp turns in its banks, which have been considerably altered before they reach Timberland* parish, where they again become more perfect. At this point rising ground is seen extending towards the right, and on advancing this will be found to form a promontory skirted by the Car-Dike, where its usually sluggish waters are enlivened by a running brook. Afterwards the natural sloping ground on the right served as one bank of the canal, while the other has been made to correspond with it artificially, for a considerable distance. (Sec. 14.)

At the end of Martin wood Timberland delph is passed, and here a modern road runs along the top of the eastern bank past the village of Martin,† an old Jacobean house called Linwood,‡ surrounded by trees, a farm house, and some cottages, built upon its edge. From this point its western bank is covered with trees, forming the edge of Blankney wood, and the eastern one is also prettily dotted with thorns. About a mile further to the north, Metheringham delph is passed, and here for a short space the Dike banks have been removed, but again are seen rising on either side of a wide channel, (Sec. 15.) until they reach the road leading to the village of Metheringham, where the former become less apparent, and the latter shrinks into a ditch; but upon approaching Nocton wood, the channel is 12 feet wide, owing to the waters of Dunston beck which here flow into it; and the flat treeless plain through which the Car-Dike has so far passed, is exchanged for a woodland scene on either side. Here its banks, although covered with trees and bushes, are very visible until they reach Nocton delph, where the eastern one emerges from the wood, but the other still continues just within its limits as far as its northen boundary marked by some rising ground called

---

* A hoard of Roman coins was found near the Car-Dike, in this parish, in 1808.

† When Martin mere was drained, no less than eight British canoes were discovered.—*Itin. Cur. Iter.*, I., *Note, p.* 16.

‡ Formerly a gold torc was dug up here, but it was immediately disposed of to a Jew, and melted up.

Abbey hills, near Nocton Hall.* Hence a road runs along its eastern bank, here for the most part much worn down, so as to be detected at times only by the lighter colour of its soil, and a long wood known by the names of Low-barf, Norman-hay, and Hanworth-spiney covers the western bank. After passing the road leading to Bardney, once so famed for its Abbey, the Car-Dike turns more towards the east, and is bordered by Branston wood, until reaching Branston delph, where a modern road runs along the western bank, which is still conspicuous from its size as it passes opposite Washingborough wood on its way to the turn to Heighington. Hence the banks run towards the east without so much as a ditch between them to represent the ancient channel, and even these are occasionally almost lost, the lighter colour of the remains of the subsoil of which they were originally made being the principal evidence of their former existence.

After diverging slightly from the Washingborough road, where the Car-Dike for a short way is almost obliterated, it may again be traced running parallel with that road on the right, until it passes behind a row of houses forming the northern portion of the village of Washingborough, and is then finally lost within a very short distance of the Witham, near the Railway Station, and opposite the village of Greetwell.

Here terminates this great work, giving access to Lindum Colonia during the Roman dynasty, and thence by the Foss-dike, another similar Roman canal, to the Trent, Humber, and Ouse. Thinking it would be interesting to give representations of the implements used by the Romans in the formation of their earth works, a group of these is given as a heading to this description of the Car-dike, taken from various authentic sources. (See page 64.)

Such are the greater Roman remains connected with the Wapentakes of Flaxwell and Aswardhurn, forming a part of their province of Flavia Cæsariensis, and reference will be made to many smaller vestiges of that wonderful people in connection with the various parishes about to be described in this volume.

---

* In cleaning out the Car-Dike in this parish, some clay moulds for casting Roman coins were discovered, in 1811, also two boats, or canoes, of a very early period. These were presented by Sir Joseph Banks to the British Museum.

General history informs us why the Romans eventually retired from Britain, whose coming was considered a national infliction, but whose departure was viewed with dismay; and then it records how another human wave, also considered as another very grave infliction, was preparing to sweep over our country before the Romans retired from it, and destined to produce far more permanent results as regards the character of its population, although not calculated to astonish us with such mighty works of art and such proofs of indomitable perseverance as were exhibited by the Romans.   To these and to the next invaders of the British soil we must shortly advert, because they also have left traces of their former occupation of that part of Lincolnshire proposed to be described.

THE SAXONS AND THE DANES.

The Saxons, coming from the shores of the Caspian across the centre of Europe in a north westerly direction, at length reached the Cymbric peninsula, and, dispossessing its former inhabitants, they gradually peopled Jutland, Schleswick and Holstein, as also the islands of North Strandt, Busen, and Heligoland or Heiligiland.*   Not content, however, with the territory they had thus boldly wrested from its earlier occupants, the Saxons were in the habit of making such frequent incursions on the coast of England, as well as of Belgium and Gaul, as to compel the Roman government to equip a fleet at Boulogne for the especial purpose of repelling their attacks; which fleet was placed under the command of the celebrated Carausius.†   A land

---

* The Saxon confederation at length reached from the Elbe to the Rhine. This people is first mentioned by name in Ptolemy's Geography, where the Saxons are described as living on the north side of the Elbe, on the neck of the Cimbric Chersonesus, and inhabiting three small islands—Lib. II, c. 11.

† Carausius, a low born Menapian, having amassed great wealth by plundering smaller naval plunderers, excited the anger or the jealousy of the Emperor Maximian, who ordered the execution of Carausius.   Upon this, the

force was also raised for the same purpose, whose chief was termed " Count of the Saxon Shore."

For two hundred years a series of petty invasions had been carried on by the Saxons before the landing of Hengist and Horsa at Ebbes Fleet; and sometimes these had assumed a serious aspect, as in the year 368, when combining with the Picts, Scots, and Attacottians, they slew Nectaridus, the Roman commander of the Saxon shore, and defied several of his successors, until Valentinian sent Theodosius as a commander, who completely subdued them for a time.

After the departure of the Romans, however, the Saxons by degrees took possession of the greater part of Britain; but it was one hundred and thirty years before the Heptarchy, or perhaps we may say the Octarchy,* of that people was established, Hengist founding the kingdom of Kent in 457, Ella that of Sussex in 477; Cerdic, Wessex, in 495; certain chiefs, Essex, in 530; and others, East Anglia, about the same date; Ida, Bernicia, in 547; Ella, Deira, in 559; and, last of all, Mercia was founded in 586.

Of the three Teutonic peoples combining in the invasion of England, the Saxons established themselves in the south, excepting Kent, the Isle of Wight, and part of the adjoining coast of Hampshire, which were seized by the Jutes from South Jutland; while the Angles, from the district of Anglen in Sleswick, settled themselves in the northern and midland portions of our island. Thus Lincolnshire was undoubtedly a portion of the Anglian province of Mercia.†

Deep must have been the sufferings of the Britons at this time, although for the most part unrecorded. Their faith in

---

intended victim boldly assumed the imperial purple, and for seven years defied the power of Rome, holding supreme power in Britain from 287 to 293.

* The number of the Saxon kingdoms varied at different periods, through the absorption of some by conquest for a time, and again by their after separation; but they were once clearly eight in number.

† This province—comprising the central portion of England—was divided into north and south Mercia by the course of the Trent; North Mercia comprising the modern counties of Chester, Derby, and Nottingham; South Mercia—Lincolnshire, Northamptonshire, Rutland, Huntingdon, parts of Bedfordshire and Hertfordshire, Buckinghamshire, Oxfordshire, Gloucestershire, Worcestershire, Herefordshire, Staffordshire, and Shropshire.

Christ, which at least some of them had embraced, derided by
the fierce heathen conquerors of their land, their dominion lost,
their hunting grounds seized, their persons enslaved; by flight
alone could they save themselves from a grinding tyranny, and
perhaps from a cruel death. Many, therefore fled from the scene
of their birth and from their lawful inheritance, to the mountains
of Wales, and to the remote wilds of Cumberland and Cornwall;
but some did not feel themselves secure until they had placed the
sea between themselves and their oppressors by emigrating to
Bretagne,* a fact still attested by its name.   Attacking the
Britons on all sides, the Saxons gradually drove them all out
like beasts from the confines of their several kingdoms, except
such as they converted into slaves and drudges.   Yet these
retired before their invaders only by slow degrees, fought with
them often and obstinately, and were occasionally victorious even
long after that period when this country had assumed a national
Saxon character; thus Exeter was only lost to the Britons so late
as the reign of Athelstan; and Gloucester, Cirencester, and Bath
not until A.D. 571; whilst they obtained a signal victory over the
people of Wessex, at Wanborough, in 581.

But a great change was now at hand; the holy leaven of
Christianity was about to exercise its benignant influence over
the Saxon kingdoms of Britain, under the auspices of the good,
as well as great Gregory of Rome, and through the instrumentality of Augustine; Ethelbert of Kent and his subjects having
embraced Christianity in 596—a happy precedent, which was by
degrees followed by all the other Saxon princes of England and
their people, of whom, Edwin of Deira introduced Christianity
into Yorkshire in 627, and shortly afterwards into Lincolnshire.
The continental Saxons, however, still remained in their heathen
condition, until Charlemagne took some steps to forward their
conversion; and we find from an exceedingly interesting letter,
written by that emperor to Offa, our Saxon king of Mercia, in

---

* Another large body of Britons emigrated to Bretagne in 664, owing to
a pestilence which terribly afflicted England and Wales at that time.   Those
that remained suffered much from the Saxons, and were visited with fire as
well as with the sword.   Bangor monastery, for instance, with its library,
was destroyed by Ethelfrith.—*Humph. Lhuyd Comm. Frag. Brit. Descrip.*
58.

777, that his efforts had met with some success, and that he offered his protection and every encouragement to all pilgrims engaged in Christian missionary work.*

It was well that the Saxons had secured some consolation for themselves, which no man could take from them, for great troubles were at hand; and as they had harried the Britons, driven them out with fire and sword from their hereditary lands, or else had enslaved them—so, now they, in their turn, were about to experience a calamity, which, though apparently not of great moment, yet eventually afflicted the whole Saxon territory, and was most severely felt, more or less, by its entire population. This plague was the Danish Invasion.

Prodigies foreboding the advent of the Danes are said by our old chroniclers to have preceded the arrival of that people; and, amongst others, that men's clothing was found mysteriously marked with the symbol of the Cross, in token that they were, by repentance, to prepare for the coming visitation.† But why were the Danes to be so deeply and so justly dreaded? They were Teutons from Denmark and Norway, of the same race with the Saxons of Britain; and yet they were about to rob, to burn, to slay, without pity and without remorse, their brother Teutons, who still used nearly the same language, dress, and arms that they did themselves. Such an act demands a reason for its perpetration; and we shall find on enquiry that there were two principal causes leading to this result. First, *Necessity;* and secondly, a *Difference as to the religious faith of the two peoples.* As the Saxons had been, in some measure at least, compelled to leave the shores of Northern Germany through the inconvenient increase of their numbers,‡ so, towards the close of

---

* Du Chesne, Script. Fr. II., p. 28.

† Chronicle of Henry of Huntingdon, Lib. IV.

‡ "Et sicut hi, qui lascivientes arborum ramos solent succidere, ut radix reliquis, sufficire poterit, sic incolæ illarum provinciarum sorte terram alleviant, ni tam numerosæ prolis pastu exhausta succumbat . . . . Inde est quod homines illarum provinciarum tantam invenerunt ex necessitate virtutem, ut a patriâ ejecti peregrinas sedes armis vindicarent; sicut Wandali olim Africam, Gothi Hispaniam, Longobardi Italiam, Normanni partem Galliæ, quam Normaniam ex suo nomine notaverunt, subsiderunt."—*Historia Monasterii S. Augustini Cantuariensis, p.* 139 (by Thomas of Elmham).

the 8th century, Denmark found that she could no longer support her enlarging population with the scanty produce of her
northern soil.* Hence her boldest and most daring sons—already
in the habit of entrusting themselves to their vessels with as
much confidence as that wherewith they trod their mother earth
—sought the coasts of more southern countries, whence corn,
cattle, and spoil of various kinds could be readily carried off by
brave adventurers like themselves. Nor had they any scruple
in committing such wrong and such robbery upon the English
soil; for, although there existed a tie of blood between themselves and the Saxons, an event had occurred tending to fill their
hearts with mingled feelings of contempt and hatred towards
their kinsmen, instead of with sympathy and affection. The
Saxons no longer believed in Odin, in the glory reserved in Val-
halla for the shedders of blood, in the banquets prepared for the
brave, in the future delight of drinking beer and strong liquors
out of the skulls of their enemies. No, they were a renegade
race, who showed mercy and pity, believed in some new and
strange superstition, whose warriors had become women, whose
children were only fit to be hurled in sport from one true hero's
spear-head to another, whose temples ought to be consigned to
the flames.

The Danes in the first instance dreamt of nothing but pirat-
ical descents on the shores of this island. Entering our great
bays, such as that of the Wash; or ascending rivers—such as
the Humber, Ouse, and Trent, until they drew near the fat
beeves and sheep of our rich alluvial lands, they pursued their
pillaging, burning, bloodstained course on land, and loaded themselves with spoil; after which, a cloud of dust betokened their
return towards the water's edge, and columns of smoke rose behind their fatal track, as witnesses of their savage depradations;
nor was it until they were emboldened by repeated successes,
that the Danish Vikingr thought of aiming at permanent territorial conquests, in addition to the migratory stimulus they
experienced at home from the redundancy of their increasing
population; but at length—just as adventurous spirits from
Spain and Portugal were always forthcoming for a voyage to

---

* Olaf's Saga, p. 97.

America, after its discovery by Columbus and others, and eventually to settle there in constantly increasing numbers—so the Danes, after repeated visits to our shores, began to take possession of the Yorkshire and Lincolnshire soil, and gradually to advance the line of their settlements by driving out all such of its former owners as resisted this usurpation.

The first recorded Danish descent upon the British shore took place in 786 under Kebright, who entered the Humber and landed with his marauding followers on its bank, when a fight ensued between them and Herman, an officer of Brightric, a local chief, who had married king Offa's daughter, which ended in Herman's death, but in the defeat of the Danes, who fled to their ships. "Peter Langtoft's Chronicle."

The next recorded Danish descent on the coast of Lincolnshire was more successful, when those Northmen, again entering the Humber and seizing all the horses they could find, advanced into Lindisse, defeated and slew the Earldorman Herbert, and marched triumphantly through Lincolnshire to East Anglia and Kent. The cruel death of Regner Lodbrog at the hands of Ælla, king of Northumbria, in 865, led to the most disastrous consequences; for as the captivity of Cœur de Lion—so plaintively bewailed by the mediæval troubadours—led to enormous sacrifices on the part of his people, and, as his death in an Austrian prison would have aroused the deepest spirit of vengeance throughout the kingdom, so the horrid details of Regner's death —no doubt exaggerated by the bards of Scandinavia*—aroused all the naturally fiery feelings of the Northmen against the inhabitants of that land where it occurred; and quickly an immense army of commingled Danes, Swedes, Norwegians, and even Russians, bent on vengeance, under the command of Hinguar and Hubbo, reached the shore of East Anglia, where they win-

---

* The *Lodbrokar Guida*, as it is termed—or poem relating to the death of this noted hero—is one of the most celebrated ancient compositions of the North. It is thought by most to have been Ragner's own composition, or that of his wife Aslauga, who is known to have been a *Schald*, or poetess. A Schald usually accompanied any important warlike expedition, for the purpose of recording its progress, and encouraging the fighting men to perform acts of valour by reminding them of the feats of their fathers. The great Canute, we may remember, was a Schald as well as a mighty king.

tered, and prepared for their intended conquest of Northumbria, by collecting from the surrounding population forced tributes of horses and other necessaries for their coming campaign.

Being on their mission of revenge, the Danes rapidly traversed Lincolnshire on their way to York. During this campaign the Northmen not only took that city, but permanently reduced Northumbria to subjection; after having completely defeated its army with great slaughter, killed Osbert, one of its princes, and wreaked upon Ælla, the slayer of their Regner, that vengeance they had vowed to visit him with—whom they first most cruelly tortured, and then finally executed.* Having secured the conquest of Northumbria, the Danes during the following year again crossed the Humber, and then either ascended the Trent, or perhaps marched through a portion of this county on their way to Nottingham, where they wintered, but whence they were forced to retire again to York, by the forces of Burhead, king of Mercia, aided by those of Ethelred of Wessex.† There they remained stationary during 868, perhaps in consequence of a severe famine that then occurred; but in the spring of the following year, the Northmen commenced their celebrated progress of blood from one extremity of Lincolnshire to the other. Landing at Humberstone, deliberately did the sword descend; slowly, but surely, was fire applied, until there was nothing left to burn. First, Lindsey suffered throughout that fatal summer, when the splendid and venerated abbey of Bardney was utterly destroyed, and all its defenceless monks were cruelly slain within its church.‡ At Michaelmas the Witham was passed; and the wail of Kesteven began, as its monasteries, churches, and villages were fired in succession, and its unresisting inhabitants of both sexes and all ages were given to the sword. Resistance, however, was at hand—the result of desperation. Osgot, the sheriff of Lincoln, took the field with 500 men, in concert with Earl Algar from Holland, who, assisted by Wibert and Leofric, raised 300 men

---

* The sons of Regner are said to have divided his back, spread his ribs in the figure of an eagle, and agonized his lacerated flesh by the addition of a saline stimulant.—*Anglo-Saxons*, by Sharon Turner, II, p. 20.

† In this campaign Earl Algar the younger, of Spalding, greatly distinguished himself.—*Historia Ingulphi*, anno 866.

‡ *Historia Ingulphi*, anno 869.

from Deeping, Boston, and Langtoft, and Toli, once a soldier but
then a monk of Croyland, with 200 of the inmates of that abbey,
and Morcar, lord of Bourn. These on the feast of St. Maurice
dared to attack the van of the invading army, and gained a
complete victory over the Danes, killing three of their chiefs,
and chasing their forces from the battle-field to their camp in the
rear. Unhappily, however, an immense reinforcement of Northmen arrived during the ensuing night at the quarters of their
defeated countrymen, headed by ten chiefs of different grades,
including Hinguar and Ubbo ;* and this coming to the ears of
the associated Lincolnshire forces, so terrified them that many
individuals fled secretly during the night, and thus most inop-
portunely diminished their already far too small numbers. Earl
Algar, however, who acted as commander-in-chief, boldly and
skilfully marshalled his little band, after having first joined
with it in offering up public prayer to God, and partaken of
the "viaticum," all that remained with him being determined
to die in defence of their faith and their country, rather than
to yield to their heathen foes. With Toli on his right, aided by
Morcar; and Osgot on his left, supported by Harding of Ryhall
and a band of young fighting men from Stamford, he remained
in the centre with his two *Seneeshals*—as Ingulphus terms them
—Wibert and Leofric, being prepared to aid either wing as
occasion required. The Danes, very early on this fatal morning, having first buried their three fallen chiefs, advanced,
burning with fury to avenge their previous loss, against the little
band of Saxon warriors they saw before them. This had been
so skilfully formed in a wedge shape, that the Danish cavalry

---

* A most extraordinary birth has been attributed to these savage chiefs
by one of the old chroniclers, in consequence of the merciless ferocity of their
deeds, Thomas of Elmham saying—"Quo tempore venerunt Hynguar et
Hubba, qui ut fertur, filii fuerunt cujusdam ursi, qui illos contra naturam de
filiâ regis Daciæ generabat ; quam Sanctus Edmundus, ob eandam causam
Daciam transiens, cum illud horribile facinus, favore cujusdam cubicularii
ejusdem dominæ, perpendisset, in camerâ noctu latitans sub cortinis infaustum
contra naturam aspiciens ursinum cum fæminâ coitum, extracto gladio ursi
caput abscidit, et mox in Angliam rediit. Ob quam causam eadem mulier,
filiis adultis retulit Edmundum prætactum patrem eorundem, quem illi homi-
nem fuisse putaverant occidisse. Et hæc fertur fuisse causa adventus illorum."

charged time after time against each of its faces in vain. Throughout the whole day did the men of Lincolnshire stand, as firmly in their triangle on the Kesteven soil, as did their fellow countrymen centuries afterwards, in squares, on the plains of Waterloo! But then the Danes had recourse to other means; they feigned a retreat; upon which, deaf to the call of their leaders, the Lincolnshire men, breaking up their position, pursued the flying host with eager impetuosity, and thus sealed their own destruction; for quickly did the Danes return, and entirely surrounded the little band that could be formed no more, slaughtering them all in turn; their six heroic chiefs, planting themselves on a slight eminence, vainly fought to the last over the bodies of their fallen followers, returning blow for blow with their raging foes, until they one after another sank, and expired, with the name of patriot as justly attaching to their memory as it does to any of the heroes of Greece or Rome. Two or three Sutton and Gedney lads alone escaped, bearing the afflicting and alarming news to the inmates of Croyland Abbey, presaging their own fate, or at least that of their stately and revered sanctuary. Theodore, the abbot, after the sad celebration of matins for the last time, dismissed all the able-bodied monks to the safe keeping of the fens, who bore away with them the relics, charters, and most precious effects of the monastery. Other articles of value, such as cups, and vessels of brass, were thrown into the cloister well; and also the large super altar, covered with plates of gold, presented by king Witlaf to the abbey, but as one end of it could not be sunk below the surface of the water, Theodore, assisted by two of his aged monks, was obliged to take this up again, and hide it in another spot. And now rapidly advancing columns of smoke, arising from the successive firing of the villages, announced the near approach of the dreaded Danes. To the altar—then, was the cry of the aged abbot; and there, fully robed, he was in the act of celebrating high mass—assisted by Elfgy, his deacon; Savin, his sub-deacon; and his candlebearers, when the heathens rushed in, and Theodore quickly fell by the hand of Osketil; afterwards all the aged priests were slain, many first suffering torture cruelly administered, to compel them to disclose the spot where the treasures of their establishment had been concealed. Of the other inmates one boy alone escaped—Tugar— saved by the younger Sidroc, who threw a Danish cloak over him as a token of his protection. The Danes then broke open all the marble tombs of the abbey, including that of St. Guthlac, in the vain hope of finding treasures in them; and at length, after three days' havoc, they set fire to the whole fabric, and continued their destructive course towards Medeshampstead (or Peterborough), Huntingdon, and Ely; and there, after defeating Earl Wilketil with his East Anglian forces, they took Edmund, its king, prisoner, whom they first bound to a tree and shot at wantonly with their arrows before his execution; after which they possessed themselves of his territory.

Such were the fatal consequences of the Saxon Ælla's cruelty towards the far-famed Regner Lodbrog; thus did the Danes accomplish the conquest of Yorkshire, Lincolnshire, Norfolk, and Suffolk. About this time, also, they appear to have established five strongholds for the future protection of the territory they had acquired, viz., Stamford, Lincoln, Leicester, Nottingham, and Derby; to which were afterwards added those of York and Chester.

In 873, a large body of Danes, after having wintered in London, advanced northwards under Heafdene, laden with much booty, through East Anglia and Lincolnshire; but on this occasion, as these districts had been previously subjugated by the Northmen, no acts of violence appear to have been perpetrated. This winter was passed by them at Torksey, the next at Repton, when, by the conjunction of their forces with those of Guthrun, Oskytel, and Anwynd, they drove out Burhed, king of Mercia, who retired to Rome, where he died.*

Up to the year 880, the Danes had simply by force of arms possessed themselves of Lincolnshire and much of the northeastern part of England; but then, Alfred ceded to them in a regular manner all the territory north of the Thames—following the Lea to its rise, and thence to Bedford and the Ouse—henceforth termed the *Danelagh;* and by another treaty, signed in 941 by Edmund the elder, and Anlaf—that prince of Northumbria who had previously fought with Athelstan the celebrated battle of Brunanburgh—all the territory north of the Watling-Street was ceded to the Danes; but whichever prince might be the

---

* Saxon Chronicle, anno 874.

survivor was to be the sole sovereign of the whole.* The rever-
sion falling to Edmund, the dominion of the Danes was thus for
a time ended; and in consequence of internal commotions in
Denmark during the middle part of the tenth century, England
reposed awhile from any fresh Danish invasions, excepting an
attempt made by Eric, son of Harald of Norway, to regain possession of Northumbria during the short reign of Edred in 946;
but Eric was defeated, and fell on the battle-field.

Under the weak unready Ethelred the Danish Vikingr again
began to ravage our shores, and in 991 he began that wretched
system of attempting to buy off the Northmen by the payment of
Danegelt, or imposts levied from his subjects wherewithal to
bribe the Danes to withhold their ravages. Then followed an
execrable act of treachery on Ethelred's part, who, without the
sword of a soldier or the policy of a counsellor, hoped to rid
himself of the Danes by their secret and simultaneous massacre,
when, in accordance with his orders, the Danes dispersed over
England, together with their wives and children—including even
Gunhilda, the Christian sister of Svein, and her boy—were suddenly slaughtered. Probably this massacre did not extend to
those parts of England, such as Lincolnshire, where the Danish
element was generally predominant, but this county shared the
lamentable results of Ethelred's deed of blood, for when the
Danish Svein came as an avenger of his people, after having
sailed up the Humber and the Trent to Gainsborough and reduced the people of Northumbria and Lindisse to submission,
leaving his celebrated son Knut behind, he advanced through
Kesteven slaying, burning, pillaging, torturing its wretched
people—not sparing even monks, who were subjected to barbarous atrocities before they were slain—and for a short time
was master of England.

Still backwards and forwards swayed the contest between the
Saxon and the Dane in this part of England, when first, through
the return of Ethelred and his gallant son Edmund Ironside,
Knut fled from Lincolnshire and took to sea again from the
Humber; but then, two years later, again invading this county
from the south, he marched through it unopposed towards

* Matt. Westm., p. 365.

Northumbria, where he established his sway, after which many contests took place between these two brave princes, until at last, after a battle fought at Assingdon, in which Ednoth, Bishop of Dorchester, and Godwin, Earldorman of Lindsey, fell, the partition of England was agreed to by Knut and Edmund, and thus Lincolnshire became an acknowledged part of Knut's dominion before he succeeded to the sovereignty of all England through the death of Edmund the following year. After Knut's death in 1035, a contest for dominion took place between his two sons Hardiknut and Harald, when the partisans of the latter were the predominant party in the North; but the only result as far as Lincolnshire was concerned, amounted to this, that dreading the coming conflict, hundreds of families from the south took refuge in our fens, accompanied by their cattle and all their portable goods. These were a terrible plague to the inmates of Croyland Abbey, in whose vicinity they located themselves in swarms, for they so eagerly and constantly entreated the monks and their servants for counsel and assistance, pouring into their ears such long stories of their fears and their woes, that the poor Brothers dared no longer shew themselves in their own cloister, nor scarcely to leave their dormitory for the purpose of joining in Divine worship, or taking their meals in the refectory. But the anchorites of the surrounding fens were still more despondent at this time, and from the same cause; one—Wulfius of Pega-land —being so worried by clamorous companies coming to his cell by night, as well as by day, that, tired of his life, he bound a bandage over his eyes to shut out from view as much of the troublesome scene around him as he could, and finally sought a more quiet retreat at Evesham. Five years later, by the death of Harald, Hardiknut became the undisputed king of England. He reigned for two years only, having first greatly injured his constitution by his excesses, and then suddenly fallen down dead when attending a marriage feast—an event which gave rise to a great change in the destiny of England, for the Danish dynasty in England had now come to an end, never to be renewed. This was a subject of great rejoicing throughout the greater part of our land, but not so, probably, in Lincolnshire and the north, where the Danish element had become so strong as almost to supersede the original Saxon basis on which it had been overlaid.

The crown was then offered to Edward, the son of Ethelred, by Godwin—the Fairfax of the eleventh century—who, after its assumption, re-established the Saxon laws of his father, abolished the burthensome tax of *Danegelt*, and banished a few of the remaining Danish chiefs; but, for the most part, he suffered the Danes that were peaceably disposed to dwell in his newly acquired kingdom without molestation, whilst they on their part submitted quietly to the mild rule of the Confessor. Thus, before long, an amalgamation of the two races began to take place, which eventually so completely blended them together, as to exhibit only some lingering traces of their original distinctive characteristics.

Throughout the long reign of Edward the Confessor the Northmen attempted no fresh invasions, although Magnus, king of Norway, sent letters to him claiming the crown of England, 1046; but after Harald's accession, the Humber once more witnessed the approach of a Norwegian fleet of vast magnitude, in accordance with the prayer of the brother of the then king of England—Tostig, who had been expelled from Northumbria during the Confessor's reign, and was so indignant with his brother Harold for declining to reinstate him in his former government, that he sailed off to the north for the purpose of persuading the kings of Denmark and Norway to join with him in an expedition against England; the former, although a connexion of his own, sternly declined his proposition, but with the latter he was more successful. Harald Hardrada had inherited a large share of the old viking spirit; and perhaps the following flattering address on Tostig's part urged him the more to undertake the proposed adventure. "The world," said Godwin's son, "knows that there is no warrior living fit to be compared with thee; thou hast only to will it, and England is thine."* In reply, the fair-haired monarch promised to equip a fleet in the spring for this purpose, as soon as the icy ports of Norway were open. Tostig then adjourned to the court of William of Normandy, from whom he received some aid; and having collected together in Flanders 60 ships, sailed for the English coast. First, he levied supplies in the Isle of Wight; thence, sailing northwards, he at length entered the Humber, and committed great depredations in

---

* Snorre's *Heimskringla*, III., p. 149.

Lindsey, until he was driven out by the Earls of Mercia and Northumbria, with the loss of all but twelve ships. In the meantime Harald had set sail with his Queen Ellisif, his daughters, his son Olaf, and his forces, in 300 ships, had touched at Shetland and the Orkneys, and was running along the Scotch shore, when Tostig fell in with him. Joining their fleets, they then in concert attacked Scarborough, which they burnt and pillaged, and afterwards boldly sailed up the Humber and the Ouse to York, where they gained a signal victory over the late conquerors of Tostig—Earls Edwin and Morcar—who retreated within the walls of York. This event compelled Harold of England to leave the southern coast, where he was watching the movements of William of Normandy and his assembling host, to give battle to his ambitious brother and his northern allies. Falling in with them after a rapid march through Lincolnshire, at Stamford Bridge, a little beyond York, he there gained a most complete victory, and slew both Tostig and Harald;* so that the remnant of their forces were thankful to fly from the scene of their disaster in twenty-four ships only, swearing before their departure never again to make war with England.

---

* Saxon Chronicle, anno 1066. A very remarkable reminiscence of this prince has recently been brought to light and in a place where it could have been least expected—viz., at Venice, Professor Rafn of Copenhagen, having ascertained that his name appears upon the large Pentelic marble Lion of the Venetian arsenal. This Lion was brought from the harbour of Piræus at Athens in 1687, by Francesco Morosini, the distinguished General-issimo, and afterwars Doge of Venice, among other trophies of his success against the Turks. On a winding scroll, on the left side of this Lion is a Runic inscription, that has long baffled the attempts of the learned to de-cipher owing to the effects of time upon the surface of the marble ; but, by the aid of casts and photographs, Rafn happily succeeded in reading this specimen of the Norse language, formerly in use throughout Scandinavia, and still retained in Iceland. It runs thus,—" Hakon, in conjunction with Ulf, Asmond, and Orn conquered this Port. These men, and Harald the Great (*i.e.* of great stature), imposed large fines, or contributions on account of the insurrection of the Greek people. Dalk remained captive in distant countries ; Egil had gone on an expedition with Ragnar into Rumania and Armenia." After a sanguinary conflict in the north, Harald (then quite a youth) fled to the south, and arrived at Constantinople in 1033, when he was only 18 years of age, and where he became Chief of the Varangian Guard under the Emperor Romanus III. He remained in the south until 1043, when

But no such vow was made by the Danes, nor did they fear to attack the new and powerful conqueror of England three years later. In 1069 the three sons of Svein, with a large force conveyed in two hundred and forty ships, entered the Humber, and reached York, where they demolished the castle, slew the Norman governor, and carried off many prisoners; after which, in defiance of the Conqueror, who marched against them, they wintered in the country between the Ouse and the Trent.*

Again, during the following year, king Svein himself sailed up the Humber, when he was joined by a large number of persons, who, either from the frequency of these invasions, from sympathy with them, or from witnessing the formidable character of Svein's forces, allied themselves with him, in the belief that he would become a second conquering Knut the Great. Advancing southwards to Ely, the fen men of that district joined them in great numbers. Thence they pressed on, intent on plunder, to Peterborough; and although accompanied by Christien, one of their bishops, they scrupled not sacrilegiously to steal all the valuables from its abbey, before they committed it and the adjacent town to the flames. These consisted of a crown of pure gold from a figure of our Lord, a beautiful footstool of the same material from under its feet, a super-altar of mixed gold and silver (that was vainly attempted to be hid in the tower), two gilt shrines, nine silver ones, fifteen great crosses of gold and silver, besides an incalculable amount of other valuables, such as money, vestments, and books. With these they retired to Ely, and,

---

he returned to his own country, at first sharing the rule of Norway with Magnus the Good, and then becoming its sole king in 1047. The above-named Ulf is a very interesting character in connection with the subject of Harald's invasion of this country, as he is recorded to have opposed that king's daring proposition most warmly, warning him of the improbability of success against the great valour he must expect to meet with in England.

The other scroll, on the right side of the Venice Lion, tells us that Harald the fair-haired was the author of both inscriptions. It is as follows: "Asmund engraved these Runes, with Asgeir, Thorleif, Thord, and Ivar, at the request of Harald the Great, although the Greeks had endeavoured to prevent it."—*Inscription Runique du Pirèe,*, par C. C. Rafn; and *Archæological Journal*, XVI., p. 188.

* Saxon Chronicle, anno 1069.

through some arrangement with the Conqueror, who perhaps at this time was not in a position to cope with them, they sailed away in a portion of their fleet; this was, however, dispersed by a great storm, which threw some of the ships on the Irish coast, and wrecked others on the Danish and Norwegian shores; whilst the author of the Saxon chronicle exultingly remarks that the only portion of the plunder that was secured—having been deposited in a church for security—perished by fire, occasioned by the drunkenness of the guard. The remainder of the Humber fleet then sailed for the Thames, where it hung about for two nights; but its commander probably hearing there of king William's strength, returned to Denmark.

The last Danish attack upon our north-eastern shore occurred 1075. In that year, Ralph, Earldorman of Norfolk, in concert with Waltheof, Earldorman of Huntingdon, Northants, and Northumberland; Roger, Earldorman of Hereford, son of William Fitz Osbert; together with several bishops and abbots of East Anglia, conspired against William; and as the mother of Roger was a native of Wales, he succeeded in bringing some Welsh forces into the field; but not content with these, he applied to Denmark for an additional body of men, and obtained his request. Knut, the son of Svein, and Jarl Hacco, were its commanders; but upon their arrival they found that their English allies had been completely dispersed, and not daring alone to face the then formidable sovereign of this island, they determined to make a foraging expedition more to the north, when for the last time the Humber saw a hostile Danish fleet, consisting of two hundred vessels, ascending its broad yellow waters on its way to York, and, after a while, again descending with the valuable spoils of its minster* stored away in their holds, and steering for the north. Another invasion, indeed, was planned in Denmark ten years later, viz., in 1085, when Knut agreed to combine his forces with those of his father-in-law, Robert, Earl of Flanders, for the purpose of making a descent upon England; and of so threatening a character was this, that King William, who was then in Normandy, quickly returned with an immense army of Normans, French, and Bretons; these he quartered

---

* Saxon Chronicle, anno 1075.

upon this nation at large, to its great distress, and even caused portions of the coast to be laid waste, where the expected invaders would be likely to land, so that they might not be able to maintain themselves with facility.*   Happily, however, for this country, a mutiny occurred on board the Danish fleet, which occasioned its return to the north; and Knut was eventually slain by his own soldiers in a church at Odensee, dedicated to St. Alban, our English saint, whose relics—or some portion at least of them—Knut had previously taken over to his own country from England.

Space will not allow comment at any length on the traces of the Danes still discernible in Lincolnshire; but perhaps it may be well to mention that there are 212 places in this county having the Scandinavian terminal of *"by,"* and that in this respect it exceeds all others; Yorkshire, although far larger in extent, and also long forming a portion of the Danish possessions in England, possessing only 167 places of the same character; while in the Wapentakes of Flaxwell and Aswardhurn alone the names of 15 parishes terminate in this Danish form.

It is impossible to distinguish Danish from Roman antiquities, as they are so nearly if not exactly alike, but the subjoined cut represents one of their bone comb-cases, discovered on the site of the Great Northern Railway Station at Lincoln.   Upon this is engraved in ancient northern lettering, "A good comb makes Thorfaster."   Two Saxon cemeteries have yielded a pro-

fusion of their weapons, vases, and ornaments, as also Sleaford

---

* Saxon Chronicle, anno 1085.   The obnoxious tax of *Danegelt* was now again revived, to furnish means for the maintenance of the defensive army levied by William, at the rate of twelve silver pence for every hundred acres of land.—*Concilia Magnæ Brit.* I., 312 ; *Wilkins.*

PLATE II.

FIG. 1.　　　　FIG. 2.　　　　FIG. 3.

FIG. 4.

FIG. 5,

FIG. 6.

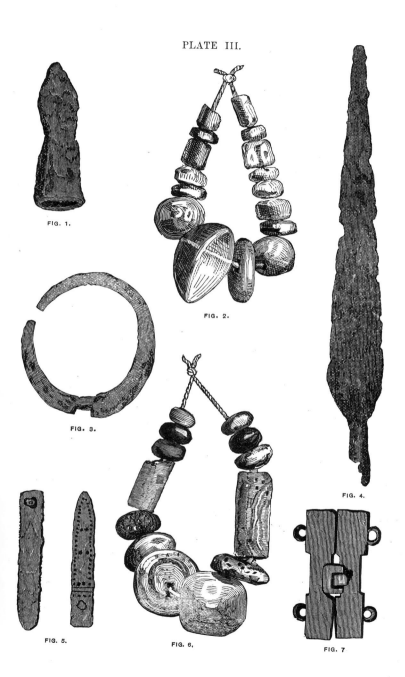

PLATE III.

FIG. 1.

FIG. 2.

FIG. 3.

FIG. 4.

FIG. 5.

FIG. 6.

FIG. 7

and its immediate vicinity. The first was discovered in 1828, lying for the most part in a field called Grey Lees, in Quarrington, on the north of the road from Sleaford to Ancaster and Grantham, but extending over some portion of the field on the other side of that road. This discovery was made through digging for gravel, on the top of which some human skeletons were found, but more remains of bodies that had been consumed by fire and partly gathered into vases. With these were also found numerous articles, such as spear heads, horse harness, fibulæ (or brooches), clasps, buckles, bead necklaces, and pins of bronze and bone. The most interesting of these are given in the accompanying Plates taken from drawings made by the skilled pencil of the Rev. Charles Terrot.

Plate II. Fig. 1 : A rough grey vase, found full of fragments of burnt bones and dark earthy matter; now in the British Museum. Fig. 2 : A vase of grey ware, scored with lines and dots forming a simple pattern. It is 7 inches high, and was got up entire, excepting a small hole made by a workman's pick in its side. It was filled with fragments of bones like the other, and is now in the Duke of Northumberland's Museum at Alnwick. Fig. 3 : Another grey cinerary vase similar to Fig. 1. Fig. 4 : a bronze harp-shaped fibula, or brooch, the pin of which is lost. Fig. 5 : a large bronze fibula of the same form. This is quite perfect, and still retains much of the cobalt blue and red enamel with which it was originally enriched. Fig. 6 : a still larger bronze fibula, bowed in the middle.

Plate III. Fig. 1 : the iron head of a small dart or arrow. Fig. 2 : part of a bead necklace, consisting of one large crystal bead and others of amber and different coloured vitreous pastes or glass. Fig. 3 : a flat oval-shaped fibula, the pin of which is lost, and also a piece of its ring. Fig. 4 : an iron spear head, now 19 inches long, but originally 3 or 4 inches longer, when its socket was complete. This was found on the south side of the Sleaford and Grantham road. Fig. 5 : two sides of a bronze tag, or small strap end, originally enclosing the end of a strap between them. Fig. 6 : part of another necklace, similar to Fig. 2, composed of variously shaped and coloured opaque and transparent vitreous pastes, or glass. Fig. 7 : a pair of bronze clasps intended to be attached to a belt. The under sides of these are represented to shew the way in which they served as a belt fastener. Their outer faces have hollows or beds minutely hatched and gilt, originally filled with transparent enamel.

Plate IV. Figs. 1, 2 and 3: bronze buckles of various sizes. Fig. 4: a group of pins; the two with their heads on the right are of bronze, the other two of bone. Fig. 5: an iron cheek-piece of a horse's bit, one end of which has been accidentally bent. Fig. 6: a bronze fragment, perhaps half of the beam of a pair of balances. Most of these articles are in the possession of Mr. Jacobson, surgeon, of Sleaford, and have been kindly lent by him for the purpose of being drawn and engraved. Many more similar articles were found in this cemetery, including duplicates of those represented, but on the whole these are the most distinctive and interesting.

As a stone, 6 feet long and 2 feet wide, was said to have been uncovered here in 1828, but that from its great weight it was not raised, the author of this volume employed one of the men who made this statement to search for it, thinking it might possibly prove to be the lid of a Roman stone coffin similar to one found at Ancaster, but the search was unsuccessful; many fragments of pottery, however, and a small brass of Valens, were found in the soil thus thrown up.

The other Saxon cemetery was discovered in 1858, when the Grantham and Sleaford railway was extended to Boston. On excavating the earth for this purpose in an ancient pasture field in Old Sleaford, lying immediately on the outskirts of the town and on the eastern side of its southern approach, the skeletons of a number of Teutons were found about eighteen feet below the surface, surrounded by darker mould than ordinary. Each skeleton was accompanied by a shield, spear head, and knife, differing in size and form, and in a fair state of preservation, the remains of the spear shafts being still distinguishable, and even the kind of wood of which they were made—viz., ash.

Plate V. Figs. 1 to 7: iron spear heads of different shapes, varying from 8 to 19 inches in length. All have a slit in their sockets, and in some of these the remains of the ash shafts once fitted into them are distinctly visible, as well as the rivets passing through them and the shafts. The length of the sockets greatly varies, as will be seen by comparing Fig. 4 with Fig. 7, both still being in a perfect state, but the spear head Fig. 3 has lost part of its socket. Figs. 8 and 9: bosses of shields, large enough to

PLATE IV.

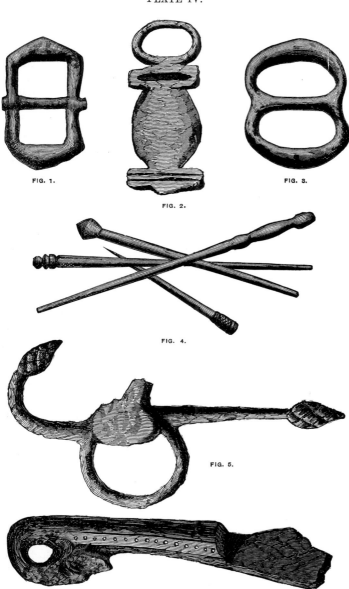

FIG. 1.

FIG. 2.

FIG. 3.

FIG. 4.

FIG. 5.

FIG. 6.

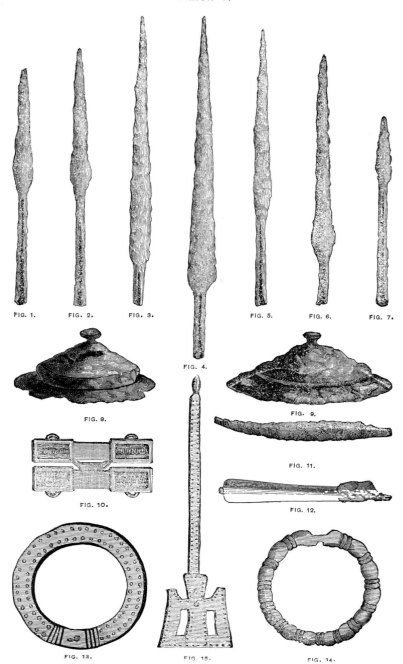

PLATE V.

FIG. 1.　　FIG. 2.　　FIG. 3.　　　　　　FIG. 5.　　FIG. 6.　　FIG. 7.

FIG. 4.

FIG. 8.

FIG. 9.

FIG. 11.

FIG. 10.

FIG. 12.

FIG. 13.　　　　FIG. 15.　　　　FIG. 14.

protect the hands of the bearers, and attached to the shield by three large rivets. The first seems to have been twice pierced either by the sword or spear of an enemy. When perfect they were 7 inches in diameter, and 4½ inches across the hollow. Fig. 10 : a pair of bronze clasps, nearly 1½ inches long, originally ornamented with enamel filling the now gilt but otherwise empty beds at its ends, and provided wth little eyes to attach these clasps to a belt. Fig. 11 : an iron knife blade, 4 inches long. Many smaller ones were found, only 3 inches long, of the same shape. Fig. 12 : a portion of a knife fitted into a bone handle, 2½ inches long, through which the ferule of the knife blade passes and just protrudes at the other end. With these weapons and fibulæ, &c., were also found a small brass coin of Valentenianus; reverse, Victory marching and the legend " Securitas Republicæ." Fig. 13 : a flat circular bronze fibula, the pin of which is gone. It is 2 inches in diameter, and is simply ornamented with minute circlets. Fig. 14 : another fibula, 1½ inches in diameter, which has also lost its pin. Its pattern resembles the classical moulding now commonly called the egg and tongue. Fig. 15 : a bronze article, 5½ inches long ; intended with a fellow to suspend a pouch from the belt of the wearer.

It would be impossible within the limits of this volume, which only professes to be one on local history, to attempt even a sketch of those general historical events which occurred subsequent to the Conquest; but their bearing upon Sleaford and its neighbourhood will be in some measure shewn by the account of each place about to be described. Then a great and disastrous change took place, which we may devoutly trust will never occur again,—a change that was only ushered in by the decisive battle of Hastings, but not completed until but very few estates remained in the hands of their former Saxon lords, and the Norman interlopers introduced by William of Normandy had by his stern will possessed themselves of the lands of England, and exercised a proud harsh rule over both Saxon nobles as well as Saxon serfs; when also Saxon bishops, priests, and monks were replaced by Norman successors, who looked down with contempt upon their new flocks, not one word of whose language they knew.

NEW SLEAFORD.

ACREAGE,
1800.

POPULATION,
3325.*

Although Sleaford is not one of the larger towns of Lincoln-shire, it may be at least regarded as one of some consideration, as it contains, with Old Sleaford, the portion of Quarrington adjoining it, and the hamlet of Holdingham, a population of 4089 souls, according to the census of 1861. It is situated as near as possible in the centre of the Wapentakes of Flaxwell and As-wardhurn, but just within the border of the former, and was enclosed in 1796. It is 115 miles from London, 18 from Lincoln, Boston, and Newark, and 9 from Falkingham. From its healthy and well chosen position, in the midst of a large agricultural district without a rival, from its well attended Fairs and Markets, and a Railway passing close by it, so as to supply an easy means of communication between it and all parts of England; it is a thriving place, whose inhabitants have reason to be proud of its beautiful Church, spacious Market-place, handsome Court-house and Corn-exchange, as well as of its general appearance; whilst the little river Slea supplies it with a never failing source of pure water, and communication with Boston, formerly of great value.

The Slea rises in Willoughby, a hamlet of Ancaster, but is chiefly fed by a more abundant spring a mile west of Sleaford, called Bully Wells, from which spot it is now navigable, and runs through what was formerly a little fen, before the Sleaford and Boston navigation was carried out, by virtue of an Act of Parliament, passed in 1792; this work took two years to com-plete, but has now been almost entirely superseded by the Sleaford and Boston Railway. The Slea divides before it approaches Sleaford, and thus necessitates two bridges in South-gate, which passes over both streams. One of these bridges formerly bore

---

* The population in this and all subsequent cases is taken from the last census.

the date 1673, and a shield with the Arms of Carre quartering Bartram, and a Baronet's hand gules on an escutcheon at the fesse point. The other was built in 1765. The Slea again becomes one stream a little to the west of the Navigation basin, and it is a remarkable fact that it very seldom freezes. For a long time the terms Old and New Sleaford were unknown, the whole being called Eslaforde in Domesday Book and Lafford in Testa de Nevill; but in the Valor Ecclesiasticus, compiled in 1535, the present distinction between them is first found, wherein they are termed Lafford Vetus and Lafford Novus, or Old and New Sleaford; but they were always distinct manors.

ANCIENT HISTORY.

Probably the advantages offered by the Slea induced some British family or families of the great Coritanian tribe to establish themselves on its bank where it first became navigable for their canoes, and certainly traces of their presence about the site of the present town of Sleaford have been detected from time to time beneath its soil, as previously described in the prefaratory notice of the Britons.

The Romans assuredly also occupied this spot, to which one of their roads directly led from their important station and town of Durobrivæ; and as the greater part of the Roman coins found here from time to time have been discovered on the southern bank of the Slea, either on the site of the Castle, or near the Old Place and Roman road and ford, we may conclude that they at least chiefly settled themselves there. But from the same evidence we can still trace them at the very source of the Slea, which no doubt they naturally often visited. A coin of Nerva was found on the Castle site in 1823, and Stukeley in his *Itinerarium Curiosum*, Iter. I, p. 9, says, that many Roman coins of the Constantine period had been found in his time about the Castle and Bully Wells, or at the spring head, as he calls it, near to which have of late years been found a dark coloured urn, containing a small implement like an awl, and more coins.

Some sept of the Angles subsequently settled on the site of Sleaford, and gave the first recorded name to the present town, viz: Slowaford.

I

Before the conquest Bardi the Saxon was the chief, if not the only owner of the land in Eslaforde, or Sleaford, and also the lord of the manors of Quarrington, Carlby, Holywell, and Corby. All these were given to Remigius, the first Norman Bishop of Lincoln, previous to the compilation of Domesday Book, and probably in connection with his removal of the seat of the See from Dorchester to Lincoln, and his erection of the then new Cathedral Church in that already ancient city. The possessions the Bishop thus acquired at Sleaford consisted of 11 caracutes of land; part of this he kept in demesne, or cultivated himself, by the aid of 3 ploughs, and 29 villans, 6 sockmen, and 11 bordars, using 4 ploughs. He had also three mills here, worth £10; 120 acres of meadow, 330 acres of marsh, and 1 acre of coppice. The whole was valued in Edward the Confessor's time at £20, but in the Conqueror's reign at £25. There were also here 2 sockmen ploughing with 2 oxen, 15 acres of meadow, and 13 acres of coppice. To this manor there also belonged some lands in Howell and Heckington, also a parcel of land within the manor belonging to Ramsey Abbey in Quarrington; while on the other hand some land in Sleaford was soke of that manor.

From Testa de Nevill, p. 321, we find that by an inquisition taken in the reign of Henry III., before Hugh de Vedasto, Alexander de Lafford, Robert de Heckington, William son of Jordan, of Ashby, Lawrence de Howell, Roger de Kelby, Thomas de Kelby, William de Kelby and others, the Bishop of Lincoln held the whole of Sleaford as an alms gift of the king. The Bishop appears to have been then holding all his lands here in his own hands, except an eighth part of a knight's fee, which he had let to William de Morteyn, by knight's service, and who had sublet it to Robert de Lafford. A subsequent inquisition reports that the Bishop of Lincoln had appropriated to himself the whole of the vill of Sleaford in burgage on the north side of the water, which was accustomed to belong to the wapentake of Flaxwell. "Hundred Rolls." In 1275, Oliver Sutton, Bishop of Lincoln, was asked by the king's commissioners by what authority he claimed to have a market, fair, gallows, waif, view of frank pledge, and hue and cry, in his manor of Lafford; in answer to which he said, that he and his predecessors had *always* enjoyed these, interrupted only by the vacation of the See. "Plac de quo war, p. 429." In 1321-2 when the Barons revolted against

Edward II., as Bishop Burghersh was probably with reason suspected of infidelity towards the Crown, the king seized the Castle of Sleaford, and placed it in the custody of Robert Lord Darcy. "Hundred Rolls." But it was soon restored to the See; for in 1330 the Bishop of Lincoln was again holding it, the manor and its appurtenances, together with the right of free warren. "Inq. p. m. 3. E. 3"; and from that time it was held by all the successive Bishops until the middle of the 16th century, and let to various persons, one of whom Sir Richard de Willoughby died seized of the profits of the suit of court there 1369, and another Thomas de la Warre, died seized of the manor in 1398. "Inq. p. m. 22. R. 2."

In the reign of Henry VII., the first of the family of Carre to which Sleaford is still so much indebted, came to reside here. This was George Carre, son of Richard, and grandson of Sir John Carre, of Hetton, Northumberland, a wool merchant, of the staple of Calais. Prospering in his trade, he bought the manor of Tetney and some lands in and about Sleaford, where he also built himself a handsome house opposite the south side of the Church, on the spot now occupied by the Hospital, and bounded on one side by a narrow street, both of which still commemorate his name. He died 1520, and was succeeded by his son Robert, to whom the family was indebted for the vast estates it subsequently enjoyed.

Henry VIII visited Sleaford, August 8th, 1541, on which day he arrived there from Grimsthorpe, where he had been the guest of the Duke of Suffolk, his brother-in-law. Sleaford is referred to by Leland, in his Itinerary, published 1546, as a town built for the most part all of stone, and having two houses that were superior to the rest, the one being the parsonage, the other the residence of the Carre's, the then possessor of which (the first or old Robert Carre) he describes as being a proper gentleman, whose father was a rich merchant of the staple. He also speaks of "the house or manor-place lately almost new-builded of stone and timber by the Lord Hussey, which standeth northward without the town." This was then probably in the king's own hands through its forfeiture in 1537, and the execution of its rebuilder. As the Castle was then habitable, probably the king was the guest of the Bishop of Lincoln; but we have no record as to this, except that on the morning after his arrival at Sleaford, August 9th, the king held a council there before he passed on to Lincoln. On his return from the North, the king again stopped at Sleaford, October 14th, coming from Nocton, where he had been the guest of Thomas Wymbysh and his wife, the only daughter of Gilbert, Lord Tailboys, the half sister of Henry, Duke of Richmond, the king's illegitimate son. On this occasion the king received at Sleaford an Ambassador of the king of Portugal, who came to treat respecting the transport of corn from England to Portugal, and then passed on to Grimsthorpe.

In 1535, the Bishop's manor here was valued by the king's commissioners at £57 4s. 0d. a year, derivable from the following sources :

	£	s.	d.
Fixed rents per annum......................	39	16	$0\frac{1}{2}$
Movable ditto ditto	0	0	6
Firm of the demesne lands per annum	3	14	8
Firm of Pasturages, with exits of the Castle, per annum.............................	7	6	2
Firm of the Market Toll there, per annum	1	13	4
Sale of One Acre and a Half of Underwood, in the Wood belonging to the Bishop, at Ropesley, year by year	1	10	0
Amount of common Fines per annum..........	2	13	4
Perquisites of the Court there, one year with another	0	10	0
	£57	4	$0\frac{1}{2}$

REPRISES OR DEDUCTIONS.

	£	s.	d.
To the Lord Hussey, Seneschal there, by letters patent, for his Fee per annum............	2	0	0
To John Mawdley, Constable of the Castle there, by letters patent, and by ancient usage and custom, being his Fee	6	13	4
To Thomas Smith, Bailiff there, by letters patent from old time, being his Fee	3	6	8
	£12	0	0

In 1550 the Manor and Castle of Sleaford were alienated by Henry Holbeach, Bishop of Lincoln, to Edward, Duke of Somerset, who exchanged them with the king for the Monastery and Manor of Glastonbury.   " Brown Willis."

It will now be advisable to advert to the history of the Castle, which is to a considerable extent connected with the history of Sleaford.

SLEAFORD CASTLE.

Little did William the Conqueror foresee that on the Manor of Sleaford which he presented to Remigius, Bishop of Lincoln, a stronghold would arise calculated to excite the jealousy of one of his successors ; yet through the disputed right to the Crown, after the death of Henry I, and the troublous time that ensued, when most of the Nobles of England built strongholds as a means of increasing their power, as well as of conducing to their personal safety, the Bishops, as temporal lords, took part in this movement ; of these, Henry de Blois, Bishop of Winchester, was in advance of his brethren, for we are told that he converted *all* his episcopal residences into Castles ; while Roger, Bishop of Salisbury, erected four such strongholds, viz., those at Sherbourne, Devizes, Malmesbury, and Salisbury ; an example that was followed by his nephew, Alexander, Bishop of Lincoln, who erected three Castles in his diocese, viz., those of Newark, Banbury, and Sleaford.

Sleaford Castle was strong in itself, but made far stronger by its water defences. An elevated bank running north and south and connecting the higher ground on one side of the Castle site with the other, always supplied a means of access to it, even when all the land around was flooded for its defence ; and while this raised causeway was necessary for the use of the Castle garrison, it could be easily defended against assailants.   Newark Castle we are told was magnificently as well as massively built, and Henry of Huntingdon says, that Sleaford Castle was in no wise inferior to it.   Protected by an outer and an inner moat, fed by the unfailing waters of the Slea, and by the little fen through which it flowed on the west, with a gate-house, or barbican, at the sole entrance to the outer and inner baily, or court, it must have been most difficult for any foe to approach it; but supposing it had stood on undefended ground, from the thickness of its massive walls it could well defy all such engines of war as were then in use, and long protect itself, almost without the aid of a garrison. In plan it consisted of a quadrangle, with square towers at its angles, walls having shallow buttresses of the usual Norman type, placed at irregular intervals, and a master tower or keep in the middle. The general ground-plan of the Castle, as far as it can now be ascertained from an examination of its site, taken by Mr. Charles Kirk, of Sleaford, is subjoined.

After Stephen had got possession of Newark Castle, through the half starvation of its episcopal builder and owner, who was compelled to order his faithful retainers holding out against the king to deliver it up, the same process recurred at Sleaford ; and thus both Castles were seized by Stephen. These, however, were soon restored to their former owner.

The next important event connected with Sleaford Castle, was the visit of another king, October 14th, 1216, not coming to seize it with a strong hand, but as a half-ruined fugitive, just escaped from the devouring waters of the Wash, when his subjects were alienated from him ; a foreign Prince was at hand, waiting to receive the Crown already more than half stolen from him, and he was sick unto death. This was John, who, although usually unstable, at times displayed the fierce courage and determined resolution of his Norman ancestors ; when, therefore, he heard that his offended barons had selected a foreign prince to be their ruler, in preference to himself, and felt that after a successful progress through England, Prince Louis of France had almost thrust him off his throne, he determined to struggle desperately in defence of his crown and sceptre. Hence, knowing the powerful effect of his personal presence, in the month of September, 1216, he had hurried from Chippenham to Cirencester, and thence successively to Burford, Oxford, Wallingford, Reading, Ailesbury, Bedford, Cambridge, Rockingham, and Lincoln, which last city he reached on the 22nd.* There he paused awhile, and thence he started on two progresses through Lincolnshire, from a desire, apparently, to make personal appeals on his own behalf to the people of this county. The first

---

* Itinerary of King John. *Archæologia*, vol. 22, pp. 159, 160.

PLAN OF SITE OF THE CASTLE, SLEAFORD.

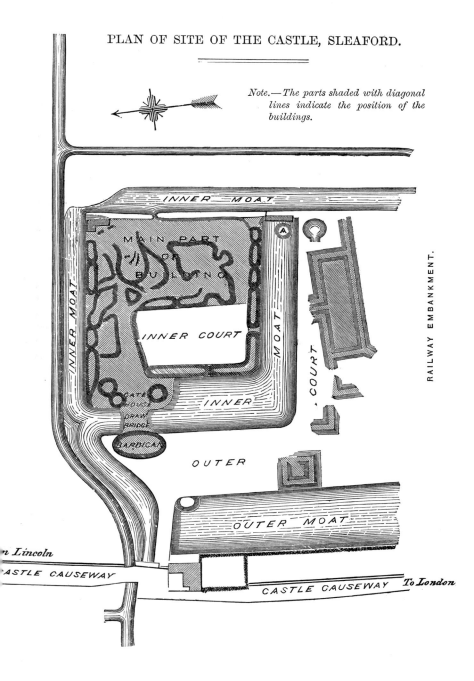

Note.—*The parts shaded with diagonal lines indicate the position of the buildings.*

RAILWAY EMBANKMENT.

INNER MOAT

INNER MOAT

MAIN PART OF BUILDING

INNER COURT

MOAT

A

INNER

COURT

GATE HOUSE

DRAW BRIDGE

BARBICAN

OUTER

OUTER MOAT

Lincoln

CASTLE CAUSEWAY

CASTLE CAUSEWAY   To London

was a short one, commencing on the 24th, during which he
stopped successively at Burton, Retford, Scotter, and Stow,
whence he returned to Lincoln on the 28th, where he remained
until October 2nd. Then he commenced a longer progress ; first
northwards to Grimsby, and then southwards to Louth, Spalding,
and Lynn, where he remained from the 9th to the 11th of October. There he heard that the expected crisis had arisen, and
that his revolted barons had taken possession of the city of
Lincoln, and were pressing his garrison in the castle hard, who
most urgently requested immediate relief at his hands. Therefore,
once again marching northwards, he arrived at Wisbeach on the
11th, and on the following morning resumed his march. Such
being the case, he must have left Sutton Wash behind him on
the right, as well as the now so called *King John's House*, before
he met with his memorable catastrophe in the Wash, as there
could have been no possible reason for his wandering in that
direction so far from the direct line between Wisbeach and Lincoln, when speed was of the utmost consequence to him. On,
therefore, he hurried, over a track of fen land, as fast as his
baggage waggons would permit, until a wide expanse of sand
was reached, intersected by shallow channels, beyond which a
distant low bank and a church tower or two indicated at least a
more hopeful travelling district, while on the right a blue streak
marked the presence of the sea in that direction. A question
probably arose as to whether that sandy plain might be safely
crossed ; but the necessity was great ; therefore the cavalry advanced, the infantry followed, and then the baggage waggons
were dragged along, deeply scoring the yielding silty surface,
and sometimes sinking still more deeply, where hollows and
channels had to be crossed, until the panting horses began to be
exhausted through their frequent and severe struggles ; and
while the shouts and goadings of the drivers were becoming
gradually less and less effective, their anxiety increased in proportion. Still the sea looked distant, yet threads of white were
drifting inland with great rapidity, whence the native fen-men,
who were compelled to assist the royal progress, knew that the
tide had turned, and that ere long all that wide space, which
intervened between them and those delicate yet insidious streaks,
would be covered with water. Deeper, therefore, did the goads
penetrate the sides of the labouring beasts ; more eagerly did the

men-at-arms aid in turning the wheels of the waggons, and especially of those containing the royal treasure, plate, jewels, and the precious vessels of the chapel; yet nearer and nearer advanced those dreaded streaks, and then the natives first cry, " We must fly for our lives ! " Still, at the king's command, one more effort is made to hurry on the now utterly exhausted horses, and especially those attached to the waggons in which were placed the crown jewels. Then it was seen, beyond a doubt, that they must leave all, and if possible save themselves, for the bank of safety in front was still distant, and those slender threads—but lately so far off—are now seen plainly enough to be foaming waves, advancing towards them with the most alarming speed. Therefore the traces were cut, the king's treasure was left to become a prey of the waters, and both man and beast, as far as possible unincumbered, rushed on for dear life's sake, and were half submerged before they escaped from the fearful dangers of the Wash.

Unwell at Lynn,* greatly excited by the news from Lincoln, and now again still more deeply moved by the irreparable loss of his regalia and treasure—in addition to having been exposed to a wet journey through a portion of the Lincolnshire fens—no wonder that King John's illness increased before he reached the shelter and repose he sought at Swineshead Abbey, the nearest place capable of affording him a temporary harbour of refuge.

There he was received with such honours and such hospitality as that monastery could command, and the king, whose feverish thirst was now great, hastened to quench it with long draughts of cyder and fruit from the monastic orchards.† From the evening of the 12th until the morning of the 14th of October, the king remained at Swineshead, during which time his illness increased, which now plainly declared itself to be an ague fit, attended by dysentery. During that time his conduct, bad though it was throughout his worthless life, has probably been unnecessarily and untruly maligned by some chroniclers ; while

---

* Stow's *Annals*, edition of 1615, p. 174.

† " The pernicious greedie eating of peaches, and drinking of newe cidar increased his sicknesse, and kindled the heate of the ague the more strongly." —*Ibid.*

that of the inmates of Swineshead Abbey has been painted in still darker colours by the same authors, and with an equal amount of untruthfulness.

John, in his wretched condition of body and mind, we can readily conceive, made use of violent and threatening language as to what he would do to reduce his rebellious subjects to submission, but he can scarcely have been so insensate as to have vowed, as is reported, that he would greatly raise the price of bread throughout England. Again, although John was undoubtedly an immoral, as well as a violent man, yet, when very ill and anxious above all things to hurry on to the relief of Lincoln, upon the success of which design his crown was almost dependent, it is not the least likely that he could have committed such an outrage upon his host, the Abbot of Swineshead, as Knyghton* has recorded; nor, on the other hand, is it credible that any of the brotherhood of that abbey should have been implicated in the foul murder of the king, during his two days' sojourn with them as their guest, even had they been greatly tried by his violent expressions or the irregularity of his conduct. John was not on the whole unfriendly to the monastic Orders, although he was sometimes rapacious in his dealings with them, as he was with the laity. The variety of ways, also, in which John's death is said to have been compassed, appears to throw the greatest doubt upon the presumed fact of his murder, and to indicate the unsoundness of those reports that arose after his death, which were probably only the offspring of idle rumours, although adopted by some of our chroniclers, and accepted by our greatest dramatic

---

* "Rex ipse Johannes ad monasterium de Swynsheaed quod a Sancto Botolpho distat per quinque leucas, hospitandi causâ declinaret. Audivit abbatem ejusdem loci pulchram habere sororem, priorissam cujusdam loci propinqui; accensusque ex more libidine, misit satellites suos ut eam adducerent ad se. Quod cum audisset abbas frater ejus, tristis admodum affectus est, noluitque a fratribus consolationem accipere. Cui dixit unus conversus suus qui curam gerebat hospitii, et familiaris, et notus domino regi, *Quidnam habes, Pater, cur decidit vultus tuus, et tristior solito est facies tua?* Cui abbas: *Sororem habeo,* inquit, *unam sponsam Christi, quam dilexi; proponit eam deturpare Rex;* et ille: *Ignosce mihi, Pater, et ora pro me, et auferam vitam iniqui a terrâ, et timorem ipsius a conversatione hominum;* cui ille: *vellem hæc,* inquit, *fili mi, non tamen licet in personam regis manum extendere."* —*Henry de Knyghton, de Event. Angl.*

bard. He was poisoned, says Ralph of Chester, by one of the white monks of Swineshead, as report says, when he was intoxicated, because he had threatened to increase the price of bread enormously throughout England ; and the poisoner perished with him.*—His death was occasioned by poison inserted in some pears, says Henry de Knyghton ;† and this was administered by a monk with the complicity of the abbot, because the king had proposed to send for the abbot's sister, the prioress of a convent in the neighbourhood, whose reported beauty had tempted him to do so. He was destroyed by venom extracted from the body of an unfortunate toad, pricked to death for the purpose, and mixed with a cup of ale administered by a patriotic monk, who, first making the accustomed assay thereof, was shortly carried off to the infirmary, where his body became more and more swollen until it burst from the effects of the poison, while the king died two days afterwards.‡

---

* " Tradit tamen vulgata fama quod apud monasterium Swynheade alborum monachorum intoxicatus est. Juraverat enim ibidem (ut asseritur) prudens, quod panem tunc obolum valentem faceret infra annum, si viveret, 12 denarios valere. Quod audiens, unus de conversis fratribus loci illius venenum confecit porrerit, sed et ipso sumpto prius viatico catholico simul cum Rege interiit."—*Ranulphus Censtrensis in Polycron*, 1. 7, c. 33.

† "Tulit pira nova quibus ipsum Regem libenter vesci sciebat, apposuit que venenum singulis præter tria, quæ cum cæteris reposita optimé denotabat. —Venit, itaque conversus ille, et applausit Regi sicut et alias facere consueverat, et dixit ei : *Placitur tibi, O Rex, comedere de fructu novo ? Placet*, inquit, *vade et affer*. Tulitque præparata pira et statuit coram Rege, et ait Rex : *Quid attulisti. frater ?* At ille : *Non venenum, O Rex, sed fructum opitimum.* Et Rex : *Comede*, inquit, *de fructu tuo.*—Moxque apprehenso uno ex piris cognitis comedit. Et Rex : *Comede*, inquit, *et alterum ;* et comedit. *Adde*, inquit, *et tertium*, et fecit sex. Nec se ulterius potuit continuere ; Rex apprehenso uno ex venenatis comedit, eadem nocte extinctus est."—*Henry de Knyghton de Event. Angl.*, 1. 2, c. 15.

‡ "The Monke that stode before the Kynge was for this worde full sory in his herte, and thought rather hee would himselfe suffre deth, yf he might ordeyne some manere of remedye. And anone the Monke went unto his Abbot and was shriven of him, and tolde the Abbot all that the Kynge had sayd ; and prayed his Abbot for to assoyle him, for he would give the Kynge such a drynke that all Englonde should be glad thereof and joyfull. Then yede the Monke into a gardeyne, and founde a grete tode therèin, and toke her up and put her in a cuppe, and prycked the tode through with a broche

Believing, however, that these reports were not founded on fact, from their conflicting character, strengthened by the result of a *post mortem* examination of the body by his friend and confessor, the Abbot of Croxton, we may reasonably conclude that his indisposition, which commenced at Lynn, was so aggravated by his hurried and agitating journey to Swineshead, and thence to this town, as to lead to its eventual fatal termination.

In vain was the king bled at Sleaford, for his disorder continued to gain ground ; and the more so after travel-worn messengers from Dover were ushered into his presence, who announced to him the certain fall of Dover Castle, within a few days, unless he could send a force to the relief of the garrison. This was, however, beyond his power; yet, although so sick, on the following morning the miserable king resumed his suffering progress, and by the aid of support did so on horseback. Whether he removed from want of proper provision for himself and followers at Sleaford, or from political reasons, is unknown, but certain it is that on the 15th he travelled to another of the Bishop of Lincoln's castles at Newark. On his way thither he probably rested awhile at Hough Priory,* where indeed Robert de Brunne records that he died, saying,

"At the abbay of Suyneshued ther he drank poyson,
At Hauhe his lef he leued, so say men of that toun."

---

many tymes, tyll that the venym came out of evry syde in the cuppe. And he toke the cuppe and filled it with good ale, and brought it before the Kynge knelynge, sayinge ; Sir, sayd hee, Wassayll, for never the dayes of all your lyfe dronke ye of so good a cuppe. Begyn, Monke, sayd the Kynge. And the Monke dranke a grete draught, and toke the Kynge the cuppe ; and the Kynge dranke also a grete draught, and so sat downe the cuppe. The Monke anone ryght went in to the farmerye, and there dyed anone, on whoas soule God have mercy, Amen. And fyve Monkes synge for his soule specially, and shall whyle the Abbaye standeth. The Kynge rose up anone full evyll at ease, and commaunded to remove the table, and axed after the Monke ; and men tolde him that he was dede, for his wombe wes broken in sundre. Whan the Kynge herde this, he commaunded for to trusse, but it was for nought, for his belly began to swelle for the dranke that he had dronke, and withen two dayes hee deyed, on the morrowe after Saynt Lukis day."—*St. Alban's Chronicle*, printed by Caxton, Anno 1502, Pars 7.

* Hough, formerly spelt Hagh, Halgh, and Howghe on the Mount. About 1164, King Henry II. gave this manor to the Abbey of St. Mary de Voto at Cherburgh in Normandy (which was founded by his mother the

But such a tradition, although not true, may very probably have arisen from the king's resting at Hough, in a dying condition, on his last earthly journey. When he reached Newark, feeling that his end was near, he immediately took measures to secure the succession of his son, Prince Henry, by causing such nobles as were with him to swear allegiance to him as his successor, and sent off letters to the principal constables of castles, and to all sheriffs, enjoining them to serve the future king faithfully. Then John sought religious consolation at the hands of the Abbot of Croxton, and committed his body to the keeping of St. Wolstan; but when the dying king was thus making ready for his transit from this world, an unexpected event occurred, that only a few days before would have elated his spirits beyond measure, but which now failed to move him. The Barons had begun to repent of their treason. Excommunicated by the Pope, and roughly treated by Prince Louis, who failed not to let them see in what light he looked upon them whenever they hesitated to obey his orders, their position was finally most alarmingly put before them by the Earl of Melun* on his death bed, who told them that as soon as Louis had established himself upon the throne of England he would treat it as a conquered country, and portion out its lands among his French subjects, just as the Conqueror had once done before. This led forty of the barons to send messengers to John, stating their readiness to return to their allegiance to him, and seeking pardon for the past at his hands; but when these arrived at Newark, they found that a similar supplication, to one far higher than any earthly king, had shortly before proceeded from the lips of him of whom they sought favour; that his ear was dull to hear their words, and that his mind was wandering, so that he fancied he saw nothing

---

Empress Maud and himself), so that here was an alien priory of some Austin canons subordinate to that foreign monastery. This cell, valued at £20 per annum, was seized by the Crown, and granted by King Richard II., first to the Priory of the Spittle on the street in this county, and then to the Carthusians of St. Ann's near Coventry. It was restored, by Henry IV., to Cherburgh, but with other alien Priories was given by Henry V. to the Priory of Montgrace in Yorkshire, and subsequently as parcel, thereof, was granted to John, Lord Russell, 33 Henry VIII.—Tanner's *Notitia Monastica*, p. 272.

* Speed's *History of Great Britain*, edit. 1632, p. 570.

but cowled monks* trooping around him; shortly after which his agitating final fears were hushed by the hand of death, on the night of the 18th of October.

As might have been expected, the unworthy followers of so worthless a king instantly began to pillage their deceased master; and he who had fared so luxuriously, and was attired so gorgeously in life, in death was stripped of everything by his servants, who, as Stow says—"left him not so much as would cover his dead carcase," and fled. True, however, to his trust, the Abbot of Croxton performed the last offices for the late king, ascertained that no poison had been administered to him* and, clothing the royal corpse in a monastic habit, conveyed it honourably to Worcester Cathedral, where the Bishop received it; and a spot near the grave of St. Wolstan was selected as a fitting one for that of King John, in compliance with his dying request.

Hugh de Welles, then Bishop of Lincoln, was away with his vassals among the rebel Barons, when his dying Sovereign thus made use of two of his Castles, as temporary places of harbour, coming as a moribund man to Sleaford Castle, and actually dying at that of Newark.

No doubt the successors of Bishop Hugh II., from time to time made use of the Castle on their journies to and from Lincoln, for which purpose it was well situated; but scarcely any records of such visits now remain. We have, however, an account of Bishop Flemming's death here, January 25th, 1820, who was such a remarkable prelate that a little Memoir of his life will perhaps be acceptable.

---

* This delusion can scarcely be deemed to indicate either John's dislike of monks, or his desire for their presence. He had indeed, during his way-ward life, dealt harshly with monks at times, but he had also proved himself to be a munificent patron of several Orders. He founded the Benedictine monasteries at Waterford and Cork, before he ascended the throne, and afterwards the grand Cistercian abbey of Beaulieu in Hampshire, the monasteries of Faringdon, Hales Owen, and Otterington; he built those of Godstow and Worhall, and enlarged a chapel at Knaresborough; while his last moments were comforted, at his own request, by the Abbot of Croxton, to whose house he left a very liberal bequest.

* "The Physitian that dis-bowled his body, found no sign of poison in it."—*Baker's Chronicle,* p. 109.

Bishop   Flemyng.

Richard Flemyng, eventually Bishop of Lincoln, was born at Crofton, near Wakefield, towards the close of the 14th century. After having received his early education in his native county, he became a student of University College, Oxford, where he distinguished himself through his attainments in Logic and Philosophy. Soon after he had taken his M.A. degree he warmly enbraced the doctrines of Wycliffe, and induced several persons of eminence to follow his example; but when he found that he had thus prevented his advancement in the church, and was tempted by the persuasions of his friends, and the offers of temporal advantages, he succumbed, and soon became at least as warm an advocate of the Roman Catholic faith, as he had been its opposer. As a clever disputant, he was selected to advocate those very doctrines he had previously condemned while still a student of the University, having in 1396 been deputed to act as one of twelve doctors as examiners and judges of Wycliffe's tenets, by all of whom they were condemned and execrated as most pernicious heresy. Promotion quickly followed. In 1403 he became Rector of Staithbourne, Yorkshire. In 1406, he was presented to the Prebend of North Newbold, in the Cathedral of York, and the next year was Proctor at Oxford. Early in 1414, he was presented to the Rectory of St. Michael's, Oxford; but resigned it later in that year, when he became Incumbent of Boston, and soon after exchanged the Prebend of South Newbold, for that of Langford, in York Cathedral.

Having attracted the favourable regard of Henry V, he was promoted by him, April 24th, 1420, to the Bishopric of Lincoln, with the sanction of the Pope. Four years later he attended the council of Sienna, convened for the purpose of opposing the Reformers, where he so distinguished himself by the power of his rhetoric, in defence of the Papal supremacy, that Pope Martin V, appointed him his Chamberlain, and selected him to fill the vacancy that then occurred in the Archiepiscopate of York; but the young King's Council, and the Chapter of York, so strongly resisted the proposed appointment, that the Pope was obliged to retract it, by a fresh Bull, and the Bishop only regained the temporalities of his vacated Bishopric through the presentation of a humble petition to the King.

In 1426, Bishop Flemyng founded a College at Oxford, built at great cost, and endowed with the Churches of All Saints, Saint Michael, and Saint Mildreds, Oxford, by virtue of a licence from the king, and termed the College of the blessed Mary the Virgin, and All Saints, Lincoln, now called Lincoln College. This was intended for the use of literary men, who were to write, preach, and dispute against Wycliffe; but eventually it languished through the premature death of the Bishop, until it was freshly endowed by Thomas Scott, or Rotherham, his successor at Lincoln, in 1471.

In 1428, Bishop Flemyng executed that decree of the Council of Constance, which ordered the exhumation and burning of Wycliffe's bones, after they had lain in the grave at Lutterworth for more than 50 years. This he did as Bishop of Lincoln, by the authority of Archbishop Arundel, in which diocese Lutterworth then was, as quaintly described by Fuller;—" He sent his officers—vultures with a quick scent at a dead carcase—to ungrave him accordingly. To Lutterworth they came, Summner Commissorie, Official, Chancellor, Proctors, Doctors, and their servants, so that the remnant of the body would not hold out a bone among so many hands, to take what was left out of the grave, and burn them to ashes, and cast them into Swift, a neighbouring brook running hard by. Thus, this brook hath conveyed his ashes into Avon, Avon into Severn, Severn into the narrow seas, they into the main ocean : and thus the ashes of Wycliffe are the emblems of his doctrine, which now is dispersed all the world over. Only two of his literary works remain, viz : his " Etymologia Anglic," and his " Orationes in Concilio Sienensi." According to the words of a contemporary biographer, " he delivered his spirit into the hands of mercy, at his Castle of Sleaford, on the 25th of January, in the feast of the Conversion of St. Paul, about two o'clock in the afternoon, according to the pleasure of the Most High." Harl. M.S. 6952." He is termed by Shelton, " one of those eminent men whose names have exalted University College, Oxford, the oldest establishment in that place." He had previously built a beautiful little mortuary chapel, attached to his cathedral at Lincoln, for the reception of his body, to which it was removed for sepulture from Sleaford. His monument still remains there beneath a vaulted canopy, between this chapel and the south aisle of the presbytery of the Cathedral. This consists

K

of an altar tomb surmounted by the Bishop's effigy in full pontifical vestments. The pillow on which his mitred head rests, is supported by figures of angels, and at the feet is a lion grasping a serpent, probably in allusion to his conflict with the holders of Wycliffe's doctrines.

Within the arched open sided tomb below, is one of those ghastly contrasts not uncommonly adopted during the 15th century, as a *memento mori*, viz : the emaciated body of the dead prelate, almost reduced to a skeleton, and stripped even of the shroud, which lies below. Formerly there were two coats of arms at the head and foot of this monument. The two first bore Barry of 6 Arg and Az, in chief 3 lozenges Gu ; on the second bar a mitre labelled Arg. ; on the third bar, a mullet Sa, and the other two had a sword point in base as a difference.

Subsequently, Bishop Alnwick either largely repaired or added to Sleaford Castle, during his episcopate, lasting from 1436 to 1450. Of his residence here we have a record in the Issue Roll 24, Henry VI, p. 453, as follows :—" Paid £5 to William Gedney, lately sent by the king's command to the Bishop of Lincoln, then at Sleaford, in the County of Lincoln, and elsewhere, to obtain a copy of the last Will of his Father Lord Henry V." And that he very often travelled between Lincoln and Sleaford when he was repairing or adding to Sleaford Castle, we have proof, from the fact of his having made a new track or road over Lincoln-heath, called the " brode way," according to testimony given at a trial between the commander of Temple Bruer—Sir Thomas Newport, and de la Launde, of Ashby ; but at length the obsequious Henry Rands, or Holbeach, was base enough to alienate much of the episcopal property to the Crown, when the Castle and Manor of Sleaford first passed into the hands of the Duke of Somerset, ever greedy for the plunder of the Church, although regarded as a Saint by the Puritans, who was eventually executed for high treason. These then reverted to the Crown, and were granted by Queen Mary to Edward Fines, Lord Clinton, afterwards the famous Earl of Lincoln and Nottingham, for his services in suppressing Wyatt's rebellion ; but he did not keep them long, for in 1559, with the consent of the crown, he sold them to Robert Carre, together with all the rights, members, liberties, and appurtenances belonging thereto, with divers lands, tenements, meadows, pastures, mills, and other hereditaments, to be held by him and his assigns of the queen for ever, for the sum of £60 a year, from the 1st day of March in that year, at the feast of Saint Michael and the Pask, in equal portions. "Pipe Rot., 29 Eliz." At this time the appurtenances of the Castle and Manor of Sleaford were very great, consisting of various other manors, lands, tenements, and rights of various kinds, a list of which is still preserved in the form of a record drawn up in 1627, by Mr. William Burton, a faithful steward of the Carre family, for the instruction of the young Sir Robert Carre, the second Baronet, then a minor, son of Sir Edward Carre, the first Baronet.

In right of the Castle, all the freeholders in Sleaford and Holdingham held their lands and tenements in burgage of its lord, although some owners of these claimed to be freeholders.

The Manor of Old Sleaford was within the liberty of the Castle, and held of it by knight's service, and its lands were purchased by Robert Carre, after the confiscation of Lord Hussey's lands. 28, Henry VIII. The following also belonged to it, viz : The Manor of Quarrington, formerly held by Stanton : The Manor of Evedon and Thursby, or Blackhills, in right of which Robert Carre had enjoyed the wardship first of Bartholomew Harby, and then of his son Daniel Harby ; respecting which right a suit had taken place in 1589, which was decided in Carre's favour. The Manors of Lessingham and Ringston were held successively by members of the Marmyon and Hesslewood families, but in 1627 the former was held by Mr. Brownlow, the latter by Mr. Bernard, who then paid the fees for both Manors. The Manor of Hougham held by two knights' fees, of the Castle, by Sir Thomas Brudnell, whose tenants did fealty to the Castle court, paid yearly fines, and acknowledged its lord's right to wardships. The manor of Boughton in the parish of Asgarby. A capital messuage in Silk Willoughby, called Dounehall, held by knight's service, formerly Thomas Hussey's, but then William Berrie's ; lands in Rippingale, Dunsby, and Stainfield, held of the Castle by rents service ; besides these the right of presentation to the Church of Quarrington belonged to the lord of Sleaford Castle, after its alienation by Bishop Holbeach, as determined by a suit instituted by Robert Carre against Bishop Barlow, who claimed his right as Bishop of Lincoln ; when Lord Cook decided that the Bishop's presentee should continue to hold it ; but, that its future presentation was to be Carre's. The Castle was certainly in good order when Leland visited it about 1545, for he thus describes it, "Withoute the towne of Sleaford standith west south west the propre Castelle of Sleford, very welle mantaynid, and it is compasid with a rennyng streme, cumming by a cut oute of a litle fenne, a lying almost flatte weste againe it. In the gate-house of the Castelle, be 2 porte colices. There is an highe toure in the midle of the Castelle, but not sette upon a hille of raised yerth." "Itinerary, Vol. I, p. 27." But during the next 50 years its demolition had in a great measure taken place. Perhaps the Duke of Somerset had commenced this, by selling the lead and timber of its roofs—always the first and most profitable act of spoliation; and then the stonework was carried off for building purposes elsewhere as required. The next we hear of its condition is a reference to " the late fair Castle at Sleaford," in a deed executed by Robert Carre, in 1604, which he would have scarcely used if he himself had destroyed it. But we are hence enabled distinctly to disprove the popular error that Cromwell battered down the Castle, as some harmless remains of it alone then existed : for much of its materials had been carried off at that time, and according to tradition, were used in the erection of the then two principal inns of Sleaford ; more no doubt followed ; but even so late as 1720 a considerable portion of the north wall and north western tower, as well as of a much larger tower, and a compound turret—perhaps the Keep—were still standing. (See Cut taken from a contemporary drawing.)

And the Rev. Edward Waterson, vicar of Sleaford, from 1781 to 1809, has left it on record that persons were still living during his incumbency who remembered the existence of the west gate of the Castle ; but now only an upturned portion of the above named north western tower remains of all its former vast stores of stone. Its walls are five feet thick, and this fragment seems likely to endure awhile still, to serve as a solitary relic of the past grandeur of Sleaford Castle. During some recent excavations on the site of the Castle, one of its keys was found, of which a cut is given below.

GUILDS.

There were several Guilds at Sleaford in mediæval times as in other towns, the chief of which were those of the Holy Trinity, or Saint Thomas, Corpus Christi, and Saint John. These were semi-religious, semi-charitable Institutions, or Corporations, intended to give aid in life, in death, and after death; but some were more especially founded to advance prosperity in trade. If rich enough each had its House, or Hall, commonly called the Guild Hall, and consisted of an Alderman, Chamberlains, and often a Chaplain, besides the brethren and sisters. They were prosperous popular Societies, possessing lands and tenements bequeathed to them, besides the proceeds of the subscriptions of their members. Their objects were to relieve the distressed, to celebrate the funerals of their deceased members with solemnity, and to have masses said for the repose of their souls. They often met for business, but once a year kept a grand Festival when they attended mass in great state, offered up especial prayers for all the brotherhood both living and dead, audited their accounts, and dined together, sometimes with unhappy results. The chaplains of these Guilds were usually the directors of those religious plays got up with great splendour by such communities, attended by the Magistrates and chief personages of the neighbourhood, and celebrated with bell ringing, singing, and playing of minstrels, and feasting. The Alderman was elected by the brethren annually, and usually the choice fell upon the senior Chamberlain of the preceding year.

The Holy Trinity Guild existed at Sleaford in 1477, but how long before that date we know not. An account book of this Guild, commencing that year, still exists, of which the following is given as a specimen of its character.

"Compotus Iohis Swynshed aldyrman, Willi Pynder, et Ricardi Franke camerariorum Gylde Sancte Trinitatis anno Dni millmo ccccLXXVIJ.

Md. that the next sonday aftyr the fest of the Trinite the yer afor wretyn, that Jon Swynshed countyd and delyveryd the day aforsayd, apon hys count to the toun of Sleford, and bredyr and systers of the Gyld of the Trinite, of the saule—scott to hym delyveryd be the hands of John Gylbert and Robert Wryght, sum iij li., xi s., ix d., of the quych sume ther remaynys in the charge of John Gylberd, iv li.

Also ther remanys in the hand of Jon Swynshed, Alderman
of the year aforsayd .... iij li xi s. ix d. ob.
Item. the increase of the Stoke .... iij li xviij s. j d.
Item. of hold soulscott .... vi li xi s. ix d.
Item. of New brodyrod ....　　xiij s.
Item. of legat ....　　vi s. iij d.
Item. for malte sold to the chaumerlayns .. xx xviij s. viij d.
　　　　　　　　Summe total .... iij li. xviij s. iij d. ob.
This ben the parcels in expens don be the sayd Aldyrman an hys chaumerlayns.
Item. Fyrst payd to the prest .... v li. v ii. viij d.
Item. payd to the dirige....................　　xx d.
It. payd to the prest for messe penys for ye
　　bredyr dyssesyd that yer .... 　　x d.
It. payd to the mynstrells .... 　　xiiij d.
It. payd to the mynstrells of Corpus day ..　　iiij d.
It. payd for the synging of the same day ..　　ij d.
　　　　　　　Summe................... v li.　x s.　xd.
Item. in expens don be the hands of the chaumerlayns in all
　　maner chargs .... iij li. xiii s. vj d.
The sume of the Stoke, althyngs countyd and aloud delyveryd to the hands of William Curwyn chosen for Aldyrman, and the next yer following is .... iij li. xvj s. iijd.
Sum totalis de claro .... iijix li. xvj s. iijd.

This Guild lasted until the dissolution of all such Institutions, when its rents and profits were made over to the Crown.

Corpus Christi Guild was famous for the magnificence with which it presented its religious plays to its brethren and visitors. and especially on Corpus Christi day. It had a property belonging to it called Nelson's lands. It existed after the confiscation of its property until 1613, under the management of the churchwardens. It is not improbable that the chapel at the west end of the south aisle of the parish church belonged to one of these Guilds, as its peculiar situation and distinct bell-pinnacle favour such a suggestion.

THE HUSSEYS.

The earliest mention of the name of Hussey in connection with Sleaford is in the reign of Richard II., when Robert Halden, Vicar of Sleaford, is recorded to have married Elizabeth daughter of John Husay, of Sleaford. Next we hear of a Sir William Hussey, knight, of Sleaford, who married a Lumley. Their son, John Hussey, of Sleaford, living circa 1441-58, married Elizabeth Nesfield, and they were the parents of a second Sir Wm. Hussey, of Sleaford, besides whom they had a younger son, Sir Robert, also settled at Sleaford, whose name occurs on a roll of knights and gentlemen employed to fix the boundaries between Kesteven and Holland, in the year 1500. Sir William was a student at Gray's Inn Hall, and through his great skill and learning rose to the top of the legal profession, and thus exalted the position of his family. He certainly continued to live occasionally in Lincolnshire, for we find his name as one of the Commissioners of Sewers for Kesteven, in 1467. He was made Attorney General, June 16th, 1471, and Chief Justice of the King's Bench, May 7th, 1481, with the allowance of 100 marks a year, an office which he continued to hold by subsequent patents of Edward V., Richard III., and Henry VII. In the reign of Richard he was appointed one of his Commissioners for treating with the King of Scotland respecting a proposed marriage between his eldest son James, with Anne, Richard's niece, and daughter of John, Duke of Suffolk. In the first year of Henry VII., he attended that king on the northern progress he made after his coronation, and three years later acted as one of the commissioners for the array of archers in the County of Lincoln, to be sent to the relief of Brittany. In the year 1490 he acted as one of the king's commissioners appointed to treat for peace between Charles, king of France, and Anne, duchess of Brittany, and did so again the year following. He was a benefactor to Pembroke Hall, Cambridge, "Leland's Collectanea," Vol. V, p. 200. After having been admitted as a Canon of Lincoln, he died September 8th, 1495, and was buried at Sempringham. A record of him, and his wife Elizabeth Berkeley, still remains in one of the windows of Gray's Inn Hall, viz., his armorial bearings, and below them this legend, " Willus Husee, miles, capitalis, Justic ad placita cora Rege, et Elizabetha uxor ejus, filia Thome Berkeley, Armigeri." His above named wife, Elizabeth, daughter of Sir Thomas Berkeley, of Wymondham, died 1505. They had four sons, John, afterwards Lord Hussey ; Sir William, Sir Robert, and George ; and two daughters :—Elizabeth, married to Richard Grey, Earl of Kent, and Mary, married to William, Lord Willoughby de Eresby. John Hussey was born 1465, and became an important public character. In 1494 he was appointed custodian of the manor of Holewell (Holywell), in Lincolnshire, and of Stretton, in Rutland, through the mainprisal of William Hussey, of London, and Thomas Archer, of Swineshead. The same year also he was appointed Sheriff of Lincolnshire. He fought at the battle of Stoke, June 16th, 1487, and at that of Blackheath 1497 ; after which he was knighted by Henry VII. In 1509, on the accession of Henry VIII., he obtained a release of all debts due to the king, dated at Oxford, May 22nd., and the same year was admitted as a Commissioner of oyer and terminer in the County of Lincoln. In 1513 he went as a captain of 328 men to the French war, previous to which he obtained letters of protection during his absence, and a license to alienate lands worth £20 a year, to the Master and Fellows of Pembroke Hall, Cambridge. Two years later as Justice of the Peace, and Custos Rotulorum for Holland, in Lincolnshire, he was called upon to attend the French queen. In 1520 he followed the king to the celebrated Field of the Cloth of Gold, accompanied him whereever he went, and jousted on the queen's side at the tourney. The next year he was made Chief Butler of England. In 1523 he attended the king, when he went to meet the Emperor at Canterbury, May 7th, and on the 3rd of November, 1530, was created Baron Hussey of Sleaford. After such services rendered to the Crown, and such rewards as he had received from Henry VIII. in return for those services (who, as a mark of his personal regard, had stood sponsor for one of Lord Hussey's children), we should have thought he would ever have remained faithful to his sovereign; but, although he aided in putting down the first popular movement against the suppression of the monasteries, and the old faith, under Dr. Mackarel, prior of Bardney, commonly called Captain Cobler, he subsequently joined with others, and especially with Sir Thomas Darcy, under whose influence he is supposed to have acted in this matter, in taking part in a similar rebellion, which cost him his life. When warned of the threatened danger of the first rising of the people of Lincolnshire, by the then Dean of Lincoln—the famous Wolsey, he directly sent the following proper instructions to some authority in command at Lincoln—perhaps the Governor of the Castle. "Cotton MSS., Vespasian F 113., fol. 116."

"In my right herty manner I recommend me unto you, Advertysing the same, that this daye at ix of the clocke in the mornyng, I had word from the Dean of Lincoln that there is a company of fals rebellious knaves rysen and gathered to gether in Lyndsey; wherefore, I will advise you, and in the King's behalf I commaunde you that ye do see the citie of Lyncoln surely kept, so that there passe no suche evyll desposed persons thorough the same : And further that ye be in redynes with suche company as ye can make, to serve the King in suppressing the same, if nede reqwyres : And that ye immediatly cause furthwith all the bowes and arrowes being in the bowers' and fletchers' hands to be taken up at a reasonable price, if ye so nede : And that ye handle this matter so discretely and secretely as ye can ; And if ye see cause that ye be not able to resist, send me word. And I shalbe redy at all tymes to assist you with suche power as I can make. And thus fare ye well. From Sleaford, this tuesday the iij^d daye of October, with the hande of

"Yours to ——

"JOHN HUSSE."

Eventually this movement became a very serious one, and 20,000 men of Lincolnshire were, as far as they could be, in arms against the king; but, backed by a large force, Henry is said to have persuaded the leaders to submit, and then addressed the rest in terms neither conciliatory nor flattering to this county, telling them that he had never read or heard that rude and ignorant common people were meet persons to discern and choose sufficient counsellors for a Prince, called them presumptuous rude commons, of a shire the most brute and beastly of the whole realm, who dared to take upon them to rule their king; and finished by ordering the poor Prior of Bardney and others to be executed.   A similar rebellion however soon broke out again, further to the north, first under Aske, and then under Lord Darcy, Sir Robert Constable, Sir John Bulmer, Sir Thomas Percy, brother of the Earl of Northumberland, Sir Stephen Hamilton, Nicholas Tempest, and others; and in this Lord Hussey joined.   All of these are said to have been offered pardon at an early stage of their proceedings on this occasion; but although their cause was hopeless, they persevered, failed, and fell into the hands of the king.   Lord Darcy and Lord Hussey were then arraigned at Westminster, before the Marquis of Exeter, High Steward of England, and were pronounced guilty of high treason, for which the former was sentenced to be beheaded on Tower-hill, and Lord Hussey shortly afterwards suffered the same fate at Lincoln.   At his death he possessed the manor of Old Sleaford and adjacent lands, and the manors of Leake, Leverton, and Skirbeck; but although his children were restored in blood 5 Eliz., they did not recover his estates.   It is a question which of his two wives he married first, but probably this was Margaret, daughter and co-heir of Sir Simon Blount, of Mangotsfield, Gloucestershire, and widow of John Bane, of Banes Court, in the same County, by whom he had Sir Charles Hussey, of Caythorpe, knighted at Morlaix, in Brittany, and Thomas Hussey, of Holton Holgate. His other wife was Anne, daughter of George Grey, Earl of Kent. For further particulars of this family see the subjoined pedigree.

On the attainder of Lord Hussey, Robert Carre bought the Manor of Old Sleaford, and the residence of the Husseys, now called "the Old Place," and it remained in the hands of his descendants until it passed into the Hervey family, by the marriage of Isabella Carre with John Hervey, the ancestor of the present Marquis of Bristol, who is now its proprietor.

THE FAMILY OF CARRE OF SLEAFORD.

The Carres of Sleford* were a Northumberland family, of Anglo-Norman origin, who removed into Lincolnshire in the reign of Hen. VII. Their chief residence in the north was Hetton, in Glendale, a few miles from the borders of Scotland.

The immediate ancestor of the Sleaford family—Sir John Carre, temp. Henry VI., married Margaret Clifford, daughter of the eighth Lord de Clifford, Lord of Hartlepool, and great granddaughter of the renowned Hotspur, of Chevy Chase, so celebrated by historians. They had several children, of whom the youngest son—James, married a sister of Lord Ogle, and was grandfather of the Margaret Carre, whose monumental brass at Pinchbeck in this county, has long been an object of interest with antiquaries.

Sir John Carre, Kt., of Hartlepool, the eldest son, was a favourite of Henry VIII. He was Squire of the Body, to the King, in 1509, and, afterwards a "Sewer of the Mouth," (an officer equivalent to that of cupbearer). The king lavished upon him many honors and estates; amongst others, a slice of the possessions of the attained Lord Lovel of Blankney, and also the rent which Lord Hussey paid to the Crown for the grant of that Barony. In 1514 the king gave him considerable estates in Yorkshire, and, in the following year, he served the office of Sheriff for that County,—on which occasion he obtained a "Grant of Standard." This Grant, dated 14 March, 1515, under the seals of Wryothesley and Yonge, Kings at Arms, was found in the archives at Sleaford, and is a most curious document. Sir John is therein described as " descended of noble lineage : " the device was a Stag's head, decorated, as it may be seen on the old monuments in Sleaford church. Sir John died at Cambridge in 1522. In his will he bequeathed his "cheyne and crosse" to Sir Wm. Compton, mentioning the love he had borne him through life : his debt to the King of 100 marks, he trusted of his forgiveness, of all or half, if his executors

---

*The greater part of the following account of the Carre family is derived from a treatise on that subject, by the late M. P. Moore, Esq., of Sleaford, published in the reports of the Associated Architectural Societies, Vol. 6.

did sue for it—and he also trusted that a small sum would content the executors of George Carre, of Sleford, for what he owed to them. His "reyment, plate, and effects," he bequeathed to his priest, and desired to be buried " afore St. John the Baptist, in St. John's College ; " thus adopting its patron saint, after the manner of Geo. Carre of Newcastle, who in his will desired that the image of St. George, that was kept in the Hall, should remain there during the life of his wife, and then be preserved "in the cupborde as an heirelome."

The nephew and heir, George Carre, of Sleaford, (who was the son of Richard Carre, by a daughter of Sir John Elmden, of the Bishoprick), was the first of whom we have any record as being settled in this place ; and it is somewhat singular that so many Northumberland families should have migrated into Lincolnshire about the same period, such as the Herons of Cressy, the Widdringtons of Blankney, the Talboys of Kyme, the Ogles of Pinchbeck, &c. George Carre established himself at Sleaford as a merchant of the staple of Calais, trading in the export of wool from Boston to the continent—the wool at that time passing down by water—(by the Old river, and through Haverholme Park) to St. Botolph's, as in the time of Edward I. The commerce was regulated by a wealthy Guild at Sleaford, called the Guild of the Holy Trinity, to early *brethyren* of which ancient fraternity we are said to be indebted for our parish church.

In these pursuits, George Carre acquired a large fortune, including the manor of Tetney on the coast, and other estates in this town and neighbourhood. He dwelt in the " Carre House," south of the church, described by Leland, (who travelled in the wake of Hen. VIII.,) as one of the great ornaments of the town. It now forms the site of the Carre Hospital.

The eldest surviving son, Robert Carre, Esq., (familiarly known as old Robert Carre,) became the founder of the great landed wealth of the family. He survived his father for seventy years, and throughout that long period, and with an unlimited command of money, he devoted himself to the continual extension of his landed possessions. He lived in eventful times, favourable to that object, especially for one whose antecedents gave him the ear of the King. Living all through the reigns of Hen. VIII., Ed., VI., and Mary, he survived to assist Elizabeth, in 1588, with a loan against the Spanish Armada. Born a catholic, he was a close observer of the Reformation; more especially of the manner in which the monastic possessions, the Chantries, Guilds, &c., were transferred to the Crown; and in that century, too, more private property was forfeited by attainder, than in any other period of our history. He purchased the manor of Old Sleaford, forfeited on the attainder of his fellow-townsman, Lord Hussey, and which estate Cranmer had granted to the Goodrich family, He also purchased the ancient Castle, manor, and great Barony of Sleaford, forfeited by the attainder of the Protector Somerset, and which had been granted to Lord Clinton, for his services in suppressing the rebellion of Wyatt. The learned editor of the Progress of King Henry with Q. Catherine Howard, through Lincolnshire, in 1541, after the rebellion in Lincolnshire, conjectures that the King rested at the Old Place, and held his councils *there*, under the erroneous impression that the Old Place then remained in the hands of the King: but it is more probable that he was received at the Castle, which was then in all its splendour " very welle mantaynid."—Moreover it belonged to Bishop Longland, who in the previous week had proudly entertained the King and all his Court, at his other Episcopal palace of Liddington, in Rutland. The precise time when this Castle was dismantled is not known. Leland classes it amongst the *Religious Houses* of the County, and probably it was left to share the fate of the Abbeys. In the grant to Lord Clinton, 1556, it is treated more as a ruin, and much mention is made of its stone, lead, and iron.

It may further be mentioned, that Robert Carre bought the manor and mansion of Aswarby and Asgarby, of his niece, the Lady Ambrose Dudley, which had devolved upon her as the daughter and heir of Lord Talboys; he also bought the manor of Rauceby, of Sir John Huddylstone, Kt., of Sawston, Vice Chamberlayne to the Kynge's Hyghnesse; the manor of Ingleby Hall, in Kirkby, of John Stanlow and Myles Bussye; another manor there, of Thos. Sleford, Esq., who had removed to Willesthorp; Cattley Abbey, and the manors of Digby and Brauncewell, with the manor and mansion of old Dunsby on the Heath, that were appurtenant to that monastery; large estates in South Elloe, of the Welby family; great possessions of the dissolved Monasteries of Haverholm, Bourn, Louth, &c.; and a well-known spot on the heath, described in those days as " the shepegate, called *Mayden House*, in Fulbec, parcel of the possessions of the late priory of Sempringham."

But it would be tedious to continue the enumeration of these purchases, which he made on most favourable terms for himself, through their doubtful titles, as having been either forfeited estates or monastic property. He was hence enabled to exhibit his patriotism in a very substantial manner at the time of the threatened Spanish Invasion, by contributing £100 towards the defence of the country, or more than all the other Lincolnshire contributors towards that fund, excepting Thomas Conye, of Bassingthorpe, who gave the same sum, most of the leading gentry giving only £25

In private life, old Leland speaks of him as " a proper gentilman." He took a prominent part in the judicial business of the county, and was an active supporter of the Lord Treasurer Burleigh, in the business of the Musters.

Robert Carre was thrice married : 1st, to Elizabeth Cawdron, (daughter of the King's Bayliff at Heckington) by whom he had seven children ; 2nd., to the widow Irby ; and 3rdly, to the widowed Lady Dymoke, the sister of Lord Talboys. He died in 1590, at an advanced age, and was buried in the church where his monument indicates.

Throughout his life, Robert Carre continued to reside in the old Carre House at Sleaford ; his three sons, Robert, Sir William, and Sir Edward, respectively occupying the Old Place, Aswarby Park, and the old Hall at Dunsby.

Of his six surviving children, the eldest daughter, Elizabeth, married Mr. Fairfax, of Swarby, nephew of Ralph Fairfax, the last Prior of Kyme. Anne, the second daughter, married Robt. Whichcote, Esq., of Harpswell, ancestor of Sir Thomas Whichcote, Bart. Ann Bridget married Richard Rossiter, of Somerby, and was the grandmother of Col. Sir Ed. Rossiter, M.P., General of all the Lincolnshire Forces in Cromwell's time, and Governor, in usurpation, of Belvoir Castle ; afterwards " a promoter of the nation's happiness," and knighted at Canterbury on the Restoration of Charles II. He married the Lady Arabella Hollis.

George Carre, the eldest son, predeceased his father, leaving by Mary Sutton, his wife, grandniece of Lord Hussey, a son, Robert, who died young, s.p., and a daughter, Elizabeth, who married, imprudently, Edward Sisson, Esq., and was disinherited.

Robert Carre, the second son, High Sheriff 1581, was Founder of the Sleaford Grammar School, and of other charities at Rauceby and Aswarby. He went as Treasurer of the Army of the North, accompanied by many Lincolnshire gentlemen, to quell the rebellion against Queen Elizabeth, got up by the Earls of Northumberland and Westmoreland. The list of " the principal officers and captaynes " included,

Ambrose Dudley, Earl of Warwick.   }   *L. L.*
Ed. Lord Clinton, Adm. of England, }   *Lieuts.*
Robert Carr, of Sleford, Esq..........*Treasurer.*
Leonard Irby, Esq......................*Muster Mayster.*
John Heneage, Esq......................*Master Harbinger.*
Captains of Horse, Dymock Nevile, St. Poll, &c.
Purveyor ....*John Death.*

Robert Carre married the widow of the great warrior, William, Lord Gray of Wilton, Lord Warden of the English Marches; and secondly, the widow of Adlard Welby, Esq., of Gedney; and died without issue in 1606.

The next brother, Sir William Carre, was knighted with his younger brother, Edward, at Belvoir Castle, on going to greet James I in his progress to take possession of the Crown of England. Sir Wm. married Bridget Chaworth, of Wyverton, who, as her monument at Ufford relates, " *served the late Queen* " *Elizabeth of most famous memory, being one of the Gentlewomen of* " *Her Majesties Privye Chamber, for the space of five and twenty* " *years; and afterwards served the most renowned Queen Anne, Wife* " *to our most gracious Soveraigne, King James, for the space of* 14 " *years, being the residue of her life.*"

Sir William died without issue in 1611, and was succeeded by his youngest brother,

Sir Edward Carre, Knight, who was created a Baronet by James I, but did not long survive to enjoy that honour. He was twice married: by his first wife, Catherine Bolle, he had no family; by the second, Anne Dyer, he left three children, Sir Robert, Rochester, and Lucy, and died in 1618. The monument, and recumbent effigies of the knight and his lady, are said to have been mutilated in the civil war, when General Cromwell and the Earl of Manchester were so " much about Sleford," and Col. Rossiter desecrated the parish church, by converting it into a stable for his troop-horses.

Sir Edward, by his will, augmented the jointure of his widow to 5000 acres—leaving her also her jewels, her coach and horses, her own riding horses, the white nag called "Gray Cawdron," and the white silver plate belonging to her own chamber; the manor of Upton he left to his daughter Lucy-Englishe; the Aswarby estates to his second son Rochester, together with the service of white silver plate; the eldest son, Sir Robert, taking the residue of the family estates, and the service of plate "all gilt," much of which had been birth-day presents from Queen Elizabeth to Sir Wm. and his lady, when in waiting at that Court.

In Sir Edward's time, the Carre estates were in the zenith of their integrity. Besides the old property in Northumberland, Yorkshire, and Hunts., and in Kesteven, (far exceeding what remains in the present day,) there were manors, advowsons, and estates in 19 parishes in Lindsey, and 24 parishes in the Parts of Holland.

The widow of Sir Edward Carre, within a twelvemonth of her first husband's death, married her countryman, Col. Hen. Cromwell, M.P., the eldest son of the veteran Royalist, Sir Oliver Cromwell, of Hitchinbroke, elder uncle of the Protector.

Sir Robert Carre, the second Baronet, on coming of age, founded the Sleaford Hospital, A.D. 1636, endowing it with estates that at the present time yield an income of £1200 a year. In very early life he married one of the daughters and co-heirs of Sir Richard Gargrave, Kt., of Kingsley Park, and Nostell, in Yorkshire. This unhappy person, "*Dick Gargrave*," was of antient family, and the owner of an immense estate, the whole of which was wasted at the gaming-table. "He could once ride on his own land from Wakefield to Doncaster," and was at last found dead, in the stable of a small inn, resting his head on the saddle of his *packhorse*. His daughter, a beautiful woman, became known in many after sorrows, as "*the Lady Mary Carr*."

Rochester Carr, of Aswarby, named after his godfather, Sir Robert Carr, Viscount Rochester and Earl of Somerset, in 1637, was found lunatic, and continued in that state for 40 years. His guardianship became the subject of fierce contention between Lady Mary Carr, for her husband on one side, and Dame Anne Cromwell and her family, on the other side. The struggle was maintained incessantly for 30 years—through the remaining years of Charles I—through the Commonwealth—and down into the reign of Charles II :—-but the Carres, having the right, were successful throughout.

The affairs of the elder brother, Sir Robert Carr, proved if possible, a greater anxiety to his wife, Lady Mary, than those of Rochester—for he too, as Fleetwood asserted, became "of very weake understanding."

Early in his married life, when he had daughters only, he made a remarkable settlement of his castle and estates upon the Earl of Ancram, conditional upon either of Lord Ancram's sons, (Lord Charles Carr or Stanley Carr) marrying one of these young ladies. This settlement, which was attested by six of the great ministers of state, was afterwards as solemnly revoked on the birth of a son. Then followed a series of settlements, in the time of Sir Robert's weakness, confiding the estates to different sets of trustees, for various family purposes—each succeeding settlement being followed by suit for breaches of trust—Lady Mary alleging "sales of estates by the trustees to themselves and their friends, at nominal prices, and rendering no account of the money: "—and notwithstanding the friendly interest taken by King Charles himself, and although the trustees were most of them Ministers of State, Speakers of the House of Commons, and Law Officers of the Crown, or of the Commonwealth, it would seem that they did take advantage of the times in which they lived, for "they could render no account, because during the war, Sleford having been an usual quarter for soldiers, they had divers times imprisoned the agents, and plundered and embezzled all their papers." Of all the trustees, the first and last friend of the Carrs, seems to have been their countryman, Algernon, Earl of Northumberland.

Sir Robert Carr died in 1667, and now "new troubles came upon Lady Mary" in her widowhood.

Sir Robert left four children, of whom, the eldest daughter, Elizabeth, married Sir William Trollope, Bart., and had an only daughter, Elizabeth Carr Trollope, wife of Charles Fox, Esq., paymaster to the Forces of Charles II, and elder half-brother of the first Earl of Ilchester, and the first Lord Holland.

Mary, the second daughter, married Sir Adrian Scrope, Kt., of the Bath, and was ' *the greate witt* ' of Evelyn's time.

L

Lucy, third daughter, was married in Westminster Abbey, to the second Lord Hollis; who in time claimed and recovered from Sir Robert Carr, for his wife's portion, the greater part then remaining of the Lindsey and Holland estates—which property he carried to the Newcastle family.

The shares of the elder sisters, were happily bought up by the first Earl of Bristol.

The only brother, The Right Hon. Sir Robert Carr, Knt. and Bart., Chancellor of the Duchy of Lancaster, was the last of this Royalist family, in the male line, that attained to man's estate. He was returned M.P. for the County in several Parliaments, as his cousin Rossiter had been in the Commonwealth. He married a sister of Bennett, Earl of Arlington, joined "THE CABAL" Administration, and was one of the favourites of Charles II. Before his death at Aswarby, in 1682, he appointed the Rt. Hon. Sir Stephen Fox, Sir Wm. Yorke, of Leasingham, and Sir Gervas Elwes, of Suffolk, to be his executors; and desired to be buried in the family vault in Sleaford church by torch light.

Sir Edward Carr, the 4th Bart., died in his minority, (when the Baronetcy became extinct)—leaving an only sister,—

Isabella Carr, the sole heir, and the last of her race, who in 1688, married John Hervey, Esq., of Ickworth Park, Suffolk, afterwards created Earl of Bristol; the ancestor of the present Marquis of Bristol.

PEDIGREE OF CARRE OF SLEFORD,

Formerly of Hetton, Northumberland.

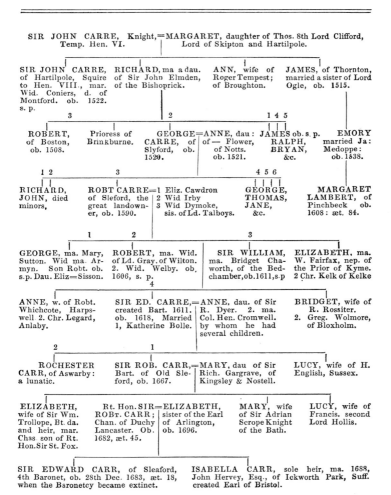

SIR JOHN CARRE, Knight,=MARGARET, daughter of Thos. 8th Lord Clifford,
Temp. Hen. VI. | Lord of Skipton and Hartilpole.

SIR JOHN CARRE, | RICHARD, ma a dau. | ANN, wife of | JAMES, of Thornton,
of Hartilpole, Squire | of Sir John Elmden, | Roger Tempest; | married a sister of Lord
to Hen. VIII., mar. | of the Bishoprick. | of Broughton. | Ogle, ob. 1515.
Wid. Coniers, d. of
Montford. ob. 1522.
s. p.
3   2   1 4 5

ROBERT, | Prioress of | GEORGE=ANNE, dau : JAMES ob. s. p. | EMORY
of Boston, | Brinkburne. | CARRE, of | of — Flower, RALPH, | married Ja:
ob. 1508. | | Slyford, ob. | of Notts. BRYAN, | Medoppe:
| | 1520. | ob. 1521. &c. | ob. 1538.
1 2   3   4 5 6

RICHARD, | ROBT CARRE=1 Eliz. Cawdron | GEORGE, | MARGARET
JOHN, died | of Sleford, the | 2 Wid Irby | THOMAS, | LAMBERT, of
minors. | great landown- | 3 Wid Dymoke, | JANE, | Pinchbeck ob.
| er, ob. 1590. | sis. of Ld. Talboys. | &c. | 1608 : æt. 84.
1   2   3

GEORGE, ma. Mary, | ROBERT, ma. Wid. | SIR WILLIAM, | ELIZABETH, ma.
Sutton. Wid ma. Ar- | of Ld. Gray. of Wilton. | ma. Bridget Cha- | W. Fairfax, nep. of
myn. Son Robt. ob. | 2. Wid. Welby. ob. | worth, of the Bed- | the Prior of Kyme.
s.p. Dau. Eliz=Sisson. | 1606, s. p. | chamber,ob.1611,s.p | 2 Chr. Kelk of Kelke
4

ANNE, w. of Robt. | SIR ED. CARRE,=ANNE, dau. of Sir | BRIDGET, wife of
Whichcote, Harps- | created Bart. 1611. | R. Dyer. 2. ma. | R. Rossiter.
well 2. Chr. Legard, | ob. 1618, Married | Col. Hen. Cromwell. | 2. Greg. Wolmore,
Anlaby. | 1, Katherine Bolle. | by whom he had | of Bloxholm.
| | several children.
2   1

ROCHESTER | SIR ROB. CARR,=MARY, dau of Sir | LUCY, wife of H.
CARR, of Aswarby : | Bart. of Old Sle- | Rich. Gargrave, of | English, Sussex.
a lunatic. | ford, ob. 1667. | Kingsley & Nostell.

ELIZABETH, | Rt. Hon. SIR=ELIZABETH, | MARY, wife | LUCY, wife of
wife of Sir Wm. | ROBt. CARR; | sister of the Earl | of Sir Adrian | Francis. second
Trollope, Bt. da. | Chan. of Duchy | of Arlington, | Scrope Knight | Lord Hollis.
and heir, mar. | Lancaster. Ob. | ob. 1696. | of the Bath.
Chas. son of Rt. | 1682, æt. 45.
Hon.Sir St. Fox.

SIR EDWARD CARR, of Sleaford, | ISABELLA CARR, sole heir, ma. 1688,
4th Baronet, ob. 28th Dec. 1683, æt. 18, | John Hervey, Esq., of Ickworth Park, Suff.
when the Baronetcy became extinct. | created Earl of Bristol.

Tradesmen's Tokens.

Various little copper tokens of Sleaford tradesmen are worthy of notice in connection with the 17th century. Four of these are represented in the annexed cuts. Fig. 1 : Obverse—James Adamson and a queen's head on a shield ; reverse—In Sleeford, 1656, and the initials I. M. A. Fig. 2 : Obverse—John Farnfield, and a shield having a chevron between 9 cloves, or the Grocers' bearings ; reverse—I. E. F., In Sleeford, 1656. Fig. 3 : Obverse—Richard Cawdron, and a shield bearing the figure of a woman, probably intended for a Queen ; reverse—R. C., In Sleeford, 1664. Fig. 4 : Obverse—Christopher Green, and a shield the same as the last ; reverse—C. M. G., In Sleaford.

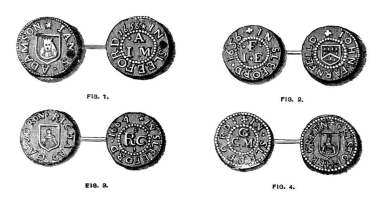

FIG. 1.

FIG. 2.

EIG. 3.

FIG. 4.

Until the reign of James I., there was no Royal copper money, which led to the use of private tokens by retail tradesmen for the mutual convenience of their customers and themselves. To meet this want, and to check what was an infringement upon the royal prerogative, royal farthing tokens were issued in 1613, and continued to be struck from that time until the close of his successor's reign ; but as this practice was discontinued during the Commonwealth, cities, corporations, merchants, and tradesmen then issued tokens in greater abundance than ever, until at length their use was pronounced illegal in 1672, and such specimens as still exist are now simply curiosities of the past.

In the last year of the 18th century an event occurred at Sleaford worthy of record from its amusing character, and as being characteristic of that period. Now, of all religious sects, the Society of Friends, or Quakers, are the most quiet and inoffensive; but in the 17th century and for some years subsequently they were violent beyond measure, and often experienced violence in return, especially from their chief opponents the Baptists. In a collision between these that occurred at Panton, in this county (as described in a curious contemporary tract), a judgment is said to have befallen one of the polemical divines in the form of a leprosy that was subsequently removed at the prayer of his opponent; and at Sleaford a remarkable disputation took place between a Baptist bearing the unenviable name of Bugg and a Quaker named Pickworth. The former, in a quixotic spirit conceiving that he was bound to contend with Quakerism in general, and provided with a certificate from certain "worshipful persons vouching for the honest and sober life of the bearer, and further discreetly asserting that he was not disturbed in his mind, or discomposed, arrived at Sleaford, August 11th, 1700. Bugg was originally a Quaker himself, and as an ardent pervert had previously disputed with Pickworth, by whom he had been challenged to a polemical contest, and was encouraged to do so by James Gardiner, Bishop of Lincoln, then holding a Visitation at Sleaford, who spoke to the clergy in his behalf. The use of the Sessions House for the forthcoming disputation was obtained from Mr. Hervey, Lord of the manor, then at Sleaford, and in it the Quaker erected a lofty platform capable of accommodating 20 persons. After lodging with the Rev. Edward Smith, then vicar of Sleaford, the next day Bugg triumphantly mounted his platform from which poor Pickworth was excluded, who could scarcely be heard from the floor; while the magistrates—Edward Payne and Robert Cawdron, took their seats as judges. Pickworth spoke first, before a crowded assembly, and then the ardent Bugg poured forth his declamations against Quakerism for such a length of time that the justices at last despairingly exclaimed in what would now be considered too familiar terms on a public occasion, "Come, Bugg, 'tis now three o'clock, 'tis time to give over, we want to go to dinner," reminding us of one of Pope's lines—

"And wretches hang, that jurymen may dine."

Eventually, however, judgment was passed as follows:—
"March 11, 170½. We whose names are hereunto subscribed, being
two of his majesties justices of the peace for the parts of Kesteven,
in the county of Lincoln, do testify, that being at a conference at
Sleeford, Aug. 25, last past, between Mr. Fran. Bugg and Hen.
Pickworth, a quaker of that town, Mr. Bugg did produce several
books, wrote by the quakers, to prove those pernicious and anti-
christian principles which he had charged them with in several
books printed by him, which he did to the great satisfaction of
the auditors, by fairly and openly reading the quotations out
of the said quaker authors; nor did the quakers then present
deny, but that the books which Mr. Bugg produced were wrote
by their own people, and fairly printed, except one which was
written by some one C. Atkinson; but it was fairly proved and
owned by some of them, that it was written by him when he was
a quaker. After some hours dispute, Mr. Bugg having made
good his charge against them, we did, in abhorrence of their base
principles, pursuant to an agreement under their hands in print,
order two of the quaker's books, in which were very scandalous
expressions, and directly contrary to the fundamentals of christianity, to be burnt in the market-place, (which books were produced by Mr. Bugg, but wrote by the quakers), and they were
accordingly burnt in the presence of many people; and indeed
several others of the quaker books deserved the same fate, but
we thought in destroying them all, we should prevent Mr. Bugg
from detecting their pernicious doctrines, and defending himself
against the quakers, which consideration preserved them; for
there were very mischievous principles contained in most of
them: in witness whereof, we have hereunto set our hands the
day and year abovewritten.

"EDW. PAYNE.
"ROBERT CAWDRON."*

Thus *burning* was the sentence, but happily not of Pickworth the Quaker, two of his pamphlets only having been
consigned to the flames at the cross in the Market-place. Of
course Bugg triumphed beyond measure, gloating over the twelve

---

* "A Narrative of the Conference at Sleeford, in Lincolnshire, Aug. 25,
1701, by Francis Bugg; sold by John Taylor, at the Ship, and R. Withers,
at the King's Head, in St. Paul's Churchyard, 1702."

Quaker teachers, a hundred of their body, and many hundreds of Christians who had listened to his redundant address, and he recorded his victory in the Evening Post, a journal of that time, and wrote a batch of fresh tracts. One of these he entitled, "News from new Rome, *i.e.* New Sleaford ;" another, "Quakerism deeply wounded, and now lyes a bleeding in Sleaford and Colchester ;" and a third, "Quakerism drooping and its cause sinking, clearly manifested from divers conferences at Banbury, Sleaford, Colchester, and Mildenhall, by a servant of the Church. F. Bugg." "Bugg's Sleaford Conference and other Tracts, by the Rev. B. Loveling, vicar of Banbury. London, 1703. B. M. Catalogue, 13 M.M. a. 1582."

Probably the last instance in Lincolnshire of the public burning of books, deemed to be of an obnoxious character, was the destruction of Tom Paine's works on the Cornhill, Lincoln, after they had been suspended awhile from the gallows; and when the Mayor and Corporation of Lincoln in their gowns, witnessed that act.

ECCLESIASTICAL HISTORY.

There was a church and a priest here when Domesday Book was compiled. The patronage of the former was in the hands of Remigius, Bishop of Lincoln, and long remained in those of his successors.

The vicarage was founded and endowed in 1274,* of which the original record still remains in the Bishop's Registry at Lincoln. From this we gather that Henry de Sinderby was presented by Richard de Belleau, Treasurer of Lincoln, and Prebendary of the church of Sleaford, to the vicarage of the same church, and was instituted by the Bishop at Lydington, on the 4th of the nones of March. The vicarage consisted of all portions and profits appertaining to the alterage by whatever name

---

* In 1252 the famous Robert Copley, or Grostete, obtained permission from the Pope to institute Vicarages in churches where there had been none so far, and to augment those that were slenderly endowed, at his pleasure. "Hollinshed's Chronicle, Vol. 3, reign of Henry III."; but Benedict de Gravesend was Bishop of Lincoln, in 1274, when the Vicarage of Sleaford was founded.

known, viz: the tythes of wool, lambs, calves, pigs, pullets, geese, curtilages, flax and hemp; also four principal oblations in the year, with other oblations of what kind soever, and oblations placed under the candles with all manner of mortuaries, and the tenths of private merchants; to it was also given the tythes of mills and fisheries, a house near the church, which Roger the chaplain formerly inhabited; and at the cost of the Prebendary a sufficient road to the said house was to be made; the vicar for the time being was to pay to the Prebendary yearly fifteen marks at the feasts of the Nativity of our Lord and St. John the Baptist by equal portions, and to serve Sleaford church by himself and another priest or deacon, and other proper ministers, and to maintain ten wax torches and one lamp burning in the church; but the Prebendary was to retain all his right of jurisdiction in the Prebend, and was to sustain all ordinary and extraordinary burdens, also to build and repair the chancel and find books and other necessary ornaments for the church, which might be needed, and the vicar extraordinary ones by a rate on his portion, found by a legal inquisition to amount to the sum of twenty marks, the aforesaid fifteen marks excepted; and no more.

From the above record it is clear that the Prebend of Sleaford existed previous to the year 1274, and most probably Remigius or one of his successors was its founder, as the patronage has always been in the hands of the Bishops of Lincoln. This was endowed with the great tithes of Sleaford, and its proceeds were valued in the King's books at £11 19s. 7d., and in 1616 at £13 a year, when the Prebendary was patron, and the number of communicants 440. " Willis's M.S., p. 37" A pension of 57s. 1d. used to be paid annually to the Dean and Chapter of Lincoln.

Upon the inclosure of the parish of New Sleaford in 1797, 500 acres of land, in that portion of Holdingham called the Anna, were allotted to the Prebendary and his lessee in lieu of the greater rectorial tithes. The Rectory at that time was held by the Earl of Bristol as lessee under the Reverend Basil Bury Beridge, then Prebendary. The lease of the Rectory shortly afterwards become vested in Richard Yerburgh, Esq., to whose son, the Rev. Richard Yerburgh, D.D., a renewed lease was granted for three lives in 1829, by the Right Rev. John Matthias

Turner, Bishop of Calcutta, then Prebendary. Upon the death of Bishop Turner, the Rectory, subject to the lease, passed into the hands of the Ecclesiastical Commissioners. In 1847 the lessee's interest in the farm at Ho`dingham Anna was sold by the late Dr. Yerburgh, to the late Anthony Willson, Esq., of Rauceby, who in 1853 acquired the fee simple by purchase from the Ecclesiastical Commissioners ; but the patronage of the Vicarage, with the tithe yard adjoining the churchyard, was reserved, and will remain in the gift of Dr. Yerburgh's family until the termination of the lease, when it will pass into the hands of the Bishop of Lincoln.

The following is a list of the Prebendaries of Lafford, or Sleaford :

Date of Institution.

Circa 1274.—Richard de Belleau
   1279.—John de Wydrington
    .—Roger de Martival
   1293.—William de Stockton
   1310.—Thomas de Bray
   1316.—Peter de Dalderby
   1322.—Luchin, alias Anthony de Flisko
   1327.—William de Exon
   1336.—Geoffery de Groppo
   1340.—William de Cusance
   1369.—John Ufford
   1376.—Thomas de la Warre
   1390.—William Halswell
   1418.—Ralph Lowth
   1432.—Richard Tone, L.L.D.
   1434.—Nicholas Clark
   1459.—Thomas Salisbury
   1460.—John Sapton
   1463.—Thomas Gauge
   1465.—Nicholas Rawdon
   1479.—Richard Langton, S T.P.
   1482.—Richard Norton, L.L.D.
   1492.—Nicholas Haleswell
   1520.—James Mallett
   1533.—Thomas Robertson

Date of Institution.

Circa 1536.—Owen Oglethorpe, S.T.P.

       1557.—John Hurd or Herd, M.D. *

       1588.—George Huddleston

       1613.—John Williams, S.T.P.

       1614.—Nicholas Greenhill

       1660.—John Mantel

       1668.—John Lee

       1670.—Thomas Meriton

       1683.—George Thomason, A.M.

       1686.—Thomas Meriton

       1712.—William Wake

       1712.—Thomas Seller, A.M.

       1737.—Henry Gibert

       1770.—Basil Bury Beridge

       1808.—Charles Proby, A.M.

       1822.—George Turnor, L.L.B.

       1824.—John Matthias Turner, A.M.

       1829.—Edward Smedley, M.A.

       1843.—John Coker, B.C.L.

       1867.—Robert Bateman Paul, A.M.

After the Commonwealth was established, the then vicar of Sleaford was expelled from his cure, and the church was desecrated, and robbed of its brass lectern and other valuables. Puritan Ministers then obtained possession of the church, of whom Richard Milward died 1656, and was succeeded by George Boheme, a Pomeranian of Colberg, born in 1628. He was ejected by the Act of Uniformity passed in 1662, when he retired to Walcot near Falkingham, where he kept a school, and was allowed to preach in the Church there by the Incumbent, until this was stopped by Bishop Gardiner because Boheme had never been ordained, and was simply a dissenting preacher. He died at Falkingham, September 9th, 1711, aged 83, and was buried there. Several suffering clergymen living at Sleaford, who had

---

* The following reference to Dr. Hurd is made in one of the Bishop's Registers. "Lafford Decanatus. Sleaford. Johannes Herd, in medicinis doctor, habet peculiarem jurisdictionem in et per totam parochiam ididem, et Dominus Georgius Cocket, vicarius institutus, habet curam animorum in eadem parochiâ, quæ consistit de villâ de Sleaford, in quâ sunt familiæ VII. atque hamlet de Holdingham, ubi familiæ xx.

been harshly ejected from their livings by the Puritans, regained possession of them, after the Restoration ; such as Thomas Gibson, first, master of the Free Grammar School of Carlisle, and then vicar of Horncastle, who, after having been deprived of his living, and imprisoned at Hull, Lincoln, and Tattershall, was elected master of the Free School at Newark in 1644. In 1650 he was appointed master of the Sleaford Grammar School by Elizabeth Lady Carre, and retained that post until the Restoration, when, accompanied by several hundred rejoicing friends, he regained possession of his vicarage at Horncastle, and was made Prebendary of St. Mary Crackpool by Bishop Saunderson. On the other hand several extruded ministers came to live at Sleaford or in the neighbourhood, such as Theophilus Brittaine, Colonel King's dissenting chaplain, who was minister of Brocklesby during the Commonwealth, but being ejected at the Restoration, turned farmer at Roxholm ; subsequently he took part in Monmouth's rebellion, and, with Nathan Drake, the then disloyal rector of Leasingham, and some others, was imprisoned at Grantham. He died 1696, and was buried at Sleaford. The vicarage is valued in the King's books at £8., and is discharged.

The following is a list of the Vicars of Sleaford, extracted from the Bishop's Registers at Lincoln : *

A.D. 1274—Henry de Sinderby.

—Richard de Bray

1313.—John de Kirkeby

1336.—Henry de Levesingham, or Lessingham

1340.—Thomas de Werdale

1343.—Richard de Hugate

1349.—John Whittlelegh

1391.—Thomas le Warre

1404.—William Smyth of Rauceby

1416.—William Penyman

1416.—William Hoghton

1432.—John Bower

* These Registers, extending from Bishop Hugh de Welles's episcopate, 1209, to that of Bishop Barlow, 1608, are extremely valuable, and in an excellent state of preservation. Those of Bishops Welles, Grostete, Lexington, Gravesend, and Sutton, constitute rolls, the others are written in large parchment volumes. The endowments of the Vicarages of the Diocese are contained in Bishop Welles's roll of Institutions, written in a small good hand.

A.D. 1467.—John Walker

1468.—Richard Mareys

1477.—Richard West

1489.—Adam Grafton

1491.—Gilbert Cowell

1515.—John Godfre

1539.—William Warre

1545.—Robert Bayt

1553.—George Cocket

1577.—Joseph Overton

1587.—Thomas Westcott

1606.—Edmund Newton

1618.—Richard Flear

1630.—Robert Alford, A.M.

1640.—Miles Long

1644.—Richard Milward

1656.—George Boheme

1660.—Henry Allen

1682.—William Wyche *

1691.—Edward Smith, A.M.

1703.—Thomas Seller, A.M.

1737.—William Seller, A.M.

1769.—Edward Smith

1780.—John Plampin

1781.—Edward Waterson, A.M. †

1809.—Richard Yerburgh, D.D.

1851.—Richard Yerburgh, B.A., the present patron of
the Vicarage.

The oldest Register of Sleaford parish commences with the
date 1575, only 36 years after the first order for keeping such
records was issued by Henry VIII. The following are a few of
the most interesting entries they contain :—

1588—Edward Barnard, gentilman, was Xtned. 1601—Two strangers,
young men, that were found kyld in our field were buried in our church-yard.
1602—A child Xtned the day of its father's burial. 1614—Two ran from
Sleaford with a license, and Mr. Morice married them. 1638—A poor stranger
boy found dead in our field. 1639—Goodwife Washingborough the elder

---

* Subsequently Rector of Silk Willoughby.

† Subsequently Rector of Quarrington.

buried.　1656—Lancellot Foster of Lincoln, gent., stabbed by a soldier, Thomas Nicholls was hanged for the same, and Mr. Foster was buried. 1662—Old Goodman Squire of Holdingham, buried.　1663—Mr. Robert Cook (burnt in his fired stable), buried.　1665—John Waite buried of the plague. 1698—A soldier kill'd and buried.　1728—A father and his child baptized together.　1751—The bell knolled for the Prince of Wales 4 hours.　1760— The bell knolled for king George II. 12 hours.　1775, was buried the wife of William Farmery, who was murdered by her son.　The above William Farmery died a few days after this melancholy fate of his wife's, having been sexton of the parish 49 years.　1817—On November 19th, the bell tolled, in minute time, from eight o'clock at night until twelve, being four hours, in consequence of the funeral of the Princess Charlotte of Wales.　1818—The bell tolled one hour on the death of her majesty queen Charlotte.　1820—On January 30th, Sleaford passing bell, after ringing as usual on the death of a male, tolled twelve hours, viz : from one o'clock in the day, as soon as the melancholy news arrived by the mail, till one o'clock in the night, for his late majesty king George III., as was the the the case with king George II.　1821— On August 8th, the passing bell tolled for queen Caroline one hour, as it did for queen Charlotte.

The following is an extract from another parish book, commencing with the year 1606, and ending in that of 1627, which is interesting as giving a list of the church goods at that time :—

1606—John Parke, Senr., and Henry Carre, Church-Wardens.　Edward Newton, Vicar.

1607—Book signed by Robert Cammock & Richard Warsope on account of goods delivered to the new Church-Wardens.

Imprimis.　In money ———— 3lb. 9s. ijd.

Item—A Comunion table, & a carpett & a table clothe.

Item—A Comunion cuppe with a cover.

Item—2 quart pewter potts, & a new pewter pott of 3 quarts.

Item—One Surplice and a Hood.

Item—One Darning Covering for a Beare, given by J. Parke, Sr.

Item—One pulpit cloth, & a cushen, given by J. Parke, Sr.

Item—One brazen Eagle.*

item—One great Beare, & 2 lesser Beares.

Item—Tree yron Hookes.

Item—One great cable rope to hoyst up Bells, & one little rope.

Item—One ould Hutch, & one ould Chist, given by Mil. Hailes.

Item—Nine pieces of yron for the Organs.

Item—One long ladder given by John Parke, Senr.

Item—One great locke.

Item—One ton of lead, One Web, & one peece of a Web.

Item—Erasmus, his paraphrase & Bullenghers Decades.

---

* Mentioned for the last time in 1622.

The Church.

This is dedicated to St. Dionysius, or as he is now commonly called, St. Denis, and is by far the most beautiful and attractive building in the town. Its west front not only at once commands attention, but has the merit of continuing to please when all its features have become thoroughly well known. This arises from the variety of its component parts quite as much as from their individual character. From the midst springs a venerable tower, which had been endangered by the insertion of arches in three of its walls and a window in the fourth, but the original solidity of which has of late years been reverentially confirmed through the varied resources summoned to its aid by a skilful architect of the present century. As in the case of Lincoln Cathedral, this, constituting a part of the original fabric, has been here retained and incorporated into a later one. It is certainly not so old as the time of Bishop Alexander, during whose episcopate it is said to have been built, and which terminated in 1147; there being more reason to suppose that it formed part of a church erected during the episcopate of Bishop Gravesend, perhaps partly at his own cost, and partly at that of Richard de Belleau, treasurer of Lincoln, prebendary of Sleaford, and patron of the vicarage. Subsequently Bishop Alnwick left 40s. to be expended on the fabric. In the south-west angle of the tower is a beautifully finished newel staircase, the whole being of the early part of the 13th century, when the Early English style was thoroughly in vogue, but when the round-headed arch was still often blended with the pointed one. The bold mouldings, the banded shafts, and the stiffly foliated capitals of the belfry window lights are well worthy of notice, as well as the angle shaft of the southern buttress. The spire is well placed upon the tower, and evidently shows how satisfactorily it is fulfilling its duty as a covering to the same. As it is one of the earliest examples of a spire remaining to us, it is the more valuable, on this account. The break in the upward run of the octangular lines near its top, where they assume a quadrangular form, is a quaint feature that is not often seen. The height of the tower and spire together is 144 feet. Of the same period with that of the tower there was once certainly a nave, and at least a south aisle. The roof pitch of the former is still indicated on the eastern face of the tower,

and the extent of the latter is marked by a piece of walling
at the east end of the present south aisle, below the plinth.   The
north doorway is also of the same date.   About 1370 the whole
of the present nave with its aisles overlapping the tower, excepting the new outer north aisle, was built.   It, like its predecessor,
had a high-pitched roof, as may still be seen.   Externally the
tower, flanked and supported by the aisles, constitutes a very
pleasing composition; and while inclined cornices honestly indicate
the slope of the aisle-roofs behind, richly carved perforated parapets above, in conjunction with central bell-cots and exquisite
angle pinnacles, give considerably increased dignity to the western elevation.   The doorway, in the end of the south aisle, originally opened into a chantry, and the numerous enriched niches
beside and above it were no doubt once filled with figures of
saints.   The beautiful gabled doorway, at the end of the north
aisle cuts into the window above it, which last is rather too large.
The figure of a female saint still remains in one of the canopied
niches of the west end of this aisle, as does another of St. Margaret in the adjacent angle turret.   The south elevation, with its
varied and delicately-moulded aisle windows, is a fine piece of
ecclesiastical architecture of the Decorated period, that any town
might be proud to possess, and one scarcely surpassed in beauty
by any in England.   On this side is a very beautiful porch
both as to design and detail.   Below is a crypt, access to which
is supplied by means of an entrance in the west wall.   This was
probably simply intended to be used as a vault.

The transept was next added, perhaps some ten or twenty
years later ; and that it was an addition not at first contemplated,
is clear from a remaining jamb of the east window of the original
south aisle.   This was long used as a school-room, but is now
purged from such desecration.

During the prevalance of the Perpendicular period the
chancel was rebuilt, the clerestory was added to the nave, with
its richly panelled and embattled parapet, surmounted by numerous crocketed pinnacles, and its moulded panelled roof within,
formerly adorned with shields bearing, Gu, a lion rampant
regardant Arg. Gu, 3 bendlets Or. and Gu, 3 goats heads erased
Arg.   " Harl. M.S.S., 6829, p. 288." Then also the present
arches were inserted in the tower, together with its stone vaulting
and its west window.   Breaks in the chancel walls, near their

junction with the nave, show where the newer work commenced, and an external weather-moulding marks the pitch of the earlier roof. The chancel will not bear any comparison with the nave, yet from the additional length it gives to the fabric its value is considerable.

A few years ago the whole of the north wall of the north aisle exactly corresponded with that of the opposite or south aisle ; but as more accommodation was required, this was pulled down and re-erected more towards the north, so as to form a second aisle, separated from the original one by a new arcade. The north elevation is much less ornate than the southern one, but yet is by no means plain. Within, a most striking improvement was effected at the same time, 1853, when this church, after having been thoroughly and most appropriately restored, at a cost of £3,500, was again opened for divine service; and perhaps no other is now better adapted to the purposes of public worship. The following are its internal dimensions, viz :—length (including the chancel), 154 feet ; breadth of the nave, 64 feet ; breadth of the chancel, 25 feet ; length of the transept, 45 feet ; breadth, 25 feet. The lofty arcades of four bays each, with their manifold mouldings and their slender clustered pillars are very admirable. Originally there were certainly chapels at each end of the south aisle, as indicated by their beautiful canopied piscinæ which remain, although their enclosing screens have long since disappeared. In the wall of what was once the westernmost chapel is a sepulchral arch, but this with the piscina adjoining are of later date than the wall in which they are inserted.

The chancel screen, with its overhanging canopy, its central projecting feature, its varied outline, and its richly-worked details—pronounced by Pugin to be one of the most perfect in England—not only constitutes an unusually beautiful specimen of mediæval oak carving, but also affords relief to the great expanse of stonework by which it is surmounted. On the north of this are two staircases—one leading to the rood-loft, the other to the transept roof, within a turret. There is also another similar staircase to the rood-loft on the southern side of the chancel arch ; but these are now blocked up by the Carre monuments at their bases, which will be subsequently described. The pulpit, with its deeply cut oak panels, rising from a stone base, is a good example of modern design and workmanship. The Decorated

M

font, at the west end of the north aisle, is the original one, but has been too freely repaired. In this part of the church a clever expedient was adopted for the purpose of strengthening the tower, in the form of a buttress, combined with an arch, the structural character of which is worthy of notice. The sedilia and east window in the chancel are fair examples of Perpendicular work. The tracery of the former is so designed as to form a large cross, which has of late years been made more conspicuous by the distinctive colouring of the glass inserted in it. Adjoining the chancel on the north side is a small coeval sacristy, now used as a vestry. There are as many as 32 windows in this church, some of which have been filled with painted glass as memorials. Several crosses within circles will be observed painted upon the walls, which were disclosed on the removal of the plaster. From their form they might have been of a much earlier period than they really are, such crosses being both cut and painted on very ancient christian churches erected within some of the heathen temples of Egypt, as reminiscences of their dedication to God's service ; but as some of these crosses appear on the walls of the chancel, they cannot be earlier than the 15th century, and are probable reminiscences of the period when the existing chancel was consecrated.

In the tower hangs a peal of eight bells, cast by Thomas Osborn, of Downham, Norfolk, in the year 1796. The weight of the tenor bell is nineteen hundred weight, three quarters, and six pounds, and is in the key E. They bear the following inscriptions :—

    1.—The Lord to praise, my voice I'll raise.
    2.—Give no offence to the church.
    3.—Peace and good neighbourhood.
    4.—Edward Waterson, vicar.
    5.—Long live king George the third.
    6.—William Kirton and George Robinson, Churchwardens.
    7.—These eight bells were cast in the year 1796.
    8.—I to the church the living call,
      And to the grave do summon all.
          Thomas Osborn, Founder, Downham, Norfolk.

Previously there were only six bells, one of which bore no inscription, but the others were thus lettered :—

    1.—A. R., founder.　Thomas Seller, Vicar.
      T. Harriman & W. S., Ch. W.　1707.

2.—Jhesus be our speede. 1600.
    Prayes ye the Lorde. 1600.
4.—God save the Church, our Queen, and Realm,
    And send us peace through Christ, Amen. 1600.
5.—This town subscribed to have me here,
    Thro him whose name below I bear.

Geo. Arnett.

Then also there were chimes connected with the works of the clock, which played at four, nine, and twelve o'clock every day. The morning bell sounds at six o'clock and the evening one at eight o'clock, representing the curfew, or couvre-few bell, ordered to be rung by the Conqueror.

The communion plate is very handsome, and is thus inscribed :—

Ex dono Annæ Ashby, Gul. Ashby de Leicestriæ, Armig. nuper uxoris. On two pieces.

Donum Parochiale.

Ex dono Dorothæ Roper, Jos. Roper, D. D. Relictæ.

Ex dono Thomæ Seller, A. M. Hujus ecclesiæ per 34 Annos nuper Vicarius, 1737.

And on a piece given by the Earl of Bristol in the year 1810. Sleaford Church.

During the fanaticism of the Commonwealth times this church is supposed to have been dealt with very gently, comparatively speaking; nevertheless, the following extract from the parish register, dated 1647, records plainly enough the general disorder that then prevailed :—" *Per totum hoc triennium bella civilia inter Regem & Parliament^m omnia turbant & perturbant, omnes constitutiones ecclesiasticas & quamplurimas politicas vertunt, & evertunt. Quid mirum si per hos annos multa omnino in hoc Registro valde imperfectè tractent^r*." Then, the painted glass of this church was destroyed, rich with the armorial bearings of several Bishops of Lincoln and those of the Hussey, Wymundham, and other families; then the seating was torn up and cast on one side, according to tradition, so as to convert it into a barrack for the Parliamentary soldiery; then its plate was not considered too superstitious to find its way into the pockets of the despoilers : then its organ was destroyed, its fine brass eagle lectern was broken up for the sake of the metal; and in fact all that could either be readily injured or abstracted, was maltreated or stolen; but perhaps we can not fairly attribute those marks of fire on the piers and arches about the chancel screen to the Puritans, as this last fortunately still remains, and was probably substituted for an older one accidentally destroyed by fire. The organ was replaced in 1772 by Mr. Edward Evans,* at a cost of £300, and has since been added to, improved, and repaired, so as to render it, at least, in some degree, worthy of the church in which it stands. Happily we live in more truly Christian days, when none would injure buildings dedicated to God's service, however widely we may still differ as to our religious principles or opinions, and when we are at least more disposed to combine for the public good than to separate in hostility.

It was probably thought that when the present Bishop of Lincoln ordained five persons in Sleaford Church last year, such an interesting sight had never been witnessed there before ; but from certain records in the Bishop's registry we find that he was then simply following the example of some of his predecessors in this respect, viz. :—" Ordines celebrati in eccl prebendal de Sleford, Non. Apr. 1432, p John Stephon, auctoritate episc, &c." " Ordines celebrati apud Sleaford, 14 Kal Jan, 1472, pr Thos. Roth, vice et auctoritate Tho epus Lincoln." " John Chambre de Corringham, ordinatur pbr 5 Kal Apr. 1479, apud Sleeford, p. Thos. Rothram, epum."

CHANTRIES.

In 1271 Thomas Blount and John de Bucham, merchants of Sleaford, founded a chantry, which they constructed in the north aisle of Sleaford church. This was dedicated to the Virgin Mary for the benefit of the founders' souls, and those of their predecessors. It was richly endowed with lands and tenements in Old and New, or Great Sleaford, Holdingham, Quarrington, Kirkby-Laythorpe and Evedon ; all of which were to be held of the founders while living, for the maintenance of a perpetual service at the altar of the chantry chapel. The chaplain enjoying

---

* The builder was Greene, of London. On the south side of the churchyard is the grave of the donor, marked by a stone thus inscribed : To the memory of Mr. Edward Evans, who died Jany. 20th, 1780, aged 58 years. He was surgeon to his Majesty's ship the Egmont, and after a successful voyage from America (being a patron of the musical science) he gave an organ to this parish, in the year 1772.

this care was, with his clerk, to celebrate a full service of the Virgin, or Mass, after the great Mass, in which he was to make especial mention of the founders of the chantry in his prayers, and this daily, unless Sunday services and other solemnities should prevent his doing so. He was also to celebrate Vespers, Matins, and other Hours of the Virgin before the said altar daily, without note, except on the principal Feasts of the Virgin, and was to take part in the canonical Hours with the parochial choir, and to aid the vicar if needed, gratuitously. The furniture of the chapel and its altar, such as the chalice, books, vessels, vestments, lights and ornaments of the same, for which the founders had made ample provision, were to be kept and maintained by the chaplain, and none were to be alienated. The presentation to the chantry was to be retained by the founders for life, but after their death, they willed that three worthy men of Lafford, elected by the community of the same, should have the power to present after having made oath that they would faithfully fulfil this duty, and then the chaplain on his part was to make oath, before the Dean and Chapter of Lincoln that he would faithfully execute his duties, and do nothing to injure the greater or lesser oblations of the parish church of Sleaford, and to repeat that oath before the Prebendary of Lafford, then Richard de Belleau, Treasurer of Lincoln. If these three should not present within 20 days after a vacancy, the Dean and Chapter were to present. If the chaplain should become unworthy or inefficient he was to be removed by the Dean and Chapter, and another appointed; but if through age or infirmity he could not fulfil his duties he was to provide a fitting assistant at his own charge. During vacancies all the profits of the chantry were to be reserved by the founders while they lived, and subsequently by the Dean and Chapter for the next chaplain. If the founders disagreed in their selection of a fresh chaplain, the Dean and Chapter were to decide the choice.

To this deed, taken in duplicate, the seals of the Dean and Chapter of Lincoln, the Treasurer of Lincoln, and the founders were attached in the chapter house at Lincoln, in the month of January, 1271. One copy was to be kept in the Treasury at Lincoln, the other by the founders. "Ex lib de ord Cant. fol. 46." At the suppression of chantries, the incumbent, Robert Walrood, then 40 years of age, had the profits amounting to £4 5s. 0d. clear, after the payment of 15s. due to the Duke of Somerset as

Lord of the Manor of Sleaford. Then also it is noted, that a toft in Old Sleaford, worth 9s. 4d. a year, belonging to the chantry had been unjustly seized by Thomas Horseman.

This chantry chapel must have been reconstructed during the 14th century, but probably in the same relative position as before, viz : at the east end of the north aisle of Sleaford church, and when it was restored, a stone plinth and part of a carved oak screen, which had stood upon it, were disclosed between the coupled pillar at the east end of the north aisle, and the first pillar westward of it, whence no doubt another screen ran across the aisle, and thus chancelled off the easternmost bay of this aisle, that constituted St. Mary's chapel.

Another chantry chapel certainly existed in connection with Sleaford church, but by whom founded and where situated, is not recorded. This was worth £3 0s. 6d. at the dissolution of chantries, out of which 10s. had to be paid as a reprise to the Duke of Somerset.

Until very lately the east wall of the chancel was plain and bare, having nothing to relieve it but two equally plain aumbry recesses, and two crosses within circles painted upon it. For a time it and the greater part of the window above had been covered by a classical oak screen, designed by Sir Christopher Wren for Lincoln Cathedral, but subsequently ejected from it, when its utter incongruity with all the beautiful Gothic features around it became apparent to the then Dean and Chapter, and it found a temporary asylum within Sleaford church; but eventually being thought equally incongruous there, it was cast out thence, as it had been from the Cathedral, and the bare wall behind it was preferred to such a cumbrous inappropriate ornament. Now, a beautiful Gothic reredos of finely carved Ancaster stone, clothes this wall as far as it requires such an application, erected in memory of the late Mr. M. P. Moore, of Sleaford, from designs by Mr. Charles Kirk. The lower part consists of an arcade with crocketed canopies and panels of Minton's encaustic tiles ; over the altar table is a very delicately diapered central panel, in the middle of which is a quatrefoil containing a cross, and above, the words " This is my body. This is my blood." carved upon a rich foliated cornice. On either side of the window the reredos rises as high as the springing of its arch, in the form of pedimented niches supported by green marble shafts, which niches will perhaps hereafter be filled with coloured figures of Angels, Evangelists, or Apostles, to obviate the coldness of its present appearance.

At the same time the space within the altar rail was paved with encaustic tiling, the upper part in memory of the late Dr. Yerburgh, vicar of Sleaford, and the lower part in memory of the late Rev. H. Manton, master of the Sleaford grammar school.

MONUMENTS.

The oldest tombstone in this church is a grey marble slab in the south aisle. This is of the 13th century, and has a border legend in detached Lombardic letters, now so worn away as to be illegible.

Of the 14th century is a small brass plate found during the recent restoration of the church, and now attached to the wall of the tower staircase at the entrance to the south aisle. This bears the following legend :—

> Quisquis eris qui transieris. sta. p lege. plora.
> Sū qᵈ. eris. fuerā qᵈ. es. pro me. precor. ora.
> Disce. qᵈ. es. et quid eris. memer esto qᵈ. morieris.

Also a grey slab in the pavement of the south aisle, which has evidently borne the effigy of an ecclesiastic with a legend plate below, and a small scroll on either side, all of which however are now gone.

Of the 15th century is this inscription neatly cut on a stone beneath the external face of the east window sill.

> Orate pro aiab Ricardi Dokke (or Cokke) & Johanne uxoris
> ejus. Johis filii eorum, & oium benefactorum, quorum aibus
> propitietur Deus Ano MCCCCº XXX.

Also another cut on the plinth below the sill of the westernmost window of the south aisle running thus :—

> Here lyeth William Harebeter and Elizabeth his wife
> Chryest Ihu graunte yem everlastyng lyfe.

Of the 16th century Holles saw many monuments which are now gone, viz : in the chancel three thus inscribed :—

> Here lyeth the body of Richard Buller, Priest, who deceased
> the 21st day of August, 1540.
> Hic jacet Rob'tus Bayt, Vicarius, qui obiit 30º die Maii,
> A'no D'ni 1553.
> Hic jacet Jo'hes Godfray, Vicarius, qui obiit 25º die Julii,
> Anno D'ni 1539. Cujus a'i'æ, &c.

There are, however, two memorials of this century still remaining, which are not mentioned by Holles, viz : a slab in the north aisle bearing a brass plate thus inscribed :—

> Here lyeth ye bodie of Rycherd Pikeworth, mercer, ye which depted this world ye XXIII daie of Julie in ye year of our Lord God MCCCCCLVII of whose soull God have mercie, Amen.

Below this is his trade mark between his initials R. P. Holles observed the only monuments of the Carre family then existing. The first was a raised tomb in the nave bearing this inscription :—

> Hic Jacet Georgius Carre et Anna uxor ejus, qui quidem Georgius obiit—Ano. Dni. 1521.

He was the first of the family who settled at Sleaford. The grey marble slab of this tomb is now laid in the floor of the chancel. It is 8 feet 6½ inches long, and 4 feet 2 inches wide. At the four angles were inserted as many brass shields, each charged with the Carre bearings. Three of these still remain, but have lost their enamel colouring. Towards the upper part were the effigies of George and Anne Carre—engraved also on brass plates. His effigy is now preserved at the vicarage, and represents him in his merchant's dress. That of his wife still remains. She is depicted in the pointed and lappeted cap, the long gown with large furred cuffs, and long pendent girdle of her period, and with her hands conjoined in prayer. Immediately below these was a narrow brass plate—now lost, on which the epitaph was inscribed, and, beneath this again a group of four kneeling sons below their father, and a corresponding group of three daughters below their mother, both of which still remain.

The other monument Holles noticed was one of alabaster, near the chancel, which still stands against the wall of the staircase leading to the rood loft in the angle between the north aisle and chancel walls, and close to the northern respond of the chancel arch. This consists of a base suggestive of an altar tomb, whence spring pilasters panelled with grey marble, supporting a flat canopy ; above this is a grey marble obelisk at each corner, and in the centre springing from some ornamental work, a circlet, on which are carved the Carre and Bartram* bearings, viz : Gu on a chevron Or, 3 mullets Sa, quartering Or, an orle Arg, surmounted by a mantled helm

---

* Barons of Mitford.

with the Carre crest, viz : a stag's head couped Arg, attired Or, and about the neck 2 bars gemelles Gu, painted, and gilt.   At the back of the recess below this canopy is a pedestal, on the front of which is a large shield bearing the same device impaling, Arg, a chevron Sa between 3 martlets, on a chief Sa, 3 cross crosslets Or.—Cawdron, for Elizabeth first wife of Robert Carre.   On either side above are small shields on which were painted the following bearings in Holles's time, but of which a portion only now remains, viz ; Arg a saltire Gu, on a chief Gu 3 escallops of the first,—Tailboys, for Robert Carre's second wife.   Arg, a bend Sa within a border engrailed of the same.—Knyvet, for Anne Knyvet the third wife.   Or, on a chevron between 3 annulets Gu, 3 crescents of the first.—Sutton, for Mary Sutton, wife of Robert Carre's eldest son George.   Arg, on a fesse France and England, a border gobony, Arg & Az.—Somerset, for Elizabeth, daughter of Henry, Earl of Worcester, the widow of Lord Grey de Wilton, and wife of Robert, second son of Robert Carre.   Fourteen closets Arg & Gu, 3 martlets 2 and 1 Sa. —Chaworth, for Bridget, daughter of John Chaworth, and wife of William Carre, Robert's third son.   Az, 3 bowls Or jessant de boar's heads Arg.—Bolle, for Catherine, daughter of Charles Bolle, of Scampton, wife of Edward, afterwards Sir Edward Carre, Robert's fourth son.   Sa, a bend between 2 cottises fleury Arg.—Kelke, for Christopher Kelke, second husband of Robert Carre's eldest daughter, Elizabeth.   Erm, two sangliers trippant Gu.—Whichcote, for Robert Whichcote, first husband of Anne, Robert Carre's second daughter.   Arg, on a bend, Sa 3 roses of the first, Rosseter, for Richard Rosseter, husband of Bridget, third daughter of Robert Carre.   This monument bears the following inscription :—

> Here lieth bvried Robert Carre, Esqvire, who by his first wife Elizabeth yᵉ davghter of William Cawdron, Esqvire, had yssve 4 sonnes & 3 davghters.   George Carre, his eldest sonne, by Marie yᵉ davghter of Ambrose Svtton, Esqvire, had yssve Robert Carre, the nowe heire livinge.   Robert Carre, his seconde sonne, first married Marie yᵉ davghter of .... Earl of Worcestr, then widdow to .... Lord Gray of Wilton, & afterwardes he married Cassandra yᵉ davghter of .... Price, Esqvire.   Willi Carre his thirde sonne, married Bridgett the davghter of Sʳ John Chaworth, Knight, one of the Gentlewoemen of yᵉ

Qveene's Maties Privie Chamber.   And Edward Carre
his fourth sonne, married Katherine ye davghter
of Charles Bolle, Esqvire.   Elizabeth his eldest
davghter, first married Willia Fairefaxe, Esqvire,
& afterwards Christopher Kelke, Esqvire.   Anne
his seconde davghter, first married Robert Whitchcote,
Esquire, & afterwards Christopher Legerde, Esqvire.
And Bridgett his third davght^r married Richard
Rosseter, Esqvire.

The first saide Robert Carre, secondlie married
Anne the davghter of S^r. George Tailboyes,
Knight, then widdow to S^r. Edward Dymocke,
Knight.   And thirdlie Anne the davghter of
Charles Knivett, and died, without yssve
by them, the xi daie of September, Anno
Domini 1590.

Above is this inscription :—

"Christus mihi vita, et mors mihi lucrum ; or, To me
to live is Christ, and to die is gain."

In a corresponding position on the southern side of the
chancel arch is a similar but grander monument, commemorating Robert Carre's fourth son, but eventually his heir—Sir
Edward Carre, Bart., and probably his second wife, Anne Dyer.
It is composed of alabaster, relieved by an admixture of grey
marble, paint, and gilding.   On a base or altar tomb are placed
the effigies of Sir Edward and his wife.   His is placed in front
upon a mattress, the end of which is so folded up as to form
a rest for the head.   He is represented in the armour and
dress of his time, with a formal ruff round his neck, and his
sword by his side.   The ankles, feet, and greater part of the
right arm are now gone.   Lady Carre's effigy is more perfect,
but although the hands are lost, we can see that these, like
those of her husband's, were raised in prayer.   She wears the
pendent veil, tight bodice—buttoned down the front, the thickly
plaited skirt, looped together, and mantle depending from the
shoulders, of the time of James I.   Her hair is crisply curled,
and her head rests upon an embroidered cushion.   Behind is a
highly ornamented dossier, or back piece, which, with its demi
returns and composite pillars at the front angles, serve to support
a flat canopy similarly enriched with carving.   On the front of
the cornice is a grey marble insertion within a carved alabaster
frame and various sepulchral emblems, and its under face is

MONUMENT OF SIR EDWARD CARR IN SLEAFORD CHURCH.

panelled and decorated with gilt roses. Above this canopy is a grey marble obelisk at each of the front angles, placed on alabaster bases, and in the middle a panel between two piers supporting a cornice, on which is a large shield bearing Carre quartering Bartram, with the Baronet's hand on a canton, surmounted by the Carre helm, crest, and mantling, filling up the rest of the panel. In the middle of the dossier is the epitaph on a black marble slab, which runs thus :—

> Here lyeth the bodye of Sʳ. Edward Carre, Knight and Baronett, who maried two wyves. The first was Katherine, davghter of Charles Boll, Esqvier, by whom he had noe issve. His second wief was Ann the davghter of Sʳ. Richard Dyer, of Stovghton in yᵉ covnty of Hvntingdon, Knight, by whom he had issve two sonnes and one davghter, vidlᵗ. Sʳ. Robert, now Baronett, Rosseter, and Lvcy, He departed this lief the first daie of October, Anno Domini
>
> 1618.

This is surrounded by a carved frame having four groups of funereal objects below, such as bones, a skull, coffin lid, book, pick-axe, shovel; and also such emblems of death as an hourglass, scythe, darts, and reversed torches. On either side are naked boys as mourners holding reversed torches, of which the lower ends alone now remain, and above are wings and an hourglass surmounted by a steelyard evenly balanced.

At the south eastern angle of the transept is a noble altar tomb composed of black and white marble, and surmounted by a grand slab of black marble. This commemorates the Right Honorable Sir Robert Carre, Kt., 3rd Bart., and Chancellor of the Duchy of Lancaster, and his young son Sir Edward Carre, 4th, and the last Bart., who died under age. It is thus inscribed on the south side :—

> Within
>
> Resteth yᵉ body of yᵉ Right Honᵇˡᵉ Sʳ. ROBERT CARR, of Sleaford, in yᵉ Covnty of Lincolne, Kt. & Barroᵗ., Chancellor of yᵉ Dvtchy & Covnty Palatine of Lancaster, and one of his Maties Most Honᵇˡᵉ Privie Covncell.
>
> Son of Sʳ. ROBERT CARR, of Sleeford, Barrᵗ. and Dame MARY his Wife.
>
> Hee married ELIZABETH BENNET, one of the davghters of Sʳ. JOHN BENNET, of Harlington, in yᵉ Covnty of Middlesex, Kt. by whome hee had issve sonns and davghters.
>
> Hee departed this life November yᵉ 14th, in yᵉ 45th yeare of his age, and in yᵉ yeare of ovr Lord, 1682, leaving behinde him only two children, EDWARD and ISSABELLA.

Hee was a gentleman of great parts, loyall to his prince, beloved of his country, and a true protestant according to the Church of England.

And thus on the north side :—

Within

Rests all that remaines of Sr EDWARD CARR, Bar^t. ye only son & heir y^t surviv'd ye Right Honble Sr ROBERT CARR, K^t. and Bar^t. whos early vertves gave jvst hopes, and most fair promises of great fvtvre perfections, for he was indeed vertvous to an example.

He dyed ye 28th of Decem^{br}, 1683, & in ye 18th year of his age, to ye great sorrow of his acqvaintance, greater loss of his family, but greatest grief of his dear indvlgent mother, who caused this inscription in memorial of him.

It is surrounded by a pavement of black and white marble, and originally had an iron railing round it. Connected with this monument is a well-executed bust of the young Sir Edward in white marble, representing him in the long curling wig of his time. This stands on a bracket beneath the north window of the transept, and is thus inscribed :—

Sir Edward Care, sonn of Sir Robert Care, the 4th
Baronet of the family.
Departed this life Decr. ye 28, 1683.

On the left is a large shield carved and coloured, bearing Lozengy Arg and Sa, a bend Sa, 3 crescents of the first, surmounted by a helm wreathed and mantled.—Gargrave. On the right is a corresponding shield bearing quarterly Gu on a chevron Arg, 3 mullets Sa.—Carre. Or, an orle Az.—Bartram. In the middle chief an escutcheon bearing a Baronet's hand Gu, and on an escutcheon of pretence

1. Lozengy Arg & Sa, a bend Sa, 3 crescents Arg.
2. Arg, on a fesse indented Gu 3 cross crosslets fitché, Or.
3. Az, a cock standing upon an escallop Gu.
4. Gu, a chevron between 3 mullets Sa.
5. Sa, 3 lioncels Gu bendwise, between 2 bendlets indented, Or.
6. Sa, a cross fleuré between 4 annulets Arg.

At the west end of the tomb is the same shield beautifully cut in white marble but not coloured, surmounted by a helm wreathed and mantled, and the Carre crest,—a stag's head couped Arg attired Or, collared with 2 bars gemelles Gu. This altar tomb was erected by Elizabeth Lady Carre, the wife of Sir Robert, and mother of Sir Edward, who seems also to have desired to record the marriages made by her husband's three sisters upon their family monument, for it originally bore four other shields, two on either side, but of which only two now remain, viz : Sa, 3 goats salient Arg with a label of 3 points as a mark of cadency,—Thorold, recording the marriage of Elizabeth Carre with William, eldest son of Sir William Thorold, of Marston, Bart.   Vert, within a bordure Arg, 3 bucks trippant Arg.—Trollope, referring to the second marriage of the same Elizabeth with Sir William Trollope, Bart., of Casewick, Az a bend Or, marking the marriage of Mary Carre, Sir Robert's second sister, with Sir Adrian Scroope, K. B., of Cockerington, and Ermine, 2 piles Sa a crescent for difference,—for Holles, referring to the alliance between Lucy Carre, Sir Robert's third sister with Sir Francis Holles, Kt. and Bart., afterwards the second Lord Holles.   All four of these impaled the Carre bearings and were surmounted by helms and crests.   Two of these however are now entirely gone, and the only remaining crest a panache, or Ducal coronet surmounted by a plume of feathers, which is the Scroope crest, now appears on the Thorold helm.

Elizabeth Lady Trollope died 1661 ; Mary Lady Scroope 1685 ; and Lucy Lady Holles 1667.

Beneath is the vault of this family whose name ought ever to be held in grateful remembrance at Sleaford.   It could formerly be entered by a doorway and steps descending into it, but is now closed.

Of the 17th century the following monuments are the most interesting, viz : a marble mural monument on the south wall of the chancel bearing this inscription :—

> Here lyeth the body of John Walpoole,
> of Whaplode, Esq., who departed this
> life Ano 1591, having no issve of his body :
> and his wife was after married to John
> Markham of Sedebroke (Sedgebrook),
> Esq., and after his decease, to Sr. William
> Skipwith, of Cootes (Coates), Knight,
> at whose cost and
> chardges this monvmt was erected, Ano
> 1631.

A slab on the north side of the chancel pavement near the vestry door bearing this legend :—

Robert Camock his remembrance of his Friend.

Here vnder lyeth the body of Richard
Warsope, woollen draper, who departed
this life the 21st of September, 1609,
Ætatis svæ 52.

Another slab in the chancel is thus inscribed :—

+

Resvrgemvs
depositvm fidei
fidelis uxoris
Milonis Long, gener'.
10 Marcij, 1664.
*Nostra autem conversatio
in Cœlis est.*

And a brass plate on the wall of the tower stairs with this legend :--

Theophili Brittaine,
cantabridgiensis allum'
ffidelis evangelii præconis
reliquiæ hic depositæ,
sunt decimo secundo die
Septembris, Anno Dom.
1696.   Ætatis suæ LXIII.

Of the 18th century two mural monuments are perhaps
worthy of notice as specimens of their period, viz : one on the
north side of the chancel towards the west end, thus inscribed :—

Near this place lies the Body of Eleanor the Wife of
John Peart Gent., who was one of the Daughters of
Robt. Cawdron Esq., and departed this life the 29th
Day of June Anno Dom 1725.   Ætatis suæ 34.

Above is a shield, bearing Arg, a bend lozengy, impaling Arg,
a chevron between 3 martlets Sa, a chief Sa charged with 3 cross
crosslets Or.   Crest a pelican and its young.

Another mural monument near to this, but on the west wall
of the chancel bears this inscription as if written upon a pendent
cloth, :—

M. S. Annæ nuper Uxoris Gul Seller hujus ecclesiæ
Preb, Jam nunc Vicarii, et Sororis unicæ Ant Taylor
de Heckinigton in hoc Comitatu Armigeri quæ obiit
14ᵘ die Januarii 1765.   Æt suæ 54ᵒ.

On a shield above are these bearings, viz : Arg a bar Erm, a
chief charged with three red roses, impaling Sa, a lion rampant Or.   Monuments of the present century in this or in any
other church will not be described for obvious reasons.

Painted Glass.

From Holles's church notes, taken in 1640, we gather that when he visited this church the following armorial bearings were painted on some of the nave windows, viz :—Or, a plain cross Vert.—Hussey, impaling Gu, a chevron between 10 cinquefoils Arg.—Barkley. For Sir William Hussey, obiit 1495, and his wife Elizabeth, daughter of Thomas Barkley, of Wymondham, Leicestershire. Az, on a chief Or a demi lion rampant Gu within a border Arg.—Markham. Quarterly Az, 3 crowns in pale Or. Arg, a cross patonce Sa. Sa, 3 shuttles Or.—Probably Shuttleworth. Gu, a cross patonce Arg. Gu, a cross patonce Erm. Az, 2 chevrons Or between 3 roses Arg.—Russel, Bishop of Lincoln. These have all now disappeared ; but in their place several of the windows have of late years been filled with modern painted glass as memorials. Unfortunately however no general scheme for the adornment of the church in this manner has been devised, so that in several instances the same subjects are repeated, and some from the Old Testament are, without sufficient reason, commingled with others from the New.

In the east window of the chancel are the following subjects, by Ward, viz : Jacob blessing his sons. Christ stilling the storm. The brazen serpent. The raising of Jairus's daughter. The raising of Lazarus. The good Samaritan ; and the Presentation in the Temple, severally commemorating the late Dr. Yerburgh, Charles Kirk, Francis and Benjamin Handley, Caroline E. Moore, Robert George Bankes, John Bissill, and John Caparn. Above are small figures of the Evangelists, and below emblems of our Lord's passion, &c. The constructional figure of the cross in the tracery of this window has been brought out by the distinct colouring of its glass. One light of the adjacent window in the south wall was the gift of Mrs. Rochfort, and is in memory of Lucy, wife of the Rev. H. Ashington, and daughter of the Rev. R. Yerburgh, D.D. The subject is : The death of Rachel. The next window, by Holland, of Warwick, was presented by the late Miss Bankes, of Heckington, in memory of her brother Captain Robert George Bankes. The subjects are : The raising of Jairus's daughter. The miracle at Cana. The raising of Lazarus, with David above and Solomon below. Christ healing the sick. Christ stilling the storm. The other south window, by the same artist, and erected by the same donor in memory of her sister Henrietta Bankes, contains these subjects : The good Samaritan. The labourers in the vineyard. The wedding feast. The good shepherd. Christ dividing the sheep from the goats. The rich man and Lazarus; and the Sower. In the opposite window, on the north side of the chancel, by the same artist, erected in memory of John, son of William and Mary Pearson, are represented : Christ raising the widow's son. Christ casting out devils. Christ feeding the multitude. The faith of the Centurion. The miraculous draught of fishes, with the figures of Abraham and Isaac at the top and bottom of light ; the figures of Joseph and Mary are also introduced in the tracery. In the quatrefoil light at the east end of the nave is a figure of our Lord in the attitude of blessing, by O'Connor, the gift of Mr. Thomas Parry. The glass of the small two-light window over the south aisle door, representing Christ blessing little children, and Christ raising the widow's son was presented by Mr. C. Drake Newton and Mrs. Warwick ; and the west window in the tower is made up of fragments of old painted glass supplemented by modern additions ; but by far the finest glass in this church is in the east window of the south aisle, placed there in memory of the late Mr. William Foster, by his friends. This is by Hardman, and represents the following scenes in the life of St. Paul : 1, His education by Gamaliel ; 2, His commission from the Sanhedrim ; 3, His preaching at Antioch ; 4, His address to Felix, and censing angels in the smaller lights of the head above.

The Lectern.

There was a brass eagle lectern in Sleaford church, referred to for the last time in 1622, previous to the unhappy Republican days of Cromwell ; but this was far too tempting a bit of metal to escape the despoiling hands of his troopers, by whom it was converted to their own use, and it long remained unreplaced ; but a few years ago an anonymous benefactor presented another lectern, which is admirable as a work of art, and most useful to those ministering and ministered to in this church.

OLD CHESTS.

There are two chests worthy of notice in this church. One of these now stands under the north window of the transept. This is of solid oak, covered with stout iron banding applied cross ways. A small portion of this chest can be opened with one key, but the remainder, having three locks, requires as many keys to open it, which were no doubt formerly in the possession of the vicar and churchwardens. The other chest is a larger and later one—also of oak, now kept in the vestry. On a small panel in front is carved the helmeted bust of a man, and above the initials R. T. This is either of the time of James I. or Charles I. It contains a beautifully worked pulpit cushion of the same date, bearing the same initials as the chest in which it is deposited. In the centre is a figure of Judith with the head of Holophernes in her hand, and the camp of his host in the back ground. The rest of the cushion is covered with flowers of the finest needle-work, and is finished with a border of the same, representing hunting scenes, birds, fruit, &c., after the style of the tapestry then in vogue, in miniature. In this chest also is a once superb altar cloth, evidently the work of some devoted lady or ladies who thought no amount of labour too great to dedicate to the service of God and his church. The foundation is puce coloured velvet, relieved by a broad border and stripes of white corded silk, fringed; the whole of these were overlaid with the finest needlework of a foliated character, and chiefly of a tint matching the velvet which these stripes so beautifully relieve; but much of this work is now dropping from its silken foundation through age. It is 10 feet 6 inches long, and 4 feet 6 inches wide.

OLD BOOKS.

In the passage leading from the chancel to the vestry is a curious old oak reading desk, containing a collection of books of Divinity, each of which is fastened to a rod by a chain sliding upon it, long enough to allow of its being placed on any part of the desk above, but intended to prevent its abstraction. The oldest volume is a black letter copy of the Paraphrase of the Gospels, by Erasmus, wanting the title and other pages. This is no doubt the volume referred to in the list of church goods given before, p. 146 ; but the other old book mentioned in it also, viz : "Bullinger's Decades," is not now forthcoming. The other volumes are :—

A brief discourse concerning Faith. 1639.

Antidote against Atheism, by Henry Moore, D.D. 1662.

A modest enquiry into the mystery of iniquity, by the same author. 1664.

Thirty-five Sermons, by Robert Saunderson, Bishop of Lincoln, with a Life of the same, by Isaac Walton. 1681.

The works of Isaac Barrow, D.D. 1683.

Homilies appointed to be read in churches in the time of Queen Elizabeth. 1683.

Forty Sermons, the greatest part preached before the King, by Richard Allstree, D.D., King's Professor at Oxford, Provost of Eton, and Chaplain to the King. 1684.

The Great Exemplar of Sanctity and Holy Life, by Jeremy Taylor. Sixth edition.

Practical Discourses, by John Scott, D.D. 1697.

Ditto, by the same author. Two vols. 1698.

The Christian Life, by the same author. Five vols. 1669.

An Exposition of the 39 Articles, by Gilbert, Bishop of Sarum. 1700.

A Companion to the Temple, by Thomas Comber, D.D., Dean of Durham. 1702.

Pearson on the Creed, an old undated edition.

THE CHURCH YARD.

This is no longer used as a burial ground, but forms an appropriate enclosure around the church, protecting it from injury. It has several times been added to, as the increasing population of the town required more room for the reverent burial of its dead.

In 1391, John Bokingham, Bishop of Lincoln, paid the king half a mark for a license to give a strip of land, 150 feet long and 8 feet wide, held of the king in burgage to Thomas le Warre, then parson of Sleaford, for the enlargement of its cemetery. Pat 15 Ric 2, dated at Westminster, July 28th, in that year.

In 1796 the church yard was considerably enlarged, by taking in a piece of ground on the north.

A simple dwarf wall formerly surrounded the church yard, and on each side of the principal entrance to it and the church itself on the west side, were lofty stone piers surmounted by representations of skulls wreathed with chaplets. This wall and these piers were removed in 1837, and replaced by the present handsome stone and iron fence supplied by public contributions. Since the church yard has ceased to be used for burial purposes, its surface has been levelled and almost all the tombstones are now laid flat so as to facilitate the mowing of the grass, which is always kept in good order, and in conjunction with the trees planted where there is room for them, presents a pleasant appearance.

THE CEMETERY.

In consequence of an Act of Parliament affecting church yards and burial grounds passed in the 16 and 17 of Victoria, the future disuse of the ancient burial place of the inhabitants of Sleaford became imperative, and it was necessary to provide a cemetery. Accordingly an appropriate piece of ground for this purpose was bought in 1856, situated on a slight eminence eastward of the town, and near to the Sleaford and Tattershall road.

At the entrance is a very pretty lodge, whence a road, having a row of pinus on either side, leads to the cemetery. This is a rectangular piece of ground surrounded by a yew hedge and subdivided by the same means. Originally it was laid out on correct principles, and thoughtfully planted with appropriate evergreen trees and shrubs, like that of Grantham, which is always so much admired; but as this was at first ill cared for, almost all the trees and shrubs died, the turf became coarse, and the walks, with ragged edges and rough surfaces, made the whole ground look miserable; and then instead of renewing the evergreen shrubs— so placed as not to interfere with interments, deciduous trees were planted as if in child's play irregularly over the ground, while the old formal walks remain to protest against such very inappropriate treatment.

THE WESLEYAN CHAPEL.

This was built in 1848 on the site of the Old Falcon Inn, in North-street, and is a neat building of yellow brickwork and Ancaster stone dressings. The architect, Mr. James Simpson, of Leeds, had some Tudor example before him when he designed this structure, but has interpolated a Perpendicular window over the doorway, and classical projecting quoins at its angles. Its internal dimensions are 75 feet by 43 feet, and, with the accommodation afforded by its galleries is calculated to seat 800 persons. Behind are vestries and class-rooms. The cost of its erection was about £2000. The builders were Messrs. Baker, of Sleaford.

The Congregational Chapel.

The original Congregational Chapel, built in 1776, was in Jermyn-street, and chiefly supplied by ministers of the Countess of Huntingdon's College, at Cheshunt; but through the liberal donation of £500 by Mr. Simpson, of Sleaford, on condition that £1000 more should be raised towards the erection of a new and larger chapel, this was effected in 1868, and by subsequent concession on his part the present chapel in South-street was erected from plans by Messrs. Habershon and Pite, of London, carried out by Messrs. Pattinson, of Ruskington. It is built of roughed stone from the Bulley-wells quarry, relieved by Ancaster stone dressings after the example of some church of the early Decorated style; but its features are of too light a character if intended to represent any real grave old church of which it is an imitation, and its clerestory of timber especially adds to its fragile appearance. Within, its fittings are neat and in good taste, and it possesses a good organ by Mr. Holdich. It is calculated to accommodate 450 persons.

The Baptist Chapel.

This was erected in 1811. It is a plain square brick edifice, situated in Old Sleaford, behind the houses facing the street on the north side of the Boston road, whence it is approached by a passage. It was opened in 1812 by Mr. William Huntingdon, and is capable of seating 250 persons.

The Primitive Methodist Chapel.

This is a red brick edifice situated on the south side of Westgate. It was built in 1814 at a cost of £725, together with a house for the minister behind it; but as this was inconvenient and an enlargement of the chapel was needed, these alterations have just been made, much to the improvement of the chapel, which can now accommodate 240 persons.

THE MONUMENT, SLEAFORD.

THE WESLEYAN REFORM CHAPEL.

This is a small unpretending brick building, on the West Bank, 27 feet long by 22 feet wide, with a gallery at one end. It was opened in 1864, and is calculated to hold 200 persons.

THE HANDLEY MONUMENT.

This stands at the southern end of South-street, and is a great ornament to the town. Designed after the manner of Queen Eleanor's crosses, its spire-like form, Gothic details, and appropriate iron fence below, render it an attractive feature. It was erected by subscription in 1851, after the designs of Mr. William Boyle, of Birmingham, and executed by Mr. W. M. Cooper, of Derby, at a cost of £1000. It commemorates Henry Handley, Esq., one of the Representatives of South Lincolnshire in Parliament from 1832 to 1841, who died in 1846, and whose statue in Caen stone, by Mr. Thomas, stands within its lower stage. Above this are two other diminishing stages, highly enriched with emblematical statuettes in canopied and crocketed niches, &c., and terminates with a crocketed spirelet. Its height is 65 feet. In front of this a supply of good water may always be obtained by the public, through a considerate gift of a pump and stone basin below it, bearing the inscription " Every good gift is from above." The accompanying plate gives a good idea of the character of this monument.

THE MARKET PLACE.

This consists of a large open space in the heart of the town, adjoining two of its principal streets, and enables the public to have an excellent view of the picturesque west front of the fine old Parish Church, the Sessions House, the Corn Exchange, and some of the principal shops of the town. Formerly a Market Cross stood here nearly opposite to the north west door of the church. It consisted, as usual, of several steps, a base, on the sides of which were carved shields, each bearing a saltire between 4 roundels with the date 1575, and a shaft springing from it. This cross was removed about 70 years ago, when for a time the base was preserved in the church, but has now disappeared. Near to it strangely stood the Stocks and Whipping

Post. In a corresponding position on the other side of the gravelled way now crossing the Market Place long remained a less religious object, viz: a stout post buried in the ground, having its head covered with an iron plate and a ring inserted in it. This was a Bull Ring, to which unhappy bulls were attached and baited by dogs for the amusement of the people. A few persons are still living at Sleaford who remember a bull being thus baited in the Market Place for the last time, about the year 1807, when at least one wretched dog was gored to death. This post was at length taken up when Royalty had long ceased to countenance such a barbarous sport, and the riotous conduct that usually attended it, as well as a growing feeling against all such brutal scenes tending to degrade the tastes and habits of the populace, led to its total disuse throughout England. A curious illustration of this once popular sport is supplied by the still existing sign of the Black Bull, in Southgate, of which an accurate

cut is given. This is carved in stone, and represents a bull in the act of being baited. Tied by a cord round its neck to a low post or stake, one dog, after the manner of its kind, hangs upon the poor brute's lip, while two others are attacking it, and a man in the dress of the 17th century is urging them on. The whole is painted with appropriate colours. Above are the initials R. M. B., doubtless those of the then landlord of the Black Bull when the accompanying date of 1689 was cut, and below is a subsequent date with the initials I. W. A Market is held at Sleaford every Monday, and five Fairs take place annually, viz: on Plough Monday, Easter Monday, Whit Monday, the 1st of October, and the 20th of October ; the last of which is the most important, and represents the day on which the old feast of the Patron Saint of Sleaford, St. Dennis, was kept, or the 9th of October, according to the old style.

From the Market Place diverge the four principal streets of the town, severally called Northgate, Southgate, Eastgate and Westgate, not because there were ever gates and walls protecting the town, but simply because these streets led towards the four cardinal points, the common Lincolnshire expression, " I am going this a gate " illustrating the use of such terms, *i.e.*, " I am going this *way*."

THE SESSIONS HOUSE.

This is a large and conspicuous stone building of the Tudor style, on the north side of the Market Place. It was built in 1829-30 at a cost of £7000, after the designs of Mr. Edward Kendall, by the late Mr. Charles Kirk. It contains a spacious Court, in which the Quarter and Petty Sessions are held, retiring rooms for the Magistrates and Grand Jury, and other apartments. In front of it is an arcade for the convenience of persons in attendance. Formerly the only receptacle for prisoners or drunkards in Sleaford was a little building still standing on the eastern edge of the church yard, and only fit for a toolhouse. This has now long since been disused as a place of detention, and in 1845 a Police Station with cells adjoining was built in a little street branching from Eastgate, at a cost of £1000, which, with some subsequent alterations and additions, serves its purpose well.

THE CORN EXCHANGE.

In 1857, the great desideratum of a Corn Exchange was supplied, after some difference of opinion as to the best site for the purpose had been brought to a happy conclusion. This stands next to the Bristol Arms, in the Market Place, and its Gothic elevation is not only handsome in itself, but one that harmonizes well with the buildings near it. It was built by shareholders on a site sold to them for the purpose by the late Miss Bankes; its interior is spacious, handsome, and well adapted to its purpose. The roof is on the ridge and furrow system, glazed on one side, and boarded on the other, so as to supply ample but not too great an amount of light to the corn buyers and sellers, for whose use it was intended. Underneath is a butter market, and attached to it are other rooms and offices. The architects were Messrs. Kirk and Parry, of Sleaford.

The Grammar School.

This was founded in 1604, by Robert Carre, of Aswarby, second son of Robert Carre, the purchaser of so many estates near Sleaford, who also exhibited a charitable disposition by acts of benevolence towards the parishes of Rauceby and Sleaford. He was High Sheriff of the county in 1581, and took part in quelling the rebellion against Elizabeth, fostered by the Earls of Northumberland and Westmoreland. He married, 1, the widow of Lord Gray, of Wilton, Lord Warden of the English Marshes ; and 2, Cassandra, daughter of William Apreece, of Washingley, in the parish of Lutton, Hunts, and widow of Adlard Welby, of Gedney, but had no issue by either, and died two years later— 1606. The school was to be called The Free Grammar School of Sleaford, and was intended for the better education of the youth and children born or living with their parents within the parishes of New Sleaford, Old Sleaford, Aswarby, Holdingham, Quarrington, North Rauceby, South Rauceby, Anwick, Kirkby Laythorpe, and Evedon. The Master was to receive £20 a year out of a freehold estate consisting of 100 acres of land in Gedney, probably acquired through Robert Carre's marriage with the widow of Adlard Welby, and the rest of its profits was to be disposed of in alms to the poor of Old and New Sleaford and Holdingham at the discretion of the Trustees, in whom this estate was vested. All went well with the school until Cromwell's time, when, according to a memorandum in its records "From 1644 until May 1646 the times were so confused in respect of warrs, that neither rents could be received, nor accounts taken up, yet the money that could be got was disposed of as appears by bills, &c.," *i.e.* was alienated from its proper application. After this the Masters again received their stipend, but at last this became so utterly insufficient that difficulty was found in securing the services of an efficient Master in Orders, and at one time the office was vacant for two years

To improve its condition, a small house and garden at the extremity of Northgate was bought for the use of the Master in 1825, and in 1834 the present Master's house and school-room adjoining were built. The school was then started again under an order of Chancery, made April 7th, 1830, and certain regulations were agreed to by the Patron and Trustees for its future management in 1835.

It is under the control of the Marquis of Bristol as the present representative of the Founder, and ten Trustees resident in Sleaford.

The following is a list of the Masters :—

A.D. 1640.—Anthony Baston
1608.—Mr. Browne
1609.—Mr. Newell
1615.—Mr. Etherington
1619.—Rev. John Kitchen
1622.—Mr. Northern
1629.—Mr. Trevillian
1635.—Rev. M. Fancourt
1638.—Rev. Edmund Trevillian
1650.—Rev. Thomas Gibson
1663.—Rev. Peter Stevens
1683.—Rev. William North
1691.—Rev. Matthew Smith
1723.—Rev. Benjamin Wray
1736.—Rev. William Gunnil
1781.—Rev. Edward Waterson
1811.—Rev. Elias Huelin
1835.—Rev. Henry Manton
1867.—Rev. C. Child

ALVEY'S SCHOOL.

William Alvey, by his will, dated 26th August, 1726, bequeathed an estate in Fishtoft to Trustees for the purpose of paying £20 annually for the education of poor children of New Sleaford, who were to be taught to read, write, sew, and knit. He also left £8 annually to educate poor children at Balderton, and 40s. a year to the Incumbents of Sleaford and Balderton to preach anniversary sermons. The residue of the income from the estate was to be divided for the benefit of Sleaford and Balderton, in the proportion of two thirds to the former and one third to the latter. The gross annual income is now £160 a year. New school-rooms and a house for the Master were erected in the Elizabethan style in connexion with this charity in 1851, at a cost of £1000 raised by subscription. These stand on a site in

East-gate, given by the late Marquis of Bristol, and each school-room can accommodate 100 children.

Several other persons left small sums in trust for the benefit of the scholars of this school; viz: Mrs. Ann Ashby, who bequeathed the interest of £20 for providing them with bibles and spelling books, in 1770, and Sir John Thorold, Bart., who the same year left the interest of £5 for the same purpose. In 1785 James Harryman became their benefactor in a different way, by leaving the interest of £100 a year to provide shoes and stockings for them.

THE INFANT SCHOOL.

In 1855 a building in Westgate, formerly used as a theatre, was purchased by subscription and converted into a school-room for young children. This is supported by subscription and a Government Grant, much to the benefit of the poorer classes of Sleaford.

WESLEYAN SCHOOLS.

These schools, adjoining the Wesleyan chapel, were erected by Mr. M. Bennison, after designs furnished by Messrs. Pattinson, of Ruskington, at a cost of £1100, and are intended to accommodate 200 children. They are built of white brick, and consist of one large school-room, 48 feet long by 30 feet wide and 17 feet high, and class-rooms, well adapted for educational purposes.

CARRE HOSPITAL.

This was founded by Sir Robert Carre, 3rd Baronet, son of Sir Edward Carre, Bart., and nephew of Robert Carre the founder of the Grammar School, on his coming of age in 1636. It was intended for the use and support of twelve poor men, three to be chosen from New Sleaford and Holdingham, two from Kirkby Laythorpe, one from Quarrington and Old Sleaford, two from Great or North Rauceby, with power to select from Little or South Rauceby if the former should not supply fitting persons, and one from Anwick, Asgarby, Little Hale and Aswarby. He endowed it with the great tithes of Metheringham and Kirkby Laythorpe, a rent charge of £20 out of the manor of Kirkby, and the site of the Hospital in Sleaford. This last is situated south of the church, on which the ancient residence of the Carre family stood—called Carre House, and described by Leland as being one of the great ornaments of the town. A portion of this seems to have constituted the Hospital until 1823, judging from a slight sketch of its appearance, when it was pulled down and the materials were used in building a chapel in the autumn of that year. Then also the road to the Navigation was altered, which previously ran through the Hospital ground. In 1844 this chapel was taken down and replaced by the present one, when the Hospital itself also was almost entirely rebuilt as it exists at present, forming two sides of a quadrangle with the chapel in the middle of the facade facing the fine old Parish Church. The following year, through the enlargement of the building, six additional poor men were provided for in accordance with a new scheme then sanctioned by the Court of Chancery. At the inclosure of Metheringham parish in 1777, an allotment was made to the Hospital in lieu of the glebe and tithes of 777 acres of land, and in 1852 the great tithes of Kirkby Laythorpe were commuted for an annual payment to the Hospital of £130 charged upon the estates of the Marquis of Bristol. In 1857, when the funds of the Hospital had accumulated to a considerable extent, an addition to the number of inmates was determined on by the Governors, and as there was not room for this on the old site a new one in Northgate adjoining the Grammar School was purchased, and a handsome building in the Tudor style erected, sufficient for the accommodation of eight extra pensioners, who now enjoy in common with their brethren of the older building the great boon bequeathed to them by Sir Robert Carre. Each of these is allowed 10s. a week in addition to their comfortable apartments, a blue cloth cloak and some coals; besides the services of a chaplain, a medical attendant, and a nurse.

The Hospital is managed by five Lay and four Clerical Governors. The former at this time are Sir T. Whichcote, Bart., H. Chaplin, Esq., M.P., Charles Pearson, Esq., H. Peake, Esq., W. H. Holdich, Esq.; the latter, the Vicar of Sleaford, the Rector of Aswarby, the Rector of Kirkby Laythorpe cum Asgarby, the Rector of Quarrington, and the Vicar of Anwick cum Brauncewell. Their annual meeting is on Whit Tuesday, when they and the Bedesmen have a dinner, vacancies are filled up, and the business of the trust is transacted.

The Union House.

This stands on the north side of the Sleaford and Tattershall Road, and is a much more pleasing building than the prison-like type usually adopted. It is of the Tudor style, and built of Ancaster stone after the designs of the late Mr. W. J. Donthorn, of London, in 1838, at a cost of £4000 ; but since then much has been done to render it more commodious. It is intended for the use of the Wapentakes of Aswardhurn, Flaxwell, Langoe, Loveden, Aveland and Boothby Graffoe, which comprise 56 parishes or townships, and is a very well managed Institution.

The Vicarage.

This is on the north side of the church, and abuts immediately upon the churchyard. The original parsonage stood at the east end of the church, as we learn from Leland, and was one of the only two very good houses he remarked on his visit to Sleaford, his words being "For houses in the towne I marked but 2 very faire, the one longith to the personage as a prebend of £16 yn Lincoln, and standith at the est ende of the chirch." This stood eastward of the present Waggon and Horses, and its representative, together with the old tithe yard, were sold in 1797 to redeem the land tax. It was taken down in 1816 and replaced by a small new house. The present vicarage house was most probably the residence of one of the chantry priests attached to the church of Sleaford, and part of it is of the latter end of the 16th century, bearing the date 1568 on its gable facing the church. It has of late been added to and improved.

Old Houses.

There are several houses still remaining in Sleaford of that style of domestic architecture prevalent in England from the reign of Elizabeth to that of Charles II. A portion of one of these now forms an adjunct of Miss Peacock's house in Northgate. All its details are not honestly its own, but it is a picturesque fragment that generally attracts attention ; and on a building in the stable yard adjoining is a very beautiful mediæval chimney shaft, brought from the old Deanery, at Lincoln.

Opposite to this is an exceedingly well-designed modern public house, called the Marquis of Granby, in which a little old bay window is inserted, brought from an ancient house that formerly stood on the site of the present Corn Exchange; and a little southward of it is another small ancient house, having a gable filled with characteristic mullioned windows.

On the east side of Eastgate, just beyond the chancel of the parish church, is a larger house of the same date. This adjoins the site of the old residence of the Carres, and perhaps was built by one of that family, although nothing is now known of its history previous to 1707, when it was bought by Mr. Austen Cawdron, whose family was connected with that of the Carres by marriage. Four years later it was sold to Mr. John Peart, of Sleaford, and in 1773 to Mr. John Brown, Mayor of Lincoln, at which time it was occupied by Sir William Moor, Bart. The next year it was sold to the Rev. John Andrews, and at his death in 1800, was sold to the grandfather of the present owner, Mr. Henry Snow. It is a picturesque gabled house, and still retains its original chimnies, one or two of its mullioned windows, and the head of a handsome doorway opening into the garden attached to it, but not now standing in its original position. Of a later period is the handsome old house adjoining the Sessions House, now constituting the bank of Messrs. Peacock and Handley.

CHARITABLE BEQUESTS.

At a date unknown, but probably at the beginning of the 17th century, John Cammocke left a house and garden in South-gate with some land in the open field beyond, the rents of which were to be applied to the embellishment of the parish church. This bequest is now represented by three tenements, a yard and garden in Southgate, and 3 acres 2 roods and 13 perches, let at £20 a year, situated on the north side of the Tattershall road. In 1631, Robert Cammocke the younger charged a farm at Harmston, now in the possession of B. H. Thorold, Esq., with an annual payment of £14; of which £5 were to be given to the Vicar of Sleaford, £4 to the Master of the Carre Grammar School, and £4 were to be devoted to the purchase of a freize gown, a pair of shoes, and a pair of stockings for five poor persons, if the fund allowed of this.

In 1657, Henry Callow left two fields in Ruskington, out of the rents of which £2 were to be paid annually to the Vicar of Sleaford, and £5 for the purchase of five gowns, five pairs of shoes, and five pairs of stockings to be given to five poor persons of New Sleaford ; after which the surplus was to be expended in the reparation of the church at the discretion of the church-wardens.

In 1681, Samuel Raulinson left a yearly rent of £5 derived from his house, called the Old Hall, in Sleaford, now a black-smith's shop, to the poor of the parish.

In 1688, Miles Long gave 20s. a year to the Vicar of Slea-ford, secured on two houses in Southgate, now belonging to Mr. Hipkin and Mrs. Green.

In 1715, James Harryman left the interest of £150, to be expended in bread for the poor.

In 1730, Margaret Kinsey and others left a small sum to be expended annually in bread for the poor, to be distributed on St. Thomas's day. This is secured on the Old Hall, now belong-ing to Mr. Hackett.

In 1784, Susannah Darwin, of Sleaford, left £100 in trust, the interest of which was to be given to the organist of the parish church.

In 1788, Ann Fenwick, of Sleaford, left £50, the interest of which was also to be given to the organist of Sleaford.

In 1835, Mrs. Anne Bankes left £400, the interest of which was to be spent in the purchase of coals and flour to be given to twelve poor women of Sleaford, and the same number of Gosberton.

In 1841, Benjamin Holmes left £100, the interest of which was to be distributed in money among the poor widows of New Sleaford, on the 15th of August every year, and was to be called Holmes's gift.

The Railway from Sleaford to Grantham and Boston.

For this great boon Sleaford is indebted to the late Mr. Herbert Ingram, M.P., for Boston, by which it is placed in easy reach not only of Boston and Grantham, but of Nottingham, Lincoln and London.

That portion of it between Grantham and Sleaford was finished and opened formally, June 13th, 1857. It is 14 miles in extent, and was made at the cost of about £8000 a mile, by Messrs. Smith and Knight. Its completion was celebrated by a grand dinner given by the Directors, in the Goods Shed of the Sleaford Station, and a general holiday in the town, when all sorts of good wishes were uttered in behalf of the new line, which have been amply fulfilled.

Subsequently the line was extended from Sleaford to Boston, when great rejoicings took place at Boston, and a first excursion trip was made by the Directors and their friends from Boston to Grantham ; after which, as at Sleaford, the day concluded with a public dinner in the Exchange Hall, under the presidency, as before, of the late Mr. Herbert Ingram, whose life has since been so lamentably lost through a calamitous accident in America.

HOLDINGHAM.

ACREAGE,
1360.

POPULATION,
142.

THIS is a hamlet of New Sleaford, lying northward of it. Its name was originally spelt Haldingham. It is not mentioned in Domesday book, nor in Testa de Nevill, perhaps because it always constituted an adjunct of Lafford or Sleaford; and the first we hear of it, is as a portion of the Bishop of Lincoln's manor of Sleaford.

It gave birth, we may presume, to Richard de Haldingham circa 1250-60, the author of a very early and curious map of the world, drawn on vellum, now preserved in Hereford Cathedral. He was an ecclesiastic of Lincoln Cathedral, who subsequently held the Prebend of Norton, in Hereford Cathedral from 1299 to 1310, during which time he no doubt produced his map. Next he was connected with the Chapter of Salisbury, and finally became Archdeacon of Berks. This map represents the various countries of the world as an island surrounded by an illimitable ocean, with Jerusalem in the centre, and is interspersed with various religious and other devices. Among these is a portrait of a horseman followed by a page holding two greyhounds in a leash, towards whom he is represented as turning, and saying, Passe avant. This is intended for Augustus Cæsar; beneath is the following reference to the artist of the map :—

> Tuz ki cest estoire ont.
> Ou oyront ou lirront ou ueront.
> Prient a ihesu en deyte.
> De Richard de Haldingham e de Lafford eyt pite.
> Ki la fet e compasse.
> Ki ioie en cel li seit done.

Which may thus be rendered in English :—

> May all who this fair history
> Shall either hear, or read, or see,
> Pray to Jesus Christ in Deity
> Richard of Haldingham and Lafford to pity
> That to him for aye be given
> Who made this map, the joy of Heaven.

The next we hear of any person connected with this hamlet is in a deed of Bishop Oliver Sutton, by which, with the consent of the Dean and Chapter of Lincoln, he manumitted William Rauceby, of Haldingham, his bondsman, and confirmed to him 5 tofts and 2 oxgangs of land in Lafford and Haldingham, which he had previously held in villanage of the Bishops of Lincoln for a rent of 20s. to be paid at the court of the manor of Lafford, and all secular services, customs, and demands for ever. This was dated and signed at Lincoln on the Thursday next after the feast of the Assumption, 1287, and was confirmed by the King, at Waltham, February 4th, 1332.

Before the enclosure of this hamlet, part of it at the angle between the Lincoln and Newark roads was called the Anna, a term possibly derived from Annachorage or Anchorage, marking the site of an ancient hermitage. On this was an enclosure surrounded by a fosse and the remains of an ancient building within it, now incorporated in the farm premises on its site.

In the 16th century there was a chapel here dedicated to the Virgin Mary, but how long it had then existed is unknown. This stood in the small pasture close bounded on the east and north by the Lincoln and Newark roads, and from a former examination of its site appears to have been 70 feet long and 30 feet wide. It had fallen into a ruinous state in Queen Mary's reign, when inquisition was made into its condition, and its reparation ensued. It still existed in Holles's time—1640, for he noted four armorial bearings painted on its windows, viz : those of Russell, Bishop of Lincoln, Hussey, Berkley, and Markham. In front of this by the road side formerly stood the octagonal base of a cross ; but this has now disappeared.

The whole of the land in Holdingham now belongs to the Marquis of Bristol through the marriage of his ancestor Mr. Hervey, with the heiress of the Carre family.

OLD SLEAFORD.

ACREAGE,
1150.

POPULATION,
372.

THIS is a small distinct parish, separated from New Sleaford on the north by the little river Slea, bounded on the west and south by Quarrington, and by Kirkby Laythorpe on the east. It was formerly the property of the Husseys, whose residence here in Leland's time was jotted down in his Itinerary as being one of the chief ornaments of Sleaford, and whose history has been previously given in connection with the general history of Sleaford. Besides the principal manor of Sleaford and its adjuncts, there was certainly another distinct manor here, eventually called Old Sleaford, although for a time both were comprised under the general name of Lafford, because both were long held by the Bishops of Lincoln, and considered as one. No doubt Old Sleaford was part of the original gift of the Conqueror to Bishop Remigius on the removal of his See from Dorchester to Lincoln, and it was let in common with his other lands to various tenants by him and his successors, or rather such portions of them as they did not require for their own use. When the distinctive terms of Old and New Sleaford begun to be used is uncertain, but such was certainly the case towards the close of the 14th century, from the evidence of the following will, proved January 19th, 1397 :—

> " 1 Sidonia Story de Veteri Lafford, on Saturday in the feast of St. Thomas the Martyr in the week of the Nativity of our Lord 1397 make my will."

> " I leave my body to be buried in the church of All Saints in the afore said vill. To the fabric of the church of Lincoln I leave 4s. 3d. To the house of St. Katharine 3s. 4d. To the fabric of the church of Old Sleaford 20s. To the church of North Rauceby 3s. 4d. To the chapel of South Rauceby in the same parish 3s. 4d. The residue of my goods I leave to my executors, and I appoint them, viz : John Storey, my son, John Gillham of Falkingham, and William Scote of North Kyrkby. The following being witnesses : John Helveston, Dominus Thomas, Chaplain of the parish and Dominus Thomas Welton." "Buckingham's Registers 451."

The Old Place.

This lies half a mile eastward of Sleaford, on the north of the Sleaford and Boston road, and is bounded on the east by the remains of the old Roman road from Peterborough to Lincoln, before it crossed the Slea near to Cogglesford mill by means of a ford, which existed until 1792. It appears to have been erected on the site of a small Roman Station, the fosse of which was probably incorporated in, or adopted as the one formerly defending the residence that subsequently was built within the area it surrounded, where many Roman coins and some pottery have occasionally been found, bespeaking its Roman occupation. About the year 1400, if not before, a house arose on this spot, apparently the work of the first of the Husseys settled at Sleaford, whose descendants certainly lived here until their estates were forfeited by the attainder of John, Lord Hussey. This was formerly represented by an interesting old mullioned window house, having a stepped gable of which the subjoined cut is a representation; but in 1822 it was unfortunately taken down and

the present farm house was erected in its stead. There are however still some portions of the old fosse remaining, and the garden wall and doorway attest the handsome character of its adjuncts.

The manor of Old Sleaford was held of the castle of Sleaford by Lord Hussey, but was purchased by Robert Carre after the attainder of that unfortunate nobleman, and thus transmitted to its present owner, the Marquis of Bristol.

ECCLESIASTICAL HISTORY.

When first we hear of the church of Old Sleaford, it had fallen into the possession of the Monastery of the "Blessed Mary of Haverholme," and was served by a vicar of its appointment. The following were some of the later vicars and the dates of their presentation by the Prior and Canons of Haverholme Priory :—

A.D. 1503.—Robertus Grayme.

1505.—Richardus Symson.

1507.—Johannes Thomason.

1535.—Galfridus Wodnot.

1538.—Robertus Walker (presented by the King.)

In Ecton's Liber Regis, the church of Old Sleaford is called a vicarage. It is said to have been dedicated to St. Giles, but from the evidence of Sidonia Storey's will, previously given, it appears really to have been called that of All Saints. This stood eastward of the Old Place, and within the farm yard of the present house representing it. Some carved stones belonging to it were found built into the chimneys of its predecessor and some of the painted glass of its windows was found in digging into the ground near to its site. It appears that Haverholme Priory appropriated to itself all the proceeds of this church, and although vicars were appointed, these served it from Haverholme without endowment. Thus when the tithes of Old Sleaford as part of the proceeds of Haverholme Priory fell into the King's hands at the dissolution, he first granted a least of them to Thomas Horseman, and subsequently sold them to Robert Carre. The parishioners, then consisting of ten families, attended New Sleaford church. Some time after, the Rector of Quarrington, thinking to benefit himself, got a presentation to the church of Old Sleaford under the great seal ; but when he found " noe manner of tythes belonging unto it he exceedingly repented him of his folly, & soe left it," as old Burton informs us in his instructions to the then young representative of the Carres. Subsequently an arrangement was made between Robert Carre and the Rector, that the latter should admit to his church the inhabitants of Old Sleaford on condition of receiving a yearly payment for the accommodation. As the Rector of Quarrington failed to get any tithes from Old Sleaford, so in the time of Bishops Chatterton and Barlow the Crown failed to get any tenths from it, after having twice tried to do so.

ANWICK.

ACREAGE,
1965.

POPULATION,
277.

THE name of this village, lying 5 miles north east of Sleaford, was spelt differently even in Domesday book, viz : Amuinc and Haniuuic, and subsequently Hanewic, Anewyke, Amwyk, and Anwyk. According to the above named ancient record Anwick was a berewick of Ruskington, and contained 6 carucates of taxable land when the Conqueror's survey was made. Ralph, the grandson of Geoffrey Alselin, had here 21 sokemen and 4 villans, cultivating the greater part of this land, also a vassal called Drogo holding 5½ oxgangs of land of him, worth 25s. Subsequently the land here was divided between the families of Alselin, or Hanselin, and de Calz. Then that of the former passed to the Bardolf family, of whom William Bardolf died possessed of the manor here 1252-4, another William in 1290, and John in 1372. The de Calz heiress—Matilda, after having given certain lands in Anwick in pure and perpetual alms to the Prior of Haverholme, left the rest to the de Everinghams, of whom Robert obtained a right of free warren over his lands in Anwick, let to John de Everingham, who sub-let them again to Walter de Anwick by knight's service. This Robert de Everingham died 1287. "Testa de Nevill, p. 318." In 1356 died David de Fletewicke, knight, seized of a messuage in this vill. In 1431 died John Tyrwhit, of Harpswell, seized of a manor here, held as of the manor of Ruskington, and ten years later died William Phelip, knight (husband of one of the Bardolf coheiresses), seized of this vill. "Inq. p. m. 9 & 19, H. 6." In 1544 the king granted a license to Edward Lord Clinton to alienate the manor of Anwick to Robert Carre and his heirs, "Harl. M.S. 6829 ; " and the next year he answered at the Exchequer for the sum of £1 10s. 11d. due from him out of the exists of the manors of Haverholme, Ruskington, and Anwick, held of the King in capite. "Pip. Rot. 283." Then we hear of a John Thompson, of Boothby, who died April 7th, 1559, seized of two thirds of the manor of Anwick, which he left partly to his widow and partly to his son Francis, who, when he died, had increased this third to one half. " Harl M.S. 6829." On the 13th of December, 1561, died Hamond Whichcote, seized of the manor of Anwick, held of the manor of Ruskington by fealty, and on the 14th of September, 1578, Robert Whichcote died possessed of it. On the 24th February, 1593, died Robert Carre, of Sleaford, seized of the manor of Anwick, leaving his uncle Robert Carre, of Aswarby, his heir, from whom it descended to the heiress of that family, and thus eventually passed into the hands of the present possessor, the Marquis of Bristol. In Elizabeth's reign there were only 30 houses in this parish. This was enclosed in 1791. Previous to the formation of the turnpike road passing through it to Tattershall and Horncastle, Anwick was difficult of access during the winter months, and all communication with places eastward of it was entirely stopped.

THE DRAKE STONE.

Many absurd stories have been told respecting this stone, the present popular name of which is said to be derived from the form its guardian spirit assumed when disturbed by a vain attempt to move it, he took flight in the form of a drake. With the assistance of the late Rev. S. Hazelwood, Dr. Oliver had this stone exposed to view in 1832, and put forth various bold statements respecting it, in which he connected it with the Druids and Druidical uses ; but in reality it bears no trace of any such application, nor even of having served as a cromlech, or sepulchral memorial. Originally it stood on the surface of the ground about half-a-mile north of the village of Anwick, or in the fifth field from the church, but some years ago was sunk to allow of the free action of the plough over it. Lately, through the kindness of the present vicar, the Rev. Henry Ashington, it was once more laid bare, and a drawing made of it, from which the accompanying cut was engraved. It consists of a large mass of dark reddish grey sandstone full of sea shells, and its partially water worn appearance clearly indicates that it has been brought here by the action of water during some long past great convulsion of nature. By its side lies a fragment that has evidently been broken off

from it. It is still however nearly 6 feet long, 3 feet wide, and the same deep. Other boulders and their fragments abound around it, proving that it is only one of a number of such stones that have been brought from a distance by water power. This stone is said to have stood upon another stone at one time, which renders it possible that it may have been used as a cromlech; but perhaps this second stone may only have been a fragment of itself, like the one now beside it, although there is no evidence whatever to suggest that it did serve this purpose, neither has man left any mark upon its surface, so that it cannot be classed with any degree of certainty among British relics. The greater part of this parish belongs to the Marquis of Bristol.

ECCLESIASTICAL HISTORY.

In 1150-60, Ralph Anselin confirmed to God, the Blessed Mary, and the Priory of Haverholme, $3\frac{1}{2}$ acres of land in the plains of this vill, which Robert, the son of Geoffrey had given them. Matilda de Calz gave to the same Priory 5 oxgangs of land in this parish, the privilege of cutting as many reeds for thatching as two men could cut annually, and liberty to fish in the Anwick waters. "Lansdown M.S. 207." Ralph, the son of Fulco de Anwick gave five parts of the church of Anwick to the same, for the benefit of his own and his wife's soul; which gift his nephew, Walter, son of William de Anwick confirmed. Another member of this family, Geoffrey, son of Roger de Anwick, gave a fifth part of the church of Anwick for the health of his own and his wife's soul. "Ibid." William, the son of Philip de Kyme, gave in pure alms to the nuns of Haverholme pasturage for their flocks in Anwick fen. "Ibid." Richard, the son of Robert, the priest of Anwick, gave one acre of arable land in Anwick to Haverholme Priory. "Holles." Alan de Cranwell gave it one toft and one bovate in Anwick which had been given to him by William de Anwick, and Ralph, the son of Robert gave it 6 selions of his own fee in this parish. "Ibid." The following also gave lands in Anwick to the adjacent Priory of Haverholme, viz: William, son of Falco de Anwick, who presented it with 22 acres of arable land of his fee in Coleland, on the east of its Bercary, for the benefit of the souls of his parents, his brother —Ralph, his wife—Emma, and his own. "Lansdown M.S. 207." Geoffrey, the son of Agnes de Anwick, who gave it all his fen land in Anwick. Walter, parson of Anwick, who gave a toft and 2 oxgangs that had been held by his mother Lina, and given him by his brother Ralph. "Holles." The firm of one tenement and 4 acres of land and pasture in the plains of Anwick were given by Robert Falkner, for the annual observance of his obit in the church of Anwick for ever; out of which·12 pence was to be paid to Robert Carr and William Thompson, and 4 pence in alms to the poor at Michaelmas—worth 7 shillings a year at the dissolution. So also 22 pence a year arising from the firm of 2 acres of meadow were given for the same purpose by an unknown person.

The following is a characteristic Will of the first half of the 16th century, connected with Anwick :—

"By Will, dated 21 Jan. 1534, I John Thompson of ye parishe of Anwick leave my body to be buried in the churchyarde of the Holly Aposteyl in the pishe of Anwick. I will to

Wm. my son a cowe, and he to be in the governaunce of
John Chamlayn. To Richd. my son a cowe, and he to be in
the governance of John Freeman. To John my son a cowe,
and he to be in ye gov^{nce.} of John Potte. To Emma my
daughter a cowe with calfe, and she to be under the
gov^{nce.} of John Skayth and Isabell my wyfe. To Isabell
my daughter 10 shepe, to Jenet my daughter a brandyd
cowe of 4 yer age. Exors John Potte and Robt. my son."

Proved 21 Ap. 1535.

The vicarage was formerly impropriate of Haverholme
Priory. In 1616, this was valued at £20 a year, and there were
140 communicants. "Willis's M.S. f. 39." It is now in the
patronage of the Marquis of Bristol. The following is a list
of the later vicars :—

Date of Institution.

   A.D. 1535.—Richard Symson.

        1590.—John Lillington.

        1593.—Robert Wilson.

        1610.—Geoffrey Wood.

        1648.—John Simpson.

        1650.—John Walker.

        1668.—Gilbert Nelson.

        1684.—Richard Disney.

        1691.—William Everingham (also Rector of Brauncewell.)

        1717.—Henry Croske.

        1730.—Robert Gardener.

        1760.—William Tongue.

        1769.—John Andrews.

        1799.—George Matthew.

        1812.—Robert Denny Rix Spooner.

        1826.—Samuel Hazelwood.

        1852.—Charles Cotterill.

        1854.—Henry Ashington.

THE CHURCH.

This is dedicated to St. Edith, and consists of a tower and
spire, a nave, north and south aisles, a porch, and a fragmentary
part of a chancel. Externally it is wholly of a good Decorated
character, except an Early English doorway inserted in the north
wall of the nave. The tower and spire are the most conspicuous
features of the fabric. Their mouldings, in common with those

ANWICK CHURCH.

of the whole church, are bold and good; and their hood mould terminals, finials, and other ornaments, spring forth most effectively, but are perhaps slightly too large. The sills of the belfry lights are cleverly carried right through the thickness of the tower walls at a very acute angle, so as to exhibit their full depth. A newel staircase is contrived in its south western angle, and curiously enough large putlog holes have long remained unstopped in its faces. It was built before the aisles, as may be seen by the manner in which their west walls are built on to the eastern buttresses of the tower. The spire scarcely tapers enough, and is rather oppressed by its three tiers of lights, and ornaments, but is a handsome feature. The pitch of the first roof of the nave is clearly marked out by its weathering remaining upon the east face of the tower, and a still higher one appears to have been afterwards added, reaching more than half way up the eastern belfry light. Unfortunately the present wretched roof is nearly flat. The aisles are low, and only a little later than the tower. Their windows are all alike, and of two lights with segmental arched heads, except those at the east ends of the aisles, which have three lights. It will be at once seen that the east end of the chancel, and its original roof are gone; a wretched modern wall and window now robbing it of its proper length, and an equally wretched low roof curtailing its due height. It once had two lights in its north wall, but one of these is stopped up. On the south side is one light that has lost its head, and a door. The porch, on the south side of the nave, has a well moulded arch without, and a richer doorway within. In the external face of the north aisle is the charming little Early English doorway before spoken of. On each side is a small pillar having a keel-shaped shaft and a small nail-head band passing round its cap; its arch is enriched with two rows of a boldly cut tooth ornament.

Within, the north aisle arcade is of the same beautiful character as the above-named doorway, which no doubt at first served in a contemporary aisle, before the present Decorated one was built. It consists of four bays, supported by clustered filleted pillars, with a little band of the nail-head ornament on their caps, and the water mould adorning their bases; the whole springing from plain square plinths. The responds have keel-shaped shafts and a bold band of the tooth mould on either side of them. The hood mould of the whole arcade is enriched with a similar band of the nail-head ornament.

The south aisle arcade—also of four bays, together with all the rest of this church, is Decorated. Its pillars spring from diagonal plinths, and have clustered shafts supporting plainly moulded arches. The tower and chancel arches are similar to these. A piscina in the south wall of the chancel near the east end indicates that there was once a chapel there.

The staircase, formerly leading to the rood loft at the south eastern angle of the nave, still remains perfect. On opening its long closed doorway in 1859, when this church was in part restored, a small mutilated sedent figure of the Virgin and child was found within. This is of Ancaster stone, painted. There also three little octagonal shafted pillars were found, which had perhaps served as supports to an altar slab. One is Norman and has a scalloped cushion cap, the others are Early English, but dissimilar in detail. The font is a plain octagonal Decorated one, and retains the staples on the edge of its bowl formerly used to fasten down the cover. Here also is an iron hour-glass stand, formerly of service, we may hope, both to the preachers and congregations. On the three bells of this church are the following inscriptions :—

1.—God save this church. 1654.

W. Thompson. T. Squire. Wardens.

2.—Grata sit arguta resonans campanula voce.

3.—Will Gladwin. Warden. 1656.

In the chancel floor is a large sepulchral slab bearing the following border legend :—" Hic Jacet corpus Thomæ Whichcote de Haverholme fili Hamond Whichcote de Dunston armigeris—vitam expiravit—die Julii Ano. Dni. 1615," and a boar's head, or the Whichcote crest, upon a shield in the centre.

Close to the porch in the churchyard is the clustered base of a shaft, once no doubt surmounted by a cross.

ASHBY DE LA LAUNDE.

ACREAGE,   POPULATION,
1298.   176.

THE name of this village, lying 6 miles north of Lincoln, has been variously spelt Aschebi, Asheby, Askeby, Eshebie and Esseby.   The principal Saxon landowners here were Aschil, from whom Ashby perhaps derived its name, and Outi.   After the Conquest Colsuein became the possessor of their lands.   These consisted of 3½ carucates subsequently reckoned as 4 carucates, of which Colsuein retained ½ in demesne.   He had 12 villans, 2 sokemen, having 1 oxgang of this land, 1 bordar with 2 carucates, and 15 acres of meadow, worth in King Edward's time 40s., but subsequently 70s.   From the time of Stephen to that of Henry VIII. two distinct manors continued to exist in Ashby.   One, constituting Colsuein's lands, and consisting of 2 knight's fees, first held of the King by the Earl of Salisbury, was let by him to Jordan de Essheby.   Subsequently the de la Hayes held this manor as the representatives of that Earl, and it continued to be held of them by the Esshebys.   The other was at first possessed by Simon Tuchet, who gave his manor and half his lands in Ashby to the knights of Temple Bruer, and the remainder to the Prior and fraternity of Haverholme.   "Testa de Nevill p. 313, and Peck's MSS."   William de Essheby, temp. Henry I., for the better security of his lands and person joined the fraternity of the Templars, and presented them with certain lands on the heath near their residence, and four oxgangs of land in Ashby on certain conditions, according to the tenor of the annexed translation of his gift-deed as recorded in "Peck's MSS. 4934," now in the British Museum.

William de Eshebie greets all the Barons and Vavassors of
    Lincolnshire (Lyndecolnshyre), as well as his friends and
    the Sheriffs, both French and English.
Know all of you, as well present as future, that I, William, did
    when the knights of the Temple received me into their

Brotherhood, and took me under their care and protection, grant by the full assent of my brothers Inhillus, Gerhard, and Jordan, and did give to God, the blessed Mary, and to the said knights of the Temple, whatever had been left me of the waste land and breure, besides that which I had confirmed to them by my former charters. And I will and grant that they may have and hold in perpetual alms all that portion of the waste land and breure, which had formerly belonged to me, situated between the way which leads from Sleaford to Lincoln, and that other road which leads from Lincoln to Stamford. I have also given and confirmed to them 4 oxgangs in Ashebie, on condition that Henry my son hold three oxgangs of these said knights of the Temple for an annual rent of 2s. This donation I have made into the hands of brother Robert Leigner, there being present witnessing the same my brothers Inhillus, Gerhard and Jordan, also Robert, Westburne, Richard the deacon, and Galfrid the priest of Gilbert de Cressy, and others.

William de Essheby was succeeded by his son Henry, his grandson Colsuein, and his great-grandson Robert, whose son—a second William, in the reign of Richard I., gave the church of Ashby to the Templars of Temple Bruer, as will be seen more fully subsequently. This son, Jordan de Essheby, was Constable of Lincoln Castle, temp Henry III., when disputes began to arise about the respective rights of the Templars and the lords of Ashby to the amount of common pasture on the heath, but were temporarily settled. He died circa 1247, and was succeeded by his son Jordan. Then the old disputes about the heath pasturage commenced again, together with a fresh one respecting the right to Ashby church. He married Alice, daughter and coheir of Sabina de Mustell, and had two sons William and John, but as they both died before him, his sister Cecilia became his heir, married to William de la Launde, of Laceby, living circa 1345, who thus transferred to him her family estates, and gave to the parish of Ashby that useful distinguishing name which it still bears. He, in his wife's right, held the manor of Ashby of the Lady Wake, Countess of Kent, wife of Edmund of Woodstock, and of the fee of de la Haye. He paid also an annual rent of 10s., as Warden of Lincoln Castle, and was obliged to give suit of court at Bardolf Hall in the bail of Lincoln every six weeks. In his time the Templars were suppressed. He was succeeded by his son William, who on attaining his majority did homage and fealty to the Lady Wake's steward for his lands in Ashby. He was one of the Commissioners of array for the parts of Kesteven for the defence of the kingdom in the King's absence, 1359. He married Isabel, daughter and heir of William de Londerthorpe, both of whom were buried at Ashby. Their eldest son, Edmund, died without issue 1387, when Thomas became their heir. His son Simon, lord of Ashby and Londerthorpe, and his wife Isabella were buried beneath tombs formerly existing in Ashby church. They had two sons, Henry, the eldest, a priest, who assigned the manor of Ashby to his younger brother Robert. He married Elizabeth, daughter of Robert Blyth, of Leadenham, by whom he had Thomas, born 1466. He was attached to the household of the Earl of Oxford, and was famous for his litigious propensities. His first dispute with the Master of the Hospitalers of Temple Bruer was respecting the right of the church of Ashby, which will be described subsequently. His next was as to an advantage he had been deprived of during his minority by Sir John Boswell, the then Master, and for which he presented him after he came of age in 1492. It appears that one John Anwick, of Anwick Place, in Ashby, married a daughter of John Gubton, of Lincoln, and by her had a son called John the younger, an idiot. The mother died, when the father married secondly Janette Cappe, of Harmston, and died soon after. Janette then took possession of Anwyke Place belonging to the family of that name, and their deeds, &c., and married John Glayston, when the idiot Anwick heir was taken from her and placed under the wardenship of Robert de la Launde, his lord superior, as a minor 8 years of age. This Robert then let Anwick Place to a relation— William de la Launde, Henry Wymbish, and others, for his own benefit, and instead of taking proper care of the little wretched idiot owner, made him over to Sir John Boswell of the Temple, as a fool for the amusement of the community at Temple Bruer. Happily for himself this poor child soon died, and then Boswell's conduct assumed even a darker hue than that of Robert de la Launde, for he persuaded Janette Glayston to give him the deeds connected with Anwick Place, and pretended to purchase that property ; but although this was proved to be untrue at a court held at Colly Weston, before the Lady Margaret—the King's grandmother, he was still able to retain it through the

poverty of de la Launde, and to enfeoff William Smith, vicar of
Ashby, and William Audelyn, of Welbourn, with it, for the
benefit of his bastard son William Bosswell by Janette (perhaps
the relict of John Anwick, and John Glayston), before he took
his departure for Rhodes, where he died. Sir Thomas de la
Launde on his accession to his father's property ought by feudal
law to have inherited Anwick Place as escheator; but he was
absent for some time with the Earl of Oxford, so that he could
not attend to this matter, and when he did do so he found that
Audelyn had died, and that Smith, after cutting down all the
timber on the estate, had allowed it and the house to go to ruin.
He then demanded possession of the property, but was refused as
he had no title deeds or other proofs to exhibit. Next he sued
Smith for trespass, who then produced the documents given by
Janette Boswell, and with these a forged Will pretended to have
been made by John Anwick, in which authority was given to
Janette to sell his property if driven to any great necessity; but
when ordered by Sir John Ormston, Chamberlain to the Lady
Margaret sitting in council to exhibit any Will proved under the
Bishop's seal, he was unable to do so, and de la Launde's right
was admitted. Finally he sued Smith at common law, got
damages in his favour, and so reduced that recreant that he
humbly urged his late opponent not to allow the Sheriff to return
him an outlaw, which entreaty was granted, and he removed his
goods from Anwick Place, gave it up to Sir Thomas de la Launde,
and paid damages to the amount of £60. "Add. MSS, 4936.
B.M." In the following reign Thomas de la Launde proceeded
against another Master of Temple Bruer,—John Babyington, for
wrongs he accused him of having committed, and as the complaint
and the answer to it are very curious and characteristic of the
period when the case was heard, the whole will perhaps be read
with interest. The former is as follows :—

The complaynte of Thomas de la Launde of Assheby against
Frere John Babyngton of the Order of St. John of Jerusalem,
Fermer of ye Comaundery of Temple (Bruer) for certeyn greet
injuries done to hym by the sd Babyngton put yn afore my Lord
Cardynall 12. H. viij. 1520-1.

1.   Piteously complayneth and shaweth unto yor grace yor
daily orator and bedeman Thomas de la Launde of Assheby, next
Bloxham, in the countie of Lincoln, gent. that,

2. Whereas yr said orator being seized in his demesnes as of fe of a parcel and a pece of ground and pasture callyd Assheby Hethe, in ye parish of Assheby, in the countie of Lincoln aforesaid.

3. Which pasture and heith yor orator and all other his tenants and all they whos estate he hath in the sd manor and their tenants at all tyme, without tyme of mind of men hath occupied and taken the profites of the seyd heyth with ther shepe and other catell, necessary for the compastryng, gayngny, and tyllyng of the seyd lande and lyfyng within ye seyd manor without impediment or let of any person.

4. Unto now of late that one Frere Babyngton of the order of religion of St. John of Jerusalem, and fermer of the Comaundery of Temple Breur in the countee aforesaid, caused his chaplyn and 16 of his servants (whose names yr sd orator knoweth not) in the Rogation days in the XI of the king that now is, to go in a riotous manner, (that is to say with billys, bowys, arrows, swords, and bucklers and order wepyns) under color of a procession about the said Hethe of Assheby.

5. And also avised and commaunded them to marke and cleyme the sd hethe to be parcell of the sd commandry of Tempull, and to put out the catell of yor sd orator and other hys tenaunts without any ryghte or title, (the whiche commaundment they did observe and kepe), but only intending by his myght of power to vex and troble yr sd orator and his tenaunts for occupying and taking the pfittes of the sd Hethe, and to cause them to avoyde from their fermes of Assheby aforesaid.

6. And farther the sd Sir John Babyngton threwith not being content immedyately after avised his sheperd to kepe VCCC shepe and LX kyne and other cattell on ye sd hethe fro the feste of the nativity of St. John Baptiste in the foresd XI yere of ye Kyng that now is, unto the feste of Allhallows next ensuying, by meane whereof not only the pasture of ye sd hethe was wasted and destroyed, but also the corn of ye sd orator growing in ye fields of Assheby to the value of X l. was destroyed and eten with the sd shepe and catell.

7. And also the sd Frere John Babyngton in the wynter season in ye sd XI yeer caused his servts to bayt with dogs ye shepe and catell of yr sd orator and other his tenaunts when they wer dryven by tempest of wether in ye nyght tyme unto the fields of Temple Breuer.

P

8.   And after they had so bayted them caused his said tenaunts to impound ye sd shepe at ye Temple aforesaid in a place full of dung and myre to ye belyes of ye said shepe.

9.   And wold not suffer delyvre of them to be made unto such tyme as yr sd orator had made a fyne with ye said Sir John Babyngton and his servaunts as they pleased.

10.   By furze (force) of the which unlawfull pinning and bayling of the sd shepe and destroying of the sd pasture, whence they shold have had relief, the shepe and catell of yr sd orator to the number of iiij C wer destroyed and lost to the hurt and damage of ye sd orator of LX *l.*

11.   And also whereas yr sd orator and his ancestors and all they whose estate he hath in the sd manor of Assheby have usyd the tyme without mynde of man to have lete wayf and stray within the said manor of Assheby unto now of late that the sd Syr John Babyngton by his myght and power wrongfully hath taken dyvers strayes wythyn ye sd manor, and causyd them to be dryven to a ferme of his called Hanford (which is about vij myle by the sade Temple) whereof ye oon half is in Nottingham shyre, to the intente that yr sd orator should have no knowledge where they wer becom.

12.   And also caused the steward of Courte of the sd Comaunderie of Temple for to usurpe and kepe a Leyte Courte within the sd manor to the use and pfitt of the seyd Syr John Babyngton, whereupon ye sd Babyngton hath usurped wrongfully of ye ryght and rialte that belongeth to our Sovn. Lord the Kyng in the said Lordshippe and manor of Assheby as chief Lord ther, the which maner all the auncesters and fore elders of the sd Thomas de la Launde holdith in chief of our sd soverign Lord the Kyng by reason of his Duchie, and Fee de Hay, and was always chief lords ther under the Kyng's grace, and hath pecebly had, enjoyed, and kept ther letes and iij weekes courts yerely fro tyme to tyme, and hath had all the penalties as felle wyth wayfs and strayes and other penalties ther paying yerely Xs of Duche rente with comon sute to the ———— —— holdyn at the Castle of Lincoln for the Duche to the utter undoyng of yr sd orator without yr gracious Sovryn to hym be shewed in this behalf, forasmuch as yr sd orator is not of power to maynteyn sute accordyng to course of comon Lawe nor none action lyeth ayt the sd Frere John Babyngton, for as much as he is a religious person, and under obedience to his prior.

13.   Wherfor the premises tenderly considered it may plase yor grace to graunte a special comission to be directed to certyn personues comaunding them by the same to call afore them the sd Syr John to answer to the premised and all other varyances between the sd partgyes to here and to determyne the thyngs concernyng the same, or els to certyfy before the kyng's most hon councell at a certain day what they have dune conceryng the same.

In answer to this petition a commission of enquiry was appointed by the King, consisting of Sir John Hussey, Knt., Robert Hussey, his brother, John Wymbish, of Nocton, William Disney, of Norton, and Richard Clerk, of Lincoln, recorder, who met at Sleaford, and received the following defence from Sir John Babyngton :—

1.   The sayd Syr John saith the sd Bille is untrue, and the more part of the matter of the same fayned by the said Thomas for the vexation of the said Syr John, without gode grounde or cause, but for answer or declaration of the truth in the premises ye sd Syr John saythe,

2.   As to any ryot, rout, or unlawful assemblie or other mysdemeanor in the sd bylle agt the Kyng's pease supposed to be done, he is nothyng gylty : and as to the residue of the sd matter conteyned in the sd byll, the said Syr John as fermor of the Comaundre sayth,

3.   That the sd Hethe, which the sd Thomas surmyseth and claymeth to be Assheby Hethe, is, and out of tyme of minde hath bene, parcell of Temple Hethe.

4.   And at such tyme as the sd Syr John entred as fermor of the sd Temple the same parcell of heth amongst others was shewn to be parcell of Temple Hethe by certain old boundes and markes not known in the said countrie, by reason whereof the sd Syr John at dyvers tymes hath had both shepe and oder bests kept upon the seyd heith in lyke manner and forme, as master Newport late comaunder of the same and other predecessors have kept on the same.

5.   And as to dryfte, the same hethe yt lay most convenient for the kepyng of the catell of the sd Syr John, but not so many kye (kine) or oder bests as he supposith in the seyd bill have bene kept there.

6.   And sayth that such as wer tho tenaunts to Sr. John's in Assheby by lycence of the sd Syr John have dyvers weite

(wet) years been suffred to come wyth ther shepe upon the same hethe and oder places adjoining amongst whom the sd Thomas as a tenaunt to St. John's hath beene lykewyse sufferid.

7. And sayth that the sd XI yere the begynnyng thereof was verrey day.

8. And the sd Syr John being at London his preste and V oder men—persons, and 3 women—persons went in procession in peaseable and devout manner about all the Temple Hethe to pray for seasonable wedder.

9. And as he understode at his comyng fro London they went upon ye sd. heyth claymd by ye sd de la Laundes, and by the old marks and bounds of the same.

10. And if any of the sd marks were removed, it was the same compas that the olde marks was, as may appere.

11. And further that the seyd Thomas takyth upon hym as chief Lord in Assheby, when ye sd Syr John supposith he is but a tenaunt, and that the lordship belongyth to the said Comaundrie.

12. But by craking and pratyng among the pore tenauntes ther the sd XI yere he toke upon hym as lorde to brake the pasture and eddyshe of the sd towne of Ashby, a day or two, or more before other tenaunts ther, by reason wherof the sd Syr John supposyth the shepe of the sd delalande dyed.

13. And also the latter end of the sd yere was so dry or droughty that it was in manner universal dethe of shepe in all places for ye same yer.

14. The same Syr John lost above VC of his shepe at Temple, which cum not into the low grounds as the sd delalaunde's did, wher few or none escapid.

15. And sayth that the sd Thomas and oder have dyvers tymes trespassed in the corne and grasse of the sd Syr John at Temple and oder besyde on ye sd heythe, which he claymeth, for the which sometimes his servaunts, if they wer nyghe ye utter borders, did peaceably dryve them oute, and if they war far wythin ye uttergates of ye Temple as a distress for trespasse, and sometyme kept them in his gresse withaul til some person cum to borow them, and to know that they had trespassed: at all which tymes ye sd Syr John never toke anything for amends of ye sd delalaunde, or any other, but in curtos maner prayed them to forbeare of eftsoons trespassyng : and, if anything wer gyften by any persone it was but some small rewarde as 1d. or ij d. or

iij if they wer a hole flock of shepe, to the person who pynned the catell as the herdsman and shepherds pay to the . . . . The remainder of these instructions is now wanting, which served as Thomas de la Launde's brief to Hugh Clarke, of Welbourn. The issue is thus described by de la Launde :—I gaf him (Hugh Clarke) to make my byll of complaynt after I was departed from London for dyvers matters of the Lord Willoughby's, and to get me a comyssion, and to be dyrect to dyverse men of worship in the cuntre, and I gaf hym vj s. viij d. to pay for the commysion and other money to pay for other charges, and also left him part of my evidences in his kepyng for to take more councill, who promised to bryng all to Lincoln at the assize time in Lent in the viij of or Lord Henry viij.   And he brought down the com-yssion, but left out Sir Christ Wyllughby tho ordered to put hym in by my bill of instructions, because he knew well he was my gode master, and wolde take for my ryght, wherfor he left hym out, and put yn Sir John Husey, his brother Robert, Wm. Dysney, of Norton, Richd. Clarke, of Lincoln, and John Wym-bush, of Norton, which dyd me no good, but was brought agt me, and so was the said Clarke yt I put my special trust to, who falsly deceyved and bewrayed all my matter to Babyngton, and made him privy to all my evidences and wrytyngs that I left wyth hym to my great hyndrance, and losse of CC markes.

Through the subsequent poverty of Thomas de la Launde, occasioned partly by his father's extravagance, partly by his own losses in law suits, his lands at Ashby passed into other hands, while about the same time his opponents at the Temple were dispossessed of theirs through the dissolution of all Hospitaler establishments.

In 1543 the King granted these to John Bellow and Robert Brockleby, and circa 1550-60 John Bussey was in possession of a manor here—probably that of the Temple.   About the same time Robert Huddleston held of the Crown a toft and grange here—called Sheepgate, situated partly in Ashby, partly in Ling-holm.*   He died 1559, and was succeeded by his son Geoffrey,

---

* Probably the same as Lingo Grange, which no doubt derived its name from the ling formerly growing upon its soil.   It consisted of an inclosure of 5 acres on the east of the Lincoln road.   Upon it once stood a Grange, but now there are no traces of this, or of the inclosure around it.

who died the following year, and another son Robert, who died 1564. About this time the de la Launde manor and its appurtenances in Ashby, and the greater part of the Temple lands were bought by Thomas York, of a merchant family, probably deriving its name from the City of York. These last are described as consisting of the manor, 10 messuages, 1 cottage, 40 acres of plough, 100 of pasture, 60 of warren and heath, a rent of £3 in Ashby, held of the Preceptory of Temple Bruer, and of the King in chief. "Harl. MSS. 757." Thomas York died September 7th, 1574, and was succeeded by his son George, who is stated to have held the de la Launde manor of the Honour of Bolingbroke by a knight's service. "Rot. Cur. Ducat. Lanc." In 1580, Ashby again changed owners, for then George York sold it to Edward King, who in 1595 built a goodly mansion there, part of which is still standing and bears that date. He was son of John King, of Long Milford, Suffolk, and held the manors and advowson of Martin and Salmonby, half the manor of Humberstone in right of his wife, besides the manor and advowson of Ashby; also lands in Leasingham, Walcot, Digby, Timberland and Rowston. He was succeeded by his son Richard King, who, by Elizabeth his wife, daughter of Anthony Colly, left a numerous family. His eldest son Anthony died before him, whence his second son Edward succeeded to his estates. He afterwards gained considerable notoriety as a Parliamentary Commander, and appears to have been an independent turbulent man living in turbulent times. He fought against the King, but would never pay taxes to the Commonwealth Government, and was desirous of defending his Sovereign's person. He was a Parliamentary Officer, but was accused of High-treason and other misdemeanors by Colonel John Lilburne when a prisoner in the Tower through his agency, viz : that he misspent the large sums of money he exacted from the county of Lincoln, that when before Newark he ordered Captain Cony most improperly to leave his command at Crowland, then endangered by the enemy, and dismissed 100 musqueteers therefrom, providently thrown in by Ireton as a stop-gap, which led to the taking of Crowland, that he protected the enemies of the Parliament and discountenanced and imprisoned its friends, that when the enemy attacked Grantham, and Major Savile—then Major of the town, commanded Colonel King to march in defence of that place, he answered that he scorned to be commanded by him and would sooner let the enemy into the town, owing to which act of insubordination the enemy entered and took the town, that he opposed himself to Lieutenant General Cromwell, that he quarrelled and fought with the committee who were men of the best estates, quality and integrity, that he was a persecutor of godly men at whom he scoffed, that he was of a turbulent and factious spirit, that he kept about 20 men around him as a life guard, to whom he gave extraordinary pay though they were exempted from all duty except waiting upon him and aiding him to alarm the country, and that he falsely styled himself Lieutenant General of the county of Lincoln. Poor Lilburne's piteous complaint seems to have been disregarded ; but as King continued to be the same turbulent man, he soon after found himself in a very difficult position, for he was arrested by order of Parliament, October 21st, 1648, "on a charge against him of dangerous consequence to the Army under Lord Fairfax." Perhaps this catastrophe calmed his spirit and cooled his Republican sympathies, for we hear no more of him until 1660, when he was elected as a representative of Grimsby in the Convention Parliament, and subsequently of the Long Parliament. He was the first to move for the restoration of Charles II., and took part in the wholesome act of disbanding the army. But his troubles were not as yet ended, for his loyalty being suspected by Sir Anthony Oldfield and Sir Robert Carre, Deputy Lieutenants of Lincolnshire, they called upon him to sign a bond of £2000, and, on his refusal, would not admit him to bail, but sent him a prisoner to Lincoln Castle, September 16th, 1665. He then appealed to the Lord Lieutenant, demanding the right of habeas corpus ; but there he was kept for 12 weeks during a time of pestilence, when through a petition to the King, in which he stated that he had ever been loyal, had promoted the Restoration, had taken the oath, and had helped to disband the army ; he obtained his release, but through Sir Robert Carre's accusations was incarcerated in the Tower, early in the following year. Then he again petitioned the King for the benefit of the Act of oblivion, for reparation of the wrong done him, and for his maintenance while in prison. "Domestic State Papers V. 135." He at last obtained his release, and died at Ashby, 1680. His lineal descendant, the Rev. John William King, is now in possession of the manor and rectory of Ashby.

ECCLESIASTICAL HISTORY.

In the reign of Henry I. William de Essheby gave the church of Ashby to the Prior and Brotherhood of Haverholme Priory ; but before long it was recovered by his family, for in the reign of Richard I. his descendant of the fourth generation, another William de Essheby, made a fresh presentation of it to the Brotherhood of Temple Bruer on condition that they provided a chaplain to perform mass twice a week in the chapel of St. Margaret, at his hall at Ashby for ever, which grant was confirmed by his brothers Inhellus, Gerhard, and Jordan.

The gift of the church of Ashby to the Templars was confirmed by Simon Tuchet, who succeeded as lord of Ashby after the death of William de Asheby's son Henry, in the reign of Stephen ; but at length its ownership was disputed by Robert de la Launde, a descendant of the Ashby's, in the reign of Henry VI. through a curious arrangement made by the second Jordan de Ashby with his son William. It appears that Jordan was in monetary difficulties, and that his son, who had acquired considerable means, fearing lest his father should alienate all his estates and rights agreed to advance him 15 marks on condition that he secured the succession of his lands to himself, also that this clause should be inserted in the deed drawn up to effect the negotiation : "Confirmavi Willo filio meo et heredi meo, et heredibus suis totum jus quod habui in ecclia de Asheby sine aliquo relevemento." But this speaks of a *past right*, and was really worth nothing, for the church had clearly been given to the Templars by his ancestor William. Then William de Ashby died before his father Jordan, who thus regained that which he had granted to his son for a consideration, after which he signed a fresh grant or confirmation of the church at Ashby to the Templars. Yet Robert de la Launde on the strength of this temporary arrangement between Jordan and William de Ashby, in the reign of Henry VI., as the then representative of the Ashby's, tried to recover it from Robert Skayfe, or Skayth, the then Master of the Commandery of Temple Bruer, to whom the Templar possessions there had been granted by the King ; but he justly failed, although Thomas de la Launde, son of Robert the claimant was naturally not satisfied, and has left this memorandum behind him of his view of the matter.—" I suppose rekoverie thereof myghte be hadde by ye means of ye lawe; and Robert Delalaunde my father sued Master Skayfe late Knight of ye Temple in his dayes, and had hym at for processe, and should have had recoverie thereof of hym, if he had lyved. But then he decessed, and so the sute was lost. Horbeit the said Master Skayfe proferred Robert my fader a grete rewarde till have been agreed with him, and he died: and this I heard ye said Robert Delalaunde my fader say, of my conscience in his life, and oon John Saynton of Lincoln was attorney for my said fader in ye said matter."

The de la Laundes no doubt were for the most part buried in Ashby church, and of these William, the first who possessed the manor in right of his wife the Essheby heiress, desired that his body might repose there, according to his will, which runs thus :—

> "On Thursday in the vigil of the Epiphany 1345 I. William de la Launde make my will. I desire that my body be buried in the church of the Holy Trinity at Essheby, to which I give my best animal for a mortuary. The residue of my goods I bequeath to Master John de Rouceby parson of the Church of Holdhm (Holdingham) to William my son and to Thomas his brother to dispose of them as they think best. Witness. William vicar of Essheby." "Bishop Beck's Reg. 102."

In 1616 the living was valued at £16 a year, when Edward King, the first of that family after its establishment here was patron, and there were 102 communicants. "Willis's MSS. f. 30."

The list of the vicars of Ashby is lamentably deficient. We only just gather the name of one from the above document in the 14th century. In 1492 Thomas Smith resigned the living, when it was given to Thomas Dalby. "Lansdown MSS. 968." For a time it is almost impossible to discriminate between the vicars of this Ashby and the several others in the Diocese of Lincoln, but after they were termed vicars of Ashby de la Launde in the books of Institutions at Lincoln, the following occur :—

A.D. 1671.—Robert Whitehead.

1681.—John Lascells.

1731.—William Jessop.

1742.—Joseph Mason.

1745.—Francis Willis (died 1782).

1791.—George King.

1822.—John William King.

The Church.

This is dedicated to St. Hybald. The earliest portions of the fabric are the tower and beautiful doorway in the north wall of the nave. These are contemporaneous Early English features. The former is a plain structure springing from a severe but well moulded base, and finished with a string thickly beset with the tooth ornament before it is surmounted by the belfry stage. In each face of this are coupled lancets, and between the northern pair is a grotesque figure, besides some heads inserted about them. Above, is a coeval string ornamented with half circlets projecting from its chamfered face, whence rises a Decorated embattled parapet having boldly projecting monsters springing from the angles and gurgoyles between them. From the midst of this rises a spire relieved only by minute lights, and terminating in an acute point, perhaps rebuilt in 1605, when Edward King restored this church. In the lower part of its western face a small Decorated window was subsequently inserted—circa 1320. Within, it opens into the nave by means of a low but effective plainly chamfered arch partly springing from circular corbels. It contains only two bells. The above-named doorway, now sheltered by a plain modern porch, is the most attractive feature of this church. Its jambs and arch are beautifully moulded ; the former is adorned with keel-shaped shaftlets, the caps of which are encircled with a delicate little nail-head band, and the latter with two bands of the tooth ornament.

The nave and chancel, except the north arcade and chancel arch, were rebuilt in 1854, after the designs of Mr. Huddleston, of Lincoln, at the cost of the present incumbent, the Rev. John William King. Previously, this arcade, once opening into a north aisle, was buried in the north wall ; but the new wall now rises just beyond it, so as to exhibit all its details. It consists of three arches springing from low clustered and filleted shafted pillars and responds—of the Decorated period. The chancel arch is a low and poor Perpendicular feature, having a four-leaved flower carved on each face of its pier pillar caps. On the south of the chancel is a modern vestry, and on the north a heating chamber.

The font is a well-designed Decorated example, having a band of effective four-leaved flowers encircling its octagonal bowl.

ASHBY-DE-LA-LAUNDE CHURCH.

When Holles visited this church in 1640, he found two monuments here commemorating Simon and Isabel de la Launde, the last of which remained in the northern part of the nave pavement until the late restoration, but is now gone. It was a slab bearing the effigy of the above-named lady with the de la Launde armorial bearings on her robe, and in the usual attitude of prayer. But portions of a Jacobean monument commemorating Edward King and his wives Mary Clopton and Elizabeth Colly still remain in the chancel. Their effigies in a kneeling position are now placed on a ledge in the north wall; opposite are those of their three daughters, Mary, Anne and Elizabeth, and of a baby in a cradle representing either Amy a fourth daughter, or Edward, only son of Edward King, by his second wife, who died an infant, all carved in the dress of their time with much care. On the eastern face of the north pier of the chancel arch is a small brass plate thus inscribed :—

> Here lyeth Edwarde Kinge, Esqvier, who died the XXIII of July, 1617. He married two wives, the first beinge Mary Clopton, one of the daughters of Richard Clopton, of Ford Hall, in the County of Suffolke, Esq. by whom he had issue two sonnes and foore daughters; the second wife was Elizabeth Colly, late wife of Anthony Colly, of Glaston, in the County of Rutland, Esq., and one of the daughters and coheires to Henry Keeble, son to S......... Keeble, by whom he had issue one ....

Below are the remains of four latin lines, begining " Quis situs hac sub mole." When Holles visited this church it had then been lately restored by Edward King, viz: in 1605, who had taken the opportunity of displaying his armorial bearings therein : Sa, on a chevron engrailed arg 3 scallops of the first, for King; impaling, Sa, a bend arg between 2 cotises dancette or, a mullet as a difference for Clopton; and King impaling Arg, 2 bars nebuly sa, on a canton gu a bend or, for Keeble. Holles also noted the following armorial bearings in the east window of the chancel, viz: Gu, 3 darts or feathered and bearded arg, for Hales. Sa, a bend arg charged with heads of rye, for Rye. Arg, a fesse dancette between 10 billets gu, for de la Launde. The communion plate consists of a silver flagon and a chalice dated 1719.

BLOXHOLM.

ACREAGE,
1298.

POPULATION,
115.

THIS village, situated a little more than 5 miles north of Sleaford, was originally called Blochesham, and then Bloxham, now unwisely changed into Bloxholm because this entirely alters the meaning of its original terminal, which simply means village or settlement, whereas the present one means island, to which Bloxholm has no true claim. After the Conquest the unfortunate Saxon possessor of Bloxham, Turver by name, was ejected, and his lands were given to Roger of Poitou. These consisted of 9 carucates and 5 oxgangs, of which he held 1½ carucate in demesne; he had 18 sokemen and 2 villans cultivating 5 carucates and 13 acres of meadow. The whole was valued at £4 in King Edward's time, subsequently at £3. Part of the land here lay within the soke of Alured's manor of Brauncewell. This consisted of 2 carucates and 3 oxgangs, connected with which were 2 sokemen cultivating half a carucate. Out of this Wigolus de Brauncewell, in the reign of Henry II., gave to Haverholme Priory a toft in Bloxham with the consent of Alice his wife, Mary, Matilda, Margaret, and Beatrix wife of William de Sares, his daughters. This gift was formally made in the King's Court, at Lincoln, in the presence of his Justices, Geoffrey, Bishop of Ely, Geoffrey, Fitzpiers, Jocelyne the Archdeacon, and Robert de Hordres. It was also confirmed by Hugo Baiocis the representative of Alured of Lincoln. He also gave the Templars of Temple Bruer another toft. The de Grelles, Gresles, or Gresleys next held the manor of Bloxham, of the honour of Lancaster, of whom Robert de Gresley, circa 1150, for the redemption of the souls of his father, mother, and all his deceased ancestors, as well as for the good of his own soul, his wife Matilda's, his sons, and for the love of God, gave in perpetual alms to God and the brethren of St. Mary at Haverholme, 3 acres, near to 10 perches he had before given them, whereon to build certain edifices and also common pasturage throughout the vill of Bloxham. This gift was made in the presence of Albert his son. In 1185, Isabella, his widow, and as such regarded as the lady of the manor during the minority of her son, became the ward of the King himself for a year, after which her wardship was given to Thomas Bassett, when Richard son of Siward, and William de Cornur were her tenants, who paid her £9 3s. 8d., besides 100s. and 12d. for corn they had sold. Her son, then 11 years of age, was placed in the King's custody, and the Barony of Gresley, put in charge of Nigel, son of Alexander de Gresley —Sheriff of the county of Lincoln. The widow was then married to Wido de Credon, by the King's order. They confirmed the grant of Robert de Gresley her first husband's father. In the next century another Thomas de Gresley—probably her son, was holding half a knight's fee and a quarter of another here of the honour of Lancaster. In 1253, William Bardolfe was holding this manor, and obtained a right of free warren in Bloxham from the crown, but in 1297 Robert Gresley was in possession of it. Previous to this both the Templars of Temple Bruer and the Priory of Haverholme had received gifts of lands in Bloxham from the Gresley's, or by their consent, for in 1275 the Prior of Haverholme was holding 8 oxgangs of land in Bloxham, given by Alexander of Bloxham 32 years before, and held of the King by him, and also 2 oxgangs given about 80 years before by Margaret, daughter of Wygratus, who had held them of John Haxhouse, and he of the King. Under the date 1304 reference is made to the Templar lands here, when Robert de Swaynesthorpe on the part of the Temple was taxed for a messuage and 12 bovates of land in Bloxham. In 1325 Robert de Gresley was in possession of the manor, whose heiress' daughter, Johanna, by her marriage with John le Warre, carried the manor of Bloxham into that family. He died in 1347. In 1360 died John Chaumberlayn, of Drax, Yorkshire, seized of the manor, and in 1371 Roger le Warre, Kt., seized of it conjointly with Alianora his wife. Then a Bardolfe again possessed it, viz : John, who died 1372, but in 1402 another Thomas de la Warre had succeeded to it. Sir Thomas West and his descendants next became its owners. He died in 1413, his son, Reginald in 1426, and his son—another Reginald, in 1451, all of whom possessed the advowson of the church as well as the manor. In 1529 died

Christopher Wymbysh, and in 1559 Richard Woolmer, both seized of the manor of Bloxholm. Gregory Woolmer then held it of the honour of Bolingbroke by the service of one knight's fee and the tenth part of another. "Rot. Cur. Ducat Lanc." In 1632 the manor passed into the hands of one who is termed the Right Worshipful Nathaniel Hubberd. Its next owner was Septimus, or Septimius Cyprian Thornton,* who also acquired by purchase the adjoining manor of Digby, and built the present Hall at Bloxham. He planted the trees skirting the road between Bloxholm and Digby, and otherwise improved his estate; but subsequently lost all his property through speculating in the South Sea Scheme, and died at Linwood Grange, at that time belonging to his uncle, Mr. Gilbert Bury. The Earl of Harrowby then bought the manor of Digby, and Lucy daughter and heiress of Lord Sherard by Elizabeth the heiress daughter of Sir Robert Christopher, bought that of Bloxholm on the death of her husband, John, 2nd Duke of Rutland, in 1771. She left it to her eldest surviving son Lord Robert Manners,† who bequeathed it to his eldest son, General Robert Manners. He died in 1823, and left Bloxholm to his brother George, who died in 1828, and bequeathed it first to his spinster sister Lucy, and then to Lady Mary Bruce, granddaughter of his eldest sister Mary, the wife of William Hamilton Nisbett, Esq., of Dirleton, county Haddington, married to R. A. Dundas, Esq., now the Rt. Honble. R. A. N. Hamilton, formerly Chancellor of the Duchy of Lancaster, the present owners of the estate.

ECCLESIASTICAL HISTORY.

John de Bloxham, a Carmelite friar at Chester, and Provincial of the Order in England, circa 1333, was distinguished for his learning and ability. He may possibly have derived his

---

* In the parish register are the following entries connected with this family: "Aug. 30. 1708. Sep. Cuprianus Thornton. Arm. Feby. 14. Sep. Cuprianus. filius Annæ relictæ Gulielmi Thornton Armigeri." When the above-named were apparently buried.

† Lady Robert Manners survived her husband and both her sons, as she died in 1829, aged 92.

BLOXHOLM HALL.

CULVERTHORPE HALL---SEE PAGE 356.

name from this place or been a native of it ; but there is no proof whatever of this, and it is more probable that he was connected with Bloxam in Oxfordshire.

The lords of the manor of Bloxholm appear to have been always the patrons of the living. The names of only a few of its Rectors have been preserved and the dates of their institutions, viz :—

A.D. 1229.—Henry Blundus, presented by Robert Gresley.
1280.—Robert de Easton.
1535.—Milo Garnett.
1616.—William Colsell.
1667.—Thomas Siston.
1670.—Thomas Sicker.
1676.—Timothy Quarle.
1680.—Henry Dixon.
1689.—Simeon Ashe.
1691.—Richard Disney.
1732.—Gilbert Smith.
1782.—Henry Pickwell.
1787.—Daniel Mackinnon.
1825.—John Mackinnon.

In 1616 the living, then in the gift of Gregory Woolmer, was valued at £20 a year, and there were 50 communicants. " Willis's MSS. f 39."

THE CHURCH.

This is dedicated to the Virgin Mary, and was originally an entirely Early English structure having two aisles and a bell-gable of that style ; but its exterior has been subsequently so altered as to conceal most of its earlier remaining portions.

The greater part of the aisle walls, as evidenced by their base-moulds, and lancet windows at their ends, and also by the lower portion of the western wall of the present tower, are of this early style. Subsequently two segmental arched Perpendicular windows were inserted in the side wall of the north aisle, and a similar window together with a flat headed coeval light were placed in the opposite aisle wall. Above these is a clerestory of the Tudor period, having three similar lights on either side.

The chancel and porch are poor substitutes for their predecessors. These, together with the roofs of the nave and aisles were erected by General Manners in 1812.

The tower also is Perpendicular, except that part of its west wall before spoken of, and was erected within the area of the older nave, but it received a new battlemented parapet under General Manners's auspices, whose armorial bearings are conspicuously carved upon the gable of the porch.

In the interior each aisle arcade originally consisted of three bays, but half of the western one on each side is now incorporated in the base of the present tower, the staircase of which is on the southern side. The pillars of both arcades are octangular and well moulded, but the caps of the southern one are rather richer in detail, having a little band of the nail-head ornament introduced into their composition. The eastern pier of the north aisle has a keel-shaped shaft. The chancel arch is a plain Early English feature.

In a vault beneath the chancel are buried the remains of Lord John James Manners, ob. 1762, Lord Robert Manners, ob. 1782, General Robert Manners ob. 1822, the colours of whose Regiment—the 30th Foot—after having been gallantly borne on the field of Waterloo and exposed to the thickest of the fire, now hang within this church as a trophy of that signal victory accorded by Divine providence to the English Arms on the famous 18th of June, 1815. George Manners was also buried here in 1828, and Lady Robert Manners in 1829.

BRAUNCEWELL.

ACREAGE,
2480.

POPULATION,
112.

THE name of this village, situated 5 miles north of Sleaford, was originally spelt Branzeuuelle and Branzewelle. In it there were 9 carucates and 2 oxgangs; of which Aldene had 2 carucates and 6 oxgangs, and Geoffrey Alselin held another carucate in demesne. Here were 13 sokemen and 3 bordars holding 4 carucates, besides 2 vassals holding 1 carucate and 13 oxgangs, $4\frac{1}{2}$ acres of meadow and 14 acres of coppice; and Alured of Lincoln had 3 villans and 2 bordars who ploughed with 3 oxen; yet the whole was only valued at 20s. in King Edward's time and subsequently at 10s.

In the 13th century John de Baiocis, a descendant of Alured, held a manor here comprising 1 knight's fee of the old feoffment, let to William de Brauncewel. At the same time Alselin's land comprised 1 knight's fee and 13 oxgangs, of which half a knight's fee was held by William Bardolf a descendant of his, who had let it to William de Anwick by knight's service; the other half, partly in Brauncewell, partly in Dunsby, was let to Alexander de Cressy, and the 13 oxgangs were held by the Templars of Temple Bruer as follows, viz: 1 oxgang and the 3rd part of another let to Clemens the Dean for a rent of 1s. 8d., which land had been given by Wigotus; 9 oxgangs let to Walter Winterhead and Walter de Bovill for 4s, of the gift of Robert de Calz; 2 parts of an oxgang let to Ainfrid for 16d., of the gift of Wigotus; 1 toft let to Roger for 2s., le present, and 4 days work, of the gift of Alexander de Cressy, and another toft of the gift of Robert de Ansewic (Anwick) let for 12d. and le present, to Vulbernus (perhaps Welbourn).

William, the son of Fulco de Anwick, gave to Haverholme Priory a toft and an oxgang in Brauncewell which Walter Winterhead held of his brother; and then we hear of the last gifts made to the Templars in 1302, when William Rivel petitioned the King to allow him to give 3 acres and-a-half of meadow in Brauncewell to the brethren of the Temple, and Robert de Swaynesthorpe gave 1 messuage 12 oxgangs and 1d. of annual rent in this vill and Bloxham to them. "Inq. p. m. 31. E. 1." The custody of the Templars property here at the suppression of their Order was given to William de Spanby. "Ab. Rot. Orig. 5. E. 2." In 1303 died John de Brauncewell, who held lands here under the son of Elias de Rabayn—then a minor. "Rot. Fin. 31. E. 1." In 1353 Norman de Swynford, Lord of Lea, gave to John his son, born 1346, and Elizabeth his wife, daughter of Edmund Pierpont, Kt., the manors of Brauncewell and Dorrington to be held of them and their heirs, but still retained a carucate of land here, of which he died seized 1386. In 1397 died John Lord Beaumont seized of a knight's fee in Brauncewell, which was held of him and his wife Katherine by John de Swynford, the Priors of Haverholme and the knights of St. John of Temple Bruer. "Inq. p. m. 20. R. 2." In 1422 died Hawise Lutteril, wife of Godfrid Hilton, first married to Thomas Belesby, grandson of William Swynford, seized of a toft here; and six years later Thomas Bleseby, her son and heir, by her first husband. In 1473 died Elizabeth, wife of John Stanley, and daughter and heir of Sir Thomas Beelsby, Kt., seized of property here. Robert Carre, of Sleaford, who died 1590, bought among other manors that of Brauncewell. In 1619 John Fisher was the tenant of the manor lands, which were then possessed by Ann, widow of Sir Edward Carre, when it appears she either thought of residing there, or expected Fisher to act as her bailiff, which he had objected to, for this odd entry still remains in an account book of the then young Sir Robert Carre: "John Fisher to pay an additional rent of £5, *if he refused to wear my Ladie*," *i.e.* to buy and sell for her. The site of the manor house is described as being on the west side of the street. From that time all the lands in Brauncewell belonged to the Carres until 1688, when, through the marriage of Isabella, daughter of the Rt. Honble. Sir Robert Carre with John Hervey, afterwards Earl of Bristol, they passed into his hands, and so into those of his descendant the present possessor, the Marquis of Bristol.

Although this place is now so small as scarcely to be called a village, there are distinct traces of its once having been much larger; for on each side of what is termed the Old Lane on the

east of the church are foundations of many buildings, apparently
of cottages, and when these are laid bare, the marks of burning
are found upon them very distinctly. No record of any great
fire here now remains ; but from the above-named reliable evidence it is quite clear that at some time or another such a
calamity must have occurred, which has reduced Brauncewell to
its present modest dimensions.

ECCLESIASTICAL HISTORY.

When Ralph Deyncourt founded Thurgarton Priory he gave
the church of Brauncewell to its Prior and Canons.

In 1446-8, John, Lord Beaumont obtained a licence to assign
certain lands here, in Kirkby and Dunsby, to a chaplain for the
purpose of performing divine service in Brauncewell church for
the good of the King's soul and his own. " Inq. ad. q. d. 24 H.
VI." An acre-and-a-half of arable land was given here by Adam
Pinchbeck for the annual observance of his obit in Brauncewell
church for ever. This was worth 20d. a year at the suppression
of chantries, and was let to Robert Burton. In 1616 the living
was valued at £13 6s. 8d., when Sir Edward Carre was patron,
Henry Holdsworth, Rector, and the communicants were 60 in
number. " Willis's MSS. f. 39." It is now with the hamlet of
Dunsby annexed to the vicarage of Anwick, and valued in the
King's books at £35 7s. The following is a list of the later
Rectors of Brauncewell :—

Date of Institution.

A.D. 1667.—Stephen Masters.
  1680.—James Troughton.
  1680.—William Wyche.
  1683.—Peter Stephens.
   .—William Everingham.
  1730.—Robert Gardiner.
  1760.—William Tonge.
  1769.—John Andrews.
  1799.—George Matthew.
  1812.—Robert Denny Rix Spooner.
  1826.—Samuel Hazlewood.
  1852.—Charles Cotterill.
  1854.—Henry Ashington.

The Church.

We know from Domesday book that a church, served by a priest, existed at Brauncewell before the Conquest. This had probably been rebuilt more than once, when its representative having fallen into a ruinous state at the beginning of the present century, it was taken down and the present small structure was erected. From the time when this took place it would be hopeless to expect to see such a church as we should now build, but it is a noteworthy fact that the nave was built entirely at the cost of a tenant of Lord Bristol's, who then farmed the land around it. It is dedicated to All Saints, and consists of a nave and miniature tower surmounted by an embattled parapet and angle pinnacles, and a small chancel added in 1855, sufficient to accommodate the few parishioners of this little place. When Holles visited Brauncewell church he observed the name Henricus de Rouceby inscribed upon one of the windows.

CRANWELL.

ACREAGE,
2506.

POPULATION,
233.

THE name of this village, situated 4½ miles north west of Sleaford, was originally spelt Cranewelle, and consisted of 12 carucates of land, belonging to Ulf. After the Conquest these lands were given to Gilbert de Gant. Here one of his vassals, Geoffrey by name, held 1 carucate in demesne, 21 sokemen had 9 carucates and 2 villans, and 5 bordars had 8 carucates and 29 acres of meadow. The arable land was reckoned at 22 furlongs in length and 7½ in breadth. This was worth 100s. in King Edward's time, but subsequently £7, Besides this there was 1 carucate and-a-half of land that had belonged to Azor, worth in King Edward's time 20s., and subsequently 10s. This was a berewick of Gilbert de Gant's manor of Falkingham, and was a separate holding let also to the above-named Geoffrey, who had 6 villans and 1 bordar cultivating 1 carucate, and 17½ acres of meadow.

St. Benedict of Ramsey, or Ramsey Abbey, possessed half a carucate of meadow land here, the gift of the Conqueror. This was subsequently held by Geoffrey Selvein, or Selvayn, when it was valued at the eighth part of a knight's fee.

In 1185 David de Armentiers, or Ermentiers, who then held the de Gant fee here had given to the Templars of Temple Bruer 6 carucates of land in Cranwell, of which Thomas de Fulbec was then holding 5½ carucates at a rent of 12s. 4d., and William de Armentiers the other half carucate at a rent of 7s., some work, and "le present," or pocket money. Besides this gift, the Templars then possessed 1 carucate of land, the gift of Robert Selvein, let at a rent of 5s. to William de Cranewell, and half a carucate, the gift of Henry Selvein let at a rent of 3s. 4d. to Falco, son of Maurice. Subsequently Galfrid de Ermentiers held the de Gant fee here, part of which he let to Adam de Cranewell, and the remainder to Humphrey de Welle, who sublet it to the Prior of Sempringham. The Templars land here was then reckoned as half a knight's fee, and held by Adam de Cranewell of Galfrid de Ermentiers, he of the de Gants, and they of the King in capite. Adam de Cranewell died 1262.

In 1286 Peter de Goushull died seized of lands here, held of John de Baiocis in right of his barony. He was followed by Ralph de Goushull, who died 1295, and Philip le Despenser the husband of Margaret de Goushull, who died 1314. Previous to this, viz : in 1299, Robert de Kirton obtained the King's licence to give to the Prior of Sempringham certain lands and tenements in Cranwell, " Inq. p. m. 27. E. 1 " ; and Robert de Carlton took the same means to be allowed to give 2 oxgangs of land and a messuage here to the Templars. " Inq. p. m. 30. E. 1." In 1330 died Margaret de Goushull, first the wife of Philip le Despenser, and then of John de Roos, and at the same time her young son and heir Philip le Despenser.

In 1376 died Henry de Beaumont in possession of the old fee of John de Baiocis.

Early in the 16th century the manor of Cranwell had passed into the hands of the ancient family of Thorold. It appears to have been purchased by William Thorold of Hough and Marston, who in the year 1541 had to exhibit his title to it and his other possessions here. He died November 24th, 1569, seized of the manor of Cranwell, 34 messuages, 30 tofts, 1000 acres of land, 120 of meadow, 200 of pasture, 500 of warren, 200 of moor, and an annual rent of 20s. in Syston and Cranwell, held of the Queen in capite.

He left his estates in Hough, Marston, Syston and Cranwell to his son, Sir Anthony Thorold, who died seized of these June 26th, 1594, from whom they have descended together with other lands, subsequently acquired, to the present head of the family. Formerly the Thorolds had a good old Hall at Cranwell, at which they occasionally resided, and Sir John Thorold, the 8th Bart., born in 1703, certainly made this his principal residence. He died in 1775. His son, the 9th Bart., established himself at Syston, but members of the family continued to reside at Cranwell until 1816. The present Sir John Thorold, Bart., of Syston Park, is lord of the manor, impropriator, and the owner of all the land, except a farm belonging to St. John's College, Cambridge. In the middle of the village is the base of an old stone cross.

Cranwell Hall was a handsome spacious stone mansion, having a lofty roof covered with tiles. On the west was a court, bounded by the stables on the south, and a row of horse chestnuts on the north, having a wide gravelled ring in the centre leading to the usual entrance of the house; and in the middle of this ring was a large lime tree, whence it was called Ring Tree Court; but the principal front was the southern one, where the hall and grand staircase were situated. The walls of these and all the principal rooms were panelled, and enriched with carving, fragments of which now most incongruously appear in the church; and their ceilings were ornamented with rich plaster decorative work. From the eastern front ran a gravelled path, bordered by box hedges, leading to a raised terrace, shaded by a row of yews.

The poor of this parish receive the benefit of £8 2s. yearly through a benefaction of Sir William and Ann, Lady Thorold, bequeathed by them in 1682, and Margaret, Lady Thorold out of a farm in South Rauceby, land in Silk Willoughby, &c., left for various charitable purposes, supplied the means of apprenticing a boy of this parish and aiding the education of its poor children.

ECCLESIASTICAL HISTORY.

According to Leland, Joel de Lincoln, a monk of Ramsey, gave to that Abbey the church of this vill on XI. Kal. Feb, (Jany. 22d.) but no year is given. Dugdale also reports that Robert de Armentiers gave a mediety of this church to the Templars, for which John, the clerk, paid during his life in the nave of the church half a mark. The extreme antiquity even of a part of the present fabric proves that there was a church here before the Conquest, although it is not made mention of in Domesday book. The Priors of Sempringham were for some time patrons of the living; but it is now in the gift of the Bishops of Lincoln. Its value having been formerly very small was first augmented by a gift of £200 from the Governors of Queen Anne's Bounty, and by a similar gift from Margaret, the then Dowager Lady Thorold, with which and £60 further added by Lady Thorold, 80 acres of land in Rauceby, together with right of commonage for 30 sheep, 4 cows, and 4 beasts were happily bought to augment the living, together with a moiety of the impropriate tithes of Rauceby; and again in 1787 the same process was repeated by a further grant from the Governors of Queen Anne's Bounty of £200, and £20 given by the then vicar, the Rev. John Pugh, with which another piece of land adjoining the first was purchased, consisting of 18 acres in Westfield, in the parish of Leasingham. It is valued in the King's books at £8, and is in the patronage of the Bishop. The list of the incumbents is very imperfect, but it is clear from the first extract that the living was once divided into two medieties, an eastern and a western one :—

A.D. 1218.—Robert de Gravel was presented to the eastern mediety.
1571.—Thomas Johnson.
1604.—Richard Flear.
1729.—Abraham Wilcox.
1744.—William Gunnell.
1771.—John Pugh.
1799.—Matthew Barnett.
1833.—George John Skeels.
1834.—Owen Davys—now Archdeacon of Northampton.
1846.—Robert Allan Scott.
1870.—John Thorold.

The Church.

So humble is the appearance of this little church that most would hardly think it worthy of inspection ; but it will well repay a visit on the part of any ecclesiologist. It is dedicated to St. Andrew, and consists simply of a nave, small porch, and chancel ; this last having a tile covered roof raised far above the flat lead covered one of the nave.

The earliest fragment is at the north east angle of the nave, where about ten feet of long and short work still remains. This may readily be of Saxon origin. Then comes the Norman aisle arcade within, perhaps added to a Saxon nave now totally gone. This consists in all of four bays, but a pier separates the western-most one from the others, and has its own distinct half-round shafted responds with plainly moulded caps and square abaci and bases. It may have served as a belfry, screened off by a partition wall, or wooden screen, from the rest of the nave. The responds and pillars beyond this pier are of the same date and character, but their caps differ as to detail, that of the western respond having volutes at its angles and stiff foliage between, its corresponding one has similar volutes, with the scalloped cushion device between, and the intermediate pillar caps are wholly of that character. The arches above have three members, the inner one being a half-round, the next a plain chamfered rectangular one, the third the same unchamfered. The hood-mould is enriched with the billet ornament.

It is clear that with the exception of this arcade and the little fragment of long and short work, the whole church was rebuilt during the Early English period, of which the following features still remain, viz: the west end of the nave with its deeply splayed lancet light, that of the aisle with its smaller lancet, and their external bold base-moulding, the large lancet in the south wall of the nave, the porch, the now crushed and mutilated chancel arch, and part of its south wall containing a doorway.

During the Decorated period the east end of the aisle seems to have been rebuilt wholly or in part from a small piece of base moulding seen there, and a good two light window of that style surmounted by a quatrefoil was inserted in the south wall, between the porch and the above-named lancet.

When the Perpendicular style was in vogue, the chancel was considerably lengthened and supplied with a three light east window of that style and a two light one in its south wall; then also one was inserted in the south wall of the nave, west of the porch, and the large angle buttress at the east end of the nave was erected.

In the 17th century the top of the Early English gable at the west end of the nave was taken down and replaced by a very incongruous successor containing a small bell, and surmounted by an obelisk finished with a weathercock. The north wall of the aisle was rebuilt about 60 years ago. The nave roof is nearly flat, and the chancel ceiled. The font is a plain Early English one, having an octangular bowl, stem, and base. When Holles visited this church there were the following shields of arms in the east window of the chancel, viz: Barry of 8 Arg & G a bend bearing a cross potent Az., St. Gilbert. Gu. 3 bars Arg a label of 4 points Az, impaling Gu, 3 cranes Arg., Cranwell, and this legend : " Orate spialiter pro aibus Willi Cranwell

Armig. et Margarete consortis sue." Also in a south window of the nave—probably the Perpendicular one, in which are still figures of angels harping, delicately drawn, these bearings, viz: Arg, a cross patonce Sa, and Arg within a border Sa, a chief Gu, over all a bend Az., Cranwell, and an address to the Virgin in latin. The condition of this church now is most miserable, and totally unworthy of the sacred purposes to which it is dedicated.

DIGBY.

ACREAGE,
2351.

POPULATION,
330.

THE name of this village, lying 6 miles north of Sleaford, was originally spelt Dicbi, and then Diggeby. After the Conquest Geoffrey Anselin obtained its lands as a gift from the new Norman King. These consisted of 12 carucates, 100 acres of meadow, and 10 acres of coppice wood; here also he had 35 sokemen. About 1150 Ralph Anselin, grandson of Geoffrey, confirmed to God, St. Mary and the Nuns of Haverholme, 6 acres of arable land in the plains of Digby that his vassal Roger had given them. The same Ralph gave 2 tofts of land here to the Templars, who also possessed a mill at Digby, given them by Saer or Sayer de Arceles, afterwards let to Ralph, the clerk of Hagworthingham, at a rent of 8s. In the first half of the 13th century the Anselin lands here comprised 2 knight's fees, both of which were then held by William Bardolf; one he kept in his own hands, half the other he let to Robert de Tilton, and half to William, son of Goisfrid, by knight's service. William Bardolf died in 1245; another William Bardolf, 1290; Hugo, 1304; Thomas, 1328-9; John, who appears to have let certain lands and tenements here to Robert de Digby, and then to Lena, wife of John Aylmer, of Digby, for which she paid a fine of 20s., 1333. "Inq. p. m. 7. E. 3." In 1335-6 William, son and heir of Robert Bate, paid the King 2 marks on his acquiring certain lands and tenements here. "Pip. Rot. 9. E. 3." In 1358 Agnes, wife of William Bardolf died, and in 1372 John Bardolf, possessed of the manor of Ruskington and its appurtenances in Digby. In 1397 died Thomas Mortymer, Kt., seized of a manor then forfeited, in 1441 William Philip, husband of one of the Bardolf heiresses, seized of this vill, and in 1454 Anna, relict of Reginald Cobham, Kt. In 1462-3, through the attainder of William Viscount Beaumont as a Lancastrian, the manor of Digby became an escheat of the crown, when Thomas, Archbishop of Canterbury, and George, Bishop of Exeter, were enfeoffed with it. In 1514 the manor of Digby was granted to Thomas Lord Howard, Admiral of England, when he was created Earl of Surrey for services he had rendered to the State. In the reign of Elizabeth a Chancery suit took place between Richard Huddlestone and William Gannock, respecting a claim of the former to a manor called Bowers Hall and 10 oxgangs of land in Digby and lands in Dorrington and Rowston that had belonged to Godfrey Huddlestone, the grandfather of the said Richard, and of the said William Gannock's wife. In 1592 died Edward Digby seized of the manor of Digby, and in 1606, after its forfeiture by his son, Sir Edward Digby, a lease of it was granted to Thomas Merry. "Domestic State Papers, James I., V. 23. N. 11." Two years previous to this the plague, or some other similar fatal pestilence, prevailed in this parish, 134 funerals having occurred here in July, August, and September of the year 1604, as appears by a memorandum to that effect in one of the old parish registers. Before 1680 Colonel Edward King had acquired the disputed estate of Bower Hall, as he died seized of it in that year, and left it to his daughter Anne who was living at Lincoln at the commencement of the next century. In 1720 this parish was enclosed, when it and the adjoining parish of Bloxholm were possessed by Mr. Thornton, who was subsequently ruined by speculating in the South Sea Scheme. Soon after it was purchased by Sir Dudley Rider, from whom it has descended to its present Noble owner the Earl of Harrowby, K.G.

A little to the south east of the church is a village cross in a more perfect state than usual, eight feet of the shaft still remaining.

Henry Young, gardener to the Duke of Rutland, who died in 1761, gave 9 acres of land in Frieston for the benefit of four poor widows of this parish and a house, each of whom was to have 5s. on St. Thomas's day, and the remainder of the proceeds of this land was to be applied to the education of eight poor children. A tablet in the church commemorates this humble benefactor.

Ecclesiastical History.

The vicarage of Digby was formerly in the gift of the Prior of Catley, and subsequently of the Carres. It was united to the

DIGBY CHURCH.

Rectory of Bloxholm in 1717, through the purchase of Catley Priory by Robert Carre, 31 Henry VIII. Reference is made to a chantry once existing here, at the time of the suppression of chantries, to which John Bell of this vill had given certain tenements in this parish, worth 2s. 4d. a year, for the annual observance of his obit in Digby church. In 1616 the living was valued at £10 a year, Edward Carre was patron, and there were 140 communicants. "Willis's MSS. f. 39." The earliest register commences 1679. The following is a list of the vicars as far as can now be ascertained :—

A.D. 1535.—John Bardock.
1616.—Henry Hackley.
1672.—Roger Brecknock.
1701.—Thomas Seller.
1705.—James Middleditch.
1711.—William Harvey.
1720.—Richard Disney.
1731.—Gilbert Smith.
1782.—Henry Pickwell.
1787.—Daniel Mackinnon.
1825.—John Mackinnon.

THE CHURCH.

This is dedicated to St. Thomas a Becket, and consists of a nave, aisles, chancel, tower and spire. The oldest feature is a late Norman doorway in the south aisle, constituting the principal entrance. This is ornamented with reticulated work and the nail-head, and was thought good enough to be incorporated into the Early English church forming the basis of the present structure. In front of this a monstrous modern porch has been built, when one of the aisle buttresses was destroyed for its sake. This aisle is for the most part Early English as declared by its base moulds and a large lancet light remaining in its west end, but the others have been superseded by two flat-headed Decorated windows in its side wall, and a three light one of the same date, circa 1320-40, in its eastern end. The north aisle is also Early English. In this is one lancet light towards the west end, and another in its western wall, also the usual north doorway, but two Decorated windows similar to those in the opposite aisle have also been inserted in the wall of this aisle. The nave is surmounted by a Perpendicular clerestory having six lights arranged in couples on either side, and an embattled parapet. The chancel walls are Early English. In the southern one are two little lancets, a square low-side window towards its western end, and a poor modern doorway, probably the successor of a better old one. In the north wall is a solitary little light or slit with a semicircular head after the Norman fashion, which, from its position might also have served as a low-side window. The east window is an after insertion, and the terminals of its hood mould are well carved ; the one representing a lady's head having broad bands of plaited hair projecting from the temples, the other a man's head in a hood, the upper edge of which is turned back from the forehead, and its under edge worked in a nebulated form.

The lower stage of the tower is Early English having a lancet in its western wall. Above this is a Decorated stage constituting the belfry. This is surmounted by a coarse but effective Perpendicular parapet and a well proportioned spire.

Within, both arcades, each of three bays, are excellent, but of different periods. The northern one is Early English. Its pillars stand upon square sub-bases, from which clustered and filleted shafts of the most delicate character spring. These have good water-moulded bases, and from their very slender character scarcely appear up to the work imposed upon them. The eastern arch above springs from a large bracket ornamented with conventional foliage, and a tuft of the same is carved above the pillar caps, at the points whence the arches spring. The westernmost bay of this aisle is separated from it by an arched division of the Decorated period, and now serves as a vestry.

The southern arcade is of the same style as this partition, and is supported by three clustered and filleted pillars.

There was once a chapel at the east of both aisles, as evidenced by an aumbry towards the eastern end of the north aisle wall, and a piscina in a corresponding position in the south aisle.

A plain massive Early English arch springing from brackets ought to throw the tower and its western lancet light open to the nave ; but this is now stopped up. In its south wall is a doorway.

Most of the old oak benches still remain. The font is a large coarsely carved one of the Perpendicular period.

The chancel arch is Early English, but the caps of its piers are most dissimilar, that of the northern one being enriched with foliage, while the other is merely moulded and has an octangular abacus.

In this arch is a Perpendicular oak screen in fair condition.

In the south wall of the chancel are two piscenæ and a small recessed Early English sedile. Opposite is an aumbry, and in the east wall are two statue brackets. When Holles visited this church he saw in what he terms the east window of the nave, *i.e.* of one of the nave aisles, this inscription : "Priez pur Johan Elmere (Almer) & Loue sa femme. Johannes Aylmer & uxor sua me fecerunt"; and in the southern clerestory windows legends recording the names of Cooke and Beecke as benefactors.

In the tower are three bells, one of which is modern, the others bear these dates and legends :—Will. Medcalf. Warden. 1656. Be God with us. 1672.

The chalice is a small silver one with a paten cover inscribed Dygbe Coup. 1569.

DORRINGTON.

THE name of this place, situated 5 miles north of Sleaford, has been variously spelt Diringtone, Dirington, Derington, Dyrington. The Conqueror gave it to Geoffrey Alselin as part of his manor of Ruskington. It consisted of 12 carucates. Geoffrey had 1 carucate in demesne, 28 sokemen, and 8 bordars cultivating 7 carucates. One of his vassals here had also 9 oxgangs of land and 1 plough. Besides these had 160 acres of meadow and 50 acres of underwood. The whole was worth 20s. in King Edward's time.

In 1185 the Templars had been given some lands here, of which Ralf the Dean held 2 oxgangs, of the gift of Walter de Dirington at a rent of 4s., Robert Winterhard 1 oxgang at 16d., Robert, the Chaplain 1 toft, the gift of Robert de Calz at 12d. some work, and "le present." Lund 1 toft at 12d., 4 hens, and 4 days work. William de Bovill 1 toft and a particule of land, the gift of Ralf de Ledenham at 12d., some work and "le present." In the 13th century Anselin's land here comprised 2 knight's fees. One of these was held by William Bardolf who let it to Robert de Dirington by knight's service. Half a knight's fee was held by the Prior of Haverholme to whom it had been given by Ralph Hamslap, and the remaining half was held by Robert de Everingham, who let it to Ralph Hamslap, he to William de Boville, and he to the Prior of Haverholme. It was of the new feoffment, and the Prior paid scutage to Robert de Everingham, who died 1237, and he to the King. In 1275 the Prior of Haverholme held a knight's fee in Dorrington the gift of Ralf de Totenhall and William Sparwe 56 years before. They had held this land of Matilda de Calz, and she of the King. In 1304 died Alicia de Scopwyk seized of this vill and the profits of its court. "Inq. p. m. 33. E. 1." In 1327 the Prior of Haverholme acquired the right of free warren in Dorrington, and two years later John de Dirington was his tenant here. In the time of the Civil War it is reported that several fugitive loyalists were hid beneath some barley straw in a barn that formerly belonged to the Todkills, and escaped the search of some of the Roundhead troops in pursuit of them, although these got upon the straw beneath which they were hid, and pierced it with their swords. William Burton, the faithful steward of the Carre family, relates that three woods in Dorrington, first the property of the Duke of Norfolk, then of the Earl of Suffolk, and then of James Standish, were bought by Sir Edward Carre, father of Sir Robert the 2nd Baronet. In the 17th century Robert Oldfield, son of Anthony of Metheringham had acquired lands here, and was succeeded by Anthony, his son, of Dorrington, who died 1666. He seems only to have had four daughters, Mary, wife of a Mr. Low, of Denby, Derbyshire, obiit February 1st, 1667, Elizabeth, Lucy, and Margaret. Of these Mrs. Lucy Oldfield left a house and garden to the clerk of the parish, situated south of Chapel Hill. The Oldfield house was that occupied until lately by the Thackers. The Enderby family lived in the old manor house, now pulled down, the Standishes in a house near Chapel Hill, and the Todkills in another house of some size; of whom Mrs. Lucy Oldfield and Edward and Thomas Standish left small sums for the benefit of the poor of this parish.

The Earl of Harrowby is now the lord of the manor and the possessor of the greater part of the land, who bought these of the late Sir Gilbert Heathcote, Bart., but Joseph Dent, Esq., is also a large landowner here, including the Rectorial lands. In the village is a cross consisting of a square base and part of an octagonal shaft 7 feet high, and a little to the north of this is a piece of ground called Play garth, left to the parish by some charitable person for the recreation of its boys and girls who used especially to assemble there on St. Bartholomew's day, after having strewed the church with rushes and decorated it with flowers. On this spot stood a remarkable old oak having fine large limbs, ascent to which was supplied by nicks or steps cut in its bole; but through long continued ill-usage by the thoughtless youngsters of the parish it at last died. The lower portion of this parish was once forest land, the trunks and stumps of many large trees having been from time to time dug up, lying from one to six feet below the surface   Some of these appear to have

R

been felled and others partially burnt. Near to one of these was found an axe head or celt.

ECCLESIASTICAL HISTORY.

After William Bardolf had acquired lands and rights in Dorrington through the Anselins, he gave a mediety of the church here to the Prior and Convent of Haverholme, and Walter de Dirington gave it the other mediety by the consent of his son John, at the same time that he gave it 2 oxgangs of land here that had belonged to Nicholas the clerk. In 1228 the Templars had acquired the right of its presentation, who in that year presented Richard de Stapelford to it. In 1574 Thomas York, of Ashby, died possessed of the Rectory of Dorrington. Next we hear of it as being in the hands of George Wolmer, viz : in 1580, and in 1617 Robert Oldfield had to shew cause why it should not be seized by the King as of the Monastery of Shelford. "Harl. MSS. f. 757." In 1616 a Mr. Brown, of London, was patron of the vicarage, then worth £10 a year, and when there were 102 communicants. "Willis's MS. f. 39." Lord Aveland is now the patron of the living. Certain tenements and lands were given by John Thien, Thomas Stenygs, and others, for the purpose of supplying perpetual lights in this church. The registers commence with the date 1653.

The following is a list of the vicars as far as can now be ascertained :—

A.D. 1228.—Richard de Stapleford.
    1535.—William More.
    1660.—John Young.
       .—John Harrison.
    1686.—Matthew Smith.
    1698.—Richard Parke.
    1726.—James Thompson.
    1737.—Francis Hetherington.
    1764.—Lawrence Wright.
    1772.—Joseph Arnall Eyre.
    1792.—Robert Blyth.
    1799.—John Maydwell.
    1823.—Zachariah Shrapnel Warren.
    1862.—William Sykes.

The Church.

The isolated position of this church on a little eminence quite apart from the village is remarkable ; but there is reason to believe that formerly some houses stood nearer to it, as connecting links between the village of Dorrington and its church. This is dedicated to St. James, and consists of a tower, nave, north and south aisles, chancel, and a modern porch and vestry. The whole was no doubt originally Early English, as evidenced by its tower and chancel aisle, the north arch arcade and side walls of the chancel which still remain, while the pitch of its former roof is indicated on the eastern face of the tower. The south aisle is low and buttressed at its angles. It is now wholly Decorated ; on the north side of the porch is a two light segmental arched window, a similar one at its east end, and a slit at its western end. Above this is a Tudor clerestory, having three windows, each of three lights, on either side, and a plain parapet. In the north aisle wall is an Early English segmental arched doorway towards the west end, and a two light Decorated window, the head of which has been restored ; besides a pretty small one of the same date in its east wall. In the south wall of the chancel is a single lancet, a plain low-side window, and a segmental arched doorway. The east wall appears to have been wholly rebuilt—circa 1330, and certainly in a very careful manner. It is flanked by angle buttresses, whence sprang pinnacles. The east window has reticulated tracery, and is well moulded throughout. Its arch is of the ogee form, and terminates with a foliated pinnacle. Above is a piece of sculpture on two stones, representing the Judgment, and in the right hand corner of which is pourtrayed the entrance of Hell, or its dread jaws. Above this is a small niche for some other sculpture, just below a beautiful gable cross. On the north side a small modern vestry has lately been attached to the chancel transeptally, and a lancet light.

The tower is a good specimen of Decorated work, once supporting a spire, but now simply finished with a plain parapet without angle pinnacles which it once had. Its belfry lights are effective from their being deeply set, and in the south west angle is a staircase contrived between its buttresses. There are two small lights in its western face, the upper one being now partly filled in by a tombstone on which a cross may be discerned.

Within, the Early English north aisle arcade consists of two wide arches springing from low pillars, and responds having keel-shaped piers. Its central pillar has a line of the tooth ornament between its four members, and the effective water mould is employed in the composition of its base. The south aisle arcade is Early English, but greatly inferior to that of the north aisle. Its central pillar is octangular in plan, and its arches are ill formed. Formerly a chantry chapel clearly existed at the east end of either aisle as indicated by a small corbel-like piscina still remaining in the wall towards the east end of the north aisle, and the remains of another within a little pointed headed niche in a corresponding position in the opposite aisle, as well as a canopied and pinnacled statue niche at its eastern end.

The tower arch piers have keel-shaped shafts flanked by outer subsidiary ones. The caps of those on the south side are plain, but their compeers are carved.

The seating, pulpit, and font are new. On either side of the east window of the chancel is an ogee arched statue niche having shafts with carved caps, and finials corresponding with the window between them, which is filled with good painted glass by Hughes, representing our Lord's birth, resurrection, and ascension. In the south wall is the low side window before adverted to, and in the opposite one a square aumbry. Here also are a few old bench ends, being remnants of the old nave seating.

Besides the parish church there was formerly a chapel here called Shefford chapel, perhaps erected by some Prior of Shelford. Its site is still called Chapel Hill, and consists of a little eminence in the village, about half-a-mile south east of the church. In 1535 reference is made to this chapel, as William More was then presented to it as well as to the church of Dorrington. Its bell— dated 1643, now in the church, shews that it was then still used, but in 1698, it was pulled down, and its materials were used to repair the church with, as both had then become much dilapidated. The bell long continued to remain in the village suspended on an oak frame, and was rung there previous to divine service in the church, in consequence of its distance from the village ; but through its misuse was at length wisely removed to the church.

There is a tradition that divine service was performed here three times a month, and only once a month at the parish church, also that on St. Bartholomew's day, its floor was strewn with rushes.

The grave stones of Anthony Oldfield and Elizabeth his wife still remain in this church. He died September 30th, 1668, and she January 16th, 1686. Here also is a handsome monument erected in memory of them and their daughters. It bears this inscription :—

> Near this place lieth interred the bodies of Anthony Oldfield, late of this parish, Gentleman, and of Elizabeth his wife, and also of their four daughters, Mary, married to John Lowe, of Denby, in the county of Derby, Esquire, Elizabeth, married to James Groundman, of the Middle Temple, London, Gent., Lucy, who died unmarried, and Margaret, married to Samuel Anderson, of Lincolnshire, Gent.
> The said Lucy Oldfield by her last Will in October, 1715, desired this monument to be erected in memory of her said father, mother, and sisters.

In the chancel pavement are the grave stones of Margaret Anderson, who died October 26th, 1697, and of her sisters Elizabeth Groundman and Lucy Oldfield, the last of whom died October 31st, 1715. On the first is a shield bearing Anderson impaling Oldfield. On the north wall of the chancel is a slab commemorating William Thacker, who died January 16th, 1783, Maria and Lucy his wives, and Elizabeth a daughter of William Thacker, and his first wife. Here also is a white marble tablet recording the death of Mrs. Elizabeth Farmer, one of the most benevolent of women, who lived for many years in Leasingham, but was buried next to her mother's grave in the chancel of this church, according to her desire.

Dorrington parish was enclosed 1787.

DUNSBY.

THIS is a hamlet of Brauncewell, situated 4½ miles north of Sleaford. From Domesday book we find that its name was originally spelt Dunesbi, and that when that record was compiled it consisted of 6 carucates. The Conqueror gave part of it to Geoffrey Alselin as an adjunct of his manor of Rusking-ton. He held 2 carucates in demesne, and here he had 13 soke-men and 1 bordar holding 1 carucate and 6 acres of meadow. The rest, consisting of 3 carucates and 6 acres of meadow, was held by the Abbot of Ramsey as soke of his manor of Quarrington. This was cultivated by 11 sokemen and 3 bordars. In the 13th century Alselin's lands were divided between the Bardolfs and Everinghams, and comprised 1 knight's fee, of which one third was held by Robert de Everingham, who died 1287, and the remainder by William Bardolf. The first was then let by knight's service to Robert Dayville, and by him to Alexander de Cressy, who was also Dayville's tenant. "Testa de Nevill."

About 1370, the manor of Dunsby constituted part of the property made over in mortmain by John Ginwell, Bishop of Lincoln, for the support of his chantry in Lincoln Cathedral; but at the Bishop's death it was sold by his executors, John de Warrsop and John de Thorpe, of Rippingale, to Robert, Abbot of Newbo, and his convent, "Lib de ord Cant, f. 385·6"; but the Abbot was charged with the payment of the amount entailed on the manor by the maintenance of Bishop Ginwell's chantry.

In 1185 Alexander de Cressy held the third part of a knight's fee here, out of which he gave 1 toft to the Templars of Temple Bruer, then let to one—William for 2s., some work, and "le present," or an offering.

In 1544 the King granted to John Bello and John Bales the Grange of Dunsby. "Harl. MSS. 6829."

Towards the close of that century the manor was bought by Robert Carre, of Sleaford, and it appears to have usually formed part of the jointure of the widows of that family. In 1595 the house upon it was occupied by Mrs. Carre, probably the third wife and widow of Robert Carre, and in 1619 it formed part of the jointure of Anne Lady Carre, widow of Sir Edward the first Baronet, who was about to reside there, when her intention was altered through her second marriage with Colonel Henry Cromwell. It then became the residence of the Death family, connected with the Carres through the Irbys. Of these, Henry Death, J.P., was buried at Dunsby in 1639, and several children of Edward Death, probably his son's, were baptised here, one of whom was christened Cromwell Death, and another, with very doubtful taste and feeling, Welcome Death! During the Civil Wars some Parliamentary troops, probably the regiment raised by Colonel King, of Ashby, took possession of the place, felled the timber round it, and left it in a half ruined condition, after which time it was never again inhabited, and the materials of the old manor house were gradually removed, so that now only portions of the garden wall and some mounds mark the site where it once stood, close to the eastern verge of the road between Sleaford and Lincoln ; while the houses around it and the chapel have also quite disappeared. The site of this old hall afforded covert for marauders on the Heath during the last century, and perhaps from the unpleasant name of the last family who occupied it a tradition survives in connexion with it: that through the rash and impious vow of the last lady of the Death family, who was long childless, she at last did give birth to a queer little son, who after awhile was suddenly whisked away from his nurse's lap and disappeared up the chimney in the midst of more than ordinary smoke !

The living was united to that of Brauncewell in the 17th century.

EVEDON.

ACREAGE,
1588.

POPULATION,
62.

THIS little village lies 3 miles north east of Sleaford. Its name was originally spelt Evedune, and subsequently Evedun. After the Conquest it was divided among several great Normans. To the Bishop of Durham was given $2\frac{1}{2}$ carucates that had been Turvert's, together with members in North and South Rauceby, Willoughby, and Kirkby Laythorpe. His vassal Colsuein had 1 carucate, 4 villans, 2 bordars having 1 carucate and 2 oxgangs, and 20 acres of meadow. Part of Earl Morkar's land here, constituting a berewick of his manor of Kirkby Laythorpe, was retained by the King. It consisted of 2 carucates, apparently in the hands of 2 sokemen, another carucate worked by 2 villans, a mill worth 5s. 4d., the site of a mill, 6 acres of meadow, 8 of underwood, and 40 of marsh.

The Bishop of Lincoln had 5 carucates, 20 acres of meadow, 100 acres of marsh, and 16 acres of underwood cultivated by 13 sokemen, soke of his manor of Quarrington. Of this Colsuein held 1 carucate, and had 4 villans and 2 bordars holding another carucate and 20 acres of meadow, and Osmund who held land under him at Quarrington, also held $1\frac{1}{2}$ carucate here in demesne for which he paid 30s. annually. Two carucates here which had belonged to Outi, a mill and 40 acres of marsh, were given by the Conqueror to Geoffrey Alselin. Another part was a berewick of Colsuein's manor of North Kyme, and consisted of 2 carucates of land sufficient for 2 ploughs ; and another portion was in the soke of Colgrim's manor of Ewerby, on which the church was situated. This land consisted of 2 oxgangs, 2 acres of meadow, 1 of coppice, and 5 of marsh.

In 1185 the Templars had acquired lands here, viz : 1 oxgang, the gift of William the son of Ranulf, let to William de Beaubrach for a rent of 2s., and 1 toft let to Pcidras for 2s., some work, and "le present."

Alexand de St. Vedasto gave 6 andenas of his meadow in Evedon lying under his brother Hugh's wood, and near the meadow of Thorold Talmuord, also 2 andenas westward of that meadow to the Prior and Convent of Haverholme. Robert de Evedon also gave to the same 5 andenas of his meadow near to the last named piece of ground.

Circa 1200 the Bishop of Lincoln's land here and at Quarrington was let to Hugh St. Vedasto. "Testa de Nevill p. 340." Circa 1270 we have from the same authority that Hugh de Nevill, Beatrice de Engleby, Alan son of Wittenden, Henry de Horningherd, and others were then in possession of lands here, of whom more will be found in the history of Kirkby. In the 14th century the family of Hardby, Hardeby, Herdeby, Herby, or Harlby had become the tenants of the Bishop of Lincoln here, of whom are mentioned a Thomas Herby, Brian de Hurdeby, to whom the King granted a license of free warren in 1331, Richard Herdeby 1419, William Hardby, who died November 4th, 1540, Brian Hardby his son and heir, Bartholomew Herdebye, who held the old episcopal manor of Robert Carre, its then possessor, as of his Castle of Sleaford, who died April 19th, 1576, and Daniel Hardby, who died in 1616.

The faithful old steward of the Carres, William Burton, in his instructions to the then young representative of that family, 1627, speaking of Evedon says: "You have wood in Evedon, contents about tenne acres, yt belong to ye Manner of Whilhull in Kirkebye. For the Timber thereof being olde, very tall, & well harted, I know that Sir William Carre, yr Uncle, was offered a Thousand Pounds." The manor of Evedon and Thursby had been bought by Robert Carre, and were held of him as the possession of Sleaford Castle by rent service. Through this right Robert Carre had acquired the wardship both of Bartholomew and Daniel Harby when minors; but this had been disputed, Burton thus quaintly recording the particulars of a suit respecting it: "About ye wardshipp of ye said Daniel, yr Grandfather had a long and chargeable suite in ye Cort of wards, wth one Tucke, an auditor of that Cort, who pretended yt there was fower oxgand of land in Thursbye, some times Blackvills, yt was held in Capite; but upon a writt of Melius inquirendo granted by ye Cort & returned, as I take it, in Michms terme anno 1589, all yr lands were again found to be held of yr Castle

of Sleaford ; and soe there was an end of yt suite, which writt &
returne being upon record, will be a speciall evidence for you if
ye like happen to come in question hereafter." Daniel Harby
had 5 sons and 8 daughters. Of the latter Anne married the
Honorable Sir Peregrine Bertie, 3rd son of Robert Earl of
Lindsey in 1631, and through the death of her brothers and elder
sisters having become the heiress of her family, she and her
husband resided at Evedon. Here their eldest son Robert was
born in 1634, but died in 1637, and also a second son, Peregrine,
born in 1638, besides a daughter, Ann, born in 1636. But at
Sir Peregrine Bertie's death in 1652, he left an only surviving
child, Elizabeth, who married William, 2nd Lord Widdrington,
of Blankney.

This parish was enclosed in 1639. The whole of it now,
together with the advowson of the Rectory, is at this time held
in trust for the Honorable Murray Finch Hatton, second son of
the late Earl of Winchilsea.

ECCLESIASTICAL HISTORY.

We have seen that there was a church here on Colgrim's
land at the time when Domesday book was compiled. The
Bishops of Lincoln were probably the first patrons, as in the 14th
century Brian de Hardeby, in 1346, the then holder of the
Bishop's lands, presented John de Roos to it, and Richard
Hardeby—termed lord of Evedon, in 1419 presented another
incumbent. "Lansd. MSS. 963. f. 213." In 1616 the living
was valued at £20 a year when the last of the Hardeby's was
the patron, and there were 86 communicants. "Willis's MSS.
f. 39." The following characteristic Will connected with a
former parishioner of Evedon will perhaps prove interesting to
some :—

> " By Will dated 19th of June 1532 I John Stele of Evedon leve
> my body to be buryed in the church yd of our Lady of
> Evedon. To Mr. William Harbe the best land of wheet.
> To Mr. John Harbe an amblyng fole. To my wyfe 4 best
> oxen, and to Janet Peikell 3 Kyen. To Robert my son 2
> bullock & a grey bald stagge. To Margaret my dorter a
> strong gwye (probably a kye or cow), and to Alice my
> daughter a gwye calf (cow calf). To my brother William
> my soul (only) horse. To William his son, and Emota his

daughter a lamb. Residue to Wm. my brother and Alice
my wife. Exor. Sir Bartholomew Ingolesby, parson of
Evedon, supervisor. Witness. John Harby. gent."

The registers of this parish really commence with the date
1562, although the oldest is headed "The Register booke of
Evedon penned in the year of our Lorde 1599." For the first
30 years the entries are made in Latin. The following is an
extract from the same:—

The Register Books of Evedon, penned in the year of our Lord 1562.—
The inventorie of all the names of such as have been baptized, &c.—A festo
Mich'is, 1562, usq. ad Mich'am festum, 1563. Ex ap^d. Lincoln, 25 Oct.
1563.—A festo Paschæ, Anno 1599, usq ad dictum festum, Anno 1600.
Isabell Alarm buried Nov. 25, and Thomas Alarm, her husband, buried Nov.
28, 1638 ; an old couple. 1662—To 2 gentlewomen travelling northward, 6d.
An hue & cry to Ruskington & Ewerby, 4d. Spent at the bonefire on the
King's birthday, 7s. Item at Sleeford among the soldiers and townsmen,
8s. 6d. Colours for the New Town soliders, 3s. Bandilerres (leathern belts),
2s. 8d. Powder and match, 10d. Musket mending, —. For training the
last day at Rossby, 2s. 4d. The soldiers at Willowby training, 5s. One
gentleman and 4 children with letter of request, 6d. 1663—An hue & cry
to Kirkby for a horse, 3d. Item, muster master, 3s. 2d. 1664—Perambulation, spent 7s. Bread & drinke, watchers all night, 6d. An hue & cry for
a grey maire, 2d. The first three months tax for the royal aid, 5d. in the
pound. Repaire of Lincoln cathedral, 8s. 2d. 1665—To 14 gipsyes, 1s.
3 maimed soldiers, 3d. A sword fourbishing, —. Edward Clarke, sen., for
whipping the dogs, 1s. 2d. 1676—Spent with the neighbours on Holy
Thursday, 6s. For two foulmords heads, 4d. William Widdrington, gent.
buried 1683,—a Roman catholic priest.

List of the Rectors :—

A.D. 1341.—John de Roos.

—Richard Flemyng, Bishop of Lincoln.

1419.—Thomas Marshall.

1535.--Bartholomew Ingoldesby.

1560.—William Cantrell.

1584.--William Glen.

1604.—Nathaniel Tuke.

1619.—John Nixon.

1664.—Edmund Thorold.

1670.—Josiah Miers.

1687.—Anthony Beveridge.

1702.—Rowland Fox.

1722.—Benjamin Rudge.

1741.—Francis Hetherington.

A.D. 1769.—Bracklay Kennett.
 1772.—Thomas Griffith.
 1773.—Thomas Treacher.
 1777.—Edward Turner.
 1804.—Edward Turner.
 1837.—Edward Pollard.

The Church.

The foundations of this little edifice, dedicated to St. Mary, must have been bad throughout, as no one of its walls is now upright, and the whole structure looks as if it might fall at any time, yet it has remained in this condition for many years. Originally it was an Early English fabric, consisting of a tower, nave, north aisle, and chancel of that style. Then a Decorated chantry chapel was added to the nave, on the south side of which the arch still remains, partly filled in with masonry, and partly with glass to light the interior in a strange fashion, and a square-headed window of the reticulated type was inserted in the north wall beneath a new head and label. Next a Perpendicular embattled parapet, angle pinnacles, and perhaps a shield on the south side, bearing a plain cross, were added to the tower; then the present wretched little chancel was built, and finally in 1809 the aisle was pulled down and its arcade filled in with masonry and glazing in the strangest manner to serve as an outer wall. Happily however its character may still be seen from such portions of its features as remain exposed to view, whence we gather that it consisted of two bays, and that it had clustered filleted pillar shafts and responds, the caps of which were ornamented with the nail-head ornament. The tower is low, and was lighted by plain coupled lancets serving as belfry windows in each of its walls, three of which still remain. At the west end was a large window, now filled in with masonry, pierced only by three small rude lights.

Within, the chancel and tower arches are Early English, the pier caps of the former are ornamented with the nail-head ornament, and shew that a screen once stood within it. The latter has plainly chamfered square piers surmounted by a roll mould and massive plain brackets, whence the arch springs. The Font is a carefully carved octangular specimen of the

Perpendicular period. On two of its panels are cut the sacred monograms I. H. C. and M. R., and on others, shields now almost smooth, but two of which bore a fesse dancette between 10 billets 4. 3. 2. & 1., for Hardeby or Harby ; another a fesse dancette between 3 lions heads erased, and a fourth a chevron between 3 escallops. There are three bells. The largest bears this inscription, "God save his church." The second, "Acknowledge me to be the Lord." The third, "We praise thee, O God;" all are dated 1745. When Holles visited this church the tomb of Thomas Hardeby still remained within it, and as he saw upon it the same shields as upon the Font with the addition of Erm, a fesse dancette, impaling a fesse between 3 griphons passant regardant, probably Thomas Hardeby was the donor of the Font. In the south window of the chancel he also saw two shields, one bearing Or, 3 griphons passant Az. 2 & 1, the other Sa, a fesse between 3 griphons passant regardant Arg. On brass plates now attached to the front of a modern gallery are the portraitures of Daniel Harby and Anne his wife, kneeling in prayer on either side of a double desk supporting devotional books. Above is a curtain, and below a chequered pavement. Behind him kneel five sons, and behind her eight daughters. On a second plate is this legend :—

"Danieli Hardeby de Evedon in Com Lincoln Armigero. Uni Justiciar Dni Regis ad pacem in Com præd."

Just did this Justice lieue, and dyinge Just
As all good Mortalls ought, sleeps here in dust ;
Blest sleepe ! where dyinge ashes do receiue,
An Heauenly body from an Earthly graue.

Filii { John. Bryan. William. Charles. Edward.	Filiæ { Elizabeth. Mary. Katharine. Mary. Susan. Ann. Susan. Judith.

On a third plate is a shield bearing Harby, impaling a fesse charged with 3 fleurs de lis. Here also is a mural monument commemorating Sir Peregrine Bertie, the husband of Ann Hardby, bearing this inscription :—

"Here lyes the bodys of Sir Peregrime Bertie, son of the Hon. Robt. Earl of Lindsey, and Lord Great Chamberlain of England, and Governor of the City of Lincoln in the Civil Wars under King Charles the First, and Anne his wife."

In the churchyard is a mediæval stone coffin with a small drain hole in the bottom, found together with its lid in digging a grave some years ago, and still exposed to view.

HAVERHOLME.

THIS lies 4 miles north east of Sleaford, and is simply termed Holm, or Island, in Domesday book, whence also we gather that Ulf had 12 carucates of land in demesne here, and the same quantity in soke; that Gilbert de Gant had 4 carucates in demesne, 28 sokemen, 28 villans, and 3 bordars having 14 carucates; and that there were 2 churches, 2 priests, and a mill worth 13s. 4d. a year. The annual value in King Edward's time was the same as it was in King William's, viz: £10, and it was tallaged at £3.

Subsequently Holm was called Hufreholme, and Hafreholm, from the situation of part of its land between two branches of the river Slea, consisting of 300 acres. Next we hear of it as being chiefly in the possession of Alexander, Bishop of Lincoln from 1123 to 1147, and of his presenting it and its appurtenances to the Abbot and Monks of Fountain's Abbey, Yorkshire, in 1137 for the good of the souls of King Henry, Roger, Bishop of Salisbury (Alexander's uncle), and others, from a desire he had to establish another Cistercian House emanating from Fountain's; but after a little band of Cistercians had come to Haverholme and settled there, suffering most probably in mind and body from the dreary swamps then around it, and had tried it for two years, they despairingly vacated it, and were compassionately settled by their considerate patron on his manor of Louth Park. Haverholme having thus reverted to the Bishop, he then gave it to the Gilbertine Order in 1139.* Tanner informs us that the

---

* "The Sempringham or Gilbertine Canone were instituted by St. Gilbert at Sempringham in Lincolnshire, A. D. 1148, and confirmed by Pope Eugenius III. This devout man composed his rule out of those of St. Austin and St. Benedict, (the women following the Cistercian regulation of St. Benedict's rule, and the men the rule of St. Austin), with some special statutes of his own. The habit of these Canons, as described in the Monasticon, is a black cassoc with a white cloak over it, and a hood lined with lamb skins. This order consisted of both men and women, who lived in the same houses,

Cistercians had made some progress in providing monastic buildings for themselves at Haverholme; but the Gilbertines, more easily contented than their predecessors, soon built a church here which they dedicated as usual to the blessed Virgin Mary, and erected all the necessary conventual buildings. The following is a translation of the Charter of Bishop Alexander, which throws much light upon the foundation of this House :—

"Our blessed God and Lord Jesus Christ, who has opened the eyes of mercy upon us, and illuminated the eyes of our mind, and inclined our heart to the necessities of his handmaidens, the faithful holy nuns, viz: of that wonderful religion, who under the guidance and learning of Gilbert the priest, are devoutly meditating in behalf of Christ and God. These nuns taking upon them a self denying life, a life holy, viz: of the monks of the Cistercian religion, are endeavouring to maintain, and indeed do maintain it; we, because they have not a place befitting their religion, have prepared by the inspection of divine grace, and given one to them, which may be sufficiently adapted to their mode of life. For we have given them the Island before called Hafreholm, which is now called and believed to be the Island of St. Mary, with all which belongs to it, in meadow and land, which is convenient for culture, and in march and in waters, and in all things even to the end of the said Island, with the 2 mills, the whole Island to be exempt and quit from all human and secular service, and to be kept in perpetual possession."

"Now to those persons, who with us had share in the same Island, we have made for that share full satisfaction, viz: to Ralf Halselin and Robert de Calz for we have given to them to their satisfaction in exchange for their part of the land one mill. And this donation, which we have made to the said holy nuns, we have confirmed and do confirm by the assent and testimony of our chapter that of the holy Mother church of Lincoln, and by the testimony of Ralf Earl of Chester, and William Earl of Cam-

---

but in such different apartments that they had no communication with each other, and increased so fast that St. Gilbert himself founded thirteen monasteries of it, viz : four for men alone, and nine for men and women together, which had in them seven hundred brethren and fifteen hundred sisters. At the dissolution there were about twenty-five houses of this order in England." "Preface to Tanner's Not. Mon. p. 19."

bridge his brother, and by the testimony of my own seal. And whatever faithful persons for the love of God, and by our prayer, shall stretch a hand of mercy to them, or shall render any benefit, or extend to them a defence against the enemies of God, and the adversaries of these nuns, we will be mindful of these persons in our prayers as much as pertains to the dignity of our order and our power, and will commemorate them in all the benefits of our Mother church of Lincoln, as also in our own, and in those of all the churches of our diocese. At the same time we will grant them to be partakers also in all those of the faithful abbots, monks, canons, priests, hermits, anchorites, and all faithful people."

"But all persons who shall wish to annihilate this our gracious favour, or to change it for worse, or to intercept its effects, or diminish them, or shall trouble these sisters or these brothers with a malevolent intention, or shall take from them by violence, or shall circumvent them by fraud, or molest them by any injury, we will, unless such evil doers truly repent and correct their errors by ecclesiastical discepline and council, condemn and curse, and anathematize them in that damnation, in which that Judas, the betrayer of God and our Lord Jesus Christ perished, and that to which the apostle Peter consigned Simon magus, and that which Dathan and Abiram deserved and suffered. Amen. Now this favour we have confirmed on the aforesaid handmaids of Christ for the comfort and advancement of our Mother Church, and for our own selves and our friends, and for the soul of King Henry and my Uncle Roger, who was Bishop of Salisbury, and for the souls of my father, my mother, and my deceased friends. Be mindful of him who is most dear to you in your prayers, that God may have mercy on you. Amen. In the year 1139 from the incarnation of our Lord Jesus Christ, I, A., Bishop of Lincoln, confirmed by this my charter the aforesaid donation, by the testimony of the aforesaid and many others." " Ex autog in bibl Cotton."

Adam Fitz-Piers, or Peter, was a subsequent benefactor to this Priory, who made the following grant in its favour :—

"To all the Sons of our Holy Mother the Church, Adam Fitz-Peter, Greeting. Be it known to you that I have given, and by this present deed confirm to the Nuns, Canons, and Brothers, at Haverholme, there serving God and St. Mary, all I had in the town of Norford, viz: one carucate of land, with all its appurtenances in wood and plain, waters, meadows, and pastures. Besides this, I will give to the aforesaid Nuns, Canons, and Brothers, for ever, one stone of wax yearly, at the feast of St. Michael, and my heirs shall do so for me for ever: All this I have given them with the good will of my wife Maud, and of my heirs, in free and perpetual alms, as is most freely given to any free religious persons, quit of all secular service, exaction and occasion, as any alms is most freely given to any religious person; and we will warrant and maintain all these things aforesaid, against all men, as our proper and special alms, saving ourselves and the reasonable service of our Lord the King. But it is to be observed, that this carucate at Norford defends itself for a fourteenth part of a Knight, and the two carucates at Kikely for the eighth part of a Knight's service. All this I have given to the aforesaid Convent of Haverholme, with my daughter Juliana and my niece Maud, for the health of all our kindred, as well living as deceased. But at my death they shall perform the service for me and my wife Maud, which they do for any Canon or Nun of their order. These being witnesses: Robert Pyron, Alexander Cressy, Robert Divell, Robert, my heir, Helias Fitz-Richard, Robert Divell, Peter Filad, Richard Such, Roger Fitz-Richard, Helias Man, Robert Pyron, Geoffry York." *

This House had also the patronage of the following churches, viz: Anwick, Old Sleaford, Ruskington, Quarrington, and Dorrington alternately, A.D. 1209. The following notices refer to the presentation to some of the above livings : "John de Kirkeby, chaplain, was presented by the Prior and Convent of Haverholme to the vicarage church of Amewyk, 1286." "Conrad de Kokenato was presented by the Prior, &c., to the church of Old Sleaford, 1245." "Alexander de Brancewelle, clerk, was presented, to the church de Querington, 1218."

It is an interesting fact that when Thomas a Becket, Archbishop of Canterbury, fled in 1164 from his angry sovereign in fear of his life, he took refuge in the hermitage belonging to Haverholme Priory, on the edge of the fen, under the guidance of a monk who knew the country, after which he returned to his own manor of Eastry in Kent. "Wilson's Notes."

---

* Dugdale's Monasticon, vol. 2, p. 264.

S

The sum of 100s. per annum—formerly payable by the Prior and Convent of Haverholme to the Dean and Chapter of Lincoln, was dedicated by them to the use of the poor chorister boys of the Cathedral. Through the manorial tenure of Religious Orders some of their houses were liable for the maintenance of the drainage of the fens in Lincolnshire and the ferries over the rivers and drains of the same, and were often complained of for not fulfilling such duties. Thus, in 1316, the Prior of Haverholme was reported as having neglected to provide a ferry boat at the "Bothe near to the Wathe mouth, which he was bound to supply for foot folks by night and by day as being a public passage for the King's liege subjects passing from Kesteven to the river Witham; also that the said Prior in right of his lands in Ewerby and Ousthorpe had neglected to maintain the south side of the water or drain from Appletreeness to Kyme, and had refused to do so, although the whole marsh of Kesteven and Holland was drowned thereby." "Dugdale's Imbanking, p. 290." In 1327, the King granted to the Abbot of Haverholme the right of free warren in all his demesne lands in Haverholme, Ruskington, Anwick, Quarrington and Dorrington.

In 1360 a disagreeable contretemps occurred in connexion with this Priory, for then Alice, daughter of John de Everingham fled from it, but was captured and brought back; upon which she was taken before the Bishop, and the case was tried by him and 12 jurors, when her declaration was believed that she had never "professed herself," or taken the full vows, and was released. This Priory was always a popular one and well conducted throughout its existence; but it was nevertheless abolished in common with all others at the dissolution of Monastic establishments, when its possessions were as follows, taken from an Abstract Roll, 30. H. 8., in the Augmentation Office:—

	£	s.	d.
Ryskington, Anwyke, and elsewhere, rent fixed from free tenants	4	13	4
Rents from tenants at mill	21	3	5
Dyrington, movable rents in	0	2	4
Ryskington and elswhere, farm of lands in	20	7	1
Holme, windmills in	5	6	8
Lesyngham, fullers mill in	1	6	8
Slyford, a mill called Tylby mill in	0	16	0

	£	s.	d.
Marston, a mill in............................	1	0	0
Ryskington, portion from the rectory............	6	6	8
Dirryngton, do. do.	2	13	4
Anwyk, tithes of the grain in	3	0	0
Laford vetus, pension in	2	0	0
Haverholme, farm of demesne lands in Notts	10	15	0
Stanton le vale and elsewhere, fixed rents........	3	14	$2\frac{1}{2}$
Thorp, rents of tenants in	5	18	8
Thorowton and elsewhere, farm of lands	0	14	2
Stanton, farm of manor in	4	14	8
Shelton, farm of house and tenements	2	13	4
Shelton, messuage and lands in	1	10	0
Warbrough, farm of grange of	1	1	8
Slaturne, farm of grange in....................	2	13	4
Thorpe, pension from	1	0	0

The seal appended to the deed of surrender represents our Lord and the Virgin Mary enthroned beneath a canopy, and under a sub-arch, a monk kneeling and a priest celebrating mass. Around is the legend, Sigill Prioris de Haverholm. This deed is dated September 5th, 1539, and by it William Hall, then Prior, and six canons gave up the Priory and all the estates belonging to it, and in return, together with some nuns, received pensions for life varying from £4 to £2 per annum. Happily the inmates of this Priory had dwindled down to a small number before its dissolution; for once it held 50 brothers and 100 nuns, for whom accommodation was provided in its more palmy days.

The site of the Priory was granted to Edward Lord Clinton, who, by the King's licence, alienated half the manor to Robert Carre in 1544, and the other half to William Thorold. "Harl. MSS. 6829." The heirs of Robert Carre and William Thorold continued to enjoy their portions of the Priory spoils for some years, of whom Sir Edward Thorold, of Hough, died seized of his part—called Haverholme Grange, in 1604, held of the manor of East Grenwich, leaving a son Alexander as his heir. The Abdys succeeded the Clintons, and next Sir John Shaw, Bart., seems to have possessed all the land in Haverholme, of whom Sir Samuel Gordon, Bart., bought it in 1763. He was succeeded by his son, Sir Jenison William Gordon, the second Bart., by whom Haverholme was bequeathed to the late Earl of

Winchilsea, Bart., on certain conditions, and is now held in trust for his second son, the Honble. Murray Finch Hatton.

All remains of the old Priory buildings above ground have long since passed away, but the house built upon its site previous to the present one was intended to be of the Gothic style and of a monastic appearance, although ill carried out, and of poor materials. The present edifice is a handsome and far better specimen of modern work, produced by casing the old house with Ancaster stone, and adding an elevated terraced garden, &c., to it. Attached to it on the south side is a large deer park in the parish of Ewerby. The cemetery of the Priory was on the east side of the present mansion, as several stone coffins containing the remains of some of the former inmates of the Priory have occasionally been uncovered here, and with fragments of painted glass and other small relics was found a little square leaden ventilator like the model of a 14th century traceried window, when certain alterations were being made at the Priory in 1854, and during the present year the foundations of a portion of the Priory buildings on the west of the house were disclosed, lying from 3 to 4 feet below the present ground level. These consisted of several courses of large dressed stones, and over an angle of these a large elm tree had grown and fallen, in some measure, indicating the time that has elapsed since the superstructure of these buildings was removed. On the east was a room 34 feet by 18 feet, next to it a small one 31 feet by 8 feet, then a larger one 32 feet by 21 feet, then a passage 4 feet wide, and finally another large room, at least 32 feet by 21 feet, but its west wall was gone. Behind this range of rooms the foundations of 4 small ones were also discovered, and of other walls south and east of them.

SOUTH KYME.

ACREAGE,
8458.

POPULATION,
1004.

THIS lies 9 miles north east of Sleaford. Previous to the
Conquest Earl Morkar possessed 4 carucates and 2 oxgangs
of land at this place, then called Chime, also 2 acres of meadow,
210 acres of wood, 700 acres of fen, and 6 fish garths worth 4s. a
year, altogether valued at £3 13s 8d. Then also there were two
churches and one priest here. After the Conquest King William
for a time retained Kyme in his own hands, but subsequently
gave it and its appurtenances in Morton, Edenham, and elsewhere,
including 14 oxgangs of land that had belonged to the Saxon
Tunne, to Gilbert de Gant, when its value had increased to £7.
All that time Egbright, a vassal of Gilbert's had half a carucate,
6 villans with another half carucate, 1 acre of meadow, 82 acres
of coppice wood, and 3 fisheries, worth 20s. in King Edward's
time, subsequently increased to 40s. The family of Kyme, no
doubt deriving their name from this place, next possessed this
manor. The first of these, William, a tenant of Gilbert de Gant's
circa 1100, was the son or grandson of a Ralph Kyme, of Bullington. His son, Simon, sometimes called Fitz-William, or son of
William, founded a Priory for nuns on his ancestral lands at
Bullington 1136, and died before 1160. He had three wives,
Agnes, who had died before 1136, Sybilla, and Beatrice, but their
respective progeny is unknown. Simon's son and heir was
Philip, a munificent benefactor to his father's religious foundation at Bullington, and also the founder of St. Mary's Priory at
Kyme, the inmates of which were to pay for the present and
future welfare of his soul, his wife's, and also for their an-
cestors and descendant's souls. He gave the church of North
Carlton, or Carlton Kyme, to found a prebend at Lincoln, the
presentation of which he reserved for himself and his descendants,
which was confirmed by his son Simon, 1208. He was Sheriff of
Lincolnshire from 1168 to 1170, and held two knight's fees under

Robert, Bishop of Lincoln. He married either Hawise, daughter and heir of Robert Fitzooth, or of Robert Deyncourt, and died at the close of the 12th century. He was succeeded by his son Simon de Kyme, who held the office of Sheriff of Lincolnshire from 1195 to 1198. He joined the Barons against King John, and was taken prisoner at Lincoln, 1217. He married Rohaisia or Rohisia, called the Rose of Bullington, daughter and heir of Robert the dapifer, or steward to Earl Percy and his wife the relict of Gilbert de Gant, and daughter of William de Romara, Earl of Lincoln. She had lands at Thornton le Moor, given her by Adam de Percy, a knight's fee in Elkington, and dowry lands elsewhere. After the death of her husband in 1219, she gave the King a palfrey for a summons against her husband's brother, William de Kyme, calling upon him to surrender her lands to her. Both she and her mother the Countess Rohaisia were buried in Bullington Priory church. Their son Philip had been on the Barons side until their discomfiture at Lincoln in 1217, when he returned to his allegiance and paid £100 for the King's pardon. He held the office of dapifer to the Percies as his grandfather had done, and married Agnes de Wallys, or Welles, or, according to Dugdale, Agnes, daughter of William Fitzallan. By her he had two sons, Simon and William, and a daughter Johanna, a nun of Bullington, for whose sake her father gave all his lands in Huttoft to that Priory. It is uncertain which of the sons was the eldest; but as Simon gave the nuns of Bullington a wood near his park there, and he is said to have been *succeeded* by his brother in a cartulary of Valle Dei Monastery, probably he was the eldest. He died without issue, 1247. William de Kyme then certainly succeeded to his family possessions and the office of Dapifer to William de Percy, paying as a relief for his inherit-ance £100 in 1256-7. He married first Matilda, or Maude, daughter of Sir Giles Thornworth, and secondly Lucy de Roos, who had in dowry the toll of all loaded vehicles coming out of Immingham, also free warren over the Thorntons and Newstead, as dowry lands of the heirs of Philip de Kyme. William de Kyme confirmed all his ancestor's gifts to Bullington Priory, and added to these all his meadows by the Trent. He died in 1259, and his heart was interred in the church of that House. His son and heir Philip, being then a minor, was assigned to the custody of Hugh Bigod by the King, and whose daughter he subsequently married. He was one of the Barons who signed the remonstrance sent to the Pope from Lincoln 1300, and in the same year procured a licence from the crown to hold a weekly market at his manor of Borwell, and also a grant of free warren in Authorpe, Billinghay, Walcot, and Metheringham. Eight years later he obtained a grant of the house of Black Friars near his family house in Thorngate, Lincoln. In 1311 he was selected with Edmund Lord Deyncourt, David Fletwyck and Lawrence Holbeach to lead the Lincolnshire levies to Roxburgh, which they were ordered to reach before July 15th in that year, a service he was the better able to perform because in his youth he had served in a previous war with Scotland, and in 1276 had supplied three knights and their attendants properly mounted for the King's service. In the Carlaverock roll he is mentioned in high terms, and as bearing a red banner charged with a golden chevron surrounded by crosslets. In 1317 he was excused from further attendance on the Scotch war on account of his advanced years, and died 1322, when he was possessed of a messuage in Thorngate, Lincoln, worth £4 a year, the manors of Kyme, Sotby, Croft, Goltho, Calceby, Muckton, Immingham, &c. His son and heir William de Kyme, born circa 1282, paid his relief for lands in Thorganby, &c., in 1324. He married Johanna, daughter of Adam Lord Welle of Hellowe, bringing as her dowry the manors of Burwell, Croft, Thorpe, and Friskney, who after the death of her husband, circa 1339, married Nicholas Lord Cantilupe, and was the foundress of the Cantilupe chantry in Lincoln Cathedral, 1358, which she endowed with the church of Leake, lands there and in Panton, Hardwick, and Stretton. Lord Cantilupe died 1355, and she in 1361. Both were buried in the Cantilupe chantry chapel in the Cathedral. On the death of William de Kyme, the last Baron, without issue, his sister Lucy, or her son became his heir. She married Robert de Humfraville, Earl of Angus, second son of Gilbert de Humfraville, Baron Prudho of Northumberland, created Earl of Angus, who died 1308, his eldest son, Gilbert, having predeceased him in 1303 without issue. Thus, Robert, 2nd Earl of Angus, inherited his father's estates as well as his wife's, or those of the de Kyme's, then consisting of lands in Kyme, Sotby, Stallingboro', Aswardby, Metheringham, Baumber, Calceby, Elkington, Immingham, Faldingworth, Bullington, &c. He died 1325, leaving a son and heir Sir

Gilbert de Humfraville, 3rd Earl of Angus, and a daughter
Elizabeth.   Sir Gilbert paid the King a fine of £10 for the profit
of the customs taken on Kyme Ea, "Ab. Rot. Orig. 16. E. 3.,"
and obtained a charter for holding a fair at South Kyme in 1344,
when he was also appointed one of the Guardians of the northern
marshes.   In 1359 the King selected him to keep the peace in
Lindsey during his absence.   He appears to have let the manor
to Sir John de Kirketon, who died 1367.   In 1379 he gave his
manor of Immingham to a religious Fraternity, and died in 1381.
His first wife was Johanna, daughter of Robert Lord Willoughby,
and his second Matilda, daughter of Sir Thomas Lacy, and his heir
after the death of her brother Sir Anthony, and who had the manor
of Croft as her dower on the death of her husband.   Subsequently
she married Henry Earl of Northumberland, and died 1399.   By
Sir Gilbert she had an only son, Sir Robert, who died before his
father, when Elizabeth, or Eleanor, daughter of Elizabeth Humfraville and sister of Sir Gilbert married to Sir Gilbert Burdon,
Boroughdon, or Barrowden, became his coheir with her uncle
Thomas de Umfraville.   She was born about 1347, and married
Sir Henry Tailboys, son and heir of Sir William Tailboys, Baron
of Hephall, Northumberland, but died before his uncle Sir
Gilbert, whence her son, Sir Walter Tailboys, succeeded to the
patrimony of the Barons of Kyme, and eventually to that of
the Barons of Hephall.   He was High Sheriff of the county in
1389-90, and the following year sold the old family residence by
Thornbridge Gate, Lincoln, commonly called Kyme Hall.   He let
the manor of Kyme to Sir Henry Grey de Wilton, and died 1417.
By Margaret his wife he had a son Walter, born 1414, who paid
his relief for his ancestor's estates in 1419, and on the death of Sir
Robert Umfraville succeeded to his lands at Riddesdale and Har-
bottle, and died, seized of the combined lands of the Kyme's,
Umfraville's, and Tailboy's, 1443.   By his wife Alice, daughter
of Humfrey Stafford, he had a son and heir, William Tailboys,
sometimes called Earl of Kyme, a distinguished Lancastrian in
the reign of Henry VI.   He was taken prisoner at Redesdale,
conveyed to Newcastle, and there beheaded, after which his
estates were forfeited, and the manor of Kyme was given to
George Duke of Clarence, 1461-2.   By Elizabeth, daughter of
Lord Bonville, William Tailboys had a son and heir, Sir Robert,
who obtained the restoration of his ancestor's estates, 1478, when

he became lord of Kyme and Redesdale, &c. He was High Sheriff for Lincolnshire 1481, and died June 18th, 1495. In accordance with his Will, dated November 16th, 1494, and proved June 19th, 1495, he was buried in the Priory church of Kyme. It runs thus :—

> "I leave my body to be buried in the north side of the choir in the Priory church of Kyme, and there I will have a tomb with a picture of me, and another of my wife, my son George, my son William, and my 2 sons Robert and John, &c., &c. Whereas a marriage is intended between George my son and Elizabeth, sister to Sir William Gascoigne, Kt., I will that my manor of Faldingworth and the advowson of the church and the manor of Rottingham, in Lancashire, be settled on my son William Tailboys for life. I will that my manors of Kyme, Newton, Hornington, and Oxton, in the county of York, be settled on Robert Tailboys my son for life. My sons John, William, Robert, and Richard, and my daughters .... I will that an obit be kept yearly for me in the Priory of Kyme, and the like obit in the Priory of Bullington, in Lincolnshire. And I appoint William Hussee, Thomas Welby, and Thomas Wymbish my executors." "Nicholas's Testamenta vetusta, p, 420."

According to his Will his obit was kept at Kyme and Bullington until the dissolution of monastic houses. By Elizabeth his wife, daughter of Sir John Heron, Kt., he had a son, Sir George Tailboys, born 1467. He was High Sheriff for Lincolnshire 1495-6, and was buried in the Priory church of Bullington. Sir George, by his wife Elizabeth, daughter of Sir Robert Gascoigne, who died in 1554, had a son Sir Gilbert, created Lord Tailboys of Kyme, by Henry VIII. He chiefly lived at Kyme, and was buried in the Priory church there on his death, April 15th, 1530. He married Elizabeth, daughter of Sir John Blount, of Shropshire. She was one of the most beautiful and accomplished ladies of the Court, but untrue to her husband, as she became the mother of a son by the King; he was born at Blackmore manor, Essex, 1519, and went by the name of Henry Fitzroy until 1524, when he was created Earl of Nottingham, and in 1533 Duke of Richmond and Somerset. He married Mary, daughter of Thomas Howard, Duke of Norfolk, and died 1536. Lord Tailboys had two sons, George and Robert, who died in their infancy, and were buried in Kyme Priory church, and two daughters, Elizabeth and

Margaret. The first thus became his heir. She had married Thomas Wymbysh, of Nocton, but was childless, and when he petitioned the King to be allowed to claim the Barony of Kyme, this was refused, and led to an important decision " that thenceforth none should use the style of his wife's dignity, but such as by courtesy of England had also a right to her possessions for the term of his life." She married secondly Ambrose Dudley, Earl of Warwick, second son of John Dudley, Duke of Northumberland. Her sister Margaret married Sir George Vernon, of Bakewell, Derbyshire, by whom she had Dorothy, married to Sir George Manners, and Margaret, married to Thomas Stanley, Earl of Derby. On the death of Elizabeth, Countess of Warwick, her family estates were divided among the descendants of her aunts, who had intermarried with the Willoughby, Ingleby, and Dymoke families, when the Castle and manor of Kyme thus passed to the Dymokes through the marriage of Sir Edward Dymoke with Anne, fifth daughter of Sir George Tailboys and Elizabeth his wife. In 1607 this Sir Edward Dymoke, Kt., and Lionel Massenberde, both of Kyme, each paid 500 marks for counsel in the Star Chamber, *i.e.* were fined to that amount. "Pip. Rot. 6. J. I." The Dymokes continued to reside at Kyme until the close of the 18th century. In 1730 the manor was sold to the then Duke of Newcastle, and in 1748 to Abraham Hume, Esq., the father of Sir Abraham Hume, Bart., from whom it descended to Earl Brownlow, and its present owner the Honble. Charles Cust.

The Castle.

From the natural value of the land constituting the manor of Kyme, a Saxon anla or hall most probably existed upon it at a very early period; and when the family of de Kyme began to live here they no doubt provided a suitable residence for their accommodation, which most probably was gradually enlarged and strengthened by themselves and their successors until it at last assumed the form of a grand moated Baronial Castle. This still remained in the reign of Henry VIII., when Leland, after having visited it, speaks of it in his Itinerary as "the goodly house and park at Kyme, belonging to Sir George Tailboys."

KYME TOWER.

Its moat still proclaims the size of its area, and happily one of its towers still remains as a monument of its past grandeur. This was spared at the beginning of the last century when all its other features were pulled down. It is an admirable piece of masonry of the middle of the 14th century, almost as perfect as when it was erected. In plan it is nearly square, with a square staircase turret attached to its south eastern angle, and is 77 feet high. It consists of a basement story, vaulted with eight plainly chamfered ribs converging to an octangular cusped panel in the centre serving as a boss, on which is a carved shield bearing Gules, a cinquefoil within an orle of cross crosslets Or, for Humfraville. The doorway giving access to this is in the inner or court yard side of the Castle, and by its side is a flat arched recess as if for a fireplace, but it has no chimney. This room is only lit by narrow slits for the sake of security, and probably only served as a cellar or office. Above this were three other rooms one over the other, reached by a newel staircase in the turret. The first of these was called the chequered chamber, perhaps from the character of its now lost pavement, and this communicated with another portion of the Castle by means of a doorway over the one below. From traces on the south side of this it is clear that a flat roofed building only as high as the lower string of its remaining tower adjoined it. This perhaps gave access to the hall, which is said to have stood on the south of this tower, and to have been adorned with carved figures of mounted knights, perhaps representing jousts. Above were two similar rooms, each supplied with a fireplace and lighted by well moulded two light windows surmounted by a quatrefoil. The roof was very low pitched, having gurgoyles on either side to carry off the water from it through the parapet walls, which are plainly embattled. 104 steps give access to this. The turret staircase is covered by richly carved stone vaulting, supported by a little central shaft. From its summit a fine view of the old Castle precincts and the vast flat tract around it is obtained, whence also Lincoln Cathedral, Tattershall Castle, and other distant objects of interest may be seen. Now, all traces of the drawbridge over the moat are lost, but these were still visible long after the destruction of the Castle. The ruined base of another tower has also been removed, which remained until the last century, and is spoken of as affording a convenient and safe

platform on which women and children stood to witness bull
baitings, then not unfrequently exhibited on the site of this once
grand residence of the Umfravilles.

THE PRIORY.

This was a House of the Black or Regular Canons of the
Order of St Augustine, Bishop of Hippo, A.D. 395. Their habit
was a long black cassock with a white rochet over it; and over
this a black cloak and hood. It was founded by Sir Philip de
Kyme, 1170, who dedicated it to the blessed Virgin Mary,
and was further endowed by his son Simon de Kyme, and others,
until its possessions became very considerable, as will be seen
from the subjoined list of these taken from a Roll in the Augmentation Office, written at the time of its dissolution in 1539 :—

	£	s.	d.
Kyme, Fixed rents in	0	6	8
Conesbye do. do.	0	4	7
Swarbie do. do.	0	10	8
Calverthorpe do.	0	8	8
Asgarby do. do.	0	1	4
Evedon do. do.	0	4	0
Esthorpe and Ywardbye do. do.	0	2	4
Anwyke do. do.	0	1	0
Dodyngton and Westborough do. do.	0	0	1
Boston do. do.	0	1	8
Wyberton do. do.	0	1	6
Kyme, Farm of a cottage and garden	2	5	8
Osburnbye, Farm of lands and tenements	2	0	0
Croston, Farm of a tenement	0	8	8
Hasbye, Farm of tenements and lands	0	11	6
Aswarbye, Farm of tenements	0	0	4
Evendon, Farm of lands	1	3	8
Eathorpe and Ywardbye, Farm of tenements and lands	0	10	0
Anwyke, Farm of lands	0	4	0
Thorp and Tilney, Farm of cottages and lands ..	7	1	4
Merton (Morton), Farm of lands	0	1	8
Billinghay, Farm of marsh	0	6	8

	£	s.	d.
North Kyme, Farm of cottages	0	6	8
Lincoln City, Farm of a toft	0	17	0
Boston, Farm of a house	2	14	4
Byker, Farm of tenements and lands	1	0	0
Quadrynge, Farm of tenements and lands	0	13	4
Horblyn do. do.	0	10	0
Dodyngton and Welbourne, Farm of tenements and lands	0	19	0
Langton, near Wragbye, Farm of lands	0	13	4
Ewerbye, Farm of Rectory	12	7	0
Swarbye, Farm of Rectory	3	0	0
Kyme, Farm of Rectory	6	0	0
Osbournbye, Farm of the manse of Rectory......	6	13	4
Medringham, Farm of the Rectory..............	7	0	0
Ewdon, Pension from the church	1	0	0
Ormesby, Pension from the rector	0	16	8
Asgarbye, Pension from the church	0	2	0
Aswarby, Pension of 1lb. of incense	0	0	6
Northome and elsewhere, Fixed rents	5	0	0
Northome, Farm of a cottage, garden, and pasture	0	16	9
Wayneflete, All Saints, Farm of pasture	0	3	4
Wayneflete, Blessed Mary, Farm of cottage and lands	0	13	10
Thorpe, Farm of lands........................	0	3	5
Fryskney, Farm of lands and marsh	0	10	0
Cokeryngton, Farm of lands	0	3	4
Crofte, Farm of lands	0	0	4
Crofte and Thorpe, Farm of Rectory............	18	0	0
Northome, Tithes of the chapel	2	0	0
Calceby, Pension from the rectory	0	13	4
Wainflete, All Saints, Pension from church	3	6	8
Immingham, Fixed rents......................	8	2	9
Immingham, Farm of lands, &c.	22	17	4
Kyme, Farm of demesne lands	2	16	10

But few names of the many Priors who ruled this House for nearly 400 years have been placed on record ; the following, however, are some of these : Jordan, circa 1195 ; Lambert, 1200 ; Henry, (called Abbat of Kyme) ; Hugh de Wayneflete, obiit 2. H. 4. ; Thomas de Bykeyre (Bicker), 3. H. 4. ; Robert de Langton, who resigned 9. H. 4.; and Thomas Day, the immediate predecessor of Ralph Fayrfax, who succeeded as Prior, March 27th, 1511, and in whose time this House was suppressed. "Harl. MSS. 5943. p. 29."

In 1450 the Priors and Convents of Kyme and Thornholm were appointed collectors of a tenth of every ecclesiastical benefice not taxed nor accustomed to pay a tenth granted to the King by the clergy, in the Archdeaconry of Stow. "Pip. Rot. 34. H. 6." The seal of the Priory bore this legend : "Sigillum Prioris et Conventus de Kima."

At the dissolution there were 10 inmates of the House, who were pensioned off through the representation and recommendation of John London, one of Cromwell's commissioners for the suppression of Monastic establishments, who especially spoke of the blameless life of the Prior, and of his being "an honest preste well estemed in his contreye." He therefore received a pension of £30 a year, and the others between £5 and £6 each a year. From another letter of London's it appears that John Heneage and two others, Wiseman and Cotton by name who acted with him, committed the custody of the Priory to Lord Tailboys's bailiff, and in 1541 the site of the house, &c., was given to Thomas Earl of Rutland, and Robert Tyrwhit ; but the whole of the site and capitular house, together with all the demesne lands, edifices, orchards, applegarths and gardens within its demesnes and circuit, the advowson of Kyme, its tithes and glebes, and certain lands in North and South Hykeham, were to be held of the King in capite." "Harl. MSS. f. 829."

In 1580 died Robert, son and heir of Sir Edward Dymoke, seized of the manor of South Kyme, 20 messuages, 1 windmill, 3000 acres of land in South and North Kyme, Dogdike, Billinghay, Skirbeck, Walcot, Swinshead, Bicker, Austhorpe, Asgarby, Anwick, and Coningsby, also the advowson of South Kyme of Lord Clinton, as of his manor of Falkingham. "Harl. MSS. f. 829." In 1616, Francis Colly was curate, and there were 300 Communicants. "Willis's MS. f. 39."

In 1646, Sir Edward Dymoke, of Kyme, was obliged to compound for his estates and settle the Rectories of North and South Kyme and Billinghay (worth £200 a year), upon the two churches or chapels whence the tithes were taken.

PERPETUAL CURATES.

A.D.   —Charles Dewsnop.
        1806.—John Bellaman.
        1837.—Henry Sidney Neucatre.
        1870.—Edward Garvey.

THE CHURCH.

This is simply a fragment of the great cruciform church of the Augustine Priory at Kyme, dedicated to the Virgin Mary by its founder Philip de Kyme, circa 1170. The greater part of its nave existed until 1805, when it was reduced to its present dimensions, and its area now comprises the south porch of the Priory church, the greater part of its southern nave aisle, and a small longitudinal slip of its nave having a wide modern gable at each end, and a uniform span roof of a common description surmounted at the west end by a little nondescript bell gable.

Its earliest feature is an elaborately carved semicircular headed Norman doorway, circa 1140. Two circular shafted pillars adorn its jambs, the inner pair having foliated caps, the outer pair scalloped cushion ones; from these spring the two members of its arched head, the one enriched with a lozenge shaped ornament worked partly on its face and partly on its soffit, the other with the dove-tailed device not uncommon in Norman work. Above these is a cable hood mould springing from dragons heads and surmounted by a lion's or a leopard's head boldly projecting from its apex. This doorway was no doubt spared from its rich character when all the contemporary work around it was destroyed and replaced by excellent Decorated work about 1360, with which it still remains incorporated. The aisle, out of which the present church was formed, evidently consisted of five bays, the porch occupying one, and four three light windows the others. Two of these still remain quite perfect, and are fine well moulded specimens of their period, having tracery of a flamboyant character. Part of a third also remains; but this has been barbarously curtailed and filled in with mullions and a transom brought from elsewhere and incongruously put together. At the west end is an equally good but smaller window of the same date, and two excellent pedimented

buttresses.   Similar buttresses appear on the south side ; and in
the one east of the porch is a carefully executed statue niche
flanked by little pillars and having a trefoiled head.   The base
mouldings are bold, and add much to the appearance of the fabric.
The side walls of the porch have been meanly rebuilt with brickwork and the commonest masonry, but the front is in a good
state of preservation.   Its well moulded archway is flanked by
buttresses, and above it is a large niche, having a trefoiled head,
in which still remain two well sculptured figures, representing
the Coronation of the Virgin.   On the right is the representation
of our Lord seated with his left hand placed upon a globe, but
the head and the other arm—probably raised towards the Virgin's
head—is now gone, as well as the upper portion of her figure.
On the lower part of the west buttress of the porch is cut this
legend, now much worn : " Orate pro anima Thos. Weston,
hujus prioratus pincerna," and without it is a much mutilated
stoup.

Within, at the west end, is the respond of the now destroyed
south arcade of the Priory church, serving to indicate precisely
its former position, and also that it was supported by clustered
pillars.

The Font is a small octangular one of the Perpendicular
period, having a blank shield cut in each face of its bowl, and is
only in part original.   In the south eastern angle of the church
is inserted a Decorated piscina having a trefoiled head.

Towards the east end of the north wall is a fragment of the
monument of Gilbert Lord Taylboys.   This consists of part of a
Purbeck marble slab, still retaining the epitaph on a brass plate
and the beds formerly filled in with the kneeling effigies of himself
and his wife, their armorial bearings, and two short legends.
The epitaph runs thus :—

> Here lyeth Gylbert Taylboys lorde Taylboys, lorde of
> Kyme, whych maried Elizabet Blount, one of the
> dowghters of ser John Blount of Kynlet in the counte
> of Shropshier, kniht, wych lord Taylboys departed
> fourth of this world the XV. day of Aprill, aº. Dni.
> MºCCCCCºXXXº., whose solle god pardon.   amen.

Gervase Holles telles us that the now wanting armorial bearings
were, Arg, a saltire Gu, on a chief Gu 3 escallops of the first, for
Taylboys, impaling Nebuly of 6 pieces Or & Sa, for Blount, surmounted by the Taylboys crest—a bull's head couped.   The

effigy of Lord Taylboys represented him in a tabard over his armour, on the body and sleeves of which appeared his armorial bearings, as did those of his lady on her mantle. When the present north wall was built, the vault containing the remains of Lord Taylboys and three children in leaden coffins was accidentally disclosed, and one of the latter was found to have been filled with a liquid serving to preserve the body in a wonderful way ; the coffin of Lord Taylboys was not opened.

At the west end is a stone mural monument consisting of two panels flanked by the figure of Death with a dart on one side, and that of Time with an hour glass and a scythe on the other. It commemorates one, who, as a poor boy of Kyme, was apprenticed to a tailor at the cost of the parish, but lived to acquire a considerable fortune in London through honest industry, and by his Will benefited his birthplace, as thus recorded by his epitaph :

> To the memory of Mr. Marmaduke Dickenson, Citizen
> of London, who dyed January ye 9th, 1711, and by his
> last will gave to ye poore of South Kyme two hund
> pounds, to be paid unto ye Minister and Churchwardens
> within twelve months after his decease, and to be by
> them laid out in a purchase of free land, and ye yearly
> income of ye same to be by them distributed unto ye
> poorst sorte of people of South Kyme, and accounted
> for unto their Jury upon December ye 21st day for ever.

In the lower panel are the following lines, in which the arbitrary use of capital letters is remarkable :—

> Kind Reader Stay, Goe Not Away,
> Your Silent Lectures Take ;
> Redeem your time, Now in your prime,
> That May You Happie Make :
> Cease not to Pray, Both nighte and day,
> God Would Repentance Give,
> That when you dye, Eternally
> You May A Crown Receive.

Holles, under the head of " Tumuli lapidei cum aere," in this church, describes the tombstone of Mary wife of Thomas Whichcote, gentleman, who died 16th January, 1591, which bore the following armorial bearings quarterly, viz : Erm, 2 sangliers trippant Gu, Whichcote. Gu, 3 lapwings Or, Tirwhit. Gu, a chief indented Or, Gronall, impaling quarterly Arg, on a bend Sa, 3 owls of the first, Savile of Newton. Or, an escutcheon within an orle of martlets Sa. Sa, a bend, in chief an eagle displayed. On a bend 3 escallops. Holles also speaks of another stone commemorating " John, son of Thomas and Mary Whichcote, deceased 15º. Sept. Anº. 1588. Ætat. 8º.," and of the representations of a man and a woman holding in their hands the armorial bearings of the Kyme family, and displaying them upon their tunics, viz : Gu, a chevron between 9 crosses botony Or.

During the unhappy contest between Charles I. and the Parliament, the troops of the latter were quartered in the old Priory church here, and did much injury to it.

In 1719, when Commissioners were appointed to inquire into the value of livings, for the purpose of taxing them, the curacy of Kyme was returned as being only worth £10 per annum.

NORTH KYME.

A SAXON of the name of Mere possessed lands in North-Chime—as it was then called, before the Conquest. These were subsequently given to Robert de Todeni, and consisted of 6 carucates of land, valued in King Edward's time at £3 13s. 8d., but after the Conquest at £7. Ivo, a vassal of Robert de Todeni, had then 3 carucates, 12 villans, and 2 bordars with 4 carucates, 50 acres of meadow, and 30 acres of wood. Outi, another Saxon, also possessed 2 manors here, consisting of 5 carucates and 2 oxgangs of land sufficient for 2 ploughs, including their appurtenances in Westby, Haydor, Evedon and Kirkby, 20 acres of meadow, 5 acres of coppice, and a fishery worth 40s. in King Edward's time. This was given to the Norman Colsuein, when it was valued at £4, and afterwards constituted the fee of de la Haye. Subsequently Simon de Kyme held it of the Earl of Salisbury, and he of the King by the tenure of a hawk. In 1315 died Gilbert de Clare, Earl of Gloucester, lord paramount of North Kyme, then computed at one knight's fee. " Inq. p. m. 8. E. 2." In 1325 William de Kyme was holding this vill of the de la Haye fee by the service of a hawk, or a payment of 2s. a year.

In 1392 died Thomas, Earl of Stafford, eldest son of Joan the heiress of the Wake family, seized of the above-named land. " Inq. p. m. 16. R. 2."

Eight years later died Matilda, wife of Henry, Earl of Northumberland, and sister and heir of Anthony Lord Lucy, seized of the manor and its members here. In the same year William, brother and heir of Thomas Earl of Stafford became lord paramount of the manor, then held by Philip de Kyme. " Inq. p. m. 22. R. 2." In 1576 this was held by Sir Edward Dymoke of the honor of Bolingbroke, and afterwards of Lord Taylboys by the old tenure of a hawk, or 2s. a year for all services. " Rot. Cur. Ducat. Lanc." In 1402-3 William Lord Willoughby was responsible to the Treasury for the sum of £20, being the value of divers goods and chattels, late belonging to Henry Percy, found in the manor of Kyme, forfeited by him for being in arms against the King. "Pip. Rot. 6. H. 4." The last great personage connected with North Kyme was the late Earl Fitzwilliam who possessed the manor, but who sold it in various lots. S. S. Muggliston, Esq., is now lord of the manor, and Mr. N. Jackson, of Tattershall, is the owner of Kyme Vacherie, once the old manor house, but now simply a modern farm house. In the village still stands part of a mediæval cross.

LEASINGHAM.

ACREAGE,
2800.

POPULATION,
381.

THIS is situated 2 miles due north of Sleaford. Its name was at first spelt Levesingham or Levesyngham, then Lesyngham, Lessingham, and now Leasingham. Before the Conquest its land was divided between the two Saxons, Barne and Outi. After that great event Barne's land, consisting of 6 carucates, was given to Bishop Remigius, who let part of it and of his manor of Ringsdon to one Adam. He had originally here 2 carucates, 16 villans, 1 sokeman and 4 bordars, to whose use was assigned 30 acres of meadow. The whole was valued in King Edward's time at £6, but subsequently only at £5. Afterwards this manor passed from Adam's grandson Elias to his four sons : Elias, Adam, Hugo and Ralph in succession, then to one of his daughters, Nichola, and then, as all these died without issue, to his sole remaining daughter, Hillaria, married to David de Fletwyke in 1240. Of these, Elias de Ringsdon granted the right of free access for vehicles through all parts of his lands in Leasingham to the fraternity of Haverholme Priory. Outi's lands here, consisting of 6 carucates, and 30 acres of meadow, were given by the Conqueror to Geoffrey Alselin as part of his manor of Ruskington. "Domesday Book." Out of these Ralph Anselin gave to God, the blessed Mary, and the Nuns of Haverholme, a toft called Goosebert, in Leasingham, together with the increase that Lefwin son of Sywar had given them, with pasture for 40 sheep, 4 animals (beasts), and 1 horse. At the same time he made a like donation to them from his lands in Ruskington, circa 1150-60. This Ralph Anselin also appears to have given the fraternity of Temple Bruer 1 oxgang of land in Leasingham, which they had let to Outi and Osmond in 1185, for a rent of 8s., some work and "le present."

In 1253-4 William Bardolf, the then possessor of the Alselin manor, obtained a right of free warren in Leasingham. He was succeeded by Hugh Bardolf in 1304, and then by John Bardolf —termed of Wermsegeye, who possessed it circa 1372. Meanwhile the Bishop's manor was held by Sir David Fletwyke, son of David and Hillaria, who was obliged to sue an impudent intruder, John Rippingale, clerk, in 1300, before he could oust him. "Lansdown MS. 204." In 1311 he was appointed to take charge of the Lincolnshire levies, and led them to Roxburgh, "Rot. Parl.," and died seized of the regained manor here and another at Ringsdon in 1356. "Inq. p. m. 26. E. 3." He left a son David—born 1349, by his wife Laura, daughter of Sir Guy Gumbard, of Rippingale, and Elizabeth his wife, daughter of Sir Roger de Colville, through which marriage the Gumbard lands, held of the Wakes, accrued to the Fletwykes. In 1420 died one of the descendants of this David Fletwyke, who married Katharine, daughter of Sir Walter Pedwardine, of Burton. In the 15th century the Bardolfs had ceased to be lords of the Alselin manor through the marriage of their heiress daughter with Sir William Phelip, who, in her right, died seized of it, 1441. "Inq. p. m. 19. H. 6." In 1454 died Anna, relict of Sir Reginald Cobham, Kt., seized of this vill—perhaps the Phelip heiress. "Inq. p. m. 32. H. 6." In the 15th century Mancerus Marmyon had probably through marriage succeeded to the Fletwyke manor here and at Ringsdon. He died 1449, and was buried at Ringsdon; his son William Marmyon also died possessed of it June 8th, 1520-3, leaving an heiress daughter Katharine. "Harl. MSS. 6827." After the dissolution of the Hospitaler or knights of St. John's establishments, Sir John Williams, first acquired the lands of that fraternity at Temple Bruer, and subsequently sold them to John Bloxholme and John Bellowe. Some members of the Hesslewood family next held the manors of Leasingham and Ringsdon of the Castle of Sleaford by knight's service, after it had been alienated by Henry Holbeche, Bishop of Lincoln; then Ringsdon, or Ringston, was sold to the Brownlow family, and the Leasingham manor was sold to a Mr. Bernard, who, in turn, sold different portions of its land to William King, Joyce King, John Morice, George Swan, Richard Glen, and others; but the Carres as possessors of the Castle of Sleaford, the ancient possession of the Bishops of Lincoln, still claimed fealty of all the tenants of the Bishop's manor of Leasingham in 1527. After Edward York, of Ashby, had sold his property there to Edward King in 1580, he bought the manor of Leasingham, and left it to his son William York, of Burton Pedwardine and Leasingham, at his death in 1681, aged 82. His son William was knighted, and represented Boston in Parliament from 1681 to 1702. He was the first of his family who lived at Leasingham, and his descendants continued to do so until the death of the last male heir—Thomas York, of Leasingham, in 1782, when his property here was inherited by his daughter Frances, the wife of the Rev. John N. Birch, Rector of Leasingham, his residence was pulled down, and his estate was divided between his four daughters.

There were formerly two village crosses here. The base or stump of one of these, termed the Butter Cross, stood in a small paddock called the Nut Yard, just opposite to the road leading to Roxholm. The other—popularly termed the Baker's Cross—stood on the rising ground north of the village, near the present turn in the turnpike road leading to Lincoln. The site of the old house occupied by the Yorks is marked by a clump of old trees and some remains of its offices, now converted into cottages. For a time this house was supposed to be haunted by an evil spirit, the very littleness and folly of whose reputed deeds ought to have assured its inmates that a mischievous wag alone was the author of them; yet the then vicar of Sleaford—Mr. William Wyche, carried on a grave correspondence with a college friend of his—a Mr. J. Richardson, of Emmanuel College, Cambridge, respecting this subject, and an account of the same was thought worthy of a place in a work called "Remarkable and True Stories of Apparitions and Witchcraft, by Henry More, D.D., with the evidence of Joseph Glanvil concerning the same," under the heading of "A true and faithful narrative of the disturbance which was in the house of Sir William York, in the parish of Lessingham, in Lincolnshire," from which the following is an extract: "In May, 1679, Sir William York being from home, there was a great noise made by the lifting up of the latch of the outmost door, which continued with great quickness and noise for the space of two or three hours, till betwixt ten and eleven o'clock in the night. His lady then being at home with few servants, apprehended it to be thieves, and thereupon they went to the door and spake to them, and afterwards winded a horn and raised the town, and upon the coming in of the town the noise ceased and they heard no more of it till May following; and then, Sir William being at London, the same noise was made at the door as before, for two or three nights together, and then they began to believe it to be occasioned by some extraordinary means. This was heard alike by twenty several persons then in the family, who looked out of the windows over the door, heard the noise, but saw nothing."

The account then goes on to state that about a month after, when Sir William was at home, this noise was heard very distinctly several times in the night. From that time to the month of October following, this nuisance appears to have continued in various ways, for we find that besides beating at the doors, windows, ceilings, &c., the chairs were taken from their places and put in the middle of the hall, which, on being set right again, were removed into a passage between the hall and kitchen, and a lighted candle, which Sir William had at another time placed in the hall, was extinguished, and the candlestick carried into the same passage. The noise is said to have sometimes resembled the carpenters and plumbers, who were there doing some repairs, at work, "insomuch that the head carpenter said that if he had not known his servants to be in the house, he should have thought they had been chopping."

A shoemaker of the name of Follet who desired to be thought a wise man and one that could read the language of the stars, was subsequently suspected of having made all these noises, &c., either for his own amusement, or in the hopes of being called in to purge the house of himself, and he grew bolder as Sir William's terror increased.

The same wretched cobbler is supposed to have terrified the daughter of William Medcalf, a farmer in Leasingham about the same time, who fancied she was bewitched by a demon or spirit in the form of a fair-haired man often seen by herself, but never apparent to any one else, who continually annoyed her by rattling her milk pancheons, turning her frumenty into hard curd, matting her hair, &c., which case of presumed witchcraft has also been gravely recorded.

Besides the Rectory, built by the late Rector, and added to by the present one, there are two pleasant residences in this village, of which the larger one, having a handsome classical elevation, said to have been brought from Dunsby when the

Hall there was pulled down, now belongs to the Rev. Oswald Fielden; the other is the pretty little house of Captain Myddleton nearly opposite to it. The Windmill House, now occupied by Henry Hammond, and situated about half way between the villages of Leasingham and North Rauceby, stands on the site of a little public house formerly existing there, where the highwaymen who formerly infested Lincoln Heath and the solitary parts of the London road used to assemble and agree upon their nefarious plans. One of these rascals was shot dead by General Manners, of Bloxholm, when attempting to rob him on his way to London. There is a very picturesque old farm house in the middle of the village. It bears the date of its erection cut on a shield inserted in the centre gable, viz: 1655, and the initals B. E. K. Originally the door was in the centre, but it now constitutes two cottages, and from its grey walls, mullioned windows, and general design, is worthy of the attention it usually receives from visitors. On the gable of another house northward of this on the higher ground, are the initials I. E. P., and the exhortation "Aspice viator et memento te mortalem esse. Anno Domini 1687." This was perhaps provided for the builder—one of the Poyntells—by the then Rector of the parish—Geoffrey Eves. There is a neat little schoolhouse here, built partly with the proceeds of a legacy left for the purpose by the late Mrs. Elizabeth Farmer, and partly at the cost of the present Rector.

ECCLESIASTICAL HISTORY.

There is no mention of the existence of any church at Leasingham in Domesday book, but before the close of the 12th century there was certainly one church here on the site of the present one, and probably a second, that of St. John the Evangelist, which we are sure subsequently stood on the rising ground north of the remaining church. There were also two separate Rectories here having different patrons, but these were united in 1726, and the living was bought by Sir John Thorold, Bart , in 1782, in whose family the patronage still remains. In 1330 David de Fletwyke obtained the King's licence to make over in mortmain 3 messuages and 3 oxgangs of land in Leasingham to a chaplain, for the purpose of celebrating divine service in the chapel of the Virgin, at Leasingham. "Inq. ad. q. d. 3. E. 3. Rot. Hun. 277."

In 1307 William, parson of Leasingham with Adam de Dunslode, chaplain, and Roger Barbdoc, gave the King £12 for a licence to assign a certain tenement with its appurtenances in the suburb of Lincoln, to the Prior and Convent of Nocton Park, to be had in mortmain.

In 1390 Stephen de Houghton, Rector of a moiety of the church of Lesyngham, left 13s. 4d. for the repairs of its chancel, "Bishop Buckingham's Memorandums, f. 371, Capit. Reg. Linc." and at the same time, with others, obtained the King's licence to amortize to the Abbey and Convent of Barling, 2 messuages, 3 acres of plough land, and 5 acres of meadow land lying in the suburb of Lincoln; also a salt pan in Quadring, and a messuage and lands in Middle and North Carlton. "Inq. p. m." In 1616 both medieties of Leasingham were in the patronage of the King, and worth £16 a year. There were then 80 communicants in each mediety. "Willis's MSS. f. 39."

The following is a list of the Incumbents as far as can now be discovered :—

Date of Institution.

Circa 1220.--William de Brauncewell.

1228.--John de Bridgeford, chaplain of Shelford Priory.

1280.—Roger de Trekingham.

1307.—William ————

1390.—Stephen de Houghton.

1394.—William de Ketell.

1535.—Christopher Huchynson, Rector of the south mediety.

1535.—John Green, north mediety.

1597.—Thomas Crook, south mediety.

1597.———— Morice, south mediety.

1614.—William Green, south mediety.

1616.—John Marris, south mediety.

1643.—William Eves, south mediety.

1662.———— Hales, ejected by the Act of Uniformity.

1680.—Gasper Justice.

1682.—Lawrence Benson, north mediety.

1682.—Wilfred Eves, south mediety.

1687.—Nathan Drake, north mediety.

LEASINGHAM CHURCH.

Date of Institution.

1694.—Matthew Smith, north mediety.
1696.—Matthew Smith, south Mediety.
1709.—Stephen Nickols, south mediety.
1720.—Nathan Drake, south mediety.
1754.—John Nevill Birch, both medieties.
1779.—Thomas Taylor, both medieties.
1784.—Friskney Gunniss, both medieties.
1838.—Ainslie Henry Whitmore.
1843.—Edward Trollope, Archdeacon of Stow.

THE CHURCH.

This is dedicated to St. Andrew, and from the evidence of a few carved stones found during its recent restoration, now inserted for their preservation in the vestry wall, it is clear that a Norman church constituted the predecessor of the present fabric. This last consists of a tower and spire, nave, south aisle and porch, chancel and vestry. Of these features the tower is the oldest, and by far the most striking. Built in part of small rubble work circa 1175, 1200, through the excellence of its ashlar framework and buttresses, it still stands firm after the lapse of some 670 years.

In its western face is a most beautifully moulded semicircular headed doorway, and just above it a circular cusped light, formerly walled up, but now opened, and faithfully restored by the aid of evidence derived from a fragment of the original cusping found among the stones used to block up its light. In addition to this a small lancet in the southern wall of the tower serves to light its lower stage. A single minute window lights the middle stage—constituting the ringing chamber, and in the upper one are coupled belfry lights, each consisting of two plain lancets having a small pointed oval above, subdivided by a pillar-mullion springing from an angular transom, instead of from the sill below. The lower parts of these are filled in with stonework of a very peculiar kind. A little interlaced arcaded ornament gives a pleasing appearance to the cornice of the tower. Above this rises a beautiful Decorated broach spire having three tiers of lights, the ornaments of which spring forth from them with effective boldness.

Within the porch is a doorway of the same date and style as the tower, being a relic of an earlier nave. Subsequently, but when the Early English style was still in vogue, the nave was rebuilt, of which a now closed north doorway, and a beautiful double lancet surmounted by a cusped circlet in the north wall are remaining features. At the east end of the aisle is a large Decorated window, near to it in the south wall a small coeval two light one, and at the west end a single light, all having cusped heads ; in addition to which a wretched debased window has been inserted in the south wall, perhaps instead of a better predecessor. In the north wall of the nave, besides the beautiful window above mentioned, there are two large Perpendicular lights, one of fair character, the other ill proportioned and weak. The porch is an ill worked Decorated one, its most remarkable features being beautifully carved figures of kneeling angels, one having a sickle in his hand, serving as the hood mould terminals. There had been no chancel for about 200 years, and a poor Perpendicular window—probably that of the destroyed chancel, was placed in the east wall of the nave. The present chancel was erected in 1863, the style of which was adopted from that of the older beautiful window still remaining in the north wall of the nave. In the eastern wall is a good three light window surmounted by three cusped circlets, and in the south wall two smaller windows of the same style, the sills of which are laid at different levels, and a small door with a good moulded head. Above is a well designed corbel table supported by crocket shaped corbels. On the north side is a lean-to vestry ; this was built of materials taken from the east wall and window of the nave—necessarily pulled down when the chancel was erected.

Within, a Decorated arcade of three bays separates the nave from the aisle, and a wide Early English arch, crushed out of shape through the weight placed upon it, gives access to the tower.

Until recently the nave with its aisle, forming nearly a square, was all the space available for public worship, for the tower arch was stopped up with masonry faced by a gallery, and no chancel at all existed ; but now through the opening of the former, and the addition of the latter, the plan of the fabric is long, rather than square ; so also the nave was low, its walls being covered with a very roughly constructed and nearly flat roof, access to which was supplied by steps descending from a doorway in the tower above it, but this now stands far below the present noble high pitched roof, and enables the ringers in the belfry chamber to see into the church. Standing at the west end, the eye passes over the newly floored central alley and a series of neat open seats towards the really grand chancel arch, the solid carved oak stalls beyond, the richly coloured tile reredos, and the east window, with satisfaction. The pulpit in the north east angle of the nave is composed of Ancaster stone, delicately carved, and is a pleasing specimen of modern art. The Font has often puzzled visitors, whose attention it naturally attracts. It has an Early English base and stem, on which is placed an octangular Tudor bowl, rudely carved with subjects apparently copied from others of an anterior date, giving it the appearance of a degree of antiquity to which it has no just claim; for, from the character of the square head dresses of the females pourtrayed thereon, and the short plaited tunics of the males, we may assign it to the reign of Henry VIII. Besides a single male figure cut on one panel, now too much mutilated to be intelligible, the following subjects are perhaps intended to be represented, viz : The marriage of the Virgin, indicated by a couple joining hands before a priest and an attendant. The temptation, or Satan fleeing from our Lord. Herodias and her daughter with the head of the Baptist. Christ crowned and bearing the wood of the cross lashed together. The entry into Jerusalem, or our Lord mounted on the ass and bearing a rod or staff in his right hand. The resurrection of the dead, or Michael with a conical cap, blowing the summoning trumpet, with the Sun of righteousness above, and two kneeling praying figures on one side below, and a single one on the other. Christ crowned and seated on the rainbow in Judgment, with the wound of the spear in his right breast, and the sun and moon above him. On the spring of the bowl beneath are the following figures at the angles, viz: a female with her arms extended, a second with her hands resting on her hips, a third holding a bag or purse, a fourth holding a distaff, an eagle displayed, perhaps the symbol of St. John, an angel holding out two scourges, and an angel holding three heads before him, perhaps intended to represent souls.

In front of the south pier of the chancel arch is a white marble tombstone bearing this inscription :—

Above this in a circular panel is a shield bearing quarterly per fesse indented, 3 lions rampant two and one ; over all, an escutcheon of pretence bearing a chevron between 3 stag's heads caboshed, the whole surmounted by a helm mantled and a demi eagle with wings elevated springing from a mural crown. Tradition reports that the Charles Medlycot thus commemorated was murdered by his servant, who subsequently confessed the deed when about to be hung for sheep stealing. An iron hour-glass stand, formerly in front of the old pulpit, still remains affixed to the eastern pillar of the aisle arcade, and a panel from the back of the same—dated 1672, is now preserved as a relic in an adjacent seat. When Holles visited this church these armorial bearings were displayed in the east window, viz : Checky or & az, Warren. Arg, 2 lions passant sa. Fletwycke, and Or, 3 chevrons gules, Clare. In a north window also, *i.e.* in the one nearest to the east end of the nave, he speaks of one having the Fletwycke armorial bearings and part of a legend—" David de ———— ———— me fecit in honore beæ Mariæ." This last is now gone ; but the former still appears in the cusped circlet of the head of this window. The lectern is of solid brass, and the standards of the altar rail are beautiful specimens of modern metal work. The terminals of the chancel arch hood mould are half angels bearing scrolls, one inscribed with the prayer—"Lord save thy people," and the other with " Bless thine inheritance." On the hammer beams of the chancel roof is this prayer : " By thy cross and passion good Lord deliver us " ; and on the labels held by the four Evangelical symbols below, the words " Holy, holy, holy, Lord God Almighty, which was, and is, and is to come." At the east end of the aisle is a piscina now partly concealed, and the remains of the usual entrance to the rood loft. Here most probably was St. Mary's chapel. In the tower are four heavy bells. Three of them bear these legends, viz : " God save the King " ; " God save his church " ; " Jesu be our speed " ; and are dated 1617, when they were recast. A very pretty little 14th century coped child's tombstone was found some years ago in the churchyard. This was as usual simply ornamented with a cross carved upon it, to indicate that a little christian child's body was once deposited below it.

NORTH RAUCEBY.

ACREAGE,
6573.

POPULATION,
744.

THIS village is situated on one of the highest spots in Lincolnshire, 3 miles north west of Sleaford, and the spire of its
church forms a land mark that may be seen for many miles around
it. Its name has been variously spelt Rosbi, Roscebi, Rousby,
Rouceby, and finally Rauceby. It, together with South Rauceby,
is made mention of in five different places in Domesday book,
and in some cases it is difficult to determine which Rauceby is
referred to. Before the Conquest the land here belonged to
Archil, a royal Thane. After that great event it was for the
most part given to Robert de Stadford, the ancestor of the
Staffords, Dukes of Buckingham; but a small portion was in the
soke of the Bishop of Durham's manor of Evedon, another in
that of Robert de Vesci's manor of Caythorpe, and a third in
that of Geoffrey Alselin's manor of Ruskington that had belonged
to the Saxon Outi. This last consisted of 6 carucates 2 oxgangs
and a half, sufficient for as many oxen, on which land Geoffrey's
grandson had 25 sokemen, 8 villans, and 5 bordars with 8
ploughs; also 1 carucate sufficient for 12 oxen, on which were 7
sokemen and 2 bordars with 1 plough and 5 oxen. Of Robert
de Stadford's land Ulsi held 3 carucates and half an oxgang,
and Osmond nearly the same quantity, of whom Siward held
11½ oxgangs. Edelo, one of Robert Stadford's vassals, had 7
sokemen and 1 villan here. Bishop Remigius had also some
land in Rauceby, and claimed more that had been Archil's; but
the jurors rejected his claim because Archil had only possessed
10 oxgangs of the demesne lands here, which he had obtained
through exchange. Before and after the Conquest the land in
Rauceby was valued at 40s.

Circa 1200-20 the Bishop of Durham's land here was held
by Geoffrey de Evermue, and consisted of a third of a knight's fee.

The Bishop of Lincoln's land, reckoned as the twelfth part of a knight's fee, was held by William Morteyn, who had sublet it to Roger Hacket. About this time gifts of land began to be made to the Templars of Temple Bruer, of which the following is a list taken in 1185 :—

Galfrid Perrun then held a tenement, the gift of Robert de Staford, at a rent of 33s. 4d.

Ulbern, 2 oxgangs and a toft, the gift of Galfrid Perrun, at a rent of 10s., 4 hens, and 4 days' work.

Jordan, 1 oxgang and a toft, the gift of Reginald de Normanville, at a rent of 4s., 4 hens, and 4 days' work.

Hermbern, $\frac{1}{2}$ an oxgang and 1 toft, the gift of the same, at a rent of 2s., 4 hens, and 4 days' work.

Peter, $\frac{1}{2}$ an oxgang and a toft, the gift of the same, at a rent of 2s., 4 hens, and 4 days' work.

Colswain Ophilio, $\frac{1}{2}$ an oxgang and a toft, the gift of the same, at a rent of 2s., 4 hens, and 4 days' work.

Thomas Kafot, 1 oxgang and $\frac{1}{2}$, and a toft, the gift of Robert de Calz, at a rent of 3s.

Anneis, mother of the last, held $\frac{1}{2}$ an oxgang of the gift of Robert de Calz, at a rent of 12d.

John, the skinner, 1 oxgang and a toft, of the same gift, at a rent of 5s., 4 hens, and 4 days' work.

Walter Holdicum, 3 oxgangs and a toft, of the same gift, at a rent of 5s.

Thomas, the provost, 1 oxgang and a toft, of the same gift, at a rent of 5s., 4 hens, and 4 days' work.

Randolf, the thresher, 1 oxgang and a toft, the gift of Walter, son of Holdewin, and a rent of 3s. 5d., 4 hens, and 4 days' work.

Picot, a toft of the gift of Henry, of the fee of Galfrid de Perrun, at a rent of 12d., 4 hens, and 2 days' work.

Walter de Nuecum, a toft of the gift of Walter, son of Haldiwen, at a rent of 12d., 4 hens and 2 days' work.

Ralf, the son of John, a toft, of the gift of William, son of Herveius, at a rent of 12d.

Roger, son of Holdanus, 1 oxgang and a toft, of the gift of Gilbert de Evermew, at a rent of 2s. and 2 days' work.

Walter Peri, a toft, of the gift of Galfrid, at a rent of 12d. "Dugdale's Monasticon."

In the 13th century Hervius Bagot, through marriage with one of the Stafford family, was holding half a knight's fee here of the King in chief, which he let to the Hospitalers of St. John. Robert de Everingham about the same time possessed half a knight's fee in this vill as the representative of Geoffrey Alselin, who had let it by knight's service to Geoffrey, the son of William, and subsequently to Randolf de Normanville.

In 1287 died Robert de Everingham, lord paramount of part of Rauceby, and in 1302 the family of St. Laudo held lands here. In 1373, Ralph Earl of Stafford, and Margaret his wife, daughter and heir of Hugo de Audeley Earl of Gloucester, were in possession of their ancestor's lands in Rauceby. In 1393, Thomas Earl of Stafford, eldest son of Joan the great Wake heiress, died seized of a knight's fee in Rauceby, "Inq. p. m. 16. R. 2," and in 1399, William, his brother and heir, was lord paramount of half a knight's fee here, then held by the knights of St. John of Jerusalem. "Inq. p. m. 22. R. 2." In 1446 died Sir Hugh Basinges, seized of a messuage and 2 virgates of land here. In 1470 died John Tiptoft Earl of Worcester, seized of the manor of Kent or Wake fee in Rauceby; and from the Inquisition stating this we gather the names given to some of the old woods in this parish, it telling us that that Earl died possessed of the third part of Kelbyehawe, Brunwood, Asshehold, or Ashholt, Hawberry-hill, and Trygoldthweyte woods. "Inq. p. m. 10. E. 4."

In 1540 died John Puller seized of land; and in 1544 the King granted a licence to Edward Lord Clinton to alienate a grange in North Rauceby to William Monson, of Carlton, and his heirs. "Harl. MS. 6829." In 1559-60 died Thomas Hussey, seized of 6 acres of arable land, 10 of pasture, and 40 of marsh in this vill, held of Robert Carre as of his manor of Sleaford by military service. "Ditto." The said Robert Carre, of Sleaford, died February 24th, 1593, seized of the manor, leaving his uncle Robert Carre, of Aswarby, his heir. "Harl. MS. 758." This, and all the other numerous lands possessed by the Carres, passed into the hands of Mr. John Hervey through his marriage with Isabella the eventual heiress of that family, and so into those of his descendant, the Marquis of Bristol, who still possesses the greater part of the land in North Rauceby.

V

ECCLESIASTICAL HISTORY.

From the time of the Conquest the advowson of the church was divided into two medieties, of which, as we have seen, Alnod, the Bishop of Durham's vassal, possessed one. At the rebuilding of Croyland Abbey after its destruction by the Danes, 84 men of Rauceby with Godscal its priest, and John its deacon, built one of the pillars of the new choir of that Abbey, by the aid of workmen and quarrymen to whom they gave 6 marks for the purpose, and paid for the carriage of the stone from their own quarry to the boat, and hired two "baidours," or carriers, to unload the stone and carry it to the Abbey site. "Peter de Blois's History of Croyland."

At the beginning of the 13th century, the Prior and Convent of Shelford Priory, Notts., was in possession of one mediety, and in the Roll of of Institutions of the time of Hugh de Welles, still preserved in the Bishop of Lincoln's Registry, we find that William de Lexington, the chaplain, was presented in 1229 to the vicarage of this mediety by the Prior of Shelford; also that it consisted of the whole altarage of that mediety, a sufficient house, and some land. Out of this the vicar was to pay 20s. annually to the Prior and Convent, and the synodals, but they undertook to pay the procuration fees to the Archdeacon, and to bear all other burdens. The vicarage was then valued at £5 a year. In 1535 we have a notice of the other mediety of the vicarage in the Ecclesiastical Survey in the First Fruits Office, taken in the 26th year of Henry VIII., when William Styrlay was vicar, and the proceeds of the vicarage were as follows:—

	£	s.	d.
For the tithes of lamb and wool per annum	4	0	0
For oblations at Easter, with other lesser oblations	0	16	8
For pigs, geese, hemp, and flax	0	2	6
For hay	0	0	12
For house with glebe	0	5	4
For the church yard	0	0	6
Total, as by the book then shown	5	6	0
Deductions in money paid to the Archdeacon of			
Lincoln in Synodals and Procurations	0	5	1
Leaving clear..............................	5	0	11
The tenth thereof	0	10	$1\frac{1}{2}$

In the minister's or bailiff's accounts of the possessions of the Priory of Shelford, 28. H. VIII., is the following notice of the liability of the then Rector:—He answers for 100 shillings for the rent of a mediety of the Rectory with all the houses built upon the same, also for a mediety of the tithe corn and hay belonging to the said Rectory, demised to William Styrlay, clerk, and Richard Carre, by indenture dated 16th February, in the 21st year of the reign of King Henry VIII., for the term of 18 years, to be paid at the terms of St. Martin and St. John equally, all reparations during the term aforesaid to be paid at the expense of the former, and the same sufficiently repaired at the end of his term, to be left and delivered up as in the indenture aforesaid is fully contained. The following is the Will of William Styrlay, dated 29th of November, 1536:—

"I, Wm. Styrlay, Vicar of Rowceby, leave my body to be buried in ye church of Rowceby. To James Styrlay, my brother, I leave my horse and saddyll, and fower quarters of barley, and 22s. of the parsone of Gedlying, and 8s. of the Vicar of Gedlyng: and to every one of Richard Carre's servaunts a shepe, and to W. Smyth a shepe: To Myles Styrlay, my brother, the residue of my shepe with a fatherbedd: and to Margaret Powtrell a kirchiff: to Sir William Tractall a gowne: to Sir Henry Edwarde my best gowne, my best typete, and a sylver spone: Item to Richard Carre all my hyves, and he to finde a lighte afore the whyte Mary, and 2 kyne, to fynde an objt in ye parishe of Rauceby, during his lyfe with my woode and my cole: to Isabell Carre, all my pewter and sylver spones, &c.: to Elizabeth Carre a quarter of malte: to Alice Styrlay a quarter of barley: to Robt. Rede my best bonat: to dame Eliz. Stanhope half a quarter of malte: Residue to Sir Hen. Edwardes, and Richd. Carre, Exors., and Mr. Geo. Cateler, supervisor, to have 11s. 3d. Proved 15th Decr., 1536, by Exors."

In the 31st year of the same reign the Rectory was granted to Michael Stanhope and Anne his wife, together with that of Westborough. In Bishop Neal's time, 1616, the vicarage was valued at £5 a year, and there were 110 communicants. "Willis's MS. f. 39."

The following is a list of the vicars of Rauceby:—
Date of Institution.
A D. 1229.—William de Lexington.

Date of Institution.

A D. 1294.—Roger de Cestrefield.

1314.—Henry de Rouceby.

1341.—Dionysius de Elsham.

1352.—Hugh de Cranewell.

1378.—Simon de Wotton.

1399.—John de Westrasen.

1401.—Robert de Hirneby.

1432.—William Smyth.

1494.—William Talbot.

.—Henry Edward.

1552.—Christopher Massyngberd.

.—William Styrlay.

1574.—Philip Tilney.

1576.—John Talbot.

.———— Greaves.

1675.—Richard Kelham.

1680.—Wilfrid Eves.

1682.—Edmund Thorold.

1710.—Thomas Spencer.

1729.—Abraham Wilcox.

1744.—William Gunnell.

1771.—John Pugh.

1800.—George Thorold.

1823.—William Verelst.

1830.—Henry Baugh Thorold.

1836.—Ainslie Henry Whitmore.

1838.—Owen Davys, subsequently Archdeacon of Peterborough.

1841.—Edward Trollope, subsequently Archdeacon of Stow.

1843.—Granville Wheler Stuart Menteath.

1854.—Charles Thoroton.

Robert Carre, of Aswarby, left £5 a year, and Margaret Lady Thorold £3 a year to be given to the poor of North and South Rauceby. North Rauceby also enjoys the privilege of sending two persons to the Carre Hospital at Sleaford, but should it fail to have fitting persons, South Rauceby enjoys this boon.

RAUGEBY CHURCH.

THE CHURCH.

The fine old tower and spire of this church, dedicated to St. Peter, resemble generally those of Sleaford church, but are a little later, or of the commencement of the 13th century. Here, as at Sleaford, the round arch is intermingled with the lancet. The very bold tooth moulding of the belfry window in the southern face of the spire, and the circular perforated finial on the gable above it are worthy of attention. The spire is not quite so heavy as that at Sleaford, and the gentle graduation of the squinches produces a pleasing effect. In the tower are four bells, thus severally inscribed :—" Hn. Badge gave this bell. Ten L. 1619." "Jesus be our speed. 1621." "Do. 1684." "Do. 1723." The southern aisle of the nave is of the Decorated period, except the porch, which is Early English. The reticulated tracery of the carefully moulded windows, and other details, gives the date of 1320-50 to this portion of the church. The variation in the size of the windows adds to its picturesqueness, and the smaller window on the eastern side of the porch is a little gem of its kind. The staircase turret at the western end of this aisle is provided with a stone cover or hood. Until a few years ago the chancel was a very poor structure, built by William Styrlay in the time of Henry VIII. This, through the liberality of the late Anthony Willson, Esq., has now been replaced by a more ornate successor from designs supplied by Mr. Teulon. Its general outline, well-pitched roof, and some of its details are good, but the window tracery, although of a more ambitious character than that of the nave, from the omission of all mouldings, has a comparatively crude look. The north elevation of the nave is of a far plainer character than the southern one, but is of the same date, and retains its old doorway externally, although now walled up within.

Inside the porch is a Decorated niche above the door, and on entering, it will be seen that there was once an Early English nave as well as a tower of that period here ; the chancel arch, that of the tower now rebuilt on heightened piers, the western respond of the north aisle, and the porch, on the capitals of the pillars of which the nail-head moulding is cut, all demonstrating this.

The south arcade, of three bays, was the next addition to the fabric, and it would be difficult to find more elegant clustered shafts than those which support its arches.

The corresponding north arcade and both aisle walls, circa 1320-50, follow. There have been chapels at the east end of both aisles, as indicated by the remains of a canopied niche in the east wall of the north aisle, and the following evidences at the east end of the south aisle, viz: a piscina, a canopied bracket for a statue, and an arched recess with splayed jambs, which originally enabled the priest officiating in this chapel to look into another formerly attached to the chancel.

Through the removal of the old pews in this aisle a low arched sepulchral recess was disclosed beneath the easternmost window of its side wall, with a piscina below a little cusped head recess. This arch is well moulded and of the same date as the aisle, circa 1330-50. Below was found a sepulchral slab which still remains there, but is of later date, and has probably been brought there from some other place in this church. It is ornamented with an incised stemmed cross, and this border legend :—

> Hic Jacet Willus ffraunk de Rauceby, qui obiit ......
> die mensis septembris Anno. domini MCCC octogesimo :
> quinto : cujus anime propicietur deus. Amen.

Close to it now lies another sepulchral slab of the same date, also adorned with an incised cross, but in this instance the cross springs from a base of carefully squared ashlar work. A round-headed doorway now supplied with a new door in the tower above the arch was probably intended for the use of the sacristan of old, who could hence see when he was to commence or cease ringing. The original pitch of the nave roof may still be discerned, through its weathering attached to the tower. About 1500 the clerestory and a flat roof were added, perhaps by William Styrlay, which certainly give loftiness to the fabric, but scarcely any increase of beauty. The former is surmounted by an embattled parapet enriched with quatrefoil panels and blank shields. Between the windows of the north aisle a large painting on the old plaster was revealed during the late restoration of this church. It was twenty feet long and five and a half wide. Within a red border a large figure remained, dressed partly in monastic and partly in priestly vestments ; the whole of the back

Hic iacet dūs willm° Stylar quondam vicari°
istius ecclesie et canonic° de Sleſſord qui obiit m°
die Menſis Decebris Anno dm M° cccc° xxvi°
cuis aie pvicietur deus Amen

ground was powdered with stars, and in front of the figure was the head of some indescribable animal or monster. The whole was executed in distemper and with only three tints, viz : Venetian red, neutral tint, and a reddish brown. In the hands of the figure were a book, and perhaps a bell. If so, it was intended for St. Anthony. The rood-loft staircase still remains quite perfect, together with its doorway that formerly communicated with the rood itself. The font is a good specimen of the Perpendicular period, having cusped panels. Most of the old oak bench ends are still doing service in the nave, and on one of them is carved a male figure in the dress of the reign of Henry VIII.

The chancel was built in the time of William Styrlay, vicar, and Henry Edward, curate of Rauceby, at a cost of £44 8s. 8d. "Holles Harl. MS. 6829." Holles observed the following armorial bearings in a window of the north aisle, viz : Gu, 3 mullets arg, a label of 3 or, Hansard. Gu, 2 bars arg, in chief 3 roundels erm. Arg, on a bend sa double cotised gu a chevron sa charged with 3 crosses botony of the first sa, a chevron between 10 crosses botony arg, Kyme. Arg, 2 bars gu, in chief 3 torteaux a bend sa, Threckingham. Arg, a chevron gu between 3 ———. Arg, a fesse between 3 cinquefoils, Powtrel. He also noted down the following sepulchral inscriptions on stones within this church near the chancel :—

Hic Jacet Willus Powtrel de Rowsby, qui obiit ... .

Hic Jacet Elizabetha quondam uxor Rici Pinchbeck, que obiit 18o die Septembris 1505, cujus &c.

There are fragments of old painted glass in several of the nave windows, and the westernmost window of the north aisle is filled with modern glass by Lavers and Barraud. The east window of the chancel is filled with glass by Hughes, representing the leading subjects of our Lord's life, and is a very good specimen of modern art. One of its south windows is also filled with painted glass.

In the middle of the chancel pavement formerly stood the gravestone of William Styrlay, canon of Shelford, and vicar of Rauceby. This consisted of a massive grey marble slab in which were set brass plates engraved with the effigy and epitaph of that canon vicar ; but most unfortunately this was broken in pieces during the process of rebuilding the chancel, and the brass plates now alone remain attached to the vestry wall. Most faithful representations of these are given in the accompanying wood cut, and the inscription runs thus in modern lettering :—

> Hic Jacet Dus Willm^s Styrlay, quondam vicaris istius
> ecclesie et canonic^s de Shelford, qui obiit iiii^o die mensis
> Decebris, Ano. Dni. M^oCCCCC^oXXXlV, cujs aie
> ppicietur Deus. Amen.

He was also commemorated by a painted glass window in the clerestory on the north side, bearing his arms, viz : Paly of 6 Arg & az, in chief a cinquefoil gu, and the inscription :—" Orate pro aia Willi Styrlay, vicarii, qui hanc fenestram fieri fecit." Here also was the grave of his curate, marked by a slab thus simply inscribed :—

> Hic Jacet Henri Edward, Curatus de Rawsby, qui obiit xi^o die
> Julii, Ano. Dni. 1552, &c.

Near to this was the grave of a noted later vicar of Rauceby marked by a slab bearing this epitaph :—

> To the memory of the Rev. John Pugh, M.A., 29 years
> Vicar of the Parishes of Rauceby and Cranwell, who
> died April 26th, 1799, aged 56 years.
> Also of Ann his wife, who died May 10th, 1780, aged
> 40 years. And of Sophia his relict, who died Sept.
> 5th, 1803.

Mr. Pugh was one of the founders of the Church Missionary Society, and a most earnest evangelical clergyman of high ministerial reputation, set as a spiritual light on Rauceby hill, in a time of ecclesiastical supineness, and resorted to by many for miles round desirous of profiting by his counsel, and receiving the holy communion from his hands, so that certain of the parishioners murmured at the cost of supplying the necessary amount of bread and wine. He was a stern disciplinarian, and insisted on public penance on the part of persons who had offended against the laws of morality; and perhaps one of the latest instances of the enforcement of penance occurred at Rauceby through the instrumentality of this evangelical clergyman, viz : in the last quarter of the last century, John Dough, a very old man, still living in 1842, having told the author of this work that he remembered a frail woman standing in a sheet during divine service in Rauceby church, as a penitential infliction, ordered by its then vicar, before he absolved her.

The gravestone of such a man should surely have been venerated and carefully preserved over his grave ; but it, like those of William Styrlay and his curate, has now disappeared, together with various mural monuments. One of these commemorated the Rev. Thomas Spencer, vicar, who died 1729, aged 55. Another, the Rev. William Gunnell, vicar, who died 1771, aged 59, his wife Mary, 1768, and their sons William and Peregrine, in holy orders. On a slab in the north aisle was the following touching inscription :—

> In memory of the Rev. John Flavell, B.A., of Clare Hall, Cambridge, and of Cleobury Mortimer, Salop, aged 23 years.
>
> This very amiable pious person was ordained Deacon at Buckden, June 11, 1797, at that time very weak in body. On the day following he came hither, and on Sunday the 18th, took his happy flight hence rejoicing in his God and Saviour.

One old monument however still remains, now erected over the entrance to the tower staircase. It bears the following very quaint epitaph :—

> Near this place are interred the Wives of Richard Jessap ; viz :
>
> Alice on Sep. 27, 1716, aged 25.
>
> And Joanna, on Aug. 31, 1720, aged 29.
>
> How soon ye objects of my love
>   By death were snatcht from me ;
> Two loving matrons they did prove,
>   No better cou'd there be.
> One child the first left to my care,
>   The other left me three ;
> Joanna was beyond compare,
>   A Phœnix rare was she ;
> Heaven thought her sure too good to stay
>   A longer time on earth,
> In childbed therefore as she lay,
>   To God resign'd her breath.
>
> In Morte Quies.

In pulling down the chancel of the 16th century it was found that many old tombstones of the 13th and 14th centuries had been used in its construction, as well as worked stones of the Early English period. These are described in the Archæological Journal, vol. 10, pp. 63 and 162.

In the churchyard is the tombstone of an ecclesiastic, on the top of which is carved his effigy, clothed in eucharistic vestments, and holding a chalice in his hands. This is of the 14th century.

At the corner of the vicarage garden where the road to Ancaster branches from the one leading to South Rauceby has long stood the base of a village cross. This has of late years been supplied with a graceful shaft and finial, and constitutes a pleasing ornament to this village.

SOUTH RAUCEBY.

THIS adjoins North Rauceby, and is a distinct parish except for ecclesiastical purposes.

The greater part of its land had belonged to Turvert before the Conquest. Subsequently his land was given to the Bishop of Durham and held of him by Aland his vassal, who had 15 sokemen, and 6 bordars; he had also half the advowson of the church. South Rauceby was valued at 70s. in King Edward's time, afterwards at 60s. Subsequently Galfrid de Evermue held the third part of a knight's fee here by knight's service of the Bishop of Durham, he of the heir of Brune, and he of the King, Roger Kachet held the twelfth part of a knight's fee of William de Mortayn, and he of the Bishop of Lincoln, and William Perun was a tenant of the Templars.

There was a chapel in South Rauceby dedicated to St. James, and in the gift of the Priory of Shelford. It stood a little to the north of this village, and on the east of the road leading to North Rauceby. Holles, about the year 1640, speaking of South Rauceby says : "In this place the church is down."

Formerly a beacon stood near to Parham Dam, and a farm house called by that name. A younger branch of the Welby family was the principal land owner in this parish during the earlier part of the present century; but before his death he sold his estate here to the late Anthony Willson, Esq., who built the present excellent house now possessed by his widow, which, by the aid of further purchases of land and judicious planting around it has become one of the most pleasing residences near Sleaford.

In the time of Elizabeth the population of North and South Rauceby was nearly alike, in the former there having then been 22 families, and in the latter 21 ; but now, although North Rauceby is sometimes called Great Rauceby, the population of South Rauceby is by far the most considerable.

ROWSTON.

ACREAGE, 1833.

POPULATION, 224.

THIS village lies 7½ miles north east of Sleaford. After the Conquest, when its name was spelt Rouestune, King Willliam gave its lands to Geoffrey Alselin, who granted a portion of them to two of his knights according to Domesday Book. In all he had 12 carucates and 150 acres of meadow, also 32 sokemen cultivating 10 carucates; but the whole was only valued at 20s.

In the 13th century Geoffrey Alselin's lands here had passed into the hands of the de Calz family, when they consisted of half a knight's fee, and an eighth part of another. These were held by the Templars through the gift of Matilda de Calz; then let by them to Philip de Rouston and Richard West by knight's service. Five oxgangs here were then held by the Chapter of Lincoln to whom they had been given by Matilda de Calz, and 2 oxgangs were held by the Prior of Catley, through the gift of Geoffrey de Calz. "Testa de Nevill." In 1275 the Prior of Haverholme held 5 oxgangs of land in this vill, 4 of which he let to Robert de la Grene for 20s. per annum, and the other to Robert Clerk at a rent of 3s. per annum. The first lot had been given to the Prior by Philip son of William de Scaupewyke, who had received it of Matilda de Calz, and she of the King; and the last was the gift of Matilda herself, some 60 years previously.

In 1287 died Robert de Everingham, lord paramount of part of this vill. "Inq. p. m. 15. E. I." In 1291 died William Fitzpiers seized of lands here. "Inq. p. m. 20. E. I." In 1321 Hugo de Tighler or Tigheler, of Lincoln, paid the King a fine of 5 marks for having acquired the manor of Rowston for life. "Ab. Rot. Orig. 15. E. 2." But this act led to litigation between him and Sir Adam de Everingham, of Laxton, and others; and although he recovered possession of the manor in 1327, by re-cognizance, was disseized of it the following year by judgment of the King's court at Lincoln. "Ab. Rot. Orig. 1 & 2 E. 3." In 1550 Richard Huddleston was holding the manor of Rowston. Nine years later Robert, son of Geoffrey Huddleston, died seized of the manor and a capital messuage here, held of the King by military service. In 1560 died Geoffrey Huddleston seized of the manor, leaving a son Robert, who lived at Pinchbeck, and died 1564. "Harl. MS. 6829." He was succeeded by his son Richard, who alienated the manor to William Ryvitt, citizen and mercer of London, by licence from the crown in 1569, except a small portion in the hands of Geoffrey Huddleston, consisting of a messuage, a cottage close containing 7 acres, called Crathe close, another called Lages or Sand close, and 16 acres of moor and marsh held of the King in chief by the service of an eleventh part of a knight's fee. "Pip. Rot. 16 J. 1." His son, John Huddleston, succeeded to these in 1618. Benjamin Thorold, Esq., is the owner of the greater part of this parish now.

ECCLESIASTICAL HISTORY.

Matilda, daughter of Robert and Sibilla de Calz, during her widowhood, and previous to 1176, gave the advowson of Rowston church to the Templars of Temple Bruer, whose House she in part founded. This gift was confirmed by her successor, Ralph Fitzpiers son of Stephen, the King's chamberlain, in 1177, and several members of the Everingham family. In 1185, Peter de Tilney paid to the Templars during his life from the church of this vill, the sum of 3 marks annually.

In Bishop Neal's time, 1616, James Rivett was patron of the living, and the number of communicants was 70. "Willis's MS. f. 39."

The following is a list of the vicars :—
Date of Institution.

A.D. 1562.—Thomas Parker.

1566.—Edmund Hickson.

1601.—Christopher Hawes.

1604.—William Northan.

1630.—John Harrison.

1686.—John Lascells.

1731.—Andrew Graham, D.D.

1759.—John Gage.

1770.—Thomas Nocton.

Date of Institution.
    A.D. 1809.—John Rawlins Deacon.
        1821.—Henry Clarke.
        1862.—Thomas Cooper Lewty.

The Church.

The original design of this church, dedicated to St. Clement, may still be clearly detected. Built at an early period after the introduction of the Early English style, it consisted then, as it still does, of a nave, a very narrow and low north aisle, a remarkably small tower, a chancel, and a chantry chapel opening into it and the aisle.

The principal doorway, nearly in the centre of the south wall of the nave, is well designed. The jambs are adorned with pillars having plain elongated caps and square abaci, whence springs a well-moulded arch; the inner member is enriched by a band of the tooth ornament on a large scale cut on its chamfer. This doorway was not originally protected by a porch, but simply stood in the middle of a slight structural projection common in Norman churches.

On the east of this is a pretty little window consisting of two minute lancets with a tiny circlet above—originally cusped—and surmounted by a delicately moulded hood-mould. On the west are the remains of a similar window, but through the removal of its mullion, &c.—probably for the purpose of gaining more light —it is now simply a wide lancet.

In the south wall of the chancel are two plain lancets, the westernmost one being set at a lower level than the other, probably to serve as a low-side window.

The east end has been rebuilt, and a very small poor little Tudor window has taken the place of the original Early English lights there. The roof is a poor modern one covered with tiles.

On the north side of the chancel is a square parapeted adjunct on the site of a chantry chapel, formerly used as a schoolroom, and now as a vestry.

About the middle of the nave aisle wall is an Early English doorway, having necessarily a very depressed head from the extreme lowness of the wall in which it is placed. A string runs along the aisle wall, which is only interrupted by the later introduction of a flat headed Decorated window, circa 1320-40,

ROWSTON CHURCH.

towards its western end. In its western wall beneath a semi-circular hood-mould is a pretty little quatrefoil light. In the west wall of the tower is a little light, and above this a single lancet with shafted jambs in each wall of the belfry chamber. This contains two small bells bearing the name of Humphery Wilkinson, of Lincoln, and the date 1622. The tower is finished with a corbelled cornice, whence now springs a coarsely executed crocketed spire, perhaps of the same late date as the east window of the chancel. The appearance of this miniature tower and spire is remarkable. The base mouldings of the former are bold and effective; and probably it was at first covered only by a pyramidal or slightly conical roof. A striking addition was made to the nave of this church during the Perpendicular period, when its former roof was removed and a clerestory added. This is lighted with four three-light windows on either side, and surmounted by an embattled and pinnacled parapet.

On entering this church the beautiful Early English aisle arcade will first attract attention. This consists of four bays. At its west end is a circular bracket springing from a small foliated pillar cap, but swelling out into a feature sufficiently large to support the spring of the westernmost arch, and is enriched with manifold mouldings. The corresponding bracket is of a similar but not identical character; it springs from a little corbel surmounted by a man's head and has a little band of the nail-head ornament encircling it. The pillars of this arcade are set upon square sub-bases, and differ greatly in treatment. The westernmost one is circular, and has simply a well-moulded circular cap and base. The second consists of a cluster of four filleted members, with a bold band of the nail-head encircling the middle of its cap; and the third has four filleted principal members of the keel-shape with subsidiary shafts between them. This is a very beautiful feature, and round the middle of its delicately worked cap a little band of the nail-head ornament is introduced. The two westernmost springing points of the hood-mould above this arcade are finished with circular bosses overlaid by a peculiar leaf resembling that of the horse-chestnut, and on the others are carved two male heads. The construction of the eastern face of the tower and its newel staircase partly projecting into the south-western angle of the nave is peculiar. On the north side at its point of junction with the aisle wall is a characteristic banded shaftlet, and in its angle nearly opposite is a shorter similar shaftlet. The Perpendicular font is, as usual, octangular in plan, and on its bowl Tudor flower devices are coarsely carved. Some slight remains of the chancel screen still stand within the Perpendicular chancel arch; but both of these features are almost smothered by a vast painted timber superstructure filling up the whole of the arch above. Through the art of a local painter this displays the facade of some Classical Building, the Royal Arms, the Tables of Commandments, &c., and finally the arms of Mrs. Millicent Neate, together with an inscription stating that she was the donor of this huge specimen of art, and also of the fittings of the church generally, in the year 1741.

The chancel, with its low ceiling and poor east window, is a most wretched feature. In its north wall is an Early English arch opening into the chantry chapel before alluded to, and also another opening into the aisle. The last is filled in with some old oak screen-work, perhaps taken from the one formerly in the chancel arch. In the north wall of this chapel is an acutely pointed recess. This appears to have been a single sedile in the 13th century, but now constitutes a cupboard. The silver flagon and paten of this church were presented to it by Anne Lady Hodgson, in 1761. She was the daughter of Anthony Thorold, eldest son of Sir William Thorold, Bart., of Cranwell, and left lands for several charitable purposes, the benefit of which is still experienced by this and other parishes.

When Holles visited this church the following armorial bearings remained in its windows, all of which have since disappeared, viz: in a south window of the chancel, Or, on a cross sable 3 bull's heads couped arg. Sa, on a chevron arg 3 mullets pierced gu between 3 pheons arg, a chief gu charged with a cross arg; and in the aisle windows, Arg on a bend sa 3 owls of the first for Savile, with the fragment of a legend:— "Savyle & Agnetis uxoris." "Orate pro bono statu Robti Hodleston & Emmotæ consortis suæ." "Orate pro bono statu Johis Inman, & Johæ consortis suæ." "Orate pro bono statu Johis Inman, & Johæ consortis suæ." "Orate pro aie Willmi Grege & Aliciæ consortis suæ." Also the effigy of St. Egidius, Ægidius, or Giles, and beneath the figure of a man and this legend: "Tu tutus a cervâ repellas cuncta proterva."

ROXHOLM.

ACREAGE,
880.

POPULATION,
61.

THIS village lies 3 miles north east of Sleaford. In Domesday Book its name is spelt Rochesham ; it has also been called Roheston, Roxton, Roxthom, Roxanne, and Roxham, now most improperly converted into Roxholm, instead of Roxham, as though it was an island instead of a hamlet. Prior to the Conquest the Saxon Aldene had 2 carucates and 6 oxgangs of land, and 40 acres of meadow here. This was given by the Conqueror to Alured of Lincoln, who let the greater part of it to his vassal Ralph, under whom were 8 villans. The remainder of the land belonged to Outi's manor in Ruskington, which was given by the Conqueror to Geoffrey Alselin. This consisted of 3 carucates and 6 oxgangs of land, sufficient for the same number of ploughs and oxen. Its value was 40s. in King Edward's time, and subsequently 50s.

In the 13th century John de Baiocis had become possessed of the manor of Roxham, as part of the Barony of that name, of whom, and probably of his heirs, several generations of the de Gowshull family held it, viz : Egidius de Gowshull who obtained a right of free warren here 1258 ; Ralph de Gowshull circa 1270, whose land was reckoned at two parts of a knight's fee ; Peter, who died 1286 ; and Ralph 1295 ; but at length it passed into the hands of Philip le Despenser, through his marriage with Margaret de Gowshull. He died 1314. By him she had a son and heir Philip, and then married John de Roos, who died 1338. She finally died in 1350, and her son Philip le Despenser also died the same year. Previous to this, viz : in 1290, William Bardolf died seized of lands here in right of his manor of Ruskington, as did Hugo de Bardolf in 1304. Then Henry de Bello Monte, or Beaumont, possessed them, who died 1376. In 1441 died William Philip, Kt., seized of the vill of Roxholm in right of his wife, one of the Bardolf co-heirs. " Inq. p. m. 19 H. 6."

W

Next Hugh Basynges, Kt., was seized of the manor here, who died 1446. "Ibid. 24 H. 6." In 1454 Anna, relict of Sir Reginald Cobham, Kt., died seized of half this vill. In 1478 died Margaret, wife of Roger Wentworth, and relict of John Lord Roos, seized of the Despenser manor here. In 1560 Simon Freeman was holding some lands in Roxholm, and in 1569 William Thorold died possessed of a fifth part of 4 messuages, 130 acres of land, 70 of meadow, 50 of pasture, and a small rent in Roxholm, leaving a son Anthony. In 1573 John Bushy and others, then in possession of the manor of Roxholm, had to prove their title to the same. Soon after, this passed into the hands of William Thompson, who, as well as five generations after him, were small squires or gentlemen here. The last of these, William, died in 1710, soon after which it was bought by Mr. Barry Neale, and subsequently by the late Wyrley Birch, Esq. It has now just again once more changed owners, having been purchased by Mr. J. M. Cole, late of Rothwell, Northamptonshire. In 1627 the Blackthorn farm in Roxholm, consisting of 126 acres of land, was in the possession of the Carre family, and had probably been bought by Robert Carre in the previous century. It is now the property of the Marquis of Bristol. The house in which the Thompsons lived still has an air of respectability about it from its mullioned windows, &c., and until very lately two very fine yew trees stood in front of it, but it is now only a farm house; and a larger house has been built upon the property.

ECCLESIASTICAL HISTORY.

There was once a chapel here, annexed to the church of Leasingham. This still existed in 1560, but has long since passed away. It probably stood close to the old manor house, but its exact site can not now be ascertained. The circular head of a tombstone, on which is cut an elaborate cross in relief, and part of an octangular shaft, each face being hollowed, were found within the last few years at Roxholm, and probably belonged to this chapel.

RUSKINGTON.

ACREAGE,
4700.

POPULATION,
1089.

THIS large village lies 4 miles north north east of Sleaford, and has the advantage of a little stream of pure water flowing through it, which divides it into two nearly equal parts. This is supplied from two sources, one rising close to the site of Dunsby Hall, near to the Sleaford and Lincoln road, the other at Brauncewell, which, after uniting westward of Ruskington, and running through Ruskington, discharges into the Sleaford canal near Haverholme.

Last year some Saxon remains were found here in digging gravel about 20 yards north east of the windmill, where many human bones had previously been found without exciting any attention, but which, from the evidence now afforded, may certainly be termed a Saxon cemetery. Here two skeletons were found that had been laid in the same grave one over the other, the skull of the lower one lying to the east, and that of the upper one to the west. With one of these was interred an iron spear head, 8 inches long, in the socket of which still remained a portion of its ash shaft, and undoubtedly of Saxon make.

In Domesday Book Ruskington is called Rechintone and Risehintone. We also gather from that record that Tochi had 12 carucates here, afterwards given to Geoffrey Alselin. He kept 2 of these in demesne, and had 22 sokemen cultivating 3 carucates and 2 oxgangs, 8 villans and 8 bordars cultivating 8 carucates, 60 acres of meadow, and 240 acres of woodland with some pasture intermixed. Its annual value in King Edward's time was £25, and subsequently double that sum; but was only taxed at £10. Drogo held 6 oxgangs of this land, worth 20s. a year, and Adestan appears to have been his tenant. Here also were 3 mills worth £4 12s. 8d. a year. It had sokes in Leasingham, Roxholm, Dorrington, Digby, Rowston, Brauncewell, Dunsby, North and South Rauceby; and berewicks in Anwick and Evedon.

Ralph, the grandson of Geoffrey Alselin succeeded to this and all his other numerous possessions, and in 1150-60 he gave to the Nuns, and Clerical and Lay Brethren of Haverholme Priory, Ruskington wood, and all the plow lands belonging to him eastward of that wood, 22 acres of land in Colelaunde, a manse on Ruskington moor, pasturage on the common for 500 sheep and 40 beasts, pasturage for all their stock throughout his fee in this vill, as much flag thatch for their houses from the marshes as they could take thence, two tofts in Ruskington, a forrery (headland) near the same, and pasturage for 60 sheep, 4 beasts, and ½ draft horses, also another forrery. This gift deed was witnessed by Humfrey the Sub-dean, and Hamo the Chancellor of Lincoln. It was subsequently confirmed by Robert de Calz in a deed quoted by Holles, and running thus :—

"Robt. de Calz and his wife to the Archdeacon, the Dean, and the Chapter of St. Mary at Lincoln, and to all the faithful of the Holy Church, health, &c.

"Whereas by advice and authority, things which have been collected in alms for the Holy Church it is very useful to confirm, we therefore implore your clemency that ye will benignly hear this Chapter, and cause it to be confirmed by your consent. Know that we have granted and given in alms to the holy Nuns of Haverholme the Grove of Ruskington and 5 acres of arable land called Ruckhill, for the souls of our father and mother, and all our relations, in free and perpetual alms, in the presence of Isabella de Ferrars, and Geoffrey the Chaplain, and John de Westboro, and others." These gifts to Haverholme Priory were subsequently confirmed, and added to by Robert and Matilda de Calz's successors at Ruskington—the Everinghams. Ralph Anselin the elder or younger also gave to the Nuns of Haverholme a foot road on his lands in Ruskington, liberty to dig for sand on his part of Ruskington moor, to repair roads with, and for building purposes, together with the right of fishery in all his waters at Ruskington and Anwick. He also gave them Robert, son of Hals, of Levesingham, his bondman, and all his chattels and homage.

Ralph Anselin also bestowed lands in Ruskington upon the Templars of Temple Bruer, which, in 1185, were let as follows : Reginald held 1 oxgang and a toft at a rent of 3s., 4 hens, and 4 days' work ; John, a parson, held a toft at a rent of 12d., 4 hens, and 4 days' work ; Adam Belle held half a toft at a rent of 20d., 4 hens, and 4 days' work; Robert, son of Ren, held half a toft at a rent of 16d., 4 hens, and 4 days' work; and Rocelinus, the smith, held a toft at a rent of 12d., 4 hens, and 4 days' work.

In the 12th century the fee of Anselin was reckoned at 2 knight's fees, when one was held by William Bardolf and the other by Robert de Everingham, both being descendants of the Anselins. Robert had then let his lands to John de Everingham, and died in 1287. "Inq. p. m. 15 E. 1." William Bardolf obtained the right of holding a market and two fairs here in 1272, and died possessed of the whole manor in 1290 ; Hugh Bardolf died in 1304, and Thomas Bardolf in 1328. Agnes, the wife of Thomas Bardolf, next held the manor, perhaps during the minority of her son John, and died in 1353. John Bardolf, of Wrymagye, died seized of the manor of Ruskington with its members in Digby, Anwick, Leasingham, Bloxholm and Brauncewell, in 1371. In 1383 William Bardolf, Kt., gave this manor and a mediety of the advowson of the church to his son Thomas and Amicia his wife, daughter and co-heir of Ralph Cromwell, "Inq. p. m. 6 R. 2," and died five years later. In 1397 died Thomas Mortymer, Kt., seized of the manor here—then forfeited, "Inq. p. m. 21 R. 2," and in 1403-4 Agnes, wife of William Bardolf, Kt., seized of a third part of it. In 1441 died William Phelip, Kt., husband of Johanna, one of the Bardolf co-heirs, who died in 1447 seized of half of this manor and its members in Dorrington, Digby, Leasingham, Dunsby, Anwick, Brauncewell and Sleaford. "Inq. p. m. 25 H. 6." In 1454 died Anna, relict of Reginald Cobham, Kt., seized of the manor. On the attainder of William Beaumont Viscount Bardolf in 1462, all his lands here were forfeited to the Crown, and consigned to the keeping of Thomas, Archbishop of Canterbury, and George, Bishop of Exeter. These were eventually restored to Lord Beaumont; but on the rebellion of Francis Lovel Viscount Beaumont in 1487, and his attainder after the battle of Stoke-upon-Trent, were again forfeited to the Crown.

As the families of Bardolf, Calz and Everingham are immediately connected with the parish of Ruskington, and reference is made to various members of the same in other parts of this volume, it will perhaps be acceptable to give a brief account of them here.

Thomas, son of Dodo Bardolf, and younger brother of a second Dodo, married Rohesia, eldest daughter and co-heir of Ralf Alselin the younger, grandson of Geoffrey Alselin, to whom the Conqueror gave the manor of Ruskington. Their son Dodo, born 1167, married Beatrice, daughter and heir of William de Warren, and possessor of the manor of Wormigay, who, after her first husband's death 1290-1, married Hubert de Burgh. William, Dodo's son, born 1195, was subsequently knighted, and held Nottingham Castle from 1255 to 1263. He was a large landed proprietor, as declared by a grant of free warren given to him in Ruskington, Roxholm, Anwick, Brauncewell, Thorpe, Digby and Leasingham, in 1252. He married Juliana, daughter of Almiric de Spencer, and Anabella daughter of Walter de Chesney, and died 1275. He was succeeded by his son William Bardolf, who married Juliana, daughter and heir of Hugh de Gournay, and died seized of 'the manors of Ruskington, Filling-ham, Westborough and Blyborough, 1296. He was succeeded by his second son Hugh Bardolf, born circa 1260, his eldest son, Roger, having predeceased him. Hugh was summoned to Parliament as Baron Bardolf from 1299 to 1302. He married Isabel, daughter and heir of Robert Aguillon, and died 1304. He was succeeded by his son Thomas, second Baron Bardolf, born 1283, and summoned to Parliament from 1307 to 1331. His wife's name was Agnes, and he died seized of the manor of Ruskington and its members, and of the manors of Westborough and Fillingham 1331, when his widow held them until her death in 1353. John, third Baron Bardolf, son of William, younger brother of Thomas, succeeded to the family estates. He was born 1313, and summoned to Parliament from 1336 to 1372. He married Elizabeth, daughter and heir of Sir Roger Damony, by Elizabeth de Burgh, and died 1372-3 seized of the manors of Ruskington, Westborough and Caythorpe, the last in right of his wife. He was succeeded by his son William, fourth Baron Bardolf, a minor at the time of his father's death, when his wardship was purchased by Sir Michael Poynings, whose daughter Agnes he eventually married. He was summoned to Parliament from 1376 to 1386. He lived at Bardolf Hall, Cay-thorpe, and in 1383 enfeoffed his son Thomas and Amicia his wife with the manor of Ruskington and half its advowson, also with the manors of Caythorpe, Wesborough and Fillingham, and left to him an additional precious legacy in the form of a fragment of the true cross set in gold. He died September 12th, 1384, and was buried in the choir of the church of the Carmelites, at Lynn. His son Thomas, fifth Baron Bardolf, born 1369, espoused the cause of Henry Earl of Northumberland, and consequently was forced to flee from England, but returning after three years, was slain at Bramham Moor in 1408, when his body was quartered and exposed in various towns, and his head was set up over one of the gates of Lincoln. He married Hawise or Amise, daughter and co heir of Ralph de Cromwell, who died March 10th, 1408-9. He left two co-heir daughters, Anne and Johanna. The first married Sir William Clifford, Kt., who died 1418, and subsequently Sir Reginald Cobham. She died childless 1454, seized of the manors of Caythorpe and Westborough, and the vills of Frieston, Normanton, Sudbrook, Willoughby, half of Ancaster, Leasingham, Roxholm, Digby and Anwick. Johanna married Sir William Phelip, created Lord Bardolf, who died June 6th, 1441. She died 1447, seized of the above-named manors and those of Doddington and Stubton. Her only heiress daughter, Elizabeth, married Sir John Beaumont in 1436, created Viscount Beaumont 1440, and slain at the battle of Northampton 1460. They had three children, Henry, who died in infancy, William, seventh Baron Bardolf and second Viscount Beaumont, and Johanna. William was born at Edenham 1439. He fought at Towton fight on the Lancastrian side, and was taken prisoner 1461, after which his estates were confiscated, but were restored to him by Henry VII., November 7th, 1485. He married Joan, daughter of Humphrey Stafford Duke of Buckingham, and secondly Elizabeth Scroop relict of John de Vere Earl of Oxford, but had no issue by either. He died October 22nd, 1506, when the Barony went into abeyance, and the Viscounty expired. Johanna married John Lord Lovel, of Titmarsh, Northamptonshire, and died before her brother Lord Beaumont. She had three children, Francis Viscount Lovel, who perished miserably at Minster Lovel after the battle of Stoke-upon-Trent, 1487 ; Johanna married to Sir Brian Stapleton, of Carlton ; and Frideswide married to Sir Edward Norreys. The Bardolf armorial bearings were Az, 3 cinquefoils or. Those of Phelip quarterly Gu & Arg an eagle displayed or in the first quarter.

Walter de Calz, Forester of the counties of Notts. and Derby, a tenant of Ralph Alselin, and most probably his son-in-law, eventually shared his lands with his grandson Ralph. His son Robert thus became the owner of half the Alselin lands in Ruskington, and of half the church which he gave to Haverholme Priory. He married Isabella, daughter of Richard Earl Ferrers, and second Sibilla daughter of Richard Bassett, and died circa 1185. He left an only heiress daughter Matilda, the famous benefactress of several Religious Orders, and foundress of the Templar House at Temple Bruer. It is thought that she had three husbands; but the first recorded is Adam Fitzpiers, lord of Birken, Yorkshire, and the second Ralph Fitz-Stephens, the King's Chamberlain. In 1222-3 her lands in the counties of Lincoln, Leicester, Notts. and York, were seized by the King on account of her non attendance during his Welsh campaign. She was buried in Brompton church, near Chesterfield, where her monument still remains. Adam and Matilda Fitzpiers had six children, viz: John, Peter, Roger, William, Robert, and Juliana. John Fitzpiers or John de Birkin, warden of the forests of Notts. and Derby, by Johanna his wife had two children, Thomas and Isabel. Thomas died without issue in 1231, when Isabel became his heir, the wife of Sir Robert de Everingham, Kt., who gave the manor of Temple Bruer to the Knights Templars, and died circa 1251. Thus the Alselin lands in Ruskington were transmitted by marriage, first to the de Calz's, then to the Fitzpiers's, and next to the de Everinghams. Sir Robert de Everingham had three sons, Sir Adam, John, to whom his mother gave the manor of Birken and advowson of its church, and Robert in holy orders presented to the rectory of Birken by his brother John. Sir Adam paid his relief for his lands 1252, and attended Edward I. into Scotland. He held a knight's fee in Claypole, which he granted to Adam de St. Lando and Roger de Cressy, and died seized of the manor of Westborough 1280-1. He left two sons, Sir Robert and Sir Adam. The first, born circa 1257, confirmed the gifts of his ancestress Matilda de Calz or Fitzpiers to the Templars, and married Lucy, daughter and heir of Robert de Thwenge, a lady of light conduct who was divorced from William de Latimer, junior, and had a natural son by Nicholas de Meinil, also called Nicholas, who acquired a Barony by sitting in Parliament from 1336 to 1343, which descended to his daughter

Elizabeth, married first to John Lord Darcy, and subsequently to Peter de Manley. Sir Robert de Everingham died 1287, and was succeeded by his brother Sir Adam, and sat in Parliament from 1309 to 1316. He alienated the manor of Westborough to a member of the Barony of Shelford in 1310. He resided at Fillingham, dispossessed Hugh de Tigler of the manor of Rouston, and died 1342. By Margaret his wife he left six children, viz : his successor Sir Adam, Robert, Alexander, Edward, Nicholas, and Margaret a nun of Brodholme. Sir Adam, born 1312, was one of the commissioners for cleansing the river Axholme, 1357, and married Johanna, daughter of John de Eyville. He died seized of the manor of Westborough in 1372 according to Dugdale, but most probably not until 1388. He had two sons William alias Adam, and Reginald. William married Alice, daughter of John Lord Grey, of Codnor, and died in his father's life-time, 1370. He had one son, Robert, who died without issue 1371, and two daughters, Johanna, born 1363, married to Sir William Elys, and had a son Robert. The other daughter, Katharine, born 1366, married Sir John Etton, and had a son Milo Etton or Elton, whose daughter and heir married John Roos. The armorial bearings of Calz are Sa, a chevron arg between 3 fleurs de lys of the same. Of Fitzpiers, Arg, a fesse az, a label of 6 gu. Of Everingham, Gu, a lion rampant vairée az & arg crowned or.

Returning to the history of Ruskington, we find that after its earlier noble possessors had passed away, one of the numerous merchant families that became prominent after the desolating Wars of the Roses, became connected with this parish, viz : Sir John Hussey, Kt., who in 1509 was appointed steward of the manor by a patent dated at Greenwich, July 27th, in that year, and had previously held that office under Lord Beaumont and John, Earl of Oxford. In 1514 the manor was granted to Thomas Lord Howard, Admiral of England, for the services he had rendered to his father, Thomas, Duke of Norfolk, at the battle of Branston. In 1528 died John Everingham, Kt., leaving a son and heir Henry, born 1507, seized of a manor here with appurtenances in Thorpe and Timberland. Sir Thomas Johnson next possessed it, and in 1544 died Thomas Johnson, of Lyndeby, Yorkshire, seized of this manor, who bequeathed it to his wife Isabel and William Skrymsher for the term of 26 years, with remainder to his son Arthur Johnson for life, Henry Johnson being his heir. "Dodsworth MS. 99. f. 234." Subsequently this Arthur Johnson was made to shew cause why he held the manor of Ruskington. "Originalia Exchequer." In 1544 Edward Lord Clinton obtained a licence to alienate the manor of Ruskington to Robert Carre and his heirs, "Harl. MS. 6829." ; but in 1556 Thomas, Duke of Norfolk, is said in the same document to have been holding the manor of the Queen in capite by free service

In 1569 William Thorold held half the manor with its appurtenances of the Queen, as did Anthony Thorold after him.

In 1659 William Watson left £2 per annum, partly to the poor, partly towards the repair of the church of Ruskington, but as this was secured on Lord Widdrington's estate, it was lost on his attainder in 1715. Mrs. Martha Chamberlain who died in 1709, and was buried in the chancel of the church during that year, left 40s. yearly for instructing 10 poor children of Ruskington ; and Ann Thorold, Lady Hodgson widow of Sir Thomas Hodgson, of Rowston, who died in 1719, left certain lands in Ruskington in trust, partly to be applied to the building and maintenance of 3 alms houses and their inmates, to consist of 3 poor women of Rowston or Ruskington, partly to put out apprentices, and partly to aid in educating the boys of those parishes.

Ecclesiastical History.

When Domesday Book was compiled there was a church served by a priest here.

At a very early period, as now, there were two medieties of the church, Robert de Calz the elder, husband of Matilda—so noted for her numerous benefactions—having given one mediety of the church here to the Nuns and Brethren of Haverholme, and towards the relief of the poor.

An acre-and-a-half of arable land in the plains of Ruskington were left by an unknown person for the support of a lamp to be kept ever burning in the church. This was appropriately called Lamp Land, and valued at 7d. per annum at the suppression, when it was held by John Brian, the vicar.

RUSKINGTON CHURCH.

In 1616 the rectory was valued at £30 a year and the vicarage at £8 a year, when the communicants were 231. " Willis's MS. f. 39."

The following is a list of the rectors as far as can now be ascertained :—

Circa 1229.—Walter de Kantebury, presented by William Bardolf.
  1535.—William Pell.
   .—John Owen.
  1616.—William Willemont, presented by the Earl of Suffolk.
  1662.—Frederick Jack.
  1668.—Edward Stokes.
  1707.—-William Wyche.
  1718.—Francis Lascelles.
  1738.—Joseph Eyre.
  1780.—Joseph Arnall Eyre.
  1781.—Irton Murthwaite.
  1794.—John Myers.
  1832.—Charles John Myers.
  1871.—Arthur Myers.
Vicars :—
  1535.—John Bray.
  1547.—John Brian.
  1616.--William Willdeton.
  1738.—Joseph Eyre.
  1781.—Joseph Arnall Eyre.
  1793.—John Rymer.
  1804.—John Nelson.
  1845.—James Heckford.
  1867.—Grover Scarr.

The earliest Register is thus entitled : " A Register book containinge all the mariages whiche haue happened within the pishe of Ruskington since the beginninge of the Raigne of our most gracious Souigne Lady queene Elizabethe."

The Church.

This is dedicated to All Saints, and consists of a tower, nave, north and south aisles, south porch and chancel. The earliest feature is the tower arch, circa 1150, which so often survives the loss of a coeval nave and chancel. Its piers rise from square stilted bases in the form of a main circular shaft and subsidiary ones having scalloped cushion caps, whence springs a semicircular headed arch of two plainly chamfered members. About 1220 the church appears to have been rebuilt, the south arcade, south doorway and chancel arch being of that period. This arcade consists of three bays, in which great variety of treatment is displayed. Its pillars and responds spring from wide circular sub-bases, and the plain elongated bells of their caps bespeak their early date in the First Pointed period. The western respond has a massive keel-shaped shaft. The pillar next to this is of a curved lozenge form, having circular shafts at the angles, and square features between them. The next pillar is a most beautiful one composed of four circular and four keel-shaped shafts, the latter having a row of the tooth ornament set widely apart on each of its faces. The eastern respond consists of a keel-shaped shaft flanked by circular filleted shaftlets, between which are rows of the tooth ornament set close together. Its cap has been beautifully foliated, but much of its ornamental work is now destroyed. The chancel arch, of the same character and date as the south arcade, is deficient in elevation, and far inferior in beauty and richness to the contemporary south doorway. Its jambs are worked into filleted keel-shaped pillars, whence springs a most richly and delicately-moulded arch, having three rows of the tooth ornament introduced at intervals between its mouldings. The next feature in order of date is the north aisle, which corresponds generally with its companion aisle, and is also Early English, but of later date and purer style, although perhaps less attractive. Its design, however, and its mouldings generally, but especially those of its clustered keel-shaped pillar bases are excellent. Its arches are plainly chamfered. In the west wall of this aisle is a little cusped quatrefoil and the head of one of the windows it originally surmounted, but the rest of this is now either destroyed or concealed by masonry filling it up. At the east end of the south aisle is a large Decorated window, and during the prevalence of the Perpendicular style two good windows were inserted in the side wall of each of the aisles, and one of three lights in the east wall of the northern aisle, still retaining some few fragments of broken glass.

At the north east angle of the nave is a rude recess in the wall, apparently occupied once by a statue niche belonging to a chapel there, and as many as six small statue brackets in the east wall of the opposite aisle give evidence of the former existence of a chapel there also. A late doorway of the Tudor or Stuart period remains in the west wall of the south side, but is now filled in with masonry, and the little subsidiary building to which it gave access is destroyed, but the weathering of its lean-to room still remains on the face of the aisle wall. The font is an octangular specimen of the Perpendicular period. On one of its panels the instruments of our Lord's crucifixion are carved, and on another appears the pillar of flagellation flanked by a sword and some other emblem, perhaps the pelican. About six feet has been cruelly abstracted from the east end of the chancel, and a plain square-headed transomed light was inserted in its new east wall of a late Tudor or Stuart character ; this is more to be regretted as the character of the chancel is otherwise excellent. It is of a pure simple Early English type, having two long lancet lights on the north side, one similar one towards the west end of the south elevation, and another shorter one nearly over a coeval door still retaining a portion of its original iron work. Besides these there is a well-moulded lancet-headed low-side window towards the west end of the north and south walls. One sedile remains in the south wall, and a fragment of another has been forced to aid in the construction of an aumbry-like recess opposite to it. A large oak chest effectively carved, of the commencement of the 16th century, now stands in the tower. Holles observed the following armorial bearings in the windows of this church when he visited it, viz : Arg a fess Az, a label of 5 points G. Everingham, impaling Az a cross patonce voided Arg, Melton, the same reversed, probably only through the accidental reversal of the shield, Everingham alone, Gules, a chevron between 10 crosses crosslet Or, Kyme, and Az 3 cinquefoils Or, Bardolf; but these are now all gone. The tower, which was originally Norman, had probably been at least partially rebuilt, and certainly was surmounted by a spire ; but unable to bear such a burden it fell in 1618, and was rebuilt in its present form, in 1620, which date is cut upon its southern face. Assistance to repair this calamity was sought for beyond the parish, of which the following record still remains in the church-wardens accounts of St. Martin's, Lincoln :—

" In 1618 the inhabitants of Ruskington obtained a brief for collecting money towarde the building of there steeple. It was presented to the churchwardens of St. Martin's, in the city of Lincoln, December ye xxvii that year, John Wallor & Robert Storr being then churchwardens."

The tower contains three bells, bearing the following legends : " God save our church, our Queen and Realm " ; " Jhs be our spede " ; " Campana sacina fiat." In 1862 this church was judiciously restored, when its former flat roof was exchanged for the present high-pitched one, and it was reseated.

A 14th century stone coffin lid surmounted by the effigy of a priest vested, now lies near the tower in the churchyard.

TEMPLE BRUER.

THE name and remains of a Templar establishment on Lincoln
Heath, which was afterwards possessed by the Hospitallers,
or knights of St. John of Jerusalem, will probably lead to a desire
for a slight sketch of those once famous Orders; so that before
describing the past history and present remains of Temple Bruer
the following little account of those Fraternities will perhaps be
acceptable :—

The famous semi-religious, semi-military order of the
Templars was founded A.D. 1118, during the period of the first
crusade, and consisted originally of nine French knights, whose
object was to protect all pilgrims on their way to the Holy
Sepulchre at Jerusalem. At first its members voluntarily lived
in a condition of the strictist poverty, depending for their sub-
sistence solely upon the alms of the faithful, and were termed
"Poor Knights"—a condition referred to by one of their seals,
on which two knights are pourtrayed riding upon one horse.
Baldwin II. assigned to them a portion of his palace at Jerusalem;
and the abbot of the adjoining convent of the Temple afforded
further accommodation for their use, whence they derived their
appellation of "Templars." In 1128 they assumed a white
mantle as their distinctive habit, with the sanction of Pope
Honorius II.; to which a red cross on the left breast was added
by the direction of Eugenius III. in 1166, when they also began to
bear the same emblem on their banners. This occurred shortly
after a more strictly religious element had been infused into the
Order by a bull of Pope Alexander III., in 1162, who then pre-
mitted the admission of spiritual members into this society,
termed "chaplains"; after which, if not before, it began to
observe the rule of the canons regular of St. Austin. The fame
of the Templars, and their feats of arms in the Holy Land, now
soon became so great, that not only many scions of the noblest
houses of France and England flocked to their standard, but
multitudes of a lower grade so earnestly begged to be enrolled

as humble members of the society that a third class was added
to it, acting as servitors to the knights ; whilst offerings were
poured into its treasury, and many broad lands were made over
to its use in various parts of Europe, so extensively, that it soon
became as celebrated for its wealth as it had been at first
remarkable for its poverty. The society was governed by a
Grand Master, aided by other officers resident in Palestine, until
A.D. 1192, and afterwards in Cyprus, and by Grand Preceptors
in other countries, each of which was termed a Province of the
Order. The Templars first obtained a footing in England in the
early part of Stephen's reign, at a spot termed "The Old Temple,"
very near the present Southampton Buildings in London ; but
removed to another site A.D. 1185, celebrated for that beautiful
circular church once connected with this Order, still called "The
Temple Church."

The wealth of the society, however, at length having led to
much corruption of character on the part of many of its members,
it began to be viewed with a jealous, and finally with a hostile
eye, as well by the nobles as by the monarchs of France and
England ; so that, all sorts of exaggerated accusations having
been brought against it, whereby it was attempted to be shown
that its further existence was dangerous to those nations, Philip
IV. of France, Sept. 12th, 1307, arrested every Templar in his
dominions, and threw them into prison, whence he brought them
to trial at intervals during the four following years with the
sanction of the Pope, when fifty-four knights were sentenced to
be burnt, and their whole property was confiscated. At the same
time Edward II. exercised nearly the same degree of severity
towards the Templars established in England, who both imprisoned their persons, and seized their estates, although he does
not appear to have put any of them to death ; and on March the
22nd, 1312, Clement V. abolished this society altogether, when
it was found to be possessed of 9000 manors and 16,000 lordships,
besides other lands, situated in various parts of Christendom.
After an interval of some years, Edward II. A.D. 1324, made a
grant of the whole property possessed by the Templars to another
similar society, termed the "Knights Hospitallers," whose origin
it will now be necessary to refer to.

Certain traders of Amalfi having obtained leave of the Caliph
of Egypt to build a church and monastery for the Latins, near

the Holy Sepulchre at Jerusalem, dedicated the establishment to St. Mary of the Latins, and committed to its inmates the care of the sick, and the poor pilgrims then resorting in great numbers to that sacred city; to which was shortly added an hospital, or reception-house, together with a chapel, dedicated to St. John the Baptist, erected through the proceeds of the offerings and gifts of more wealthy pilgrims made to the community. But it was not until the Christians became masters of Jerusalem that the Hospitallers formed themselves into a distinct society; at which time, A.D. 1099, Gerard and others, who then were the curators of the sick of this hospital, took a vow that they would perpetually defend the Holy Sepulchre, wage war against the infidel, and observe the rule of St. Austin; they then also began to assume a white cross, which they wore on their breasts as the badge of their new Order. From this time they were termed Knights of the Hospital, or of St. John, from their patron saint; and in 1154 they procured a bull in their favour from Anastasius IV., the predecessor of that distinguished and sole British pontiff, Adrian IV., whereby they were exempted from the payment of tithes on all their lands, wherever situated, on the ground of their having been bequeathed to them for the support of the pilgrims and the poor; and by the same bull Anastasius forbade the publication of all episcopal interdicts, suspensions, or excommunications in any of the churches belonging to their Order; allowed them to have divine service performed in their churches with the doors shut, even in places that were under a general interdict; to receive priests and clerks to officiate in their churches from what diocese soever they came, and to keep them even without the consent of their respective Bishops, as being subject to none so long as they continued with them, except their Chapter and the Apostolic See; to have their churches and altars consecrated, their clerks ordained, and the sacraments administered by the Bishop of the diocese, if he should be willing to perform those functions without fee or reward, but if he required the least acknowledgment, to avail themselves of the services of any other Bishops they should think fit; and, lastly, he confirmed to them all the lordships, lands, and territories they possessed, or ever should acquire, on either side of the sea, in Asia or in Europe, but forbade the knights, after they had taken the cross and made their profession, to return to the world, or to enter any other religious Order. Raymond de Podio was at this time Grand Prior of the Order; but he and his knights appear to have so presumed upon these extraordinary marks of the Papal favour, that only two years afterwards, viz: in 1156, when Adrian had succeeded to the Papal chair, Pulcher, Patriarch of Jerusalem, attended by six Bishops, went to Rome in person, although nearly 100 years of age, for the purpose of pouring out a series of bitter complaints against the Hospitallers, wherein he accused them of having abused the Papal privileges, insulted him and his Bishops, and engrossed all the benefactions of the faithful; so that they besought him to rescind, or at least to modify, the bull of his predecessor. Pulcher, however, does not appear to have obtained his request, although the subject was discussed in council for several days; and it is curious to find that Temple Bruer, amongst other old possessions of the Hospitallers, after the lapse of so many centuries and the occurrence of great religious and political changes, still remains exempt from the payment of tithe, and until very lately from episcopal jurisdiction, as being extra parochial.

After the expulsion of the Christians from Palestine, the Knights retreated to Cyprus, but succeeding in conquering the island of Rhodes from the Turks, they then established themselves there so firmly that no Sultan for a long period was able to dispossess them of their spoil; until, at length, A.D. 1522, Solyman II. advanced in person against the island with an immense force, and after a siege of six months obliged its brave defenders to capitulate. And now they were in great danger of extermination, as most of the princes of Europe, when they heard of the fall of Rhodes, were on the point of seizing the Hospitallers' lands in their respective dominions; but this blow was averted by a hurried visit of the then Grand Master, L'Isle Adam, to the principal courts of Europe, who, by his urgent appeals, not only saved the property of the Order, but obtained an asylum from the Emperor, Charles V. for the Knights, who then conceded Malta to them, which was to be held by the tenure of an annual presentation of a falcon. L'Isle Adam and the Hospitallers took possession of their new rocky home in 1530, after which they were commonly called the Knights of Malta, and immediately began to fortify that island, to import earth from

Sicily to lay upon its stony surface, and adopt other means to render it productive; so that under their nurturing care, the vine, the orange, and other fruit trees, together with some vegetable produce, quickly sprang up. But war against their old infidel enemy was still their chief occupation; and from this strong and beautiful retreat, their galleys continually swept the sea in quest of Turkish spoil; nor did they often return into port without a captured Turkish vessel in tow, or Turkish property in their possession.

Roused by such repeated injuries, and especially by the capture of a ship of 20 guns, richly laden, belonging to one of his chief officers, Solyman, who still reigned, raised a force of 30,000 men, which he dispatched to Malta, in 180 galleys under the command of Mustapha, one of his best generals, with the intention of driving out the Knights from that island, as he had done from Rhodes. The fleet arrived off Malta, May 18th, A.D. 1565; and then followed that celebrated siege, so well known in the annals of history, and so amply described by many authors, especially by Prescott in his History of Philip II. Then it was that Jean Parisot de la Valette, the most famous Grand Master, after the loss of the fortress of St. Elmo—in the capture of which 8000 Moslem troops fell—caused Mustapha their commander to exclaim, "what will not the parent cost, when the child has cost me so dear?" This hero, after the exhibition of feats of prowess, rarely if ever surpassed, at length received the succour of 11,000 men sent by the Emperor to his relief, under Don Garcia de Toledo; when after one more struggle in the open field, wherein Mustapha was twice unhorsed and nearly taken prisoner, the Turks retreated from their intended prey utterly baffled and defeated. After Valette's death, the Knights of St. John still continued for some time to harass the Turks, by the aggressive expeditions of their galleys; but they gradually assumed more peaceful habits, until at length the Order was dissolved at the close of the last century by the fiat of Napoleon, when he visited Malta on his way to Egypt; the last Grand Master then retiring to Germany with a pension, and most of the Knights accepting commissions in the French army.

Such was the end of this once illustrious Order, at first fostered by Godfrey de Bouillon and Godfrey, the crusader kings of Jerusalem, the provincial establishments of which were termed

Commanderies, to distinguish them from the Preceptories of the Templars, and whose chief, or Prior, took precedence of all Barons in Parliament.

There were three Preceptories in Lincolnshire; one at Willoughton, near Kirton in Lindsey; another at Aslackby, near Falkingham; and the one termed Temple Bruer, near Sleaford, now under our notice. This is situated ten miles south of Lincoln, and one mile east of the High Dyke, or nearly in the centre of Lincoln Heath, whence it derived its appellation of Templum de la Bruere, or Temple on the Heath, now shortened into Temple Bruer. It was first founded by the Lady Elizabeth de Calz, according to a record in the "Additional MSS. B. M. 4936," on land given for the purpose by William de Ashby, as Tanner says previous to the year 1185, "Notitia Monastica, p. 274," and probably about 1134, but certainly in the reign of Henry II., as the occupants of the new Preceptory on Lincoln Heath obtained from that King a charter for holding a market every Thursday on their manor. Their first possessions were various parcels of land given them by landowners of Rowston. Elizabeth de Calz gave them the advowson of the church and 25 oxgangs there, Robert de Everingham the manor of that vill and some appurtenances, Philip de Branston 25 oxgangs, and Gilbert de Cressy 2 quarantines of heath, and pasturage for 500 sheep in the same parish. Their next benefactor appears to have been Walter Lord D'Eyncourt, who gave them 6 bovates of land, a toft, 3 shillings, 4 hens, and 4 days' work in Scopwick, which grant was amplified by his descendant, John D'Eyncourt, in 1175, by the gift of 1 barcary and 2 carucates of land in that parish. Several landowners of Rauceby were also early benefactors of the Templars on the Heath, viz : Galfrid de Perun, a tenant of Robert de Stafford, who gave them a whole knight's fee there valued at £15 a year, and a carucate of land valued at 48s. a year ; Geoffrey de Evermue, an oxgang of land he held of Baldwin de Wake, he of the Bishop of Durham, and he of the King ; Ralf de Normanville, an-oxgang-and-a-half ; and Galfrid de Rouceby, 3 oxgangs. "Rot. Hund., p. 278." Simon Tuchet was another important early benefactor of the Templars, who gave them a knight's fee in Ashby which he held of Ralf Pagnell, and he of the King. In 1258 the Templars obtained a licence from Henry III. for holding a market at their manor of Breuere every Wednesday instead of on Thursday as before, "Lit. Pat. Julii 20, 43 H. 3.," and also of holding an annual fair for three days at the feast of St. James. The same year they attached their seal to a deed connected with an exchange of lands with Henry de Colville, when Robert Sutton was their Preceptor. This seal, according to Holles, was of a circular form, having an Agnus Dei and flag as a device, surrounded by the legend "Sigillum Militis Templi." For the better security of their house, they obtained a license "34. E. 1," to build a strong gate-house, no doubt consisting of two circular towers with a stout door and portcullis between them. By degrees the Templars of Temple Bruer acquired many other possessions and rights, viz : from the Crown, 5 carucates of land and a rent of 14s. in Navenby, a knight's fee and an oxgang of land in Leasingham, 3 carucates of land in Carlton, given by Elias de Amundeville, and other smaller lots ; a toft and 20 acres of land in Ormsby, given by Hugh de Caythorpe, and other lands situated in Normanton, Navenby, Grantham, South Witham, Ingoldsby, Hacconby, Metheringham, Dorrington, Dunsby, Quarrington, and Hecking-ton, besides 2000 acres of heath lying around the Preceptory with two granges upon it, amounting in all to upwards of 10,000 acres, besides tenements at Grantham (including the Angel Inn there), Blankney, Metheringham, Kirkby Green, Evedon, Scop-wick, Timberland and Billinghay. They also possessed the advowsons of Caythorpe and Normanton, given by William de Vesci, a mediety of that of Cranwell, given by Robert de Armen-tiers, that of Ashby, given by Jordan de Ashby, that of Gedney, given by Matilda de Engaine, a mediety of Wyn, given by Galfrid de Cleypole, the advowson of Bottelbrigge, given by Robert de Gimiges, that of Sibthorpe, given by Ralf and Robert Malebisse, that of Drystoke, given by Gilbert de Dristoke, that of Friseby, given by Jordan Foliot, and a mediety of that of Willoughton, given by Simon de Cansy, besides the advowson of Rowston, the gift of the foundress—Matilda de Calz. They also claimed the rights of amerciament, waifs, and fines in the vills of Sleaford, Evedon, Ewerby, Blankney, Metheringham, Scopwick, Kirkby Green, Billinghay and Timberland, and exemption from all the services to which their lands had been subject before they had passed into their hands, and from the payment of all taxes and tithes.

No doubt the Templars were sometimes covetous and extortionate, notwithstanding their original vow of poverty, a curious instance of which is recorded in one of the Hundred Rolls, p. 280, under the date 1270, viz: a complaint of one Adrian Lewin, of Rowston, that Robert de Stratton, then Preceptor of Temple Bruer, had compelled him to supply him with half a mark of silver to enable him to purchase a Roman gold coin, termed a denarius, that had been found by one Catherine de Foston, and which he ardently longed for. One of the rules of local Preceptories, however, was that after paying for the cost of their maintenance out of their common fund, they were bound to transmit the surplus annually to the Grand Master of the Temple in London ; and they professed to desire that if any Member of their Order died possessed of wealth his money should be buried with him in unconsecrated ground with the imprecation "Thy money perish with thee." In the early part of the 13th century the first recorded dispute between the Templars and the Ashby's arose about the pasturage of 300 sheep on the Heath, which was settled in 1221 ; but a similar one about the pasturage of 408 sheep, 8 oxen, and 100 hogs, about 26 years later, which was settled in 1247, and from that time these continued to arise during their occupation of Temple Bruer and that of the Hospitallers, as described in the history of the parish of Ashby, whose contentions with the De la Laundes, the successors of the Ashbys, were fully as frequent and violent as those of their respective predecessors.

Both the Templars and the Hospitallers were accustomed to hold Tournaments at Temple Bruer, until this practice was forbidden by a writ of Edward II. in consequence of the disturbances that had been occasioned by them ; but one of the latter Order was certainly worse employed in the 15th century, although under the highest ecclesiastical authority, viz : John Seyvill, who acted as a Papal Procurator of indulgences under Alexander V., and his successor, from the evidence of a still-existing form of indulgence or absolution he granted to Henry Marshall and his sisters, dated at Temple Bruer, 1412, two years after the death of Alexander.

In 1260 Amadeus was installed as Preceptor, "Bp. Welles' notes" ; circa 1270 Robert de Stratton was Preceptor; in 1282 Robert de Turville ; in 1290 Guido de Foresta; and in 1300

William de la More—the last Preceptor of Temple Bruer, and Grand Prior of all England. In 1307, Edward II. who had just ascended the throne, summoned the Grand Master to his first parliament ; and two months afterwards, sent a writ to John de Cormel, sheriff of Lincolnshire, commanding him with a sufficient force, to seize both the persons and property of the Templars. This was accomplished January 10th, 1308, and William de la More and his knights were carried off to Lincoln, and imprisoned in Claxlede Gate and other city prisons. There they were kept until November 25th, 1309, when they were tried in the Cathedral Chapter-house, and accused of blasphemy, infanticide, cruelty, the most atrocious debauchery, &c., divided into many counts ; but it was their wealth that was wanted ; Fuller saying, "Their lives would not have been taken, if their lands could have been got without ; but the mischief was, the honey could not be got without burning the bees." Eventually, however, they did escape with their lives, but were stripped of all their estates, which were seized by the King. An account of these was taken by Thomas Burnham, and they were committed to the charge of William de Spanby. In 1324 the King granted them to another Order, that of the Hospitallers, or knights of St. John of Jerusalem, a slight sketch of whose origin has been already given, when Temple Bruer thus became a Commandery of that Order, and remained such until the suppression of all their Houses in 1535. Its estates were then granted to Hamond Sutton in fee for an annual rent of £22 10s. 0d., and the whole, including the salaries of the Members of the Order, according to an account of John Sutton, its treasurer, was valued at £183 10s. 0d., or according to Dugdale at £184 6s. 8d.

The names of the following Commanders have alone been preserved, viz :—

A.D. 1364.—John Percley.

1430.—William Hulles.

1432.—Robert Mallore.

1441.—Robert Botyll.

1460.——— Skafe.

1469.—John Langstrother.

1471.—William Turnor.

1477.—John Weston.

1484.—John Roswell.

A.D. 1503.—Thomas Newport.

1509.—Thomas Docwra.

.—John Babyngton.

In 1541 Henry VIII. granted the site and capital messuage of the Hospitallers of Temple Bruer with its appurtenances, messuages, and 2000 acres of land around it to Charles Brandon, Duke of Suffolk, to be held of the crown in chief. "Harl. MS. B.M. 6829."

In the course of the same year the King paid Temple Bruer a visit in person, on his way towards the north, for the purpose of holding a conference with his nephew, the young King of Scotland, and pacifying the people of Yorkshire and Lincolnshire after the suppression of their Monasteries. The King had held an early council at Sleaford, Tuesday, Aug. 9th, and the same day dined at Temple Bruer on his way to Lincoln, accompanied by his unfortunate Queen—Catherine Howard, the Dukes of Norfolk and Suffolk, the Earls of Oxford and Southampton, the Bishop of Durham, and others. Leland visited Temple Bruer the following year, viz: in 1542, who says, "Itin. vol. 1, f. 32": "There be great and vast buildings, but rude, at this place, and the este end of the temple is made *opere circulari de more*." The church must have been preserved for another century, for Holles in his "Church Notes" gives a long list of the coats of arms then emblazoned on its windows—including those of Cromwell, Tateshall, D'Eyncourt, Ufford, Beke, Mowbray, Beaumont, Bardolfe, Cantelupe, La Warre, Welles, Zouch, Grey, Savile, Middleton of Fulbeck, Roleston, Babington, &c.; besides the following : Erm, a chevron Sa. Or, on a cross Sa, 5 bull's heads couped Arg, impaling Sa, on a chevron Arg 3 mullets G between 3 pheons of the 2nd, over both a chief extended G charged with a cross Arg. Arg, a chevron between 3 eaglets Sa. G, a chevron Erm, a bordure engrailed Az. Az, 2 reynards passant Or. He also speaks of a tomb here, commemorating Dorothy, wife of Roger Rolston, who died January 18th, 1529, and having these bearings displayed upon it, viz: Party per fesse G & Arg, a lion passant in chief Arg, in base a cinquefoil pierced Az —Rolston, quartering—a chevron between 10 martlets Sa, impaling Arg, 10 torteaux, in chief a label of 3 Az—Babington. Buck published an engraving of this church in 1726 ; but it perished within the next period of fifty years, for, when Gough visited it, nothing

TEMPLE BRUER.

but a tower and a few vaults then remained—the former of which still happily exists, although in a sadly mutilated condition, and but for a strong bracing of iron work would probably have fallen.

This is of the Early English period, and was probably, erected about the middle of the 13th century. Its total height is 51 feet, and it contains three stories; the entrance was on the north side, and is now walled up, whilst a modern substitute has been broken through on the opposite side, under an interpolated window of the Perpendicular period. The interior of the vaulted basement story is richly decorated on the south and west sides with a series of well moulded arches, once supported by circular shafts, of which but one now remains. Under the south-eastern-most arch is a piscina; the level of the two next arches is slightly higher than that of the others, from which arrangement there is but little doubt that this apartment was used as a chapel, and that the altar stood in the centre of the arched recess at its east end. It still retains its original vaulted roof, and was lighted by a window on its east, west, and south sides. A newel staircase in the north-west angle leads to a chamber above, which is lighted by three lancet windows, and was once vaulted like the one below; then to a low room above, and, finally, to the roof, which was surrounded by a parapet, a small portion of which still remains at the south-west angle of the tower. The corbel table of the south elevation, and of the flat buttresses on the north and west fronts, are of a very effective design. See accompanying plate, giving a section of this tower from a drawing by Mr. J. Padley.

The elevation of the circular church, built so appropriately after the model of the Holy Sepulchre at Jerusalem, in common with that of the Temple in London, of Little Maplestead, Essex, St. Sepulchre's, Cambridge, and St. Peter's at Northampton, is now quite gone; but the bases of its pillars still lie below the soil, a little to the west of the tower, and were laid bare for the last time in the year 1833, under the superintendence of Dr. Oliver, from whose account of Temple Bruer, published by the Lincolnshire Topographical Society, the following particulars are gathered: "The circular church was 52 feet in diameter within, and was supported on a peristyle of eight cylindrical columns, with massive bases and capitals, and a series of circular arches profusely ornamented with zigzags and other Norman enrich-ments, forming a circular area, which occupied exactly one half of the diameter; and the aisle, or space betwixt this colonnade and the exterior walls occupied the other half. The aisle, it appears, had a groined roof; and a portion of it on the north side contained the tomb of the founder. On the west was the principal door of entrance, with an ascent of stone steps, and a magnificent porch, the foundations of which remain perfect. In the floor are two coffin-shaped stones, one plain, the other charged with a cross botony in relief." This circular church was certainly united, either by an extension of the fabric or by a cloister, to the still-remaining tower, as may be seen in Buck's view of Temple Bruer, published in 1736, and in the plan given in Dr. Oliver's Paper on this place, referred to above; whilst the clustered column and bracket on the north side of this last, still present visible evidences of its former existence at that point. Here also two stoups will be observed on the left of the tower entrance. Beneath the tower, and other portions of the remains, various vaults were discovered (probably cellars) connected by passages, seven feet six inches high, arched over above, running under the cloister, &c., giving rise to the popular belief that a subterranean communication existed between this establishment and Wellingore. Dr. Oliver also discovered many human remains in his researches, which is not surprising, as there was certainly a burial garth here, from which has lately been extracted a much worn monumental slab, or coffin lid (still remaining on the premises) having the effigy of a recumbent Ecclesiastic cut upon it. A portion of one of the old vaults is yet visible, now used as a saw-pit, and another spot sounds hollow, so that further sub-structures may hereafter be discovered. The whole of the ground in the vicinity of the tower abounds with evidences of the extent of the buildings once existing here; portions of columns, ribs, and other worked stones having frequently been turned up, of which a few still remain; whilst a pretty little Decorated window, doubtless derived from the ruins, is inserted in the gable of the adjoining farmstead. There is also a remarkably fine well here, nine feet in diameter, never known to be dry—perhaps a legacy from the knights of St. John; and in another well, discovered during the last century to the west of the Temple site, three bells of large dimensions were found. Two mounds existed, until lately, in an adjoining close; but these were probably only archery butts, and upon their removal no signs of any deposit were disclosed. One of the Temple boundary stones stood, until 1776, by the side of the High Dyke, as recorded by Stukely, who says, "Iter. 5, p. 87" "Over against Temple Bruer, is a cross upon a stone, cut through in the shape of that borne by the Knights Templars;" but this has since been removed, or destroyed. He also adds, "Some part of their old Church is left of a circular form as usual." In 1628 the Earl of Dorset, then the possessor of Temple Bruer, disposed of it to Richard Brownlow, Esq., of Belton, and through the marriage of Alice, daughter of Sir John Brownlow, with Francis North Earl of Guildford, passed into his hands. He sold it to the ancestor of the present owner of Temple Bruer, Henry Chaplin, Esq., M.P., of Blankney.

WILSFORD.

ACREAGE,
2900.

POPULATION,
641.

THIS village lies 5 miles west of Sleaford, and is bounded on the west by the Ermine street, where some of its houses immediately face those on the other side of that ancient road in the parish of Ancaster.

Its name was originally spelt Wivelesforde. Here Siward had 12 carucates of land, rated at 9 carucates. Azor and his brother held 6 bovates of this and a mill, subject only to military service. Gunfrid, or Geoffrey of Cambrai, had 3 carucates in demesne, 12 sokemen with 3 carucates, 6 villans and 2 bordars having 6 carucates; and the church had 2 bovates, 45 acres of meadow, and 20 of underwood. This was valued before and after the Conquest at £4, and taxed at 20s. Subsequently Bishop Remigius bought the manor for the church of St. Mary at Lincoln. Four carucates here, rated at 3, together with 9 sokemen and 2 bordars, were soke of the manor of Sedgebrook. This had belonged to Godwin, but was granted to Robert Mallet, and comprised in the Honour of Eye, in Suffolk, and subsequently possessed by the Uffords and Poles, Earls of Suffolk. In the reign of Stephen, Hugh de Evermue or Wake, held the manor of Wilsford, and founded an alien Priory here. Haverholme Priory possessed three oxgangs-and-a-half of land in Wilsford, the gift of John, the son of William de Odenby and Elizabeth his wife, besides certain tofts, and the villans on this land, together with their families and chattels. About the middle of the 13th century the Honour of De la Haye in Wilsford and Ancaster, constituting a quarter of a knight's fee, was held of Earl Richard by the Prior of Haverholme Priory, half a knight's fee of the Honour of Eye was held by Peter de Mallet, and a similar portion of land was held by William de Vesci of the King.

From the "Inquisitiones post mortem" of the 14th, 15th, and 16th centuries, we find that Ralph, son of Walran de Mortimer died in 1325, seized of a messuage in Wilsford, 60 acres of land, 5 of meadow, and 10 of wood, valued at 112s. Robert de Ufford, Earl of Suffolk, in 1348, seized of the fee of the Honour of Eye, and his successor of the same name in 1369. Sir Henry de Scroop, seized of part of the same Honour in 1393. Michael de la Pole, slain at Harfleur, Sept. 14th, 1415, and his son, also called Michael, slain at Agincourt on the 25th of October following, both being lords paramount of the same portion of Wilsford ; also William de la Pole, Earl of Suffolk, in 1449.

The picturesque old house close to the parish church, was formerly occupied as a hunting-box by the then Duke of Rutland, but is now simply a farm-house. Probably it was built by Sir Charles Cotterel, an accomplished gentleman attached to the court of Charles II., and who was born at Wilsford.

The land in this parish now principally belongs to Messrs. Myers, Parkinson, and Calcraft, and Captain Willson.

ECCLESIASTICAL HISTORY.

There was a church at Wilsford when Domesday Book was compiled. In the reign of Stephen, Hugh de Evermue, or Wake, founded a Priory here, which he attached to the famous Benedictine Abbey of Bec in Normandy, and endowed it with 9 carucates of land in this place, when a number of its monks came over to secure the profits of this gift. "Testa de Nevill." During the war with France in 1369 this, with all other alien Priories, was seized by the King of England, but its own Prior was appointed its custodian as long as the war lasted, at the annual rent of 6 marks. " Pipe Rolls 45. E. 3." At this time he had a right to hold a market and fair at Wilsford. In 1397 Thomas Holland, Earl of Kent, the King's half brother, obtained a grant of the Priory and all its possessions and bestowed it upon the Abbey of Bourn. "Inq. p. m. 20 R. 2." When, at the petition of the Commons the King took possession of all alien Priories, John Oudeby was the clerk of Wilsford Priory. At the dissolution as parcel of Bourn Abbey, its lands were granted to Charles Brandon, Duke of Suffolk, " 30 H. 8," who died seized of them 1545.

The following is a list of the rectors :—

Date of Institution.

A.D. 1661.—William Letts, presented by Lord Rockingham.

1676.—William Barriffe, ditto.

1691.—Lewis Smith,   ditto.

.—Stephen Atton.

1721.—Chamberlain Atton.

1731.—Watson Tookey.

1734.—John Lowth.

1753.—Thomas Mirehouse.

1758.—John Image.

1762.—John Richard Middlemore.

1770.—John Richard Middlemore.

1771.—Thomas Marsham.

1791.—John Middleton.

1831.—Charles Brackenbury.

1849.—George Bugg.

1852.—John Parkinson Bayly Younge.

THE CHURCH.

The tower and spire of this church, dedicated in honour of St. Mary, produce a pleasing effect. The proportion between the two is far better than that of Ancaster, and the boldly projecting gurgoyles beneath the parapet of the tower add much to its appearance ; but on a nearer examination the weakness of the spire-lights and other details become fully apparent.

The south aisle was once wholly Early English. The pitch of its first roof will be seen at the east end, above a lancet window there. Close to a similar window, in the nave wall beyond the aisle, is some ancient long and short masonry, forming the south-eastern angle of the nave. During the prevalence of the Perpendicular style this aisle was renewed, and a clerestory was added to the nave, both of which were then surmounted by embattled parapets and pinnacles, the bases of which alone now remain. Over the porch arch is a shallow niche that once probably contained a sculptured representation of the Virgin and Child. Near the porch is a plain low-side window. The chancel is essentially Early English, to which subsequent additions have been made. In its south wall are two lancet windows and a

WILSFORD CHURCH.

Decorated one nearest to the nave. The whole design of the east end with its well developed angle buttresses and its very beautifully traceried window is excellent. In the north wall there is only room for one lancet window before the commencement of a chantry chapel, which now forms a prolongation of the north aisle. In the east end of this there is a large Decorated reticulated window, and a smaller window in the lateral wall. In the north aisle proper is another Decorated window and a doorway. Between the windows of the clerestory are four canopied niches which produce a good effect, but prove to be of a weak design when examined closely. Pinnacles appear to have risen above the parapet here as on the other side of the clerestory.

In the interior, the north-east angle of the original nave will be inspected with much interest. It is composed of long and short work, and corresponds exactly with the south-east angle of the nave before alluded to, and which still remains an external feature. These must be either of Saxon origin, or of Saxon workmanship, during the early Norman rule.

Adjoining this very interesting feature are a pair of Norman pillars, carrying a pointed arch of a later period, and adorned with the nail-head ornament. This opens into what was a chapel, where a piscina, credence, and the supporters of the altar slab still remain. The Early English north aisle arcade has lofty cylindrical pillars and wide semicircular arches. The pillar capitals, with their brackets to support the outer members of the arches above are of a peculiar type.

The arrangement of the south aisle arcade is curious. This is of the Decorated period, and consists of one very large arch and a smaller one ; nearly above which, is the outline of another archway that appears to have opened into the nave, as it is certainly not a constructional one, although now filled in with masonry. What this can have been for is perplexing, unless it was for the accommodation of a recluse, whose chamber might possibly have been constructed over the eastern portion of the south aisle. Below was certainly a chapel, the piscina and aumbry of which still remain. In the last was found much charcoal, when it was opened during the late restoration of this church. The chancel is said to have been *re-built* by a former rector of the name of Warde, in 1479, according to the inscription upon his gravestone : but the word *restored,* or *repaired,* would have been more correct, as the east window and one of the side ones are the only remaining features of the above-named period, the rest being very considerably older.   The chancel arch is supported by pillars on elevated bases.   In the sill of the south-eastern window, which has been lowered for the purpose, is a double piscina.   One bowl is plain, and its drain passes horizontally through the wall behind it; the other is fluted, and has the usual perpendicular drain.   Here also is a credence.

HANDBECK.

THE name of this hamlet, attached to Wilsford, was originally spelt Handebec, or Handebeck, and sometimes Hanebeck. The Vescis and Clintons are the first recorded proprietors of land in Wilsford, but in the 12th century the Templars had acquired a footing here, Osmund Ferling in 1185 having given an oxgang to that Order in Handbeck, let for a rent of 2s. a year, 4 hens, and 2 day's work, and another benefactor having given another oxgang and a toft, let at 2s. a year.

The Vesci fee here in the 13th century was reckoned at half a knight's fee, then held of the King by William de Vesci, and let by him to John Colman. Early in the same century the Clinton lands in Handbeck were reckoned only at the tenth part of a knight's fee, when they were held by Henry de Clinton, and let to Osbert, son of Nigel. In 1240 their value was reduced to the twelfth part of a knight's fee, when they were held by Roger de Kingerby of the King in chief, and let to Robert Croc. "Testa de Nevill."

In 1584 John Bucke bought Handbeck Grange of Sir Henry Sidney. He was Provost Marshal in the expedition to Cadiz in 1596 under the Earl of Essex, when he was made a knight. He married Eleanor, daughter of John Wymarhe, of Gretford, and died November 20th, 1596. His son Sir John Bucke was Sheriff of the county in 1619, who, after his marriage with Elizabeth, daughter and heir of William Green, of Filey, resided at Filey, and died 1648. Their eldest son, John, was created a Baronet December 22nd, 1660, and died 1668. He married first, Anne, daughter of John Style, of Winteringbury; and subsequently, Mary, daughter and sole heir of William Ashton, of Tengrey, Beds., by whom he had a son, Sir William, who married Frances, daughter of Daniel Skinner, of London, and died August 15th, 1717. Their son, Sir Charles Bucke, born 1692, married Anne, daughter of Sir Edward Sebright, of Besford, Worcestershire, and died June 20th, 1729; and lastly their son, the second Sir Charles, born January 31st, 1721, died without issue by his wife Mary, daughter of George Cartwright, of Ossington, Notts., June 7th, 1782, and was the last male heir of his family. He was buried in Osbournby church, where his sisters erected a monument to his memory. The Bucke armorial bearings were Lozengy Or & Az, a canton Ermine. Crest, a portcullis. There are now no remains of the residence of this family in Handbeck, which now belongs to John Archer Houblon, Esq.

WAPENTAKE OF ASWARDHURN.

THE boundaries of this Wapentake have been mentioned at the commencement of the History of Sleaford, &c. It contains the following parishes and hamlets, which will be described in their alphabetical order, viz: Asgarby, Aswarby, Aunsby, Burton, Culverthorpe, Dembleby, Ewerby, Hale, Haydor, Heckington, Helpringham, Howell, Kelby, Kirkby, Osbournby, Quarrington, Scredington, Spanby, Swarby, Swaton, Welby, Willoughby (Scot), and Willoughby (Silk).

Since the description of the Wapentake of Flaxwell has been printed, a new census has appeared, which of course varies from that of 1861—so far quoted. It will be well therefore to give the population of the parishes already described according to this later record, or the census of 1871 here, which is as follows:—

POPULATION OF THE FLAXWELL WAPENTAKE
ACCORDING TO THE CENSUS OF 1871.

New Sleaford	3592
Old Sleaford	397
Holdingham	143
Anwick	324
Ashby	161
Bloxholm	84
Brauncewell	139
Cranwell	219

Digby	307
Dorrington	495
Evedon	71
Haverholme	11
Kyme North and South	1221
Leasingham	390
Rauceby	691
Rowston	233
Roxholm	115
Ruskington	1156
Temple Bruer	149
Wilsford	647

The population of the parishes in the Wapentake of Aswardhurn will be given according to the census of 1861 and of 1871.

ASGARBY.

ACREAGE,
838.

POPULATION,
1861—80.   1871—92.

THE name of this place, situated 3 miles east of Sleaford, was at first spelt Asgerebi, then Asgerbi and Asgardby, now shortened into Asgarby. After the Conquest it was given to Gilbert de Gant, and consisted of 3 carucates of plough land and 80 acres of meadow, upon which were 20 sokemen and 2 villans.

About 1200 its land was reckoned at the fourth part of a knight's fee, held by Simon de Kyme, when Mauger de Asgurdby and others were tenants here. "Testa de Nevill." In the 16th century Lord Tailboys, of Kyme, was holding land in Asgarby; and in 1553 died Blasius Holland the younger, seized of a messuage, 60 acres of plough land, and 20 of pasture in this vill, which he held of the heirs of Lord Tailboys. "Harl. MS. 757." Soon after Robert Carre of Sleaford purchased the manor of Asgarby and the smaller one of Boughton connected with it, which last he sold to Sir Edward Dymoke; but he subsequently became re-possessed of it, and left the whole, together with ap-purtenances in Monkthorpe and Brothertoft to his cousin, Robert Carre, from whom they have descended to the present owner of the same, the Marquis of Bristol. This parish was enclosed in 1688.

ECCLESIASTICAL HISTORY.

The church here was given to the Prior of Bridlington in the reign of Pope Eugenius III., by whom that gift was confirmed. In 1416 Agnes, the wife of John Wright, of Asgarby, bequeathed her body to be buried in the cemetery of the church of St. Andrew here, to the fabric of which she left 4s. Robert Toterowe of Bughton (*i.e.* Boughton in this parish), by his will dated on the feast of St. Praxidis the Virgin 1450, bequeathed his body to be buried in the church of Asgarby, to the high altar of which he left 12d., and for ornaments of the said altar 13s. 4d. To the high altar of the Cathedral church of Lincoln 20d., and to its fabric 40d. Besides which certain lands and tenements here were given by an unknown person for the support of two lamps in this church for ever. " Cot. MS. Tib."

In 1616 the value of the living was £31, Edward Carre was the patron, and there were 60 communicants. " Willis's MS. f. 39." The following is a list of the rectors :—

Date of Institution.

A.D. 1292.—John de Malden.

1315.—Hugo de Harewood, presented by the Prior of Kyme.

1616.—William Williams, presented by Edward Carre.

1662.—Richard Bull.

1662.—John Kennington.

1663.—Samuel Sutton.

1681.—Thomas Meriton.

1687.—William Pearson.

1732.—Charles Hervey.

1735.—Gascoigne Wright.

1777.—Edward Mills.

1821.—William Andrew Hammond.

1823.—John Smith.

1829.—John Morgan.

1844.—Henry Ashington.

1854.—Henry Anders.

The Church.

This is dedicated in honour of St. Andrew. The height and size of its tower as compared with the rest of the fabric, and the smallness of the spire in proportion to it, are the features that most attract attention at a distance.

Here was an Early English chancel, of which the south door-way and the piscina inside, are all that remain. The lower part of the tower, the arcades of the nave, and the whole south aisle are of the Decorated period, and the masonry is remarkably substantial and perfect. The remainder of the church is of the latest period of the Perpendicular style.

ASGARBY CHURCH.

BLOXHOLM CHURCH---SEE PAGE 211.

In the interior, the solidity of the tower-arch, the old stair-case to the roodloft, the brackets and aumbries at the east end of the aisles, and the bracket on the north side of the chancel-arch, are worthy of notice.

The easternmost bay of both aisles has been chancelled off to form chapels, as evidenced by incisions in the caps of the pillars at those points. In the northern one is a piscina and two rude statue brackets. On the north wall close to one of these a painting has recently been discovered. This consists of the figure of a kneeling angel in an alb and red stole, upon a green mound surrounded by a rope-like border. The ground is dark red, powdered partly with Tudor roses, partly with a foliated device in a lighter red. Above is this legend upon a scroll :— "Intercede p. nobis ad dnm reginam ; " and below upon another scroll : " Orate p. aia henrici Tirrwyt," as far as this last word can be deciphered ; but the middle letters are entirely gone, and the others are injured. Most probably this painting was intended to appear in connexion with an image of the Virgin Mary that formerly stood on the adjacent bracket.

In Holles's time in the east window of the chancel were the arms of Umfraville and Tailboys. In the south window, Gules, 3 livery pots Arg, for Bland, and the legend " Orate pro animâ Stephani Muston et Agnetis uxoris ejus." In the north window, the portrait of a man holding a shield, bearing S. a chevron between 3 escallops Arg, and the legend " Orate pro aia Willi Kingsman et Elizabethæ consortis suæ." In the tower window this legend : " Iohes More & Margareta uxor ejus." On a stone tomb in the choir was this epitaph :—

> Es testis, Christe quod non jacet hic lapis iste
> Corpus ut ornetur, sed spiritus ut memoretur.
> Istuc qui graderis, senex, medius, puer, an sis,
> Pro me funde prœes quia sic mihi fit venie spes.
> MCCCCLX.

And on another :—

> Orate pro aia Willi Fish & Johanne uxoris ejus.

On the wall of the eastern chapel is a monument bearing this legend :—

> Carolus primogenitus Johannis Butler de Baketon (Boughton) obiit xviio die Maii MDCIII. Ætatis suæ viii.

And above, a shield bearing a chevron charged with 3 covered cups between 3 demi lions crowned with a martlet as a mark of cadency, surmounted by a horse's head erased, as a crest.

On the north wall is this curious epitaph :—

> Here lyeth the body of Mrs. Cecily Sutton, late wife of Mr. Samvel Sutton, Rector of this church, who upon ye 2nd daye of December, anno 1680, ætatis suae 62, was gathered to the Spirits of the Just that are made perfect.
>
> I liv'd, I lov'd, I gave to the poore,
> I'm dead, I'm blest, I'm mist therefore.
> Hic requiscit in spe beatae Resurrectionis.

Over the tower arch is a characteristic memento mori of the last century, viz: a figure of Death as a skeleton with a scythe erect over his head, and an hour glass. Above is the precept, " Redeem the time," below, the counsel, " Prepare to die."

This church has lately been well and carefully restored.

ASWARBY.

THE land in this parish, situated 4½ miles south of Sleaford, at first called Aswardebi, was reckoned at 9 carucates, according to Domesday Book, but only at 4½ carucates and 1 bovate for taxation. Here also were 180 acres of meadow. Of this Gilbert de Gant was then holding 4½ carucates and 1 bovate, and also the above-named meadow land; Wido de Credon was holding a smaller portion, and Ralph, the priest of Aswarby, another. At the beginning of the 13th century Simon de Kyme was holding the de Gant lands here, reckoned at one knight's fee, "Testa de Nevill," and in 1336 William de Kyme was their possessor. In 1334 Richard Whitwell and others obtained the King's licence to give certain lands in Aswarby, Swarby and Willoughby to the Dean and Chapter of Lincoln, "Inq. ad. q. d. 27 E. III.;" and in 1381 Gilbert de Umfraville, Earl of Anjou, died seized of the manor of Aswarby conjointly with Matilda his wife. "Inq. ad. q. d. 8 R. II." In 1421 died Sir Gilbert de Umfraville seized of this manor, which he held of the Honour of Bolingbroke. "Inq. p. m. 9 H. 5." In 1462 Edward IV. granted the manor of Aswarby to Sir John Fogge, after the attainder of Sir William Tailboys; but it was subsequently restored to that family, and eventually inherited by Lady Ambrose Dudley, the daughter and heir of Gilbert Lord Tailboys, who sold it to her uncle, Robert Carre, of Sleaford, from whom it descended to his sons in succession, and then to his grandson Rochester, son of Sir Edward and brother of Sir Robert Carre, who held it of the Earl of Lincoln, as of the Castle of Falkingham at an annual rent of 6s. 8d. "Harl. MSS. 758." On his death as a lunatic, the manor reverted to his brother Sir Robert, and then passed to his son the Right Honourable Sir Robert Carre, and his young grandson Sir Edward Carre, who died under age in 1683. The manor was sold by Lord Carre Hervey to Sir Francis Whichcote, Bart., in 1723, whose descendant, the present Sir Thomas Whichcote, still possesses it.

Sir Jeremy Whichcote, the 1st Baronet, created 1660, was Solicitor General to the Prince Palatine, and Warden of the fleet during the Commonwealth. He married Anne, daughter and heir of Joseph Grave, Esq., by whom he had a large family and was succeeded by his eldest son, Sir Paul, 2nd Bart., who married Jane, daughter and coheir of Sir Nicholas Gould, Bart. He died in 1721, and was succeeded by his son Sir Francis, 3rd Bart., M.P. for Cambridgeshire. He married, first, Mary, only daughter of Joseph Banks, Esq., of Revesby, and secondly, Frances, daughter of Edward Hall, Esq., and relict of Sir Nevill Hickman, Bart., of Gainsborough. He died in 1775, and by his second wife left as his heir Sir Christopher, 4th Bart., who married Jane, daughter and coheir of Thomas Whichcote, Esq., Harpswell. He died in 1785, and was succeeded by his son Sir Thomas, 5th Bart., High Sheriff for Lincolnshire in 1790. He married Diana, daughter of Edward Turnor, Esq., of Panton and Stoke Rochford, and died in 1828, and was succeeded by his son Sir Thomas, 6th Bart., who married Lady Sophia Sherard, third daughter of Philip, 5th Earl of Harborough. He died in 1829, and was succeeded by Sir Thomas, the 7th and present Bart., who married, first, Marianne, daughter of Henry Becket, Esq., and secondly, Isabella Elizabeth, daughter of Sir Henry C. Montgomery, Bart., by whom he has one daughter.

Aswarby Hall is a large mansion, a small part of which is of some antiquity; the park and grounds around it are flat, but well timbered. The cottages in the village and the buildings on all the farms are of an excellent description, clearly indicating that they belong to a wealthy landowner who desires that his estate should be well maintained. Formerly a medicinal spring, mentioned by Camden, was of some note, but its fame has now entirely passed away.

Ecclesiastical History.

There was a church here at the time of the Conquest, served by a priest called Ralph, who held 3½ carucates of land in Aswarby, the profits of which were divided into two parts.

Aswarby Church.

Gilbert de Gant became the possessor of these by the gift of the
Conqueror, and they subsequently passed into the hands of the
Priors of Kyme.

In 1225 Adam de Aswardby was elected Abbot of Bardney
Abbey, over which he presided for 12 years. In 1616 the value
of the rectory was £40 a year, and Sir Edward Carre was the
patron. " Willis's MS. p. 39." The following is a list of the
rectors :—

Date of Institution.

A.D.   .—Gilbert de Byham, presented by the Prior of
            Kyme.
1263.—Hugo de Heckington.
    .—Robert Daunce, died 1460.
    .—Stephen Scarbruth (Scarborough), died 1537.
    .—William Jones, died 1580.
    .—William Williams, died 1616.
1660.—William Wood.
1680.—Francis Hopes.
1714.—John Mason.
1748.—William Bassett.
1754.—Richard Brown.
1777.—Nathaniel North.
1814.—John Hanmer.
1818.—Francis Whichcote.
1850.—Christopher Whichcote.

The old rectory house stood on the south side of the churchyard,
but was taken down when the present one was substituted for it.

THE CHURCH.

This is dedicated in honour of St Dionysius or Dennis, and
consists of a tower and spire, a lofty nave, a north aisle, porch
and chancel. On examining its various features it will be readily
seen that the whole fabric has been more or less completely
rebuilt at two distinct periods, and also that this operation was
repeated some 30 years ago. From the evidence of the fine old
doorway within the porch on the north side of the nave, and the
font, we are assured that a church stood here when the Norman
style of architecture was in the act of being exchanged for that

of the Early English. The first feature is a very beautiful specimen of its kind. The head is semicircular, and the whole consists of three members supported by as many pillars on the jambs below. The inner pair and the corresponding moulding above are thickly banded, and the foliated caps of the others vary in their treatment in common with them. Besides being beautifully and effectively moulded, the head of the doorway is enriched with two series of four-leaved flowers. The font is a large and curious one of the same period. It resembles a circular stone well-head, to which are attached four pillars at equal distances, the foliation of each cap being prolonged so as to trail over the adjoining surface of the bowl. This and the before-mentioned doorway are of the last quarter of the 12th century. Next we have some Decorated work in the aisle and its arcade. This last consists of three clustered and filleted pillars and their responds, supporting four well-moulded arches. The aisle is lighted by a two-light window at each end, and two others towards the east end of its north wall. How far the older church here succumbed to this newer style can not now be ascertained; but it also in turn was afterwards considered inferior to the subsequent Perpendicular style, when the greater part of the present fabric was erected, viz : the south elevation of the nave, a chancel preceding the present one as evidenced by the present chancel arch, the clerestory with its range of six windows on either side, and the tower and spire. These last are imposing at a distance, although it will at once be seen that the latter is not well set upon the former, and that its apex has been restored in a clumsy manner, while on a nearer view the usual weak details of the Perpendicular style will detract from the merit of both tower and spire.

About 30 years ago the chancel and porch were rebuilt; two Decorated windows, copied from others in this church, were inserted in the south wall of the nave, and it was re-roofed and re-seated. In the present year the chancel, separated from the nave until the restoration of the fabric by a carved oak screen, has been supplied with handsome seats for the choir. The staircase formerly leading to the rood loft still remains at the east end of the aisle with a handsome piscina near it, and a plain one opposite, indicates the former existence of a chapel there. There are three bells in the tower.

The following memorials were observed in this church by Holles, viz: in a window of the chancel, Gu, a cinquefoil pierced within an orle of cross crosslets Or—Umfraville, repeated twice. Above the sedilia in the chancel, Arg, 3 escutcheons Az—Lowdham, and Gu, 3 lucies hauriant Arg—Lucy. On the chancel screen—once richly gilt—he saw, Gu, a chevron between 10 cross crosslets Or—Kyme, Arg, a saltire Sa on a chief Gu 3 escallops of the first—Tailboys ; also Umfraville and another. Of these, the shields bearing Umfraville and Tailboys still remained upon the panels of the western face of the screen until its removal ; and in a south window, probably of the chancel, this legend :—

> Orate p. aiabus Dni Roberti Daunce et Johanne uxoris eius.

Also a stone slab bearing this inscription :—

> Hic Jacet Dns Robertus Dawnce quondam Rector istius ccclie, qui obiit xxviii die Januarii, An Dni MCCCCIX cuius anime ppicietur Deus. Amen.

In the north aisle was a stone slab bearing this epitaph : —

> Hic Jacet corpus Willi Jones qui obiit ixº die Octobris Aº Dni MDLXXX. Vana. Deum. requiem. sprevit. amavit. habet.

Also near the door—probably the southern one—another slab thus inscribed :—

> Hic Jacet Willus Dymson, et Johanna uxor ejus, qui obiit Vto. die Augusti Ano Dni MDLVIII, cuius aie ppicietur Dius. Amen.

All of these are now gone. The only monument of any interest still preserved here, excepting quite modern ones, is a marble tablet in the chancel commemorating Francis Hopes, a former rector, who died 1704, and his wife Christiana, whose daughter, of the same name, was the second wife of Sir Stephen Fox, by whom he had a son, Stephen, created Earl of Ilchester.

AUNSBY.

ACREAGE,
1200.

POPULATION,
1861—140. 1871—139.

THIS parish lies 5 miles south west of Sleaford. Its name was formerly spelt Ounesbi or Ounesby. According to Domesday Book its land consisted of 7 carucates, 2 bovates of inland, 70 acres of meadow, and 6 acres of underwood, upon which were 25 sokemen, when that computation was taken. Part of it lay within the soke of Wido de Rembrudcurts' manor of Scot Willoughby. In the 12th century Cristina Belet or Ledet held one knight's fee here of the King, when she had let it to Nicholas do Ounesby by knight's service. "Testa de Nevill." Subsequently through the marriage of Lucy, daughter of Michael Belet, with John Pigot, it passed to the the Pigot family, of whom John, son of Baldwin de Pigot, knight, of Dodington, sold the manor and all its appurtenances in 1318, to William de Baiocis, clerk, who derived the means of making this purchase through the will of Robert de Lasey or Lucy, Treasurer of Lincoln Cathedral. Five years later he left it in trust to Richard de Hiltoft, John de Bratingham, and Robert de Luda, chaplains and vicars of the choir of Lincoln Cathedral, for the purpose of making it over to the Dean and Chapter, on condition of their finding three chaplains to say masses for their souls and those of all the faithful, with the consent of William de Waure, who held the manor of Sir William Latymer, by each of whom, and by William Latymer, son of Sir William, consent was given to this deed. "Lib. de ordinationibus cantariarum, f. 146," and "Pip. Rot. 17 E. 2." The validity of this transaction however was questioned by John Pigot in 1326, and the manor was transferred according to his will, but charged with a small annual payment of 13d. for the purpose of saying masses for the souls of his above-named executors on their anniversary day. Subsequently the Prioress of Stixwold became possessed of lands here, held by Anna, widow of John Slidolph, who died June 1st, 1525.

These consisted of 300 acres of arable land, 60 of meadow, and 60 of pasture ; besides a rent of 6s., 4 messuages, and 4 cottages. " Harl. MS. 758."

ECCLESIASTICAL HISTORY.

The Prior of Croxton at one time held the patronage of Aunsby church, but his right was disputed in 1305 by Baldwin Pigot, who claimed it through the marriage of his grandfather, John Pigot, with the daughter of Michael Belet, who thus acquired not only all the vill of Aunsby, but also its advowson, according to his statement. How the dispute was settled is not recorded. In 1371 some property in Aunsby was given by Canon Richard Whitlock towards founding two chantries in Lincoln Cathedral for the benefit of the soul of the donor, and that of the King—Edward III. In 1376 a payment from the manor of this vill was given to a mass priest towards saying masses for the soul of John Ginwell, Bishop of Lincoln.

In the 14th century William Pilet, of Scredington, founded a chantry at Aunsby according to the following record :—An agreement by indenture was entered into between the Dean and Chapter of Lincoln on the one part, and William Pylet, of Scredington on the other, in 1384, by which the former and their succesors were to find a chaplain to celebrate divine service in the parochial church of Aunsby, in Kesteven, in the chapel of St. Nicholas, for the souls of Walter de Ounesby, his father and mother, brothers, sisters, kinsfolks, friends, all his benefactors, and all the faithful, for ever. The chaplain was also to pray for the good estate of William Pilet and Margery his wife while they lived, and for their souls and those of all their kin, friends, and benefactors when they died; he and his successors were also bound to celebrate every week in the chapel of the blessed Mary at Croketon (Croxton), viz : on Wednesday and Saturday, for the souls of the same. For this service he was to receive a competent salary from the lands and tenements which had formerly belonged to the said Walter at Aunsby and Croxton as was agreed upon between the said Dean and Chapter and the chaplain, and in such a way that the said chantry was never to cease, so long as the said lands and tenements were found to be adequate for the support of the burdens of the same ; but whenever that was not the case, the chaplain was to celebrate for the said souls according to the quantity and the portion of the value of the possessions ; or he was according to his discretion to pray, or perform other good works, as often as those possessions sufficed for the finding of a chaplain, when he was bound to perform the aforesaid services. The seals of the Dean and Chapter, and of William Pilet were affixed to this indenture in the Chapter house at Lincoln, on the Saturday after the feast of St. Bartholomew, 1384. "Lib. de ordinat. cant. f. 355."

At the suppression of chantries the incumbent was 72 years old, and had no other preferment. The profits were then as follows : An annual rent of £2 13s. 4d. issuing from all the lands, tenements, and hereditaments soever belonging to the Dean and Chapter, payable at the feast of St. Mary the Virgin and St. Michael, and a cottage in the tenure of John Austyn, rented at 3s. ; also the firm of a tenement and 12 acres of land lying in the vill and plains of Aunsby, let to John Bydell, and payable as above, 12s. Out of these emoluments 3d. was paid to the Duke of Suffolk as to the monastery of Nocton Park. The goods were valued at 12d., and the jewels weighed 5 ounces. The chaplain received a pension of £3 5s. 2d.

The following is a list of the rectors of Aunsby :—

Date of Institution.

A.D. .———— Armstrong.
1670.—Richard Calcroft.
1671.—William Colthurst.
1692.—Robert Fish.
1694.—Henry Williamson.
1709.—William Bass.
1711.—Benjamin Stokes.
.—Robert Sampson.
1721.—John Adcock.
1753.—Emanuel Langford.
1778.—John Baker.
1786.—George Hickes.
1800.—Michael Thorold.
1836.—Arthur Leapingwell.
1856.—Octavius Luard.

AUNSBY CHURCH.

The Church.

This is dedicated in honour of St. Thomas a Becket, and from the age of some of its features, and the beauty of others, well repays investigation on the part of ecclesiologists. It would scarcely be suspected that the whole of the beautiful early Decorated tower and spire had been entirely re-built very lately, from the excellent and careful manner in which this operation was carried out. The details of the spire-lights are delicately finished, and a crown-like finial of a later period surmounts the legend of " Ave Maria," cut in separated letters just below it. The slits for lighting the tower stairs are curiously contrived. The aisles partly overlap the chancel, and the southern one, of an early Perpendicular character, is very pleasing ; above the sills proper of its windows is a structural filling-in, or stone panelling.

Within, the Norman north arcade with the varied and pendent details of its pillar capitals is striking. This was in a most dangerous condition, partly from a rash incision made through its eastern end, for the purpose of giving access to the rood loft, and partly from the failure of its foundations ; but it has now been set in order very satisfactorily. When the modest Perpendicular aisle beyond was built, it was not carried on so far eastward as its predecessor, from the evidence of a piscina now seen externally in the chancel wall, whilst its present east end cuts off a portion of the wall opening into the chancel. The piers of the chancel arch are Norman, but these have been subsequently surmounted by a later arch. At the east end of the south aisle was formerly a chapel, enclosed by a coped wall four feet high, and having a stone bench within, evidences of which still remain ; here is also a rude bracket piscina. The east window of the chancel is new. The fine old Norman font, at the other extremity of the church, has a remarkably good effect there.

Gervase Holles observed the following memorials in Aunsby church when he visited it, viz., this fragment of an epitaph :—

Priez pour lalme Walter de Ownsby q. dona ....

On a brass inserted in the wall :—

Orate pro anima Christopheri Hogekinson quondam
.... manerii de Ownesby, qui obiit xx° die
Decembris, Anno Domini MDXCIIII.

Z

On the base of a stone tomb on the left hand side of the chancel :

Johannis Colthirst, patris Johis, qui vixit 1600.

A flat stone still remains in the pavement of the chancel, having this inscription :—

Here lyeth the body of............ Calthurst, Gentleman of Ownsby, who was buried 2 day of December, Anno Dni, 1627.

BURTON PEDWARDINE.

BEFORE the Conquest Adestan and Azor were the principal
Saxon landowners here. Subsequently their lands were
bestowed upon Wido de Credon and Ivo Tailbois. The first of
these new Norman lords allowed the unfortunate Adestan to
retain 10 carucates of what had been his own land as tenant of
the same, who had 30 sokemen and 9 villans. Of the rest,
reckoned at 17 carucates, he retained in demesne 5 carucates.
Besides these plough lands there were 120 acres of meadow, 12
bordars having 11½ carucates of land, and a mill worth 2s. a
year. The whole annual value in King Edward's time was £6
and subsequently £8, tallaged at 40s. Ivo Tailbois's land here
was mixed up with other land in Ewerby Thorpe. It consisted
of 14 carucates of land. Part of this was occupied by Azor, who
had 3 villans under him, and 2 bordars having 2 carucates of
plough land, 300 acres of underwood, and 13 acres of meadow.
The annual value in King Edward's time was 30s., subsequently
20s. Gilbert de Gant also possessed 2 carucates in this parish
belonging to his manor of Falkingham. Wido de Credon, of
Bretagne, whose family name subsequently assumed the form of
Croun, received from the Conqueror in return for the services he
had rendered him, lands in 60 parishes of Lincolnshire and
others in Leicestershire. The chief seat of his barony was at
Freiston, where he built a residence for himself. His manor of
Burton consisted of 10 carucates of plough land, 120 acres of
meadow, and a mill worth 2s. a year. It had also appurtenances in Heckington, Aswarby, and Mareham. Wido himself
had 3 carucates, 30 sokemen, 9 villans, and 12 bordars cultivating
11½ carucates. The whole was worth £6 in King Edward's time,
subsequently £8, and was tallaged at 40s. It is doubtful whether
Wido's eldest son Godfrey, the first Prior of Freiston, succeeded
him, but certainly his second son Alan eventually became his

heir. He was called "Open door" from his great hospitality, and was Grand Steward of the Household to Henry I., by whom he was summoned to Parliament as Baron Credon. He founded Freiston Priory 1142, and when Crowland Abbey was rebuilt he laid one of its foundation stones, and placed upon it the gift of the church of Freiston. He died 1150, and was buried on the north side of the high altar of that famous Abbey. By his wife Muriel de Bellechamp he had a son Maurice, made Governor of Anjou and Maine by Henry II. He married Clarissa, or Isabella, sister to William de Valence, who after his death married the Duke of Burgundy.

Their son Wido succeeded, who accompanied Richard I. to Palestine, and was present when the treaty took place between Richard and Tancred, 1190. He was a benefactor to Haverholme Priory and to the Templars. He married Isabella, daughter of Thomas Bassett and widow of Albert de Gresley. Their heiress daughter Petronilla de Credon married William de Longchamp, son of William Abbot, of Crowland, and nephew to the Bishop of Ely. At this time both manors in Burton were held by the de Credon heiress, who then possessed here 5 carucates of the old enfeoffment, 4 oxgangs of which were let to Lambert de Quaplode, and a similar quantity to Peter Angevin. "Testa de Nevill, pp. 322, 340." She subsequently married Henry de Mara or de Meris, and lastly Oliver de Vallibus, by whom she had a son, John de Vallibus, who inherited his mother's manor of Freiston, and died circa 1280. Henry de Longchamp succeeded to the Burton manor. He married Sibilla, daughter of Thomas de Herrigrande, Earl of Suffolk. He gave lands in Burton to the Abbot of Crowland in perpetual alms, and two days before his death 2 oxgangs of land in Hale, together with his body for burial in Crowland Abbey.

He had a son William, living 3 E. 2; but who died before him, so that his only daughter Alice became his heiress, married to Roger Pedwardyn or Pedwardine* son and heir of Walter

---

* He derived his name from Pedwardine, a small lordship containing about 700 acres in the parish of Brampton Brian, Herefordshire. Most probably he possessed that lordship, and certainly his family was connected with it, as one of its members was called Brian in the 14th century, and Christopher, son of Roger Pedwardine, High Sheriff of Lincolnshire, 1430-1,

Pedwardine and Maude his second wife, daughter of John Lyngayne. Thus the manor of Burton passed from the Creon family through that of Longchamp to Roger Pedwardine, whose name is still associated with this parish. In 1312 Roger Pedwardine alienated the manor to Bartholomew de Baddlesmere for a payment of £20 a year, "Ab. Rot. orig. 5 E. 2," and five years later paid the King a fine of £10 for a licence to do so again "Pip. Rot. 11 E. 2"; but this was only a temporary alienation, as he certainly lived at Burton the greater part of his life after his marriage, and died 1340 seized both of it and of the manor of Clipstone, Northamptonshire, in right of his wife, who had inherited it from John de Lacy, Earl of Lincoln. He was succeeded by his son Roger, who married Agnes, daughter and co-heir of Philip Darcy, of Nocton, and died 1368. This son and heir, Walter, knighted 1358, enjoyed the manor of Burton with its members by the service of one barony, half the manor of Nocton and the advowson of Flixborough, as parcel of the barony of Darcy, the manor of Thorntoft, in the parish of Leake, of the Honour of Richmond, and the manors of Friskney, Croft, and Dalby. He married Isabella, daughter and heir of Sir Robert Hilton, and Mary, his wife, daughter of Sir Marmaduke Tweng, and died June 11th, 1405.

Thomas de Roos, of Hamlake, next possessed the manor of Burton as a descendant of Oliver de Vallibus or Vaux, third husband of Petronilla de Croun. His son John de Vallibus having left two co-heir daughters, the second of whom—Maude—married William de Roos, lord of Hamlake and Freiston. Thomas de Roos died 1415, and was succeeded by his son and heir, John de Roos, who died 1421. The manor of Burton then reverted to Sir Robert Pedwardine, who married Elizabeth, daughter of Robert or Edward Pierpont. John Auteyn, of Burton, granted all his lands and tenements here to Sir Robert by a deed dated December 7th, 19 R. 2. He died April 26th, 1432. His eldest son, Walter, lived at Thorntoft, but died before his father, possessed of that manor, and lands in Friskney and

---

is termed of Brompton, *i.e.* Brampton, in a contemporary deed, as if he retained some rights or interest in that lordship. Pedwardine is still connected with the title of a noble family, the Earl of Kirkwall being also Baron Hay, of Pedwardine, and sitting in the House of Lords as such.

Wrangle, and was buried in Friskney church. He married, first, Katharine, daughter of John Ingleby, of Ripley, Yorkshire, and secondly, Katharine, daughter of Sir John Markham, of Notts., the widow of Matthew Leake.

Their son, Roger, accompanied the King to France, and was Sheriff of Lincolnshire, 1441-2. He paid his relief for half the manor of Stanley, in Westmoreland, 1439, and the same year was fined for not taking up the order of knighthood. He was also fined 40s. for an improper return of a brief connected with Hamond Sutton, of Burton. He married Beatrice, daughter of Matthew Leake, and his own step-mother. Their son, Christopher Pedwardine, of Brompton, Salop, succeeded, who alienated all his lands in this parish. Thomas Daniel, a Lancastrian, next possessed it together with the advowson of the church, but forfeited it on his attainder in 1464 ; when it was granted to Sir William Hussey. Then for the last time we hear of the name of Pedwardine in connexion with Burton, when Sir Walter Pedwardine paid his relief for the whole barony of Darcy, and for the lands of Elizabeth, late wife of Sir William Hussey, including the manor of Burton.

In 1552 Sir Thomas Horsman, of Mareham, obtained from the King a grant of the manor—commonly called Hussey's lands, forfeited for high treason, and some land that had belonged to Swineshead Abbey. "Harl. MS. 6829." He died November 26th, 1610, and was succeeded by his nephew Thomas, who married Mary, daughter of John Tredwaye, of Easton, North-amptonshire, and died possessed of the manor of Burton and Mareham grange, April 2nd, 1631.

Grants of Mareham to the Horsmans were repeatedly made, viz: in 1531, 1542, 1551-2, and 1564, who held it of the Crown by military service. "Harl. MS. 6829." Sir Thomas Horsman let Mareham in 1565 to Thomas Fulbeck, who lived there until his death, and subsequently to Simon Hall. At Thomas Horsman's death his lands at Burton and Mareham passed to his daughter, the wife of Sir Charles Orby, Bart., then to his brother Sir Thomas, and lastly to his daughter and heir the wife of Robert Hunter, Esq. The estate then descended to his son Thomas Orby Hunter, Esq., who sold it to Mr. Benjamin Handley, about 1808. Subsequently it was inherited by Henry Handley, Esq., M.P. for the Southern Division of Lincolnshire, and then by his son Captain Handley, who sold the estate to the present owners of the same in 1864.

Three acres of land in Spanby were left by an unknown person to the parish of Burton. This is now let for £6 a year, and after augmentation by the parishioners, is distributed to the poor on St. Thomas's day.

Some members of the Yorke family, descended from a merchant, probably deriving his name from that of the city of York, lived here towards the close of the 17th century and during the following one. The present principal landowners are, Sir Thomas Whichcote, Bart., Retford Hospital, the Rev. B. Snow, Mr. Erasmus Tomlinson, Mr. Millns, Mr. G. Hercock, Mr. Farrant, and Mr. Ward.

ECCLESIASTICAL HISTORY.

There was a church here when Domesday Book was compiled, and a priest serving it. Wido de Credon gave certain lands in Burton to God and St. Nicholas for the good of the souls of King William and Queen Maude, that the Lord might grant him success in life, and bring him to a good end.

In 1114, Matilda, daughter of Alan and Muriel de Croun, after laying the fifth stone of the east wall of the choir of Crowland Abbey, placed upon it the title to the patronage of Burton church.

In 1191, Henry de Longchamp, son and heir of Petronilla de Croun, gave to the altar of the blessed Mary at Burton, in the presence of his brother William, and to the vicar ministering there, 3 acres of arable land in Burton, to provide a wax candle of half-a-pound weight to be burnt every festival upon the altar at mass time, and to insure the saying of a weekly mass at the altar for his soul and the souls of his heirs and all the faithful, when the said candle was to be lighted. Any vicar neglecting these conditions was by power of the grant subject to distraint on the part of the donor and his heirs. He died 1274, when his heart was buried before the above-named altar. "Inq. p. m. 3 E. 1." Alice, daughter and heir of Henry de Longchamp, and wife of Sir Roger Pedwardine, after her death 1330, was buried on the north side of the above-named chapel near her father's heart. In grateful memory of his last wife, Sir Roger rebuilt this chapel and the greater part of the church to which it was attached; but the parishioners rebuilt the south aisle and the chapel of St. Nicholas attached to it. He was aided in this work by a Papal Bull granting an indulgence of 520 days to all who would contribute towards it. Sir Walter Pedwardine, grandson of Sir Roger, by his will, dated 1404, bequeathed his body to be buried in the chapel of the Assumption of the Virgin Mary, at Burton, near to his parents, and left to it a ruby coloured vestment (*i.e.* a chasuble) with its orphrey, two silver phials, six pounds of wax to make two torches to be placed at the head and foot of his corpse on his burial day, and nine ells of russet cloth to cover the same, which was afterwards to be given to three poor persons. "Repingdon's Register, 6 b."

In 1616 the vicarage was valued at £26 13s. 4d. a year. "Willis's MSS. f. 39."

The following is a list of the vicars of Burton as far as can be ascertained :—

Date of Institution.

A.D. 1280.—John de Puson, presented by the Abbot of Crowland.

1616.—William Westhall, presented by Thomas Horsman.

1643.—Samuel Lee, indicted for high treason at Grantham for taking part with the Parliament, and afterwards ejected from his living by the Act of Uniformity in 1662.

1663.—Jeremiah Goodknapp.

1681.—Peter Bold.

1702.—John Sedgwick.

1717.—Edward Jones.

1732.—Philip Sedgwick.

1737.—James Dove.

1738.—William Nickolls.

1744.—William Gery.

1787.—William Braithwaite.

1800.—Lewis Jones.

1833.—Henry Cheales.

1837.—Henry Handley Brown.

1859.—Benjamin Snow.

THE CHURCH.

The church, dedicated in honour of St. Andrew, known to have been rebuilt by Sir Roger Pedwardine and the parishioners 1330-40, consisted of a central tower, a nave, transeptal chapels, aisles, and a chancel. This remained until 1802, when a sad catastrophe occurred through the previous long neglect of the ancient fabric. Then, as the tower shewed evident signs of weakness, the materials of the chapel of St. Nicholas were taken to build up a large pier against its south-eastern angle, and a girdle of iron was thought sufficient to ensure its stability in conjunction with this pier; but when the workmen were employed in putting up scaffolding for this purpose the upper portion of the south-western angle of the tower suddenly fell, partly upon the roof of the church, but principally upon that of the south aisle, so as almost entirely to destroy it. The rest of the tower and its bells still stood, but for safety's sake were pulled down, and the next year the whole of the church, except St. Mary's chapel, was taken down, and a very poor successor erected in its place. This consisted simply of a small nave having semicircular headed windows and a little tower scarcely higher than the roof of the nave, whilst the remainder of the materials of the old church served the purpose of aiding the construction of a farm house in the parish.

Holles observed the following armorial bearings in the windows of the old church, viz : in the east window of the chancel, G, 2 lions passant or—Pedwardine, and Lozengy or & gu—Croun. In an upper north window Pedwardine thrice again, one shield having the difference of a label of 5 arg. In a south window Pedwardine, and Or, 3 crescents gu each charged with a plate—Longchamp. Also the Pedwardine crest twice— out of a crown gu, a lion's paw or. In a window of St. Mary's chapel he saw depicted the two heiresses of Burton in a kneeling posture, viz : Petronilla Croun with her bearings on her robe holding up a shield charged with those of William Longchamp, her husband; and Alice Longchamp, similarly pourtrayed, holding a shield charged with the bearings of her husband— Roger Pedwardine.

Very lately this church has been again entirely rebuilt, when the interesting little 14th century chapel was once more spared.

It now consists of a small nave and chancel, substantially built in the Decorated style, with a little bell-cot surmounted by a crocketed spirelet above its western gable and a pretty cross on the eastern one. The nave is lighted by two single-light windows in the southern wall, three similar ones in the north wall, and a good three-light window at the west end. At the east end of the chancel is a three-light window. The roofs are substantial and well-pitched.

In pulling down the former church several portions of Norman tombstones, having the intertwining ornamentation of that period carved upon them were discovered, as well as part of a hood-mould ; also some pieces of Early English work, all of which have been inserted in the west wall of the new church for their preservation. The base of one of the pillars of the old fabric, found at the same time, is now used as a credence on the north side of the chancel. There were also found at the same time fragments of a beautifully carved font and part of a church-yard cross.

St Mary's chapel, now serving as a vestry, is an interesting relic of Roger Pedwardine's church. It has good base mouldings and angle buttresses enriched with pedimented crocketed niches, and a well-moulded three-light window in its north and east walls. In its west wall is an arch formerly opening into the north aisle of the old church, and another on the south communicating with the present church. This had been filled up when Sir Thomas Horsman or his family took possession of this chapel for a burying place, and a little new door made by its side to provide access to it, but has now been very properly restored.

In the north wall of this chapel still remains a well-moulded sepulchral arch, beneath which is the grey marble tombstone of Alice Pedwardine, once adorned with her bust engraved upon a brass plate inserted in it, flanked by two shields, no doubt originally charged with the Longchamp and Pedwardine bearings. It still retains the greater part of the following border legend :—

> Dame Alis de Pettewardine gist icy.
> File de Longchampe S. Henri.
> Deu de sa alme eyt merci.

Here also was the effigy of a lady, with angels supporting a cushion beneath the head, and a dog at the feet, but this had disappeared previous to 1815.   There still however remains an ancient slab in the floor of this chapel that once had a brass border legend with the evangelical symbols at its angles, as well as the more ambitious monument of Sir Thomas Horsman, now erected against the west wall of the chapel.   This consists of a base, or altar tomb, on which is placed the effigy of Sir Thomas in armour, with the head reposing on a cushion and the hands upraised in prayer.   In front are black marble pillars with gilt capitals, supporting a canopy, and behind is a reredos, the whole being for the most part of alabaster.   On two black marble tablets is the following epitaph :—

Memoriæ sacrum.

Thomas Horsmannus, eques auratus, Thomæ Horsmanni armigeri quondam domini huius manerii et Elizabetæ unius filiarum et coheredum Roberti Hussei militis, filius et hæres ab ineunte adolescentia liberaliter institutus a latere fuit ornatissimo viro Gulielmo Baroni de Burghley summo Angliæ thesaurario, postea in famulitium Reginæ Elizabethæ adscriptus, per 40 annos serenissimæ Reginæ ministravit, et pregustatoris munere perfunctus fuit.

Vir summa fide, eximia constantia morumque probitate insignis xxvjo die Novembris, anno Domini 1610 ab hac luce migravit plenus dierum atq. cum in corpore per 74 annos tanquam migraturus habitascet.

Hujus memoriæ Thomas Horsmanus, Armiger eius e fratre Nepos et hæres hoc monumentum charissimæ pietatis ergo dicavit.

Above are the Horsman armorial bearings.   In the pavement near this is a slab commemorating his nephew, Thomas Horsman, Esq., and his wife, whose arms, effigies and epitaph were engraved on brass plates inserted in it ; but of these the effigy of the lady and the epitaph above now alone remain.   The former is well cut and represents Mary Horsman as usual in a devotional attitude and grave costume, with a veil over her head and falling behind, and in a cloak having a thickly pleated short cape round her shoulders.   The epitaph runs thus :—

Here lieth interred the bodie of Thomas Horsman, Esqvire, who was Lord of this towne.   He tooke to wife Mary, the davghter of John Tredwaye, of Easton, in Northamptonshire.   He departed this life the 2 of Aprill, in the Yeare of our Lord 1631.   Whose wife in her pious memorie erected this memoriall.

Formerly there were three bells belonging to this church, one inscribed "W. Eden, C. W. I. N. cast me 1591," and another "M. Collingwood cast me 1671," which are now gone, but the third remains, and is thus inscribed : "Cum voco ad ecclesiam venite 1604." A beautiful little piece of ironwork, used as a grating or ventilator in the door formerly opening into St. Mary's chapel, still remains here.

A tablet erected in memory of a Mr. William Yorke is now placed in the vestry of the new church, or St. Mary's chapel, and bears this inscription :—

> Within this chancell lyeth ye body of Mr. William Yorke, late of Lessingham and formerlie an inhabitant of the parish, who departed this life March 16, 1681, in ye eighty second yeare of his age. He married Elizabeth, daughter and one of the co-heirs of Mr. Simon Walgrave, who lyes here interred with him, by whom he had issue 3 sonnes and 6 daughters, Mary, John, Anne, Elizabeth, Thomas, Elizabeth, Sarah deceased and here likewise buried ; Philip, now wife of Mr. Edward Browne, * of Horbling ; and Sir William Yorke (now living at Lessingham), who married Penelope, daughter of Mr. Richard Samvell, of Gayton, in ye County of Northampton, by whom he had issue 6 sonnes and 2 daughters, Penelope, William, Samvell, Thos., Francis, Wenman, Philip, Richard, whereof Samvell, Francis and Richard lye here buried.

A black marble slab commemorating another William Yorke lies in the chancel pavement, just below the step of the sacrarium, and is thus inscribed :—

> Wilhelmus Yorke, Arm : filius Wilhelmi Yorke de Lessingham, Equitis : obiit 2do. die Janvarii Ano 1725.

Above is a circlet containing a shield bearing the Yorke Arms, impaling those of Elizabeth Oates, of Pontefract, his wife, surmounted by a mantled helm, and a Griffin's head erased for a crest.

On another mural slab in this church is this inscription :—

> To the memory of Ann ye wife of Thomas Smith, and the daughter of Mr. Joseph Thorold, of Boston, who died October 12, 1727.

---

* The founder of the free school of Horbling in 1691, from whom was descended the late wealthy Edward Brown, of Stamford.

MAREHAM.

THE name of the land so called in Burton parish was spelt Marham and Marnham, as well as Mareham, in former days. This was probably derived from the name of some former occupant, as it never constituted a separate hamlet of Burton, but was simply a grange belonging to Haverholme Priory. Its buildings were protected by a square enclosure surrounded by a bank and ditch, of which there are remains on the eastern side of the Roman road passing by it, now called Mareham lane after this old Monastic grange.

After the dissolution of Monasteries, Mareham was granted by Henry VIII. to Thomas Horsman, the husband of Elizabeth, daughter and co-heir of Robert Hussey. He was succeeded by his son, Sir Thomas Horsman, brought up in the famous Lord Burghley's family, and subsequently a courtier at Queen Elizabeth's court. He died November 26th, 1610, aged 74.

The after possessors of Mareham are recorded in the preceding history of Burton.

CULVERTHORPE.

THIS is a hamlet of Haydor, lying $5\frac{1}{2}$ miles south west of Sleaford, called Ledvlvetorp in Domesday Book, and subsequently Cudtorp, Cudetorp, Culverthop, Thorpe, and now Culverthorpe. When that record was taken Tor and Aschil had $5\frac{1}{2}$ carucates of land here, and Conded and Anschitel, two of Colsuein's vassals, had 4 carucates, 7 villans, 10 bordars, and 1 sokeman. Here also was a church and a priest. It was valued in King Edward's time at £4, and the same subsequently.

Circa 1200, Richerus de Billingburgh and Adam de Buckminster held in this vill, of the fee of La Haya, 6 oxgangs of land then in possession of Gerard de Kamville, by the service of one knight's fee. The canons of Kyme at the same time held the like quantity of land, partly in this vill and partly in Dodington, of the fee of the Earl of Chester, through the donation of Philip de Kyme. Robert de Hasceby was then holding one knight's fee of Gilbert de Gant, situated partly in Culverthorpe and partly in Swarby; and Wido de Croun had in this vill, in Kelby, and Swarby, the third part of a knight's fee, then held by Alan de Thorpe. "Testa de Nevill."

In 1338 Sir Bartholomew de Burghersh, the brother of Henry Burghersh, Bishop of Lincoln, had acquired either the whole manor or the greater part of it, and obtained a grant of free warren over his lands here. "Dugdale."

In 1610 Sir Edmund Bussy, Kt., of Haydor, conveyed to William Lister, of Rippingale, a messuage, its yards, gardens, and 344 acres of land, with the consent of Frances his wife and Miles his son and heir for the sum of £1850; and in 1619 Miles Bussy, of Oseby, his son, gave a bond to William Lister connected with the release of certain lands abutting upon his estate in Culverthorpe, and occupied by William Barbolt and Robert Coggles. This William Lister was desirous of securing more than he was justly entitled to through his purchase, viz: a piece of land at Culverthorpe belonging to the prebend of

Haydor, as evidenced by this crafty letter addressed to a Mr. Towne, of Sudbroke, probably a land surveyor or agent :—

"Mr. Towne. I w^{d.} 'mend me hertilie unto you. I pray you sett down under yr hand with this my letter, and send it me againe by this bearer. The lands which doe belong to the prebend of Haydor y^{t.} le within the grounds in Culverthorp which I bought of Sir Ed. Bussy, and as neare as you can conjecture the contents of the lands, yt I may know how much there is of it. And I praye you kepe your knowledge thereof to yourselfe, & do not disclose it to any person, for I w^{d.} not have it known to any person yt you can sett forth the land. And so resting myself assured of yr kindness herein, I rest

"Your Loveing frende,

"WILLM. LISTER.

"Downe Hall, this 24 March, 1619.

"To his loveing frende Mr. John Towne at his house at Sudbroke these."

The reply was short and explicit, viz :—

"Sir,—As I take it there is within ye groundes xiiij Landes, and as I gese them to conteane in quantitei betwene thre or foure acres. From Sudbroke this 26 March, 1619.

"Yrs to my power,

"JOHN TOWNE."

In 1658 William Lister and Mary his wife and William their son granted a lease of the house and lands at Culverthorpe to John Colthurst and Mary his wife for a term of 21 years, at an annual rent of £21.

In the reign of Charles II. the manors of Culverthorpe and Haydor passed into the hands of the Newton family, of whom John Newton was created a Baronet in 1661, whose estate was valued at £3000 a year, and was thrice the representative in Parliament for the borough of Grantham. He was succeeded by his son, the second Sir John, in 1699, and he by his son, Sir Michael, who was made a Knight of the Bath in 1725, and was twice M.P. for Grantham. Through the early death of his only son, on his decease in 1743, his estates, amplified by a large one left him by his uncle Sir Michael Wharton, were inherited by his sister Susanna, the wife of William Eyre Archer, Esq., M.P. for Berks., whose son Michael took the name of Newton ; but he dying without issue in 1803, his estates were inherited by his sisters, and subsequently by the present owner, John Archer Houblon, Esq.

THE HALL.

This is built in the Italian style, and consists of a central feature with a high-pitched roof, and wings, intended to have been connected with other subsidiary buildings, or pavilions, and is a pleasing specimen of that style. Within, is a remarkably fine drawing room, adorned with a curious painting of Sir John Newton and his family equipped for hunting, by Wootton, and several portraits of the Newtons. Here also is a fine staircase, the roof of which was probably painted by Laguerre, a pupil of Verrio's.

Formerly there was a chapel here dedicated in honour of St. Bartholomew, to which Holles apparently refers when he speaks of "Or, a cross patonce" that he observed at Culverthorpe. Now there is a little classical building east of the hall which was used for divine service until the death of Mr. Michael Newton.

DEMBLEBY.

ACREAGE,   POPULATION,
1071.   1861—51. 1871—78.

THIS little village is situated 6 miles south west of Sleaford.
Its name was spelt Delbebi in Domesday Book, whence we
gather also that Gouchil's manor here was given to Colsuein, but
that he was allowed to retain 10 bovates of land reckoned as 1
carucate, and that Rainald, a vassal of Colsuein, had 1 carucate
here, 4 sokemen, a bordar having another carucate and 16 acres
of meadow and 20 of underwood, the whole being valued before
and after the Conquest at 20s.

A portion of this parish was within the soke of Gilbert de
Gant's manor of Falkingham. This consisted of 12 bovates,
reckoned at 1 carucate ; he also had here 20 sokemen and 3
bordars having 3 carucates, 18 acres of meadow, and 16 of
underwood. Wido de Credon also had 2 carucates, reckoned at
6 bovates, and of 1 sokeman and 2 villans having 1 carucate, 14
acres of meadow and 20 of underwood as soke of his manor of
Osbournby. About 1200 Gilbert de Gant's land was reckoned
as the fourth part of a knight's fee—then in the tenure of Gilbert
de Lekeburne—but subsequently as one third only, when it was
held by Henry de Lekeburne of William de Dyve. At the same
time the said Henry de Lekeburne also held the de Credon or
Croun land here, of Henry Camerarius, and he of Petronilla de
Croun, when it was valued at one fourteenth part of a knight's
fee. The said Henry obtained a grant of free warren over all his
lands here 1312-13. One fifth part of a knight's fee in Dembleby,
of the fee of de la Haye, was held by William de Dembleby of
William Lungspee, the de la Haye heir. Adam Pescam also
held some land here of Gerard de Kamville, valued at one
fourth part of a knight's fee. "Testa de Nevill." At the beginning
of the 14th century the de Gant fee in this vill passed by marriage
into the hands of John de Bussey, who died lord paramount of
this soon after, viz : in 1305. "Inq. p. m. 34 E. 1." His son,

AA

John de Bussey, next inherited them. In 1321 William de Twynge and Matilda his wife held one messuage and a carucate of land of John Hundset, her first husband, which land was afterwards held by Richard Brown, of Osbournby. In 1338 Henry de Legburne and Robert his son did homage to John Bussey for half a knight's fee they held of him. "Harl. MS. 1758." In 1372 John de Rouceby did homage to William de Bussey in the hall at Hougham for one fourth part of a knight's fee in Dembleby, and the next year John Goldsmith did the same as his successor. In 1397 John Lord Beaumont died seized of the same quantity of land held of him and Katharine his wife by Sir John Bussey, also of one twentieth part of a knight's fee held by William Spaine. "Inq. p. m. 20 R. 2." In 1428 died Johanna, widow of Sir Robert Byron, seized of messuages and lands here, "Inq. p. m. 5 H. 6," and in 1520 died John Stanley possessed of the manor of Dembleby, who left it to his son William, then a minor. "Harl. MS. 756." In 1576 Sir Richard Pell, descended from the Pells of Water Willoughby, and knighted July 23rd, 1603, held lands here of the fee of the Honour of Bolingbroke, formerly held by William de Twenge, and afterwards by Robert Manall. He died April 19th, 1607. By his second wife, Katharine, daughter of Sir Anthony Meeres, he left a son and heir, Anthony, who lived at Dembleby, and was knighted May 24th, 1608. He bought the office of the King's Master Falconer, and in 1624 obtained an increase of the salary attached to it of £300 a year. He married Elizabeth, daughter of Sir William Willoughby, of Carlton, Notts., and had four sons, Richard, William, Anthony, John, and two daughters, Katharine and Anne. The present owner of the manor is T. R. Buckworth, Esq.

Ecclesiastical History.

A rood of meadow land in the plains of Dembleby was left by an unknown donor for the support of a lamp in Dembleby church for ever. This, at the suppression of such endowments, was valued at 6d. a year. The rents also of two tenements in Aslackby, amounting to 2s. a year, were given for a similar purpose. On the other hand two messuages in Dembleby were given by Thomas Wymbish in 1478 to the Priory of Nocton Park. "Inq. p. m. 18 E. 4."

In Bishop Neale's time the living was valued at £16, when Richard Tomlinson was rector, and Sir Anthony Pell patron.

The following is a list of the rectors :—

Date of Institution.

A.D.   .—Thomas Watson.
1662.—George Campion.
1670.—Richard Moore.
    .—Benjamin Stokes.
1721.-—John Jones.
1731.—Wyat Francis.
1780.—Joseph Mills.
1804.—Thomas Mills.
1856.—James Tillard Bonner.

The Church.

Until lately a small ancient church, dedicated in honour of St. Lucy, existed here. This was chiefly of the Early English style, but possessing some Norman features, and some of later date. As the whole was in a very dilapidated condition, its almost entire re-building was requisite, when it became a question whether the distinct features of the old fabric should be retained and restored, or whether one or other style should predominate in a new church. The latter plan was finally adopted, and with the exception of the old Norman chancel arch, the present church is entirely new, and built in a corresponding Norman style. It is a solid well-built structure having a bell-gable at the west end, a spacious porch, and a chancel terminating in an apse ; the roofs of both nave and chancel are covered with Staffordshire brindled tiles.

Within, it is neatly seated, and the whole now constitutes a creditable place of worship for the parishioners. The font is a very elegant late Norman one, consisting of a square base, a sexagonal stem ornamented with the chevron mould from top to bottom, having an enriched scalloped cap supporting a small square bowl, the faces of which are enriched throughout with a delicate diapered pattern cut upon them.

EWERBY.

ACREAGE,
2789.

POPULATION,
1861—473. 1871—461.

THIS village lies 4 miles north east of Sleaford, and was conjoined with Ewerby Thorpe, or Austhorpe, when Domesday Book was compiled, in which the former is called Bergesbi, Grenesbi and Leresbi, the latter Oustorp. Subsequently the name of Ewerby was spelt Ywarby and Iwaṛdeby or Iwardby, and that of Oustorp—Ousthorpe.

In Ewerby were, according to the same authority, 2 carucates of land rated at 3 carucates, 24 acres of meadow, and 20 of underwood; also 9 sokemen, and 9 bordars having 4 carucates.

Previous to the Conquest the lands here belonged to Leofric, Earl of Mercia, and were at that time in the hands of his widow the famous Godiva, sister of Thorold of Bucknall and Sheriff of Lincolnshire. Subsequently they were distributed between Gilbert de Gant, Remigius, Bishop of Lincoln, and Colsuein. Previous to 1185 the Templars had obtained a considerable estate in Ewerby, which was then let to various tenants. Circa 1200-10, Gilbert de Gant's fee, constituting the fifth part of a knight's fee, was held by Alured de Ywarby; and the Bishop's, consisting of half a knight's fee, was held by Nicholas Fitzwilliam. At the same time Osbert, son of Nigel, held 2 carucates of land of the fee of Henry de Quenton, then underlet by him to Nicholas and Walter de Hoyland. In 1337 died Roger de Kerdeston, seized of a manor in Ewerby, and twenty-four years later, Ranulph de Rye was lord of this vill and its hamlet—Ousthorpe. He gave to Sir Alexander Aunsel a windmill here, together with suit of all the holders of rents and tenements in Ewerby and Ousthorpe. "Lansd. MSS. 863." In 1383 Peter de Malo-Lacu died, seized of certain lands and tenements here. In 1397, John, Lord Beaumont, seized of the fifth part of a knight's fee let to the Lady de Welles, and a similar quantity let to John Aunsel. In 1451, Constance, widow of Sir John Bigod, seized of half the manor, and ten years later her son and heir Sir Ralph Bigod. In 1453, Elizabeth, one of the heiresses of the Hebden family, and relict of Sir Thomas Dymoke, died seized of half of the manor, then held of the Duchy of Lancaster. This was forfeited on the attainder and decapitation of her son Sir Thomas in 1470, but recovered by his widow, Margaret, who died eleven years afterwards. In 1515 died Sir Ralph Bigod, possessed of a manor here; and in 1521, Edward Skipwith, seized of another, leaving a daughter, Margaret Tempest. Four years later Maurice Berkeley died, also seized of a manor in Ewerby; upon the death of whose son and heir, his sister succeeded to it, who died in 1583. Haverholme Priory was enriched with lands in Ewerby, viz: two acres of meadow, the gift of Simon the son of Stephen de Horbling; ten-and-a-half of meadow, situated between Ewerby wood and the lake made by Bishop Alexander, also a certain marsh called Otrisholm, *i.e., Otter's Isle,* containing ten acres, the gift of William the son of Ulf, for the benefit of his parents' souls, which gift was confirmed in the Chapter-house at Lincoln in the presence of many witnesses. " Gervase Holles."

In the 17th century Sir Henry Packenham was possessed of lands here, of whom Burton, the Carre steward, records, that Robert Carre had bought 4 acres of wood besides a great store of ashes and elms in hedge rows. In 1661 Richard Rothwell, created a Baronet that year, possessed lands at Ewerby, but dying without issue in 1674, the Baronetcy became extinct. His armorial bearings were Arg, 3 chevrons engrailed Az, each charged with 3 plates Or, a crescent Sa in dexter chief for a difference. In 1667 Henry Pell bequeathed a sum of £10 a year, a house and garden towards the maintenance of a schoolmaster here who was to teach the poor children of the parishes of Ewerby, Evedon, Asgarby, and Howell. The present principal landowners here are the Honourable Murray Finch Hatton, and T. P. Tindale, Esq.

Ecclesiastical History.

There was a church and a priest here when Domesday Book was compiled. Subsequently the patronage of the former belonged to Kyme Priory.

The following are some of the gifts made at various times to the church of Ewerby :—In 1327 Master William de Baiocis, parson of Iwardeby, for a fine of one mark, obtained the King's license that John Scarle, of Lincoln, might give one messuage and the moiety of another, with its appurtenances in this vill, situated close to the rectory manse and the church, and assign it to the said William, to be held by him and his successors, parsons of that church, for ever, for the enlargement of the manse or rectory. "Ab. Rot. Orig., 10 Edw. 3."

In 1352 Sir Alexander Aunsel and others petitioned the King for a license to give John de Haburgh one rood of land for the enlargement of the cemetery of Iwardby, at a cost of 6s. 8d. "Inq. p. m., 26 Edw. 3."

Three acres of land and some tenements in Ewerby were left by a person, whose christian name was Hugh, for the annual observance of his obit for ever. These lands were let for 12d. a year by the churchwardens, of which half went to the vicar, and the other half was expended in bread and pottage given to the poor on the obit day. "Cotton. MS." Two acres of land, let for 10d. a year, were left by a person of the name of Gibson, for the purpose of keeping his obit, of which 1d. went to the vicar, and the remainder was distributed in the form of bread and pottage for the poor. Two other acres, let at 8s. 3d. a year, were left by an unknown person for a similar purpose. "Ibid."

In 1616 the King was patron of the church, and Edward Bowman, vicar, when the vicarage was worth £8 a year, and there were 280 communicants. The registers commence with the year 1562.

The following is a list of the incumbents :—

Date of Institution.

A.D.   .—William de Baiocis, circa 1327.
          .—Richard de Ouingham, rector, died 1396.
          .—Richard Tupler or Typler, rector.
          .—Edward Bowman, circa 1616.
1639.—Henry Bryerly, vicar.
          .—Ciprian Day.
1669.—Roger Smyth.
1677.—Silvester Leech.
1732.—Matthew Alexander.

EWERBY CHURCH.

Date of Institution.
A.D. 1735.—Joshua Dewsnop.
1769.—Charles Dewsnop.
1806.—John Bellaman.
1837.—Edward Pollard.

The Church.

This is dedicated in honour of St. Andrew, and is a most beautiful example of a Gothic church entirely built in one style, and with very little variation. The promise of excellence held out by the distant view of the beautiful broach spire is abundantly fulfilled on a near approach. The perfect masonry of the whole fabric, the depth of the mouldings, and the vigour of its carved ornaments (among which may be noticed the figure of a boat), are very striking. The original entasis of the spire, 172 feet high, is best seen on the western face, where it least suffered when struck by lightning in 1810, whence its outline is now somewhat distorted. Besides this, the fabric consists of a nave, north and south aisles, south porch, and chancel. The chapel at the east end of the north aisle, and the east gable of the chancel with the sedilia and piscina, are the earliest portions as to style, and there is a simpler character about them than in the later work. The acute point of the west window of the north aisle, the moulding of the north door, and the carving of the outer arch of the porch all deserve attention. Unfortunately the nave has lost its original high pitched roof.

Internally there is no chancel arch, nor any other separation between the nave and chancel than a noble screen, of the same date and character as that in Sleaford church. Another screen, enclosing the chantry chapel on the north side, is exceedingly valuable as being one of the earliest remaining examples of such features. Within this chapel, the corbels for the altar slab and a piscina are still visible; but its chief feature is the tomb and effigy of its founder, Sir Alexander Aunsell. This monument is remarkable as having been formerly overlaid with rich ornamental work, of which portions yet remain. On the effigy the chain mail of the gorget is thus represented, and the breastplate was similarly covered with a fretted wavy pattern, very like the tracery of the windows. The arch above was overlaid with stars, flowers, and interlaced figures, and the wall behind was covered with bands of lozenges having a flower in the centre, as on glass quarries. On the pediment above is carved a shield and tilting helmet.

There are two shields represented in stained glass in the east window of this chapel, one bears Threckingham, the other, Or, 2 chevrons Gu within a bordure of the same, a label of 5 Az. The bowl of an old Norman font is now serving as a base to its successor of the Decorated period. The panels of this are enriched with carvings resembling traceried windows surrounded by borders of diapered work.

Passing through the fine old carved oak chancel screen the desolate condition of the chancel becomes the more painful to the eye. In the south wall are three canopied sedilia and a piscina, and behind the altar table is an aumbry or locker. The table itself is made of fen oak and was presented by the late Sir J. W. Gordon, Bart. In the north wall is another locker.

Gervase Holles observed the following armorial bearings in this church, viz : in the south window of the chancel, Arg, 2 bars Gu, in chief 3 torteaux over all a bend Sa. repeated twice—Threckingham. In a north window of the nave (or north aisle), the effigy of a man kneeling, having on his surcoat and a shield in his hands, Barry of 6 Or & Az, a bend Gu—Gant. In the west window of the north aisle, Arg, 2 chevrons Gu, a label of 5 points Az. and Threckingham. In the tower window, Or, 2 chevrons Gu a label of 5 Az, and Gu, 2 chevrons Or a label of 5 Az. In the east window of the north, or Aunsell chapel, where they still remain, Threckingham, and Or, a chevron Gu within a bordure of the same, a label of 5 az. Formerly there was this legend below : " Stephanus Capellanus de Iwardby me fecit " ; and in another window of this chapel, the effigy of a man kneeling, having on his surcoat and shield the Threckingham bearings.

In this chapel he further observed the tomb and effigy of Alexander Aunsell, before described, but when the now blank shield above it bore, Erm, on a fesse Gu 3 crosses botony Or. He also saw the following epitaphs on tombstones or slabs, viz., on one in the chancel :—

Hic Jacet Ricus de Ouingham, quondam Rector istius ecclesie, qui obiit xº die Aprilis Ano Dni MCCCXCVI cuius aie ppicietur Deus. Amen.

On another :—

Ricus Tupler, Rector.

And the following in the nave :—

Hic Jacet Willus Broun, qui obiit xvi⁰ die Augusti Ano Dni MCCCCLXIV cujus aie ppicietur Deus. Amen.

Hic Jacet ———— Glouer, qui obiit xx⁰ die Februairi Ano Dni MDV cujus aie ppicietur Deus. Amen.

Hic Jacet Johannes Boulle, qui obiit iid⁰ die Octobris Anno Dni MDV cujus aie ppicietur Deus. Amen.

Also over the chancel arch :—

Pray for ye welfare of Mrs. Joane Gibson.

On a mural tablet in the chantry chapel is this inscription :—

To the memory of Henry Pell, &c., ob. Novr. 1667. By his last will he gave out of his lands at Ewerby and Kirkby ten pounds towards the maintenance of a schoolmaster to teach the poor children of Ewerby, Asgardby & Howell, and a cottage at Ewerby for a school house for ever, & 2 grey gouns yearly for two poor widows of Ewerby.

Cloaths for the body, learning for the mind,
So here a friendly helper in each kind.
And which doth crown his charitable deed,
He doth this when & where there is most need.

On a fragment of a slab in the chancel is cut a chalice reversed and a label bearing a now illegible inscription.

Here also are the tombstones of two former incumbents of Ewerby, the one bearing this memorial :—

Depositum Roger (Smith) nuper Vicarus 1677 ;

the other :—

Revd. Matthew Alexander, Rector, obiit 1735.

In the church yard is the base of a cross, erected by a former rector, which once bore this legend : " Sumptu Rectoris fuit hæc crux facta Johannis Hauburgh, mœroris expers sit in omnibus annis " ; and four shields bearing severally Three lions passant—England. A lion rampant. Three lucies hauriant. A cinquefoil between 8 cross crosslets—Umfraville. At the back of the head of the cross were figures of the Virgin, St. Peter, and St. Paul.

There are four bells in the tower, thus inscribed : —

1.—All laude and praise
  Be unto God alwaise.   1616.

2.—John Bulliman, William Tindale, Ch. Wardens.
  T. Osborn.   Downham.   Norfolk fecit 1783.

3.—Ihesus be our spede.

4.—Henry Penn.   Fusore 1710.

EWERBY THORPE.

THE name of this hamlet has been variously spelt Ousthorpe, Oustorp, Housthorpe, and Owesthorpe ; but was often simply called Thorp, or Torp. Part of it was originally Earl Morkar's land, afterwards an appurtenance of the King's manor of Kirkby Laythorpe. Another portion, that had belonged to the Saxon Tunne, was subsequently given to Gilbert de Gant as an appurtenance of his manor of Kirkby Laythorpe. This consisted of 3 carucates of land, upon which stood the church, and attached to which were 9 sokemen and 9 bordars cultivating 4 carucates, and of 24 acres of meadow, and 20 acres of coppice wood. Eddiva possessed a small manor here, consisting of 3 carucates and a half, and 1 oxgang. This was given by the Conqueror to Colsuein, besides 44 acres of meadow and 23 of coppice. The whole was worth 36s. in King Edward's time and subsequently 30s.

Circa 1200 Gerard de Camville held lands here in right of his wife, the De la Haye heiress, by the service of one knight's fee ; which lands were let to William de la Launde. " Testa de Nevill."

In 1262 Robert de Tibbethot, Kt., granted to Sir John de Rye all his manor of Houstorp, in the vill of Ewerby, to be held by him and his heirs as Reginald de la Launde once held it of Sir Richard de Haye, by paying to him and his heirs one pair of gilt spurs or 6 denarii at the feast of St Botolph. Dated the 46th year of Henry III, 1262. "Dodsworth's MS."

In 1325 John de Rye held the manor of Ousthorpe of the fee of de la Haye, and died seized of it 1335-6. " Inq. p. m. 9 E. 3."

In 1453, Elizabeth, a co-heiress of the Hebden family and widow of Sir Thomas Dymoke, Kt., died seized of half this manor, held of the Duchy of Lancaster. " Inq. p. m. 31 H. 6."

In 1470 by the attainder and execution of Sir Thomas Dymoke, half the manor in his possession was forfeited. " Inq. p. m. 10 E. 4." But it appears to have been given back to his widow, Margaret Dymoke, who died seized of this in 1481, " Inq.

p. m. 20 E. 4," and her descendant, Robert Dymoke, held this still by the service of one knight's fee.

The following will of a yeoman of Ewerby Thorpe, who died in the 16th century, is so characteristic of that period as to be worthy of record :—

"By my Will dated 14th June, 40 Eliz. I Michael Stennett, of Austrop, Yeoman, leave my body to be buried in the parish church of Ewrebee. To my son Augustine Stennet £60, and as he has grown to be of small government and little discretion, I will the said money to be kept in custody of Thomas Stennet and George Stennet my sons, and not to be paid him unless he marry some honest discreet woman, and live according to his friends advice, otherwise the legacy to be void. To my daughter Elizabeth Stennet 80 shepe at Ruskington and £80, and, if she die under age and unmarried then to be divided among the rest of my children. To Thomas Swyer a cowe and 40s. when of age. To widow Hooton of Antwicke 10s. To my three daughters Agnes Garwell, Grace Swier, and Johanna Pierson each 2 angells in gould or 20s. To Michael Stennet a cubborde in my hall, with table forms, &c., all the glass in my house, and the pales and gates on my grounde, ce to dire,* my steepefate, hare cloth, howels, herse herk, cribes, planchers, and beast howses, after the death of Johanna my wife. To Elizabeth Swan a ewe hogge. To my sd wife Johanna, the lease I have of Master Pagnam for her life, the remainder to my said sonnes Thomas Stennet and George Stennet. To my son George £7. Residue to my wife Joan, whom I make my Exix, and Thomas Stennet and George Stennet my sonnes, my supervisors. To my brother William Stennet's children 8s. To the poor of Ewerby and Austrop 2 seams of barley and 2 seams of pease. To William Thorles and William Hides 12d. each.

"Mem. That I now will that Thomas my son have all the lease of Master Pagnam after my wife's death, for that I stand doubtful my said sonnes will not agree for the division thereof. My son George to have 6 acres of arable land out of the same for himself. Witnesses : John Crudock, Henry Bennet, Edmond Kendall, Thomas James Tyson, &c. Debts owing the testator : Thomas Swier, of Ruskington, £4 ; Master Thomas Whichcote, 40s. ; Holledge Lief, 15s. ; Ralf Newton, 12s. Proved 12th of June, 1600, by Johan Stennet exix."

---

* A failure in an unnecessary attempt to introduce the French expression "c'est a dire."

GREAT HALE.

ACREAGE,
5633.

POPULATION,
1861—1059.   1871—1086.

GREAT Hale lies 6 miles east south east of Sleaford, and 1 mile south of Heckington. According to Domesday Book, when that record was taken there were 10 carucates of land here, rated at 8½ carucates, upon which were 38 sokemen. These were given to Gilbert de Gant as soke of his manor of Kirkby Laythorpe, of which Ralph, one of his vassals, was then holding 3 carucates in demesne.

Circa 1200 the de Gant lands here were reckoned at a twelfth part of a knight's fee, and were held by John de Hal or Hall. He had also another part of a fee here held by Hugo de Neville, surnamed crassus, or the fat. His son Henry de Nevill gave 5 tofts and 3 oxgangs of land in Great Hale for the purpose of finding a lamp to be lit every day before the body of our Lord in the church of the blessed Mary at Haverholme. He died in the beginning of the reign of Henry III.

In 1220 Oliver de Vas or Vaux had in Hale, Heckington, and Scredington, the third part of a knight's fee, held of him by Simon Camerarius ; a little later Gilbert de Gant is reported to have held in Great Hale 3 carucates of land of the King, then let to William de Dive, whose sub-tenant was Hugo de Nevill, and Simon de Hall. " Testa de Nevill."

In 1247 Hugo de Nevill, son of Henry, of Great Hale, made an agreement with Henry de Longchamp, of Burton, and his heirs, that he would never hunt in his warren without his leave ; which leave, however, would be granted at his request to himself personally from the nativity of the blessed Virgin to pentecost provided he should send either his esquire or some other messenger to the house of Henry de Longchamp to obtain leave of his officers, and if these should not be in the way, having provided himself with the testimony of two or three men of Burton, that he had done so, he might go to the said warren and hunt in the plains without leave.

The said Henry de Longchamp, lord of Frieston, four days before his death gave 2 oxgangs of land in Great Hale along with his body for burial to the Abbey of Swineshead, presenting a charter of seizen by one of his vassals, and ordering him to expel thence two female tenants of the same that the land might be ploughed directly for the benefit of the Abbot. In 1327 by virtue of this act, John, the son of Elye, the cooper, held this land under the Abbot of Swineshead. "Inq. ad. q. d. 1 E. 3."

In the 21 E. 3, Thomas Howard gave divers lands in Great Hale to William Auncell, who with Alice his wife transmitted them to their son William, 34 E. 3 ; but previous to this Hugo de Bussey as the heir of one of the descendants of Sir John de Dive, had become lord paramount of a portion of this vill as a part of the Barony of Gant, which he held of the King. He was succeeded by his son John de Bussey, who held lands here, in Dembleby, Skellingthorpe, and Fenton, amounting to two knight's fees. "Lansdown MS. 863, f. 189."

In 1397 died John, Lord Beaumont, seized of the third of a knight's fee in Great Hale, held of him and Katharine his wife, by John Bussey : but in 1463 these lands, constituting the manor of Hale, and held in succession by the Beaumonts and Bardolfs, were forfeited by the attainder of William, Lord Bardolf. "Inq. p. m. 3 E. 4."

The Husseys next acquired them, of whom Robert, the first possessor, died May 28th, 1545. His son and heir, Thomas, held the manors of Great and Little Hale of the Duke of Norfolk, as of his manor of Heckington, and various messuages, one of which he held of the Queen as of her manor of Swineshead. Dying without issue 1559-60, he divided his estates between his sisters and their issue. On the 29th of January, 1609, died Charles Hussey, of Honington, seized of these manors which he held of the manor of Heckington, leaving them to his son and heir, Edward.

In 1629, Elizabeth, wife of Sir Thomas Horsman died seized of a manor here, which she left to her son, Thomas.

The present principal landed proprietors here are the Marquis of Bristol and Colonel Packe.

GREAT HALE CHURCH.

ECCLESIASTICAL HISTORY.

The church of Hale was given to that of St. Lazarus without the walls of Jerusalem by Simon de Gant and Alice his wife in the presence of King John, who confirmed the gift in 1208. In 1314 the King (Edward II.,) granted a license to Robert de Asheby enabling him to mortmain 2 messuages, 1 croft, and 36 acres of meadow in Great Hale, Little Hale, and Heckington, to a chaplain to celebrate divine service in the church of St. John of the Baptist at Hale, for the soul of the said Robert, the souls of Richard, his father, Auline his mother, Robert de Kyrington, and John Elys, chaplains, William de Tye, and all faithful people. " Pat. Rot. 7 E. 2."

In 1345 the Abbot of Bardney obtained the King's licence to appropriate the church of Great Hale to the use of that Abbey. "Inq. ad. q. d. 18 E. 3."

In 1634, when Sir Nathaniel Brent, vicar general, visited this church, he found it without a chancel although the impropriator, Robert Cawdron, was worth £200 a year. "Dom. State Papers, V. 274."

The following is a list of the vicars of Hale since 1561 :—
Date of Institution.

A.D. .—Samuel Saunders.
.—Thomas Schockey.
.—J. Pearson.
.—J. Manby.
.—Benjamin Deacon.
1700.—Richard Parke.
1727.—Richard Can.
1758.—William Harding, senr.
1775.—William Harding, junr.
1794.—William Benwell.
1796.—Richard Bingham.
1858.—Frank Sugden.

THE CHURCH.

This is dedicated in honour of St. John the Baptist, and is a fine spacious edifice, although now deprived of its chancel. The tower is by far the oldest feature. This is perfectly plain, without any plinth or string courses, and appears to have been always plastered within its quoins. In the western and southern faces of its lower stage is a small semicircular-headed light, the arch of the latter being moulded; and in the stage above is a little keyhole slit, the head of which has been mutilated. In the upper stage is a coupled semicircular-headed belfry light in each face with a circular shaft between them, having a scalloped cushion capital, supporting a long saddle impost. In the north east angle of the tower is a narrow newel staircase lighted by four slits, and it is surmounted by a poor Perpendicular embattled parapet, and eight coarsely cut crocketed pinnacles.

The nave has been deprived of its original roof, the pitch of which is indicated by its weathering on the eastern face of the tower.

The south aisle is late Early English, and has a good boldly moulded plinth, and buttresses finished with pedimented caps. At the west end is a three-light intersecting lancet window now foreshortened through the introduction of a modern doorway below it. In its south wall are five similar windows of larger size, and a spacious porch having a wide well-moulded arch and pillared jambs. Within, is a doorway of a plainer character, and above it a little niche. At the east end is rather a weak four-light Decorated window. From the absence of parapets on the aisles and the nave, as well as from the loss of its roof, this church suffers much in its external appearance.

At the east end of the nave the outline of the chancel arch may be seen, against which are built buttresses; within this is a poor window feebly copied from the design of one of the south aisle windows, and below it a stopped-up Tudor doorway. The north aisle has a well-moulded plinth and good buttresses, but of a later character than the southern one. At the east end is a good deeply-moulded four-light window, and in the side wall four three-light windows and a doorway with pillared jambs similar in design to the arch of the porch attached to the south aisle.

Within, a plain semicircular-headed arch, relieved only by a simple cornice on either side, gives access to the tower from the nave. Originally the nave was lofty as well as spacious through the breadth of its aisles. Its arcades, of five bays, are supported by circular-shafted pillars rising from square bases, and their arches consist of two plainly chamfered members, and a hood mould. The last pair of arches towards the west are narrower than the others. There was a chapel at the east end of both, as evidenced by an aumbry and a piscina still remaining in the usual position there. On the south side of the chancel arch was the rood loft staircase, part of which still remains, and the old oak chancel screen now cuts off the westernmost bay of the north aisle, to serve as a lobby. A similar arrangement exists in the south aisle, to provide a vestry, on the plaster wall of which has been ingeniously painted a copy of the real screen opposite, by some local artist. The font is an octangular one. In each face of its bowl is a cusped-headed niche having a border of quatrefoils above and on each side of it. Holles mentions the following armorial bearings which he saw in a north window of the church when he visited it, viz : those of Clare, Warren, de Gant, Beaumont, Vere, and Deyncourt. Here also he saw England and France ancient, Latimer, and Goldesburgh or Goldsboro'—Az, a cross fleureé arg. Towards the east end of the north aisle are several monuments of the Cawdron family. The oldest of these is a small mural one of white marble between the two easternmost windows of this aisle ; on this are represented Robert Cawdron and his first wife in a kneeling position above, and his two subsequent wives below. It bears the following epitaph :—

> To the sacred and perpetuel memory of Robert Cawdron, of Little Hale, in the Coun. of Linc., Gent : who departed this life ye 30 day of December, 1665. Ann Ætat sue LVI, being 3 times married : first unto Katherine daughter of Edward Netham, of Ilston in ye count of Leicest. Gent. 2dly· unto Susanna Faukenbridge, relict of Richard Gamble, Gent. Lastly unto Elizabeth Sansome, ye relict of John Woods, Gent., now living, which said sorrowful widow out of tender affection she beareth to her deceased husband caused this monument to be erected at her own proper charge and cost, this 20th day of May, 1668.

The memory of ye just is blessed, but ye name of the wicked shall rot.

The body of this Robert Cawdron was buried beneath the sepulchral slab of an ecclesiastic of the 14th century. This is of grey marble and was once adorned with a stemmed cross spring-

ing from a lion at the base, a bust of the priest it commemorated
and a border legend, engraved on brass plates, all of which are
now lost, but the initials R. C. and the date 1665 were interpolated upon it, when it was used to cover the remains of Robert
Cawdron by his third wife.

On a small white marble mural tablet, next to this on the
right, are the incised effigies of Robert Cawdron, Ann, his first
wife, daughter of Edward King, of Ashby, Eleanor, his second
wife, 9 sons, 6 daughters, and 5 children who died in infancy.
These are ranged in a kneeling posture behind their parents
praying on either side of a central desk, while the dead infants in
their grave clothes lie beneath these, each accompanied by a
skull as an indication of their death.   Below is this inscription :—

> Memoriæ sacrum.
> Roberti Cawdron Armig vitæ integeri in egenos
> largissmi in patriam fidissimi, uxores duas habuit,
> Iam. Anna nota Edwardi King, Armigeri, que peperit
> et 10 filios et 6 filias. 2 Maria, viduam Iohannis
> Austen generose, e qua 3 filios et unam filiam.
> Mortuns est die II Martii Aᵒ· 1652. Ætatis sue 73.
> Eleanora filia obsequentessmo· parenti amantissimo
> lugens posuit.   Antonius filius fecit.

On the other side of the first-named Robert Cawdron's monument is a stone tablet in which a brass plate is inserted
commemorating Anne Cawdron, first wife of the first Robert
Cawdron, and below is a second plate set in a stone, recording
the death of Francis Cawdron.   Eastward of these is another
mural monument commemorating a third Robert Cawdron, which
is thus inscribed :—

> Here lyeth the body of Robert Cawdron, Esq., who by
> Sarah his wife, youngest daughter of Sir Edward
> Hussey, of Welbourn, Baronet, had issue one daughter
> Elizabeth.   He departed this life October ye 18th,
> 1728, in the 41 year of his age.

Another daughter of Sir Edward Hussey is also thus commemorated in this church :—

> Here lieth the body of Mrs. Sarah Smith, wife of
> Weston John Smith, Esq., of this parish.   She was
> the youngest daughter of Sir Edward Hussey, Bart.,
> of Welbourn, in this County, who departed this life
> the 17 of May, 1767, in the 80 year of her age.

LITTLE HALE.

LITTLE Hale always appears to have been associated with Great Hale, as it is at present.

Circa 1200-10 Gilbert de Gant was holding a sixth part of a knight's fee here, then in the tenure of Simon Camerarius. "Testa de Nevill."

In 1418 died Thomas Geene, Kt., of Norton, Northants., seized of a capital messuage here. "Inq. p. m. 5 H. 5."

In 1590 died Robert Carre, of Aswarby, seized of the manor of Little Hale, which he had bought with many others.

In 1603 died William Callis, yeoman of this place, seized of lands and tenements here, having a young son and heir, William. "Harl. MSS. 758."

In 1629 died Elizabeth, wife of Thomas Horsman, who held this manor, leaving a son and heir living—Thomas, born 1615.

William Burton, the faithful steward of the Carres, thus instructs his young master, Sir Robert Carre, 2nd Bart., in 1627, respecting Little Hale. "This is a manor whereof divers free tenants hould their lands by rents service : You have there not above 14 acres of inclosed land ; all ye rest of yor lands, being arable & meadow, lie in ye open fields, intermixt with ye freeholders ; and part of them have bin so long held by freeholders, together with their owne landes, that they cannot be distinguished there from ye other ; soe you may by incrochments & concealments be much wronged in this place, and likewise in Great Hale, if yor officers look not ye better about them. I hold it therefore very requisite that a survey be taken of all yor lands & meadows in those 2 Townes."

Subsequently the Cawdron family was established at Little Hale for some time. Now the principal landed proprietors here —as in Great Hale—are the Marquis of Bristol and Colonel Packe.

HAYDOR.

ACREAGE,
3700.

POPULATION,
1861—466. 1871—447.

THIS village, the name of which was originally spelt Heidure, lies 6 miles south west of Sleaford.

After the Conquest 4 carucates of land in this parish lay within the soke of Wido de Credon's manor in Swaton, and a smaller portion belonged to Colsuein's manor of North Kyme. This last was afterwards held by Petronilla de Croun, who let it to Henry Camerarius, and he to Richard de Thuschit, with the exception of 4 oxgangs held by Walter de Rudestager of the mother church of Lincoln, 3 oxgangs belonging to Haydor church, and half an oxgang held by the "Hospital at Lincoln," all of which were free from scutage.

Circa 1200-20 Robert de Pickworth held 3 carucates here of the Constable of Lincoln, by the service of half a knight's fee, and Henry de Longchamps 5 carucates of the fee of Gant. Subsequently this last fee was held by the Bishop of Worcester, for a daughter of Henry de Longchamps, who was probably his ward, and afterwards by the family of Dyve. After the death of the last Gilbert de Gant without male heirs, his lands here were granted by the Crown to John, son and heir of Hugo de Bussey, of Hougham, in 1307. About the same time a family of the name of Gloucester was resident at Haydor; of whom Hawise, the wife of Sir Walter de Gloucester, quitclaimed for herself and heirs to the Dean and Chapter of Lincoln, all right she had to some tenements in Lincoln, through their enfeoffment by her son, Walter de Gloucester. This grant was signed at Haydor in 1324, in the presence of several knights. "Lib. de Ordinat. Cant." Previous to, or during the year 1338, Sir Bartholomew Burghurst, or Burghersh, (the brother of Henry Burghersh, Bishop of Lincoln), had obtained the manor of Haydor, and a grant of free-warren over its lands. He died seized of the said manor in 1356, leaving a son and heir, Bartholomew, born in

1336. "Dugdale, and Inq. p. m. 26 E. 3." A branch of the great house of Scrope next became lords of this manor. In 1391 died Sir Roger de Swillington, seized, conjointly with Margaret his wife, of a messuage and 2 carucates of land in Haydor, as of the castle of Falkingham. He assigned to the Dean and Chapter of Lincoln an annual rent of 20 marks, arising from his manor of Haydor and lands in Haceby and Braceby. That body also received an annual payment of £4 5s. 8d. from the profits of the churches of Haydor, and Waltham, Bucks., towards the support of a prebendary of Lincoln. Sir Roger left a daughter and heir, Margaret, wife of Sir John Gray, who died 1429, in possession of Southwood and certain rents at Haydor. In 1397 died John, Lord Beaumont, seized, conjointly with his wife Katherine, of half a knight's fee, then held by him of William Disney. When Ralph, Lord Cromwell, founded his college at Tattershall, he gave 16 acres of wood at Haydor, for its support, together with an annual rent of £4 13s. 4d., derived from tenements here and at Burton. A descendant of the Busseys was still resident at Haydor in 1587, in the person of Edward Bussey, who was fined £50 to the Star Chamber for some offence he had committed. " Pip. Rot., 29 Eliz." Perhaps Leland referred to this gentleman when he says, " Itin., i, 29," " One Bussey, coming of a younger brother of the house of Busseys of Hougheham, dwelleth in an old place at Haider, that he and his parents hath of a fee farm, of the church of Lincoln."

The site of that old place is still clearly indicated by the remains of its moat; and a few other relics have survived its destruction. Among these is a large figure of a female playing upon a musical instrument, carved in stone, now built into a garden wall on the north side of the church, where the old manor house of Haydor formerly stood.

The antiquary Leland, in his Collectanea, speaking of Haydor, says: "Bussey that was so great in Richard the Second's days, and was beheaded at Bristol, although he had his principal house or manor place at Hougheham, about three miles from Grantham, yet resided sometimes at this place also." But full two centuries before the time of Richard II., viz: the 29th and 30th of Henry I., we find that a Hugo de Bussey was Sheriff of Lincolnshire; and that in the 35th of the same reign, a John de Bussey held of the King two knight's fees in capite, as of the barony of Gant. Again, a William Bussey was Sheriff of Lincolnshire the 47th of Edward III., and a John Bussey de Hather held that high office in the 7th, 9th, and 14th of Richard II. This John Bussey was one of the six Commoners, who, with, twelve Lords, were, on the dissolution of Parliament, A.D. 1398, elected as a committee, and invested with the whole power of the Lords and Commons : but in the general insurrection in the month of August, in the following year, occasioned by the return of the Duke of Lancaster, he, with others of Richard's ministers, threw themselves into Bristol for security, and, on the surrender of that place to the Duke, was, together with others, led to immediate execution without any previous trial.

The following notes ralative to the ancient family of Bussey, transcribed from a vellum book of devotions, formerly belonging to some of that family, formerly in the possession of the late Mr. Edward James Willson, of Lincoln, may not improperly find a place here :*

30. Julii. Obitus Joh'is Bussy, militis, qui obiit apud Bristowe A'no D'ni m,ccc,lxxxix.

21. Octob. Hic natus est Johannes filius et heres domini Johannis Bushi, anno domini m,cccc,22†

Hic natus est Hugo filius et heres Joh'is Bussy A'o D'ni m,cccc,liii.

21. Jan. Obitus Domine Katerine Bussy, que fuit uxor Johannis Bussey, qui quidem Joh'es fuit heres D'ni Joh'is Bussy, qui obiit apud Byrstowe in anno regni Richardi secundi xii., &c. Katerine obiit in A'no D'ni m,cccc,lvi, et in ——— regni Edwardi iiii.

4. Mar. Obitus Joh'is Bussy, militis, qui obiit Hogham A'o D'ni m,cccc,lviii. Iste Johannes fuit filius et heres Joh'is Bussy, qui obiit apud Bristowe pro Ricardo Secundo, in anno regni sui xii.

---

* These Notes are written in the margins of those leaves which contain the annual calendar, at the beginning of the volume ; making up a family register.

† This entry is written in a most exact manner, apparently by the person who wrote the book itself. The last two figures in the date are the earliest Arabic numerals in this register.

28. Jan. Obitus Edmundi Perpont* qui obiit in die sancte
Agnetis supradicto, A'o D'ni m,cccc,lxxxv. A'o regni
Henrici septimi primo.
26. Jan. Obitus Johannis Bussy filii iij. Tho. Bussey, militis,
de Hogham, et dictus Johannes obiit apud Scotter, A'o D'ni
m,cccc,lxxxvii, et regni Henrici septimi, tercio. Cujus
anime propicietur deus, amen.
16. Feb. Obitus Magistri Willi. Bussy, filii Joh'is Bussy, militis,
ac rectoris de Hogham, and Winfield in com. Derbii, A'o
D'ni m,cccc, nonagessimo iij.
5. Aug. Obitus D'ne Eliz. Bussy uxoris Johannis Bussey, milits,
& filie Laurencii Barkeley. Anno D'ni m,cccc, nonagessimo
quarto. Cujus auime propicietur deus, amen.
Jun. 6. Isto die natus est Edwardus Bussy filius Edmundi
Bussi, A'o m,d,xi, & A'o H. viij. tercio.
24. Decemb. Edwardus Bussy filius Edwardi Bussy, natus fuit
apud Haidor vicessimo quarto die Decembris, Anuo D'ni
1552.
Octob. Isto die nata erat Elizabetha Bussy filia Johannis Bussy
apud Wythecoke in A'o D'ni 1558.
Primo die Januarii natus fuit Johannes Bussy filius Johannis
Bussy apud Haidor, anno domini 1559.
2. Feb. Isto die obiit Henricus St. Poolle apud Wythcoke, in
A'o D'ni 1559.
15. Mar. Isto die natus fuit Edmundus Bussy filius Johannis
Bussy apud Haydor, in A'o D'ni 1562.
Anna Bussy filia Johannis Bussy, nata fuit apud Haidor vicessimo die Septembris, anno domini 1563.
Bridget Bussey filia Johannis Bussy, nata fuit apud Haidor
octavo die Januarii, anno domini 1565, eodemque die
baptisata fuit Jana Bussy filia ipsius Johannis, A'no D'ni
1576—1577.
Francis Bussy filius Johannis Bussy, natus fuit apud Haidor
vicessimo die Aprilis, anno domini 1567.
Christopher Bussy filius Johannis Bussy, natus fuit apud Haidor
undscimo die Aprilis, anno domini 1568.
Mary Bussy filia Johannis Bussy, nata fuit apud Haidor secundo
die Aprilis, anno domini 1570.

---

* This probably was some relative of the Bussey family.

Isto die (27. Novemb.) obiit Edmundus Bussy, apud Willow, filius Edwardi Bussy, anno domini 1570.

Charles Bussy filius Johannis Bussy, natus fuit apud Haidor undecimo die Maii, anno domini 1572.

Brudnell Bussy filius Johannis Bussy, obiit apud Haidor decimo die Maii, anno domini 1578.

Isto, quarto viz., die Octobris an'o dom. 1580, baptizatus fuit Andrew Bussy filius Johannis.

15. die Aprilis, A'o regni Elizabethe 28, 1586, natus fuit Rawley Bussy filius Johannis Bussey, qui fuit filius Joh'is Bussey de Hather, armigeri.

Nupta fuit [Elizabeth Bussy, born 1558] Johanni Babington de Rampton in com. Nottingha', arm. per quem habuit nullum exitum, nisi vnicum filium vocatum Johannem, natum Hador mense Januarii, 1587, A'o regni Elizabethe regine, &c., vicessimo nono.

Johannes Babington obiit apud Rampton anno domini 1588, mense Aprilis.

Edwardus Bussy filius Edmundi Bussy, natus fuit apud Rampton, in com. Nott'. quarto die Novembris, A'o D'ni 1590.

Milo Bussy filius E'di natus fuit apud Haydor xix die Augusti, anno domini 1592.

Elizabetha Bussey filia Edmundi Bussy, nata fuit apud Haydor xi Augusti, 1593.

Elizabeth Bussy filia Edmundi Bussy, nata fuit apud Haidor 14. die Julii, A'o D'ni 1594.

Francisca Bussey filia Edmundi Bussy, nata fuit apud Haidor 29. die Aprilis, A'o Regni Regine Elizabethe 30. A'o D'ni 1596.

Jane Bussy filia Edmundi Bussy, nata fuit apud Haidor 12. Julii, 1597.

Edmundus Bussy filius Francisci, natus fuit apud Rampton tercio die Augusti, anno d'ni 1597.

Elizab. Bussye fiilia Milonis Bussye, nata fuit apud Haidor vicessimo die martii, anno domini 1609.

Ecclesiastical History.

There was a priest and a church at Haydor when Domesday Book was composed. In the reign of Henry III. 4 oxgangs

here were held by the Chapter of Lincoln Cathedral, then let to
Walter de Rudestayn; the church of Haydor was endowed with
3 oxgangs, and a hospital at Lincoln held half an oxgang, probably that of St. Catharine. Formerly the vicarage of Haydor
with Kelby was a peculiar, under the jurisdiction of the prebendary of Haydor with Walton instead of that of the Archdeacon of Lincoln. The following is a list of the incumbents:—
Date of Institution.
    A.D. 1361.—Thomas de Appelby, presented by Galfrid le
        Scroop, Canon of Lincoln.
    1585.—Leonard Towne.
    1599.—Robert Rambody.
    1604.—Francis Quiningbcrow.
    1628.—Richard Northam.
    .—Henry Peight.
    1675.—Isaac Carter.
    1688.—Joseph Wild.
    1726.—Robert Lamb.
    1747.—Emanuel Langford.
    1778.—John Baker.
    1786.—George Hicks.
    1800.—Michael Thorold.
    1836.—Arthur Leapingwell.
    1856.—Gordon Frederick Deedes.

THE CHURCH.

The general appearance of this church, dedicated in honour
of St. Michael, is imposing, partly arising from its advantageous
situation on a little eminence, and partly from the character of
its features. The spire sits well upon the tower, but the angle
pinnacles of the latter are over heavy. There was clearly at one
time a Norman church here, as indicated by a small arch of that
period, now inserted over the staircase doorway of the tower.
Then succeeded an Early English fabric, the chancel of which still
remains, together with its lateral lancet windows. The tower
arch, together with the lower portion of its northern wall, are
also Early English. During the Decorated period the whole
of the nave was re-built, and the pitch of its roof is still manifest.
The aisle windows are for the most part of the reticulated type

so common in this district, but the tracery of two of these in the south aisle varies from the usual principles observed in designing such features for the purpose of forming crosses. The east end of this portion of the church has been made to serve as a chapel, the remaining piscina of which has a drain of a singular character. Here was an entrance to the rood loft, but there appears to have been another on the opposite side of the nave, from the evidence of a doorway on the north side of the chancel arch. The font, of the same period as the nave, is pleasingly adorned with shallow carving, resembling traceried windows. In the north aisle windows is some old glass of the reign of Richard II., which has lately been carefully repaired. The westernmost one contains figures of the then three favourite patron saints of England, viz : St. Edward, St. George, and St. Edmund. Below are three shields ; of these the central one is modern ; both the others bear Gules, a bar argent., for Scrope, with a label of three points over all, as a difference. The second window contains figures of St. Vincent, St. Lawrence, and St. Stephen ; the third, modern representations of Melchisedec, Moses, and Elias. In the border of one of these windows the letter M is frequently interspersed with the other ornaments of the same, and probably refers to St. Michael, the patron saint of this church. Some fragments of the old painted glass are now misplaced, such as a figure of our Lord in glory, and a head of Christ, which are inserted below figures of angels. The nave was subsequently surmounted by the present Perpendicular clerestory, which no doubt adds dignity to the fabric by increasing its elevation, but is in itself a plain and unattractive feature. Within the porch is a Decorated niche over the doorway ; it has a stone roof supported on plain ribs, and a staircase, which formerly gave access to a room above.

In a small chapel on the north side of the chancel are two small "hagioscopes," looking towards the chancel altar, also a curious old carved chest ; but the most conspicuous objects here are a number of marble monuments recording the deaths of members of the Newton family, formerly the wealthy proprietors of Culverthorpe Hall, whose last male heir was cut off in a very extraordinary manner. The marble slab that covers his infantine remains is thus inscribed :—

Here lyeth the body of John Lord Viscount Coningesby, son of Sir Michael Newton, Bart., Knight of the Most Honble. Order of the Bath, and Margaret, Countess of Coningesby, his wife : who was born the 16th day of October, 1732, and dyed the 14th day of January, 1732-3.

Hence we might naturally suppose that this little heir of the united wealth and titles of his parents simply died of one of the ordinary complaints to which infants are subject; but it was one of the strangest misadventures that in reality cut off this hope of the house of Newton. During the eighteenth century a fashion prevailed of keeping large monkeys as pets, and the Countess of Coningesby unhappily followed that foolish fashion; afterwards a far nobler and more precious pet became hers in the form of a lovely baby; but in about two months' time she was again childless, for her monkey, during the temporary absence of its nurse, stole the infant from his cradle, and absconded with him. Upon her return, the nurse wildly pursued the flying monkey with its precious burthen. Upstairs scrambled the beast, and then, frightened by her screams, he dropped the stolen infant, and nothing remained for the wretched parents to do but to weep and to wail over the child, and to commit the remains of this last little Viscount Coningesby to the grave. The truth of this story has been doubted from the existence of a note in the parish register stating that the body of this unfortunate infant was brought from London for burial at Haydor; but the incident related may have occurred in London just as well as at Culverthorpe, and it depends not upon mere untraceable tradition, but upon reliable oral authority.

A white marble monument of the Countess, by Rysbrach, is also in this chapel.

HECKINGTON.

ACREAGE,
5049.

POPULATION,
1861—1725. 1871—1865.

THIS large village lies 5 miles east of Sleaford and on the turnpike road between it and Boston. The parish is 6 miles long and 1½ broad.

Its name was at first spelt Eschintune, then Hechintune, and next Heckintone, before it assumed the present form of Heckington. Morkar, Turchil, and Algar the deacon, were the chief Saxon landed proprietors here before the Conquest, but subsequently Colsuein obtained a grant of lands here, together with appurtenances in Helpringham, Howell, and Kirkby Laythorpe. Of this, Ralph Paganel claimed 6 oxgangs which had been Algar's, but the jury of the Wapentake disallowed it. Gilbert de Gant received 3 carucates of arable land, 100 of meadow, and 3 fisheries worth 5s. 4d. a year. The King retained Morkar's land as an adjunct of his manor of Kirkby Laythorpe. Wido de Credon obtained 4 oxgangs of plough land and 3 of meadow as an adjunct of his manor of Burton. The Bishop of Lincoln 2 oxgangs of plough land and 3 of meadow as of his manor of Sleaford, and Robert de Vesci a small portion of land as parcel of his manor of Steveninge, in the parish of Swineshead.

In the reign of Henry III. the fifth Gilbert de Gant was holding 5⅓ carucates of the King; of which he had given the twelfth part of a knight's fee to Lawrence de Howel, the same quantity to Robert de Heckington, and the twentieth part of a knight's fee to Thomas Anglicus. At the same time Simon de Hall held, of Petronilla de Vallibus, 4 oxgangs of land by the service of 40d. and a scutage of 40s.; when also William de Latimer held the third part of a knight's fee of William de Vesci. "Testa de Nevill, p. 321-2." On the death of the above-named Gilbert, in 1298, his fee in Heckington accrued to the Crown together with other lands; for, having no issue by his wife, Laura, sister of Alexander de Baliol, he bequeathed these to the then King, Edward I. "Inq. p. m. 26 E. 1," and "Pip. Rot. 30 E. 1." Whether the tenants gained by this transfer we know not, but certainly the last of the de Gants was in the habit of illegally impounding his neighbours cattle through his over anxiety to preserve the game on his manor of Hecking-ton, and he also in a most arbitrary manner ordered a high road between Hale park and Garrick to be closed and certain fences to be levelled, because this interfered with his hunting.

The great family of Beaumont next obtained the manor of Heckington through a grant from the King to Henry de Beau-mont 1310-11. Twenty years later, viz: August 19th, 1330, he probably had the honour of receiving the then young King—Edward III.—at Falkingham and at Heckington, on his way to Clipston; who, while at the last place, signed several important deeds, among which was a grant of the customs of wool, hides and skins, at Boston, to Robert Stamford, clerk. "Pat. Rot. 4 E. III." In 1463 the manor of Heckington was forfeited to the Crown through the attainder of William, Viscount Beaumont, and given to Sir William Hastings, who died in 1484; but on the accession of Henry VII., that attainder was reversed, and his estates were restored to him. He died childless, 23rd Henry VII. The manor then accrued to Lord Willoughby de Broke, from whom it descended through marriage to the Duke of Suffolk in 1540. Henry, Lord Cobham, was the next possessor of the manor, who with his brother George Broke conspired against James I., for which they were tried and found guilty of high treason in 1603. George Broke was beheaded for this; but Lord Cobham was respited; and after having suffered much from poverty, died January 24th, 1618-19. His life was spared through his abject excuses, in which he most meanly laid the blame of his conduct upon others, and especially upon his own brother; but he pleaded for mercy in a more legitimate manner, viz: by reminding the King that his royal father had been his baptismal sponsor, and that his own father had suffered imprison-ment on account of the King's mother, the unfortunate Mary of Scotland. Lord Cobham was betrayed by his steward, named Mellows, in whom he thoroughly confided. Sir William Cobham, K.B., nephew of Lord Cobham, was his heir, who although restored as to blood, never obtained the title of Lord Cobham.

On his death without issue, circa 1643, Sir John Broke, or
Brooke, often called Sir John Cobham, son of Sir Henry,
Ambassador to Spain, France, and Germany, succeeded to part
of his grandfather's estates in accordance with his will. From
his loyalty to the Crown the title of Lord Cobham was bestowed
upon him and his heirs male, through letters patent to that
effect, dated at Oxford, January 3rd, 1644. Tradition relates
that this Lord Cobham, through his manorial rights in Heckington over its then uninclosed lands, so overstocked them as nearly
to deprive all others of their privileges, whence they were induced
to give up 600 acres of land at the east end of Heckington fen to
him in lieu of his rights. By his first wife Anne he had no issue.
After her death 1625-6, he married Frances, daughter of Sir
William Bamfield, knight, by whom he had an only son, born
1636, who died young, so that he died without leaving issue,
when he was upwards of 90 years of age. His widow, Frances,
Lady Cobham, survived him 17 years, and was buried in Surfleet
church 1676 where her monument still remains. The residence
of the Cobhams stood on the south side of Heckington, and its
stables and other buildings remained standing near an old fishpond until towards the close of the last century. On the death
of Lady Cobham, Sir Peter Frazier, in right of his wife, succeeded
to the Cobham estate in Heckington, who is stated to have
removed the furniture and pictures of the Cobham family to
Cressy hall, in the parish of Gosberton.

In a field near the old hall stood a tumulus called the Butts
hill, from its having long been used as an archery butt ; but
from the discovery of a part of an urn, several socketed spear
heads and many fragments of human bones within it, when it
was levelled in 1815, there is no doubt but what it was originally
either a British or Saxon barrow ; subsequently several skeletons
deposited in a regular manner accompanied by some fragments
of iron were found in digging for gravel in a small field near to
the spot where this tumulus stood.

Besides what may be called Cobham hall, there were two
other old houses of some consideration in this parish,* viz : that
belonging to Winkhill manor, and Holmes house. The family
of Winkhill, long resident in Heckington, gave their name
to the south aisle of the church, either because they were
benefactors to the same, or worshipped there. Their residence

stood half a mile north east of the village, within a moated area consisting of about an acre of land, the only approach to which was over a bridge on the western side. It was pulled down in 1780. It had a spacious porch in front with a room above it. Over the door was a shield bearing Erm and Fretty quarterly, on a chief a mullet, surrounded by an oak wreath, which shield was inserted in a new house built on the site of the old one by Mr. Christopher.

Holmes house stood on the east branch of the Carre dike in this parish.

Heckington fen was enclosed in 1764.

The present principal landed proprietors here, are Messrs. Godson, and Mr. William Little.

ECCLESIASTICAL HISTORY.

There was a church and priest at Heckington when Domesday Book was compiled. The profits of the former were given by Simon de Gant and Alice his wife in 1208 towards the support of the church of St. Lazarus outside the walls of Jerusalem, which gift was confirmed by King John. The patronage thus exercised was inherited by Simon de Gant from his ancestor, the first Gilbert de Gant, who obtained it as an appanage of a berewick in Heckington, belonging to his manor of Kirkby Laythorpe. Although the claim of Ralph Paganel with respect to some land that had belonged to Algar the Deacon was disallowed, he appears to have possessed some other lands here, for in the 15th century his descendant, John Pouger, of West Rasen, was patron of a chantry chapel at Heckington dedicated to the Virgin Mary and St. Nicholas. Its founder was then unknown, but the rents of certain lands and houses in Heckington had been given for the support of a chaplain, who was to pray for the founder and others, and to celebrate divine service in this chapel. From an indenture dated February 21st, 1545, we find that the endowment of the chantry then consisted of a messuage, " a common er le farre fenne," i.e. a right of commonage, 40 acres of arable land and 8 of meadow, then let to Thomas Morell for 20 years, at a rent of £2 to be paid at the feasts of St. Michael and the blessed Virgin. " Cott. MS. Tib." Several cottages and small parcels of land in Heckington were given by various persons for the purpose of having their obits observed in the parish church—as they vainly hoped—for ever. For instance, one of them gave 12d., the rent of a cottage, for this purpose, 4d. of which was to be given to the priest celebrant, and 8d. to the poor in alms on the obit day ; and another left 2 acres of land in the plains of Heckington, worth 8d. a year, half of which was to be given to the priest and half to the poor on the obit day. Others left lands, &c., for the support of lights to be kept burning, as they also vainly hoped, for ever, in Heckington church ; but in every instance it is somewhat remarkable the name of the donor has now been forgotten.

Since the time when the patronage of Heckington church was given to the Abbot and Convent of Bardney Abbey it has been served by vicars. The following is a list of the incumbents :

Date of Institution.

A.D. 1218.—Henry de Colevile, chaplain of the chantry of St. Nicholas in Heckington church, presented by Henry de Colevile, with the consent of the Abbot and Convent of Bardney.

.—Simon the chaplain.

1241.—Robert de Caden.

1292.—Simon de Baston.

1307.—Richard de Pottesgrave, presented by Edward I. during a vacancy in the Abbey of Bardney.

1400.—Robert de Somerby.

1401.—Henry Yorkfleet.

1423.—Christopher Estwode.

1509.—John Doghson.

1510.—Henry Cartorge.

1520.—John Green, presented also to the chaplaincy of St. Nicholas.

1535.—Henry Gaskyon.

1540.—George Metcalffe.

1562.—William Cawtrell, presented by Queen Elizabeth.

1577.—Thomas Morley,   ditto.

1606.—Robert Tatther, presented by James I.

1610.—Thomas Noke.

1611.—Robert Lussher.

1618.—Robert Sanderson.

1619.—Richard Harrison.

HECKINGTON CHURCH.

Date of Institution.

A.D. 1636.—Robert Sharpe.

1646.—John Duckling.

1660.—Robert Sharpe.

1666.—Edward Whiston.

1670.—Anthony Beridge.

1686.—Edward Gheast.

1694.—William Tunstall.

1712.—Thomas Townsend.

1717.—Joseph Greenhill.

1741.—Wyatt Francis.

1754.—William Nottingham.

1783.—Robert Benson.

1822.—Henry Bristowe.

1833.—Charles De la Cour.

1861.—George Thomas Cameron.

The parish registers commence Michaelmas, 1559. The entries for about 150 years are made in Latin, and beautifully written.

THE CHURCH.

This is dedicated in honour of St. Andrew, and has been justly entitled the Queen of village churches. The great starting point of its history is the year 1345, when the Abbot and Convent of Bardney obtained the royal licence to appropriate the church of Heckington to their own use. "Inq. ad. q. d., 18 E. 3." Soon after that date the present grand structure was probably commenced, the size of which, as compared with the former population of Heckington, clearly indicates the different principles on which our forefathers built churches to those now usually prevalent. When the eye is at liberty to examine the features of this church, after having been awhile absorbed by its spaciousness and beauty, it will readily be seen that its plan consists of a tower and spire, a south porch, nave and aisles, transepts, chancel, and adjoining vestry, with an undercroft beneath it. The whole fabric is very nearly of the same period, and was constructed between the years 1345 and 1380. The north transept and aisle are of an earlier style than the rest, as will be seen externally from the character of their base-mouldings and other evidences.   Why this should be so we cannot tell, unless one of the Pougers of W. Rasen, the then patrons of the chantry previously alluded to, supplied the means for the reconstruction of that chantry when the remainder of the fabric had become dilapidated, and thus led the way to the rebuilding of the whole. In 1310 Henry de Bellomonte, or Beaumont, obtained a royal grant of the manor of Heckington, and was probably, in consequence, one of the principal promoters of the above-named good work.   After the building of the north transept and aisle had been completed a short pause appears to have ensued ; but then a grander work was planned and commenced, viz : the re-building of the whole remaining portions of the church in a still more ornate and beautiful manner.   From the time of this re-commencement of the work it was apparently carried on gradually until its completion in the early part of the reign of Richard II., when the porch, forming an integral portion of the south elevation, was certainly erected, from the evidence of the bearings displayed upon one of the shields there.   Presuming that the nave of this church was erected through the instrumentality of its clerical patrons, there is actual evidence to prove that a former vicar, Richard de Potesgrave, erected the chancel, but probably by the aid of Sir Henry de Beaumont ; and that he dedicated it to the Virgin Mary, St. Andrew, and All Saints, the following legend in Holles's time remaining in one of the windows apparently shewing this :—

> Ricus de Potesgrave—istius ecclie hoc cancellum fecit
> in honore beæ Mariæ, Sti Andreæ & oim Stor., Ao
> Dni mccco. ——.

Holles also intimates that the recumbent effigy placed beneath an arch in the north wall of the chancel is that of the same personage.   We should have been glad to have seen the features of one through whose instrumentality so fine a structure as the chancel of this church was built, but unfortunately the face of Richard de Potesgrave's effigy has been almost entirely destroyed ; hence we can now only mark the richness of the priestly eucharistic vestments in which it is appropriately habited.   Some years since this monument was removed and the grave below was searched.   In addition to the remains of a body that were then disclosed, an article was found with them which was pronounced

to be a "candlestick," but in reality this was the stem of a
chalice, the bowl of which had partly perished.

At a distance the effect of the tower and spire is not so
perfect as that of the same features at Ewerby, the spire
here being a little too slight and the tower pinnacles too heavy,
while the flying buttresses connecting these pinnacles with the
spire appear to serve as ties to the pinnacles rather than as
supports to the spire. But when approached the massive features
and grand repose of this tower, its perfect condition and the
beautiful tone of its colouring are especially striking. In a niche
of one of the southern buttresses a statuette still remains, indicating the character of the remainder with which this church was
formerly richly adorned. From the eagle cut on the pedestal
of this figure we may presume that it was intended to represent
St. John. A female head at this angle, turned towards that
of a Queen on a larger scale, has a most charming expression,
that has retained all its original freshness since the days
of Edward III. The whole southern elevation of this church is
one of the finest examples of Decorated work after it had attained
its full perfection, and previous to the period of decadence, which
soon followed. The noble base mouldings, the freely flowing
tracery of its aisle windows, the range of the large clerestory
lights above, the numerous canopied niches, the beauty of some
of the boldly projecting sculptured ornaments, and the strange
grotesqueness of others, the crocketed pinnacles, the enriched
parapets, and the beautiful porch, together combining to present
one of the most triumphant examples of the power of Gothic
architecture, as applied to the production of a parish church, that
we possess. One bay of the nave, eastward of the transept, being
without an aisle, has a peculiar effect, and gives variety to the
composition. A beautiful turret staircase surmounted by an
equally beautiful pinnacle, constitutes the south-eastern angle of
the nave. The south transept, usually termed the "Winkhill
aisle," corresponds with the remainder of this elevation as to its
windows, &c., but is surmounted by a closed panelled parapet of
inferior beauty to that of the chancel, and of a later date. The
original oak trussed rafter roof still covers the porch. This is
exceedingly rich in canopied and crocketed niches, as well as in
other sculptured ornaments ; its whole contour also is most
pleasing. Just below the gable apex is a niche, once filled with

a sculptured figure ; immediately below is a small shield bearing the arms of England supported by little angels, and on either side, at a lower level, are carved kneeling angels, apparently bearing the emblems of the crucifixion, and also the presumed arms of Edward the Confessor adopted by Richard II., and of St. Edmund. The southern elevation of the chancel is exceedingly fine, with its three large flamboyant windows, its rich open parapet, and its grand angle pinnacles. The doorway, partly taken out of one of the windows, is surmounted by a finial of unusual beauty, and the sculptured ornaments grotesquely jutting out from the walls give additional power to the composition ; among these is a boat, on the gunwale of which sits a knight bearing a shield charged with two bars and three mullets in chief, also a dragon with a curiously knotted tail, a demon seizing a woman, a pig and other animals. The chancel gable contains a grand window filled with freely flowing tracery, and is most efficiently supported by its massive buttresses. At the east end are fine angle pinnacles. The vestry attached to the north side of the chancel, is surmounted by two perfect pinnacles, whence the other mutilated ones could be readily restored in accordance with their original design. The arched aperture in the east end below is simply the window of the undercroft, the tracery of which has been destroyed. The northern elevation of this church is not so rich as the southern one, but is beautifully designed. Although the north aisle, formerly called the "Riby quire," and the north transept are of rather an earlier character than the rest of the fabric, it is remarkable that the northern clerestory windows are of a later type than the southern ones.

After having wondered awhile at the size and general grandeur of the interior, it will be perceived that the arcades are of a date ranging between 1360-80. Here, as at Sleaford, are double columns, or responds flanking a short piece of walling between the nave and transept arches, an expedient that gives no additional strength at those points, and is inferior to simple columns. The font stands in a conspicuous position, as at Boston, and one that is appropriate in the case of a large church like this. The upper parts of the niches of this font are shallow, and could not be deepened lest they should cut into the bowl. Probably sculptured subjects originally concealed this defect. In the eastern wall of the north transept are evidences, both externally

HOLY SEPULCHRE IN HECKINGTON CHURCH.

and internally, of the former existence of two chapels there, together with their altars. Two piscinæ and a locker still remain which belonged to one of these chapels, and part of a piscina and of a Perpendicular screen connected with the other. The south transept was once screened off from the nave and its aisles, so as to form two more chapels. Three enriched sedilia, having detached pillars with foliated capitals, together with a piscina belonging to one of these chapels, remain in the south wall of this transept. On the south side of the sacrarium are three sedilia enriched with beautiful sculptured work to a most unusual extent. In the centre above are figures of our Lord and the Virgin, and on either side of these, others, both of which apparently represent St. Barbara with the heavenly suggested tower. On the right is a figure of St. Catherine with the wheel, on the left, one of St. Margaret with the Dragon. On the cornice above is a range of angels, some of whom guard the crowns of the holy persons below, and others are ready to administer spiritual food to them.

The delicate vaulting within the canopies of the sedilia recesses is admirable, as well as the sculptured ornaments generally, but the admixture of grotesques with the other legitimate figures and enrichments does not accord with our present taste, although very prevalent during the 14th century. Under the window, beyond the sedilia, is a beautiful double piscina surmounted by a crocketed gablet, the label of which terminates in little figures, one of whom holds a vessel, perhaps suggestive of purification. The finial of this piscina consists of a richly foliated feature, that has been restored by a sincere lover of such fair specimens of Gothic art as the one now under examination. Nearly opposite is one of the finest Easter Sepulchres remaining in England. Below are sculptured the sleeping Roman guard, clothed in the armour and bearing the shields of soldiers of the 14th century. In the centre above is the recess, in which the Host was solemnly deposited on Good Friday, where it remained until an early hour on Easter Day; but in some cases our Lord's entombment and resurrection were enacted by means of a temporary sepulchre, and through the medium of the priests and their subordinates, as is still the case at Ober Ammergau, in Bavaria, which has of late attracted so much attention. On either side of the aperture are carved the guardian angel, and the three Marys; above is the figure of our Lord freshly risen, together with censing angels. Such are the principal features of this beautiful work of art, every portion of which is further enriched with subsidiary ornamentation; but here, as in the case of the sedilia opposite, some grotesque figures have been unmeaningly introduced, together with some heads on a larger scale than the other ornaments, with very questionable taste.

As the exact character of the mediæval Office of the Sepulchre is but little known, it is here subjoined, together with a translation. The original constitutes a MS. Ordinary of the Church of Rouen, whence it was extracted by Du Fresne, and is contained in "Vetusta Monumenta, vol. iii." :—

Finito tertio responsorio officium sepulchri celebratur. Tres diaconi canonici indui dalmaticis et amictis, habentes super capita sua ad similitudinem mulierum, vasculum tenentes in manibus, veniant per medium chori, et versus sepulchrum properantes vultibus submissis dicant pariter hunc versum, *Quis revolvet nobis lapidem?* Hoc finito, quidam puer quasi angelus indutus albis et tenens spicam in manu ante sepulchrum, dicat, *Quem quæritis in sepulchro?* Mariæ respondeant, *Jesum Nazarenum crucifixum.* Tunc angelus dicat, *Non est hic, surrexit enim,* et locum digito ostendens. Hoc facto, angelus citissime discedat, et duo presbyteri de majori sede in tunicis intus sepulchrum residentes, dicant, *Mulier, quid ploras, quem quæris?* Medius trium mulierum respondeat ita, *Domine, si sustulisti eum, dicite.* Sacerdos crucem illi ostendens dicat, dicens, *Quia tulerunt Dominum meum.* Duo residentes dicant, *Quem quæritis, mulieres?* Mariæ osculentur locum, postea exeant de sepulchro.

Interim quidam sacerdos canonicus in persona Domini, albatus cum stola, tenens crucem, obvians eis in sinistro cornu altaris dicat, *Maria:* quod cum audierit pedibus ejus citissime se offerat, et alta voce dicat, *Cabboin,* (Rabboin). Sacerdos innuens dicat, *Noli me tangere.* Hoc finito sacerdos in dextro cornu altaris iterum appareat, et illis transeuntibus ante altare dicat, *Avete: nolite timere.* Hoc finito se abscondat, et mulieres hoc audito lætæ inclinent ad altare conversæ ad chorum, et hunc versum cantent, *Alleluia, Resurrexit Dominus, Alleluia.* Hoc finito, archiepiscopus vel sacerdos ante altare cum turibulo incipiat alte, *Te Deum laudamue:* et sic neupma (pneuma) finiatur.

At the end of the third response the office of the sepulchre is thus performed. Let three Canon Deacons, robed in dalmatics and amices, having on their heads women's attire, carrying a little vessel, come through the middle of the choir, and hurrying with downcast looks towards the sepulchre, let them together say, *Who shall roll away this stone for us?* This over, let a boy, dressed in white, like an angel, and holding a wand in his hand, say before the altar, *Whom seek ye in the sepulchre?* Let the Marys answer, *The crucified Jesus of Nazareth.* Then let the angel say, *He is not here for He has risen,* shewing the place with his finger. This done let the angel very quickly depart, and let two priests, in tunics, from the higher seat sitting within the sepulchre say, *Woman, why weepest thou, whom seek ye?* Let the third woman answer thus, *Sir if thou hast taken him hence tell us.* Let the priest shewing the cross, say, *Because they have taken away my Lord.* Let the two seated priests say, *Whom seek ye, women?* Let the Marys kiss the spot; afterwards let them go forth from the sepulchre. In the mean time let a priest cadon, representing the Lord, in albe and stole, holding a cross, meeting them at the left corner of the altar say, *Mary:* Which as soon as she has heard, let her fall quickly at his feet, and with a loud voice say, *Rabboni.* Let the priest, restraining her, say, *Touch me not.* This over, let the priest appear again at the right hand corner of the altar, and let him say to those passing across before the altar, *Hail, fear not.* This done, let him hide himself, and let the woman hearing this, gladly bow before the altar turned towards the choir, and let them sing this verse, *Hallelujah, the Lord hath risen, Hallelujah.* This done, let the archbishop or the priest with the thurible say aloud, *We praise thee, O Lord;* and thus let the office be finished.

The little building on the north side of the chancel, now used as a vestry, contains a piscina, which has led some to suppose that it necessarily was used as a chapel in days of old ; nevertheless it probably only served as the sacristy to the church, where the sacramental vessels were washed in part, as well as near the altar.   Below is a vaulted undercroft, thought by some to have been the chamber of a guardian priest, whose private chapel was above it ; but it was more probably used as a store room.

Besides the tomb of Richard Potesgrave, already mentioned, Holles observed two others in the chancel ; one of marble commemorating Henry Asty, knight, who died in 1383, the other of stone commemorating his wife Alice, and thus inscribed :—

> Hic Asty fossa nunc Alicie tenet ossa,
> Propter eam stantes hic vos estote precantes.

Holles also recorded the following then existing epitaphs, viz., on a brass plate :—

> Here lyeth John Cadron, ye which deceased 20 Nov.,
> 1488.   For Goddes love pray for me.   Thou wotest not
> what nede I have to thee.   For charitie say a Pater
> noster and an Ave:

Another commemorating Henry Cadron, who died 1503, and his wife Elizabeth.   A third of one of the same family, who died 1554, having a brass plate thus inscribed :—

> Here lyeth W[m]. Cawdron, sometime Baylyf of Heck[n].

Also two more placed over the graves of this William Cawdron's two wives, Margery Meres, who died 1509, and Elizabeth, who died 1556.   In the south transept he saw epitaphs recording the names of Robert Marshall, Stephen Boston, and William Lyndsey, and others near the chancel commemorating John Dogson, who died 1510, and Robert Thornburgh, who died 1487.

Besides these there still remains in the south-eastern angle of the south transept a slab having a deeply sunk quatrefoil, within which is the carved bust of a civilian of the time of Edward III., represented in a hood, and a tunic with tight sleeves ornamented with rows of minute buttons ; and in the same transept another that once evidently commemorated a knight and his lady in the butterfly head-dress of the time of Edward IV.

This church was also rich in painted glass, of which much remained in Holles's time.   In the chancel he observed the following armorial bearings, viz :—Az, semè of fleurs de lys a lion rampant Or, a bend gobony Arg & Gu—Beaumont, and the legend: " Sire Henry de Beaumont Dnus de Heckington Ano 5⁰. Ed. III." The same without the bend. Or, a cross Sa— Vesci. Erm, on a cross Gu a crown Or, repeatedly. Gu, 3 crowns Or, and the effigies of a knight and his lady bearing the Beaumont shield of arms. In a south window of the chancel the Beaumont and Vesci bearings were again displayed. The aisle windows of this church were also enriched with painted glass, in the east window of one of these, given by Simon Baston, vicar of Heckington, about the year 1300, the Beaumont bearings again appeared; also Az, 3 crowns Or; and in the one over the porch was displayed the effigy of a benefactor said to be a de Gant. Only a few fragments of all this glass now remain, and these have unfortunately been gathered up into one window in an unintelligible melange.

In the church-yard is the base and shaft of a stone cross.

HELPRINGHAM.

ACREAGE,   POPULATION,
3089.   1861—912. 1871—911.

THIS village lies 7 miles south east of Sleaford, and is remarkable for the height and beauty of its church tower and
spire, which may be seen for miles round in every direction.
Originally it was called Helpricham, and its land before the
Conquest belonged wholly or in part to the Saxon Eilric, who
had 7 carucates, 3 bovates, 9 bordars, 13 villans, and 15 acres of
meadow here, worth £13 in King Edward's time and £12 in the
Conqueror's reign. Subsequently this was divided into several
parcels, of which Robert de Vesci received 3 carucates, which he
held in demesne, also 13 villans, and 9 bordars having 15 acres
of meadow, valued at £3 in King Edward's time ; Gilbert de Gant
3 carucates and 2 bovates, as soke of his manor of Falkingham ;
Ivo Tailbois 6 bovates, 3 sokemen, 1 bordar, and 1½ acre of
meadow ; and Colsuein 2 bovates, 2 acres of meadow and 1
villan, berewick of Heckington, stated to be in a manner waste,
perhaps through frequent inundation.

In the 13th century the de Gant fee comprised half a knight's
fee, and was held by Simon de Kyme. In the reign of Henry
III. Margery de Greley and John de Hayled stopped up a drain
called Cheges dyke, between Helpringham and Swineshead to
their own advantage, but to the great detriment of the public,
who could obtain no redress from Peter le Brus, the Sheriff's
Bailiff. About the same time a poaching case was tried and lost
by William le Latymer before the Royal Commissioners, who
accused William Ward of hunting with harriers over his domain
here, where he had the exclusive right of free warren, and killing
4 hares regardless of prohibition, whereby he had forfeited £10 ;
but the verdict of the jury was in favour of the defendant.

In 1322 the fee of Philip de Kyme here was held by Thomas
de Wyke, who, in right of his wife, descended from the Dribys,
became tenant of that fee. In 1322 died Gerard de Chancy

seized of rents and tenements here ; in 1387 William de Bardolf, knight, lord paramount of two parts of a knight's fee here. In 1436 John Kevermond, husband of Matilda heiress of the Monbouchers, seized of half a manor ; and in 1451 Isabella Burgh, another Monboucher heiress, seized of the whole manor. In 1522 died Maurice Berkeley, one of the heirs of Sir Thomas de la Launde, possessed of a manor here. "Harl. MSS. 756." Subsequently Elizabeth, sister and heir of John Berkeley, died seized of the manor, leaving a son and heir, Robert. In 1568 Robert Levesley and his wife were made to shew by what title they held a manor in Helpringham—perhaps that of Knott Hall—and in 1595 died Robert Packenham also seized of a manor here.

The family of Cawdron next appear to have been land-owners here, of whom Edward Cawdron died in 1621. This parish was enclosed in 1773. Its principal land-owners now are Lord Willoughby de Broke, and Messrs. Pearson, Cragg, Tomlinson, Thorold and Barnes.

ECCLESIASTICAL HISTORY.

There was a church here before the Conquest endowed with 4 bovates of arable land and 4 acres of meadow, apparently in Deeping, which belonged to Azor. Subsequently it was possessed by the Abbot of Bourn. In 1328 Lambert de Threckingham obtained the King's licence to give 37 acres of plough land and 3 acres of meadow, partly in Helpringham and partly in Little Hale, for the support of a mass priest in Helpringham. "Inq. p. m. 2 E. 3." The Abbots of Bourn were accustomed to pay 10s. a year as a pension to the Dean and Chapter of Lincoln for the church of Helpringham. In 1616 Anthony Newlove was the patron of the vicarage when it was valued at £10 a year, and there were 320 communicants. "Willis's MSS. f. 39." In 1621 Edward Cawdron left to the churchwardens £20, the interest of which was to be given to the poor of the parish of Helpringham on St. Thomas's day. "Parish Register." In 1663 Robert Cawdron left by will 40s. a year out of the tithes of Little Hale to the vicar of Helpringham for ever, for a sermon to be preached on the anniversary of his funeral.

The parish registers commence with the year 1559, from which the following entries are selected :—

The church corne was sould by the chuchwarden in 1576, for £7 13s. 4d. In 1580 the Bull Dale (by estimation 2 acres), was let to John Smyth for 10s. and he to keep the Bull. 1605.—Money given towards the buiinge of Mr. Fox his Booke of Acts & Monuments, for the Towne.—Henry Twell, 10s.— William Morrice, 6s. 8d. 1606.—The south aisle repaired by the parish. Before that Mr. Robert Crebell claimed the quire at the east end thereof, as belonging to Thorpe Latimore. 1610.—24. June, being midsummer day, the greate bell fell down as the people were ringing, & brake through the high bell-chamber, & strucke thorow the stone floor into the ground 3 quarters of a yard ; which was throwe one of her yndyrons breaking, and had no hurt at all to her. 1621.—Mr. John Cawdron payd to the Churchwardens £20, given by his father, Edward Cawdron, Esquire, the use whereof is to be distributed to the poor on St. Thos. day. 1662.—Mem. It is agreed that every £20 assessed shall find a horse for a dragoon man, and if he shall be out two days together, then the party whose horse they shall have, shall be excused when it shall come to their turn agayne. 1673.—No Churchwarden shall relife no manner of persons except they have Sir Edward Lake hands. No Churchwarden shall pay above twopence for a fulmard's head. 1675.—The church corn sold for £13.

The following is a list of the vicars of Helpringham as far can be ascertained :—

Date of Institution.

A.D. 1227.—Henry de Sandwick, presented by the Abbot of Bourn.

1263.—Richard de Munaton, presented by Hugh Bigot.

1272.—William de Northbury, presented by the Executors of Hugh Bigot.

1535.—Edmund Preston.

1559.—William Burneby.

1570.—Anthony Newlove.

1608.—William Barnes.

1631.—John Foster.

1660.—John Duckeing.

1671.—Benjamin Deaken.

1707.—Robert Smith.

1716.—Samuel Galley.

1769.—Isaac Cookson.

1784.—John Moore Brooke.

1799.—Thomas Mitchinson.

1836.—Thomas Mitchinson.

1855.—Frederick Latham.

The Church.

This is dedicated in honour of St. Andrew, and from the loftiness of its tower and spire, which may be compared with those of Heckington, Ewerby, and Asgarby, is a conspicuous object for miles in every direction around it; nor will it be found less attractive when approached, from the beauty of its architecture and the perfection of its masonry, to which time has only given a charming tint instead of effecting any injury.

The oldest portion is the chancel. This is a good sober Early English structure, now rather overpowered by the larger and later work of the nave and tower, besides having been robbed of its original high-pitched roof as evidenced by the wall between it and the nave, and the sad way in which the head of its east window has been mutilated through the substitution of the present roof for its original one. On either side nearest to the nave is a single lancet serving as a low-side window, and two coupled lancets, the easternmost on the south side being placed at a higher level than the other on account of the sedilia partly placed below it within; between these is a priest's door. The lowering of the gable at the east end, and the necessary mutilation of the window below was a barbarous act, and especially as it may be seen from its pillared jambs and other remaining details that it was originally an excellent one.

About 1340 the whole of the rest of this church was rebuilt. On the west is a fine tower of three stages, having angle buttresses rising in lofty lines, and with scarcely even a minute flaw in any of its stones. In the lower stage is a most beautiful doorway, the jambs of which are enriched by four pillars, on either side supporting as many well-moulded members constituting the arch above. In the next stage is a three-light window having flowing tracery in its head, and in the upper one a plainer two-light window of a stiffer character, the whole being surmounted by a plain parapet and square crocketed Perpendicular pinnacles. At the south-west angle is a projection containing a circular newel staircase giving access to the top, from which rises a good lofty Perpendicular spire closely crocketed, having little flying buttresses at its base connecting it with the angle pinnacles. In the western faces of the aisles are windows similar to the lower one in the tower between them.

HELPRINGHAM CHURCH.

Both elevations of the nave are nearly alike, in each aisle are four three-light windows and a doorway, but the windows of the south aisle have reticulated tracery, and those of the northern one cusped heads, but are of the same date. The doorways seem to have been originally precisely alike, both having some effective cusped carved work in the upper part of their pediments, two pillars on each of their jambs and well-moulded arches of the same date and character as that in the tower, but in front of the southern one a poor debased Perpendicular porch was subsequently added. In both the clerestory walls are four Decorated lights coeval with those of the aisles, and three projecting gurgoyles, the whole being surmounted by an embattled parapet, and on its gable is a very beautiful cross. At the south-east angle is a staircase turret giving access to the south aisle roof, and also formerly to the rood loft, the doorway to which still remains within. This turret assumes an octangular form above, and in it is a pretty little slit filled in with stone lattice work. It is finished with an embattled parapet and a crocketed pinnacle. Within, the tower arches are perhaps the most beautiful features of the fabric. The noblest of these opens into the nave, the other two communicate with lateral features opening by means of other arches into the aisles. These arches are now boarded up, but it can be readily seen how beautiful this portion of the church would be if they were set free from their present incumbrances. The nave is spacious and lofty. On either side is a fine aisle arcade of four bays supported by three clustered pillars and their responds, but the clerestory above is covered by a poor roof in bad condition.

At the east end of each aisle was, as usual, a chantry chapel, the piscina and aumbries of which still remain. The former are alike, each having a pedimented and crocketed head, and the usual circular drain within a niche below; that of the south chapel is in the usual place, viz., at the east end of the south wall, close to an aumbry in the east wall; that of the north chapel is against the respond of the north arcade; in the adjoining north east angle of this aisle is a statue bracket, and near to it an aumbry.

The font is a very interesting one of the Early English period. It has a square base, from which rises a circular bowl supported by four octagonal shafted pillars. An arcade of narrow

and acutely arched arches enriched with the nail-head ornament
runs round three quarters of the bowl; but the fourth part is
differently treated, half of it being ornamented with foliated work,
the other half with a representation of the Holy Lamb and
banner, in front of which is a pendent object, perhaps a divine
ray, or the censer of an angel above; but as the whole surface
of this font is covered with many coats of washes and paint, the
last intended to represent marble, it is impossible at present to
determine positively what this object is.

The chancel arch is low and poor; but in front of it stands
a good Perpendicular carved oak screen. Within, as well as
without, the substitution of the present low pitched roof for the
original one is greatly to be regretted. On the south side is a fine
range of Early English sedilia. These have circular shafted
pillars dividing them and bold trefoiled arched heads with a
semicircular hood mould above each, and also a piscina adjoining
these sedilia on the east, and incorporated with them. In the
chancel is a large oak parish chest bound with many iron bands
having fleur de lys terminals.

Holles observed the following armorial bearings in a north
window of this church, viz: Gu, 3 chrevronels Or, a label of 5
Az.—Clare. Gu, 3 waterbougets Arg.—Roos. Arg, 2 bars Gu,
in chief 3 torteaux, over all a bend Sa.—Threckingham, with
this legend, "Dominus Lambertus de Threckingham me fecit";
also Arg, a chief Gu. Sa, a cross engrailed Or, a label of 3
points Arg.—Ufford, and Gu, a cross patonce Or.—Latimer. He
also saw in a south window here Latimer again and Gu, a chevron
between 10 crosses botony Or.—Kyme. These are now all gone,
but on a small brass plate attached to the north wall of the
chancel is this memorial legend :—

> Here lieth the boddie of Anthonie Newlove, the elder,
> patron of the Vicaridge of this churche of Helpringham,
> whoe departed this world ye fift daye of October, 1597.

It appears that he was a mercer of Helpringham from the
evidence of his tokens, a cut of one of which is given on the
adjoining page, but he was lay rector of Helpringham, 12th
Elizabeth, when he was called upon to show how he had become
possessed of this, from the following unclassical entry in the

Exchequer Originalia :—" De Antonio Newlove occasianato ad
ostendum quo titulo tenet Rectoriam de Helpryngham in com.
Linc.''

In the pavement of the chancel are slabs commemorating
William Cawdron, who departed 1615, a second William, who
died 1719, and a third who died 1720 ; and in the registers are
other records of this family.

The bells are thus inscribed :—

1.—Daniel Hederby, Foundʳ, 1758.   J. Springthorpe, C.W.

2.—All glory be to God on high.   1707.

3.—Praise the Lord.   1600.

4.—Anthony Newlove, Rector.   William Barnes, Vicar.
Omnia fiant ad gloriam eccl.   1608.
All men that heare my mournfull sound,
Repent before you lye in the ground.   1627.

THORPE LATIMER.

THIS hamlet of Helpringham lies three quarters of a mile south east of it, and was originally part of the Saxon Eilric's possessions, subsequently given to Robert de Vesci. In the time of his descendant, Eustace de Vesci, circa 1200, his land here was reckoned at the seventh part of a knight's fee, let to Thomas de Latimer, a descendant of William de Latimer, surnamed the interpreter, who came from the Welsh border and became a tenant under John de Vesci, in Helpringham and its hamlet Thorpe, at a yearly rent of 48 marks, from which family Thorpe had derived its additional name of Latimer as early as the reign of Edward I. William de Latimer obtained a charter enabling him to hold a market and fair on his manor of Helpringham and Thorpe. He also enjoyed the right of free warren there, and other privileges. "44 H. 3." He married a daughter and co-heir of Roger de Lumley, and by her had a son William, summoned to Parliament as Lord of Corby, 28 E. 1., and died seized of the manors of Helpringham and Thorpe in 1303. He was succeeded by William, 2nd Baron, his second surviving son by his second wife, Alice, daughter and co-heir of Walter Leydet, who died 1 E. 3., leaving by Sibilla his wife, widow of William de Huntingfield, a son, William, the 3rd Baron. He died 1336, and left by Elizabeth his wife, daughter of Lord Botetourte, who died 1384, a son, William, the 4th Baron Latimer. He enjoyed the right of acting as High Almoner at the Coronation of Richard II., as the inheritor of certain lands that had belonged to William Lord Beauchamp. He died May 28th, 1384, and by Elizabeth his wife left an only surviving child, Elizabeth, the second wife of John Lord Neville, of Raby. By his will he bequeathed all his lands in trust for the young Lord Neville and his heirs, on condition that they should bear the arms of Latimer—Gules a cross fleury Or.—his executor being Richard de Ravenser, Archdeacon of Lincoln. At this time the Latimer lands, thus transferred to Lord Neville, consisted not only of the manors of

Helpringham and Thorpe Latimer, but of lands in Bicker, Heckington, Donington, Swineshead, Swayton, Beckingham, Syston, and Gipple, being parcel of the old Vesci fee. Their son, John, was summoned to Parliament as Lord Latimer from 1405 to 1431. He married Maude, daughter of Thomas Lord Clifford, Countess of Cambridge, who died in 1446, without issue. This led to another change in the destiny of the manor of Thorpe Latimer, for it then passed into the possession of Elizabeth Melville, sister and co-heir of the second John Lord Melville, or Latimer, and wife of Sir Robert Willoughby, by whose descendants it was in succession inherited, viz: Sir John, his son a second Sir John, and then Sir Robert, who was a claimant of the Barony of Latimer in the reign of Henry VII.; but although he did not obtain that title, he was created Lord Willoughby de Broke in 1492, and his descendant is still lord of the manors of Helpringham and Thorpe Latimer.

The site of the ancient residence of the Latimers and their descendants is still clearly indicated by a moated inclosure containing about half an acre.

HOWELL.

ACREAGE,
1453.

POPULATION,
1861—80. 1871—86.

THIS village lies 5 miles east of Sleaford. Its name was formerly spelt Huulle, and Huwell, sometimes shortened into Well. Before the Conquest Colsuein's berewick here, which had soke in Kirkby, consisted of two-and-a-half oxgangs of land ; and another part of this vill was a berewick of his manor in Helpringham. Other lands, that had been Morkar's, were afterwards appropriated by the Conqueror to himself as an adjunct of his manor in Kirkby. Five carucates and 3 oxgangs were within the soke of the Bishop of Lincoln's manor of Sleaford, and were cultivated by 10 sokemen and 7 bordars, for whose service the Bishop provided a priest, and a church endowed with 31 acres of land. One carucate and half an oxgang belonged to Gilbert de Gant's manor of Falkingham, and other lands to his manor of Kirkby Laythorpe. A family of the name of Howell were at an early period tenants of the Bishop's and of Gilbert de Gant, of whom were Walter de Howell, who was fined 40s. by the King for some transgression " Pipe Rolls, H. 2.", Gilbert, circa 1200-10, and Sir Richard de Howell, who was the Bishop's tenant in the 13th century. In 1282 John de Neville died seized of lands here, " Inq. p. m., Edw. I." ; and in 1397, John, Lord Beaumont, seized conjointly with Katharine his wife of a twelfth part of a knight's fee in Howell. " Inq. p. m., p. 2, 20 Ric. 2." During the 14th century the Hebdens became lords of this vill through the marriage of Sir Richard de Hebden with the Howell heiress ; and in a similar way it was acquired by the Dymokes of Scrivelsby, in the year 1448, through the marriage of Sir Thomas Dymoke with Elizabeth Hebden. By the attainder and decapitation of Sir Thomas Dymoke in 1470 the manor was forfeited ; subsequently however it was restored to that ancient Lincolnshire family, who possessed it for a considerable period ; but from the evidence of the parish terrier it had passed into the hands of Joseph Edmonds, Esq., before 1707, as he was then lord of the manor and owner of nearly all the land in the parish. He was succeeded by his son, Sir Joseph, who assumed the name of More through his marriage with Henrietta Maria More. One of their sons was baptized at Howell, 1737, and another the following year. Next the manor passed into the hands of Sir William Smith, Bart., one of whose family—perhaps a brother— the Rev. Edward Smith, rector of Howell, married the widow of Sir Joseph Edmonds More, by whom he had a son and a daughter. The Rev. William Holland next possessed the manor. Then Mr. J. C. L. Calcraft bought it, who sold it in 1803 to a Mr. Ingall and a Mr. Vessey, from whom it passed to the present proprietors.

ECCLESIASTICAL HISTORY.

The Howells and Dymokes were the first recorded patrons of the living ; but it, together with the manor, was forfeited on the attainder of Sir Thomas Dymoke, and subsequently seems to have followed the fortunes of the succeeding lords of the manor. In 1616 the living was valued at £30 a year, and there were 84 communicants. " Willis's MSS. f. 39." In 1707 the curate in charge, Thomas Tonstall, was paid at the rate of 5s. 6d. a Sunday. " Howell Terrier." On the 12th of June, 1416, Nicholas de Hebden, of Gosberton, made his will to this effect :—

"In nomine Dei. Amen. I, Nicholas Hebden, of Gosberkirke, Knt., leave my body to be buried in the chancel of the parochial church of Howell. I give to the fabric of the church 20s. To the fabric of Claypole 20s. To the high altar of Gosberkirke, for tythes forgotten, 20s. To each of the orders of friars in Boston 20s., to be distributed on the day of my burial. That there shall be 5 wax candles weighing 10lbs. shall be burning around my body at my exiques with 6 torches. The residue of my goods, my Exors., viz., the lady Katharine my wife, Master John Boterill, And de Gedney, John Flete de Frampton, Thomas Spenser of Somercotes, and Richard Melton of Howell, shall dispense for the good of my soul. Proved by Katharine, his relict." "Repingdon's Reg. 139."

The following is a list of the rectors :—

Date of Institution.

A.D. 1218.—William de Benningworth, presented by the Bishop because the then patron, William de Howell, was excommunicate.

.—Hugh de Cleypole.

1322.—John de Strettonhill.

1349.—Robert de Howell.

1355.—Theophilus Guido Leterill.

1361.—Thomas de Luda (Louth).

1371.—Thomas de Languon.

1384.—John Humfrey.

1412.—Thomas Newton.

1417.—Edward Langford.

1418.—Ralf Langford.

1420.—Nicholas Gibthorpe.

.—William Stephenson.

1424.—John Spencer.

1448.—John Croxby.

1460.—John Gygar.

1490.—William Gygar.

1493.—Robert Baldwin.

1521.—Thomas Stukeley, or Southley.

1524.—William Merike.

1525.—Henry Mallett.

.—Samuel Saunders.

1574.—Robert Wells.

1616.—Charles Weldale.

1650.—Thomas Roe, ejected during the Commonwealth (see "Walker's Sufferings of the Clergy, p. 345").

1667.—Edward Carter.

1681.—Henry Greenhill.

1709.—William Jones.

1713.—Joseph Greenhill.

1740.—John Richardson.

1749.—Edward Smith.

1780.—William Holland.

1812.—George Holt.

1828.—George Savile.

1840.—Henry Handley Brown.

HOWELL CHURCH.

Date of Institution.
1859.—David Hunter.
1864.—John S. Dolby.

The Church.

This is dedicated in honour of St. Oswald, and consists of nave, north aisle and chantry, porch and chancel. At the west end is a very beautiful double bell-gable. The inner door of the porch is Norman. The arcade between the north aisle and nave, although it has semicircular arches, is decidedly Early English. There is also a diminutive lancet window of the same period, at the west end of the north aisle. The chancel and bell-gable are Decorated. The window in the north aisle chapel and south side of the nave are Perpendicular. On the remaining bell is this legend :—" Tobie Norris cast me, 1666."

At the east end of the chancel lies the altar slab, which bears the usual five crosses. On the upper step of the ascent to the altar was cut this injunction :—" Hic Deum adora." There is also a double locker projecting curiously from the wall.

In the chapel adjoining are the corbels of an altar slab, a locker, and brackets for images, and in the western gable of this chapel there is a quatrefoiled opening which formerly gave light above the roof of the Early English aisle, traces of which may be seen both here and at the west end.

Above the porch entrance the following bearings are cut upon a shield, viz., Ermine, 5 fusils in fesse—for Hebden, impaling a bend, charged with rye ears—for Rye.

On the panels of the font are other shields charged with the bearings of Hebden, Hebden impaling Rye, Lutterell, A chevron between 3 chaplets and a bend between 6 martlets. This font was the gift of Richard de Hebden, who died in 1373. In the east window of the north aisle are two shields, one bears Argent, 2 bars Gu, in chief, 3 torteaux, over all, a bend sable—Threckingham. The other, Or, 2 chevrons Gu, with a label of 5, within a border, Gu. Beneath the subjects of this window was formerly this legend, "Stephanus Capellanus de Iwarby me fecit."

A monument of the time of James I. bears the following inscription :—

Sir Ch. Dimok, of Howell, secᵈ son to Sir Ed. Dimok
of Screelsby, knig., champion to yᵉ crowne of England,
and his wife Margaret, widow to Mr. Anthony Butler
of Coates.

Holles observed a stone tomb near the altar, bearing this border legend, viz:—

> Hic Jacet Magister Johnes Croxby, quondam Rector-
> istius eclie, qui obiit— die —— mensis Ao dni MCCCC,
> —— cuj aie per Deus.

This still remains; it was prepared in the rector's life time, blank spaces being left in the inscription to record the date of his death, which however was never supplied. In the centre, beneath a canopy, is an incised effigy of John Croxby in eucharistic vestments, with his hands upraised in prayer.

In the chapel adjoining is a low well moulded and cusped sepulchral arch, beneath which is the tombstone of a lady of the 14th century, in a veil and wimple, and a young child, whose busts are sculptured in arched recesses. The hands of both are, as usual, upraised in prayer. In the nave is an incised slab, with this inscription:—

> Hic Jacet Ricardus Boteler de Howell, qui obiit primo
> die Januarii, Anno Domini MoCCCCLVII, et Matildis
> uxor ejus que obiit vio die Augusti, Anno MCCCLVI,
> quorum animabus ppicietur Deus. Amen.

On a stone tomb Holles saw this epitaph:—

> Hic Jacent Ricardus de Hebden miles, qui obiit xxvo
> die Aprilis Anno Domini MoCCCLXXIII, cujus anime
> ppicietur Deus, et —— quondam uxor Ricardi de
> Hebden militis, que obiit xv die —— Anno Dni
> MCCCLIII. Cujus anime propicietor Deus.

At the head of the tomb were two shields, the one on the right bearing, Arg. a bend Sa between 6 mullets of the same—Lutterell; that on the left, Erm, 5 fusils in fesse, Gu—Hebden, impaling Gu, a bend Erm—Rye. On the side was a shield bearing Hebden alone, and at the foot one bearing Arg. a chevron between 3 chaplets Gu; the other, Erm, 2 bars Gu, a bend Sa. Holles has also recorded these epitaphs:—

> Hic Jacet Willielmus filius Nicholai de Hebden militis
> et Catharine uxoris sue, qui obiit Anno Domini
> MoCCCLXXXVI.

In the north choir :—

> Hic Jacet Ricardus Spenser   }   Conjuges qui obierunt
> Hic Jacet Emota Spenser   }   8º Hen. 6ᵗᵒ*
>
> Hic Jacet Ricardus Whitead, qui obiit xxvii die mensis
> Septembris, Anno Domini MₒDVIII. Cujus anime
> ppicietor Deus. Amen.

Also figures of St. Peter and St. Andrew. In the chancel a large incised slab still remains bearing this inscription :—

> Hic Jacent Nicholaus de Hebden, miles qui obiit xix
> die mensis Aprilis A.D. MCCCCXVI, cujus aie propi-
> tictur Deus, et Katerina ejus uxor, quœ obiit xxvii die
> mensis Novembris An. Dom. MCCCCXXVII.

On the cross in the church yard is this inscription :—

> Orate pro anima Johannis Spenser Rectoris ecclesie-
> istius. I.H.C."

---

* They endowed the chantry chapel in which their remains were buried.

KELBY.

ACREAGE,
990.

POPULATION,
1861—99. 1871—87.

THE name of this place, situated 5½ miles south west of Sleaford, was originally spelt Chileby or Chillebi. Previous to the Conquest the land here chiefly belonged to the Saxons Aslac, Britric, and Achil, all of which was given to the Norman Bishop of Durham by the Conqueror, and held of him by Remigius, Bishop of Lincoln, and Colgrim. Some land of the priest Aschil's at the same time passed away to Wido de Credon, as a member of his manor of Swarby, which, together with its appurtenances in Thorpe, was reckoned as the third part of a knight's fee, circa 1200-10, when it was held by Alan de Thorpe. At the same time the Bishop of Durham's land here and in Rauceby constituted two parts of a knight's fee, and was held by Geoffrey de Evermue, who also held 1 carucate in Kelby of the fee of Gant, for the service of the third part of a knight's fee. In the 13th century the fees of Durham and Gant were held by Hugh de Wake, and of him by Geoffrey de Evermue when the fee of Croun had diminished to 1 oxgang, which was let by Petronilla de Croun to Henry Camerarius, by him to Robert de Thorpe, and by him, again, to Roger de Kelby. "Testa de Nevill."

Towards the latter part of the 13th century the great family of Wake had become lords paramount of Kelby, of whom Baldwin died 1282; Thomas Wake de Lyddel, 1350; Blanch, his wife, 1381; and Johanna, Princess of Wales, the mother of Richard II., 1384, all successively seized of the manor of Kelby. Thomas Holland, Earl of Kent, next held it, but forfeited it by his attainder in 1400. In 1449 died Sir Henry Grey, possessed of land here; in 1473, Elizabeth, wife of John Stanley, and daughter and heir of Sir Thomas Belesley, in possession of other lands; and in 1532, William Armyn, who held some land that had formerly belonged to the Priory of St John of Jerusalem.

THE CHURCH.

It is not known in honour of what Saint this church was dedicated. It is a small and modest looking fabric, but possesses some features that are well worthy of examination. The tower and spire at the west end were re-built a few years ago; yet evidences of the original Early English character of the former are still apparent in the form of the buttresses at its base and the angle shafts of its upper stage. The nave arcades were also built during the prevalence of the same style. The windows of the south aisle are very beautiful, and among the remains of the painted glass in that at the east end, is a small figure of an angel censing. The aisle is vaulted with stone, and on the corbels are very quaintly carved sculptures. At the east end is a niche and a bracket. The construction of the north aisle is curious, and almost suggests the notion that there may have been another aisle beyond. The chancel has been re-built, and has now only a piscina, conjoined with a credence, worthy of attention. The clerestory is Perpendicular on the north side, but has been re-built on the south side. The font is a plain Early English one. The old Perpendicular oak benches, from the evidence of the dress of the figures cut upon some of them, are of the time of Henry VIII.

KIRKBY LAYTHORPE.

ACREAGE,
2357.

POPULATION,
1861—218. 1871—230.

THIS village lies 2 miles east of Sleaford. Originally its name was spelt Kircheby or Chirchebi, and to distinguish it from other villages of the same name, that of Ledulvetorp was super-added, probably derived from Ledulve or Ledulph, one of its Saxon lords. This adjunct was subsequently altered into Leilthorp, Laylthorp, and finally Laythorp, sometimes shortened into Torp or Thorpe. Thus the fresh mode of spelling the name of this place—Kirkby la Thorpe—is clearly wrong.

Here Earl Morkar had 4 carucates of land, afterwards rated at 5 carucates and called the King's manor, as the Conqueror retained this for himself. It was valued at £4 before the Con-quest, but at £8 in King William's time, who kept 1 carucate in demesne, and had 14 sokemen cultivating 1 carucate, and half the profits of the church.

Besides this there was another manor that had belonged to Tunne, consisting of 4 carucates, rated at 3 carucates 3 bovates. This, with very many other lands, was given to Gilbert de Gant as soke of his manor of Folkingham, who had 5 carucates in demesne here, 8 villans cultivating 2 carucates, and 120 acres of meadow. Its value in King Kdward's time was £18, and subsequently £25.

Circa 1250, three parts of a knight's fee, termed that of De la Haye, was held by the Earl of Salisbury, who had let it to Beatrice de Engleby. He also possessed one knight's fee and the tenth part of another fee here, which he let to Simon de Kyme, and he to Alan Fitzwilliam. At the same time Rosea de Verdon held two parts of a knight's fee of the honour of Lancaster, who fulfilled her service to the King through the medium of William de Lancaster. The fee of Gant, comprising one-fourth of a knight's fee of the old enfeoffment, was held by Hugo de Neville of Gilbert de Gant. The fief of Durham was held of the Bishop by Henry de Horningend. Adam de Cranwell also possessed lands in Kirkby Laythorpe at that time, who died 1257. "Inq. p. m., 40 H. 3." Previous to 1185, the Templars had acquired lands here, at which date Gerard held 1 oxgang, the gift of Alan the son of Nigel, for a rent of 5s., le present, and four days' work. Azer held another oxgang of the same donation, on the same terms; William Parisiensis half an oxgang, the gift of William Grim, of Asgarby, at a rent of 18d.; and Herwardus, 1 toft, at a rent of 6d.

Circa 1325 the Prioress of Grace Dieu was holding four parts of a knight's fee here, Thomas de Multon, the royal manor with its members in Kirkby, Evedon, Heckington, and Howell, together with the advowson of a mediety of the church of St. Dionysius at Kirkby, and William the son of Thomas (*i.e.* Thomson) 2 carucates and 1 messuage by the service of three parts of a knight's fee, of William de Kyme. In 1402 half a knight's fee was held by Ralph Copledyke of the fee of Lancaster. In 1497 Mary, daughter and heiress of Neville of Scotton, one of the representatives of the Deyncourts, of Knapthorpe, and relict of John Bussy who was decapitated at Bristol, died seized of Ingleby manor in this parish, and of others at Morton and Willingham. "Inq. p. m., 6 H. 4." In 1444 Beatrice de Ingleby was holding one knight's fee in this vill and Evedon. "Claus. Rot., 22 H. 4."

After the Dissolution, the property possessed by Catley Priory and Grace Dieu monastery, in Kirkby, was sold to John Bellow and John Broxholm, 22nd May, 1545; a capital messuage here had been sold to John Bellow and John Bales the previous year. "Harl. MSS., 6825."

Robert Carre, of Aswarby, bought an estate here, apparently called Spalding hall, in 1566, of Thomas Sleford, of Willesthorpe, that had belonged to Thomas Skynner; and in 1559 he bought another estate at Kirkby called Ingleby hall, of John Stanlowe, of Stickford, and Edmund Bussey, of Silk Willoughby. At his death, September 3rd, 1590, he left these and all his other estates to his cousin Robert Carre, from whom they have descended to the present proprietor, the Marquis of Bristol.

Some Saxon remains have at different times been discovered in this parish, among which is the little vessel of which a cut is given. This is of grey ware, 3¼ inches high and 4 inches in diameter, the lines upon its outer surface consisting of a series of minute markings made by some little pointed implement. It was filled with fragments of human bones when found.

Another relic found at Kirkby consists of a little pair of iron shears or scissors of the usual Saxon form. A cut also is given of these of the size of the original.

Another ancient article, of the mediæval period, was also found half a mile east of the Old Place, but in the parish of Kirkby. This is the iron head of a large arrow, 3½ inches long, a portion of one of its barbs having been broken off. See accompanying cut.

ECCLESIASTICAL HISTORY.

There was a church here before the Conquest. The Conqueror retained half its advowson with one of its manors for himself; and probably from that early period there were two medieties of the living, but certainly there were subsequently two benefices and two churches here, the one being dedicated to St. Dionysius or Denis, which still exists; the other to St. Peter, in the patronage of Sempringham Abbey, so early as Bishop Welles's episcopate. These were united in 1593, but the rectorial rights of the latter having passed into monastic hands were alienated at the dissolution, and in 1636 were purchased by Sir Robert Carre, who bestowed them upon his hospital at Sleaford. Soon after this the northern church of St. Peter was pulled down, and its sole relic now is the bowl of its font. This is an octangular specimen of the Perpendicular period, having panelled faces with a blank shield in the centre of each. It was long used as a sink in a small farm house, but has now been rescued from such degradation and stands in front of the parish school-house as a reminiscence of the lost church. The rectory of Kirkby Laythorpe was consolidated with that of Asgarby, April 1st, 1737, when the Rev. Gascoigne Wright was incumbent.

The following is a list of the incumbents as far as can now be ascertained :—

Date of Institution.

A.D. 1535.—Henry Norton.
     1535.—William Downes.
        .—Valentine Tangelly.
        .—John Maheris.
        .—Thomas Willesdon.
        .—William Follarby.
     1630.—Robert Garland.
     1661.—Edward Dix.
     1670.—Thomas Meriton.
     1690.—William Pearson.
     1732.—Charles Hervey.
     1735.—Gascoigne Wright.
     1777.—Edward Mills.
     1821.—William Andrew Hammond.
     1823.—John Smith.
     1829.—John Morgan.
     1844.—Henry Ashington.
     1854.—Henry Anders.

The Church.

Formerly there were two churches in this parish, one of which was dedicated to St. Peter, and is now destroyed. The vicarage of the remaining one, dedicated to St. Dionysius or Denis, was endowed in the time of Hugh de Welles, A.D. 1209, and was subsequently possessed by the Prior of Kyme. The two livings were consolidated in 1593, when William Carre was the patron,* after which St. Peter's church was pulled down.

The plan of the small remaining church is very simple, consisting of a low tower, nave, north aisle, south porch and chancel; yet small as the fabric is, we have here features belonging to each of the four periods of Gothic Architecture. The doorway represents the first or Norman period, and has a plain solid tympanum with the billet-mould both on the outer and inner chamfer of the hood-mould above it. On the voussoirs of the arch the letter M, or perhaps the monogram of V. M., and crosses have been cut, or scratched, at some subsequent time in a systematic manner. The humble arcade of four bays, and the wall of the nave are of the Early English period; the latter still retains one of its original lancet windows on the west side of the porch, and the remains of a similar one the other side of it. The chancel is also of the same period; but this has been lately rebuilt, when the old lateral windows were inserted in the fresh walls, and a new one was erected at the east end. All of these windows are filled with modern painted glass by Lavers and Barraud. The aisle wall, a flat-headed window opposite, the greater part of the tower, and portions of the nave roof are Decorated.

The original form of the last-named feature will be understood from a remaining intermediate principal, on which the nail-head ornament is cut. Fragments of some delicately painted coeval glass will be observed in the aisle windows, including a shield bearing Arg, a chevron gu, between 3 trefoils vert—for Sleaford. The entrance to the rood loft has been preserved; but it will be seen that there is no chancel arch, and that the height of the chancel is the same as that of the nave. Of the Perpendicular period, are the porch with its good old oaken roof, the chancel screen, some of the bench ends, and, externally, the tower lights and parapet. For many years the lead, covering a portion of the roof, has been allowed to slip downwards by slow degrees, and to curve over the walls below in a somewhat unprecedented manner.

---

* At this time Hugh Davyas was the incumbent, but as the dates of the institution of several of the incumbents about this time are not known, his name is not inserted in the list before given.

OSBOURNBY.

ACREAGE,
1400.

POPULATION,
1861—613.   1871—606.

THIS village lies 6 miles south of Sleaford. Its name has been variously spelt Esbernesbi, Osbernedebi, Osbernebi, and Osburnby. After the Conquest a manor here was given to Wido de Credon by the Conqueror, together with its appurtenances in Dembleby and Willoughby. This had belonged to the Saxons Aluric and Adestan, the former of whom was allowed to remain as the tenant of 3 carucates of land, rated at 2 carucates. Then also Vitalis, a vassal of Wido's, held 1 carucate, and had 1 sokeman holding another carucate, 5 villans and 3 bordars holding 1½ carucates and 24 acres of meadow, valued in King Edward's time at 40s., afterwards at £6. Wido had also more land here constituting an appurtenance of his manor of Swaton. Ralph Pagnell claimed the right of sac and soke over the lands that had belonged to Aluric, but when examination of this claim was made by the Wapentake, although not conceded, they pronounced that Ralph had a right to be supplied with one horse from Aluric's land whenever he went on military service. Here Gilbert de Gant had 5½ carucates, rated at 4 carucates, lying within the soke of his manor of Folkingham, upon which were 16 sokemen and 6 bordars. Circa 1200 this was reckoned at half a knight's fee, then held by Simon de Kyme, and let by knight's service to Hugh Bussey, Philip d'Arcy, John de Somercotes, and Richard de Saltfleetby. "Testæ de Nevill." In the reign of John or of Henry III. Sir Philip de Kyme confirmed to the nuns of Bolyngton his serf Reginald of Osbournby, together with some land he had held of him, which William, son of Richard, steward of Sir Philip's father, had given them, when he assumed a religious habit. This land was then let by the nuns of the above-named House together with other parcels they possessed here, to Walter, son of Reginald de Osbournby.

In 1301 Hugh, son of Lambert de Bussey, sued the Prior of Kyme for lands in Osbournby of which he had been unjustly deprived, and died seized of certain rents here in 1305. "Inq. p. m., 34 E. 1." In 1325 John Surdival was holding two thirds of the manor of the de la Haye fee here, together with its appurtenances in Newton and Threckingham, by the service of an eighth part of a knight's fee, and John Drewe, of Wyvill, the other third with its appurtenances in Newton, Swarby and Manthorpe, by the service of the fifth part of a knight's fee. Then also Adam de Braceby and Philip de Duneby were holding other smaller portions of land in Osbournby. In 1371 certain lands here were given to the Dean and Chapter of Lincoln for the purpose of endowing two chantries in the Cathedral, by Canon Richard de Whitwell, for the good of his own soul, and that of King Edward III. "Pat. E. 3." In 1388 died Thomas Tryvett, knight, lord of Scott Willoughby, seized of certain messuages and lands in Osbournby; and in 1417 the relict of Thomas, Earl of Kent, also possessed of lands here, which were then divided among the co-heirs of her husband. "Inq. p. m., 2 H. 6."

Circa 1458-61 Nicholas Wymbish died, seized of the manor of Osbournby conjointly with others. He had bought it of Robert Stevenot, clerk, in 1451, when it was valued at five marks. In 1478 Thomas Wymbish petitioned the King for a licence to give the manor to the Prior of Nocton Park. "Inq. p. m., 18 E. 4." In 1576 one Wasteneyes held some land in Osbournby by the service of half a knight's fee of the Honour of Bolingbroke. At the same time Robert Carre held other lands here, which, with appurtenances in Newton, Swarby and Manthorpe, comprised the fourth part of a knight's fee.

This parish was enclosed in 1705, by virtue of a private Act of Parliament for enclosing the open fields and wastes here, at Newton and Scott Willoughby.

With the exception of some small lots of land belonging to Lord Aveland, Mr. Cragg, of Threckingham, and others, the whole lordship now belongs to Sir Thomas Whichcote, Bart., who, in 1846, built a handsome school-house here for the benefit of the parish.

Ecclesiastical History.

We gather from Domesday Book that there was a church at Osbournby and a priest serving it when that work was compiled. Half of its profits were given by the Conqueror to Wido de Credon. Subsequently 15 selions of land in Handbeck, worth 8d. a year, were given by an unknown person for the support of a light for ever in this church; and other lands and tenements by another person for a similar purpose. Three acres of land were also given by a third unknown person for the observance of his obit here. This land was worth 2s. 8d. a year, of which 1d. was to be given to the Dean and Chapter of Lincoln, 13d. to the priest, and 18d. to the poor. Maria Hall gave two acres here for her obit, and William Johnson and another gave a cottage and lands in Osbournby for the same pupose.

In 1616 the vicarage was valued at £8, and a lady of the Rigden family was patron. There were then 60 communicants according to Bishop Neales' record. Now, the glebe consists of 111 acres, and the patronage of the vicarage is in the hands of Hulmes's Trustees. It has been augmented by the Governors of Queen Anne's Bounty assisted by a private benefaction, through which the vicar possesses 32 acres of land in Dorrington. The following is a list of the vicars :—

Date of Institution.

A.D.   .—Miles Whole, vicar in 1616.
        1682.—George Dickens.
        1720.—John Burman.
        1730.—John Denison.
        1763.—Isaac Cookson.
        1784.—Robert Drury Rye.
        1797.—John Corrie.
        1836.—John Pearson.
        1863.—Thomas Molineux Jackson.

Of these the Rev. George Dickens inserted the following practical advice to his successor in 1717, at the end of one of the parish register books :—

> Keep in sheep a good stock, yr lambs do not sell,
> And then at Osbournby you may live well.
> Rear most of your pigs, keep 4 or 5 cowes,
> And you may maintaine a pretty frugal good house.

EE

The Church.

This is dedicated in honour of S. S. Peter and Paul, and possesses some points of considerable interest. Its oldest feature is the font. This is octangular in plan and of a late Norman period. It stands on a plain solid base, and is enriched with intersecting arcading, in which the nail-head ornament is introduced. Next in date comes the tower, which, from the flatness of its buttresses, the character of its simple bold base mouldings, and other details, appears to be of the first quarter of the 13th century. In the south west angle is a staircase, access to which is supplied by an ogee arched doorway within. In the west face of the lower stage is a small lancet window, to which much effect is given by the great thickness of the tower wall. Little slits alone light the next stage, and the upper one was partly re-built during the Decorated period. In this are four two-light belfry windows of that time, now sadly mutilated by the excision of their mullions and tracery, apparently simply for the purpose of filling up the whole of their apertures with louvre boards. Within, the arch opening into the nave is now filled in with masonry, but the cap of its southern pier is partly exposed to view. The extent to which the foundations of this tower failed at an early period is especially evidenced by the outward thrust of its contemporary northern aisle respond. From the base of this feature we gather that it was at first semicircular in plan, then mutilated, and that finally its upper portion was made to agree with a subsequently added Decorated aisle. The corresponding pier on the south side of the arch is of a similar character, but not so massive, and has an octangular cap.

About 1320 the present nave, south aisle, porch, both arcades, and the chancel were re-built in an excellent manner, but all the roofs of that period are now unfortunately gone. Each arcade consists of five bays supported by clustered filleted pillars. The hood-mould terminal at the east end of the northern arcade represents the head of a female with a wimple. The porch, towards the west end of the south aisle, is large and handsome. It has double buttresses at its angles, and a well-moulded arch giving access to a similar doorway forming the principal entrance to the church. The internal faces of its side walls above the seats are adorned with good arcading, having ogee arched

OSBOURNBY CHURCH.

heads and crocketed hood-moulds ending in foliated finials. In the side wall of the south aisle are three three-light windows, one of these and another at the east end have reticulated tracery. Here was clearly a chapel, from the evidence of a piscina in a square recess towards the east end of the south wall, and two statue brackets opposite, close to the doorway formerly giving access to the rood loft, the staircase of which still remains. The north aisle is of a poor Perpendicular character, and its side wall now leans considerably outward. In this is a doorway towards the west end, and three three-light windows ; its east window is of the same kind. Here also was a chapel, the piscina of which still remains in a square recess close to the eastern pier of the north arcade ; a large debased statue bracket, on which are cut two shields bearing crosses, now inserted between the first and second windows from the west of this aisle, probably belonged to this chapel. A good many very richly carved old oak bench ends still happily remain in this church. All of these are elaborately ornamented, and on some are figure subjects. One represents the always popular contest of St. George and the dragon. In this instance the Saint is represented in a suit of plate armour and a salade. Part of his broken lance is below, and with his sword upraised he is about to despatch the prostrate dragon beneath his horse's feet ; from the mouth of the monster protrudes a barbed tongue, and its tail also is furnished with a smaller head and a venemous-looking tongue, or sting. Another subject is a sarcastic grotesque, representing a fox in a pulpit preaching to a goose and goslings. A third represents Adam and Eve with the fatal tree between them and bushes on either side. A fourth, a King placing his hand upon a conventional tree or bush. A fifth, a lady in a helmet-like head-dress and mantle, holding an open book in her left hand, between two boys, one of whom holds a closed book in his left hand and upraises the other, and the second, standing in front of a chair, also holds an open book in one hand. Smaller figure subjects are also carved upon some of the heads of these bench ends, one of which may be intended for that of Boaz and Ruth.

The chancel arch is Perpendicular, and a little in front of this is the lower part of a carved oak screen of the same period. Owing to the lowering of the roof of the chancel a fine four-light Decorated window at its east end has been decussated, much to its injury. In each of its side walls are three coeval two-light windows, and a priest's doorway in the southern one. Here are three sedilia of great beauty, separated from one another by pillars, and surmounted by ogee arches crocketed and terminating in foliated finials, grotesque heads being placed at the terminals of the hood-moulds. Eastward of these is a piscina with a cusped drain, in the south wall, and opposite is an ogee arched aumbry formerly provided with two shelves.

Holles records that when he visited this church the following armorial bearings appeared in one of its south windows, viz:— 1, Percy; 2, Manley—Or, a bend sa; and these in the east window : 1, Bussey; 2, Kyme; 3, Limbury—Arg, 3 cinquefoils pierced gu. 4, Marmyon; but only a very small fragment or two of these now remain.

In the chancel are several monuments of the family of Buck. One of these commemorates Frances, daughter of Sir William Buck, Bart. Above are his armorial bearings on a lozenge, viz : Paly bendy a canton arg, and below, this inscription :—

> Francisca Buck, spinster Gulielmi Buck de Haceby
> Grange, in Com. Lincoln, Equitis Aurati filia. Ætat 27.

A slab in the chancel pavement bears a shield, on which are cut Buck, impaling a chevron engrailed between 3 lions rampant, in chief 3 buck's heads couped, surmounted by a Baronet's helm with a portcullis as a crest. Below is this inscription :—

> H. S. E.
> Dna Diana Buck, Gulielmi Buck de Haceby Grange,
> in Com. Lincoln, Equitis Aurati conjux. Defuit e
> vita ætat 51. 1711.

On the south wall is a white marble tablet with a large urn of the same material above it. On this is the following record :—

> Sir Charles Buck, Bart., of Haceby Grange, in the
> County of Lincoln, was born 31 Janry., 1724, died in
> London, June, 1782. He married, April 20th, 1758,
> Mary, eldest daughter and co-heiress of George Cart-
> wright, of Ossington, in the County of Northampton,
> Esqre., by whom he had no issue ; his widow and
> sisters, Anne, widow of Ambrose Isted, Esqre., of
> Ecton, in the County of Northampton, and Katharine,
> widow of Sir Henry Inglefield, Bart., of White Knights,
> in the County of Berks., his co-heiresses, consecrated
> this marble to the memory of their excellent and
> lamented friend, the last of his name.

In the church-yard is a stone recording the murder of Thomas Pinder, a poor apprentice of this parish, by a chimney sweep, 1784-5 ; but he was buried at Colsterworth where that foul deed was committed.

QUARRINGTON.

ACREAGE,
1268.

POPULATION,
1861—299. 1871—340.

THE name of this parish has been spelt Corninctune, Currmington, Kermington, Querrington, Quarringdon and Quarrington. Before the Conquest Bardi, Joel of Lincoln (a monk of Ramsey Abbey), Earl Morkar, and Archil were the principal landowners here.

After that great event Remigius, Bishop of Lincoln, received Bardi's lands at the hands of the Conqueror. These consisted of 9 carucates, 2½ oxgangs of land, connected with which were 32 sokemen and 15 bordars cultivating 7½ carucates, besides 60 acres of meadow and two mills worth 16s. Of this Osmund held 2 carucates in demesne worth 60s. a year, and Hugh Rufus 1 carucate in demesne and another carucate worth 25s. a year. Remigius also claimed some land in the hands of Archil in Quarrington through a mortgage he had upon it, but this was disallowed by the men of the Wapentake. One oxgang here lay within the soke of Earl Morkar's manor of Kirkby Laythorpe.

Joel of Lincoln, a monk of Ramsey Abbey, in the reign of the Confessor, gave a manor consisting of 1 carucate and 6 oxgangs of land in Quarrington to the Benedictine Abbey of Ramsey, together with its appurtenances in Sleaford and Dunsby. The first consisting of 1 carucate, 1 sokeman and 2 villans, cultivating 1 carucate, and also 27 acres of meadow ; the second of 6 carucates, 11 sokemen and 3 bordars cultivating 3 carucates besides 6 acres of meadow. The whole was valued in the Confessor's time at 40s., subsequently at £4. "Ex. lib. Anniv. Rams."

Ogerius, or Osgar Brito, had 5 acres of meadow, 8 of coppice, half a carucate and 4 villans in Quarrington as an appurtenance of his manor of Morton ; Waldin Brito claimed 14 acres here as of his manor of Willoughby, but this claim was not allowed.

Circa 1200-10 Hugh de St. Vedasto, or Vedeto, held of the Bishop of Lincoln a knight's fee in Quarrington and Evedon, and

Galfrid Salvein held the Abbot of Ramsey's lands, viz : 8 oxgangs reckoned at the eighteenth part of a knight's fee and 2 other oxgangs. "Testa de Nevill, p. 321."

Of the Vedeto family, Amicia, wife of Hugh de St. Vedasto, died possessed of lands and tenements here in 1253, and Beatrix de Cundy gave to Haverholme Priory 1 oxgang of land and a toft in Quarrington ; when she became a nun, her son, Alexander de Vedeto, gave the sisterhood she joined 1 oxgang and 20 acres of land, 1 toft, and 1 croft of three acres in this parish, and a William de St. Vedeto gave them an annual rent of 13d. Both the Bishop of Lincoln's and the Abbot of Ramsey's lands in Quarrington long remained in the hands of their successors ; but at length Henry Holbeach, 33rd Bishop of Lincoln, alienated his lands and the living in 1547 to the Crown, whence they passed into the hands of the Duke of Somerset. Subsequently these were given by Queen Mary to Lord Clinton, who sold them to Robert Carre in 1559, and they are now possessed by the Marquis of Bristol.

In 1691 Widow Timberland lived in the manor house of Quarrington.

The appearance of this quiet little village, lying around its well cared for church, is very pleasing. The old parsonage house was burnt down in 1760, during the incumbency of the Rev. George Ray, through the discharge of a gun up the chimney for the purpose of clearing it, when a spark falling upon the thatched roof below ignited it, and only a fragment of the house was preserved. The new parsonage is a comely and suitable clerical house, built by the late rector, the Rev. H. T. C. Hine, in 1845.

About the time of the enclosure of this parish, in 1796, it having been thought that coal might exist below the surface, search was made for this in a valley about half a mile south of the church, near the western side of the turnpike road from Sleaford to Folkingham ; but although no coal was found, the boring for it produced an abundant flow of water which has never since ceased to be of service, not only at its source, but in the parishes of Burton, Helpringham and Swaton.

Two stone crosses formerly existed in this parish. The shaft of one of these, about five feet high, stood near the toll gate on the Sleaford and Folkingham road. Half a mile nearer the village was the other, on a spot called after it—Stump Cross Hill—

marked by a small plantation. Latterly its circular head alone remained which had a cross carved on both its sides.

ECCLESIASTICAL HISTORY.

There were two churches in this place when Domesday Book was composed, the one standing, we presume, on the site of the only remaining church, the other not far distant, and probably in a farm yard now occupied by Mrs. Cubley, all remains of which have long since passed away.

Joel of Lincoln gave a church here to Ramsey Abbey, of which he was a monk; and Henry Salvein, or Henry de Cranwell, probably a descendant of Galfrid Salvein, and the tenant of the Ramsey Abbey lands here, gave the other church to Haverholme Priory, for the good of his soul and that of Julian, his wife. In 1412 Olivia, wife of John Rossen, of Quarrington, bequeathed her body to be buried in the cemetery of St. Botolph's church, at Quarrington, and left 12d. to its rector and 12d. to the church. "Rep. Reg. 68." The same year, Joan, wife of William Ward, of Quarrington, left her body to be buried in the same place, leaving to the church two stones of wool, &c.; Robert Timberland, chaplain, being one of her executors. "Rep. Register, 78." In 1464, Margaret, widow of Roger Catelye, of Quarrington, left a tenement in Quarrington to Thomas, her son, chaplain of Sleaford church, and his heirs, besides one lectur (lectern) entire, six vases of amber, her best brazen pot, a patella (dish), and six silver spoons, on condition that he should say a mass for her soul. She also left to the church of Lessingham 20d.; the same to the chapel of Roxham; to Trinity guild in Sleaford church 12d.; to St. Anne's guild in the same church 6d.; and the same to St. Christopher's guild there. "Rep. Reg." The price of two acres of land in the plains of this parish, worth 8d. a year, was given by an unknown person to the churchwardens for the maintenance of a light for ever.

In Elizabeth's reign there were 17 families in Quarrington, and 120 communicants.

There are no marriage entries from 1642 to 1648 in the parish register, during which time marriages were performed by magistrates and regarded simply as civil contracts.

The flagon and paten were the gift of Sir Robert Carre, Bart., whose arms they bear, viz : Carre impaling Bouchier with an annulet for a difference.

About 1800, a stone coffin found in the church-yard, for some time served as a trough in a neighbouring farm-yard.

In 1616 the living was valued at £30 a year, when John Nixon was rector, and the patronage was contested for by the Bishop of Lincoln and Edward Carre. The following is a list of the incumbents of Quarrington as far as they are known :—

Date of Institution.

A.D. 1218.—Alexander de Brauncewell, presented by the Prior and Convent of Haverholme.

1248.—William de Foxton, presented by the Master of the Order of Sempringham and the Prior and Convent of Haverholme.

1269.—Richard de Herton, Canon of Lincoln, presented by Richard de Gravesend, Bishop of Lincoln.

1280.—Augustin de Stane, presented by the same.

.—Thomas Hill.

1405.—Richard Birket.

.—John Percy.

1431.—John Spaldyng.

1535.—Robert Yonge.

1558.—Robert Barton.

1575.—Robert Hichcock.

1611.—John Nixon.

.—Thomas Bouchier.

1636.—Edward Trevillian.

1646.—Thomas Appleby.

1684.—John Kelsall.

1689.—Edward Thomas.

1691.—Thomas Graves.

1725.—George Ray.

1772.—William Thomas Hervey.

1792.—Edward Waterson.

1801.—Henry St. John Bullen.

1805.—Robert Willoughby Carter.

1810.—C. J. Blomfield—afterwards Bishop of London.

1820.—William Stocking.

1821.—Isham Case.

Date of Institution.

A.D. 1825.—Robert Willoughby Carter.

1826.—Samuel Forster, D.D.

1843.—Henry Ashington.

1844.—Henry Thomas Cooper Hine.

1861.—Frederick William Shannon.

The Church.

The tower of this church, dedicated in honour of St. Botolph, is a medium specimen of the Decorated period, the southern face of which is varied by a slight projection and a line of little lights indicating the position of the belfry staircase. The spire is sadly out of proportion with the tower, and looks as if it had slipped down within it. This unpleasing effect was slightly mitigated when pinnacles sprang from each corner of the tower parapet, yet the want of union between it and the spire must always have been very apparent. The masonry of the nave generally is very indifferent, yet its southern elevation is attractive from its three large windows filled with varied and beautiful tracery, of which the central one is the largest. At a little distance the doorway appears to be of a more ancient date than it really is. This arises from the extreme obtuseness of its arch, as its mouldings and details belong, like the rest of this fabric, to the Decorated period. Until 1812 a very miserable chancel was to be seen here, erected by Bishop Blomfield, who was the rector of Quarrington from 1810 to 1820, before he succeeded to the See of Chester. The present chancel is a good example of modern taste and skill ; its east end terminates in a quinquangular apse, in each face of which is set a window with slightly varied tracery. The base mouldings are divested of all crudeness of outline, and are of a solid character, while the masonry throughout is pleasing to the eye and structurally excellent. The carving of the hood-mould terminals, the designs of which are borrowed from nature, is excellent. The north aisle of the nave was re-built upon the old foundations some years ago ; this is now agreeably relieved by the gable of a new vestry which communicates with the chancel as well as with the aisle.

In the interior, the aisle arcade is the earliest portion of the nave. It consists of three bays, the westernmost one of which is

QUARRINGTON CHURCH.

wider than the others, and its arch something lower, which gives a very awkward appearance to the whole. One capital only has been moulded, the others having been left in an unfinished state. The arches are very obtusely pointed, which, in conjunction with the plain capitals below them, might mislead a casual observer as to their date. At the east end of this aisle has been a chapel, as indicated by a bracket, and a singularly small piscina. A few of the old carved Perpendicular bench ends are still existing. The font, of the same period, is a poor one, without a base, and the stem of which is a strangely coarse feature.

In the churchyard is a beautiful monument cross forming an appropriate ornament in this quiet resting place of the bodies of the faithful dead, as well as a memorial.

On a slab formerly inserted in the chancel wall was this inscription :—

> Hic infra situs est Thomas Appleby, A.M., qui post-
> quam hanc ecclesiam per annos septem et triginta
> summâ cum vigilantiâ rexerat. mortalitatem exuit vi :
> id : Martii. anno Dom : MDCLXXXIIIᵒ. Ætatis suæ.

Below was a low tomb observed by Holles, the slab of which still remains in the pavement. On this were carved several shields bearing a chevron between three turrets.

The following quaint epitaph on a mural slab formerly appeared on the south wall of the former chancel :—

> Consecreted to the memory of his deare Father Thomas
> Bouchier, borne at Hanborow, in the County of Oxon :
> a worthy Divine and sometime faithful Preacher in
> this Church. A man of singular integrity and piety,
> who (changing this fraile life for eternity) expired
> Sept. 18. A'o Ætatis 67. et Sal : Jesu, 1635.

> The patterne of conjugall love, the rare
>   Mirror of father's care ;
> Candid to all, his ev'ry action pen'd
>   The copy of a friend ;
> His last words best ; a glorious eve (they say)
>   Foretells a glorious day.

> Erected and composed with
> teares by his pensive Sonne, James Bouchier.

On a slab, formerly over the arch of the porch, was this epitaph :—

> To the memory of his dear father, mother, wife and children. Here under lyes ye Bodyes of these, who are here named. Will : Chester, Gardiner, Bury'd April 1st, 1662, and the wife of Will : Chester, Bury'd Feb. 2. 1662. Alice ye wife of Henry Chester, Bury'd Jany. 30. 1667.
>
> | Will : Chester. | Alice, Bury'd April 10. 1671. |
> |---|---|
> | Bury'd Jany. 24. | Elizabeth, Bury'd July 12. 1681. |
> | 1668. | Elizabeth, Bury'd Sept. 2. 1682. |

SCREDINGTON.

ACREAGE,
2530.

POPULATION,
1861—397. 1871—394.

THIS village lies 4 miles south of Sleaford. Its name was spelt Scredintune, Scredincton, Skrediton, and Screddington, before it became fixed as Scredington. It used also to be termed Scredington cum Northbec. Before the Conquest the Saxon Leuric was the chief if not the only landowner here; but after that great event part of its lands was given to Robert de Stafford, and part to Gilbert de Gant in connexion with his manor of Folkingham. Circa 1200-10 Henricus de Stafford held 12 oxgangs of land here of the King in capite, and a few other small portions, but the greater part of Robert de Stafford's land had then passed into the tenure of the de Crouns. Originally this consisted of only half a knight's fee of the old feoffment. Subsequently, Petronilla, the heiress daughter of Wido de Croun, let part of it to Robert Auteyne and part to William de Latimer. She married first William de Longchamp, then Henry de Mara or Meris, and lastly Oliver de Vallibus, Vas, or Vaux, who in right of his wife let a third part of a knight's fee in Scredington to Simon Camerarius, and a whole knight's fee to Simon de Markham.

In 1328 Sir William Latimer, whose ancestors had held land under the de Crouns by knights service, obtained possession of their manor here, and died seized of it in 1336. "Inq. p. m., 9 E. 3." In like manner, Elizabeth, his widow, subsequently married to Sir Robert Ufford, knight, died seized of it in 1384. "Inq. p. m., 7 R. 2." Their heiress daughter, Elizabeth, married Robert Lord Willoughby, so that when he died 1396, he was seized conjointly with his wife of this manor. The following year John Lord Beaumont died seized conjointly with his wife Katharine of the manor, which they had let to the Prior of Sempringham and William Disney. The next possessor was Elizabeth, daughter of John Lord Nevill, the heiress grandaughter of William, 4th Baron Latimer, and wife of Sir Robert Willoughby. In 1404 died John Nevill Lord Latimer, and in 1447 Matilda, his widow, who subsequently married the Earl of Cambridge. So also in 1469 died George Nevill Lord Latimer seized of this manor. The next possessor of it we hear of was Robert Lord Willoughby de Broke, who died 1502, and left the profits of the same and of his manor of Helpringham partly to a mass priest of the church of Hoke, Dorsetshire, to pray for his soul and the souls of his wife and parents, who was to have ten marks a year for his services for twenty years, and partly in alms to fourteen poor persons for the same time.

We must now return to the de Gant fee. In the beginning of the 13th century Gilbert de Gant held one knight's fee of the old feoffment in Scredington, formerly let to Thorold, but then to William de Dive, who had sublet it to Robert Auteyne. He also possessed the sixth part of a knight's fee, let to Walter de Threckingham, and by him to the same above-named Robert Auteyne. The Amundevilles previously held the land subsequently in the tenure of the Anteynes; but on the marriage of Margaret, daughter of Jolland Amundeville with John de Auteyne, this land was made over to them ; and in the year 1215 their son Robert was cited to answer for his not having paid the fine due from him as heir of Agnes de Amundeville, which he denied he was, and refused to pay ; but one of his descendants, Hamo, and his son were still more unfortunate, for when the former was Sheriff of the county, 1260, it appears he became indebted to the King for £1000 ; and in 1287, when he died, his lands in Scredington were seized on account of this claim, and thus lost to his son William ; but on his engagement to pay the debt they were restored to him by the King's command in 1289.

The de Gants continued to be lords of this manor until 1307, when, on the death of the last Gilbert de Gant without male heirs, his fee in Scredington was granted to John, son and heir of Hugo Bussey, of Hougham. After this time it is impossible to trace the ownership of the lands in Scredington ; but in 1523 died Richard Hobson seized of the manor of Scredington, held of that of Folkingham, and therefore no doubt the old de Gant fee. He was succeeded by his young son, then only three years old. In 1615 the manor was in the possession of Rochester Carre, and held by him of the Crown. "Harl. MS. 758."

ECCLESIASTICAL HISTORY.

In 1349 the firm of this vill was granted by the Dean and Chapter of Lincoln to Richard Whitwell, Canon of Lincoln, as a reward for having continued to reside and fulfilled all the duties of the Dean and Chapter during the preceding year with another Canon, Ralf de Ergom, when all the others had fled to their respective livings to avoid contagion during the prevalence of a pestilence. He was also rewarded with the grant of other lands in Haynton, by the Dean and Chapter for his life, on condition of the payment of a mark as a nominal rent for the same. He died 1371, and gave certain property in Scredington to the Dean and Chapter, perhaps that which he had received from them for the purpose of endowing two chantries in the Cathedral for the benefit of his own soul, and that of Edward III. "Pat. Rot., 45 E. 3."

In 1535 the church of Scredington was valued at £7 6s. 8d. ; out of which a pension of £1 6s. 8d. was to be paid in augmentation of the vicar's stipend ; Thomas Smith then being vicar ; and also 6d. a year to the churchwardens for the support of a lamp. " Val. Eccl."

In 1581 died Sir Robert Tirwhitt, knight, seized of the rectory of Scredington.

In 1616 the value of the living was £13 6s. 8d., when it was a peculiar of the Dean and Chapter of Lincoln, Richard Rochford was patron, and there were 140 communicants. " Willis's MS., f. 39." The following is a list of the vicars :—

Date of Institution.

A.D. 1743.—John Stephen Masson.
1776.—Samuel Masson.
1786.—John Wilson.
1849.—William Grice.
1851.—Joshua Waltham.
1861.—Edward Stirling Murphy, who has since assumed the name of Berry.

THE CHURCH.

This church, dedicated in honour of St. Andrew, has just been partly re-built and so much restored that at first sight it

looks like an entirely new one. Previously it consisted of a
little modern tower most improperly built within the nave, which
last had so flat a roof as to be invisible, a small chancel with a
high-pitched roof covered with red tiles, a north aisle, and a
south porch ; but the whole was in such a dilapidated condition
as to require extensive reparation. Now, the aisle, an Early
English doorway within the porch, its Decorated arch, one of the
nave windows, and a few other relics are still doing service ; but
the west end, the whole of the south elevation—including the
porch, and the chancel have been rebuilt of roughened stones ;
and at the west end of the south wall of the nave adjoining the
porch stands an octagonal bell turret surmounted by a spirelet.
Both nave and chancel are now covered by high-pitched roofs,
and brindled tiles.   At the west end of the aisle is a little
coupled lancet, and in its north wall a doorway and three later
windows, each having three cusped lights and low arched heads.
At the west end of the nave is a three-light Perpendicular
window, and at the east end of the chancel a similar one-of four
lights.   Within, the old Decorated aisle arcade of three bays still
remains, the easternmost bay of which serves as a vestry, and
opens into the chancel by means of an old debased arch, and into
the aisle by another arch.   The font is an Early English one of
the plain tub form.   Here are two stone altar tombs.   One of
these formerly stood under an arch of the aisle arcade, but has
now been placed at the west end of the nave.   It is of a plain
solid character, but its sides are relieved by square panels containing quatrefoils and blank shields.   It bears the following
inscription upon a small brass plate :—

> Hic Jacet Willus Pylet de Scredyngton qui obiit xxviii⁰
> die Junii Anno dni Millo CCCC tcio. cui aia ppiciet.
> ds. Amen.

Against the aisle wall is the other altar tomb placed within a
mural recess, and below a cusped arch ornamented with foliated
crockets above.   On the front are three plain quatrefoils containing blank shields, and on the slab above is the effigy of the
person commemorated, viz., Thomas Wyke, rector of Scredington,
who, according to Holles, was connected with Manchester, and
was living 17 R. 2.   He is represented in eucharistic vestments
with his head on a tasselled pillow placed diagonally upon

another, and his feet against a dog. The hands are upraised, and perhaps originally held a chalice ; but these are now so broken that this cannot be determined. Out of the mouth of the dog at the foot of the effigy proceeds a wide label bearing a legend which Holles could not wholly decipher, nor can this be satisfactorily accomplished now, viz :—

> Meminere thome Wyke, rector, p.................
> Gaudia de .... tumulus que car (or cor) ....

Holles seems also to have met with the name of "Rici Scarlet" on some tombstone here.

SPANBY.

ACREAGE,
1019.

POPULATION,
1861—75. 1871—115.

THIS village, the name of which was variously spelt Spanebi, Spanesbi, Spanneby and Spannby, lies 6 miles south of Sleaford. From Domesday Book we find that 3 carucates of land in Spanby were in the soke of Colsuein's manor of Ulvesbi, or Welby, and that these were rated at 2 carucates; besides which, there were 20 acres of meadow and 12 sokemen. Here also was a berewick of Bourn consisting of 6 bovates, rated at 4 bovates, and 18 acres of meadow, valued before and after the Conquest at 10s. Of this, Oger then held 1 carucate and the meadow land in demesne.

In the 13th century Colsuein's land had become part of the de la Haye fee, then held of the King by William Longspee, the representative of that family, and consisted of half a knight's fee. Christiana Ledet held this of him, and let it to John, son of William Foliot, a kinsman of the de la Hayes. "Testa de Nevill." William Foliot gave to Bolyngton Priory his vassal Ailrick, surnamed the chaplain of Spanby, his wife, chattels, house, buildings, a toft, a croft, an oxgang and 32 acres of land, a meadow, and pasture for 60 sheep formerly held at the rent of a mark by the said Ailrick. In like manner Richard Foliot gave Ralph, son of Heine, one of his vassals together with 4 oxgangs of land in Spanby to the nuns of Bolyngton. Another member of this family, Paganus Foliot, gave to the Templars an oxgang of land, circa 1185, let at 2s. a year, some work and "le present."

In 1325 Hugo de Spanneby was holding 20 oxgangs in Spanby by the service of half a knight's fee of the de la Haye fee, and in 1331 John de Spanneby obtained the right of free warren in Spanby.

In 1410 died Elizabeth, widow of John Holland, Earl of Kent, seized of half a knight's fee here, and in 1417, Alice, Countess of Kent, possessed of the same. In 1428 died Elizabeth, widow of John de Nevill, knight, seized of half a knight's fee here.

In 1509 died Arthur Spanby possessed of the manor of Spanby with its members in Billinghay and Walcot, " Harl. MS., 756," and in 1540 the King granted to Robert Dighton, of Sturton, certain messuages and tenements here that had belonged to Bourn Abbey to be held of him by knight's service. " Harl. MS., 6829."

The manor and about half the land in this parish now belong to the Trustees of the late Mr. W. Cragg. The rest belongs to Sir Thomas Whichcote, Bart., Robert Kelham, Esq., Captain Smith, of Horbling, Captain Cragg, the vicar of Walcot, J. Conant, Esq., Mr. D. Bellamy, and the Trustees for the poor of Burton Pedwardine.

ECCLESIASTICAL HISTORY.

The vicarage of Spanby was consolidated with that of Swaton in the reign of Henry VIII., as recorded in the " Liber Regis.," and perhaps before that time.

The following is a list of the vicars of Spanby :—

Date of Institution.

A.D.　　　.—Thomas Wallis.
1662.—Peter Saunders.
1663.——— Waring.
　　.—John Spademan.
1681.—Joseph Holton.
1697.—Jonathan Whaley.
1702.—John Spriggs.
1729.—William Ducros.
1744.—John Stephen Mason.
1777.--Samuel Mason.
1786.—James Pigott.
1813.—John Shinglar.
1828.—Thomas Darby.
1840.—Henry Knapp.

THE CHURCH.

This was originally a small church, dedicated in honour of St. Nicholas, and apparently built during the second half of the 13th century ; but it has since been considerably curtailed by the shortening of its nave at the west end, the destruction of both its aisles and a chantry chapel on the north side of the chancel, besides the lowering of its roof; yet, although most unpromising at first sight, is not without considerable architectural value, and certainly might be made a very comely edifice.

The only subsidiary features of the south elevation are a doorway and one window in the nave. The first is inserted in the western arch of the lost aisle arcade, and is coeval with it, so that it was most probably simply taken from the aisle wall on its removal and inserted in its present position. The second is a small debased square headed window out of which the mullions have been cut. Both within and without the outlines of the aisle arcades may be plainly seen in the present external walls. These are of two bays supported by a central octangular pillar and corresponding responds. In the chancel is a comparatively large east window, consisting of two lancet lights with a solid heading between them. In the south wall is an arch that once opened into a chapel; and in the northern one a large semicircular-headed arch that gave access to another chantry chapel, now filled in with masonry, in which a small Decorated window is inserted, perhaps derived from one of the lost aisles; a similar one was also placed in the easternmost arch of the nave arcade. The original west end of the church, whether consisting of a tower or simply a wall surmounted by a bell-cot, has been pulled down and replaced by a poor comparatively modern wall cutting off a portion of the nave. This is surmounted by a wooden cage-like structure, supported in part by timber props, and containing a bell. Within, besides the arcades before spoken of, and the arch in the north wall of the chancel, there are two slender octangular shafts between the nave and chancel which are too light to carry a chancel arch; but may have supported a rood beam, or been connected with a wooden screen. The roofs of both nave and chancel have been so lowered that they are not seen externally, and spoil the appearance of the interior. The font is a remarkable specimen of the Early English period. Its stem consists of a central feature flanked by four pyramidal octangular shaftlets, and its bowl of a solid octangular block with its edges slightly chamfered. In the south wall of the chancel is a little trefoil-headed niche containing a piscina.

Holles noted only one fragmentary epitaph here, viz :—

Hic Jacet Johannes de Spanby, qui obiit ....
Ano Dni MCCCCXVII. cujus anime ppicietur Deus.
Amen.

Since then another slab has been revealed of nearly the same date, having a pleasing stemmed cross rising from a stepped base or calvary, and a fragment of a border legend, having the date of MCCCCXIIII., and the same termination as the other.

SWARBY.

ACREAGE,
954.

POPULATION,
1861—162. 1871—175.

THIS village lies 4 miles south of Sleaford. Its name is spelt Swarrebi in Domesday Book. After the Conquest Wido de Credon obtained land here with appurtenances in Kelby, Marston and Harrowby, of which Vitalis, his vassal, held a carucate. He had also 16 sokemen and 3 villans cultivating 2½ carucates, and holding 80 acres of meadow and 80 of underwood. Here Aluric held 4 bovates of land rated at 2 bovates, Godman 6 bovates, rated at 3½, and Odo the arbalist, or crossbow man, 1 carucate, 20 acres of meadow, 12 of underwood, and the third part of the church, worth 10s. a year.

Subsequently the de Credon manor was inherited by Petronilla de Credon, or Croun, when Hugo de Boothby was one of her tenants, who sublet his land to Ralf de Normanton, and Henry Camerarius held another smaller portion, which he sublet by knight's service to Robert de Thorpe, i.e. Culverthorpe. Circa 1200-10 Gilbert de Gant's fee was held by Robert de Haceby, and that of Croun by Alan de Thorpe. "Testa de Nevill." Robert de Newton held 2 oxgangs here of the Earl of Salisbury, who sublet it to Ralf de Normanton, and subsequently to William de Lunda. In 1397 died John Lord Beaumont, seized conjointly with his wife, Katharine, of one knight's fee in Swarby, held by William Disney. In 1417 died Alce, relict of Thomas, Earl of Kent, and daughter of Richard, Earl of Arundel, seized of lands and tenements here. "Inq. p. m., 2 H. 6."

In 1544 the King granted to John Broxholme the lands, the rectory, a chapel and a messuage here, that had belonged to Kyme Priory. In 1545 died Charles Brandon, Duke of Suffolk, seized of the manor of Swarby. In 1550 Christopher Kelke held of the King the rectory of Swarby, a capital messuage, a mill and certain lands in Swarby and Culverthorpe. "Harl. MSS. 6829." William Fairfax next obtained the rectory and advowson of Swarby, a columbary (dovecot), a garden, 100 acres of plough land, and 40 of pasture, held of the Queen, leaving a daughter, Elizabeth, as his heir. "Harl. MSS. 6829." In 1560 Simon Freman was holding lands in this place; and in 1574 George Fairfax obtained a licence to alienate all his lands, together with the advowson of the rectory and vicarage of Swarby, to Richard Fairfax, but he did not carry out this design, as he died seized of the rectory and vicarage of Swarby in 1635, leaving a son, Christopher, as his heir. In the beginning of the following century Robert Carre had obtained the fee of the Castle and Honour of Bolingbroke here, latterly held by the family of Hermyn by the service of the fourth part of a knight's fee. "Rot. Cur. Ducat. Lanc."

ECCLESIASTICAL HISTORY.

In 1533 Walter Gyldyn, vicar of Swarby, bequeathed his body to be buried in the chancel of Allhallows, or All Saints, in Swarby.

From the foregoing account it will be seen that in the 16th century the rectory of Swarby, which had belonged to Kyme Priory, passed successively into the hands of John Broxholme, Christopher Kelke, and William Fairfax; also that it was subsequently inherited successively by George and Christopher Fairfax.

In 1616, when George Fairfax was the patron, there were 94 communicants. "Willis's Church Notes, f. 39."

In the tower Holles observed this legend: "John Thurseby of thy soul God have mercy," and adds that this John Thurseby was thought to have been a vicar of Swarby. The following is a list of the vicars :—

Date of Institution.

A.D.   .—Walter Gyldyn, vicar 1533.

    1731.—Richard Brown.

    1795.—Thomas Dawson.

    1804.—William Turner Broadbent.

    1818.—Francis Whichcote.

    1823.—John Hannar.

    1830.—Christopher Whichcote.

    1851.—Christopher Whichcote.

The Church.

The modest little church, dedicated in honour of St. Mary and All Saints at Swarby, possesses some peculiar features. It consists of a tower, nave, north and south aisles, porch and chancel. The tower, of a late Perpendicular period, with pinnacles at its angles, is covered with a stone pyramidal roof, and surmounted by a pinnacle. The form of the parapet is unusual, partaking somewhat of the character of the cloven battlemented parapets common in northern Italy. Each pair of belfry windows is covered by a clumsily contrived hood-mould. The nave and aisles are now under one roof; to effect which, it was deemed necessary to lessen the width of the aisles and to decapitate their windows; an expedient that must be termed a most barbarous one. The southern aisle is Perpendicular, the northern one, Decorated. The windows here have double sills, or a filling-in of panelling, as at Aunsby. The door of the south aisle, and a portion of a crocketed label over its east window are worthy of notice. The chancel has been partly re-built, but it still retains one low-side Early English window in its south wall. The porch arch is also of this period. Within, there is but little worthy of notice. At the east end of the north aisle is a bracket supporting a portion of a seated figure cut in stone, and probably intended to represent Our Lord; the old rood staircase remains on the north side of the Perpendicular arch, and a portion of the Early English font.

In the chancel are the remains of a richly canopied niche. In the churchyard, at the east end of the south aisle of the church, is a mutilated recumbent effigy, and here formerly was a tombstone, erected in memory of two children, and bearing the following quaint inscription:—

> Beneath this earthly tomb there lies
> Two of the world's best roses ;
> Pray God to take their souls
> To Abraham and to Moses !

SWATON.

ACREAGE,
3150.

POPULATION,
1861—299. 1871—336.

THE name of this village, lying 9 miles south east of Sleaford, has been thus variously spelt, Suavintone, Suavitone, Swaunetone, Swaueton, Swauton and Swayton.

Before the Conquest Adestan, Auti, and Aluric were the Saxon landed proprietors here. After that great event the Conqueror gave Adestan's lands to Wido de Credon, with its members in Horbling, Haydor and Osbournby. Auti's lands, having soke in Haceby, and those belonging conjointly to Alsi, Adestan and Aluric—three Saxon brothers—to Colsuein; and two oxgangs of land, constituting a berewick of Caythorpe, to Robert de Vesci, afterwards held of the King by William de Vesci, and let to William de Latimer.

In 1185 Matilda, daughter of William de Verdun and relict of Richard de la Hay, then 57 years of age, was a ward of the King, and had this vill in dowry. Upon it were 3 ploughs, 60 sheep, 10 swine and a boar, worth £30 a year and capable of being considerably augmented. She had five daughters, one of whom was married to Gerald de Camville, another to Richard de Humer, and a third to William de Rollos. Of these sons in law Gerald de Camville succeeded to the manor of Swaton, and was in possession of it circa 1200 as parcel of his barony. "Testa de Nevill." In the 13th century William de Longspee held in capite 9 carucates and 2 oxgangs of land in this vill, in demesne, by knight's service of the old feoffment. By a grant dated at Perth, January 4th, 1282, Henry de Lacy, Earl of Lincoln, and Margaret Longspee his wife, obtained a charter of free warren over their lands in Swaton, a grant to hold a market at Swaton every Friday, a fair of four days continuance, viz: on the vigil, day, morrow, and day after the morrow of the feast of St. Michael, or the three last days of September and first of October; and another fair also of four days continuance on the vigil, day, morrow, and day after the feast of St. Thomas.

In 1311 this Henry de Lacy died seized conjointly with his heiress wife of this manor of the honour of Lancaster. " Inq. p. m., 4 E. 2." Alice de Lacy, Countess of Lincoln, gave and confirmed to God and the church and Canons of Barlings her manor of Swaton of the fee of de la Hay, by a charter dated at York on the 10th of July, 1322, " Ex cartular. Abb. Barl. Lib. Cott., f. 178," and by a licence dated at Newcastle-upon-Tyne, October 30th, 1334, the King allowed the Abbot and Convent of Barlings to give and assign 60s. a year out of their manor of Swaton and the advowsons of the churches of Sudbrook in Lincolnshire, and Middleton in Oxfordshire, to Henry de Burghurst, or Burghersh, Bishop of Lincoln. " R. Pat E. 3 m. 10."

In 1345, when an enquiry was made respecting the extent of the liberties of Barlings Abbey, it was found that its Abbot and monks were in poseession of a manor in this vill ; and they then obtained the privilege of holding a view of frank pledge in that manor, the profits of which were worth 2s. " Inq. p. m., 19 E. 3."

On the 14th February, 1557, died William Middleton seized of a capital messuage, 14 oxgangs of land, and one toft called " le cottes," held of the King in capite. By Grace his wife he left a son John as his heir, whose wife's name was Elina. " Harl. MS. 757." The following is the will of this William Middleton, given as a characteristic example of a Yeoman's will of the close of the 16th century, dated November 17th, 1599 :—

> " I William Middleton, of Swaiton, gent., leave my body to be buried in the church yard of Swaiton. I will that Mr. Francis Lumley be paid £20, and that Richard Needham be paid 20s., and Britton, of Grantham, the clothier, be paid 40s., and my uncle, Thomas Middleton, of London, as appeareth by his books, 18s., and to my brother, John Middleton, 20s., and to my brother in law, Nicholas Boole, £10, and to my father in law 13s. 4d. I give to Jane, my wife, £20, 4 kine, 4 mares, 6 quarters of peas and 4 of barley, and half of my household stuff, and the other half I will my wife have to discharge my sd Exix. of the portion of Elizabeth Boole, her sister. To my son, William Middleton, £130, and all my right in 2 farms in Swaiton called Luncheion House and Townsend House. And whereas I have sold the said lands to the Earl of Lincoln, and bound myself for the matter of the assurance, wherefore there is a sute commenced against me in the King's Bench,

and order given by the said Court that the Earl should accept the assurance, I will my supervisors set aside £100 of my said portion to pay into the Court the same amount. I give to my said son William the land mortgaged to me in Spalding, late belonging to John Middleton, my uncle, and if my said uncle redeem them, I will my son William have the £50, for which they are mortgaged. I give to Elizabeth, my daughter, £50, when 18. To my daughter Mary, £50, when 18. To my sister, Anne Middleton the elder, 40s. To Humphrey Middleton, my brother, 10s., to buy him a bible, and one baie yearling fillie. To my brother, Daniel Middleton, a black trotting colte. To my sister, Elizabeth Middleton, 2 french crowns at her marriage. To Robert Middleton and Joan his sister, each 20s. To Anne Middleton, my aunte, 40s. at her marriage. To Henrie Middleton, of Helpringham, 10s., which he oweth to me. To my father in lawe my birding piece, and my half of his caliver with the office. To my mother my bible and two of my best books that I have not bequeathed. To my cousin, John Coste, a black ambling mare, and to his wife two bookes of the said sorte of my bookes. To every of my god-children 12d. To everie of my servants 12d. To John Shepard 12d. To the poor of Swaiton 6s. 8d. Of Osbournby 5s. To the town of Horbling 5s. To good wife Berne one booke called Mr. Grencham his works. My supervisors to have my sons portion, &c., &c., till he be 21. Residue to Suzanna my daughter, whom I make executrix, and my friends, Thomas Middleton, of London, my unkell, Walter Audley, my unkell, Mr. Hugh Middleton, of London, gold-smith. Francis Braiham, of Swaiton, gent., and Richard Whittingham, of Horbling, gent., supervisors. Witnesses : Richd. Needham, William Hatfield and Wm. Cham.

The present principal landed proprietors here are J. Lee Warner, Esq., of Walsingham Abbey, who is lord of the manor and the owner of the greater part of the land. The vicar, who has in all 247 acres, and Mrs. Rasen, the impropriator and patron of the living, who possesses 175 acres ; but Lord Willoughby de Broke, and the Trustees of the late Mr. W. Cragg, of Threcking-ham, have also a few acres in this parish.

ECCLESIASTICAL HISTORY.

In the reign of Henry I. certain profits of the lordship and church of Swaton were given to the monks of Essay, in Nor-mandby, by Robert de la Hay. " Dugdale's Monasticon."

For a long time the Dean and Chapter of Lincoln received 40s. a year from the Abbot and Convent of Bardney as a pension, derived from this place.

The annual rent of an oxgang of land lying in the plains of this parish, containing about 10 acres, originally let at 5s. per acre, was left by an unknown person for the observance of his obit in the church of Swaton for ever, when a part of the money so left was to be given to the poor.

In Bishop Neale's time, 1616, the living of Swaton was valued at £30 a year, when the Earl of Lincoln was patron, and there were 208 communicants. " Willis's MSS., f. 39."

1662, when the Act of Uniformity was passed, John Spademan, an M.A. of Magdalene College, Cambridge, then minister of the parish, as he is called, took the oath required of all the clergy of the church of England; but soon after relapsed, and resigned his benefice. He then settled at Rotterdam and became the pastor of an English congregation there, where he ministered to certain students and assisted their studies, but subsequently returned to England and became a co-pastor with another non-conformist minister, and died in 1708. The following is a list of the vicars as far as can now be ascertained :—

Date of Institution.

A.D.

.—William Gregge, died 1488.

.—Edward Hassell, living 1616.

.—Thomas Wallis.

.—John Spademan, ejected 1662.

1662.—Peter Saunders.

1663.——— Waring.

1681.—Joseph Holton.

1697.—Jonathan Whaley.

1702.—John Spriggs.

1729.—William Ducros.

1744.—John Stephen Mason.*

1777.—Samuel Mason.

1786.—James Pigott.†

---

* This vicar and his successor, Samuel Mason, lived at Spanby in a house now belonging to Sir Thomas Whichcote, Bart.

† Although vicar for many years, his name nowhere appears in the parish register, whence he was doubtless one of those non-resident incumbents with which this parish was so sorely afflicted formerly.

SWATON CHURCH.

Date of Institution.
   A.D. 1813.—John Shinglar.
       1828.—Thomas Darby.
       1841.—Henry Knapp.

THE CHURCH.

This is dedicated in honour of St. Michael, and is a remarkably beautiful cruciform fabric, all the features of which are most carefully executed. Here no doubt once stood a Norman church, of which an arch springer still remains incorporated in the easternmost arch of the present north aisle. During the Early English period the tower was re-built, which has a good vaulted roof within it, and subsequently, but within the same architectural period, the chancel. When the Decorated period was prevalent, the fine nave, aisles, north porch, and transepts were erected, or in the first half of the 14th century; and finally some additions were made to the fabric during the Perpendicular period. The tower is surmouuted by a Perpendicular upper stage, having a battlemented parapet and crocketed angle pinnacles; and at the south-eastern angle is an octangular turret staircase finished with a pyramidal cap. The character of the chancel, built of two kinds of stone, is pure and grave. It has three good lancet lights in each of its side walls, and the middle one on the north side is shortened to admit of the introduction of a semicircular-headed doorway below it. In the east wall is a beautifully moulded two-light window with a cusped circlet above. The Decorated work of the nave and transepts of this church is so exquisitely designed and elaborately moulded as to be comparable with the very best specimens of the same period, but most unfortunately much of this has been most barbarously treated. The west window of four lights, with its pile of reticulated work above, is especially beautiful. This is flanked by a smaller two-light window of the same character on either side, constituting the west windows of the aisles. From the elevation of this end of the church it will be seen that both nave and aisles are covered by one roof, after the manner of Lombardic churches; but this arrangement is in part concealed by the application of grand buttresses shoreing up the ends of the aisle arcades, besides others at the angles; and also by the returns of the battlemented aisle parapets. Attached to the south aisle is a fine porch having an excellent outline, and a well-moulded arch and doorway within it. West of this is a large beautiful window of three lights vigorously but delicately moulded, with reticulated tracery in its head, but unfortunately the corresponding window on the other side has lost all its tracery. In the side wall of the north aisle are two similar windows with a small door between them. Both aisles are surmounted by battlemented parapets. Each of the transepts had also a similar three-light window; but the southern one has now been most injurously deprived of its original tracery and filled in with mullions and transoms of a most debased character; besides which its gable has been lowered in a most miserable way.

The interior is lofty and spacious. The aisle arcades are uniform, and consist of three bays each, supported by fine clustered pillars. The nave was re-seated, and the interior well restored, partly in 1851, partly five years later, through the efforts of the present incumbent, the Rev. H. Knapp. At the west end of the north aisle stands the font upon two steps. This is an unusually beautiful specimen of the Decorated period. Its shaft is encircled by eight little pillars, and at the angles of the base of the bowl are ball flowers; each of its panels also is enriched by nine four-leaved flowers in high relief. Both transepts constituted chantry chapels. The southern one, dedicated to St. John, and formerly called the south choir, still retains its piscina and aumbry; and here is the entrance to the tower staircase, also a handsome old carved oak parish chest. It has a four-light window, and is the only one in this church having so many, except the western one. As a choir of the Virgin Mary in this church is alluded to by Holles, perhaps the north transept chapel was dedicated in her honour. Here is another and more ornamental piscina than the one in the opposite transept. It was found elsewhere, and inserted in its present position; but most probably belonged to this chapel originally.

On the wall space over and on each side of the chancel arch was a series of paintings representing scenes from the life of our Lord. These were divided from one another by borders ornamented with a trailing foliated pattern. Above were four subjects representing the closing events of Christ's sojourn on

earth, viz : " His mockery by the soldiers," " His blind folding,"
" His flagellation," and perhaps " His bearing the cross on the
way to Calvary," but this last was much mutilated. Below was
a large compartment coloured red and powdered with stars, and
on either side two more subjects, one above the other ; those on
the left representing the crucifixion and burial of Christ, those
on the right his resurrection, and probably his ascension ; but only
a small part of this last was left. The remains of the chancel
screen, originally a very handsome canopied one, now serve as a
screen in the south transept. Passing through the tower into
the chancel, in its south wall is a large arched recess, within
which are two piscinæ having shallow lobated bowls.

Holles observed in this church the armorial bearings of
Meschines, Earl of Lincoln, Warren, Lucy, Bohun, Beauchamp,
Ròs, Vere, Lacy, Holland, and Richard, Earl of Cornwall ; but
of these only three now remain on shields placed upside down in
the westernmost window of the north aisle, viz : those of Warren,
Vere, and Bohun. He also saw a tombstone in the chancel thus
inscribed :—

> Hic Jacet Dus Wills Gryge, quondam Vicarius istius
> ecclesie, qui obiit xiv° die Februar Ano Dni
> MCCCCLXXXVIII, cujus aie ppicietur Deus. Amen.

Also in the south transept the effigy of a man with his legs
crossed, said to have been intended for Arthur de Spanby. Both
these are now gone ; but the recumbent effigy of a lady of the
14th century, executed in stone, has since been found and is
placed near the font at the west end of the north aisle. She is
represented in the gown, veil, and wimple of her period, with
the hands, as usual, upraised in prayer.

WELBY.

THIS village lies 8 miles south west of Sleaford. Its name has been variously spelt Ulvesbi, Wellebi, Welleby, and Welbye, before it assumed its present shortened form of Welby.

Adestan, the Saxon, possessed the greater part of the lands here, and Queen Editha the rest. Subsequently Adestan's lands were given by the Conqueror to Wido de Credon, and he retained Editha's in his own hands as parcel of his manor of Great Ponton. Circa 1200-10 Robert de Rok was holding a knight's fee and-a-half here of the de Credon or Croun fee. Later in that century Petronilla de Vaux was the possessor of the fee, when the Abbot of de Valle Dei was holding 8 oxgangs and-a-half of her, the inmates of the Hospital at Lincoln, 5 oxgangs and-a-half, for which they paid scutage, also Hugo Selveyne and Thomas Rok.

Here was also another fee, viz : that of Clinton, of which Osbert de Ingandelby (Ingoldsby) and the Abbot of de Valle Dei each held the twenty-fifth part of a knight's fee in the 13th century. The remainder of Welby was then held in pure and perpetual alms of the socage of Grantham. "Testa de Nevill."

Circa 1323 Roger de Lunderthorpe (Londonthorpe) and Isabel his wife paid the King a fine for seizen of certain lands in Welby. "Pip. Rot., 17 E. 2."

In 1330 Lambert de Threckingham and Walter his brother did the same upon their acquisition of a rent of 22s. 2d., charged on lands in this vill, belonging to William de Welleby. In the same way Roger de Londonthorpe with Margaret his wife paid a fine to the King on their acquisition of a rent of 10s., charged on lands here and at Ancaster. "Pip. Rot., 4 E. 3."

In 1479, Thomas Scott, Bishop of Lincoln, and others, petitioned the King for a licence to give certain property here to the Dean and Chapter of Lincoln. "Inq. p. m., 19 E. 4."

In 1538 the Priory of St. Katharine had a house and 3 tofts here, then held by Alice Novill and Robert Brown on a lease of 31 years, at a rent of 20s. a year ; and also other land let to Thomas Watson.

In 1545 Charles Brandon, Duke of Suffolk, died, seized of the manor of Welby, and in 1613-14 John Longland, seized of a capital messuage and lands here, which he left to his son, Francis. "Harl MS., 4135." Francis Longland appears to have died soon after, for in 1618 Richard Longland, also termed son and heir of John Longland, paid 5s. for his relief for a capital messuage, some cottages, 100 acres of land, $4\frac{1}{2}$ of meadow, and 12 of ings in this vill, held of the King in chief. "Pip. Rot., 18 J. 1."

The manor and the whole of the land in this parish, excepting the glebe, now belongs to Sir Glynne Earle Welby Gregory, Bart., whose ancestors probably derived their name from that of this place.

ECCLESIASTICAL HISTORY.

A small sum was left by Robert White for the observance of his obit in Welby church for ever, arising from the rent of two tenements in the village, besides 22d. to be given yearly to the poor on the same day. The sum of 3s. 4d. was left by Edward Bust, or the annual rent of two cottages in Welby for the observance of his obit ; and also a similar small sum by another person for the same purpose, derived from two other cottages, then let to John Drewyre at 3s. 4d. a year.

In 1616 the living was valued·at £25, when the Prebendary of South Grantham was the patron, and the number of communicants was 57. "Willis's MS., f. 39."

The following is a list of the rectors :—

Date of Institution.

A.D. .—John Robinson, rector in 1616.

1661.—Lawrence Jones.

1663.—Thomas Lodington.

1691.—Samuel Forster.

1730.—Christopher Robinson.

1750.—Robert Cane.

1771.—Basil Cane.

1775.—William Dodwell.

GG

Date of Institution.

    A.D. 1833.—Charles Bethel Otley.
    1867.—William A. Frith.

THE CHURCH.

Originally this church, dedicated in honour of St. Bartholomew, was wholly of the Early English period, when it was of the same length as at present, but its nave was narrower. The greater portion of the present tower and chancel walls are still of that style ; and within, the western aisle respond demonstrates that it also had a north aisle like the present one. Perhaps the low upper stage of the tower, and certainly its lights and the spire above—now wanting a finial—are additions of the Decorated period. The aisle was re-built, and widened at a later time ; but the pitch of the preceding one may still be seen in the west wall of its successor, built apparently in the latter part of the 14th century. Whether there was ever a south aisle we cannot now tell ; but about the year 1500 the whole of the present south elevation of the nave was re-built as handsomely as the taste and skill of that time allowed of, yet in a coarse, showy manner, and has a peculiar look from having two ranges of lights and an unusually large porch in the centre, surmounted by large crocketed pinnacles, and an octangular turret at its west end, containing a newel staircase formerly leading to the rood-loft. The whole is finished with a richly worked parapet, having blank shields in its cusped panels, and crocketed pinnacles above little piers placed between each of the upper tier of windows. These are three-light windows, six in number on either side, and below on each side of the porch is a wide four-light window. In the south wall of the chancel are three little lancets having hood-moulds enriched with the dog-tooth ornament. These have of late been restored when a new corbel table was added above. The roof is tiled. At the east end is a small Decorated window inserted at too low a level in the old Early English wall. The present aisle overlaps the chancel so as to cover an originally external lancet window in the chancel wall, now constituting an internal one between the chancel and the eastern part of the aisle, serving as a vestry. Adjoining this window is a chantry chapel arch. The original aisle arcade, with the exception of its western respond before alluded to, is of a date circa 1500, and consists of four bays. In the eastern respond is a minute niche, intended to hold the preacher's hour-glass in days of old. The chancel arch is of the same date as the aisle arcade. In the north wall of this last are traces of what appears to have been a sepulchral arch. In the upper part of the nave walls are coarsely carved brackets, from which the timbers of a former roof formerly sprung ; the present one is quite flat, and very plain. The arch of the small doorway in the tower is remarkably ill-shaped. The rude old oak bench ends are still doing service. The chancel screen is of a good character, and clearly had a canopy, of which, however, no fragments now remain. The entrance to the rood loft once existing above this is at a remarkably high level. The font is a small octangular Perpendicular one. Some few fragments of old painted glass still remain intermixed with modern glass in the little east window, including a pretty little roundel with a lion's head in the middle.

In the churchyard is a curious stone tombstone of the 14th century, representing the upper part of a lady in a veil, cut in a deeply-recessed quatrefoil, with the hands upraised in prayer. Below, her feet are shown, and on one side an infant in a shroud is represented, perhaps indicating that its mother died in child-bed.

Holles observed in a window of the north aisle the device of a purse and the words "Nay je droit" within a circlet often repeated. Also a stone tombstone in the chancel bearing this epitaph :—

> De Billesfield natus Jacet hic Robert tumulatus, hujus et ecclesie quondam Rector fuit ille, qui obiit Vto. Kal mensis Martii Ano MCCCCLXVII.

" Church Notes, Harl. MS., 6829."

SCOT, or WATER WILLOUGHBY.

ACREAGE,
530.

POPULATION,
1861—19. 1871—23.

THIS is a very small village, lying 6 miles south of Sleaford. After the Conquest Leuric's manor here was given to Wido de Reeinbudcourt. This consisted of 3 carucates and 2 oxgangs of land, 30 acres of meadow, and 28 of coppice wood. It also had soke in Aunsby. Wido had 2 ploughs in demesne, 10 sokemen holding 10 oxgangs of land, and 3 bordars having 2½ carucates. Besides which the priest here had 37½ acres of land. The whole was worth £7 in King Edward's time, but subsequently only £4, and was taxed at 20s.

In the 13th century Christina Ledet held two parts of a knight's fee in Willoughby, of the King. She let this land to Michael Belet by the usual tenure of knight's service, and he sub-let it to Simon de Nevill and Peter de Cormory. "Testa de Nevill."

In 1309 Roger de Morteyne appeared at the manor house of Silk Willoughby, and owned that he held of John of Hougham the fourth part of a knight's fee in Scot Willoughby by homage. "Harl. MSS., 1756."

In 1388 died Thomas Tryvett, seized conjointly with his wife Elizabeth of a manor here. "Inq. p. m., 12 R. 2."

In 1458 died Nicholas Wymbish, seized conjointly with Thomas Wymbish, of Lincoln, Thomas Kirkgate, chaplain, John Eylston, of Lincoln, and William Beaufo, of Willoughby. They had purchased it of Robert Stevenot, clerk, in 1451, and it was valued at four marks. "Inq. p. m., 1 E. 4." Three years later died another Nicholas Wymbish, clerk, seized of this manor; and in 1478 Thomas Wymbish and others petitioned the King for a licence to give it in mortmain to the Prior of Nocton Park. "Inq. p. m., 18 E. 4." At a later period the family of Pelle possessed the manor and a residence here, of whom Sir Anthony Pelle, knight, of Dembleby, sold these to Sir John Brownlow in

the reign of James I., for £5506. The manor is still possessed
by the present representative of that family, the Earl Brownlow,
but a few mounds alone mark the site of the old hall.

Ecclesiastical History.

The priest's lands here, after the Conquest, were subject to
a customary rent of 16d. per annum due to Wido de Reeinbudcourt as lord of the manor. Various bequests were made to the
church of this place by unknown persons, viz : 8d. per annum,
derived from the rent of two selions of land in the plains of this
vill, for the support of a lamp always to be kept burning in the
church, and the rent of half-an-acre of land in the plains of
Dembleby for the same purpose. The following also were
benefactors to this church, viz : William Wynliff, who died 1415,
and bequeathed his body to be buried in the church of St.
Andrew in this place, to the fabric of which he left a bequest,
viz : to its campanile, or steeple, half-a-quarter of barley, to its
font half-a-quarter, to its crucifix and the lights of its sepulchre
half-a-quarter, the same to the fabric of the church of the blessed
Mary of Lincoln, to the altar 12d. and for tythes forgotten, two
quarters of barley to the parochial chaplain. To Robt. Vozon,
senr., three over mattresses, and to the son of the same one
common mattress. To the senr. Robt. three over mattresses and
half-a-quarter of barley. To Agnes, daughter of John Vozon,
two over mattresses. To Alice, daughter of Thomas Vozon, one
over mattress and half-a-bushel of barley. To Thomas Vozon
one bushel of barley. To Wm. Vozon half-a-quarter of barley.
To Wm., son of Robt. Norris, one sheep. To Matilda, wife of
Wm. Mergery, one buculam. To Thomas her son, one buculam
and half-a-quarter of barley. The residium to Joan, my wife,
to Wm. Mergery, John Mergery, John Vozon, and Richard
Duxworth, exors. Proved, May, 1416. "Repingdon's Registers."

John Bardney, who died 1416, and bequeathed his body to
be buried in the cemetery of the church of St. Andrew, left to
the high altar of this church six quarters of barley, and to the
steeple of the same church one bushel of barley ; to Adam
Bardney, his father, ten quarters of barley ; to Wm., his brother,
one quarter and one gown with the cape ; to Thomas, his
brother, one quarter of barley, some peas, his gown, best cape

and duplicate; to Margaret, his sister, six quarters of wheat and
some peas; to Joan, the sister of Agnes, the same; to Margaret,
the mistress of his household, one quarter of barley; to the
chaplain of the parish of Quarrington, 6d. The residue to
Thomas, his brother, and to his executors. "Repingdon's
Register, 156."

In Bishop Neale's time, 1616, the living was valued at
£13 6s. 8d., when Miles Whale was rector, John Townley,
patron, and there were 22 communicants. "Willis's MSS., f. 39."

The following is a list of the rectors :—

Date of Institution.

A.D. .—John Armstrong.
1668.—Richard Moore.
.————— Cuthbert.
1682.—James Seaton.
1691.—Anthony Barnes.
.—Richard Moore.
1716.—Genge Dickins.
.—John Dickins.
1720.—William Cawthorne.
1740.—Richard Palmer.
1805.—Honourable Henry Cust.
1861.—Octavius Pyke Halsted.

THE CHURCH.

This is dedicated in honour of St. Andrew, and although
small, is quite large enough for the few inhabitants of the parish.
It was re-built in 1826 with the materials of its predecessor, and
is covered by an ordinary slated roof. It consists of a small nave,
lit by a single Tudor window on each side, and of a consonant little
chancel, having a two-light window of an ordinary Early English
design at the east end. The whole is of a most unpretending
character, and in good repair. It still retains two relics of an
earlier period, viz: a bell, hanging in a bell-gable at the west
end, and a plain tub-shaped font, apparently of the 13th century.

SILK WILLOUGHBY.

ACREAGE,   POPULATION,
2450.   1861—237.   1871—258.

THIS village lies 2 miles south of Sleaford. Its name was
originally spelt Wilgebe, then Wilebi, Wylebi and Wilaby;
subsequently it was called North Willoughby to distinguish it
from Scot, or Water Willoughby; and lastly Silk Willoughby,
in reference to its hamlet of Silkby. This last was also called
North Willoughby, and formed a separate hamlet until 1337,
when it was still termed Silkby in a deed of that date; but before
1494 Willoughby and Silkby were conjoined; for in a deed of
presentation to the rectory of that year, this parish is termed
North Willoughby, alias Silk Willoughby; which is simply a
shortening of its more correct title, viz: Silkby cum Willoughby.
Silkby was that part of the parish lying eastward of the turnpike
road, but its boundaries are now unknown. Here, according to
Domesday Book, were 10 carucates of land, reckoned as 5 carucates for taxation, 29 sokemen and 1 bordar having 6 carucates,
140 acres of meadow, besides 24 other acres. After the Conquest
Archil was allowed to retain 2 carucates, rated at 1 carucate; but
the greater part of the land was given by the Conqueror to the
Bishop of Lincoln, whose vassal, Ralph, held 2 carucates under
him. He had also here 5 villans and 2 sokemen having 2 carucates and 30 acres of meadow. In King Edward's time it was
valued at 30s., and subsequently at 50s. Part of this vill was
within the soke of the Bishop of Durham's manor of Evedon,
and had belonged to Turvert, the Saxon. During the reign of
Henry III., Peter de Brus, the King's bailiff of the Wapentakes
of Aswardhurn and Flaxwell lived at Silk Willoughby, who was
a great oppressor. He purposely held his courts at Sleaford at
the most inconvenient times in order that he might fine persons
for non-attendance, and among his various acts of tyranny the
following are recorded :—He seized a horse from Walter, son of
Ralph, of Heckington, worth half-a-mark, and pined it to death

because the owner refused to redeem it by a fine of 2s. He
forcibly seized three quarters of malt worth 18s. from the
premises of Richard Asky, of Howell, and demanded a fine of
3s. 10½d. for its restitution, which, not being paid, the barley
was kept. He also seized a horse from the same person who
was forced to pay 9d. for its restitution, and kept a cow he had
seized of Ralph, of Howell. His servant, Robert, of Haydor,
took two young beasts from William Mackurness, of Ewerby,
and he only gave them up for a payment of a mark of silver.
He also interfered very much to his own profit when others were
dishonest; for hearing that a servant of Walter de Holgate, of
Asgarby, had sold one of his master's oxen to Robert, a servant
of John de Evedon, but had not delivered it, he seized the said
ox himself and kept it with its other spoils at Willoughby. At
length, however, when an inquisition was about to be held
respecting his nefarious doings, in 1275, he absconded, and was
heard of no more. " Dr. Oliver's MSS."

In the 13th century the Bishop's land here, constituting two
parts of a knight's fee, was held by Osbert Selvein, and subsequently by his son, Robert Selvein. Being a minor, 11 years
of age at the time of his father's death, he became a Royal ward,
when his property in this vill, arising from the profits of 2
carucates in demesne, a rent of the farm, and 200 sheep, was
valued at £11 and half-a-mark. Jouleyn de Evermewe received
the rents of the same for the King, together with 1 pound of
cumin, 1 pound of pepper, and 2 pennies; and Richard Brito and
Robert de Hardress took 111 skeps of corn, worth £9 17s. 0d.,
probably the rent in kind, from Willoughby to the Castle of
Lafford. Part of this vill lay within the soke of Gilbert de
Gant's manor of Folkingham, reckoned as the sixth part of a
knight's fee, and held circa 1200-10, by Thomas de Silkby.
Subsequently this was reckoned at half a knight's fee and the
eighth part of another, held by Robert de Wilgheby, when also
a quarter of a knight's fee held of Gilbert de Gant by William
de Dyve, and let by him to Theobande de Stikeswaulde. " Testa
de Nevill."

In 1185 the Templars possessed a small property here, consisting of 1 oxgang and a toft, the gift of one Alfred, let to
Richard, the mason, at a rent of 6s. and 4 hens; also a toft, the
gift of Robert de Wilhebi, let at a rent of 2s. and a present. In

1307 the fee of Gant here fell into the hands of Hugo de Bussey, upon the death of the last Gilbert de Gant, who died lord paramount thereof, 1305, and left it to his son, John. We next hear of the family of Armyn, Aremyn or Ermyn, in connection with Silk Willoughby. They were descended from a younger branch of the family of St. Laudo, and resided at Osgodby long after they had obtained lands at Silk Willoughby ; but upon the marriage of William Armyn with one of the Everinghams, they lived at Willoughby.

In the 14th century William Armyn, Bishop of Norwich and Chancellor of England, was the possessor of lands in North Willoughby and Silkby, over which the King gave him and his heirs the right of free warren in 1331. He was born at Aswarby, and first became Chaplain to the King, then Prebendary of York and Wells, Keeper of the Rolls, and Deputy to John, Bishop of Norwich. He took part with Queen Isabella against the unfortunate Edward II., and when the See of Norwich was vacant, through her influence he was promoted to it, by the Pope, in 1325. At this time he was with the Pope in Italy ; and on his return the King was so angry at what had occurred that he ordered him to be seized ; but after having remained concealed for a time, he received the Royal pardon and was admitted to his See, November 9th, 1326. The next year, when the Government had fallen into the hands of the Queen and Prince Edward, Bishop Armyn was made Chancellor of England and Treasurer. When near his end he gave £200 for the purchase of lands to support two chaplains, who were to say masses for his soul for ever. He died at Sheering, near London, March 27th, 1336, after an episcopate of 11 years, and was buried in the cathedral church of Norwich. William Armyn, his nephew, did homage to John de Bussey as lord paramount the following year for the fourth part of a knight's fee he held in Willoughby. " Harl. MS., 1758." He was succeeded by another William Armyn, living in 1402, and his descendants, of whom, William, son of Thomas, died 1498, and Margaret, his wife, in 1506. Another William in 1532, a third in 1557, seized of the manor and its appurtenances, held of the Crown, and lastly, Bartholomew Armyn, who, according to the parish register, was baptized in 1596, and died seized of the manor here and lands in Haceby, held by the service of half a knight's fee. " Rot. Cur. Ducat. Lanc."

The armorial bearings of the Armyns were : Erm : a saltire engrailed G. on a chief G. a lion passant, Or.

We must now return to the record of other possessors of lands in Silk Willoughby. In 1395 died John, Lord Beaumont, seized of half a knight's fee held by William Armyn, and an eighth part of a knight's fee held by John de Bussey. " Inq. p. m., 20 R. 2."

In 1409-10 the King granted to William Loven in fee the manors of Silk Willoughby and Dembleby by military service. " Pat. Rot., 11 H. 4."

In 1441 died Sir William Phelip, knight, husband of the Bardolf heiress, seized of the manor of Silk Willoughby; and in 1454, Anna, widow of Sir Reginald Cobham, knight.

In 1478, Henry, son of Henry Rochfort, of Boston, quit-claimed his manor here to John Stanlow, of the City of Lincoln, and Mayor in 1484. His son, William Stanlow, died seized of the manor of Silk Willoughby, held of Lord Beaumont, of Folkingham, 1496. By Dorothy Thimbleby, his wife, he had a son, John, who died seized of the manor of Stickford, held of the Duke of Suffolk, in 1554; and by Margaret, daughter of Augustine Porter, of Belton, left an only daughter and heir, Ellen, married to Thomas Darnell, of Thornholme.

The Stanlow armorial bearings were : Arg. a bend G. charged with 3 mullets of the same; a canton G. 2 mullets Arg. palewise.

In 1604 died Edward Thorold, seized of this manor, leaving a son and heir, Alexander.

In a small thatched house formerly standing here was inserted a late Perpendicular doorway, having an ogee crocketed arch ending in a foliated finial, and a pinnacle on either side. This probably came from Silkby chapel; above were inserted carved representations of the principal productions of a smith's forge, of a subsequent date. Here also was a small Tudor window head, made to serve in part as the frame of a panel; in which was placed a carved Tudor rose and subsequent rude additions, consisting of lion supporters, a dog and a snake.

The chapel of Silkby was situated about a quarter of a mile westward of the parish church, close to the northern side of the lane diverging from the turnpike road, nearly opposite to the rectory, and its site is marked on Speed's map, published in 1610.

It stood close to the old residence of the Stanlows, and long after its desecration retained its arched windows and usual ecclesiastical buttresses, &c., even when used as a stable and cowhouse, having a thatched roof. It has now totally disappeared, but some large stones used as a bridge at Broadwater were always called Silkby stones, and perhaps were relics of Silkby chapel.

In this village stands the base of a mediæval stone cross, together with a small portion of its shaft. On the sides of the former are carved the evangelical symbols. See accompanying cut.

The Earl of Dysart is now lord of this manor and owner of almost all the land.

ECCLESIASTICAL HISTORY.

Here was a church served by a priest when Domesday Book was compiled. Subsequently Gilbert de Gant possessed a fourth part of the church. On the 29th January, 1494, John Stanlow presented William Oldham, priest, to the church of this vill; which presentation was confirmed by John Willes, residentiary official, the See of Lincoln being then vacant. " Lansdown MS., f. 968."

In Bishop Neale's time, 1616, the living was valued at £40 a year, and there were 40 communicants. " Willis's MS., f. 39."

The following is a list of the rectors :—

Date of Institution.

A.D. 1271.—Philip de Wylerby.
1290.—Hugo de Wylerby.
1300.—Philip de Wylerby.
1308.—William de Spanby.
1323.—William de Colleby.
1333.—Robert de Tymparon.
1368.—Thomas Malbys.
1473.—Symon Stalworth.
1483.—Augustine, Abbot of Thame.
1494.—William Oldham.
1535.—Robert Cottinghame.
1562.—Ralph Syar.
1577.—Hugo Tuke.
1627.—Matthew Lawrence.
1647.—Lawrence Sarson.
1661.—John Leigh.
1682.—John Leigh.
1693.—William Wych.
1718.—Samuel Hutchinson.
1753.—Robert Carter.
1760.—Thomas Manners.
1813.—Joseph Jowett.
1856.—Jacob Montagu Mason.

THE CHURCH.

The distant effect of the tower and spire of this church, dedicated in honour of St. Dionysius, or Denis, is perfect, and

SILK WILLOUGHBY CHURCH.

continues to be nearly so when viewed more closely, and even critically examined. Their respective proportions are good, and they are admirably blended together. He who erected this tower, apparently about the middle of the 14th century, must assuredly have been a master of his art, and we can still perceive how boldly he could design, and how freely he could execute what he had conceived. Its belfry lights, shaded by a deep framing of moulded members placed in orderly succession, shine out from that setting in especial beauty, while the steep slope of their sills fully indicates the great solidity of the walls in which they are placed. From the high stilting of the little pillars worked in the jambs of these lights, their real bases at first sight appear to constitute bands, and the lengthy supports below a continuation of the pillar shafts. All the mouldings and numerous carved decorations that start with so much freedom from the tower masonry confirm us in our high opinion of that nameless architect's power. But perhaps he did not live to complete the work, for a great change is apparent in the character of its uppermost features, which must surely have been added by a far more feeble hand. The open parapet, for instance, is comparatively weak and poor, while the angle pinnacles, and the wretched little flying buttresses springing from them, seem to have been set up in child's play when compared with the masculine spirit of the work below. The spire, however, runs up in tapering graceful lines higher and higher, until they meet beneath an appropriate foliated finial that has been lately added as a crowning ornament to the whole. The level of the nave walls and that of the chancel roof, being identical, gives an unpleasing outline to the body of this church, and the extraordinary height of the present aisle walls is a serious defect. This arises from an ill-advised but not original arrangement of the roof which covers the aisles as well as the nave without a break, as at Swaton and Swarby. The windows in the south aisle are of the reticulated type, common in this district, but always pleasing. Within the porch is a remarkably good doorway, two of the mouldings of which are filled with the ball-flower ornament. The hood-moulding is terminated with heads of a Bishop and a King, the latter probably being intended to represent Edward III. Above this doorway is a little richly worked canopied niche for a statue, and on the right side of the porch a stoup. The chancel is wholly Perpendicular, of rather a poor character. The windows of the north aisle are also poor, and very inferior to those of the south aisle. Beneath the large weak central one was formerly a small late doorway, the arch of which was partly worked out of the window-sill above it. On each side of this are the displaced capitals of a Norman doorway built into the aisle wall, and constituting evidences of the former existence of a church here at a much earlier date than the present one.

On entering the nave, probably built about 1320-50, it will be observed that the foreign ambition of securing great height for the fabric was the leading object the architect had in view. Seldom are such lofty arcades found in churches of this size even in Lincolnshire, and should they be cleansed from their present coatings of paint and wash, and the warmth of colour that their natural material possesses be exhibited, they would indeed be most beautiful. At the east end of the north aisle has been a chapel, from the evidence of an aumbry there, and perhaps the little doorway, before spoken of as having existed beneath the central window of this aisle, opened into that chapel. Here is a sepulchral slab inserted in the pavement, having four roundels incised upon it ; two of these still contain the simple but appropriate words, " Jesu mercy." The bowl of the fine old Norman font is remarkably striking. The greater part of it is adorned with boldly-cut interlacing arcades formed of a cable pattern, as are the shafts of its coupled pillars with their cushion capitals ; within the small spaces between the intersections of the arches are carved varied and characteristic ornaments. About a third portion of the bowl is left plain, excepting three ornamental circlets, which were perhaps intended to suggest the idea of the three co-equal and co-eternal Persons of the Holy Trinity, in whose name christian baptism is administered. Almost all the old poppy-headed bench-ends of this church are still doing service in their original places, and are pleasing both as to design and the rich colour with which age has invested them. The pulpit is enriched with much of the shallow surface carving prevalent in the reign of James I. A light carved oak Decorated screen stands beneath the chancel arch. Above, the doorway of the rood-loft staircase shows at what a high level it was placed. The chancel, always very inferior indeed to the nave, now has an additionally weak appearance, owing to the inclination of its

FONT IN SILK WILLOUGHBY CHURCH,

LINCOLNSHIRE.

ABOUT two miles from Sleaford, near the centre of the county of Lincoln, is the respectable village of Silk Willoughby, through which passes the great road from London to Lincoln and Hull. The Church, like most others in this district, is remarkable for its beauty, especially the tower, which is terminated by an elegant stone spire, probably raised about the middle of the fourteenth century: the Church is a very fine specimen of the pointed style of architecture. The Font is of a much older date, and bears indubitable evidence, both in sculpture and character, of being the production of artists of no inconsiderable talents about the time of the Norman conquest. The form of the base is circular, composed of four receding plinths of masonry, the arrangement of which has been much disturbed by time and accident; the uppermost course serves as a fascia, sustaining the body of the Font; this is of a cylindrical form, in diameter about four feet, and in height three; it is surrounded by an arcade of interesting arches, supported by a colonnade of double pillars, ornamented with spiral lines or cable-laid carving, the whole crowned with an astragal. The baptistry is very large, which being a characteristic of all ancient fonts, seems to indicate that our forefathers considered immersion as the true form of baptism, and a necessary mode to be observed even in the admission of infants into the pale of the Christian church.

The annexed Print also represents a back view of one of the long seats with which the areas of village churches in this neighbourhood were formerly furnished.

walls, and still more so from its wretched roof. The windows are not unfavourable specimens of the period, although not so expansive as was then usual. There are three sedilia with divisional shafts and pillars, the capitals and finials of which have been cut away, and on the south side of the sacrarium is a piscina. In the east wall is a long, shallow, weak niche for a statue, which now looks doubly weak owing to its declension from the perpendicular.

In the east window of the chancel Holles observed the following bearings :—Paynell,—G., 2 chevrons Arg., impaling Everingham,—Arg., a fesse Az. a label of 5 G. Meres,—G., a fesse Az., between 3 waterbougets Erm. impaling Everingham. Armyn,—Erm., a saltire engrailed G., on a chief G. a lion passant Or. impaling Everingham. Stanlow,—Arg., 2 chevrons G. charged with 10 mullets Or, on a chief of the 2nd, 3 falcons volant of the 3rd impaling Bussey,—Arg., 3 bars Sa.

He also noticed the following sepulchral inscriptions on grave stones here :—

> Hic Jacet Willus Armyn, Junior, miles qui obiit xvi⁰ die Octobris Ano Dni MCCCCLXVIII, cujus animæ ppicietur Deus. Amen.

> Hic Jacet Thome Ermyn, filius et heres Willi Ermyn de Osgodby, qui obiit —— die ——— Ano Dni MCCCCXCVIII, cujus animæ ppicietur Deus. Amen.

> Hic Jacet Margaretta uxor Willi Ermyn de Osgodby Dni de North Willoughby, que obiit xx⁰ Septembris Ano Dni MDVI, cujus aiæ ppicietur Deus. Amen.

And Sa, 3 conie's heads erased Arg.

> Hic Jacet Willus Armyn Dnus de Osgodby, qui obiit xxiii⁰ die Septembris, Ano Dni MDXXXII, cujus animæ ppicietur Deus. Amen.

> Hic Jacet Johes Stanlow de Silkeby Arm, ac Dominus Ville, qui obiit xxvii⁰ Die Junii Ano Dni MCCCCIX.

> Hic Jacet Johanna, uxor Willi Stanlow, et quondam filia Johis Bussy Militis que obiit ———.

There are three bells ; the first is thus inscribed : " Jhs. be my speede " ; the second : " Behold and see the parson and wifes act of Willoughbe " ; the third : " Spedlie to God, John Norris made me, 1685."

PARISHES

BEYOND THE BOUNDARIES

OF THE

WAPENTAKES OF FLAXWELL AND ASWARDHURN.

———————•———————

ALTHOUGH Creasey's History of Sleaford and its neighbourhood did not include notices of all the parishes within the
Wapentakes of Flaxwell and Aswardhurn, it described some
lying *beyond* these, viz. :—Ancaster, in Loveden Wapentake ;
Billinghay, with its hamlets of Dogdike and Walcot, in Langoe
Wapentake ; and Folkingham and Threckingham, in Aveland
Wapentake. Hence it was desired that descriptions of these
should also appear in this volume, although such an arrangement is irregular ; but as the remaining portion of the present
volume can be readily detached from it, and used in the future
description of those parts of the county to which they of better
right belong, they are allowed to appear as a supplement in the
present volume.

ANCASTER.

ACREAGE,
2800.

POPULATION,
1861—682. 1871—646.

THIS very interesting village lies 6 miles west of Sleaford, in the Wapentake of Loveden, and on the western edge of the Ermine Street, the opposite one being in the parish of Wilsford. That great Roman road has been already described in the earlier part of this volume ; we have now therefore only to describe Roman Ancaster, or such remains of the Roman period as it still possesses, and that have from time to time been discovered on its site.

The terminal of the name of this place, being the Saxon form of the Latin *castrum*, at once proclaims it to have been a stronghold at a very early period, while from the character of the earthwork partly incorporated in the present village, and other vestiges of its ancient occupants, we are sure that these remains may be attributed to Roman labour, and that they were nearly connected with that great Roman road called the Ermine Street, or, more commonly, the High Dyke. Ancaster is, almost beyond doubt, the *Causennæ* of the Antonine Itinerary, situated at a convenient distance between *Durobrivæ* (Castor), and *Lindum*, or Lincoln, stated to be 30 miles distant from *Durobrivæ*, which is nearly correct, and 26 miles from *Lindum*, an error which may easily have arisen through the interpolation, of an extra Roman numeral by one of the transcribers of the Itinerary, whereby XVI. has been converted into XXVI., the real distance being 14 miles. Some, however, have thought that this was the Roman station of *Crococolana*, now usually assigned to Brough ; but Horsley and most modern archæologists have confidently come to the conclusion that Ancaster stands on the site of *Causennæ*, originally a military station on the Ermine Street, and around which a small Roman town subsequently sprang up.

It may deserve mention that Ancaster has been supposed by Mr. Hatcher, and some who have accepted the pseudo Itinerary

HH

ascribed to Richard of Cirencester, to be the *Causennæ, Corisennæ,* or *Isinnæ* of that compilation, (compare Iter III. and Iter XVII.) between Castor and Lincoln. Mr. Dyer, in his elaborate Commentary on the Itineraries, seems disposed to agree with those authors in regard to Ancaster, whilst he points out the discrepancy in the distances stated in the fictitious *itinera.* The spurious character of the above-named Itinerary has been so fully set forth by Mr. Mayor in his edition of the writings attributed to Richard of Cirencester, and recently issued in the Series of Chronicles, under direction of the Master of the Rolls, that it is needless to examine in detail the supposed occurrence of Ancaster in the deceptive *Diaphragmata.*

Besides its contiguity to the Ermine Street, this station possessed several advantages—such as a sheltered position removed from full exposure to the bleak wilds of the open heath around it, and its proximity to a spring, now called the Lady Well, on the south, and a streamlet of excellent water that never dries up, running along its northern boundary; besides which, access to it was supplied by a remarkable natural fosse or narrow valley, cloven as it were through the adjoining eminence on the south, by means of which troops could leave or enter the station privately. The station consisted of about nine acres of land, constituting a slightly irregular parallelogram, the eastern side of which is 520 ft. long, the western side 545, the northern and southern sides 445 ft.; the whole being surrounded by a fosse 50 ft. wide and 10 ft. deep. Parts of this fosse are still perfect, and the whole is easily traceable. Its character may be best seen towards the eastern end of its southern face, where it remains nearly as it was left by the Romans. Within was a wall defended probably at the angles by circular towers, the one at the north-western point still being represented by a well defined circular mound, whence we may presume that the other angles were similarly strengthened, as at Lincoln and Richborough. See the accompanying ground-plan.

No remnants, however, of the walls of this station now exist above ground, and at first we might conclude, from Leland, that he thought it never had been walled; but he subsequently says : "The area wher the Castelle stood is large, and the dikes of it appere, and in some places the foundation of the waulle;" whilst

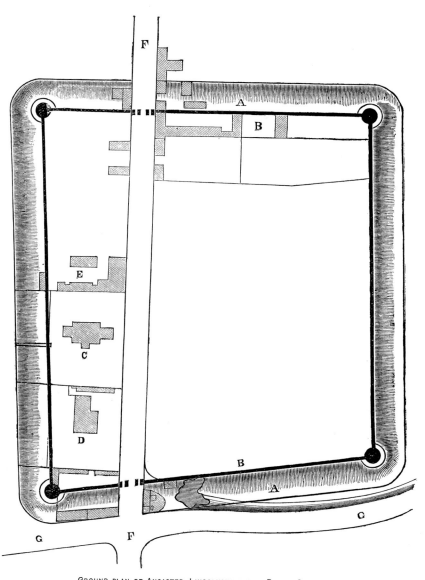

GROUND-PLAN OF ANCASTER, LINCOLNSHIRE, THE ROMAN CAUSENNÆ.

A. Foss of the Roman Station, width 60 ft., depth 10 ft. B. The site of the Roman Wall. C. Ancaster Church. D. The Parsonage. E. The Hall. F F. The Ermine Street, leading northwards towards Lincoln. G G. The Road from Grantham to Sleaford.

Stukeley says,*—"I suppose Ancaster to have been a very strong city intrenched and walled about, as may be seen very plainly for the most part by those that are the least versed in these searches." Since then considerable remains of the walls have been found from time to time below the surface, both on the north side in the bowling-ground attached to the Red Lion public-house, and on the west side, where the large stones of a very wide wall, running along the top of the fosse within the churchyard, and doubtless constituting the foundation of the Roman wall, were discovered in 1831.

The area thus enclosed is irregularly intersected by the Ermine Street, about three-fourths of the space sloping upward from it towards the east, now divided into one large and several small grass closes, the above-mentioned Red Lion Inn, and a few cottages standing next to its eastern boundary; the remainder consists of level ground, on which stand, as shown in the accompanying ground-plan, the vicarage, the churchyard, and a house belonging to the Calcraft family. Of the Roman town which subsequently grew up around the station, considerable remains have been from time to time disclosed. Its houses probably chiefly stood on either side of the Ermine Street, just as those of the modern village do now; beyond these there may have been detached villas of other colonists. The cemetery and its *ustrina*, or burning-place, stood about a hundred yards from the southern wall of the station, and on the eastern side of the Ermine Street. On approaching Ancaster, therefore, during the Roman dynasty, many sepulchral memorials were no doubt seen on either side of it; after the manner of that series of similar monuments which fringed the great *Via Appia* before it passed under one of the gates of Imperial Rome, or that between which visitors to Pompeii approached that once lovely town.

---

* Stukeley, Itin. Cur. V., p. 86. Horsley, Brit. Rom., p. 432, cites the notices of Ancaster given by Stukeley, and considers it to be the *Causennæ* of the Itinerary. He mentions that "some speak of mosaic pavements discovered there." Salmon, in his New Survey of England, vol. i. p. 247, alludes to the Roman defences of Ancaster, but places *Causennæ* at Brough Hill. Reynolds is of opinion that its position was at Boston. Iter. Brit., p. 261.

Here some skeletons have been found, and many cinerary vases of grey or dull red ware, the character of which indicates that the Saxons as well as the Romans made use of this cemetery. About forty of these vases, slightly ornamented with scored patterns, were disclosed a few years ago ; all of them were filled with burnt human bones, and had mostly been deposited in pairs, but without any lid or other covering. Unfortunately they had not been buried deep enough to ensure their preservation, so that most of them fell to pieces on exposure to the air ; but two fragments of triangular-shaped bone combs and a few Roman coins were found here, which had no doubt been deposited in some of these cinerary urns, and subsequently half of such a comb was found in a similar vase of grey ware, containing burnt bones, of which a cut is subjoined representing it in a restored condition.

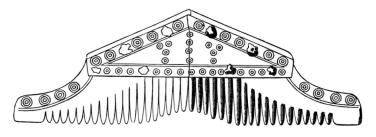

BONE COMB FOUND IN A SAXON CINERARY URN FROM THE CEMETERY NEAR ANCASTER.

In a field a little to the south-west of Ancaster, and called the Twelve-acre-close, a Roman stone coffin was found a few years ago, through the grating of a plough against its lid. It contained the skeleton of a male, but nothing else. It was deposited in a north and south direction. Although rudely formed, it still retains the marks of the oblique Roman tooling upon its surface. Its head is rounded, thus resembling some Roman coffins found at Bath, and it was covered by a slab 4 in. thick. In length it is 6 ft. 10 in. ; in width 2 ft. 2 in. at the head, diminishing to 1 ft. 10 in. ; in height 1 ft. 3 in. ; depth of the cavity 1 ft. $\frac{1}{2}$ in. ; thickness of the cover 5 in. This coffin is now in the churchyard at Ancaster. See cut on next page.

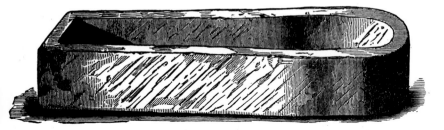

ROMAN COFFIN OF STONE FOUND NEAR ANCASTER.

Leland, in his Itinerary, commenced about 30 Henry VIII., 1538, gives the following particulars regarding the old town:— "Ancaster stondith on Wateling as in the High Way to Lincoln; it is now but a very pore strete having a smaule Chirch. But in tymes past it hath bene a celebrate Toune, but not waullid as far as I could perceive. The building of it lay in lenghth by South and North. In Southe ende of it be often founde in ploughing great square stones of old buildinges and Romane coynes of brasse and sylver. In the West end of it, were now meadowes be, are founde yn diching great vaultes. The area wher the Castelle stoode is large, and the Dikes of it appere, and in sum places the foundation of the Waulle. In the highest ground of the area is now an old Chapel dedicate to S. Marie, and there is an heremite."* And he relates local traditions of treasure trove near the station :—" An old man of Ancaster told me that by Ureby, or Roseby,† a plough man toke up a stone, and found another stone under it, wherein was a square hole having Romaine quoin in it. He told me also that a plough man toke up in the feldes of Harleston,‡ a 2 miles from Granteham, a stone under the wich was a potte of brasse, and an helmet of gold, sette with stones in it, the which was presentid to Catarine Princes Dowager. There were bedes of silver in the potte, and writings corruptid."§

---

* Leland Itin., vol. i. f. 30.

† Ewerby is about four miles east of Sleaford; Rauceby is on the north-east of that town, and about a mile from the Roman Way.

‡ Harlaxton, south of Grantham.

§ Leland Itin., *ut supra*, f. 31.

William Harrison, in his Description of England, written about 1579, and prefixed by Holinshed to his Chronicles, bears witness also respecting the remains of the Roman town at Ancaster, which then existed, and the coins there found.* "It seemeth that Ancaster hath beene a great thing, for manie square and colored pavements, vaults, and arches are yet found, and often laid open by such as dig and plow in the fields about the same. And amongst these, one Uresbie, or Rosebie, a plowman,† did ere up, not long since, a stone like a trough, covered with another stone, wherein was great foison of the aforesaid coins." Stukeley mentions that the Castle Close was full of foundations in his day, appearing everywhere above ground, the existence of which is still very plainly indicated during dry seasons by the parched appearance of the grass above them. Here prodigious quantities of Roman coins have been found, both formerly and in modern days. Stukeley observes that, for thirty years before his time, many people in the town had traded in the sale of these, procuring them chiefly from the Castle Close, and from a spot south of it towards Castle Pits; "but they are found, too, in great plenty," he adds, "upon all the hills round the town, so that one may well persuade one's self that glorious people sowed them in the earth like corn, as a certain harvest of their fame, and indubitable evidence of their presence at this place. After a shower of rain the schoolboys and shepherds look for them on the declivities, and never return empty."‡ These vestiges are still found, not quite so plentifully as of old, but occasionally in large hoards; in the year 1841, a mass weighing twenty-eight pounds was brought to light in digging a hole for a post, in front of Mr. Eaton's house, close to the edge of the Ermine Street. They chiefly consisted of small brass coins of the Emperors Gallienus, Postumus, Victorinus, Claudius Gothicus, Quintillus, the Tetrici, and Aurelianus. Two-thousand-and-fifty of these were sent to the Numismatic Society for inspection, and are noticed in its pro-

---

* Historical Description of England, Holinshed's Chronicles, edit. 1586, vol. i. p. 217 ; ch. 24. Of Antiquities found.

† Namely, a Rauceby labourer. This tale seems to have been copied, somewhat incorrectly, from Leland.

‡ Stukeley, Itin., Cur., Iter. V., p. 81. A view of Ancaster is given from a drawing by Stukeley, taken July 20th, 1724.

ceedings.* Very great must be the number of unrecorded coins discovered here, now dispersed, and never to be again recognized as having issued from the soil of Ancaster; a list, however, of such as have without doubt been found here is subjoined. This extends over more than three hundred years, viz. : from the time of the Emperor Claudius, who assumed the purple A.D. 41, to that of Valens, who died A.D. 378, and includes specimens of the Emperors and Empresses : Claudius, Otho, Vespasian, Domitian, Trajan, Antoninus, Faustina, Lucius Verus, Commodus, Severus, Julia Mæsa, Valerianus, Gallienus, Salonina, Postumus, Victorinus, Marius, Tetricus, sen., Tetricus, jun., Claudius Gothicus, Quintillus, Aurelianus, Probus, Maximainus, Constantius Primus, Helena, Theodora, Maxentius, Constantinus Magnus, Constans, Magnentius, and Valens.

The most interesting object found at Ancaster is one connected with the religious worship of its Roman occupants. Wherever the light of Christianity has been wanting, it is not surprising to find men in all ages believing in the existence of various gods, who could control events and the fortunes of men. Such was the belief of the Romans ; and many altars, dedicated by them to the Fates, and to Fortune, have been discovered in this country ; while others are inscribed in honour of Nymphs, as having especial influence over groves and springs ; and still more to the Genii or Spirits supposed to preside over particular spots, as well as over particular classes, and persons-- such as legions, cohorts, or the reigning emperor. Even these, however, were not sufficient to satisfy the religious feelings of a portion of the Roman legionaries, who, building upon the pleasing foundation of a mother's love and sympathy for the weak or wanting, conjured up the shadowy existence of certain protecting female deities, termed "Deæ Matres," whose office it was to watch over the interests of particular provinces of the empire in the first place, but also over particular spots, such as stations, houses, or fields. In vain shall we search for any allusion to these protecting Mothers in the works of classical authors, or for their representation in marble or stone, amongst the antiquities of Southern Italy, although they were certainly

---

* Numismatic Chronicle, vol. v. p. 157.

introduced into Britain by the Roman legionaries.* In France and Germany, however, under the term of "Matronæ," such representations are not rare. We may therefore conclude that the reverence paid to these deities arose from a Teutonic creed, to which the soldiers levied from these countries still fondly clung, after they had been removed by the will of Cæsar from their native lands, and that their worship may have been subsequently adopted by other troops. These Protecting Mothers are represented, on an altar found at Cologne, as three draped sedent figures, with flowing hair, and having baskets of fruit on their knees. Also, on a bas-relief found at Metz, dedicated to their honour by the "Street of Peace." They, in this instance, appear in a standing position, but holding fruit in their hands,† whilst in this country specimens of either sculptures or altars cut in their honour have been found in London, Lincoln, York, Durham, and at several points along the line of the great Roman Wall in the north, including one group seated on a triple *solium* at Minsteracres.‡ They were supposed to be benevolent dispensers of plenty ; and it is interesting to mark how some worshippers invoked the unknown Mothers of the new localities in which they were stationed, to be their peculiar guardians and benefactors, whilst others still trusted to their own original or "transmarine" Mothers, for protection, or good fortune, on a foreign soil.

---

* At Avigliano, between Susa and Turin, a remarkable sculpture has been recently found, representing five female figures, with a dedication to the *Matronæ.* No other example of such a deviation from the normal number of three *Deæ Matres* appears to have been noticed. See a communication from the Padre Garrucci to the Society of Antiquaries, and the note by Mr. Wylie on the worship of the *Matronæ*, Proceedings of the Soc. Ant., second series, vol. iv. pp. 287-293.

† L'Antiquité Expliquée, Supp. vol. i. p. 85. A singular sarcophagus with a sculpture of the *Deæ Matres*, exists in the Museum at Lyons, and has been figured by Mr. C. R. Smith, in his Coll. Ant., vol. v., p. 8. See also his detailed Remarks on these Mythic personages, Joun. Brit. Arch. Assoc., vol. ii. p. 239 ; Roman London, p. 33. A detailed essay on "Les Déesses-mères," by M. Granges, is given in the Bulletin Monumental, vol. xxi., 1856.

‡ The Roman Wall, by the Rev. J. Collingwood Bruce, LL.D., p. 403. See also his observations on this class of deities in the Lapidarium Septentrionale, p. 16, where a well preserved example, found at Newcastle-upon-Tyne, and now in the collection in the Castle there, is figured. The dedication in that instance is *Deabus Matribus tramarinis.*

In digging a grave at the south-eastern corner of Ancaster churchyard, in the year 1831, a very interesting specimen of the personification of the "Deæ Matres" was discovered, apparently occupying its original position. A large stone, about 6 ft. in length by 4 ft. in breadth, formed a base, upon which was a rough intermediate stone, and then the above-named figures, looking towards the south. The deities are seated on a "*sella longa*," united below, but having three separate circular backs above. Their hair reaches to their shoulders, and their dresses are carefully gathered up round their necks as well as their waists. The workmanship, though rude, is effective, and some pains have been bestowed in endeavouring to represent the various folds of the dresses, &c. One figure holds a flat basket or measure on her knee with her right hand ; the central one supports with both her hands a similar basket, filled with fruit, on her lap ; the third holds a smaller basket containing some doubtful object in her left hand, and a small patera in her right hand. The head of the central figure is wanting, and the others are rather mutilated. The group is 1 ft. 7 in. in length and 1 ft. 4 in. in height. See subjoined cut. Towards the southern end

GROUP OF DEÆ MATRES.

of the base in front of these deities, and upon a wrought stone, 15 in. square and 5 in. in depth, was placed a small pillar

1ft. 8in. in height, surmounted by a circular slab 9in. in diameter, forming a support for a diminutive incense altar, 1 ft. in height and 5 in. in width. In front is a plain panel; on one side are carved some of the sacrificial requisites, viz., a *capis* or jug, and a *patera ;* and, on the other, a hand grasping a ring—the emblem of eternity. On the top is a shallow cavity, or *foculus.* The mouldings have been considerably injured by the lapse of time, but their classical character may still be distinctly recognised. See subjoined cuts.

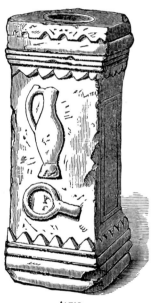

ALTAR.

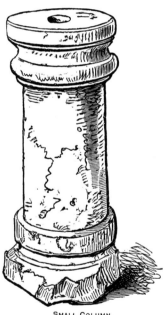

SMALL COLUMN.

Ancaster was so attractive in Stukeley's opinion that he, with the aid of Maurice Johnson, the first Secretary, and afterwards President of the Gentlemen's Society at Spalding, succeeded in forming a Society of Literati, which he proposed should meet there twice a year in the assize weeks. Johnson had suggested Sleaford as the place of assembly, but Stukeley, after a conference with the members of his own locality, wrote the following letter to Johnson, addressed to him at "the Widow's Coffee House," Devereux Court, Strand, and dated February 15th, 1728 :—" I told them of the scheme projected between you and me ; they approve of it much, but desire the place may be Ancaster, where we shall not be so much exposed to vulgar observation, and have as good accommodation. 'Tis not above five miles out of yr way, and all heath road, which is but an hour's ride, beside 'tis a Roman castle seated in the very bosom of the most delightful heath imaginable. I admire the place every time I see it. I shall meet you there on the Thursday of the assize week, by noon." Accordingly the first of these meetings was held at Ancaster, on the 14th of March, 1728, and from the MS. Minutes of the Spalding Society, vol. ii. p. 4, we learn that a paper by Stukeley was then read, "which was highly approved by the Society, being very ingenious, pertinent to the occasion, and much to the honor of this Society and that design." In it he endeavoured to prove that Lundenthorpe and not Trekingham (as the vulgar tradition will have it) was the scene of the famous battle between Algar, Earl of Holland, with his fen forces, and the Danes, which took place September 22nd, 870. Stukeley thus congratulated the society upon their assembling at so interesting a spot, saying,— " If we consider the place of our meeting, we are within the walls of an old Roman city, upon the most considerable of their roads in the Island of Britan, viz., the Hermen Street. Many are the Roman Emperors and innumerable the legions that have marched past the door in their journies northward to guard the Scottish frontiers, and we may truly be said to be on classic ground."

On a commanding eminence in the adjoining parish of Honington is a strongly entrenched earthwork, pronounced by Stukeley to be a " *castrum exploratorum* " of the Romans, but this must certainly be of British origin, as it in no respect resembles a Roman camp.* It consists of an area containing about an acre and a quarter of ground, of irregularly quadrangular form,

---

* A ground plan is given, in Camden's Britannia, edit. Gough, vol. ii. pl. lviii. See also Stukeley, Itin. Cur., Iter V. p. 81. In a letter from Stukeley to Roger Gale, Jan., 1727-8, he states that coins were found very frequently at Honington, and that he had recently received several. Bibl. Top. Brit., vol. iii., Reliqu. Galeanæ, p. 51.

surrounded by a triple vallum and a double fosse, occupying two more acres. The area, as shown in the section with the accompanying plan, is about 3 ft. 6 in. above the level of the surrounding field. The average height of the outer vallum is 3 ft., that of the other two 7 ft , but the level of the enclosed space is 3½ ft. above that of the bottom of each fosse. The width of the inner vallum is 19 ft. 4 in., of the middle one 27 ft. 4 in., of the outer one 15 ft. 4 in. As the slope of each vallum can be easily surmounted, perhaps there were no regular entrances to the central area, but there are slight depressions at four different points through the valla, which may or may not be of subsequent formation. The whole remains in a very perfect state, a portion only of the outer vallum having been partially cut away at two points.

This earthwork was undoubtedly occupied by the Romans, for in 1691 an urn containing a peck of Roman coins was discovered within its area, and subsequently two other urns were found full of coins, a score of which were presented to Stukeley in 1728. Amongst these he names a large brass of Agrippa, another of Julia the daughter of Augustus, and one of Magnentius. Fragments also of spears, bridles, and swords, had been ploughed up not long before his visit to the place in 1724.*

In June, 1865, a Roman kiln was brought to light at Ancaster, close to the eastern side of the Ermine Street, and a little to the north of the village, through the construction of a mill by Mr. Bruce Tomlinson.

In form the kiln was oval, 5 ft. long and 4 ft. 6 in. wide at the bottom, gradually increasing to 6 ft. by 5 ft. 6 in. at the top. The floor was composed of rude stone slabs, the sides were built of neatly cut stones 3 in. in thickness, each course being slightly set back as the work was carried up, so as to produce the desired increase of the size of the kiln above. The lower courses were in good preservation, and the stones resembled bricks, from their uniform bright red colour and general appearance, but on examination proved to be marl-stone profusely abounding with fossil shells, chiefly consisting of the *Rhynchonella tetraedra*, and a species of *Terebratula*. Such marl-stone containing a profusion of the same liassic *Brachiopoda* is found in the adjacent parish of

---

* Camden, Britannia, edit. Gough, vol. ii. p. 359.

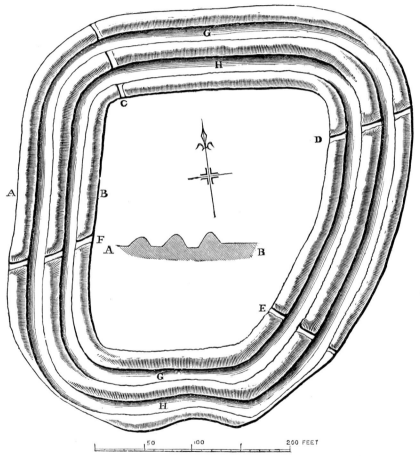

PLAN OF THE ENTRENCHMENT ON HONINGTON HEATH, LINCOLNSHIRE.

(From a Survey by Mr. Thomas Ogden, taken in 1854.)

A. B. Section of the Works on the west side.   C. D. E. F. Four Entrances, shown by depressions in the triple vallum.   G. The Outer fosse, width about 12 ft.   H. Inner fosse, average width 12 ft.   The area within the inner vallum is about 1¼ acre.

Barkstone, so that the Romans had not far to go for a supply of material suitable for this purpose. From their wonderful practical intelligence they appear to have used this compact crystalline rock for the construction of a kiln or oven, as being so well adapted for exposure to a continual high temperature. Portions of the same rock, in a half calcined state, have been found from time to time by the borders of the Roman road on the outskirts of Stamford, and its use seems to have been continued, as pieces of the same marl-stone or " red rock," as it is locally called, from the colour it has acquired through exposure to heat, are often found among the foundations and debris of the older buildings of Stamford.

The entrance to this very ancient kiln had been previously disturbed; but its site was filled with oolitic stones of the kind for which Ancaster is so noted. Some pieces were blackened and others partly reddened, through exposure to fire. Close to the kiln were found numerous specimens of Roman pottery of the usual pale red, grey, and cream-coloured wares. Among these were portions of gracefully shaped vases and pitchers, one of which has the three-lobed mouth and small handle often seen in the choicest examples of the Roman *capis*. Representations of three of these, presented to the author of this work by Captain Tomlinson, are given below. A few small coins were also found

ROMAN POTTERY FOUND NEAR ANCASTER.

II

intermingled with these relics, including one of Arcadius, several of Constantine the second, and others, but none of particular interest. A group of six or seven skeletons was also discovered deposited in a regular manner, but unaccompanied by any vases or other ancient relics.*

Passing northwards out of Ancaster, the Ermine Street is very conspicuous, both from its width and embankment, particularly at those spots where it surmounts the successive undulations of the heath before alluded to—now, however, universally invaded by the plough, and dwarf stone walls inclosing a succession of vast fields.

About a quarter of a mile north of Ancaster, and close to the western edge of the Ermine Street, was found a small milliary,† referred to at page 48. The base has evidently been broken off, otherwise the now uncertain appellation of the adjoining station might very possibly have been ascertained from this stone beyond all doubt; for thus the milliarium discovered near Leicester, and now preserved in the museum of that town, not only denotes that it was set up in the reign of Hadrian, but that it marked the second mile from *Ratæ*, or Leicester. A milliarium found at Castor also bears a similar dedication to the same emperor, which I here allude to for the purpose of dispelling any idea that might be formed of fixing the date of the formation of the *Via* itself from such slender evidence on its borders, although so intimately connected with it; as we might hence be led to suppose that the line at Castor was formed between the years 117 and 138, and that at Ancaster between 306 and 337. Doubtless these milestones were renewed from time to time by the official *Curatores Viarum*, either when the older ones had been injured by the lapse of time or by accident, and also when it was wished to pay a compliment either to a reigning or a passing emperor, in whose honour the new ones would of course be inscribed, although such would have no connection with the formation of the line.

---

* Twenty-second Report of the Architectural Society of the Diocese of Lincoln ; Associated Architectural Societies' Reports, 1865, vol. viii. part i. p. 11.

† This milliary was found near the spot where the Roman kiln and other relics have recently been brought to light, but on the other side of the ancient *Via*.

Among other small Roman articles found here, in 1861, was a beautiful little bronze fibula, shaped like a horse's foot, and illustrating, as it is believed, the manner in which the Romans shod their horses. See cuts below, representing both sides of this curious little relic, of the same size as the original.

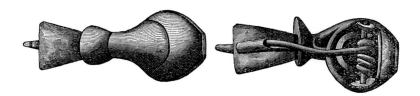

MEDIÆVAL HISTORY.

It is a remarkable fact that ancient as Ancaster is, no mention is made of it in Domesday Book, unless it is included in the record of Willoughby, now constituting a hamlet of Ancaster. Perhaps after its evacuation by the Romans their buildings were burnt down, according to the usual fate that befel them, and the place for a time was deserted. This seems to be confirmed by the omission of its name under any form in Domesday Book, and although Ancaster is now so very much larger than Willoughby or its other hamlet—Sudbroke—even in Queen Elizabeth's reign it contained only 9 families resident there, whilst Willoughby contained 8, and Sudbroke 7.

After the Conquest Robert de Vesci appears to have obtained a grant of the land in Ancaster, together with most of that in Willoughby. When Testa de Nevill was composed William de Vesci held half the fee of Ancaster. In 1185 the Templars possessed a small quantity of land here, which had been partly given them and partly acquired by exchange, and the Prior and Convent of Haverholme held the fourth part of a knight's fee of the honour of Eye. In the 14th century the Uffords, Earls of Suffolk, held the fee of the honour of Eye, of whom Robert the elder died in 1348, and Robert the younger in 1369. The De la Poles next succeeded to that earldom and to the possession of the above-mentioned honour; of whom Michael, the elder, was slain

at Harfleur, and Michael, the younger, at Agincourt, in 1415.
A William de la Pole also died in 1449. During the 14th century
the Bardolfs possessed half of Ancaster, which eventually
devolved upon two co-heiresses of that family, one of whom
married Sir William Clifford, who died in 1418, and the other,
Sir William Philip, who died in 1441.

The following notices are gathered from the Inquisitiones
post mortem. In 1406 died Stephen le Scrope, of Masham,
seized of 1 croft and 1 oxgang of land, described as being " in
the plains of Wildeforde and Ancaster; " also of the suit of court
of the honour of Eye. In 1454 died Ann, relict of Sir Reginald
Cobham, seized of half of the vill of Ancaster. In 1458 Hamon
Sutton, of Burton, was a landowner here, as we find that he conveyed certain property of his at Ancaster at that time, to Hugo
Tapton, clerk, Thomas Dymoke, and others. He died in 1467.
In 1593 died Henry, Earl of Derby, husband of Margaret, grand-
daughter and co-heiress of Charles Brandon, Duke of Suffolk,
seized of the manor of Ancaster. Subsequently Robert, Lord
Willoughby de Eresby, a lineal descendant of Katharine
Baroness Willoughby de Eresby, and her husband, Richard
Bertie, was created Duke of Ancaster and Kesteven. His title
was inherited by four of his descendants, but on the death of
Brownlow, the fifth Duke of Ancaster, without male heirs, that
title became extinct.

The parish was enclosed in 1773. The present principal
landed proprietors here are J. N. Calcraft, Esq., and Frederick
Allix, Esq.

Ancaster gives its name to the beautiful freestone, formerly
derived from this parish ; but the present Quarries are actually
situated for the most part in the adjacent parish of Wilsford.

ECCLESIASTICAL HISTORY.

Of the two churches spoken of as being in Willoughby in
Domesday Book, one probably stood in Ancaster, and was served
by one of the two priests, also mentioned in that record. At all
events a church existed in Ancaster when Testa de Nevill was
compiled, for it is recorded that this was given by William de
Vesci to Malton Priory, Yorkshire, before 1262 ; and the charter
conferring it, as contained in Dugdale's Monasticon, sets forth

ANCASTER CHURCH.

that the said William de Vesci so gave it, and all its belongings in pure and perpetual alms for the benefit of the souls of his father, mother, and ancestors, as well as for that of his own soul, by the counsel and advice of Robert, Bishop of Lincoln. On the higher part of the field opposite the east end of this church, in Wilsford parish, once stood a hermitage and the chapel of St. Mary. Formerly the vicarage house of Ancaster consisted of a small thatched tenement adjoining the churchyard on the south, in lieu of which a good modern house was erected by the late incumbent, the Rev. Z. Warren, in 1842.

The older registers of this parish are lost, and the list of its vicars is exceedingly poor, the following being all that are recorded:—

Date of Institution.

A.D.   .—Richard Carter, vicar in 1535.*
         .—Richard Gate, vicar in 1605.
         .—William Frazier, vicar in 1738.
         .—Wyat Traits, vicar in 1743.
1769.—Joseph Hall.
1814.—John Jowett.
1841.—Zachariah Shrapnell Warren.
1861.—John Primatt Maud.

THE CHURCH.

This is dedicated in honour of St. Martin, and is a very interesting structure. It consists of a tower and spire, nave, aisles, south porch and chancel. As in so many instances, when broach spires fell into disuse, there is an unpleasing disproportion between the tower and spire of this church. The former is a fair specimen of the Decorated period. The staircase is at the south-western angle of the tower, where the slight projections it occasions in the external stonework are supported by corbels worked into singular little figures.

The south aisle is Decorated, having one pointed and one segmentally arched window. The porch arch is Early English, as will be seen from its mouldings and the remains of the capitals

---

* In 1690 the living was sequestered, and the Rev. William Foster appointed curate.

below, although these are in a sadly mutilated condition. Probably this mischief was wrought when certain restorations took place in 1717, referred to with some pride by a churchwarden's inscription above. The head of the doorway within is formed by a plain bold trefoil. During the Perpendicular period, the clerestory with its coupled windows was superadded to the nave, and both it and the aisle-wall below were surmounted by embattled parapets enriched with cusped panels, blank shields, and pinnacles, which produce a rich general effect.

The nave gable carries an ingenious and not unpleasing combination of a cross and pinnacle.

The north aisle is plain. It was first Norman and then Early English, from the evidence of the little lancet window at the west end, and the remains of the north doorway, the tooth moulding of which may just be discerned on either side of the modern masonry within it; but subsequently its outer wall was heightened, a flat-headed Decorated window inserted in its north wall, and another very pretty one in its eastern end, within an archway that once opened into a chantry chapel attached to the chancel, of which the evidences still remain. At the junction point of this aisle and the chancel, the old entrance to the rood-loft may still be seen.

The carcase of the original Norman chancel and some of its features have survived many periods of reparation, such as its bold corbel table, the flat buttresses at the east end, and the outlines of the two semicircular-headed windows, originally inserted in its eastern wall. These last were destroyed when the present reticulated east window was inserted, apparently during the second quarter of the fourteenth century. On the south side of the chancel are two Decorated windows, and the usual doorway.

Within, by far the most attractive feature is the massive Norman north aisle arcade. This may have extended another bay westward before the present tower was built. The increasing richness of this arcade ornamentation, as it advances eastward, is remarkable. The first arch is quite plain, the second is boldly moulded, the third is covered with a checquered pattern, and the fourth is enriched with the characteristic zigzag.

Over the tower arch is a doorway, with a bracket below, originally intended for the use of the Sacristan, who could thence see when it was time to cease ringing the bell or bells.

The south aisle arcade of three bays, with its lofty arches supported on octangular pillars in combination with surrounding banded shaftlets, is Early English, as indicated by the character of its unmoulded and elongated pillar caps.

The chancel arch corresponds with the character and date of the southern arcade. Below it are portions of the chancel screen now forming parts of pews. On the south side of the altar is a plain recessed credence, and on the north two aumbries, one of which is of unusually large dimensions, and had two shelves within it.

The font is a beautiful circular one of the Transitional period; it is surrounded by an intersecting arcade of a Norman character, but the foliated capitals of the shafts supporting that arcade, and the nail-head moulding upon it indicate that a newer style was beginning to be introduced when this font was made.

The tower contains four bells, thus severally inscribed :—

1.—The date. 1607.
2.—My roaringe sounde doth warning give,
   That men can not heare always lyve.
3.—All men that heare my mournfull sound,
   Repent before you lye in the ground.   1602.
4.—I will sounde and resounde unto thy people, O Lord,
   with my sweet voice, to call them to thy word.   1602.

In this church Holles observed a raised tombstone with this legend, "Hic Jacet Johes de Willugby." Also in a north window, the effigy of a knight holding a shield charged with Arg, a bend Gu a border checky Or and Az.

There are several modern painted glass memorial windows in this church, presented by different members of the Allix family of Willoughby Hall, viz., the eastern one, by Wailes, representing the Crucifixion, Resurrection, and Ascension of our Lord, erected in memory of the late Charles Allix, Esq., and Mary his wife; a small one in the north wall of the chancel, having the four Evangelical symbols within circlets in its two lights, and the Holy Lamb above, by Dobbelaer, of Bruges; and a small lancet at the west end of the north aisle, having a figure of Religion below, and the subject of the Ascension above, within pointed ovals, by Wailes, commemorating Mary Catherine, wife of the late Colonel Allix.

In the churchyard there are two memorials of ecclesiastics. On both are cut the effigies of priests, one of whom is represented with his hands raised and joined in prayer, the other holding the sacramental chalice.   A mediæval stone coffin for an adult, and a diminutive one for a baby, are also preserved in this churchyard.

Attached to Ancaster are the hamlets of Willoughby and Sudbrook.   The first of these lies westward of Ancaster, and is sometimes called West Willoughby, to distinguish it from other places of the same name.   In Domesday book mention is made of it in conjunction with Frieston and Normanton and the manor of Caythorpe, then held by Robert de Vesci.   It is now the property of Frederick Allix, Esq.

Sudbrook was included in the fee of William de Vesci, of whom William de Burle held half a knight's fee in the reign of Henry III.   "Testa de Nevill, p. 323."   The greater part of the land in this hamlet now belongs to Frederick Allix, Esq.

BILLINGHAY.

Acreage,   Population,
3530.   1861—1403. 1871—1499.

THIS parish is situated 9 miles east of Sleaford. Its name
is spelt Belingei in Domesday book, Billingeie and Bilingeia in Testa de Nevill, and subsequently Belingey, Bellinggeye,
Bylinghay and other ways, but now Billinghay. Formerly it was
famous for its fisheries, from the great extent of fen and pools
within its boundaries, and the village in winter was not unfrequently surrounded by a dreary waste of waters. In this parish
the remains of a forest once covering the whole of its fen land
are frequently disinterred, consisting of innumerable roots and
sometimes the trunks of trees now blackened by age, but often
still quite sound. Here also several British dug-outs or canoes
formed of single logs have been discovered, a fine flint axe head,
the two bronze leaf-shaped swords described at p. 29 of this volume,
the vase Fig. 4, Plate I., and various other relics of the British,
Roman and Saxon period.

Before the Conquest, Sweyne, or Svein, had been the lord of
the land at Belingei and its fisheries; subsequently it was given
to the Archbishop of York, together with land in Walcot that had
also belonged to Sweyne, the whole being valued at £4 before the
Conquest, and £4 5s. afterwards. It consisted of 12 carucates of
land when Walchelin was the Archbishop's tenant or vassal, two
of Sweyne's sons had 2 carucates as his tenants, and 3 villans and
4 sokemen had 4 more carucates. There were also 16 acres of
meadow and the before-mentioned 3 fisheries. Circa 1185, the
Archbishop's lands in Billinghay and Walcot consisted of one
knight's fee, held by Peter de Bilingeia, who died that year,
having a son and heir—Peter, then 15 years of age. He gave
one toft here to the Templars, let to Clement the dean for 12d. a
year, and had paid £6 10s. 8d. as rent, for lands without the
demesne, which last, when supplied with 2 ploughs, and stocked
with beasts, sheep and pigs was valued at £11 0s. 8d. Hence

the Archbishop raised the rent of his lands to £16 after the death of the first Peter de Bilingeia.

Next we hear of this vill being in the hands of the king for 3 years and a half (probably during a vacancy of the See of York), when Ralph de Huntingdon was appointed receiver of the rents, &c., by Laurence, Archdeacon of Bedford, Roger Arundel, and William le Vavassur, the guardians of the Episcopal temporalities. The first year he received £15 16s., from a certain freeman, a pair of golden spurs, and a pound of pepper from another, and 6s. 8d. as arrears. The second year he received £18, besides the accustomed spurs and pepper, and the third nearly the same. During this period, 1179 to 1184, William Bassett, as Sheriff, received a fee of 70 shillings from the estate "de auxilio vicecomitis."

The widow of Peter de Bilingeia, through the death of her husband, became the king's ward, and was either the wife or mistress of William Talun, on which point certain jurors could not ascertain the truth. Next we hear of William, son of Peter de Bilingeia, as holder of his patrimonial fee in this vill and Walcot, of the feoffment of the Archbishop of York. "Testa de Nevill."

In the 13th century the Goushull family for a time succeeded that of Bilingeia or Billinghay here, of whom Egidius de Goushull obtained the right of warren in this parish 1258, and Ralf de Goushull in 1265 ; but in 1306 Walter de Billingeye died seized of the manor, leaving a son John, then only 4 years old, when enquiry was made whether the king could assign his wardship to any one he pleased without prejudice, and the report was in the affirmative. "Inq. ad. q. d. 34 E. I." The next year Philip de Chauncy—perhaps the custodian selected by the king, died seized of the manor. "Inq. p. m. 35 E. I." It was next held by Sir John de Meaux, who did homage for it to Archbishop Greenfield in 1307, and to Archbishop Melton in 1318. He was still in possession of it in 1331, when he obtained the right of free manor in Billinghay and Walcot from the king.

In 1307 we also first hear of the fee of de la Hay, or Haya, in this vill, when it belonged to William Earl of Salisbury, the inheritor of the de la Hays, who let it to Simon de Kyme. "Testa de Nevill." Philip de Kyme died seized of the manor here 1322. He, with Peter son of Henry de Billinghay, gave certain marsh lands in this parish to Kirkstead Priory, and Philip de Kyme 40 acres of marsh, for the good of his own soul and that of Hawise his wife.

In 1385 died Nicholas Monbouchier, Kt., seized of the manor of Billinghay and Walcot—"Inq. p. m. 8. R. 2."; and in 1417 Ralph, brother and heir of George Monbouchier, paid the king 10s. for his relief for the manor and its appurtenances in Walcot, &c. "Inq. p. m. 4. H. 5." One of his coheir daughters—Matilda, married John Kevermonde, and the other—Isabella, J hn Burgh, each of whom thus obtained half the manor of Billinghay, which they held of the king John Kevermonde died in 1435, and Isabella Burgh in 1451. "Inq p. m. 29, H. 6."

In 1544 George Welles purchased certain messuages, lands and tenements in Billinghay of Robert Dighton by the king's licence. He died 1588, and left a son and heir, Robert Welles, then 22 years old. In 1564 Henry Standish became lord of the manor, but soon after it passed into the hands of the Dymokes of South Kyme.

The parish was enclosed in 1777.

The following list of charities connected with Billinghay was formerly displayed within the church:—Alexander Bellamy gave £4. John Robinson, in 1621, £2. Henry Smith, senior, in 1660, £10. Nicholas Dickinson, in 1675, £2. Richard Marshall, in 1697, £5. Francis Robotham gave, in 1681, £5; the use of which to be distributed by the overseers, among the poor of Billinghay, at Christmas and Easter for ever.

The present principal landowners are, Samuel Wheat, Esq., Captain Willson, the Trustees of the Grantham School, and Miss Ladds; but there are also numerous small freeholders.

Ecclesiastical History.

The church here was given to Catley Priory by Peter de Bilingey in the reign of Stephen, and when the king's Commissioners visited Billinghay in 1535 it was valued at £13 14s. per annum. Subsequently it was held by Walter Aiscough, of Blyborough, of the queen in chief, who died seized of it July 4th, 1560. "Harl. MSS. 6829 and 756."

In 1616 the living was valued at £16 per annum. The patron was Sir Edward Dymoke, and there were 360 communicants. Earl Fitzwilliam is now the patron.

The parish registers commence with the date 1627, and the entries for some time are made in Latin. The following extract from an old parish book describes a perambulation of the parish boundaries, which was formerly a useful ceremony before the exact limits of each parish were distinctly defined by means of awards:—

"Sep. 30th, 1742. Rid the bounds of the parish, and did the same last year, about a month before this time, with most of the principal inhabitants who had rid it several times before.

"The dam is the bound of the manors of Billinghay and Walcott to the south-west. From the northward it abutts on the north-west side of the hedge and dike between Thorpe inclosure and Walcott common field, as far as the Slade bottom, where there is a boundary on the east side of the hedge. From thence to the fen gate there are several boundaries, some twenty yards east of the hedge between Thorpe and Walcott field, which we opened afresh, for they are holes dug in the ground and filled with coggles, and so in time would be grown up if they were not to be opened now and then. From the far end of Walcott field we crossed over Thorpe Tinleys to Tinley Wheel, which is the most remarkable boundary; from thence we went, in a straight road, past three posts to the bottom of the fen, the lowest of which posts stands on the west side of Whip Dike, and about two hundred yards east of the north-west corner of the Odds, and very near the Odds dike. The other two posts stand in a road from this to Tinley Wheel, in a low place in the fen called Whip Dike, to which place the Fenreeves and Dikereeves of Billinghay and Walcott have, time immemorial, and at this time, when the fen is not drowned, driven all trespassing stock to the common field of Billinghay, which if not owned are stray-marked and turned over to the lord of the manor of Billinghay. And the parishioners of Billinghay have, time immemorial, and do at this time, and every year when the fen is not drowned, go a processioning to the aforesaid bounds, without any let, hindrance, or molestation whatever, to my own knowledge for these five years last past, and according to the account of all the ancient inhabitants, the Dikereeves have not been disturbed for driving the stock, or the parishioners in their processioning to the aforesaid bounds time immemorial.

"ROBERT HEWITT, Vicar."

The following also are interesting entries in the parish books. "1746. One hundred and thirty-two persons had the small pox between May-day and Martinmas, of whom two only died." "1758. Wheat sold this Xmas at 24s. per quarter." In the beginning of 1747 an infectious and fatal distemper began to appear among the horned cattle of this parish in common with many other places. Of this cattle plague 700 beasts died immediately about the village of Billinghay, and 1500 altogether in the parish; a few escaped the infection, and about one in seven recovered from it. "This year (1748) the infectious distemper among the horned cattle quite ceased in this nation, for which God's holy name be praised."

A new vicarage was built here in 1827.

The following is a list of the vicars, as far as can now be ascertained:—

Date of Institution.

A.D. 1294.—Germanus de Brampton.
1324.—William de Wranby.
1329.—William de Hexham.
1342.—William de Bilingeye.
1349.—Richard de Gardiner of Burton Pedwardyne.
1349.—John Halden de Navenby.
1368.—William de Navenby.
1376.—Thomas de Wilington.
1383.—John de Botisford.
1401.—John de Cumberton.
1418.—Thomas Darley.
1422.—Thomas Brodding.
1448.—Thomas Welby.
1464.—John Rosby.
.—John Foster.
1497.—Thomas Wilkynson.
1507.—Thomas Lyster.
1535.—William Taylboys.
1545.—Thomas Smithmantle.
1577.—Ralph Palframan.
.—William Wood.
1666.—Francis Rowbotham.
1680.—Richard Kelham.
1683.—Crispus Glosse.

A.D. 1687.—Henry Blaxley.
1721.—Thomas Squire.
1760.—John Lancaster.
1785.—William Strong.
1832.—Edward C. F. Jenkins.

THE CHURCH.

This is dedicated in honour of St. Michael, and consists of a tower and spire, a nave, north and south aisles, south porch, and chancel. It is inferior in character to several of the neighbouring churches, but, in common with almost all others, possesses some features of interest. The earliest portion of the fabric is the lower part of the tower. Internally this is small, but the walls are unusually thick, giving a better effect to a little lancet window in its western face, through the increased depth of its splays. The arch between it and the nave consists of two members plainly chamfered, supported by keel-shaped piers springing from square bases. To this tower the present nave and its aisle arcades were subsequently added. Both of these are of four bays. The north aisle arcade is supported by three octangular shafted pillars and their responds. Its arches are ill formed and its mouldings rudely worked. The wall of this aisle, having become extremely dilapidated, was rebuilt in 1858, when a Perpendicular window at the west end was again made use of, and in a buttress near to this is a stone bearing the date 1668, marking the time of some other reparation of the fabric. The south arcade and aisle, of a good Decorated character, are in every respect very superior. The former has well moulded clustered and filleted shafts, rising from plain octangular bases, and its arches are far better formed and moulded than those of the opposite aisle. All its windows have segmental arched heads, and are well moulded. At one end is a three-light window, and at the other a four-light one. Attached to this aisle is a coeval porch, now in bad condition through the failure of its foundations, whence its walls incline outwards to the great detriment of its appearance. Its arch piers have filleted shafts, and some of its remaining features show what was its original character. Within is a plainly moulded doorway. West of this is a two-light window; east of it, first a narrow light, and then a window of three lights. The chancel is Decorated. In the south wall is a

BILLINGHAY CHURCH.

priests' doorway, west of this a two light window, and east of it first a narrow two light and then a three light window. The hood mould terminals of all these windows are of the conventional mask type inherited from the Early English period. In the east wall is a four light window the tracery of which has been restored. The base moulds and buttresses of the nave and chancel are good, but some of the latter require restoration. The sudden stopping of the plinth on the north side of the chancel, and the character of the wall westward of this, indicate that there has been some building attached to it, such as a chantry chapel or sacristy. During the Perpendicular period the clerestory was added. In each of its walls are four two-light windows, and three large grotesque gurgoyles, one on the south side representing a horse's head, bridled. Between these windows the ends of the tie beams protrude, which for their protection from the weather are now covered with lead. A plainly coped parapet surmounts the clerestory walls. Two large buttresses were applied diagonally to the western angles of the tower during the 14th century, and the upper part of the tower and the spire, superadded in 1787, are reported to have been built of stone brought from Metheringham Hall. This superstructure, from its date, is almost necessarily of a very poor character. Within, the old Perpendicular roof still remains. This is relieved by coarse but effective colouring and carved bosses, &c. On the south side of the chancel arch was the staircase to the rood loft, with a doorway above and below. Until lately a beautiful carved oak Perpendicular screen stood in front of the chancel arch, but only portions of this now remain in the tower. The font stands at the west end of the north aisle without a base. It is an octangular specimen of a late Decorated period, coarsely carved. There was clearly a chantry chapel at the east end of the south aisle from the evidence of a remaining piscina there. This consists of a lobed shallow basin having a boss in the middle, with little drain holes round it, within a little ogee arched niche. In the chancel, the sill of the window on the south side is lowered to serve as a sedile, and close to it was a piscina, now filled up. Nearly opposite is a small aumbry. On either side of the east window are small statue brackets.

Holles only observed one armorial bearing in this church when he visited it, viz., Or, 2 bars Gu, in chief 3 torteaux—for

Wake. This was no doubt in one of the windows. He also saw three slabs in the chancel, the first of which bore this inscription :

> Hic Jacet Johannes Foster, quondam Vicarius istius ecclesie, qui obiit xiv° die Maii Anno Domini MCCCCXCVII, cujus anima ppie Deus.

The second :—

> Hic Jacet Thomas Wilkinson, Rector............qui obiit obiit... ....MDVII.

The third :—

> Of your charity pray for the soul of Sir William Tupholme, parson of........ ......

Another slab, formerly in the south aisle, and now in the chancel, commemorated another incumbent, on which the words " Vicarius de Bylengay" still remain.

On a brass plate in a slab formerly in the nave was this inscription :—

> Here lyeth ye body of Mr. Francis Forster, who died Aug. 13, 1654, Ae 30.

This slab is probably the grey one now in the porch, but the bed only of the brass plate originally inserted in it now remains. On the north wall of the chancel are two small monuments commemorating a former vicar of Billinghay and his wife. The first bears this inscription :—

> To the memory of Robert Hewitt, Vicar of Billingay, who died May 13, 1760, in the 59th year of his age.

The second is thus inscribed :—

> To the memory of Mary ye wife of Robert Hewitt, Vicar, (and daughter of John Wilkinson, of South Kyme,) who died on the 14th day of October, 1746, in the 31 year of her age, and lyes below in the same grave with her four children (viz.) James, Mary, John and Robert, who died in their infancy.

Above is a shield, bearing Az a chevron engrailed Gu between 3 owls impaling Gu, a fess Vairy 3 unicorns Or.

The chalice of this church is of Elizabeth's reign, and rather larger than was then usual.

CATLEY PRIORY.

This House was founded by Peter de Bilingey, or Billinghay, in the reign of Stephen, for nuns and monks of the Order of St. Gilbert of Sempringham. It stood in the parish of Billinghay, and was dedicated to the Virgin Mary. The following is a translation of the charter of its foundation, long preserved in the Court of Exchequer, and inspected by Henry IV., in the 8th year of his reign.

"To all the faithful in Christ, Peter son of Henry de Bilingeya, health. Know that I have given, granted, and by this my present charter confirmed, to God and the blessed Mary, and the holy men of the order of Sempringham, and their brethren clerks and laics, in free pure and perpetual alms whatever I had, have, or shall henceforth by any right be able to leave, with the island called Cathely and in the marsh of Walecote as far as the old water course near the marsh of Diggeby, for them to dwell in that island, and there to serve God for ever, with all belonging to it, and all commodities, viz., with the wood and land, the plain, the meadows, the pastures, marshes, with the waters, fisheries, ditches, and all the like that had been made on the said island of Catheley; also the windmill on the said island, and the whole of the dam that has been made near the mill, all the drain or river banks on either side, with the whole course of the water upon the soil of my fee, viz., from the Mykelmore of Thorp on either side as far as Ulfbarne-Rouke towards Bilinghey, and with the whole of the fishery of the same mill dam within the said metes in pure alms; also with the conduit of water for all their necessary uses, in whatever part they please, as well outside of my fee as within it, according as they may think good at all times for their convenience and for the time of the year, without any impediment and claim either by myself or heirs for ever. I have also given them the site of the grange between Walcote and the marsh, with its enclosure and ditches, and with cultures of arable land, lying near the grange, one of which is called Southcroft, and the other Westcroft, with free inlet and outlet through my fee everywhere; also 2 carucates of land in the territory of Walecote, with 3 tofts in the same vill, and all their appurtenances, also the pasture in my marsh of Gubian for their animals of whatever kind they may be, to be there fed, and also the site of its vaccary (cow pasture) in the same pasture.

KK

" Besides also I have given to these nuns and their brethren one culture of arable land, called Calkecliffe in the territory of Coldecote, along with 3 other cultures of land and² 2 cultures of meadow in the same territory, one of which lies at Hallegarth-dyke, and one near Billingey Dyke : 2 cultures of this meadow lie in a certain spot below Walecote on the north part, which is called le Meire and a third is called Crocked and Turlany, abutting upon Bilingedyke, which Osbert, priest of Corby, formerly held to farm of my father.

" I have given also to them and to their brethren, the church of St. Andrew at Billingey to be taken and possessed for their own proper use, also 6 oxgangs of arable land in the territory of Billingey with all appurtenances, 2 tofts in the said vill, and the chapel of Walecote, without burden, because it is annexed to the same church ; also half a carucate of land in the plains of Billingey, and 2 oxgangs which Gerard held, with their tofts and other appurtenances. In like manner I have given and granted to the same fuel and covering sufficient for all their necessary uses, without let, in all the marshes and commons belonging to the vill of Billingey and Walecot, also a pasturage for 200 sheep in the territory of Walecot, and for 200 sheep in the territory of Billingey. All the aforesaid, with all their appurtenances and commodities within the vill and without everywhere in my fee, and free inlets and outlets, I have given and confirmed to them without retainment in free, pure and perpetual alms for the souls of my ancestors and heirs. And I and my heirs guarantee all the aforesaid to the said nuns and to their brethren clerks and laics, and will defend them against my lord the king and all my lords, and all men for ever. In the presence of these witnesses, Roger the dean of Scalby, Robert the clerk of Scorton, Henry de Marton, William Vaullger, Roger the clerk, and the whole parish of Bilynghay."

Peter de Bilinghay, son of the founder, confirmed the aforesaid donations to the sisters and brethren of Catley Priory, and superadded an acre of land in Billinghay situated on the eastern part of his barcary called Wych just outside the fosse. He did this for the health of his own soul and the souls of his wife, father and heirs, in the presence of William son of Ralf de Ledenham, Adam Blundus, of Lincoln, and John his brother, John son of Hugh Flamang, Wygot the vintner, John Rufus,

Thomas the chaplain, Godfrid the priest, William son of Thomas of Digby, Henry the provost, Ralf de Fantenei, Roger de Sempringham, Roger the clerk, Roger the priors' boy, Galfrid of the hospice, Thomas son of William de Paris, Fulk the son of Maurice, Robert provost of Bilyngey, and other men of the vill. Cheshunt Nunnery, Herts, was originally dependent on Catley Priory, but this was disassociated from it and given to Benedictine nuns by Henry III. Catley Priory ranked high among the Gilbertine houses in Lincolnshire, being inferior only to those of Sempringham and Haverholm. The number of its inmates was limited to 85 monks and 60 nuns. It possessed the remains of St. Bega, and was gradually enriched with gifts of other lands and property, which are thus enumerated in an abstract Roll of the Priory, 30 Henry VIII., taken after its dissolution, and now preserved in the Augmentation Office.

	£	s.	d.
Billinghay, Timberland, &c., Rents fixed and at will in	17	18	9
Walcote, farm of cottage in	0	4	0
Timberland and Dygbye, farm of lands in	0	1	10
Kyrkby, farm of a meadow in	0	3	4
Saltby, farm of toft and lands at	0	3	4
Byllinghay, farm de les Dales	0	8	0
Waltersdyke, &c., farm of tenements	1	2	8
Walcott, farm of toft lands, &c.	0	5	0
Engilby, farm of toft lands, &c.	0	8	0
Saxilby, farm of toft and lands at	0	10	0
Lincoln, farm of a garden in	0	1	8
Scoppyc, farm of a grange in	1	2	0
Scawpwyk, farm of a messuage and lands at	1	13	4
Rowston, farm of lands at	0	7	0
Dygby, farm of a mill	1	10	0
Catley, farm of demesne lands at	4	0	0
Byllinghay, farm of rectory of	5	0	0
Dygby, farm of rectory of	4	0	0

At the suppression its gross income was £38 13s. 8d., or £33 18s. 6d. clear, and an impression of its seal is attached to the deed of surrender, dated 25 Sep. 30 H. 8., or 1538, which is now in the Augmentation Office. Its device is a figure of the Virgin and Child with a kneeling monk below; the legend is s. PRIORATVS

DE CATTELE.   William Swyfte, the last Prior, and several of the brothers received pensions, also at least one nun, of whom in 1553, one Swyth received £6 a year, Thomas Weste £2 13s. 4d., Christopher Huddesonne £2, and Margaret Boswell £2 13s. 4d. "Brown Willis's Abbeys, vol. 2. p. 117." In 1539 the king granted to Robert Carre, of Sleaford, the demesnes of the Priory, the church, certain messuages and 72 acres of land in Walcot field, lands lying in Billinghay, Walcot, Thorpe, North Kyme, Dorrington, Rowston, and Digby, Catley wood and Catley mill, together with the watercourse supplying and belonging to the same, the pastures and the premises belonging to the Priory, to be held of the king in capite.   "Harl. MS. 6829."

The Priory buildings covered a large space of ground, and stood in a pasture containing about 40 acres surrounded by fen, conveniently supplied with water by a little brook.   Not a stone of its walls now remains above ground, but in 1775, when the foundations of some of these were taken up to build a cottage within its area, the pavement of the church was discovered about 6 feet below the present surface together with remains of its aisle arcades and several monumental slabs.   One of these had a richly foliated cross incised upon it, and a border legend.   It was for some time left exposed on the spot where it was found, but eventually served as a hearthstone in the kitchen of a neighbouring house.   Fragments of painted glass were also found on its site at the same time.

DOGDIKE.

THE name of this hamlet attached to Billinghay, formerly spelt Dokedyke and Dockdike, lies by the Witham, and adjoins Chapel Hill. It seems always to have followed the fortunes of Billinghay, and thus in olden days belonged to the Kymes, Umfravilles, and Tailbois. Either in the reign of Henry II. or Richard I. Philip son of Simon de Kyme gave the nuns of Bolyngton licence to fish in his waters at Dogdike between Winstanton and Bradware. They were allowed by this grant to employ 4 fishermen with 2 "battells" (small boats) and 2 "hamalls" (nets) for two days in the year; one when they were going to attend the great Chapter at Sempringham, and the other when they passed the said waters on their return.

There was formerly a chapel here dedicated to St. Nicholas, of which mention is made in 1310, when Gilbert de Umfraville, Earl of Angus, made over his manor of Great Stretton to Richard de Ravenser, Archdeacon of Lincoln, first for the purpose of celebrating his obit in Lincoln Cathedral, and then, among other things, of providing a priest to perform divine service in the chapel of St. Nicholas at Dogdike for the health of king Richard II., his own, and that of Matilda his wife while living; and for their souls, those of Edward III., queen Philippa, queen Isabella, and all deceased believers. This priest was to be paid 10 marks a year for his services, and nominated by the lords of Kyme; but should any of these neglect to do so within 15 days of a vacancy the then Archdeacon of Lincoln was to nominate another priest to this chaplaincy. At the suppression, William Saunderson was chaplain, then 60 years of age, and had no other cure.

The following were the sources of the endowment of the
chapel at Dogdike :—   £   s.   d.

The firm of the mansional house there with appurtenances, one barn, 2 enclosures containing 20 acres of fenne grounde, 2 little
enclosures called the Osier Garthes, in the
tenure of the said William Saunderson, at
will   5   0   0

Ten acres of land in Immingham in the tenure of
Thomas Myssonden, Esqre., at will for an
annual rent of   1   6   8

One toft in Soteby with 10 acres of meadow and
pasture in Sotebye aforesaid, in the separate
tenure of Richard Rigleton and John Fawt,
at will   1   5   4

A certain annual rent of £6 13s. 4d. from the demesnes of Sturton, Co. Lincoln, parcel of the
possessions of Lord Tailbois 6 13   4

To this is annexed the following memorandum :—" The inhabitants situated nighe and about the said chauntrie have used tyme
out of mynd as a parish church, and been wont to here the service
within the chapell of the same chauntrie, and to have their
children christened there. And that the same waye from the
said towne of Dokdyk unto the church which is their parish
church, is so overflowed and drowned with water in the winter
season that the inhabitants of the saide town of Dockdike, being
60 houseling people, cannot passe to their said parish church
without great danger. And that there is no other possession
within the said Towne of Dockdyke that belonge to the said
chauntrie, saving only the said chapel, being one covered with
thack and tyle, which were convenient to be reserved for the
causes aforesaid."

This chantry chapel was still standing when Holles made
his Church Notes, for he noticed the following inscription upon
a stone within it, viz. :—

> Of yr charity pray for the sawle of Sr William Tup-
> holme, Parson of Waydingham, and Chantry Priest of
> Dockdike, wch departed this life ye 7th day of January,
> 1530.

In 1565 there were 53 families residing at Dogdike.

WALCOT.

THIS second hamlet of Billinghay is situated two miles north of that village. Part of it is fen, from which large trees that have long been submerged are occasionally dug up lying from one to four feet below the surface. One of these, raised in 1811, contained nearly three hundred feet of timber, and under another a little to the south of this was found an axe. On the edge of the higher ground of this hamlet were formerly several tumuli, probably marking the graves of British chiefs, but these have now all been levelled. Originally Walcot belonged to Sweyne the Saxon, and was termed his Inland or demesne land. After the Conquest it was given to the Archbishop of York, and consisted of 8 carucates of land sufficient for 6 ploughs, 15 sokemen and one villan and 50 acres of meadow. Here also Walter de Aincourt had 4 carucates of land, sufficient for the same number of ploughs, and 7 sokemen, belonging to his manor of Branston.

Circa 1270 the fee of the Archbishop of York in Billinghay and Walcot consisted of 20 carucates. In 1295 died Ralf de Goushull seized of lands in Walcot. "Inq. p. m. 23. E. 1." In 1314 died Philip le Despenser, seized conjointly with Margaret de Goushull his wife of certain lands and tenements in this vill. "Inq. p. m. 7. E. 2." His widow then married a de Roos, and died 1350. "Inq. p. m. 23. E. 3." The same year also died her son—Philip le Despenser by her first husband. In 1451 died Isabella Burgh, one of the co-heiresses of Monboucher, seized of the manor ("Inq. p. m. 29. H. 6."); and in 1556 died Thomas Thornbeck seized of lands and tenements in Billinghay and Walcot ("Harl. MS. 758."), leaving two co-heir daughters, Margaret and Elizabeth. In the time of Elizabeth there were 40 families here, and 17 at Waterside. About the middle of the last century Richard Smith, Esq., was the owner of Walcot, who sold it to the then Earl Fitzwilliam, and he to Anthony Peacock, of South Kyme, in 1787. The present principal proprietor is J. Wheat, Esq. The hamlet was enclosed in 1779. Part of this hamlet, from its situation on the bank of the Witham, has long been called Waterside, to which reference has already been made. There are several farm houses and cottages distant nearly three miles from the village of Walcot. Previous to the enclosure of this hamlet its lowland portion was often covered with water during the greater part of the year, and abounded with ducks, coots and other water fowl, as well as with fish, affording maintenance to many families, who also derived profit from its reeds; but the value of the land now reclaimed from its natural wild condition has been greatly increased by that process.

At an early period there was a chapel at Walcot dedicated to St. Oswald, which was given by king John to Spalding Abbey. It was situated in the middle of the village, and consisted of a nave and chancel with a bell-cot for two bells at the west end, and had a carved oak chancel screen and oak seats. It was annexed to the church at Walcot; but having been disused after the death of the Rev. John Lancaster in 1784, was pulled down, and its bells sold about the year 1790. This was a most improper proceeding, and the more so as in the present century the need of a church or chapel here gradually became more pressing through the increase of the inhabitants of Walcot, and the more conscientious feelings of both minister and people, until, through the zealous exertions of the present vicar of Billinghay, the Rev. Edward Jenkins, a new church was erected at Walcot in 1852. This is a neat unpretending structure, built of white brick, and capable of accommodating 250 persons.

FOLKINGHAM.

ACREAGE,
1861.

POPULATION,
1861—650. 1871—696.

FOLKINGHAM is a small market town in the Hundred of Aveland, lying 9 miles south of Sleaford, and the same distance north of Bourn.

Its name is spelt Folchingeham in Domesday book, and Fokingham by Leland, whence Folkingham seems to be the more correct way of spelling it than Falkingham, which is now ordinarily adopted.

Ulf was its Saxon lord before the Conquest, who had 12 carucates of land here, valued at the unusually large sum of £50. It was given by the Conqueror to Gilbert de Gant, together with its appurtenances in Laughton, Lenton, Pickworth, Haceby, Dembleby, Threckingham, Stow, Walcot, Billingborough, Birthorpe, Aslackby, Ingoldsby, Scredington, Burton Pedwardine, Helpringham, Osbournby, Aswarby, Silk Willoughby, Aisby, Kirkby Laythorpe, Little Ponton, Honington, Hough, and Cranwell. When Domesday book was compiled Gilbert held in demesne 5 carucates here, and had 24 villans, 5 sokemen aud 9 bordars having 7 carucates. He also possessed the church of Folkingham, a mill, worth 10s. 8d. a year, 100 acres of meadow, and 80 of underwood. The whole was valued at £40 a year, and assessed at £50 a year.

Gilbert de Gant, the son of Baldwin, Earl of Flanders, and nephew to Queen Matilda, accompanied the Conqueror in his expedition against England in 1066, and was amply rewarded for his services, by the grant of one lordship in Berkshire, two in Oxfordshire, three in Yorkshire, six in Cambridgeshire, two in Bucks, one in Hunts, five in Northamptonshire, one in Rutland, one in Leicestershire, one in Warwickshire, eighteen in Nottinghamshire, and a hundred and thirty in Lincolnshire, constituting a barony of which Folkingham was the chief.

This Gilbert was at York in the year 1069, when it was destroyed by the Danes, being one of the few Normans who escaped their fury. He died in the time of William Rufus, and was buried at Bardney Abbey, which he had restored after its destruction by Inguar and Hubba. He was succeeded by Walter, his son and heir, who, when very aged, had a command in that famous battle against the Scots at Northallerton (commonly called the battle of the Standard), when, by his eloquent speech and prudent conduct, the English army was so encouraged, that the Scots were utterly defeated. This Walter founded the Priory of Bridlington, in Yorkshire, and added to the buildings and revenues of the Abbey of Bardney. He died in the fourth year of Stephen's reign, leaving issue Gilbert, Robert, and Geofrey. Gilbert, his heir, was with King Stephen at the famous battle of Lincoln, in 1142, and there taken prisoner when quite a youth by Ranulf, Earl of Chester, who compelled him to marry Roheis, his niece, daughter and heir of William de Roumara, Earl of Lincoln, whereby in her right he afterwards acquired the title of Earl of Lincoln. He founded the Abbey of Rufford in Nottinghamshire, A.D. 1148, to which, as well as to several other religious houses, he was a great benefactor, and dying in the year 1156, was buried in the Priory of Bridlington, where he had been baptized and brought up, leaving two daughters, Alice the wife of Simon de St. Lis, Earl of Huntingdon and Northampton, and Gunnora. But neither of them having any issue, their inheritance reverted to their uncle Robert de Gant. He in the fourteenth of Henry II., paid £11 6s. 8d. towards the cost entailed by the marriage of the King's daughter; and died in the third or fourth year of Richard I., leaving by his first wife, Alice daughter and heir of William Pagenel, an heiress daughter, who married Robert, son of Robert Fitz Harding, by whom she had a son, Maurice de Gant, who died childless 14 Edward III., when his lands were inherited by Gilbert de Gant, son of the last named Robert by his second wife, Gunnora, the niece of Hugh de Guornay.

This Gilbert, surnamed the Good, possessed sixty-eight knight's fees, when the levying of the scutage of Scotland took place in his time. He died 1242.

His son, Gilbert, succeeded, who payed £100 for his relief, had livery of the lands which he held of the King in capite; and

38 Henry III., paid £137 1s. 4d. for sixty-eight knight's fees, towards the aid for making the King's eldest son a knight. By an inquisition taken in the latter part of the above reign, it appears that this " Gilbert de Gant then held in Folkingham twelve carucates of land. except four bovates, belonging to the Prior of Sempringham and the Abbot of Bardney, and that it was then a capital barony manor in the county of Lincoln." "Testa de Nevill, p. 321." He died at Folkingham in the year 1274, and was buried in the Priory of Bridlington, leaving issue Gilbert (another son, Robert, having died before himself), and three daughters, viz., Margaret, wife of William de Kerdeston ; Nichola, wife of Peter de Mauley; and Julian, who died unmarried. He was commonly called Gilbert the Fifth, and married Lora, sister of Alexander de Baliol ; but having no issue, constituted King Edward I. his heir. He died 1298, when Roger, son of William de Kerdeston, then twenty-four years of age, and Juliana de Gant, sister to the said Gilbert, then forty years of age, were found to be his heirs.

The manor of Folkingham appears to have remained in the King's hands until the first of Edward II., when Henry de Beaumont, in consideration of the great services he had rendered to his father, Edward I., obtained a grant in fee, of the manors of Folkingham, Edenham, Barton-upon-Humber, and all the knight's fees belonging to Gilbert de Gant, which Lora his widow held in dower. During the reign of Edward III. he had many honours conferred upon him ; and was summoned to Parliament as a baron from the second of Edward II. to the sixth of Edward III., and from that time to the fourteenth of the same reign as Earl of Boghan, when he died.

John, his son and heir, succeeded him, who, on his father's death, had livery of his lands, but never used the title of Earl of Boghan, and died soon after, viz., 16 Edward III.

Henry, his only son, succeeded, who was born in Brabant 14 Edward III., and whose legitimacy was ratified in Parliament the 15 of the same reign. He did homage for his lands nine years later, and was summoned to Parliament from the 36 to the 42 Edward III., the year before his death.

His son John, when only eight years old, next became lord of the manor of Folkingham ; who, after making proof of his age, and doing homage, had livery of his inheritance 6 Richard II.

He was summoned to Parliament from 6 to 17 Richard II., and died full of honour three years later.

His son Henry, then only 16 years old, was made a knight at the coronation of Henry IV., and had an allowance of robes for that ceremony. He died 1 Henry V., having had summons to Parliament from 5 to 14 Henry IV.

John, his son and heir, who was only four years old at his father's death, succeeded, and on making proof of his age, 9 Henry VI., had livery of his father's lands. He was in high favour with that King, and, in consideration of his great merits and special services, was advanced to the honour of a Viscount, being the first person ever dignified with that title in England. He procured a charter in connection with his manor of Folkingham 27 Henry VI., such as return of writs and all precepts, assize of bread and ale, right of sac, soc, waif, estrays, felon's goods, treasure-trove, felo's de se, escapes, gallows, pillory, wrecks of sea, &c. Having acquired higher honours than any of his ancestors had done, in gratitude to his Royal benefactor, he bravely adventured his life in his service against the Yorkists, and was slain at the battle of Northampton, 38 Henry VI.

He was succeeded by William, his son and heir, who, adhering to the Lancastrian interest, shared the hard fate that befel that family; for being taken prisoner at Towton Field, 1 Edward IV., he was attainted, when several of his manors were given to Lord Hastings; but after Henry VII. obtained the crown, he recovered these, and his attainder was reversed, 1 Henry VII., in which year he had summons to Parliament, by the title of William Viscount Beaumont, and lived to the 23 Henry VII., but died without issue.

The manor of Folkingham then reverted to the Crown, when Edward VI. exchanged it, certain rents and farms in the parish of Birthorpe, the manors of Aslackby and Lee, the parsonage of Stow, and chapel of Burford, for the manors of Powick, Hanley, and Pixhand in Worcestershire.

Subsequently the manor belonged to R. Winne, Esq., then, with the exception of a few freeholds, to the late Sir Gilbert Heathcote, Bart., and is now the property of the Rev. T. Heathcote.

Formerly Folkingham consisted of little else than a mass of irregularly built thatched cottages, and in the middle of the market-place was a large pond, the edges of which were encumbered with piles of timber. Nearly opposite to the Green Man public-house stood the Market-cross, Butchery, and Town Hall.

Through the removal of all encumbrances from the market-place, and the rebuilding of the shabbiest houses around it, the present appearance of Folkingham is pleasing, and it possesses the advantage of several springs of excellent water on its outskirts, viz, one on the south-west called Pearson's spring, another on the south called Dunn's well, and a third on the south-east called Swallow pit, always thought to rise and fall with the level of the Trent, as so many other wells and springs of the central part of Lincolnshire are said to do. In a meadow west of the town are two mounds which may have been barrows, although a mill subsequently stood upon one of these.

There is a school, which was founded A.D. 1714, by the Rev. Richard Brocklesby, who gave a moiety of the rents, issues, and profits of certain lands in the parish of Pidley, in the county of Huntingdon, to be yearly and for ever paid to a fit and proper person, by his trustees, to teach the poor boys of Folkingham their Catechism, and the Holy Bible. This charitable donor left also, a house and premises in Stamford; one half of the rents, issues, and profits arising therefrom he directed should yearly and for ever be applied towards clothing the poor boys of this school.

In the year 1716, Peter Richier, M.D., of the bail of Lincoln, and Mary his wife, gave, by deed, a rent charge of £10, to certain trustees therein named, to be yearly and for ever paid out of a messuage or tenement and certain lands, lying in Pointon, to the master of the Free School of Folkingham, for the time being, as an augmentation of his salary.

The school was formerly kept in the Church, but Mr. C. E. Welbourne, who was elected master in 1810, built at his own expense, a spacious school-room, and house for the reception of boarders.

Besides these charitable gifts to the Free School, Thomas Arpe, A.D. 1657, gave, by deed, £50, and Lot Male £20, to the poor of Folkingham, which sums were subsequently laid out in the purchase of fourteen acres of land for their benefit.

Folkingham has seven annual fairs, viz., on Ash Wednesday, Palm Monday, May the 12th, June the 19th, July the 3rd, the Thursday after old Michaelmas, and November the 22nd. The market is held on Thursday.

A curious custom long prevailed at Folkingham in connection with Stow Green Fair, and which has only died out in the time of some still living. This was the placing of three halberts at the doors of as many houses in Folkingham on the evening before the commencement of the Fair, as a summons to their owners to keep the peace during the whole time of its continuance; but as the more respectable inhabitants gradually declined to perform this service, and there was no power beyond that of ancient custom to compel them to do so, the halberts thus fell into the hands of persons more likely to break, than preserve the peace, and hence ceased to be given out from the blacksmith's house where they were kept when not required for service. No doubt this custom was a relic of a manorial service, perhaps in the first place required of the De Gants as lords of the manor, and then carried out by deputy.

The following is a list of the later incumbents.

Date of Institution.

A.D. —Loth Male.
    1662.—Abraham Page.
    .—Richard Brocklesby.*
    1702.—Thomas Ixen.
    1720.—Richard Tollar.
    1779.—John Fountaine.
    1787.—John Moore Brooke.
    1799.—William Tait.
    1814.—Thomas Hardwicke Rawnsley.
    1861.—George Carter.

THE CASTLE.

The site only of this ancient stronghold of the de Gants and Beaumonts now remains. This was protected first by an outer moat enclosing a space consisting of ten acres of ground, and then

---

* He was licensed to preach in the whole diocese, but was deprived of his living as an adherent of the so-called Pretender, through an Act of the 13 and 14 William III., entitled "An Act for the further security of his Majesty's person, and the succession of the Crown in the Protestant line, and for extinguishing the hopes of the pretended Prince of Wales and all other Pretenders, and their open and secret abettors."

FOLKINGHAM CHURCH.

by an inner one, within which now stands the House of Correction on the east side of the town, erected in 1808, but since greatly improved and enlarged at different times. Numerous foundations have occasionally been found on the site of the Castle, and especially in 1813, when part of its sewer was discovered 12 feet below the surface. It was composed of fine stone about 3 feet square, and seems to have carried the sewage into the moat on the north side of the Castle. Coins also have occasionally been found upon its site, Leland visited this Castle, and thus alludes to it in his Itinerary, vol. I, p. 27.: "From Grimesthorpe to Sempringham a V miles, and a mile thens sumwhat inwarde on the lifte hond is the Castell of Fokingham, sumtime the Lord Bardolphe's, since the Lord Bellemonte's, now belonging to the Duke of Norfolk: it hath bene a goodly house, but now it fallith onto ruine, and it standith even about the egge of the fenne." There is a tradition that the picturesque old house with a flight of the steps before the door on the east side of the market-place and near the bottom of it, was built for one of the Clinton family with materials derived from the Castle; but it can hardly be older than the time of Charles I. It was formerly occupied by the Eastland family.

The Church.

This is dedicated to St. Andrew, and from its position on an eminence north of the town, and its lofty tower is a beautiful as well as a conspicuous object. Besides this tower it consists of a nave, north and south aisles, a south porch, chancel, modern vestry and organ chamber. The oldest feature is the Norman pier of an arch in the north wall of the chancel, originally opening into a chantry chapel of that period. This has a keel shaped shaft and a round supplemental one with scalloped cushion caps. During the Decorated period the arch it supported was replaced by a much wider one, and a corresponding pier of that style was erected. This arch has of late years been opened, and gives access to the present organ chamber. The south wall of the chancel comes next. This has no base mouldings, and is quite plain, but its date is still marked by the character of its remaining coupled lancet window, having a cusped circlet above it, associated with another eastward of it with Decorated tracery.

After this come the early Decorated nave arcades, consisting of three bays supported by two octagonal pillars and their responds, and a well moulded doorway within the porch. The aisles are of a later Decorated style, excepting the extreme ends, and have good base mouldings. The southern one is lit by a three-light square headed window at the east end, two similar windows in the south wall east of the porch, and a smaller two-light one westward of it. In the north aisle are two more of these windows and a segmental arched one between them with flamboyant tracery. The clerestory, of the same period, is lighted by three two-light windows having segmental arched beads on either side. But the great feature of this church is the Perpendicular tower, remark·able as an excellent specimen of its time, and for the wonderful perfection of its stonework, in which no flaw or failing can be detected. This opens into the aisles as well as into the nave by means of arches, and is handsomely vaulted with stone below the ringing chamber. It consists of four stages supported by buttresses lessening through breaks as they rise. The strings are unusually severe, being simply projecting square features plainly chamfered. The lower stage of the west elevation has good base mouldings, and a handsome doorway, the head of which is enriched with cusped panelling and blank shields. In the next stage is a large carefully executed window of four lights divided by a transom, and in the buttresses on either side are finely carved canopied statue niches. Above is a little quatrefoil light. In the third stage is a small two-light transomed window, and in the fourth a large belfry window composed of two coupled lights below a ogee arched hood mould. The tower is finished with a band of quatrefoils, a panelled embattled parapet, eight pinnacles and intermediate ornamental features giving it a very rich effect. The upper stages of the three other elevations are similar to the western one, but a gigantic clock-face painted on the south wall injures its appearance. It contains five bells, and in the south west angle is a staircase lit by little slits close to the adjacent buttresses. The latest ancient feature of this church is a debased Perpendicular porch, circa 1500. It has a rudely vaulted roof of a very low pitch, and above is a chamber intended for the use of the priest, supplied with a fire-place, and lighted by a small window in the front and another in each side wall. It is finished above with an embattled parapet and angle pinnacles. The head of the gable is surmounted by a cross, and just below this is a statue niche. A little staircase turret in the angle between the west side of this porch and the south aisle gives access to the chamber above and to the aisle roof. Within, the area of the tower and the westernmost bay of each aisle, probably added when the tower was built, were formerly boarded off to constitute a schoolroom, and in front of the tower arch was a gallery, when to enable the master to obtain a better view of his pupils, the piers of the southern tower arch were cruelly cut away, but have now been restored. At the east end of the south aisle was a chantry chapel from the existing evidence of a crocketed ogee arched piscina at the east end of the south wall, and the remains of a statue bracket in the east wall. On the north side of the western end of the chancel wall is a doorway leading to the roodloft, and the corresponding upper one remained until the restoration of this church in 1863. Close to this is a remarkably fine carved oak Perpendicular screen, rich in design and delicate in execution. Some of the old oak benches of the nave are now doing service as chancel seats.

In the south wall of the chancel are two handsome Decorated sedilia adorned by round shafted pillars having carved foliated caps ; and here an old copy of Fox's Book of Martyrs was chained to the wall until the restoration of the fabric, while opposite was an old oak arm chair of a stiff form and square back, in the middle of which was carved the bust of a man in a flat cap, of the time of Henry VII. ; but this also is now gone. Close to the east side of the sedilia is a small square aumbry, and then a piscina having an ogee arched head. Towards the north side of the east wall is a larger square aumbry, and nearer to it in the north wall a still larger one. The east window is filled with good stained glass by Mr. H. Hughes, representing the Birth, Crucifixion, Resurrection and Ascension of our Lord in its four lights, and our Lord in glory in a cusped circlet above.

From Holles we gather that there were formerly various memorials of the dead in this church, almost the whole of which have now perished. Near the font was the effigy of a religious person (probably a brass), and elsewhere inscriptions over the graves of Emot Gilson and Thomas Beverley. He also mentions two armorial shields cut in stone and surmounted by two tilting helms and their mantling, which still remain on either side of the nave door within the porch. The one on the left, if tinted, would have borne Az, 3 garbes Or, for Ranulph le meschin Earl of Chester; the one on the right, Az, semi of fleurs de lis, a lion rampant, over all a bend gobony Arg and Gu, for Beaumont.* In the tower window he noted the bearings of Beaumont and Bardolph—Az, 2 cinquefoils pierced Or; also Beaumont quartering Chester, and Clinton quartering Say, within a garter, for Edward Earl of Lincoln. In a north window of the nave and in the chancel, Beaumont again, and in an east window of the same—perhaps of the south aisle, Jerusalem, Beaumont repeated and the effigy of John de Newcastle, or as he terms it, "effig Johis de la Novel Kastel." Now, there are no memorials of any general interest.

Attached to Folkingham is the hamlet of Laughton, consisting of 1136 acres of land, the vicarage of which is consolidated with the rectory of Folkingham. When "Testa de Nevill" was written this place was held of the king by Baldwin Wake, who granted it to Hugh de Ringsdon, one of whose tenants was Adam de Lotton, who held half a knight's fee of him in Laughton and Aslackby. It once possessed a church, which stood in a hollow west of the turnpike road, but of this there are now no remains. Although Laughton was so small, it appears to have been formerly divided into two minute manors called East and West Laughton, upon which seventeen families were residing in the reign of Elizabeth.

---

*The arms of the Earl of Chester are thus connected with the De Gants, the former lords of Folkingham. Lucy daughter of Ivo Taillebois and Lucy daughter of Algar Earl of Mercia and sister of Morcar, had three daughters, Lucy, Beatrice and Matilda. Of these, Lucy married first Roger de Roumara Earl of Lincoln, and subsequently Ranulph Earl of Chester, by the first of whom she had William de Roumara Earl of Lincoln, and by the second Ranulph meschinus. Beatrice married to Ribald of Middleham, and Matilda to Hugh Fitz Ranulph, by whom she had Roheis, who was thus daughter of the heiress Lucy Countess of Lincoln and Chester and first cousin to Ranulph le meschin Earl of Chester, by whom she was forcibly given in marriage to Gilbert de Gant, who thus in her right succeeded to the Earldom of Lincoln and Chester. The arms of de Beaumont commemorate the after lords of this manor, the first of whom, Henry de Beaumont, received a grant of it from Edward II. in the first year of his reign.

THRECKINGHAM.

ACREAGE,   POPULATION,
1466.   1861—189.   1871—183.

THE name of this village was originally spelt Trickingeham
and Trekingham. It lies 6½ miles south of Sleaford, and
is situated within the Wapentake and the Deanery of Aveland.
The branch of the Ermine-Street from Caistor, or Durobrivæ,
to Lincoln, under the modern name of Mareham-lane, passes close
by its eastern side, and another very ancient road from the coast
to the west, formerly called Salters'-way, and now the Bridge-end
road, or Holland road, skirts its northern limit. Here many
Roman coins have at different times been found ; but it is
chiefly interesting from its connection with that great historic
event—the decisive and bloody battle between the Danes and
the Saxons A.D. 869, which took place at Threckingham, although this in no wise led to the adoption of its present name, as
has been suggested and commonly believed, because it seemed so
natural, viz., that it was first called Laundon, but after the above-
named battle—Trekingham, through the fall of three Danish
kings or chiefs and their burial here on that occasion.

A portion of the land in this parish is called Danes field, or
Danes hill, in commemoration of this Danish victory, and a large
mound or tumulus still remaining a little to the west of the church
probably marks the spot where some of the slain were buried,
while other mounds that formerly existed here have now been
levelled.

When Domesday book was compiled the manor of Threckingham belonged to the Benedictine Abbey of Ramsey, but it only
appears to have possessed 4 oxgangs of land here, rated at half
a carucate, and 1 villan cultivating it. The whole was valued
before and after the Conquest at 5s. This was because the
greater part of the land here constituted a berewick of the manor
of Newton near Horncastle. Of this Colsuein possessed 2½ carucates taxed at 14¾ oxgangs, 1 sokeman, 5 villans and 3 bordars

cultivating 1½ carucates. Odo Arbalistar, or the crossbow man, possessed 10 oxgangs, and the third part of 2 other oxgangs, 2 sokemen cultivating 2 oxgangs of this land, and 5 villans and 1 bordar cultivating 1 carucate. He also had the 6th part of the advowson of St. Peter's church at Threckingham, the 3rd part of that of St. Mary and the 3rd part of half a carucate belonging to it. Ulviet, who held under the king 5 oxgangs and the 6th part of two more, cultivated by 1 sokeman and 3 villans, the 12th part of the advowson of St. Peter's church, the 6th part of that of St. Mary, and the 6th part of 4 oxgangs of land belonging to that church. The Bishop of Durham possessed 5 oxgangs and the 6th part of 2 others, also 1 sokeman, and 3 villans cultivating half a carucate, the 12th part of the advowson of St. Peter's church, and the 6th part of 4 oxgangs belonging to St. Mary's church at Threckingham. Two oxgangs of land here also lay within the soke of Gilbert de Gant's manor of Folkingham. Subsequently Gilbert de Gant appears to have acquired the greater part of the land in Threckingham, from the evidence of Testa de Nevill. A family deriving their name from that of this place afterwards became the principal tenants here; of whom Walter de Trikingham held the 5th part of a knight's fee of Robert Marmyun and he of Gilbert de Gant, also the 20th part of a knight's fee directly of the great Gilbert himself, who in his turn held his lands here and elsewhere of the king. He also possessed the 5th part and the 4th part of a knight's fee, held of him by Hugh de Trikingham and Matilda his mother; besides 5 oxgangs held by John Gumbard. Subsequently the de Crouns inherited these lands, of which William Pedethen held the 6th part of a knight's fee in Newton and Threckingham of Petronilla de Croun, the heiress of that family, and Robert de Newton three parts of a knight's fee. After this Gerard de Kamvill possessed a knight's fee in Newton and Threckingham, which he granted to William de Osbournbi.

In the 14th century the Trekingham family were the resident if not the actual lords of this parish, of whom besides the above named Walter and Hugh, was Lambert, a justice of the Court of Common Pleas in the reign of Edward I. and Edward II., John de Trekingham, Sheriff of the County in 1334, another Walter, and a Robert, who the same year represented the County of Lincoln in Parliament, also another Lambert, a Baron of the Exchequer in 1341.

Elias de Trekingham, a monk of Peterborough and a Doctor of Divinity at Oxford, who wrote a chronicle, dating from A.D. 626 to 1270, was probably a member of this family, and certainly derived his name from this place.

In the reign of Elizabeth there were 31 families resident here; and in that of Charles I. the plague, or some other grievous pestilence, appears to have visited Threckingham from the evidence of a still existing inscription upon a stone inserted in the wall of a farm house, viz., "Vorax pestis Threck^m soevire mese maio 1646. Robert Gaton."

In the 17th century a family of the name of Fisher resided here, but they eventually removed to Grantham Grange, and in 1722 Francis Fisher represented the borough of Grantham in Parliament. Now, the Rev. Thomas Heathcote is lord of the manor of Threckingham and the owner of most of its land, the other principal proprietors being S. N. Rudge, Esq., and William Cragg, Esq. In the "Gentleman's Magazine," vol. 61, p. 193, mention is made of one Richard South, the son of a tailor of Threckingham, who at 6 years of age could with ease carry a weight of 20 stones, and was subsequently seven times married, but survived all his wives.

ECCLESIASTICAL HISTORY.

It has been already stated that there were two churches here, severally dedicated in honour of St. Peter and St. Mary, when Domesday book was compiled, and that parts of their endowment were in the hands of various laymen. The Bishop of Durham and Ulviet had equal shares of these, belonging to Newton, for each had a 6th part of the land belonging to St. Mary's church, and the 6th part of an extra piece consisting of 4 oxgangs belonging to it; also a 12th part of that belonging to St. Peter's church. Another holder of these lands was Odo Arbalistar, or Balistarius (the crossbow man), who was then the possessor of a 6th part of St. Peter's lands, and the 3rd part of St. Mary's, together with a 3rd part of half a carucate also belonging to it.

Subsequently the rectorial tithes were given to the Monastery of Burton Lazars, Leicestershire, and the vicarage, founded and endowed before 1209, was in the patronage of that Monastery.

Reference to this is made in Bishop Welles's Register, who was consecrated 1209.   "Trikingham vicaria in ecclesia de Trikingham quæ est Fratrum Sancti Lazari de Burthon consistit in toto attagis absque aliqua diminutione, cum tofto in quo nunc vicarius residen ; et ipsi Fratres Sancti Lazari procurabunt hospitium Archidiaconi, et sustinebunt in perpetuum omnia alia onera præter sidonalia quæ tantum vicarius solvebit annuatim ; et valet vicarius V marc, et eo amplius." On the 10th of February, 1555, Queen Mary, for a fine of 100s., demised to Anthony Pickeringe, Gent., the tithes of Threckingham and their appurtenances for 20 years at the annual rent of 100s.   "Harl. MS."

The vicarage is now in the patronage of the Rev. Thomas Heathcote.   The registers commence with the date of 1572.

The following is a list of the vicars :—

Date of Institution.

 A.D. 1240.—Reginald de Wistow.*
   1261.—Richard de Mackworth.
   1262.—Thomas de Trikingham.
   1286.—Geoffrey de Swayfield.
   1320.—Hugo de Toller.
   1349.—Robert Templer.
   1352.—Thomas de Brampton.
   1367.—Richard Gamul.
   1400.—Nicholas Frost.
   1406.—William Smith.
   1420.—John Tyas.
   1423.—Thomas Loper.
   1440.—Richard Sleaford.
   1452.—William Tundies.
   1452.—Robert Lord.†
   1453.—Robert Baxter.
   1491.—William Dorain.
   1506.—John Lancaster.
   1557.—Robert Nelson.‡

---

 * Presented by the Master and Brethren of Burton Lazars, as were all the subsequent incumbents down to John Lancaster, in 1506.
 † Deprived the following year.
 ‡ Presented by Queen Mary.

THRECKINGHAM CHURCH.

Date of Institution.

A.D. 1561.—John Gray.*
1597.—William Brown.
1610.—Henry Wallewell.
1612.—Samuel Askeron.
1630.—Thomas Lambe.
1642.—William Douglas.
—Thomas White.
1662.—John Marshall.
1677.—Henry Brerewood.
1703.—Robert Kelham.
1752.—Charles Potter.
1759.—John Towers.
1803.—David Henry Urquhart.
1829.—Charles Spencer Ellicott.

THE CHURCH.

This is dedicated in honor of St. Peter, and no doubt stands upon the site of the one called after that Apostle in Domesday book. It is a fine structure, which from its elevated position may be seen for many miles round, and consists of tower and spire, nave, north and south aisles, south porch, and chancel.

A Transitional church clearly once represented the earlier one referred to above, from the character of the greater part of the present chancel, and the western respond of the north aisle. In the eastern wall of the chancel are three circular headed windows separate without, but connected by an arcade within, the pillars of which, with their square abaci and simple vigorous roll mouldings, are good specimens of their kind. Towards the east end of the north wall is a single semicircular headed light, and opposite to it a corresponding one in the south wall as far as its jambs and head are concerned, but externally looks like an entirely late window of two lights having a square head, which is only in part seen within. Another arched headed window and a small door were also inserted in the south wall, but the first of these is now filled in with masonry. All three walls of the chancel are relieved by three coeval strings. On the north side,

---

* Presented by Queen Elizabeth.

westward of the window above spoken of, was an arcade of nearly the same date that once opened into an adjoining chapel. This consisted of two very wide and beautifully moulded semicircular arches supported by a central circular shafted pillar having a boldly foliated cap and two responds. The greater part of this is now imbedded in the masonry of the wall it once simply supported, but part of it is still exposed within, and serves to sustain the first portion of the north aisle arcade of the nave. The chancel and nave are covered by a continuous modern low pitched roof as there is no chancel arch, nor difference in elevation between them. The next feature as to date is the lower part of the tower. This is now of three stages supported by good buttresses, and constitutes a grand feature; but at first only the two lower ones were built, reaching just above the ridge of the nave roof. In the western face of the tower stage is a large lancet, and smaller ones are irregularly inserted above. After a considerable pause the upper stage and broach spire were added, which add so much to the character of the whole fabric. This is wholly of excellent ashlar work, and the details of its shafted belfry lights are most carefully carried out. In the spire are three ranges of lights, and towards its summit the run of its lines is broken by a projecting feature, as at Sleaford church and elsewhere, before it attains its greatest elevation, viz., 144 feet. Unfortunately it lost its finial many years ago, which very much spoils its appearance, and in 1871 the whole fabric was much shaken and injured by lightning.

In the south aisle are four good three-light windows having foliated intersecting tracery; the easternmost one has a flat head, and above is a good plain parapet. Attached to this is a beautiful porch, the interior of which is relieved by plain arcading on either side, in the middle arches of which are small two-light windows. The doorway within has a well moulded arch, and the door itself is enriched with very beautiful ironwork. At the western angle of this aisle is a square staircase turret, on which is a dial bearing this inscription :—" Sic vita," and " The gifte of Edmund Hutchinson, Gentleman."

The north aisle is of later date, circa 1325-30, and inferior in every respect. It is low, and has no base mouldings or parapet. In it are five small three-light windows all alike, and a good doorway.

The aisle arcades are supported by circular shafted pillars, excepting the last pair eastward; these consist of clustered ones, and the westernmost pillar of the south aisle has an octagonal shaft, and corresponds with the responds of this aisle, which appear to be of earlier date than their circular compeers. These last have beautifully moulded caps deeply undercut, and one of them together with those of the clustered pillars are enriched with a minute band of the tooth mould. The arches are of two orders, one plain, the other moulded with a hood-mould above. The aisle roofs, as well as those covering the nave and chancel are wretched. At the west end of the north aisle close to the Transitional respond above mentioned and partly concealed by a modern vestry wall, is a little lancet with a moulding above, now filled in with masonry. The tower arch, with its manifold mouldings and massive character, is a beautiful feature. Near this stands an Early English font, circular in plan, and having its bowl enriched with shallow arcading; on the chamfer of the base is the half destroyed legend of "Ave Maria gratiæ plena." Some of the old carved oak bench ends are still doing service.

In the north wall of the north aisle is a plain square aumbry, and in the southern one of the chancel are two adjoining recesses; one covered by a very flat arch and flanked by a Transitional pillar contains a plain piscina placed on one side of the base of the recess; the other apparently served as a large aumbry.

The silver communion flagon and chalice were given in memory of William Fysher by some relation in 1676, according to the tenor of a Latin inscription upon them.

In the tower are three bells, two of which bear the name of the founder, T. Norris, and the date, 1660.

At the west end of the south aisle now stand three large stone coffins and their lids in a very perfect condition. Originally they were probably sunk below the pavement of some part of this church or its lost chantry chapel so as only to expose their lids slightly raised above the pavement. These were long regarded as the coffins of the three Danish kings or chiefs who fell at the first battle of Threckingham; but as they are of a later date by some 500 years, and of a distinctly christian character, they can scarcely now be thought to have any connection with those heathen chieftains who perished A.D. 870, and whose followers would certainly not have buried them in a christian church or cemetery and in coffins bearing conspicuously upon them the chief symbol of the christian faith. Two of these coffins have flat lids, but that of the third one is slightly coped. All have stemmed decorative crosses cut in relief upon them, and on each side of the stem of one of these crosses the remains of an inscription may be seen, said by Holles, who saw it when it was more legible, to run thus :—" Hic intumulatur Johannes quondam d^s de Treckingham." Perhaps, therefore, this once held the remains of John de Treckingham who filled the office of Sheriff in this county 1334; but certainly all three of these coffins are of the earlier part of the 14th century.

Besides these, there are two slabs surmounted by the effigies of a knight and his lady, well cut in stone, now placed upon a modern low base at the west end of the nave in front of the tower arch. He is represented with his head resting upon two cushions, his hands upraised in prayer and his legs crossed, indicating his christian faith and vow, with two small lions at his feet. He is clothed in a *coif de mailles* covering the head, a hauberk of mail covering his body, arms, and hands, the former being strapped round his brows, and the latter round the wrists. The thighs, legs, and feet are covered with *chausses* of mail, the knees by *poleynes* or genouillieres, probably made of boiled or hardened leather. Over this armour is a long flowing surcoat confined round the waist by a narrow strap, and below this, a broad studded sword-belt, to which the sword, in a similar studded sheath, is attached on the left side. A small heater-shaped shield hangs on the left arm by means of two straps; and upon it are cut his armorial bearings, viz., Arg, 2 bars Gu, in chief 3 torteaux, over all a bend S. On the heels are spurs strapped round the ankles. The effigy of the lady is very elegant. She is represented, like her lord, in the attitude of prayer and with her head resting on two cushions, but at her feet are two little dogs. She is clothed in a kirtle having tight sleeves with the usual row of miniature buttons upon them, and over this a long flowing gown; over the gown is a mantle fastened across the breast by a strap. But little of her hair is seen, as a veil covers her head and falls on either side upon her shoulders; her chin and neck are covered by a wimple or gorget. Holles considered that these commemorated Lambert de Trekingham, a Justice of the Court of Common Pleas in the reigns of Edward I. and II., and his wife, and he is probably right in his opinion, as the armour and dress of these effigies are of that period.

At the east end of the north aisle is a white marble mural monument commemorating some members of the Fisher family, surmounted by a shield charged with their armorial bearings. Holles observed the following shields in the windows of this church when he visited it, viz., in a north window, Arg, 2 bars G. in chief 3 torteaux, over all a bend S.—Treckingham; Or, 2 chevrons G within a bordure of the same—Clare; G. 3 water bougets Arg.—Ros; Barry of 6, Arg. and Az.—Grey. In a west window, Arg. a fesse between 3 cootes S.—Coote. In the chancel the same impaling Arg. a fesse dancettè between 3 talbots' heads erased S. Also, G. a chevron between 3 fleurs de lis Arg.—Pickering, then lately set up, as he states.

STOW.

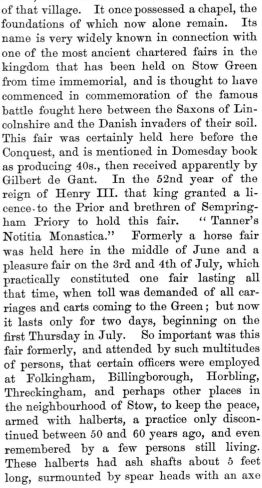

THIS little hamlet of Threckingham is bounded on the west by Mareham lane, and lies about half a mile south-west of that village. It once possessed a chapel, the foundations of which now alone remain. Its name is very widely known in connection with one of the most ancient chartered fairs in the kingdom that has been held on Stow Green from time immemorial, and is thought to have commenced in commemoration of the famous battle fought here between the Saxons of Lincolnshire and the Danish invaders of their soil. This fair was certainly held here before the Conquest, and is mentioned in Domesday book as producing 40s., then received apparently by Gilbert de Gant. In the 52nd year of the reign of Henry III. that king granted a licence · to the Prior and brethren of Sempringham Priory to hold this fair. " Tanner's Notitia Monastica." Formerly a horse fair was held here in the middle of June and a pleasure fair on the 3rd and 4th of July, which practically constituted one fair lasting all that time, when toll was demanded of all carriages and carts coming to the Green; but now it lasts only for two days, beginning on the first Thursday in July. So important was this fair formerly, and attended by such multitudes of persons, that certain officers were employed at Folkingham, Billingborough, Horbling, Threckingham, and perhaps other places in the neighbourhood of Stow, to keep the peace, armed with halberts, a practice only discontinued between 50 and 60 years ago, and even remembered by a few persons still living. These halberts had ash shafts about 5 feet long, surmounted by spear heads with an axe head and spike at the back of this below, as represented in the accompanying cut. Further reference to these halberts will be found in the account of Folkingham, p. 510.

The greater part of the land in Stow now belongs to the Rev. Thomas Heathcote, but one farm and a cottage are in the hands of the Crown.

GENERAL INDEX.

GENERAL INDEX.

GENERAL INDEX.

FLEMYNG, Bishop of Lincoln, 116 ; birth at Crofton in the 14th century, 116 ; a student at University College, Oxford, ib. ; embraced Wycliffe's doctrines, ib. ; promotion in the church, ib. ; Bishop of Lincoln, ib. ; Papal Chamberlain, ib. ; founded Lincoln College, Oxford, 117 ; executed the decree of the Council of Constance, which ordered the exhumation of Wycliffe's bones, ib. ; died at Sleaford Castle, and buried in Lincoln Cathedral, ib. ; monument in Lincoln Cathedral, 118.

FOLKINGHAM—General history, 505 ; Folkingham the more correct way of spelling this name than Falkingham, ib. ; Ulf, the Saxon lord before the Conquest, ib.; Gilbert de Gant, possessor after the Conquest, ib.; Folkingham in old times, 508 ; the water supply, 509 ; the school, ib.; the fairs, ib.; a curious custom in connection with Stow Green fair, 510 ; list of incumbents, ib. ; the castle, ib. ; Leland's reference to the castle, 511 ; the church, ib.; Holles' account of the monuments, 513.

FOLLET, a shoemaker at Leasingham, supposed to have been the cause of the disturbance in the house of Sir William Yorke, 268.

GEORGE III., an anecdote of, 4.

GRANTHAM—Discovery of Roman coins and other relics, 45.

GRAY'S INN HALL—A record of Sir William Hussey, Chief Justice, 124.

HALE MAGNA—General history, 369 ; ecclesiastical history, 371 ; list of vicars, ib, ; the church, ib.

HALE PARVA—General history, 375.

HALFPENNY HATCH—Discovery of two Roman vases, 77.

HANDBECK—General history, 325.

HARBY—Monumental brass of Daniel, in Evedon church, 241.

HAVERHOLME PRIORY—Proceeds of the church of Old Sleaford, possessed by, 184 ; general history, 242 ; given to the Cistercians of Fountains Abbey, 242 ; reverted to the Bishop of Lincoln, ib. ; given to the Gilbertines, ib. ; translation of the charter of Bishop Alexander, 243 ; Adam Fitz-Peter's grant in favour of the house at Haverholme, 244 ; churches in its patronage, 245 ; possessions of the Priory at its dissolution, 246 ; its seal, 247 ; later owners of Haverholme, ib. ; description of the present mansion, 248.

HAYDOR—General history, 376 ; ecclesiastical history, 380 ; list of incumbents, 381 ; the church, ib.

HEATH—Description of, 2 ; its dangers, ib.

HEBDEN, Nicholas de, of Gosberton—A copy of his will, 407.

HECKINGTON—Discovery of Roman coins, 76 ; general history, 384 ; ecclesiastical history, 387 : list of vicars, 388 : the church, 389.

HELPRINGHAM—General history, 397 ; ecclesiastical history, 398 ; list of vicars, 399 ; the church, 400 ; mercer's tokens, 402.

HENRY VIII., visit of to Sleaford, 105.

HIBALDSTOW—Roman entrenched camp, coins, and pavements, 57.

HOLDINGHAM, 180 ; Richard de Haldingham, ib. ; chapel there, 181.

HONINGTON—Discovery of Roman coins and fragments of weapons, 46 ; the British camp, 479.

HORKSTOW—Roman tesselated pavements, 61.

HORSMAN, Sir Thomas—Monument in Burton church, 351.

HOWELL—General history, 406 ; ecclesiastical history, 407 ; list of rectors, 408 ; the church, 409.

HUMBY, LITTLE—Discovery of Roman pottery and coins, 45.

HUSSEY—Earliest mention of the name in connection with Sleaford, 123 ; Sir William Hussey, Chief Justice of the King's Bench, 123 ; a record of him and his wife in Gray's Inn Hall, 124 ; John Hussey, Sheriff of Lincolnshire, ib. ; attended Henry VIII. at the Field of the Cloth of Gold, ib. ; created Baron Hussey of Sleaford, ib. ; rebellion in Lincolnshire

GENERAL INDEX.

through the suppression of monasteries, 125 ; letter of Lord Hussey, ib. ; joins the rebellion in the North, 126 ; beheaded at Lincoln for high treason, 126.

JOHN, King of England—Visits Sleaford Castle, 108 ; his catastrophe in the Wash, 109 ; illness at Lynn, 110 ; removal to Swineshead, 110 ; incredibility of the story that he was poisoned at Swineshead, 111 ; bled at Sleaford, 113 ; journey to Newark, ib. ; death there, 114 ; burial at Worcester, 115.

KELBY—General history, 412 ; the church, 413.

KIRKBY LAYTHORPE—Discovery of Roman coins, 76 ; general history, 414 ; list of incumbents, 417 ; the church, ib.

KYME, NORTH—Roman camp, 77 ; general history, 263.

,, SOUTH—General history, 249 ; the Umfravilles, how the manor became theirs, 251 ; the castle, 254 ; the Priory, 256 ; rent roll of the Augustines, ib. ; perpetual curates, 259 ; the church, ib.

LANGTOFT—Discovery of Roman coins, 74.

LAUGHTON—General history, 514.

LAWSUIT between Thomas de la Launde, of Ashby, and the Knights Templars of Temple Bruer, 196.

LEASINGHAM—General history, 265 ; ecclesiastical history, 269 ; list of incumbents, 270 ; the church, 271.

LELAND—Reference to Sleaford, 105 ; Sleaford Castle, 120 ; Temple Bruer, 316 ; Haydor, 377 ; Ancaster, 473 ; Folkingham, 511.

LINCOLN—Discovery of a Danish comb case, 98.

LINCOLNSHIRE—On the arrival of the Romans, 27 ; invaded by Knut, the Dane, 92 ; number of places having the Scandinavian terminal "by," 98 ; number in the Wapentakes of Flaxwell and Aswardhurn, ib.

LITTLEBOROUGH—Roman ford over the Trent, discoveries of urns, coins, altars, and many curious relics, 54.

MAREHAM—General history, 353 ; Mareham lane, why so called, 39 and 353.

MONUMENTS in Sleaford church, 155-62 ; Anwick, 192 ; Ashby-de-la-Launde, 207 ; Dorrington, 233 ; Evedon, 241 ; Kyme, 260 ; Leasingham, 273 ; North Rauceby, 282-5 ; Asgarby, 331 ; Aswarby, 337 ; Aunsby, 341 ; Burton Pedwardine, 350 ; Ewerby, 364 ; Great Hale, 374 ; Haydor, 383 ; Heckington, 395 ; Helpringham, 402 ; Howell, 409 : Osbournby, 424 ; Quarrington, 431 ; Scredington, 436 ; Spanby, 441 ; Swarby, 444 ; Swaton, 451 ; Welby, 455 ; Silk Willoughby, 467 ; Billinghay, 496.

MORTON—Discovery of Roman coins, 75.

NEWARK—Death of King John, 114.

NEWLOVE, Anthony, a mercer of Helpringham, his monument in the church, 402.

NOCTON—Discovery of clay moulds for Roman coins, 81.

OSBOURNBY—General history, 419 ; ecclesiastical history, 421 ; the church, 422.

PETERBOROUGH—Discoveries of Celtic implements and Roman coins, 73 ; pillage of the abbey by the Danes, 96.

PONTON, GREAT—Roman vaults, pavements, etc., found here, 45.

POTTERHANWORTH—Roman pottery found here, 41.

PUGH, Rev. John, vicar of Rauceby, one of the founders of the Church Missionary Society, 284.

QUAKER Controversy at Sleaford, 138.

QUARRINGTON—Description and cuts of Saxon remains found in a Saxon cemetery there, 99 ; general history, 426 ; ecclesiastical history, 428 ; the church, 430.

RAUCEBY, NORTH—General history, 275 ; ecclesiastical history, 278 : list of vicars, 279 ; the church, 281.

GENERAL INDEX.

GENERAL INDEX.

GENERAL INDEX.

WILLIAM FAWCETT, PRINTER, SLEAFORD.